December 2013

Steve,

Enjoy!

Peter Miller

NATIONAL GEOGRAPHIC

WHO'S WHO IN THE BIBLE

Unforgettable People and Timeless Stories From Genesis to Revelation

Jean-Pierre Isbouts

NATIONAL GEOGRAPHIC
WASHINGTON D.C.

CONTENTS

Page 1: An early 20th-century stained glass window from Canterbury Cathedral depicts King Solomon and the Queen of Sheba. Pages 2-3: "Adam and Eve in Paradise" is the work of Flemish painter Peter Paul Rubens (1577–1640). Opposite: "Moses Before the Burning Bush" was painted by Italian artist Domenico Fetti (1588–1623) around 1614.

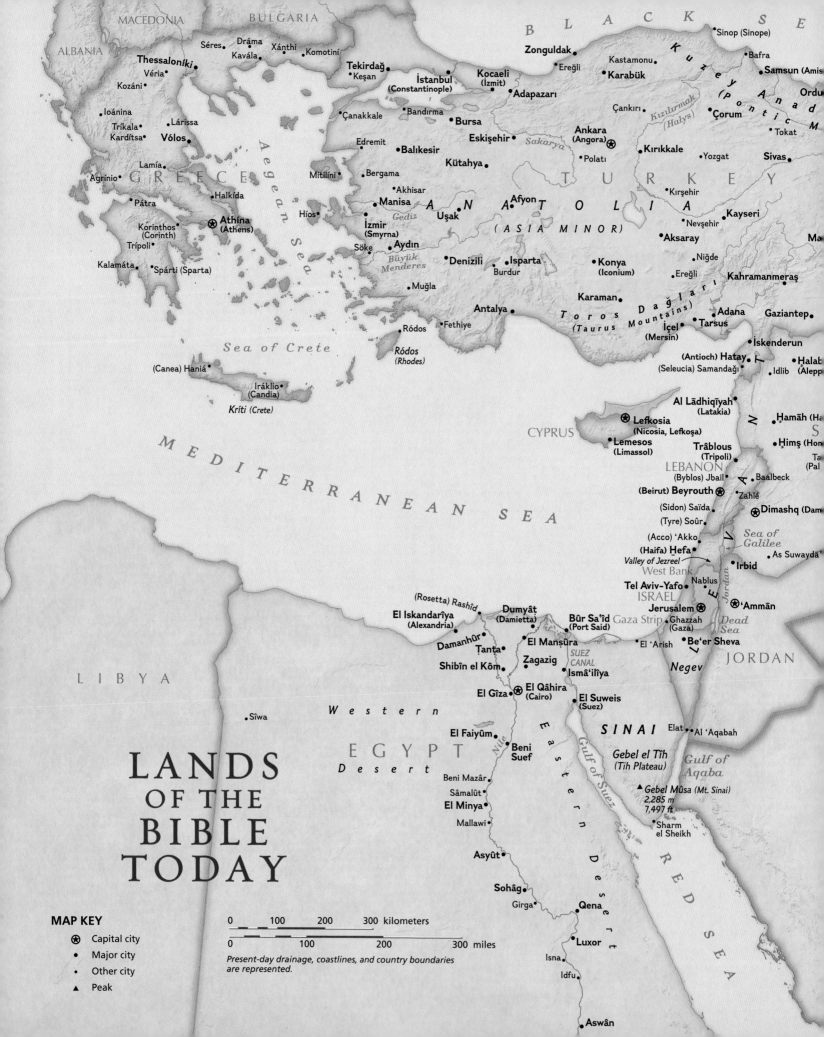

LANDS OF THE BIBLE TODAY

MACEDONIA
BULGARIA
BLACK SEA
ALBANIA

Séres
Dráma
Xánthi
Komotiní
Sinop (Sinope)
Zonguldak
Ereğli
Kastamonu
Bafra
Samsun (Amis

Thessaloníki
Kaválaa
Tekirdağ
Kocaeli (İzmit)
Karabük
Ordu

Véria
Keşan
İstanbul (Constantinople)
Adapazarı
Çankırı
Kızılırmak (Halys)
Çorum
M

Kozáni
Bandırma
Bursa
Ankara (Angora)
Polatı
Kırıkkale
Tokat

Ioánina
Çanakkale
Eskişehir
Sakarya
Yozgat
Sivas

Tríkala
Lárissa
Edremit
Balıkesir
Kütahya
Kırşehir

Kardítsa
Vólos
Bergama
Akhisar
Afyon
ANATOLIA
Nevşehir
Kayseri

Agrínio
GREECE
Mitilíni
Manisa
Uşak
(ASIA MINOR)
Aksaray

Lamía
Híos
İzmir (Smyrna)
Denizili
Isparta
Konya (Iconium)
Niğde

Halkída
Söke
Aydın
Burdur
Ereğli
Kahramanmaraş

Athína (Athens)
Pátra
Korinthos (Corinth)
Trípoli
Muğla
Karaman
Toros Dağları (Taurus Mountains)
Adana
Gaziantep

Kalamáta
Spárti (Sparta)
Antalya
İçel (Mersin)
Tarsus
İskenderun

Aegean Sea
Gediz
Büyük Menderes
Fethiye
(Antioch) Hatay
Halab (Aleppo)
(Seleucia) Samandağı
Idlib

Sea of Crete
Ródos
Ródos (Rhodes)
Al Lādhiqīyah (Latakia)
Ḥamāh
S

(Canea) Haniá
Lefkosia (Nicosia, Lefkoşa)
Ḥimş (Hom
Ta (Pal

Iráklio (Candia)
Kríti (Crete)
CYPRUS
Lemesos (Limassol)
Trâblous (Tripoli)
Baalbeck

MEDITERRANEAN SEA
(Byblos) Jbail
(Beirut) Beyrouth
Zahlé
Dimashq (Dam

LEBANON
(Sidon) Saïda
(Tyre) Soûr
Sea of Galilee

(Acco) 'Akko
(Haifa) Ḥefa
As Suwaydā

Valley of Jezreel
West Bank
Irbid

(Rosetta) Rashîd
Dumyât (Damietta)
Tel Aviv-Yafo
Nablus
Jordan

El Iskandarîya (Alexandria)
Bûr Sa'îd (Port Said)
Gaza Strip
Jerusalem
'Ammān

Damanhûr
El Mansûra
Ghazzah (Gaza)
Dead Sea

Tanta
Zagazig
El 'Arish
Be'er Sheva
JORDAN

Shibîn el Kôm
Ismâ'ilîya
Negev

LIBYA
El Gîza
El Qâhira (Cairo)
El Suweis (Suez)

Sîwa
Western
SINAI
Elat
Al 'Aqabah

El Faiyûm
Beni Suef
Gebel el Tîh (Tih Plateau)
Gulf of Aqaba

EGYPT Desert
Beni Mazâr
Gebel Mûsa (Mt. Sinai) 2,285 m 7,497 ft
Sharm el Sheikh

Sâmalût
El Minya
Nile
Eastern

Mallawi
Gulf of Suez
Desert
RED SEA

Asyût

Sohâg
Girga
Qena

Luxor

Isna

Idfu

Aswân

MAP KEY

⊛ Capital city
• Major city
• Other city
▲ Peak

0   100   200   300 kilometers
0   100   200   300 miles

INTRODUCTION

EVEN AMID THE RAPID SOCIAL CHANGES OF THE 21ST CENTURY, the Bible remains a book of enduring beauty and relevance in modern society. While for some it constitutes the bedrock of faith, for others it serves as a moral compass to the human experience; still others consider it the cultural foundation of Western civilization. Regardless of how we use the Bible, one of the reasons for its enduring appeal is that it describes men and women with whom we can identify. The Bible is fundamentally the story of families—of men and women who set out to fulfill their destiny, guided by the hand of God. It is the very human quality of these stories, with their themes of love and faith, of hope and conflict, that continues to resonate with us to this day.

That is why an updated directory of biblical characters is timely. Indeed, this *Who's Who in the Bible* is conceived not only as a comprehensive guide to the people of the Bible but also as an introduction to the social, cultural, and political context of the worlds in which they lived. In that respect, this *Who's Who* is different from other publications in that it depicts the lead characters as part of a continuous story and historical framework. This is particularly significant because of the frequent duplication of names throughout the Bible. People known as Jonathan, Simeon, or Mary appear many times throughout the biblical narrative. By organizing these characters as part of a chronological narrative, rather than in alphabetical order, we can better understand their unique role in the unfolding of events.

Consequently, this book is organized in five chapters, inspired by the division of the *Tanakh*, or Hebrew Scripture (the "Old Testament" in Christian parlance) as well as the New Testament, with a focus on those books that feature leading characters in the Bible:

CHAPTER 1: FROM GENESIS TO DEUTERONOMY
This chapter tells the story of the principal characters of the **Law** *(Torah),* the first division of Hebrew Scripture, also referred to either as the Mosaic Law, the Five Books of Moses, or the *Pentateuch* (Greek for "Five Scrolls"). It includes the Books of Genesis, Exodus, Leviticus, Numbers, and Deuteronomy. The principal figures in this chapter, from Adam to Noah, and from Abraham to Moses, take us from the stories of Creation to the Great Flood, and from the sojourn in Egypt to the Exodus to the Promised Land. This narrative section is followed by a comprehensive alphabetical directory of characters in this part of the Bible.

CHAPTER 2: FROM JOSHUA TO KINGS
Chapter 2 follows the stories from the division known as the **Prophets** *(Nevi'im),* which includes the books of the so-called *former* prophets (Joshua, Judges, Samuel, and Kings) and the *latter* prophets (including Isaiah, Jeremiah, Ezekiel, and the Twelve Minor Prophets). This chapter follows the lead characters of the epic saga of Israel's monarchy, from the Settlement in Canaan (the Promised Land) to the split of Solomon's realm into

The "Transfiguration" by Raphael (1483–1520) was completed by his pupil Giulio Romano after the artist's death in 1520.

Ramses II is shown smiting his enemies in this colored limestone relief, which dates from the New Kingdom, 19th Dynasty (1292–1190 B.C.E.).

Northern and Southern Kingdoms. The chapter ends with the capture of Jerusalem by the Neo-Babylonian King Nebuchadnezzar in 586 B.C.E. and his destruction of the Jerusalem Temple a decade later. This narrative is also followed by an alphabetical directory of characters in this part of the Bible.

Chapter 3: From Chronicles to Maccabees

Chapter 3 identifies leading characters in the third division of Hebrew Scripture, known as the **Writings (Ketuvim)**. Among others, this includes the Books of Chronicles, Proverbs, Job, and Daniel, ending with the Books of Maccabees. While not organized as a chronological composition, similar to the other two divisions, some of the Writings do help us to place leading figures in their proper historical context. To begin with, the Books of I and II Chronicles (a parallel history of the Books of Kings) as well as the Books of Ezra and Nehemiah take us into the Persian era (537–332 B.C.E.). The Books of Maccabees then continue the story into the Greek period under the Ptolemies and Seleucids. Though not included in the Jewish canon, the Maccabees do appear in a Greek translation known as the *Septuagint*, which in turn formed the basis for the Christian Old Testament; therefore, Maccabees are included in most Christian Bibles. This chapter ends with the restoration of the Jewish kingdom under the Hasmonean dynasty, followed by a comprehensive alphabetical directory of characters in this part of the Bible.

Chapter 4: The Four Gospels

Turning now to the New Testament, this chapter describes the leading individuals in the Gospel stories, from Jesus' birth through his ministry, Passion, and Resurrection, based on the works of Matthew, Mark, Luke, and

John. The first three books are often referred to as the Synoptic Gospels (from the Greek word *synoptikos*, meaning "seen together") given their obvious similarities, in contrast to the Gospel of John. Beginning with the reign of King Herod the Great and ending with the Disbelieving Thomas, this chronological narrative weaves together material found in all four Gospels, while placing the events in the context of historical events and archaeological findings. Other sources, such as the Gnostic Gospels and the Jewish Mishnah, provide additional insights into the stories. This biographical narrative is then followed by an alphabetical directory of the characters in the Gospels.

CHAPTER 5: FROM ACTS OF THE APOSTLES TO REVELATION

The last chapter traces the growth of Early Christianity as described in the other books of the New Testament, including Acts of the Apostles; the Epistles written by Paul and other Church leaders; and the Book of Revelation. Here we will encounter leading characters such as James, Paul, and Barnabas, and also emperors such as Claudius and Nero; kings such as Herod Agrippa I and II; and Roman procurators including Antonius Felix and Porcius Festus.

This chapter is followed by an Epilogue on the Christian persecutions during the Roman Era, which culminated in the formal acceptance of Christianity as a "tolerated" religion by Constantine the Great in 313 C.E. The narrative is followed by an alphabetical directory of characters in this part of the New Testament.

In trying to follow the canonical division of Hebrew Scripture, we have made some exceptions for purely narrative reasons. For example, the prophets Haggai and Zechariah belong to the section of the Prophets *(Nevi'im)* treated in Chapter 2, but since their work takes place during the post-exilic Restoration in Judah, their story is featured in Chapter 3. Similarly, the Book of Ruth is part of the Writings *(Ketuvim),* but chronologically, her story belongs in the treatment of Chapter 2.

A continuous time line runs on the bottom of the page throughout the narrative sections of the book, from the earliest signs of civilization to the emancipation of Christianity by Constantine the Great—a span of some 10,000 years. The markers in this time line refer to the emergence of civilizations, the span of royal dynasties, or the construction of cities or key monuments as attested by archaeology and historical research. As far as the dating of biblical events is concerned, it has proved to be very difficult to identify actual dates for biblical events before the reign of King David and Solomon; even then, much of the biblical chronology is subject to debate. For consistency's sake, however, we have used the principal time line markers of biblical figures and events as established by previous books published by the National Geographic Society, including *The Biblical World* (2007). This time line will therefore begin to offer specific dates for biblical figures with the reigns of Israel's kings, starting with King Saul.

This book is written for a general audience that is interested not only in the biblical context of these stories but also in their attestation by history, archaeology, and art. Both the main text and the *Who's Who* dictionary segments are richly illustrated with more

This red granite figure of Pharaoh Sobekemsaf I is one of the few royal statues from the 17th Dynasty (1580–1550 B.C.E.). The pharaoh reigned in Thebes during the Hyksos period.

than 432 color reproductions of paintings and artifacts from the Early Stone Age through the 19th century. We have taken great care to select the most beautiful depictions of biblical scenes and figures, featuring not only works by celebrated artists such as Michelangelo, Raphael, Rembrandt, Titian, and Leonardo da Vinci but also more recent works by artists such as Lawrence Alma-Tadema, Frederic Leighton, and James Tissot.

The stories of the Bible are inseparable from their unique cultural and geographical setting. Throughout this book, the narrative will take us to the major civilizations of the ancient world: Egypt, Assyria, Babylonia, Persia, the empire of Alexander the Great, and the world of Imperial Rome. The book therefore includes detailed, authoritative maps prepared by the cartographic staff of the National Geographic Society. Large maps are further illustrated with break-out images of key locations.

At the same time, sidebars in the main text shed light on everyday life in biblical times. These sidebars cover such topics as farming, marriage, and motherhood, kings and queens, language and Jewish customs, as well as recent discoveries in the Holy Land.

Who's Who in the Bible is deliberately written from a nondenominational perspective. It does not conform to any particular theological orientation, but rather treats the texts as historical documents, so as to appeal to the broadest possible readership. The same perspective applies to the question of whether the people in the Bible were, without exception, historical characters or whether some names and stories are rooted in local myth or biblical legend. No scholar will ever question the Bible's moral and religious significance, but many authors have challenged the Bible as a reliable source of historical information. In recent decades, specifically, some biblical archaeologists have expressed doubt about the Bible's fundamental historicity, particularly with regard to the Late Bronze and Early Iron Age periods. *Who's Who in the Bible* takes no position in this debate. It treats every biblical character as a specific individual, based on the information provided by the Bible as well as ancillary sources. These sources range from ancient tablets that record the deeds of Egyptian, Assyrian, or Persian rulers to the works of the first-century Jewish historian Josephus and other Roman documents.

As far as the language of the Bible is concerned, the Hebrew Scriptures have come down to us in Hebrew (with certain segments in Aramaic), or in the case of the Septuagint, in a translation in Greek. The New Testament is also written in Greek, using a common patois known as *koinè*. In this book, all English translations have been taken from the 1989 New Revised Standard Version translation (NRSV) of the Old and New Testament.

As is now common practice, this *Who's Who* uses the nondenominational temporal indicators of B.C.E. (Before the Common Era) instead of the traditional B.C. (Before Christ), and likewise C.E. (Common Era) rather than A.D. (*Anno Domini*, or Year of the Lord) to identify dates in history. This book will also follow the practice of many New Testament scholars who, for lack of a better word, refer to the territories of Judea, Samaria, and Galilee—the former kingdom of Herod the Great—as Roman "Palestine," even though, strictly speaking, these lands were not called as such until after the suppression of the Second Jewish Revolt in 135 C.E.

I sincerely hope that *Who's Who in the Bible* will serve readers throughout the English-speaking world as a comprehensive guide to the people of the Bible, while also providing an introduction to the social, cultural, and historical framework of the life and times in which they lived. ❧

— Jean-Pierre Isbouts
Santa Barbara, California

The majestic frescoes of the Vatican's Sistine Chapel ceiling were executed by Michelangelo Buonarroti (1475–1564) between 1508 and 1512.

ABOUT THIS BOOK

National Geographic Who's Who in the Bible is conceived as a modern guide to the people of the Bible, using both a chronological narrative as well as a set of five alphabetical directories, organized by chapter. This design facilitates both reading for pleasure as well as its use as a reference by biblical students, researchers, and clergy. The book is divided in five chapters, inspired by the organization of Hebrew Scripture (which Christians call the Old Testament) according to the Jewish canon, as well as the composition of books in the New Testament. Each chapter provides a chronological narrative, highlighting the biographies of lead characters in the story.

Each chapter ends with a comprehensive dictionary of the people featured in this part of the Bible. Depending on the significance of the individual in the story, these entries range from brief descriptions to article-length biographies. Every entry also includes relevant references to the biblical source.

Throughout the Bible, many characters share a name—one reason this book is organized in five different chapters, so as to position each individual in the context of the proper story. When a name is shared, the entries are numbered in order of their appearance in the Bible.

The narrative text and dictionary entries of each chapter are illustrated with more than 400 photographs of paintings, artifacts, and archaeological sites from the Near East. Each illustration is captioned to explain its significance. To sustain the chronological thread of the narrative, a time line runs on the bottom of the page. This time line offers a global overview of events, drawing from historical, cultural, and political developments in the world of Antiquity.

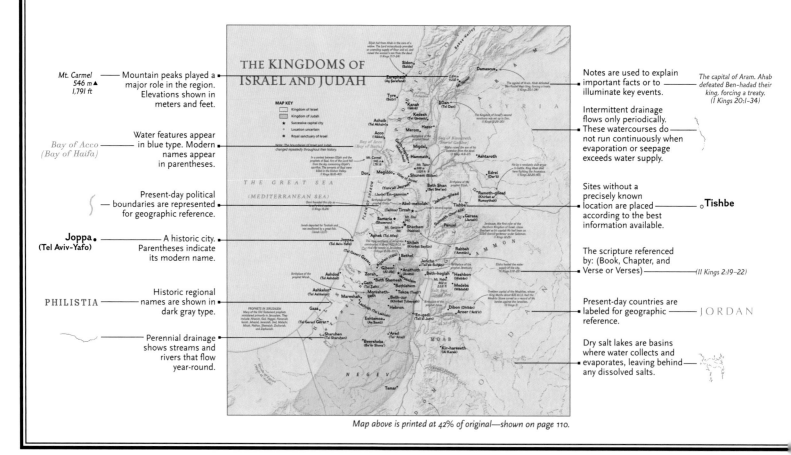

Map above is printed at 42% of original—shown on page 110.

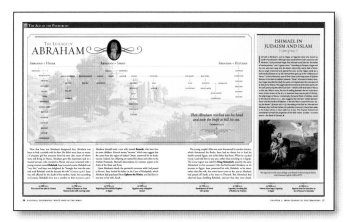

CHAPTER OPENERS: Each chapter opens with a brief introduction that describes the origin of the books and stories described in this chapter. This is followed by a biographical narrative featuring the key characters in this part of the Bible. A time line at the bottom of the page highlights the most important events of the era, and pull quotes define key themes in the Bible or other ancient texts.

SIDEBARS/FAMILY TREES: Throughout each chapter, special sidebars describe what life was like for peoples of the Bible, from the Stone Age through the Roman period. These sidebars focus on farming, trade, food, childbirth, burial customs, and other fascinating aspects of daily life in ancient lands. In addition, family trees trace the family relationships of key figures, such as the children of Jacob, or the royal dynasty of King Herod the Great.

MONTAGES: Every chapter features a montage of representative objects, figures, and art from a biblical period, ranging from the Bronze Age to the Christian era. These beautiful objects not only convey the unique creative skill set of the period but also give us a glimpse of its fashion, practices, and aesthetic sensibilities.

WHO'S WHO DICTIONARY: The second part of each chapter consists of a comprehensive alphabetical dictionary of men and women in this segment of the Bible. These entries range from brief descriptions to more lengthy biographies. Each entry starts with the meaning of the name, if it is known, and includes references to the actual Bible text.

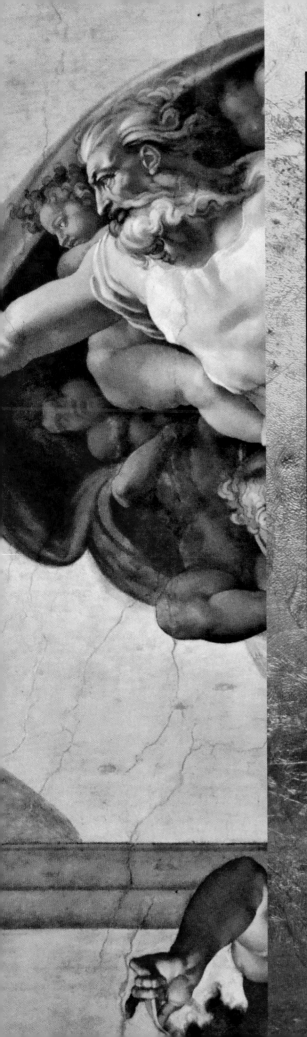

FROM GENESIS TO DEUTERONOMY

Then God said, "Let there be light";
and there was light.
And God saw that the light was good;
and God separated the light
from the darkness.
God called the light Day,
and the darkness he called Night.
And there was evening and
there was morning,
the first day.

GENESIS 1:3-5

"The Creation of Adam" by Italian artist Michelangelo Buonarroti
(1475–1564) was probably completed around 1512.

THE CREATION TO THE EXODUS

Who Wrote the Torah?

THE COLLECTION KNOWN AS THE Torah or "Law" forms the first five books of Hebrew Scripture—the "Old Testament" in Christian parlance. Also known as the "five scrolls of Moses" (or *Pentateuch*), it includes the stories of Genesis, Exodus, Leviticus, Numbers, and Deuteronomy—from the creation of the Earth to the dramatic rescue of the Hebrews out of Egypt and the arrival of the Hebrews to the edge of the Promised Land.

Paramount in the collection of the Torah is the story of Genesis. As the Bible's first book—known as *Beresh't* in Judaism (meaning "in the beginning," the book's first three words)—it sets forth some of the key themes of the Bible. These include the role of God as creator of the universe and the principal force of moral justice, and the promise of a covenant between God and his people, so they may dwell in peace and prosper.

At first, the scope of the book is universal, encompassing the primeval history of Earth and all its living creatures. Soon, however, the narrative narrows down to a series of patriarchal stories, beginning with Noah and culminating in the journeys of Abraham, Isaac, and Jacob, which take the story into Egypt. This sets up the Book of Exodus for its dramatic climax: God's deliverance of his chosen people from the clutches of Pharaoh.

The remainder of the Torah, including the Books of Leviticus, Numbers, and Deuteronomy, is concerned with the legal and ritual precepts of Judaism. It is this "Law," which includes case law and regulations for purity, worship, and sacrifice, that would sustain Hebrew identity through its many trials to come.

Tradition holds that Moses wrote the Law, based on revelations from God. Most scholars, however, agree that the stories of the Bible probably emerged over many centuries. According to one theory, known as the Documentary hypothesis, the Pentateuch was woven together by skilled redactors from four separate sources.

Dutch artist Rembrandt van Rijn (1606–1669) painted this portrait of Moses holding the Ten Commandments around 1659.

The oldest strain is named "J" or *Yahwist,* because it refers to God with the four-letter name (or *tetragrammaton* in Greek) of YHWH, possibly pronounced *Yahweh* (or *Jahweh* in German). This tradition is primarily concerned with the history of Judah, the Southern Kingdom, after the split of Solomon's realm, and possibly dates to the ninth or eighth century B.C.E.

A second major strain is known as "E" or *Elohist,* because this source refers to God as *El* or its plural, *Elohim.* E probably originated in the Northern Kingdom, and therefore represents the perspective of the North.

The third source, known as "D," is associated with the Book of Deuteronomy and may be the document discovered by the priest Hilkiah in the archives of the Temple around 622 B.C.E. (II Kings 22:8). Deuteronomy is preoccupied with worship at the Temple in Jerusalem, the capital of the United Monarchy and then of the Southern Kingdom, centered in the tribal territory of Judah. It is therefore likely that this tradition originated in Judah.

In addition, many sections in the Pentateuch deal with issues of purity, rites of sacrifice, and other cultic concerns. This source has been identified as "P" for "priestly source," and was arguably composed by a priestly group during or after the Babylonian exile, which began with the destruction of the Jerusalem Temple in 587 and ended in 539 B.C.E. The seamless integration of these four sources is a testament to the skill of the redactors who composed the Pentateuch, believed to have taken place during and after the reign of King Josiah (640–609 B.C.E.).

As the overture to this story, Genesis opens with the origins of mankind. Once all of creation was in place, God decided to make man and woman, so that they could tend to Earth's great beauty, "and watch over it" (Genesis 2:15). The first couple was called **Adam** and **Eve**.

LEADING FIGURES IN THE BOOKS OF
GENESIS THROUGH DEUTERONOMY

This panel of the "Expulsion from Paradise" shows Adam and Eve being evicted from Paradise. It was painted by Italian artist Giovanni di Paolo (1403–1482) around 1435.

ADAM

Adam was created when God "formed man of the dust of the ground, and breathed into his nostrils the breath of life; and man became a living soul" (GENESIS 2:7). Thus, Adam was created from soil, as is reflected in his name; while Adam means "man," the root *adama* in Hebrew means "earth."

The Lord then planted a garden in Eden, with "every tree that is pleasant for the sight and good for food," and in this garden "he put the man whom he had formed" so that Adam could dwell there and find nourishment (GENESIS 2:8-9). The meaning of the word *Eden* is uncertain, although a Babylonian cuneiform tablet uses "Eden" as a term for "uncultivated plain"; other scholars see the Aramaic word for "well-watered" as its source. Many centuries later during the exile, when the Genesis tradition came under Persian influence, the Garden of Eden acquired a new name: *Paradise.* The term is rooted in the Old Persian word *pardis,* which means "walled (or protected) enclosure," usually referring to parklike estates maintained for the king's comfort.

The Garden of Eden was green, lush, and filled with water, fed by a river of four branches: the Pishon, the Gihon, the Tigris, and the Euphrates (GENESIS 2:10-14). The rivers Tigris and Euphrates still exist today, but the location of the first two branches remains a mystery. Several scholars have tried to place Eden in northern Arabia or somewhere along the African coast; the land of Cush, through which the Gihon ran, is often associated with Ethiopia.

The Garden of Eden had many trees, and Adam was encouraged to eat from every branch, except the so-called "tree of knowledge of good and evil. "In the day that you eat of it," God warned, "you shall surely die" (GENESIS 2:17). As long as Adam was content to live in a state of perpetual innocence, all of his physical needs would be met.

Adam was soon given an important task. The world was teeming with animals, but none had been named yet. It fell on Adam to choose an appropriate name for every species that God presented to him (GENESIS 2:20). Giving something or someone a name in ancient cultures implied *acceptance.* When Abraham "names" **Ishmael**, the child of his concubine **Hagar**, he implicitly accepts Ishmael as his son. Hence, by naming the elements of Creation, Adam welcomed and embraced all of the living creatures and gave them their place in nature.

But Adam was lonely. He could see that even the lowliest species numbered both males and females, and he keenly felt the need for

ca 9500 B.C.E.	ca 9000 B.C.E.	ca 8300 B.C.E.	ca 8000 B.C.E.
Prehistoric villages in Jericho and rest of Canaan	Goats and sheep are domesticated in ancient Persia	Beginning of the Neolithic (New Stone Age)	First evidence of cultivated wheat in the Levant

a companion himself. God recognized this, and caused Adam to fall into a deep sleep. He then took one of Adam's ribs from him, which he fashioned into a woman, who was called Eve (GENESIS 2:21-22). In Genesis, the creation of Adam and Eve is told in two distinct stories, which the redactors of the Torah skillfully wove into one narrative.

EVE

In Western art, Eve is usually depicted as a beautiful young woman. And, indeed, Adam was delighted with his new mate. They were both naked, but their innocence prevented them from experiencing shame, or knowing good and evil.

Soon, however, a serpent came slithering onto the scene. He approached Eve and asked her, "Did God say, 'You shall not eat from any tree in the garden?'" (GENESIS 3:1). No, Eve told the serpent, "we may freely eat of the fruit of the trees in the garden, but of the fruit of the tree which is in the garden's midst, God told us we cannot eat of it, nor even touch it, lest you die." The serpent then slyly revealed *why* God didn't want Adam and Eve to partake from

A Babylonian planisphere—found at Nineveh, Assyria, and inscribed with cuneiform text—shows a schematic representation of constellations in eight separate segments.

the tree: "for God knows that on the day you eat thereof, your eyes shall be opened, and you shall be as gods, knowing good and evil" (GENESIS 3:3-5).

The meaning of this story may be that by pursuing knowledge and science, man becomes conscious of himself and his role in the universe, but loses his innocence in the process. Immortality, on the other hand, offers life without death, but a life devoid of self-awareness and free will.

Eve succumbed to the serpent's temptation. She ate from the tree, and made sure that Adam did as well. "And then," says Genesis, "the eyes of both of them were opened, and they knew that they were naked" (GENESIS 3:7). To cover their shame, they sewed fig leaves together as garments.

God confronted Adam over what he had done. Adam tried to shift the blame to his young wife, and by extension to God: "This woman whom you gave me," he said, "she gave it to me" (GENESIS 3:12). God thereupon questioned Eve, who sought to pass the blame to the serpent. For this transgression, they were evicted from Paradise. God told Eve, "I will greatly multiply your sorrow and your conception; in pain you shall bring forth children." And to Adam

THE GOD OF GENESIS

The idea that Genesis was composed from multiple narratives is evident in its conception of God. One tradition, believed to be the book's oldest, refers to God as YHWH, the so-called "tetragrammaton" that was probably pronounced as *Yahweh*, a form that will return in the Book of Exodus. Pious Jews often paraphrase the name as *Adonai*, given that God's name may not be spoken out loud; in English, this is usually translated as "the Lord." The worship of YHWH was closely associated with the Southern Kingdom of Judah and would ultimately become the dominant form in Judaism. It is YHWH who insists on being recognized as the only God:

Anonymous artists made this mosaic of God creating the firmament of heavens in the narthex of the Basilica di San Marco in Venice around 1200.

"I am the Lord [YHWH], that is my name," God tells Israel in Isaiah; "my glory I give to no other, nor my praise to idols" (Isaiah 42:8). Other Genesis strands use the word *El* or *Elohim* (the plural of "El") to denote God, a tradition that may have originated in Canaan. According to tablets from Ugarit, a major cult center of Syria-Canaan, a deity named *El* was revered as the supreme head of all gods, known collectively as *Elohim*. Some scholars have suggested that *El* of Genesis was worshipped as the principal god, but without denying the existence of other gods, including Canaanite deities associated with fertility and the harvest. ■

A detail from the San Marco mosaics in Venice depicts the "living creatures" in the water and "birds above the earth" from Genesis 1:20.

THE CREATION STORY

The Creation narrative, filled with evocative descriptions of primordial earth, ranks as one of the most beautiful stories in the Book of Genesis. Many of these motifs may have been borrowed from Mesopotamian and Babylonian archetypes, perhaps because these themes were already familiar to the earliest audience of Genesis. For example, the idea of heaven and earth emerging out of a void by divine command, followed by the separation of day and night and the creation of living things—all in a span of seven days—is also found in the Babylonian creation epic, perhaps as old as the 18th century B.C.E. The tree as a symbol of intelligent life returns in Assyrian mythology, while the devious role of the serpent is reminiscent of the *Epic of Gilgamesh*, where a snake steals a plant that confers immortality. The Genesis Creation story also has close parallels in the Qur'an, the holy book of Islam, which is based on revelations to the Prophet Muhammad in the seventh century C.E. "[God] created the heavens and the earth in six periods of time, and He is firm in power," according to sura, or chapter, 7 (QUR'AN 7:54). The Jewish, Christian, and Muslim traditions, however, diverge about the interpretation of "the seventh day," which God ordained as a day of rest. For the Jewish tradition, the Sabbath runs from Friday sundown to Saturday sundown. For Christians, it is Sunday. For Muslims, however, the holy day of prayer (*Jumu'ah*) is Friday, based on the tradition that Adam was created on Friday. ■

God said, "cursed is the ground for your sake; in toil you shall eat of it all the days of your life." Indeed, "In the sweat of your face you shall eat bread, till you return to the ground; for out of it you were taken: dust you are, and to dust you shall return" (GENESIS 3:16-19).

The Eden story underscores the fact that human existence is merely an "exile" from a primordial state of divine perfection. Indeed, the "fall of man," the expulsion from the Garden, marks the loss of innocence that was only redeemed by God's later covenant with Abraham and Moses.

Devoid of their earlier childlike innocence, Adam and Eve became aware of their nakedness—and sexual attraction. They became man and wife. In due course, Eve gave birth to her first son.

CAIN

Eve named her firstborn **Cain**. This is one of the wordplays of which Genesis is so fond, for *qayin* means "that which has been acquired or produced." Indeed, upon giving birth, Eve said, "I have produced a man with the help of the Lord" (GENESIS 4:1). As soon as Cain grew up, he followed in the footsteps of his father and became a farmer. Traces of the oldest crops found in Israel suggest that the early Israelites cultivated olives, palm dates, figs, and grapes, as well as pomegranates, nuts, and some cereals. Olives were prized as food but also as the source of olive oil, which was used for cooking, as fuel for lamps, or as a condiment for bread. Grapes were used to make wine, while dates and figs were enjoyed as confectionaries, or processed into honey.

Cain's brother **Abel**, on the other hand, grew up to become a shepherd. Tending sheep or goats in large herds emerged as the other main form of domestication. Such pastoralism forced the shepherd and his family into a nomadic lifestyle, because no single field or well could sustain a large herd for very long. As such, the occupations of Cain and his brother place the story squarely amid the growing tension between farmers and shepherds, between "settled" tribes and nomads, who were at odds in the dry climate of the Levant.

ABEL

After Cain, Eve "bore his brother Abel," says Genesis, "a keeper of sheep." (GENESIS 4:2) The name "Abel" means "emptiness," a reflection of Abel's many days roaming aimlessly with his flock through great stretches of empty, uncultivated land. And then "in the course of time," says Genesis, the two brothers presented their offerings to God. Abel's offering was of the "firstlings of his flock, their fat portions," while Cain's was "of the fruit of the ground" (GENESIS 4:3-4). This is the first time the Bible makes reference to

ca 7000 B.C.E.	ca 6700 B.C.E.	ca 6600 B.C.E.	ca 6500 B.C.E.
Production of pottery from clay begins	Durum wheat (pasta) is grown in Anatolia (Turkey)	Woven mats are made in Ammon, today's Jordan	Domesticated cattle is kept in Anatolia (Turkey)

animal sacrifice, which in later centuries would develop into the Israelite sacrificial cult, centered on the Temple in Jerusalem. Quite possibly, it reflects some of the earliest traditions of sacrifice, common in Sumer as well as in Syria-Canaan, to appease the gods and ensure a fertile harvest.

But all was not well. The Lord accepted Abel's animal offering, but Cain's fruit of the earth was not to his satisfaction (GENESIS 4:3-5). The Bible does not offer an explanation for God's favoritism; it may simply reflect the intense rivalry between farmer settlements and nomads over natural resources, such as wells and grassy fields.

Cain was incensed over the incident. God warned him that "sin is lurking at the door; its desire is for you, but you must master it" (GENESIS 4:7). But Cain did not heed God's counsel. He lured his brother Abel to a field and killed him. This terrible event takes place without any preamble or argument; it is, quite simply, the first instance of homicide in the Bible. God then questioned Cain on the whereabouts of his brother, which prompted the famous reply, "I do not know; am I my brother's keeper?" (GENESIS 4:9).

To punish Cain, God cursed him from the earth, and cast him from the land where his family lived. He became a fugitive, stripped of his tribal protection. Cain pleaded with God, saying that "my punishment is greater than I can bear!" Bereft of his clan's sanctuary, "anyone who meets me may kill me!" (GENESIS 4:14). This verse suggests that many other people already inhabited the earth, and that therefore this episode took place many generations after the time of Adam and Eve. Here, too, we may see different traditions at work.

God decided that one murder is enough, and that the killing of Abel should not lead to a vicious cycle of familial revenge. Though Cain was condemned to roam the world as an outlaw, he would not be harmed. "Whoever slays Cain," said the Lord, "vengeance shall be taken on him sevenfold." And to

underscore the fact, "God put a mark on Cain, so that no one who came upon him would kill him" (GENESIS 4:15).

Cain eventually settled in a land east of Eden named Nod, quite literally "the land of naught," a place of aimless wandering. There, he married a woman who would bear him a son named **Enoch**. Cain then "built a city, and named it Enoch after his son Enoch" (GENESIS 4:17).

Enoch is the first reference in Genesis to "a city," which suggests that at this time, farmer settlements had grown to encompass large walled communities. Genesis tells us that among those who descended from Cain was a man named **Jabal**, "the ancestor of those who live in tents and have livestock," meaning nomadic tribes. His brother was named **Jubal**; "he was the ancestor of all those who play the lyre and pipe" (GENESIS 4:20-21). A lyre and flute were among the objects that British archaeologist Sir Leonard Woolley found in 1922 in a tomb near Tell al-Muqayyar, north of Basra in today's Iraq.

SETH

Genesis tells us that Adam and Eve had other children as well. After Abel's death and Cain's flight to Nod, Eve gave birth to a son named **Seth**, "when Adam had lived one hundred and thirty years" (GENESIS 5:3). Some sources believe Seth means "substitute," whereas others see the root of the word "founder." Seth then became the father of **Enosh** and a long line of descendants; many of these names are similar to the genealogy ascribed by Genesis to Cain's son Enoch (see The Lineage of Adam, p. 24). One of these descendants was a man named **Noah**, son of **Lamech**.

A sixth-century Byzantine mosaic from the Basilica of San Vitale in Ravenna, Italy, depicts Abel bringing his offering of a "firstling of his flock" to God.

At this point in the history of mankind, says Genesis, "people began to multiply, and daughters were born to them." In one of the more mysterious passages of

ca 6400 B.C.E.
Earliest known metallurgy in the Near East

ca 6300 B.C.E.
Cultivation of corn (maize), beans and peppers begins in Mexico

ca 6100 B.C.E.
Production of domesticated bread wheat grows in Asia

ca 6000 B.C.E.
Widespread rice cultivation in Thailand

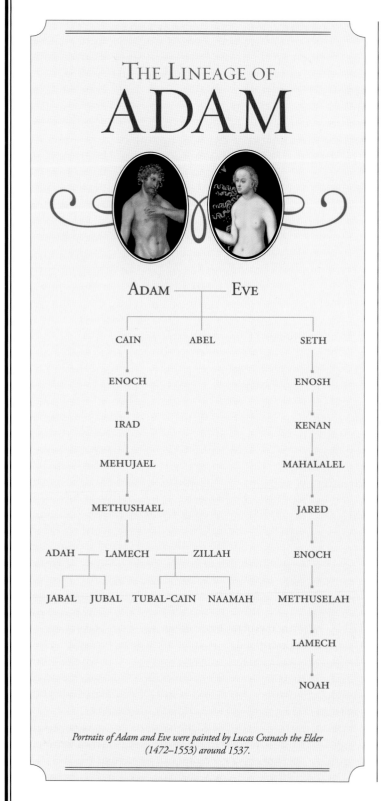

THE LINEAGE OF
ADAM

ADAM ——— EVE

CAIN   ABEL   SETH

ENOCH   ENOSH

IRAD   KENAN

MEHUJAEL   MAHALALEL

METHUSHAEL   JARED

ADAH —— LAMECH —— ZILLAH   ENOCH

JABAL JUBAL TUBAL-CAIN NAAMAH   METHUSELAH

LAMECH

NOAH

*Portraits of Adam and Eve were painted by Lucas Cranach the Elder
(1472–1553) around 1537.*

the Bible, Genesis refers to the appearance of "sons of God" who "saw that [the daughters] were fair, and they took wives for themselves" (GENESIS 6:2). What exactly is meant with "sons of God" is not clear. One interpretation holds that the verse, quite possibly under the influence of Mesopotamian myths, refers to demigods who cohabited with mortal women. Their offspring, says Genesis, were known as **Nephilim**, and as such they would return in the Book of Numbers, as giants living in Canaan (NUMBERS 13:33). One of the Dead Sea Scrolls (4Q417), however, refers to the Nephilim as children of Seth, whom God had condemned. This may support the view that "sons of God" refers to fallen angels who crossed the great divide between heaven and earth; "Nephilim" may be rooted in the Hebrew verb "to fall." Indeed, the phrase is also used in the Book of Job, where it clearly refers to angels (JOB 1:6; 2:1).

Despite—or perhaps because of—the presence of these Nephilim, who were "warriors of renown," God soon discovered that "the wickedness of humankind was great in the earth." He decided to destroy his creation, "people together with animals . . . for I am sorry that I have made them" (GENESIS 6:5-7). Only one man found favor in the eyes of God. His name was Noah.

NOAH

The meaning of the name "Noah" is not entirely clear. In the Jewish tradition, "Noah" is believed to derive from *niham,* meaning "he gave comfort to his people," whereas in the Islamic tradition, *Nuh* (based on the verb *naha*) is believed to mean "he wailed for his people."

God chose Noah and his family as the only humans to be saved from the coming cataclysm. The instrument of their rescue was a boat, a very large ship made of gopher wood, covered in pitch. God provided detailed specifications of how this ark should be built: "the length of the ark three hundred cubits, its width fifty cubits, and its height thirty cubits. Make a roof for the ark, and finish it to a cubit above . . . And of every living thing, of all flesh, you shall bring two of every kind" (GENESIS 6:15,19).

*Two and two, male and female, went
into the ark with Noah, as God had
commanded Noah.*

GENESIS 7:9

ca 5700 B.C.E.	ca 5200 B.C.E.	ca 5100 B.C.E.	ca 5000 B.C.E.
Trade in obsidian emerges in Near East	**Beginning of Ubaid culture in Mesopotamia**	**First appearance of metal tools**	**First evidence of sailing ships in Mesopotamia**

Did such large ships exist? Wall paintings and later tomb models suggest that large cargo ships did ply the waters of the Nile as early as the Old Kingdom in Egypt (ca 2500 B.C.E.). It is interesting to note, however, that Genesis makes no provision for either a rudder or a sail, which some scholars believe may indicate that the ark was not meant to be navigated, but merely carried by the waters under the protective hands of God.

For 40 days and nights, Genesis continues, God sent down rain, "and all the fountains of the great deep burst forth, and the

Irish painter Daniel Maclise (1806–1870) created this impression of "Noah's Sacrifice" between 1847 and 1853.

windows of the heavens were opened" (GENESIS 7:11-12), a description that some scholars interpret as the reversal of the original creation sequence, in which the waters were separated. Noah and his wife, as well as their three sons with their wives, were slowly carried up in the ark, together with "every wild animal of every kind."

The waters then swelled so high that even the mountains were covered. Only after 150 days did God cause a mighty wind to blow over the earth, and the waters subsided. Eventually, the ark came to rest "on the mountains of Ararat" (GENESIS 8:4). "Harê Ararat,"

ca 5000 B.C.E.	ca 4500 B.C.E.	ca 4300 B.C.E.	ca 4236 B.C.E.
Yangshao culture in China produced painted pottery	Beginning of the Chalcolithic (Copper Stone Age)	Presence of farming villages in Egypt	First date in the Egyptian calendar

STORIES OF THE FLOOD

Stories of great floods—and of survivors who were rescued by gods—abound in the old Babylonian literature. In the 18th century B.C.E. "Atrahasis Epic," man was molded from clay by a goddess named Mami. But the humans became too noisy, so the earth god Enlil decided to destroy mankind with a great flood. One deity, the water god Enki, took pity on a man named Atrahasis and told him to build a boat. He was to fill it with all of his possessions, including animals and birds. Then, "after for seven days (and) seven nights the flood had swept over the land," the tablet says, "Utu came forth . . . (and) Ziusudra opened a window of the huge boat."

In another Babylonian account known as the *Epic of Gilgamesh*, Gilgamesh's ancestor Utnapishtim also faced the threat of a flood. "The world teemed," Utnapishtim said, "the people multiplied, the world bellowed like a bull." Fortunately, the god Ea had vowed to protect him. Utnapishtim was given detailed specifications about a boat he was supposed to build, similar to those provided to Noah: "These are the measurements of the barque as you shall build her . . . Let her beam equal her length, let her deck be roofed like the vault that covers the abyss; then take up into the boat the seed of all living creatures." Scientists believe that these flood stories could be linked to the unpredictable flooding of the Euphrates and the Tigris, swollen by runoff from snow and rainfall in the northeastern mountains of Turkey. Numerous other suggestions have also been put forward, including a cataclysmic breaching of the Black Sea about 7,500 years ago. ■

A Babylonian tablet from ca 1635 B.C.E. relates part of the Atrahasis epic, which includes accounts of a creation and a flood.

the plural of "mountains of Ararat," has often been mistaken for the singular "Mount Ararat," the name given to the tallest mountain on the border of Turkey and Armenia. Mount Ararat is in fact a volcano, which rises to an elevation of some 17,000 feet. The place is a favorite destination for many Christian tour groups, but the exact location of the mountain described in Genesis is uncertain. The Book of Jubilees, one of the Dead Sea Scrolls, states that the ark came to rest on a different peak in the Ararat mountain range, called Lubar.

Noah opened the window of the ark and sent out a raven, which flew "to and fro." He then sent out three doves in succession. The first could not find a resting place and returned to the ark. The second one flew back with an olive leaf in its beak, and the third never returned. Noah then decided it was safe to set foot on earth (GENESIS 8:6-12).

In gratitude for their deliverance, Noah built an altar and sacrificed a specimen "of every clean animal and of every clean bird" as burnt offerings. God then pledged to never again destroy mankind. He entered into a covenant with Noah and his successors, reiterating his original blessing to Adam while anticipating the future covenant with Moses on Mount Sinai. "Be fruitful and multiply, and fill

A gypsum figure of a woman in prayer dates from around 2400 B.C.E.

the earth," God said, and as a visible sign of his covenant that "the waters shall never again become a flood to destroy all flesh," he placed a rainbow in the clouds (GENESIS 9:15-16).

NIMROD

According to the Genesis story, the sons of Noah—**Shem, Ham**, and **Japheth**—then became the progenitors of the people of the earth, as described in a lengthy Genesis genealogy known as "The Table of Nations." The children of Japheth, for example, are described as the inhabitants of Greece and Asia Minor, whereas the descendants of Ham would populate North Africa, Canaan, and Mesopotamia. Shem, meanwhile, became "the father of all the children of Eber," which some authors have linked to the Akkadian/Egyptian name *apiru* or *habiru,* meaning "sand dweller" or "migrant," and possibly the root of the word "Hebrew" (GENESIS 10:21). Indeed, Shem's branch would ultimately produce **Terah**, the father of Abraham, and through his line, the 12 tribes of Israel.

Another notable name in the Noah genealogy is that of **Nimrod**, son of **Cush** and great-grandson of Noah. Genesis presents Nimrod as a powerful man, "the first on earth to become a mighty warrior . . . a

ca 4100 B.C.E.	ca 4000 B.C.E.	ca 4000 B.C.E.	ca 3760 B.C.E.
Egyptians smelt copper ore mined from Sinai	First use of plow pulled by a draft animal	First evidence of farmer villages in Britain	Creation of the world according to the traditional Jewish calendar

> *When the bow is in the clouds, I will see it and remember the everlasting covenant between God and every living creature of all flesh that is on the earth.*
>
> Genesis 9:16

mighty hunter before the Lord," though his actual warlike exploits are not described (Genesis 10:8-9). Some authors have tried to identify him as a deity in Mesopotamian mythology, such as the chief god Marduk (who created the earth in seven days), or the Sumerian King Gilgamesh.

Nimrod then founded a kingdom in the land of Shinar; the prophet **Micah** would later associate this with the empire of Assyria (Micah 5:6). Indeed, Genesis implies that Nimrod went on to establish the cities of Babel, Erech, and Accad in this land. Erech is usually identified as the Sumerian city of Uruk, whereas Accad is associated with a city known as Agade, later called Akkad, the capital of the Akkadian Empire founded by King Sargon (2334–2279 B.C.E.). The remains of these prehistoric settlements have been excavated in today's Iraq.

It is in Babel that Genesis sets the next part of the story. Babel is probably the great city of Babylon, reportedly founded in the 1860s B.C.E. by the Amorites, a group of people who originally hailed from Syria-Canaan.

This was a time, says Genesis, when "the whole earth had one language and the same words," and the people of Babel developed the technology of making bricks from baked clay (Genesis 11:1). What to do with this invention? Like many other nations in human history, both ancient and modern, they strove to reach for the skies. "Come," they said, "let us build ourselves a city, and a tower whose top may reach unto heaven; and let us make a name for ourselves" (Genesis 11:4).

This did not remain hidden from God for long. "The Lord came down to see the city," says Genesis, "and the tower which the children of men had built." Rather than destroying this monstrous structure, God decided to "confuse their language there, so that they will not understand each other's speech" (Genesis 11:5,7). Confused, unable to communicate, the proud builders left the

city and were scattered abroad. For the Bible, this is the meaning of the name "Babel"—using one of the many double entendres in the Genesis tradition—because the Akkadian word *bab-ili* refers to "gate of the gods," while *balal* in Hebrew means "sowing confusion," like the English "babble."

TERAH

Nine generations after Noah, Genesis continues, there lived a man named Terah, who at the age of 70 became the father of three sons. He named them **Abram** (later renamed **Abraham** by God), **Nahor**, and **Haran** (Genesis 11:26). Haran died before his father, but Abraham and Nahor survived, and they both took wives; Abraham married Sarai (or **Sarah** as she would be called later) while Nahor married **Milcah**.

Genesis places Terah's family in "Ur of the Chaldeans." Though the identification is not without controversy, most scholars accept that the Bible is referring to Ur of ancient Sumer, located in today's Iraq. As early as the beginning of the fourth millennium B.C.E., this was the region where farmer settlements began to coalesce into true urban centers, producing cities such as Uruk, Lagash, Kish, Nippur, and Ur. The reason was the fertility of the great alluvial plain, watered by the Euphrates and Tigris Rivers through an elaborate irrigation network.

But Terah did not stay in Ur. He took his family, including his sons and their wives, as well as Haran's son **Lot**, and traveled northeast, to the city of Haran in northern Mesopotamia, in what is today's southern Turkey (Genesis 11:31). Genesis doesn't tell us the reason for this move, but perhaps it is related to the fall of Ur's Third Dynasty, near the end of the second millennium B.C.E., as a result of foreign invasions. The most powerful of these invaders were the Amorites, who

SATAN AND EVIL

Genesis, and indeed much of the biblical tradition, depicts the human experience as a struggle between good and evil, symbolized by the forbidden tree in the story of Paradise. Whereas God represents all that is good, Satan personifies the forces of evil—and evil temptations; some scholars believe the serpent in the Garden of Eden is Satan himself. The meaning of "Satan" in Hebrew is "opponent, adversary." In the Christian tradition, Satan is more closely identified with the "devil" (from the Greek *diabolos*, "vilifier"). As such, Satan rules over demons that seek to challenge Jesus at every turn (e.g., Matthew 16:23). Satan is also identified with Lucifer, an archangel in the pseudepigraphical tradition who broke with God to establish his own dark universe; in the Qur'an, he is referred to as *Iblis*. In Revelation, Satan is portrayed as the principal opponent of all who obey God's commandment; for this he is thrown into the "lake of fire" (Revelation 20:10). ■

ca 3600 B.C.E.	ca 3500 B.C.E.	ca 3500 B.C.E.	ca 3400 B.C.E.
Sumerian farmers develop irrigation network	Invention of the wheel in Mesopotamia	Copper in use in Thailand	Invention of potter's wheel in Mesopotamia

would later lay the foundation for the Babylonian Empire.

Terah's decision to travel to Haran made sense because it was the northernmost city in Mesopotamia, perched on the principal trade routes to Egypt; Haran, or *harranu* in Akkadian, means "crossroads." Whether Terah had planned to stay there indefinitely, together with his retinue of relatives, servants, slaves, and livestock, is not clear; Terah died while tarrying in the city. The leadership of the clan now passed to his eldest son, Abraham.

The stepped pyramid of King Djoser (ca 2650–2575 B.C.E.) in Saqqara, Egypt, is the oldest surviving structure built entirely of stone.

THE WORLD IN 3000 B.C.E.

The beginning of the Early Bronze Age (3300–2100 B.C.E.) is often considered a watershed in the evolution of mankind. In Mesopotamia, the culture of Sumer was reaching its first apogee in the city-state of Uruk, known as *Erech* in the Bible, nurtured by the fertile lands along the Euphrates and the Tigris. The earliest forms of writing emerged here, prompted by the need to document a growing trade in the surplus of crops. Through daily use, these pictograms evolved into some 600 character symbols, known as *cuneiform* script. In 2900 B.C.E., the region was struck by a great flood. In its wake, the city of Ur took over as the center of Sumerian culture, which in the centuries to come would produce the first sciences, such as astronomy and mathematics, as well as the invention of the wheel.

A new culture was also emerging along another major river, the Nile Valley in Egypt. Around 3300 B.C.E., Egypt's rural fiefdoms had allied themselves in two separate kingdoms: Upper and Lower Egypt. Two hundred years later, a king named Menes (or Narmer) unified these two kingdoms and founded Egypt's First Dynasty (3100–2890 B.C.E.). His son Hor-Aha then established a capital in Memphis, which would eventually produce a civilization that remained largely intact for the next three thousand years— an achievement unparalleled in human history. ■

ABRAHAM

God then called upon Abraham and said, "Go from your country and your kindred and your father's house to the land that I will show you. I will make of you a great nation, and I will bless you, and make your name great" (GENESIS 12:1-2). The reference to "kindred" may either suggest that Terah had family in Haran, or that Abraham left a large part of his clan behind. In the years to come, Abraham's grandson **Jacob** would travel back to Haran in search of a spouse, because many members of his tribe still lived here.

Thus, Abraham traveled down to Canaan, together with his wife Sarah, and his nephew Lot, for Sarah was still childless. In a cultural sense, Canaan—the future land of Israel—formed part of a region that modern scholars referred to as "Syria-Canaan," encompassing much of today's Lebanon, Israel, the Jordan River Valley, and Sinai. Economically, the region was dependent on Egypt, in part because of the caravan trade that passed along Canaan's coastal region. Assuming that the story of Abraham is set in the early second millennium B.C.E., the region had recently suffered from a sustained drought, while trade was damaged by political turmoil in Egypt during its First Intermediate Period (2125–1991 B.C.E.). This is to some extent reflected in the Genesis story. After Abraham built an altar in Shechem and Bethel, in the northern highlands, a famine forced him to continue south to Egypt.

As soon as Abraham entered Egypt, the Bible tells us, "the Egyptians saw that [Sarah] was very beautiful." Her beauty was even reported to Pharaoh. Abraham had anticipated this, and had urged his wife to "say you are my sister, so that his life would be spared" (GENESIS 12:12-14). The result was a rather unseemly affair between Sarah and the king of Egypt, who in gratitude heaped presents on Abraham. God, however, afflicted Pharaoh's house with great plagues, and soon the king discovered that Sarah was actually Abraham's wife. She was dismissed, and the family was permitted to return to Canaan (GENESIS 12:17-20).

Egyptian bread cakes from the New Kingdom have been remarkably preserved, thanks to the area's dry climate.

The Egyptian sojourn had made Abraham a very wealthy man; Pharaoh had allowed him to keep his many gifts. As a result, his livestock had swelled beyond the capacity of the local pastures, which were far less fertile than those in Egypt. There was strife among the shepherds. Abraham had little choice but to split his holdings between him and his nephew Lot. Lot left for the irrigated plains of Jordan, close to the Dead Sea, and settled

ca 3372 B.C.E. First date in Mayan calendar	ca 3350 B.C.E. Rise of the Minoan Civilization in Crete	ca 3300 B.C.E. Beginning of the Early Bronze Age	ca 3300 B.C.E. First clay tablets in cuneiform document trade in Mesopotamia

in a place called Sodom. Abraham eventually settled in Hebron, located in the southern part of today's West Bank.

"The Sacrifice of Isaac" by Italian artist Michelangelo da Caravaggio (1573–1610) depicts an angel stopping Abraham from sacrificing his son. It was painted around 1603.

HAGAR

The separation from Lot left Abraham without an heir. Because Sarah was barren, the question of who would succeed Abraham as head of the clan became urgent. According to Mesopotamian custom, Sarah selected a slave girl named Hagar, and told her to lie with Abraham so as to procure a son. Hagar was Egyptian; she formed part of the slave booty given by Pharaoh. Just as Sarah had served as surrogate wife to the Egyptian king, so too would Hagar now serve as a surrogate for Abraham (GENESIS 16:1-2).

Hagar conceived and promptly looked down on Sarah with contempt, for she had suddenly become an important personage. Sarah retaliated by dealing with her harshly, forcing the young girl to run away into the desert. An angel found Hagar at an oasis near Shur, somewhere between Beersheba and the Egyptian frontier, and persuaded her to return. "You . . . shall bear a son," the angel told her; "you shall call him Ishmael, for the Lord has given heed to your affliction" (GENESIS 16:11). "Ishmael" is a contraction of *El* (God) and *shama'* (hears), meaning "God hears

ca 3200 B.C.E.	ca 3100 B.C.E.	ca 3050 B.C.E.	ca 3000 B.C.E.
Candles are used in Egypt	**Narmer unifies Upper and Lower Egypt**	**Construction of the great ziggurat of Ur**	**Megiddo is leading city-state in Canaan**

①　Ur The partially reconstructed ziggurat of Ur (21st century B.C.E.), built of sunbaked mud bricks, looms over the ancient site of Ur in today's Iraq.

②　Beersheba Ancient Beersheba, excavated near Tel es-Sheba in the southern Negev, still contains city dwellings from the Middle Iron Age (1000–900 B.C.E.).

③　Hazor Hazor, which was excavated by Yigael Yadin in the mid-1950s, was already an important fortress in the 18th century B.C.E.

④　Harran The modern-day village of Harran in today's Turkey, located close to ancient Harran, still has mud-brick houses in the shape of beehives.

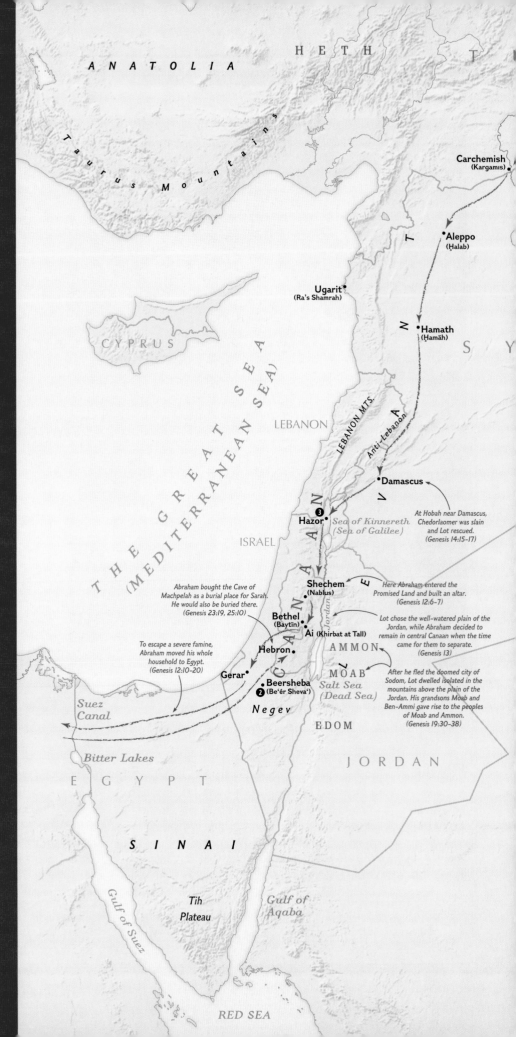

ANATOLIA

HETH

T

Taurus Mountains

Carchemish
(Kargamış)

•Aleppo
(Halab)

Ugarit•
(Ra's Shamrah)

•Hamath
(Hamāh)

S
Y

CYPRUS

THE GREAT SEA
(MEDITERRANEAN SEA)

LEBANON

LEBANON MTS.

Anti-Lebanon

•Damascus

At Hobah near Damascus,
Chedorlaomer was slain
and Lot rescued.
(Genesis 14:15–17)

Hazor•　③　Sea of Kinnereth
(Sea of Galilee)

ISRAEL

Abraham bought the Cave of
Machpelah as a burial place for Sarah.
He would also be buried there.
(Genesis 23:19, 25:10)

Shechem•
(Nablus)

Here Abraham entered the
Promised Land and built an altar.
(Genesis 12:6–7)

Bethel•
(Baytin)
Ai• (Khirbat at Tall)

Jordan

Lot chose the well-watered plain of the
Jordan, while Abraham decided to
remain in central Canaan when the time
came for them to separate.
(Genesis 13)

To escape a severe famine,
Abraham moved his whole
household to Egypt.
(Genesis 12:10–20)

Hebron•

AMMON

Gerar•

MOAB

Beersheba
(Be'ér Sheva')　②

Salt Sea
(Dead Sea)

After he fled the doomed city of
Sodom, Lot dwelled isolated in the
mountains above the plain of the
Jordan. His grandsons Moab and
Ben-Ammi gave rise to the peoples
of Moab and Ammon.
(Genesis 19:30–38)

Negev

EDOM

JORDAN

Suez
Canal

Bitter Lakes

E G Y P T

S I N A I

Tih
Plateau

Gulf of
Suez

Gulf of
Aqaba

RED SEA

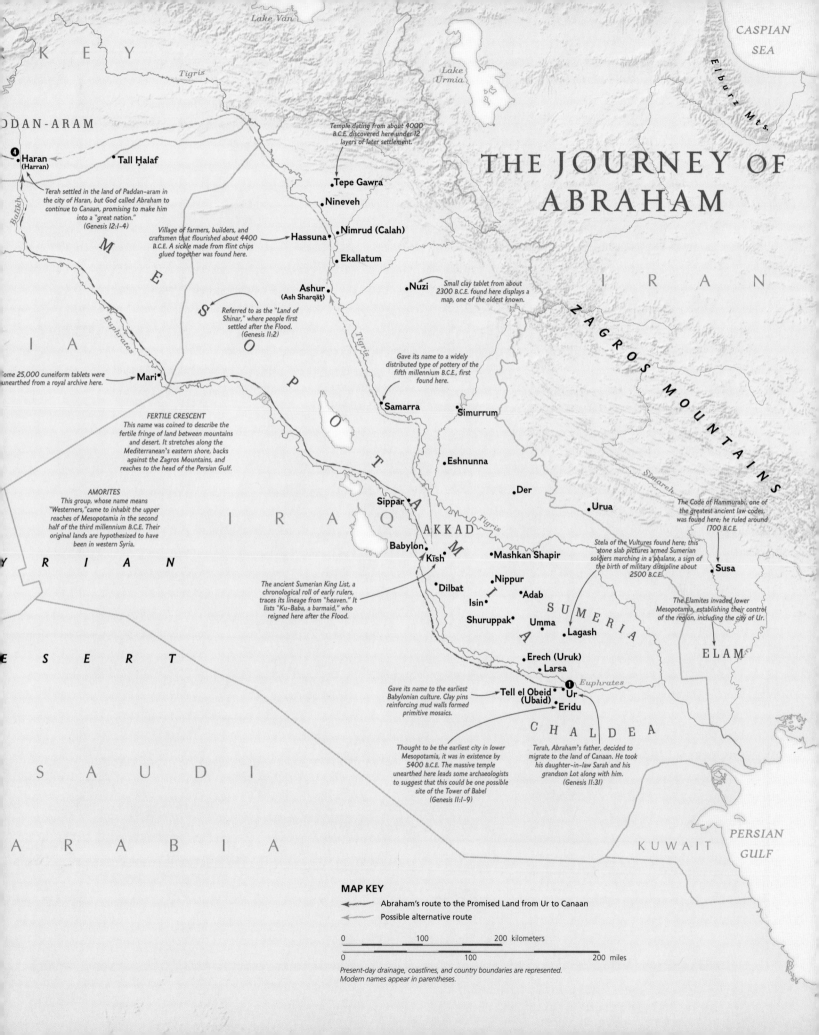

CASPIAN
SEA

Lake Van

Tigris

Lake
Urmia

Elburz Mts.

THE JOURNEY OF
ABRAHAM

DDAN-ARAM

❹ Haran
(Harran)

• Tall Ḥalaf

*Terah settled in the land of Paddan-aram in
the city of Haran, but God called Abraham to
continue to Canaan, promising to make him
into a "great nation."
(Genesis 12:1-4)*

*Temple dating from about 4000
B.C.E. discovered here under 12
layers of later settlement.*

• Tepe Gawra

• Nineveh

*Village of farmers, builders, and
craftsmen that flourished about 4400
B.C.E. A sickle made from flint chips
glued together was found here.*

• Nimrud (Calah)

Hassuna

• Ekallatum

I R A N

Ashur
(Ash Sharqāṭ)

• Nuzi

*Small clay tablet from about
2300 B.C.E. found here displays a
map, one of the oldest known.*

*Referred to as the "Land of
Shinar," where people first
settled after the Flood.
(Genesis 11:2)*

ZAGROS MOUNTAINS

Euphrates

*Some 25,000 cuneiform tablets were
unearthed from a royal archive here.*

• Mari

*Gave its name to a widely
distributed type of pottery of the
fifth millennium B.C.E., first
found here.*

• Samarra

• Simurrum

FERTILE CRESCENT
*This name was coined to describe the
fertile fringe of land between mountains
and desert. It stretches along the
Mediterranean's eastern shore, backs
against the Zagros Mountains, and
reaches to the head of the Persian Gulf.*

• Eshnunna

AMORITES
*This group, whose name means
"Westerners," came to inhabit the upper
reaches of Mesopotamia in the second
half of the third millennium B.C.E. Their
original lands are hypothesized to have
been in western Syria.*

I R A Q

• Der

• Urua

*The Code of Hammurabi, one of
the greatest ancient law codes,
was found here; he ruled around
1700 B.C.E.*

• Susa

Tigris

Sippar •

AKKAD

Babylon •

*Stela of the Vultures found here; this
stone slab pictures armed Sumerian
soldiers marching in a phalanx, a sign of
the birth of military discipline about
2500 B.C.E.*

• Mashkan Shapir

*The Elamites invaded lower
Mesopotamia, establishing their control
of the region, including the city of Ur.*

Kīsh •

*The ancient Sumerian King List, a
chronological roll of early rulers,
traces its lineage from "heaven." It
lists "Ku-Baba, a barmaid," who
reigned here after the Flood.*

• Dilbat

• Nippur

• Adab

Isin •

SUMERIA

ELAM

Shuruppak •

• Umma

• Lagash

• Erech (Uruk)

• Larsa

Euphrates

❶ Ur

*Gave its name to the earliest
Babylonian culture. Clay pins
reinforcing mud walls formed
primitive mosaics.*

Tell el Obeid •
(Ubaid)

• Eridu

CHALDEA

*Terah, Abraham's father, decided to
migrate to the land of Canaan. He took
his daughter-in-law Sarah and his
grandson Lot along with him.
(Genesis 11:31)*

*Thought to be the earliest city in lower
Mesopotamia, it was in existence by
5400 B.C.E. The massive temple
unearthed here leads some archaeologists
to suggest that this could be one possible
site of the Tower of Babel
(Genesis 11:1-9)*

S A U D I

KUWAIT

PERSIAN
GULF

A R A B I A

MAP KEY

◄— Abraham's route to the Promised Land from Ur to Canaan

◄— Possible alternative route

| 0 | 100 | 200 kilometers |

| 0 | 100 | 200 miles |

*Present-day drainage, coastlines, and country boundaries are represented.
Modern names appear in parentheses.*

THE TOWER OF BABEL

The story of the Tower of Babel has often been linked to the presence of large stepped pyramids in ancient Mesopotamia, known as *ziggurats*. One such structure stood in the fourth-millennium Sumerian city of Uruk (*Erech* in the Bible). A thousand years later, another square pyramid rose in Ur, dedicated to the moon god Nanna. This ziggurat, now partly restored, still stands at Tell al-Muqayyar in southern Iraq. Quite possibly, this pyramid formed the inspiration for the Tower of Babel story.

One Sumerian myth explicitly links a ziggurat tower to linguistic confusion, as does the story of Babel in Genesis. According to this myth, King Enmerkar of Uruk was building a huge ziggurat when a shortage of materials compelled him to demand supplies from tributary lands. To ensure that they heeded his royal order, he beseeched the god Enki to punish anyone who refused his decree by robbing them of the ability to speak the kingdom's language.

The story of the Tower of Babel also appears in the Qur'an. Here, the building project was instigated by two fallen angels, Harut and Marut, condemned to serve time in Babylon's prison. While in captivity, the angels began to study the art of magic, including the skill to build a vast monument. The people of Babylon were seduced by their magic and agreed to the tower's construction. When God intervened, he created confusion by sowing "discord between man and wife," and the people "learned what harmed them, not what profited them" (QUR'AN 2:102). ■

This painting of "The Tower of Babel" was completed by the Dutch artist Pieter Brueghel the Elder (1530–1569) in 1563.

ca 2900 B.C.E.	ca 2900 B.C.E.	ca 2800 B.C.E.	ca 2700 B.C.E.
Massive flooding in Mesopotamia	Sumerian pictographs evolve into symbols for words and numbers	First construction of Stonehenge in Britain	Hieroglyphic writing emerges in Egypt

(me)." What's more, the angel said, God would "so greatly multiply your offspring that they cannot be counted for multitude"—a promise that would soon be made to Sarah's future son **Isaac** as well (GENESIS 16:10-12).

Hagar returned and gave birth to a son, as the angel had foretold. When Ishmael turned 13, God reappeared before Abraham to reaffirm his covenant; Abraham would become "the ancestor of a multitude of nations." To seal this covenant, God told Abraham to circumcise himself as well as Ishmael, and all the male members of his household. Ever since, each male baby born to Jewish parents is circumcised on the eighth day after birth.

SARAH

Abraham then received three foreign visitors—according to rabbinic tradition, God, accompanied by two angels—who gave Abraham some astonishing news about his wife, Sarah. God said, "I will bless her, and moreover I will give you a son by her" (GENESIS 17:16). Abraham then "fell on his face and laughed, and said to himself, 'Can a child be born to a man who is a hundred years old? Can Sarah, who is ninety years old, bear a child?' " (GENESIS 17:17). Later, when the same prophecy was revealed to Sarah, she too burst out laughing. "After I have grown old, and my husband is old," she said, "shall I have pleasure?" God replied, "is anything too wonderful for the Lord?" (GENESIS 18:12,14).

As God had promised, Sarah did conceive. She bore a son and named him Isaac (or *Yishaq*), which means "he who laughs." This,

French artist Jean-Baptiste-Camille Corot (1796–1875) painted "Hagar in the Wilderness" in 1835. The setting's serene harmony against the harsh reality of the dying child created a sensation at the Paris Salon.

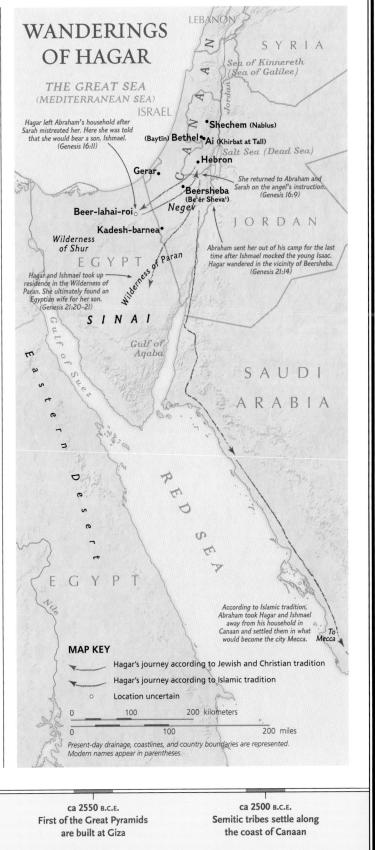

WANDERINGS OF HAGAR

THE GREAT SEA (MEDITERRANEAN SEA)

LEBANON
SYRIA
Sea of Kinnereth (Sea of Galilee)
ISRAEL
CANAAN
Jordan

Hagar left Abraham's household after Sarah mistreated her. Here she was told that she would bear a son, Ishmael. (Genesis 16:11)

•Shechem (Nablus)
(Baytīn) Bethel •Ai (Khirbat at Tall)
•Hebron
Salt Sea (Dead Sea)
Gerar•
She returned to Abraham and Sarah on the angel's instruction. (Genesis 16:9)
•Beersheba (Be'ér Sheva')
Negev
JORDAN
Beer-lahai-roi○
Kadesh-barnea•

Wilderness of Shur
Abraham sent her out of his camp for the last time after Ishmael mocked the young Isaac. Hagar wandered in the vicinity of Beersheba. (Genesis 21:14)

EGYPT
Wilderness of Paran

Hagar and Ishmael took up residence in the Wilderness of Paran. She ultimately found an Egyptian wife for her son. (Genesis 21:20-21)

S I N A I

Gulf of Aqaba
Gulf of Suez

Eastern Desert

SAUDI ARABIA

R E D   S E A

E G Y P T
Nile

According to Islamic tradition, Abraham took Hagar and Ishmael away from his household in Canaan and settled them in what would become the city Mecca.
To Mecca

MAP KEY

⟶ Hagar's journey according to Jewish and Christian tradition

⟶ Hagar's journey according to Islamic tradition

○ Location uncertain

0 ___ 100 ___ 200 kilometers
0 ___ 100 ___ 200 miles

Present-day drainage, coastlines, and country boundaries are represented. Modern names appear in parentheses.

ca 2700 B.C.E.	ca 2630 B.C.E.	ca 2550 B.C.E.	ca 2500 B.C.E.
Silk production from silkworms begins in China	Stepped pyramid is built at Saqqara	First of the Great Pyramids are built at Giza	Semitic tribes settle along the coast of Canaan

At the set time I will return to you, in due season, and Sarah shall have a son.

GENESIS 18:14

however, raised an urgent question: Whom would Abraham recognize as his heir? Ishmael could claim his right as Abraham's firstborn, but Isaac could claim greater legitimacy. The *Code of Hammurabi,* an ancient law code from the 18th century B.C.E., states that the firstborn of the first wife could be entitled to preferential treatment. God resolved the dilemma by stating that "my own covenant I will establish with Isaac," even though Ishmael was assured that he, too, "shall be the father of twelve princes, and I will make him a great nation" (GENESIS 17:20-21). History would bear this out; Islam claims Ishmael and his covenant with God as the source of its own faith tradition.

With Isaac's position secure now, Sarah urged her husband to "cast out this slave woman with her son." Abraham, advanced in age, could not resist his wife's entreaties. He gave Hagar some bread and a "skin of water," and sent her on her way (GENESIS 12:10). After several days of aimless wandering in the Negev desert, south of Beersheba, Hagar was hopelessly lost and collapsed near some shrubs. Ishmael lay dying.

Fortunately, God took pity on her. "Do not be afraid," said an angel of the Lord. "Come, lift up the boy and hold him fast with your hand, for I will make a great nation of him" (GENESIS 21:17-18). God then opened Hagar's eyes, and she saw a well nearby. They were saved.

In the years to come, Genesis tells us, "The boy lived in the wilderness and became an expert with the bow. He lived in the wilderness of Paran" (GENESIS 21:20-21). *Paran* was the name given to the northeastern part of the Sinai Peninsula, a region centered on the oasis of Qadesh Barnea, a mere seven-day march from the Egyptian border. So it was to Egypt that Hagar went when the boy reached maturity, and she "got a wife for him from the land of Egypt" (GENESIS 21:21).

LOT

The two angels who brought Abraham the news of a son had another, far more ominous mission: to punish two cities, Sodom

The angel leads Lot and his daughters to safety in this depiction of "The Burning of Sodom" by Jean-Baptiste-Camille Corot from 1857.

ca 2500 B.C.E.	ca 2400 B.C.E.	ca 2296 B.C.E.	ca 2200 B.C.E.
Sumerians introduce standard weights for use in trade	Chinese astronomers record observations of sky based on Equator	Chinese record first observation of a comet	Akkadian Empire reaches its zenith

and Gomorrah, for their sinful ways. Abraham's nephew Lot, however, still lived in Sodom. When God broke the news to Abraham, Abraham—not surprisingly—rushed to Sodom's defense. Would the Lord still destroy the city if ten righteous men were to be found there? "For the sake of ten," says God, "I will not destroy it" (Genesis 18:33).

But this pledge was rapidly overtaken by events. As soon as the two angels were lodged in Lot's house, Sodom's male population rushed to the place with the intent of abusing Lot's guests sexually, though some contemporary commentators view the sin of the people of Sodom to have been not lust but inhospitability. To placate the lustful crowd, Lot offered his daughters instead, but it was to no avail. The angels then struck the men outside with blindness, so that they could not find the front door.

With the wickedness of Sodom so clearly exposed, the city was irrevocably doomed. The next morning, the angels bundled Lot and his family out of the city. Lot had urged his sons-in-law to leave as well, but they didn't take the threat seriously and decided to remain. Lot and his wife, as well as his two unmarried daughters, fled to a nearby township called Zoar. As dawn broke, God rained down "sulfur and fire" from heaven; both cities and the surrounding countryside were destroyed (Genesis 19:25). Lot's family had nearly reached safety when Lot's wife, unable to contain her curiosity, decided to turn. She "looked back, and she became a pillar of salt" (Genesis 19:26). Today, visitors can still admire a 65-foot-tall pillar of salt on the southern shore of the Dead Sea, jutting out from Mount Sedom, named after the biblical Sodom. Archaeologists have uncovered several third-millennium B.C.E. settlements in the area, including Bab edh-Dhra (which some have identified as Sodom), Safi (perhaps the biblical Zoar), and Numeira, sometimes associated with Gomorrah. These settlements were quite possibly destroyed by a series of earthquakes, which geologists believe devastated the Dead Sea area around 2000 B.C.E. The presence of tar along the southern shore may recall the note in Genesis that the valley of Sodom was "full of bitumen pits" (Genesis 14:10).

Lot's daughters, meanwhile, were despondent. With all the cities in the region destroyed, they despaired of ever being able to bear children. They lay with their father, after they had served him wine until he passed out. Both daughters conceived and gave birth to a son: Moab, the ancestor of the Moabites who lived in the region north of today's Amman, capital of Jordan; and Ben-ammi, "the ancestor of the Ammonites to this day" (Genesis 19:37-38). The Ammonites lived in the region south of Amman, along the Dead Sea. Some scholars believe that this story served to disparage the origins of Moab and Ammon, with whom the later kingdoms of Israel were often at odds.

Isaac

Isaac grew to become a healthy boy, but God decided to put Abraham to a test. He told Abraham, "take your son, your only son Isaac, whom you love, and go to the land of Moriah, and offer him there as a burnt offering on one of the mountains that I shall show you" (Genesis 22:2). With a heavy heart, Abraham complied, but just before he struck the blade to kill his son, an angel intervened. Relieved beyond words, Abraham offered a ram instead.

NOMADS AND FARMERS

"**M**esopotamia" is a Greek word that means "the land between the two rivers." These two rivers were the Euphrates and the Tigris, both major bodies of water that originate in Turkey and navigate the thousand miles of dry plateau of ancient Iraq before emptying themselves in the Persian Gulf. This river system, so unique in the parched climate of the Middle East, is believed to have been a key factor in the transformation of Mesopotamia into a leading civilization. For millennia, families sustained themselves by hunting game, or finding edible crops that grew in the wild. Eventually, some tribes discovered that they could take control of their destiny by growing crops or husbanding animals themselves—a process known as *domestication*. Several other factors contributed to this process, including the growth of the local population, as well as important climate changes around 8500 B.C.E. Settlement, however, involved a certain vulnerability: Water from a well, animals, seeds, or crops were always prone to theft. This is why early farmers often formed communities, sometimes protected by an earthen wall, which in due course evolved into mankind's first cities.

Others decided to gather domesticated animals in large quantities, in *herds*. This forced them into a nomadic lifestyle, because no single plot of land could sustain a large herd. These nomads would therefore travel from field to field, ever in search of fresh pastures. Because wells and fertile fields were jealously protected, there was tension between nomadic families and rural settlers, which is reflected in the stories of Genesis. ∎

Sumerian farmers pour milk in large vessels in this relief from the Early Dynastic period (2900–2350 B.C.E).

ca 2200 B.C.E.	ca 2201 B.C.E.	ca 2100 B.C.E.	ca 2000 B.C.E.
Sumerians introduce the 12-month, 360-day calendar	Map of Lagash is oldest map of a city	Queen Semiramis builds tunnel underneath the Euphrates	Amorites invade Mesopotamia

THE LINEAGE OF
ABRAHAM

ABRAHAM + HAGAR

ISHMAEL — ?
↓
NEBAIOITH
↓
ABDEEL
↓
MISHMA
↓
MASSA
↓
TEMA
↓
NAPHISH
↓
MAHALATH
↓
KEDAR
↓
MIBSAM
↓
DUMAH
↓
HADAD
↓
JETUR
↓
KEDEMAH

AHOLIBAMAH — BESHEMATH — ADAH — ESAU
↓   ↓   ↓
JEUSH   REUEL   ELIPHAZ
↓
JALAM
↓
KORAH

ABRAHAM + SARAH

ISAAC — REBEKAH

JACOB — LEAH   ZILPAH
↓   ↓
REUBEN   GAD
↓   ↓
SIMEON   ASHER
↓
LEVI
↓
JUDAH
↓
ISSACHAR
↓
ZEBULUN
↓
DINAH

Now that Isaac was Abraham's designated heir, Abraham was keen to find a suitable wife for him. He didn't want Isaac to marry a Canaanite girl but someone from his own clan, most of whom were still living in Haran. Abraham gave this important task to a trusted servant, who traveled to Haran and soon returned with a young woman named **Rebekah**, Isaac's second cousin. Rebekah was "very fair," and Isaac was delighted; he "brought her into the tent, and took Rebekah, and she became his wife" (GENESIS 24:67). Isaac was still affected by the death of his mother, Sarah, but according to Genesis, Rebekah's love was a comfort to him (GENESIS 24:67).

Abraham himself took a new wife named **Keturah**, who bore him six more children. *Keturah* means "incense," which may suggest that she came from the region of today's Oman, renowned for its frankincense. Indeed, her offspring are named for places and tribes in the Arabian Peninsula. Ishmael's descendants, by contrast, appear to be Arabs of the Sinai and Syria.

Upon Abraham's death, the patriarch's covenant with God passed to his son. Isaac buried his father in the Cave of Machpelah, which Abraham had purchased from **Ephron the Hittite**, and laid him to rest next to his wife, Sarah.

ca 2000 B.C.E.	ca 1980 B.C.E.	ca 1975 B.C.E.	ca 1950 B.C.E.
First use of iron plow in Canaan	Palace of Knossos in Crete features baths with running water	Beginning of the Middle Kingdom in Egypt	Egyptian army subjugates Canaan

ABRAHAM + KETURAH

ZIMRAN

JOKSHAN

BILHAH — RACHEL

MEDAN

DAN   JOSEPH — ASENATH   MIDIAN

NAPHTALI   BENJAMIN   ISHBAK

MANASSEH   SHUAH

EPHRAIM

*Then Abraham reached out his hand
and took the knife to kill his son.*

GENESIS 22:10

The young couple's bliss was soon threatened by another famine, which threatened the flocks. Isaac had no choice but to lead his family toward Egypt, just as his father had done. When he reached Gerar, God told him to stay put, rather than traveling on to Egypt. The Gerar region was ruled by **King Abimelech**, possibly the same Abimelech (or his successor) who had befriended Abraham on *his* journey to Egypt. Isaac presented his wife, Rebekah, as his sister, rather than his wife, lest some harm come to her, just as Abraham had passed off Sarah as his sister to Pharaoh. But Abimelech had observed Isaac fondling Rebekah, and saw that they were clearly

ISHMAEL IN JUDAISM AND ISLAM

Ishmael is Abraham's son by Hagar, an Egyptian slave who served as Sarah's handmaiden. Although Isaac would inherit God's covenant with Abraham, God promised Hagar that Ishmael would also be "the father of twelve princes," and "a great nation." According to Genesis, Hagar and her son were sent away into the desert, where they nearly died of thirst. But an angel intervened and opened her eyes, so that Hagar could see a well nearby (GENESIS 21:15-18). Ishmael then grew up in the "wilderness of Paran," in the northeastern part of Sinai, close to the large oasis of Qadesh Barnea. In the Islamic tradition, however, "Paran" is located in Arabia. Here, too, Hagar searches frantically for water, running between the mountains of al-Safa and al-Marwa. The angel Gabriel intervenes by striking the earth with his staff, producing the well of ZamZam—which is still venerated in Mecca to this day. What's more, the rite of walking between the two mountains seven times, known as the *sa'y*, is reenacted every year as part of the hajj, the pilgrimage to Mecca. Interestingly, the Jewish Book of Jubilees, dated to the second century B.C.E., also suggests that Ishmael "settled between Paran and the borders of Babylon, in the land that is toward the East, facing the desert" (JUBILEES 20:11-13). According to the Qur'an, Ishmael and Abraham then built the Ka'bah, the cube-like structure in Mecca that today is the holiest shrine in Islam (QUR'AN 2:125). The Prophet Muhammad considered Ishmael the progenitor of the Arab nation, as does—to some extent—the Book of Genesis. ■

The angel comes to the rescue of Hagar and Ishmael in this painting by Italian artist Francesco Coghetti (1804–1875).

| ca 1950 B.C.E. | ca 1860 B.C.E. | ca 1800 B.C.E. | ca 1800 B.C.E. |
| Development of wheel with spokes | Legendary founding date of Babylon by Amorites | Hebrew clans begin migrating to Egypt | Egyptian texts list Jerusalem as one of Canaan's city-states |

CHAPTER I: FROM GENESIS TO DEUTERONOMY 37

This painting titled "Jacob Meets Rachel at the Well" was painted by Scottish artist William Dyce (1806–1864).

Two nations are in your womb, and two peoples born of you shall be divided; the one shall be stronger than the other, the elder shall serve the younger.

GENESIS 25:23

husband and wife. He gave orders that no one should harm either one (GENESIS 26:11).

Isaac and Rebekah then settled in the area and set about to restore the wells that Abraham had originally dug. As his herds grew, Isaac began to prosper, but tension with local shepherds (Genesis refers to them as "Philistines," though these tribes would not reach Canaan for many centuries) forced him to move away. He settled in a valley where his servants eventually found water and Isaac called it "Shibah." "Therefore," says Genesis, "the name of the city is Beer-sheba to this day" (GENESIS 26:33).

REBEKAH

For a long time, Rebekah remained childless just as her mother-in-law Sarah had been. Isaac prayed to God on his wife's behalf, and his prayers were answered. Rebekah conceived twins, but the children struggled within her. God told her that her twins would each become an ancestor of a great

THE BINDING OF ISAAC

The story of the sacrifice of Isaac, known as the *Akedah* in Judaism, is told skillfully with great sensitivity for Abraham's distress. Indeed, why would God ask a man to sacrifice his own child? One reason might be that child sacrifice was widely practiced in Syria and Canaan. During his war with the kingdoms of Israel and Judah, for example, the king of Moab "took his firstborn son who was to succeed him, and offered him as a burnt offering on the wall" (II KINGS 3:27). Child sacrifice was also practiced in the Phoenician cult of Ba'al, and in the Valley of Hinnom below Jerusalem (JEREMIAH 32:25). Perhaps the purpose of the story in Genesis is that Abraham's God utterly rejects such practices. Muslims celebrate the event during the festival of Eid Ul-Adha, the "Feast of the Sacrifice," when Muslim families around the world slaughter and roast a cow or ram. During the Jewish festival of Rosh Hashanah, the shofar, the traditional ram's horn, is blown, because God allowed Abraham to sacrifice a ram instead of Isaac. ■

people, but those two nations would be frequent enemies.

Indeed, when she gave birth, the two boys were very different. **Esau**, clearly the stronger of the two, was covered in red hair—a wordplay that identifies Esau as the forefather of Edom, the land of the Edomites below the Dead Sea; he grew up to become a fearsome hunter. **Jacob**, on the other hand, was a gentle lad who gripped Esau's heel at birth; the root of the word *ya'aqov* is *'aqev*, meaning "heel." Growing up, Jacob preferred to stay in his tent or tend to his father's flocks. The tension between the boys may be another reflection of the typical Stone Age rivalry between hunter-gatherers and shepherds. And whereas Isaac loved Esau the most ("because he was fond of game"), Rebekah's favorite was Jacob (GENESIS 25:28). She soon began to plot how Jacob could inherit the birthright—*bekorah,* the rights of the firstborn son to their father's heritage—even though he was their second-born. For God had made a prophecy, while her children were still in her womb, that "the elder shall serve the younger" (GENESIS 25:23).

ESAU

One day, when Jacob was cooking a tasty stew, Esau came in from the field and said, "Let me eat some of that red stuff, for I am famished." Jacob quickly said, "First sell me your birthright." Esau, ruled by the rumbling in his belly, agreed (GENESIS 25:30-33).

Rebekah knew that this would not stand, so she came up with a ruse. She cooked her husband's favorite stew of meat and told Jacob to give it to his father, pretending to be Esau. Because Jacob was smooth skinned, she covered his hands and neck with fleece from sheep, and gave him one of Esau's coats. Isaac,

ca 1780 B.C.E.	ca 1760 B.C.E.	ca 1750 B.C.E.	ca 1720 B.C.E.
Multiplication tables appear in Babylonia	Putative date of the Code of Hammurabi	Egyptian geometry calculates volume of a truncated pyramid	The Hyksos, Semitic nomads, overthrow Egypt's Middle Kingdom

38 NATIONAL GEOGRAPHIC WHO'S WHO IN THE BIBLE

MOTHERHOOD IN THE BIBLE

Motherhood plays a major role in Genesis. Though pregnancy is obviously of crucial importance for the patriarchal lineage, thus securing God's promise of a great nation, it is by no means assured. Both Abraham's wife, Sarah, and Jacob's wife, Rachel, struggle with infertility, and only an intervention from God gives them the children they so desperately want. The struggle with barrenness also inflames the tension with their rivals: Hagar in Sarah's case, and Leah in Rachel's. In fact, it is Jacob's overt favoritism toward Rachel that prompts God to open Leah's womb, but keep Rachel's closed (GENESIS 29:31). The "unloved" Leah then bears seven of Jacob's children—six sons, Reuben, Simeon, Levi, Judah, Issachar, and Zebulun; as well as a daughter, Dinah. But in the end, Rachel's love is redeemed, and she gives birth to Joseph, Jacob's favorite and a pivotal character in Genesis' dramatic climax, as well as Jacob's youngest son Benjamin. Taken together, Jacob's two wives and concubines present him with 12 sons, who will become the forefathers of the 12 tribes of Israel, sealing God's covenant.

The importance of producing children was so urgent in the Early Bronze Age that if a woman was barren, it was *her* responsibility to find a surrogate mother. Sarah's decision to take her handmaiden Hagar into Abraham's tent is echoed in Babylonian laws, which stipulate that if a bride has not borne children within two years of her wedding, she must purchase a slave woman to produce a child for her husband. ∎

---

who was nearly blind, touched Jacob's arms, smelled Esau's scent on his coat, and readily gave Jacob his blessing, granting him his birthright (GENESIS 27:27-29).

Naturally, as soon as Esau found out, he was furious. But Rebekah quickly sent Jacob away to Haran, to safety. In retaliation, Esau—who had already taken three wives outside of his clan—now took another, **Mahalath**, who was none other than the daughter of his father's rival, Ishmael. Nevertheless, after many years had passed and Jacob had returned from Haran with his wives and children, the brothers reconciled, close to the spot where the Jabbok River joins the Jordan (GENESIS 33:4). Still, in the centuries to come, Edom and Israel would often be at war.

JACOB

One night, while traveling to Haran, Jacob fell asleep and dreamed of a ladder going up into heaven. At the top stood God, reaffirming his covenant with Abraham that now would pass on to Jacob: "The land on which you lie I will give to you and to your offspring" (GENESIS 28:13). When he woke up, Jacob anointed the stone on which he'd slept with oil, and called the altar *bet'el* or Bethel ("the House of God"). Bethel would continue to serve as an important sanctuary,

The stela of Merneptah (ca 127 B.C.E.), from Pharaoh's funerary temple in Thebes, contains the only reference to "Israel" in ancient Egyptian sources.

particularly during the time of the Northern Kingdom of Israel.

Jacob continued on to Haran, where he fell in love with the "beautiful and lovely" **Rachel**, daughter of his cousin **Laban** (GENESIS 29:17). Laban warmly welcomed him to his family, but asked a steep price for Rachel's hand in marriage: Jacob would first have to work as a shepherd for seven years, tending Laban's flocks. When that time was fulfilled at last, Jacob spent his wedding night, only to discover at dawn that it wasn't Rachel, but her elder sister Leah whom Laban had delivered to Jacob's tent. Laban explained that according to tribal custom, the oldest daughter should be married first (GENESIS 29:26). If Jacob wanted to marry Rachel as well, he would owe Laban another seven years of labor.

In time, Jacob was able to acquire a flock of sheep, camels, and goats of his own. But tensions within the clan, particularly between Jacob and Laban's sons, compelled Jacob to return to Canaan with his wives and handmaidens, who also served as Jacob's concubines. By this time, these women had borne him 11 sons and one daughter.

While traveling south, close to the Jabbok River, Jacob came upon a stranger who challenged him to a struggle. The two wrestled all night; the word "wrestled" (*ye'abeq*) is another of Genesis' wordplays, using Jacob's name (*ya'aqov*) and that of the river (*yabboq*). The fight lasted all night and continued even after

---

ca 1700 B.C.E.
Phoenicians develop the 22-letter alphabet

ca 1650 B.C.E.
Rhind papyrus reveals the extent of Egyptian mathematics

ca 1628 B.C.E.
Volcano of Thera explodes, covering Mediterranean in ash

ca 1595 B.C.E.
The Hittites sack Babylon; end of the Old Babylonian Kingdom

CHAPTER I: FROM GENESIS TO DEUTERONOMY **39**

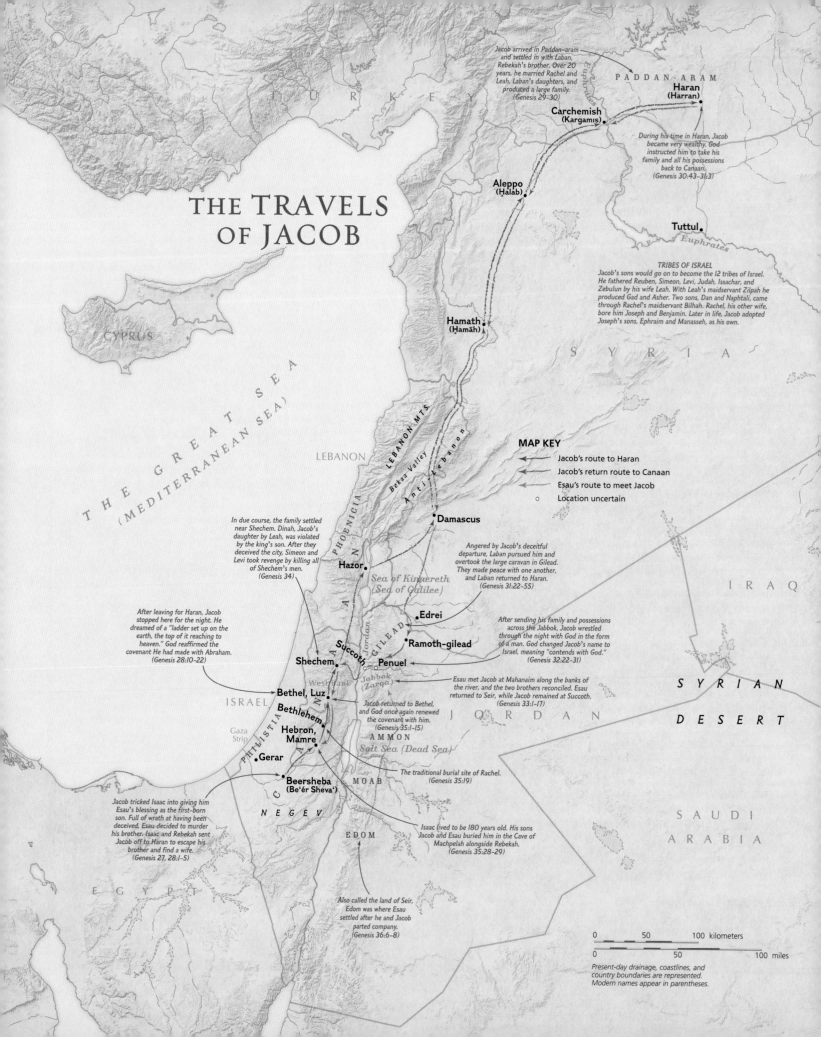

THE TRAVELS OF JACOB

PADDAN-ARAM

Jacob arrived in Paddan-aram and settled with Laban, Rebekah's brother. Over 20 years, he married Rachel and Leah, Laban's daughters, and produced a large family. (Genesis 29–30)

Haran (Harran)

Carchemish (Kargamış)

During his time in Haran, Jacob became very wealthy. God instructed him to take his family and all his possessions back to Canaan. (Genesis 30:43–31:3)

Aleppo (Ḥalab)

Tuttul

Euphrates

TRIBES OF ISRAEL
Jacob's sons would go on to become the 12 tribes of Israel. He fathered Reuben, Simeon, Levi, Judah, Issachar, and Zebulun by his wife Leah. With Leah's maidservant Zilpah he produced Gad and Asher. Two sons, Dan and Naphtali, came through Rachel's maidservant Bilhah. Rachel, his other wife, bore him Joseph and Benjamin. Later in life, Jacob adopted Joseph's sons, Ephraim and Manasseh, as his own.

Hamath (Ḥamāh)

S Y R I A

TURKEY

CYPRUS

THE GREAT SEA (MEDITERRANEAN SEA)

LEBANON MTS.

Beḳaa Valley

Anti-Lebanon

LEBANON

PHOENICIA

MAP KEY

← Jacob's route to Haran
← Jacob's return route to Canaan
← Esau's route to meet Jacob
○ Location uncertain

Damascus

In due course, the family settled near Shechem. Dinah, Jacob's daughter by Leah, was violated by the king's son. After they deceived the city, Simeon and Levi took revenge by killing all of Shechem's men. (Genesis 34)

Hazor

Sea of Kinnereth (Sea of Galilee)

Angered by Jacob's deceitful departure, Laban pursued him and overtook the large caravan in Gilead. They made peace with one another, and Laban returned to Haran. (Genesis 31:22–55)

Edrei

Ramoth-gilead

I R A Q

After leaving for Haran, Jacob stopped here for the night. He dreamed of a "ladder set up on the earth, the top of it reaching to heaven." God reaffirmed the covenant He had made with Abraham. (Genesis 28:10–22)

GILEAD

Jordan

Succoth

Penuel

After sending his family and possessions across the Jabbok, Jacob wrestled through the night with God in the form of a man. God changed Jacob's name to Israel, meaning "contends with God." (Genesis 32:22–31)

Shechem

West Bank

Jabbok (Zarqa)

S Y R I A N

Bethel, Luz

Esau met Jacob at Mahanaim along the banks of the river, and the two brothers reconciled. Esau returned to Seir, while Jacob remained at Succoth. (Genesis 33:1–17)

Bethlehem

CANAAN

ISRAEL

Jacob returned to Bethel, and God once again renewed the covenant with him. (Genesis 35:1–15)

J O R D A N

D E S E R T

Hebron, Mamre

Gaza Strip

PHILISTIA

AMMON

Salt Sea (Dead Sea)

Gerar

The traditional burial site of Rachel. (Genesis 35:19)

Beersheba (Be'ér Sheva')

MOAB

Jacob tricked Isaac into giving him Esau's blessing as the first-born son. Full of wrath at having been deceived, Esau decided to murder his brother. Isaac and Rebekah sent Jacob off to Haran to escape his brother and find a wife. (Genesis 27, 28:1–5)

N E G E V

Isaac lived to be 180 years old. His sons Jacob and Esau buried him in the Cave of Machpelah alongside Rebekah. (Genesis 35:28–29)

S A U D I ARABIA

EDOM

E G Y P T

Also called the land of Seir, Edom was where Esau settled after he and Jacob parted company. (Genesis 36:6–8)

| 0 | 50 | 100 kilometers |
| 0 | 50 | 100 miles |

Present-day drainage, coastlines, and country boundaries are represented. Modern names appear in parentheses.

Jacob's thigh was injured. At long last, the stranger—an angel of the Lord, or perhaps God himself—relented, declaring that henceforth Jacob would be known as "Israel" ("he who prevails with God") (GENESIS 32:28). Just as Jacob had struggled with God, so too would the nation of Israel wrestle for centuries with its obedience to the Lord. Jacob decided to call the place "Peniel" ("God's face"), saying, "I have seen God face to face" (GENESIS 32:30).

The "unloved" Leah bore seven of Jacob's children—six sons, **Reuben**, **Simeon**, **Levi**, **Judah**, **Issachar**, and **Zebulun**, as well as a daughter, **Dinah**. Jacob's concubine **Bilhah** gave birth to **Dan** and **Naphtali** (GENESIS 30:3-8), while another slave, **Zilpah**, gave him **Gad** and **Asher** (GENESIS 30:9-13). Jacob's overt favoritism toward Rachel had prompted God to keep Rachel's womb closed but Rachel's love was ultimately redeemed when she gave birth to a boy named **Joseph**, Jacob's favorite (GENESIS 29:31). Together with the sons of Joseph, **Manasseh** and **Ephraim**, these 12 men would become the forefathers of the 12 tribes of Israel, sealing God's covenant.

DINAH

Soon after Jacob's family had resettled near Shechem in Canaan, his daughter Dinah decided to go to the surrounding villages to meet the local women. On her way, she was seized and raped by **Shechem**, the son of the local ruler named **King Hamor**. Shechem, however, fell in love with Dinah. King Hamor intervened with Jacob, and asked him to allow the two youngsters to marry. Hamor even suggested that Jacob's clan and the local Canaanites should intermarry freely; "give your daughters to us, and take our daughters for yourselves" (GENESIS 34:9), he said. Jacob agreed, apparently with the consent of Dinah's brothers, on the condition that the local population be circumcised. Hamor agreed to do this.

JACOB'S SONS

But in truth, Jacob's sons were deeply aggrieved by their sister's rape, and were plotting their revenge. Three days after the male population of Shechem was circumcised and the men were "still in pain," two of Jacob's sons—Simeon and Levi—entered the city and killed all the males by the sword (GENESIS 34:26). The other sons then followed and engaged in wholesale plunder, while Dinah was forcibly taken from Shechem's house.

Jacob was deeply aggrieved when he heard the news. The massacre acutely threatened the fragile peace between his clan and the local Canaanite population. But, his sons retorted, "Should our sister be treated like a whore?" (GENESIS 34:31).

God told Jacob to move away and settle with his family in Bethel. While still on the road, Rachel went into labor and gave birth to Jacob's youngest son, named **Benjamin**. But the labor was hard, and Rachel died in childbirth. Jacob buried his beloved wife near Bethlehem, and set up a pillar on her grave (GENESIS 35:20).

With Rachel gone, Jacob's sons no longer hid their resentment of the way their father pampered Rachel's first son, Joseph. Oblivious to his brothers' feelings, Joseph inflamed their envy even further by

"Jacob Receives the Bloody Coat of Joseph" was painted by the Spanish artist Diego Rodríguez de Silva y Velázquez (1599–1660) around 1630.

having dreams in which he appeared to be placed above his brothers (GENESIS 37:6-8). Jacob then brought Joseph a rare gift, a beautiful coat "with long sleeves," erroneously translated in the King James Bible as a "coat of many colors," which was a rare luxury for shepherds. Furious, the brothers decided to do away with Joseph.

A perfect opportunity to do so arose when the brothers were tending their flocks in the valley of Dothan, and Joseph came up to see them. Some brothers wanted to kill him instantly, but Reuben and Judah suggested a lesser penalty. A caravan of merchants was passing by on its way to Egypt—an interesting detail, for one of the

ca 1550 B.C.E.	ca 1549 B.C.E.	ca 1500 B.C.E.	ca 1500 B.C.E.
Pharaoh Ahmose steadily ousts the Hyksos from Egypt	Pharaoh Ahmose ascends throne, founds the 19th Dynasty	Growing conflicts between Egypt and Hittites in Canaan	Emergence of pictograph writing in China

This vivid wall painting of a boy leading cows from the tomb of Nebamun in western Thebes is dated around 1356 B.C.E.—*New Kingdom, 18th Dynasty.*

main trade routes of the Bronze Age did pass through the valley of Dothan on its way toward the Mediterranean. The brothers stripped Joseph and sold him to the traders as a slave for 20 shekels or "silver pieces" (GENESIS 37:28)—which, according to Leviticus, was the going rate for a mature male slave (LEVITICUS 27:5). But what to tell their father, Jacob? The brothers agreed on a plausible story: Joseph had an unfortunate accident. By way of evidence, they spilled goat's blood on Joseph's garments and brought them back to their father. Jacob was devastated. "I shall go down to Sheol to my son, mourning," he said, referring to the netherworld (GENESIS 37:35).

JOSEPH

Upon their arrival in Egypt, the merchants sold Joseph to **Potiphar**, a captain of Pharaoh's guard. Joseph soon won his master's trust and was put in charge of the household. But Potiphar's wife—Genesis does not list her name, but in the Qur'an she is called Zuleikha—was attracted to him and even tried to seduce him (GENESIS 39:6). When Joseph declined her advances, she covered her tracks by denouncing him to her husband. Joseph was promptly thrown in prison, where he met two prominent inmates, the royal baker and cupbearer. One night, these men had disturbing dreams. The cupbearer saw three branches: "Pharaoh's cup was in my hand; and I took the grapes and pressed them into Pharaoh's cup." The baker, meanwhile, dreamed of three cake baskets poised on his head, and birds were eating from them. Joseph accurately explained their meaning: The baker was put to death, but the cupbearer was restored to his position (GENESIS 40:10-14).

Two years passed, until Pharaoh himself had a strange dream: He saw seven fat cows coming out of the river, which were then devoured by seven thin cows. None of the king's magicians could explain the meaning. Fortunately, the cupbearer remembered Joseph's gift for divining dreams. Summoned from prison, Joseph explained the dream as a warning of great famine: Egypt's seven years of plenty would be followed by seven years of drought. "Now therefore," Joseph concluded, "let Pharaoh look for a man discreet and wise, and set him and let him appoint officers over the land, and let them gather all the food of those good years that come"

ca 1473 B.C.E.	ca 1458 B.C.E.	ca 1455 B.C.E.	ca 1450 B.C.E.
Hatshepsut becomes Egypt's first female pharaoh	Thutmose III assumes sole control of Egypt	Thutmose III leads first of 16 campaigns into Canaan	First appearance of water clocks in Egypt

(GENESIS 41:33-35). "I am Pharaoh," said the king, "and all my people shall order themselves as you command" (GENESIS 41:40). Thus, the Hebrew slave, the son of Jacob, became the grand vizier of Egypt.

Archaeologists have tried in vain to find historical evidence of Joseph's elevation to grand vizier, which was tantamount to the position of prime minister. A number of scholars, however, have linked the story of Joseph's ascent to the turmoil of the Second Intermediate Period (ca 1780–1550 B.C.E.). When the death of King Amenemhet III left Egypt bereft of a legitimate successor, nomadic immigrants from Syria and northern Canaan rose in rebellion. Their power slowly spread across the Nile Delta, so that by the late 1700s B.C.E., they all but controlled Lower Egypt, pushing Egypt's aristocracy into exile in the city of Thebes. The Egyptians called these nomadic chieftains "Hyksos" *(Hikau-khoswet),* meaning "desert princes." Their first king was Sheshi, who established the 15th Dynasty (1663–1555 B.C.E.). Because the Hyksos kings were of Semitic origin, with ties to Canaan, they would have welcomed talented young men like Joseph into their administration.

There is another important clue that may corroborate this thesis. The Hyksos established their court in Avaris, which today is identified with the site of Tell el-Dab'a. The city was located in the heart of the region identified by scholars as the biblical Goshen—the same territory where four centuries later, the Book of Exodus would place Joseph's descendants, the Israelites, enslaved in bondage.

Genesis tells us that Joseph successfully stored a portion of the harvests over the next seven years, so that when the famine did occur, people from all over the Levant streamed to Egypt to buy food (GENESIS 41:57). Among these were Joseph's brothers. They met with Joseph, but did not recognize him. Joseph then put his brothers to a test: He gave them all the food they could carry, but secretly hid a precious goblet in the bag belonging to Benjamin, his youngest brother. As they approached the frontier, the goblet was discovered; Benjamin was arrested and brought back to the capital. Judah, the same brother who had sold Joseph to the merchants, pleaded with the grand vizier for Benjamin's life, not knowing that

And looking up they saw a caravan of Ishmaelites coming from Gilead, with their camels carrying gum, balm, and resin, on their way to carry it down to Egypt.

GENESIS 37:25

this powerful man was Joseph. Hearing Judah's plea, Joseph could no longer restrain himself. He ordered all his servants out of the hall, and cried, "I am *your brother*, Joseph, whom you sold into Egypt. But don't be distressed, or angry with yourselves, because you sold me here; for God sent me before you to preserve life" (GENESIS 45:5).

The brothers tearfully embraced. Jacob, their father, and all their wives, servants, and livestock were brought from Canaan. Pharaoh granted them land in the region of Goshen, "the best part of the land" east of the Nile Delta, there to live in peace (GENESIS 47:11). With their settlement in Egypt, the story of Genesis comes to a close.

THE THREE PILGRIMAGE FESTIVALS

The three Jewish festivals of Passover *(Pesach),* Weeks or Pentecost *(Shavuot),* and Booths *(Sukkot)* were ordained in the Book of Exodus (EXODUS 23:14-17; 34:18-23). After the completion of Solomon's Temple, these became pilgrimage festivals to be celebrated in Jerusalem.

Passover, or *Pesach,* commemorates the release from bondage in Egypt, when Hebrew homes were "passed over" by the angels of the Lord sent down to slay the firstborn sons in Egypt. The festival's highlight is the symbolic Passover meal, or *Seder.* Bitter herbs including parsley, chicory, and radishes, for example, serve to remind the table guests of Israel's bitter time in Egypt (EXODUS 1:14). They also eat unleavened bread, known as matzah, because the fleeing Israelites could not wait for the bread to rise.

The Weeks, or *Shavuot,* festival celebrates the day God presented the Torah to the nation of Israel at Mount Sinai. Shavuot (also known as "Pentecost," a Greek word meaning "fiftieth") takes place 50 days, or seven complete weeks after Passover. It is also associated with the harvest season, which in ancient Israel began with the harvest of barley during Passover and ended with the seven-week harvest of wheat during Shavuot, when pilgrims brought the first fruits *(Bikkurim)* of the land to the Temple in Jerusalem.

The autumn festival of Tabernacles or *Sukkot,* which lasts seven days, commemorates the tents in which the Israelites lived during their long trek through Sinai (LEVITICUS 23:42-43). During this holiday, which is popular with children, special prayers are read and meals are taken under an outdoors *sukkah,* or tent, which is erected for this purpose. Many Orthodox Jews also sleep in these improvised huts. ■

A large brass plate by 20th-century Israeli School was made specifically for use during Passover.

"The Finding of Moses" was painted in 1904 by British painter Sir Lawrence Alma-Tadema (1836–1912) at the occasion of the opening of the Aswan Dam in Egypt.

THE TEN COMMANDMENTS

The Ten Commandments, also known as the Decalogue (from the Greek *deka logous,* "ten terms"), are often considered the first comprehensive code of ethics in human civilization. Although elements of the Ten Commandments are also found in Egyptian and Babylonian laws of the time, they are unprecedented in their scope, covering fundamental precepts in faith ("You shall have no other gods before me"); work ("Six days you shall labor . . . but the seventh day is a Sabbath"); marriage ("You shall not commit adultery"); parental relations ("Honor your father and your mother"); law ("You shall not murder . . . You shall not bear false witness"); and social relations ("You shall not covet . . . anything that is your neighbor's"). The Ten Commandments are listed twice in the Bible, in Exodus as well as in Deuteronomy, with slight variations in the order and number (EXODUS 20:1-17; DEUTERONOMY 5:6-21). Together with the other 603 regulations found in the Torah, the Ten Commandments provide the essential ethical framework for the relationship between God and mankind, and the behavior of human beings toward one another. What's more, the Law applies to all, regardless of status, tribe, or gender.

According to Jewish tradition, the two tablets containing the Ten Commandments were placed in the Ark of the Covenant, a gold-plated wooden box measuring 4.3 by 2.6 feet. Whenever the people settled down in camp, the Ark was put in a special tent, called the Tabernacle. After Solomon built the Temple in Jerusalem, the Ark was placed in the inner sanctum, known as the Holy of Holies. ■

Italian artist Guido Reni (1575–1642) painted this portrait of "Moses with the Tablets of the Law."

ca 1400 B.C.E.	ca 1375 B.C.E.	ca 1365 B.C.E.	ca 1353 B.C.E.
Stonehenge in Britain assumes form it has today	Sunflowers appear in North America	Glass is invented simultaneously in Egypt and Mesopotamia	Akhenaten assumes throne and shifts capital to Amarna

MOSES

As the Book of Exodus opens, a new king had risen over Egypt "who did not know Joseph." This pharaoh became concerned that the descendants of Jacob, still living in Goshen, were too numerous (EXODUS 1:8-9). He forcefully conscripted them as slave labor, and ordered them to build "supply cities, Pithom and Ramses, for Pharaoh." Egyptian records confirm that the 19th Dynasty (1293–1185 B.C.E.) launched a major military program to reassert Egypt's power in the Levant. As part of this effort, King Seti I (ca 1290–1279 B.C.E.) built a new garrison city, which his successor, Ramses II (ca 1279–1213 B.C.E.) would call *Pi-Ramesses-Meri-Imen* ("The House of Ramses the Beloved of Amun"). Pi-Ramesses has been identified with a *tel* or mound near Qantir, north of Cairo. Ramses also built a second city dedicated to his personal patron, Atum, called *Per Atum,* quite possibly the biblical Pithom.

According to Exodus, when the Hebrews continued to multiply, Pharaoh ordered even more drastic measures: Every newborn male infant was to be drowned in the river (EXODUS 1:22). Around this time, a young couple from the tribe of Levi, **Amram** and **Jochebed**, had a baby. In order to save him from roving Egyptian patrols, Jochebed, in an echo of the story of Noah's ark, "got a papyrus basket for him, and plastered it with bitumen and pitch" (EXODUS 2:3), then set the baby afloat on the river. Jochebed and Amram also had an older daughter named Miriam, who was told to stand on the riverbank and ensure that no harm would come to her infant brother.

Eventually, Pharaoh's daughter discovered the basket. She was overcome with pity and took in the baby. Miriam rushed to the scene and said, "Shall I go and get you a nurse from the Hebrew women to nurse the child for you?" Pharaoh's daughter accepted her offer, so Miriam fetched her mother to serve as the child's nurse; thus, Moses and his mother were reunited. Eventually, Pharaoh's daughter adopted the child and named him Moses, "because I drew him out of the water" (EXODUS 2:10). The Hebrew verb *moshe* means "to draw out."

However, *mose* or *moses* was also a very common Egyptian patronymic, as in *Tutmoses,* meaning "son of Tut."

Moses grew up at Pharaoh's court, but he never lost a strong sense of kinship with the Hebrew slaves. When he saw an Egyptian overseer beating one of the Israelite workers, he killed the Egyptian and buried him (EXODUS 2:12). Word of this deed reached the ears of Pharaoh, forcing Moses to flee into the Sinai Desert. Eventually he reached a well in the Midian, where he met a group of young girls who were being harassed by shepherds. Moses intervened, and in gratitude he was invited to dine with the girls' father, a man named **Jethro**. Moses remained with Jethro and married one of his daughters, **Zipporah**. She presented him with a son named **Gershom**, a wordplay on the Hebrew *ger-sham,* meaning "an alien (in the land)" (EXODUS 2:22).

According to Genesis, the Midianite tribe traced its origins to a son of Abraham's second wife, Keturah. The Book of Exodus identifies Jethro as a priest, which may imply that the Midianites had remained faithful to the God of their forefathers. Indeed, it is during his sojourn in Sinai that Moses first encounters God in the form of a burning bush. "I have observed the misery of my people who are in Egypt," God's voice called out to him; "I have heard their cry on account of their taskmasters" (EXODUS 3:1-7). God then charged Moses to lead the Israelites out of bondage and bring them to the Promised Land. Moses demurred; he felt powerless to take on such a challenging mission. In response, God gave him the power to conjure magic signs. He also told Moses to use his brother **Aaron** as his spokesman, because "he can speak fluently" (EXODUS 4:14).

A statue depicts the youthful King Ramses II (1279– 1213 B.C.E.)—New Kingdom, 19th Dynasty.

Moses and Aaron dutifully set out for Egypt, where they requested an audience with Pharaoh. Unfortunately, their pleas to release the Hebrew slaves fell on deaf ears. Enraged, Pharaoh orders his taskmasters to "no longer give the people straw to make bricks, as before," but to let them "gather straw for themselves,"

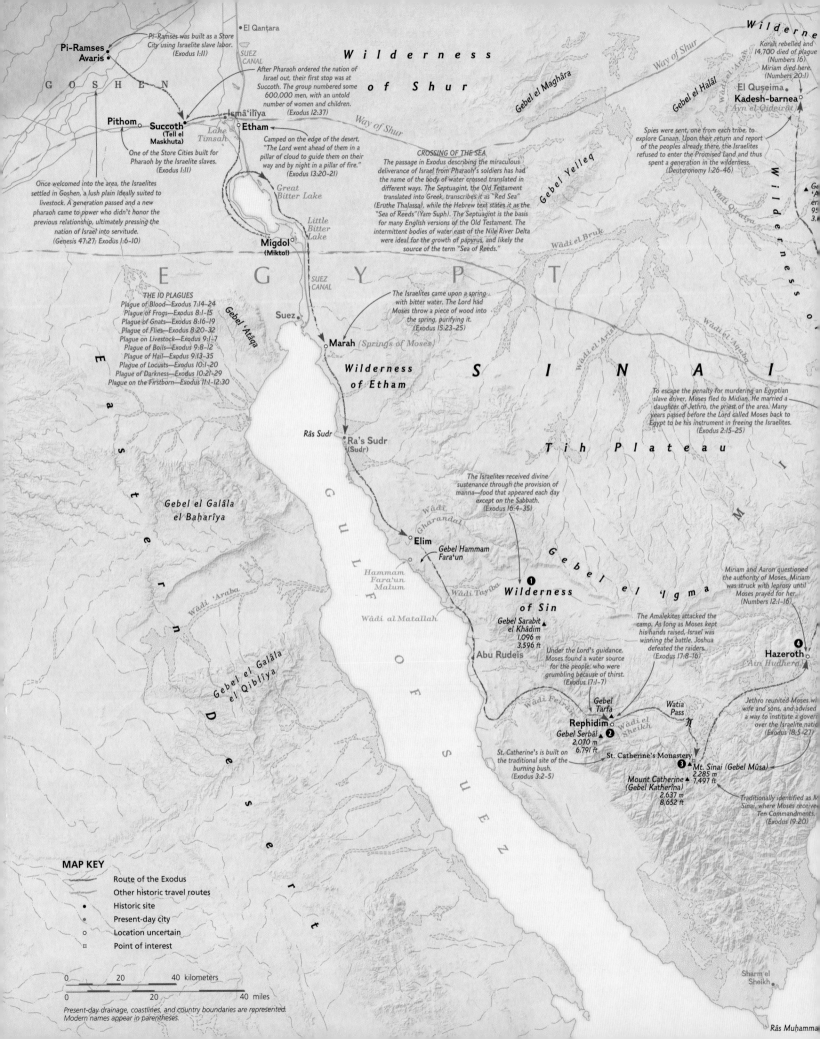

Pi-Ramses / Avaris

PI-Ramses was built as a Store City using Israelite slave labor. (Exodus 1:11)

El Qantara

W i l d e r n e s s

Korah rebelled and 14,700 died of plague (Numbers 16). Miriam died here. (Numbers 20:1)

W i l d e r n e s s   o f   S h u r

Way of Shur

G O S H E N

After Pharaoh ordered the nation of Israel out, their first stop was at Succoth. The group numbered some 600,000 men, with an untold number of women and children. (Exodus 12:37)

SUEZ CANAL

Isma'iliya

Pithom

Succoth (Tell el Maskhuta)

One of the Store Cities built for Pharaoh by the Israelite slaves. (Exodus 1:11)

Etham

Lake Timsah

Camped on the edge of the desert, "The Lord went ahead of them in a pillar of cloud to guide them on their way and by night in a pillar of fire." (Exodus 13:20-21)

Way of Shur

Gebel el Maghâra

Gebel el Halâl

El Quseima

Kadesh-barnea ('Ayn el-Qideirât)

Spies were sent, one from each tribe, to explore Canaan. Upon their return and report of the peoples already there, the Israelites refused to enter the Promised Land and thus spent a generation in the wilderness. (Deuteronomy 1:26-46)

Once welcomed into the area, the Israelites settled in Goshen, a lush plain ideally suited to livestock. A generation passed and a new pharaoh came to power who didn't honor the previous relationship, ultimately pressing the nation of Israel into servitude. (Genesis 47:27; Exodus 1:6-10)

Great Bitter Lake

Little Bitter Lake

Migdol (Miktol)

CROSSING OF THE SEA
The passage in Exodus describing the miraculous deliverance of Israel from Pharaoh's soldiers has had the name of the body of water crossed translated in different ways. The Septuagint, the Old Testament translated into Greek, transcribes it as "Red Sea" (Eruthe Thalassa), while the Hebrew text states it as the "Sea of Reeds" (Yam Suph). The Septuagint is the basis for many English versions of the Old Testament. The intermittent bodies of water east of the Nile River Delta were ideal for the growth of papyrus, and likely the source of the term "Sea of Reeds."

Gebel Yelleq

E G Y P T

THE 10 PLAGUES
Plague of Blood—Exodus 7:14-24
Plague of Frogs—Exodus 8:1-15
Plague of Gnats—Exodus 8:16-19
Plague of Flies—Exodus 8:20-32
Plague on Livestock—Exodus 9:1-7
Plague of Boils—Exodus 9:8-12
Plague of Hail—Exodus 9:13-35
Plague of Locusts—Exodus 10:1-20
Plague of Darkness—Exodus 10:21-29
Plague on the Firstborn—Exodus 11:1-12:30

Gebel 'Atâqa

SUEZ CANAL

Suez

The Israelites came upon a spring with bitter water. The Lord had Moses throw a piece of wood into the spring, purifying it. (Exodus 15:23-25)

Marah (Springs of Moses)

Wilderness of Etham

S I N A I

To escape the penalty for murdering an Egyptian slave driver, Moses fled to Midian. He married a daughter of Jethro, the priest of the area. Many years passed before the Lord called Moses back to Egypt to be his instrument in freeing the Israelites. (Exodus 2:15-25)

Râs Sudr

Ra's Sudr (Sudr)

Tih Plateau

E a s t e r n

Gebel el Galâla el Baharîya

The Israelites received divine sustenance through the provision of manna—food that appeared each day except on the Sabbath. (Exodus 16:4-35)

Wâdi Gharandal

Elim

Gebel Hammam Fara'un

Hammam Fara'un Malum

Wâdi Tayiba

Wâdi al Matallah

Gebel el 'Igma

Miriam and Aaron questioned the authority of Moses. Miriam was struck with leprosy until Moses prayed for her. (Numbers 12:1-16)

① *Wilderness of Sin*

Gebel Sarabit el Khâdim 1,096 m 3,596 ft

Abu Rudeis

The Amalekites attacked the camp. As long as Moses kept his hands raised, Israel was winning the battle. Joshua defeated the raiders. (Exodus 17:8-16)

Under the Lord's guidance, Moses found a water source for the people, who were grumbling because of thirst. (Exodus 17:1-7)

④ Hazeroth ('Ain Hudhera)

Jethro reunited Moses with wife and sons, and advised a way to institute a government over the Israelite nation. (Exodus 18:5-27)

G U L F   O F   S U E Z

Gebel el Galâla el Qiblîya

Wâdi 'Araba

Wâdi Feirân

Gebel Tarfa

Watia Pass

Rephidim ②

Gebel Serbâl 2,070 m 6,791 ft

Wâdi el Sheikh

St. Catherine's is built on the traditional site of the burning bush. (Exodus 3:2-5)

St. Catherine's Monastery

③ Mt. Sinai (Gebel Mûsa) 2,285 m 7,497 ft

Mount Catherine (Gebel Katherîna) 2,637 m 8,652 ft

Traditionally identified as Mt. Sinai, where Moses received the Ten Commandments. (Exodus 19:20)

D e s e r t

MAP KEY
— Route of the Exodus
— Other historic travel routes
• Historic site
▪ Present-day city
○ Location uncertain
⊡ Point of interest

0   20   40 kilometers
0   20   40 miles

Present-day drainage, coastlines, and country boundaries are represented. Modern names appear in parentheses.

Sharm el Sheikh

Râs Muhammad

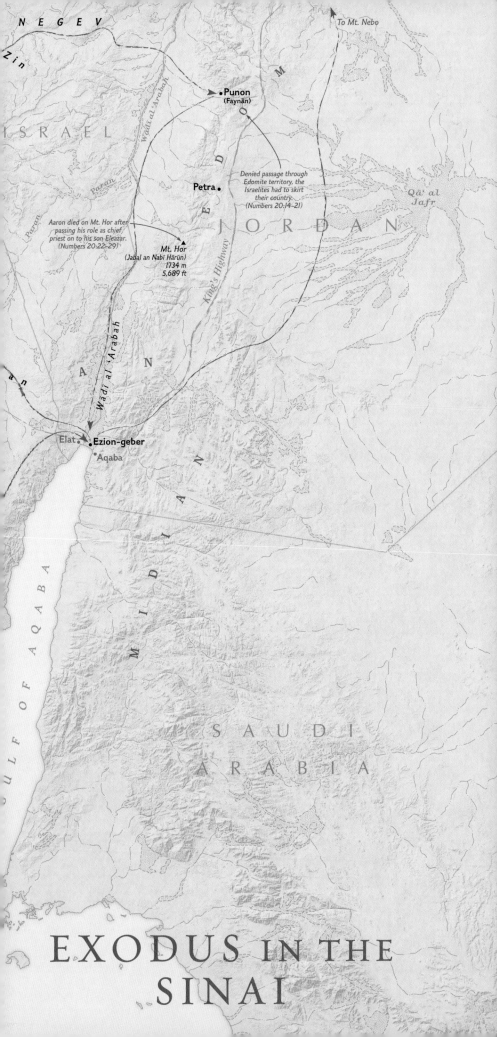

NEGEV

To Mt. Nebo

ISRAEL

Punon
(Faynān)

Petra

E D O M

J O R D A N

Qā' al
Jafr

Denied passage through
Edomite territory, the
Israelites had to skirt
their country.
(Numbers 20:14-21)

Aaron died on Mt. Hor after
passing his role as chief
priest on to his son Eleazar.
(Numbers 20:22-29)

Mt. Hor
(Jabal an Nabī Hārūn)
1734 m
5,689 ft

King's Highway

Wadi al 'Arabah

Elat
Ezion-geber
Aqaba

M I D I A N

S A U D I
A R A B I A

GULF OF AQABA

EXODUS IN THE SINAI

❶ Wilderness of Sin The Book of Exodus places the vast, moonlike surface of the wilderness of Sin "between Elim and Sinai."

❷ Rephidim This large palm grove in the lush oasis of Wadi Feiran is often associated with "Rephidim" in the account of the Exodus.

❸ Mount Sinai (Jebel Musa) The summit of Mount Sinai (or Jebel Musa in Arabic) is traditionally associated with Mount Sinai, where Moses received the Tablets of the Law.

❹ Hazeroth (Ain Hudhera) The Israelites may have passed through this steep canyon on their way to Hazeroth, today known as Ain Hudhera.

though the daily quota of finished bricks would remain the same (EXODUS 5:7-8).

To punish Pharaoh, God sent a series of plagues to bend Pharaoh's will. The river Nile turned to blood, killing its fish and making its water undrinkable. Thousands of frogs covered the land, soon followed by gnats and flies. Hailstorms ravaged the fields and destroyed the harvest; whatever remained was consumed by locusts. Then the land was cast in darkness.

But only the tent plague finally broke Pharaoh's resistance. All of Egypt's firstborn males were to be slain. To ensure that God's angels would bypass the Hebrew families, each Israelite family had to slaughter a lamb, roast it, and brush its blood on "the two doorposts and the lintel of the houses in which they eat it." The families should eat it "with your loins girded, your sandals on your feet, and your staff in your hand," ready to leave at a moment's notice. This moment, said God, should henceforth be celebrated as "the Lord's Passover" (12:6-11). That night, the firstborn sons in every Egyptian family were killed.

Pharaoh relented at last. "Take your flocks and your herds," he told Moses and Aaron, "and be gone" (EXODUS 12:31-32). Exulted, Moses led the Israelites of Egypt, but Pharaoh soon had second thoughts. He gathered his chariots and gave chase, catching up with the Hebrews near a place usually translated as the "Red Sea," though the actual translation of the Hebrew *Yam Suph* is "Sea of Reeds." Quite possibly, this may refer to the Bitter Lakes, located midway between Egypt and Sinai. Moses spread his hands and a strong eastern wind forged a path through the waters. As soon as Pharaoh's chariots tried to plunge after them, the waters returned and Pharaoh's army drowned, prompting Miriam to lead the women in a hymn of praise (EXODUS 14:28).

Moses then led his people into Sinai. Surprisingly, he did not lead them straight into the Promised Land of Canaan, which could be reached via a coastal road known as the "Way of the Philistines,"

Then Moses, the servant of the Lord, died there in the land of Moab, at the Lord's command.

DEUTERONOMY 34:5

French Baroque artist Poussin (1594–1665) painted the "Adoration of the Golden Calf" in 1629.

or a land route straight across Sinai known as the "Way of Shur." Instead, he took them south, back to Mount Sinai and the Midianite tribe of Jethro and Zipporah. Three months after their departure from Egypt, having overcome many deprivations, Moses reached Mount Sinai. Here, God handed him the Ten Commandments, the cornerstone of the Law that would guide the Israelites from this time forward. God's covenant with Abraham, Isaac, and Jacob had become tangible; the tribe of Israelite refugees was now a nation.

AARON

The Bible's portrayal of Aaron is that of a conflicted personality. Although Aaron served Moses as his second in command, Aaron was actually three years older than Moses. Aaron had married a woman from the tribe of Judah named **Elisheba**, and had four sons by her. In Egypt, Aaron was Moses' faithful companion; he attempted to impress Pharaoh with magical signs, such as changing his rod into a serpent and inducing many of the plagues. As a reward for his service, Aaron was anointed as Israel's first high priest, while his tribe of the Levi was chosen for priestly service (EXODUS CHAPTERS 28–29). But when Moses tarried on Mount Sinai for days on end, and the Israelites grew impatient, Aaron's resolve collapsed. According to Exodus, they "gathered around Aaron and said to him: 'Come, make gods for us, who shall go before us'" (EXODUS 32:1). Rather than remaining steadfast in his faith, Aaron gave in.

ca 1290 B.C.E.	ca 1279 B.C.E.	ca 1274 B.C.E..	ca 1270 B.C.E.
Putative date of the first garrison city built by Israelites on orders of Seti I	Seti I is succeeded by Ramses II	Battle of Kadesh between Ramses II and the Hittites	Putative date of second garrison city built by Israelites on orders of Ramses II

He ordered the people to collect all the gold in their possession, and used it to create a golden calf for worship. He then ordered a great feast, and all the Israelites "rose up to play" (EXODUS 32:6).

The choice of this idol was no accident. A calf or bull, symbol of virility and strength, is associated with the Canaanite *El,* and such idolatry would persist well into the period of the divided monarchy. King Jeroboam I of the Northern Kingdom of Israel, for example, commissioned two golden calves for the sanctuaries of YHWH in Bethel and Dan, to serve as the Lord's attendants. Some scholars believe that Aaron's golden calf was not meant to displace God, but to make him more tangible to the impatient Israelites, using Canaanite iconography.

When Moses descended from Mount Sinai, he was so incensed by this pagan image that he smashed the stone tablets of the Law and ordered 3,000 males to be put to death. Moses had to ascend Mount Sinai again so that the stone tablets could be written once more (EXODUS 34:2).

JETHRO THE PRIEST

Prior to his sojourn on Mount Sinai, Moses was reunited with his wife and son, as well as his father-in-law, Jethro the priest. Jethro was impressed with the delivery of the Israelites from Egypt. "Now I know that the Lord is greater than all gods," he said (EXODUS 18:11). Jethro then counseled Moses to create a proper organization, ruled by laws, to manage the unruly Israelites. "You must teach them ordinances and laws," he said. "Moreover, you must select out of all these people able men, who worship God, men of truth . . . to rule over them as officers and judges" (EXODUS 18:20-21). The Book of Numbers intimates that Jethro, now called Hobab, then served as a guide for the Israelites, to lead them out of Sinai and into the Promised Land. But that journey would last another 40 years, enabling the Hebrew slaves to become a strong, trained force before their invasion of the Promised Land.

THE PROMISED LAND

The Promised Land was a strip of land known in prehistoric times as Canaan, wedged between the Mediterranean and the Arabian desert, carved by highlands, coastal plains, and low valleys, and watered by the great river Jordan. Much of Canaan's topography, however, was more suitable for nomads than farmers. Only the Jezreel Valley, also known as the Plain of Esdraelon, was suitable for broad-spectrum agriculture, deriving its water from numerous springs as well as two small rivers, the Kishon and the Harod. As a result, the Jezreel and the coastal plains were stoutly defended by the Canaanites during the Israelite incursion, leaving the Hebrew tribes little choice but to settle in the central highlands. The Jezreel also served as a natural crossroads of caravan routes between Egypt and Mesopotamia, defended by a fortress city called Megiddo. Megiddo then became the *Har Megiddo* or "Armageddon" in the Book of Revelations as the place of the final battle between good and evil at the end of time. ◼

Moses would never see that Promised Land, except from afar. On the eve of the Hebrews' crossing of the Jordan, the Book of Deuteronomy tells us, he went up Mount Nebo to behold the valley of the river and the hills of the Promised Land beyond. And there he died, to be buried in an unmarked grave (DEUTERONOMY 34:6).

PHARAOH

The identity of Pharaoh in the Moses story has been much debated, but many scholars are inclined to accept that Exodus has King Ramses II in mind. The reference to the Israelites building the cities of Ramses and Pithom (or *Pi-Ramesses* and *Per-Atum* in archaeological parlance) is an important indication. So is the fact that the very first reference to "Israel" appears on the Victory Slab of Pharaoh Merneptah, one of Ramses' sons. This monument is dated around 1207 B.C.E.—which suggests that the Exodus story is set in a period prior to the reign of Merneptah, between 1280 and 1220 B.C.E. While there are no Egyptian records of the Exodus, there is ample documentation of Semitic immigrant workers in Egypt, who may have drifted back to Syria-Canaan in the 13th century.

British painter Sir Lawrence Alma-Tadema (1836–1912) painted "The Death of the First Born" in 1874.

ca 1259 B.C.E.	ca 1256 B.C.E.	ca 1236 B.C.E.	ca 1212 B.C.E.
Egyptian treaty with the Hittites; first peace treaty in history	Temples at Abu Simbel are completed	Ramses II launches invasion of Nubia	Ramses II dies; is succeeded by Merneptah

Sumerian artifact
The so-called "Royal Standard of Ur" is one of the most important artifacts of the Sumerian period. Dating from around 2600 B.C.E., it depicts scenes of war and peace, and features the wheel-borne wagon, a Sumerian invention.

Fertility goddess
This figure of a fertility goddess found in Syria is dated to the Middle Bronze Age (2000–1550 B.C.E.).

Gold relief cup
This beautiful gold cup featuring griffins and bulls was found in the royal cemetery of the ancient city of Marlik, today's Iran, and dates from the Late Bronze Age, 14th century B.C.E.

Canaanite necklace
The faience beads and pendants in this necklace betray a strong Egyptian influence. It was found in the Fosse Temple of the Canaanite city of Lachish, dating from the Middle Bronze Age (2000–1550 B.C.E.).

Gold leaf pendants *This lavish woman's headdress was recovered from the Royal Tombs of Ur (ca 2600–2400 B.C.E.). It features gold leaf pendants interspersed with beads of carnelian and lapis lazuli.*

Statue of human likeness
This clay statue of an unidentified god from the Old Babylonian period (1800–1750 B.C.E.) reveals the growing confidence of sculptors with the human figure. The yellow of his headdress and necklace suggests gold, while the vertical beads were colored red to suggest carnelian.

TREASURES OF THE BRONZE AGE

The beginning of the Early Bronze Age (3300–2100 B.C.E.) is often considered a watershed in the evolution of mankind. In Mesopotamia, the culture of Sumer was reaching its apogee in the city-state of Uruk, known as Erech in the Bible, nurtured by the waters of the Euphrates and the Tigris. In 2900 B.C.E., the region was struck by a catastrophic flood. In its wake, the city of Ur took over as the center of Sumerian culture, which in the millennium to come would be absorbed in the Akkadian Empire, and subsequently in the Babylonian Empire founded by King Hammurabi around 1760 B.C.E.

Another major civilization was emerging along the river Nile in Egypt. Around 3300 B.C.E., Egypt's fiefdoms had coalesced into two separate kingdoms: Upper and Lower Egypt. Two hundred years later, a king named Menes, or Narmer, unified these two kingdoms and founded Egypt's 1st Dynasty (3100–2890 B.C.E.). However, Egypt and its vassal regions—including Canaan—suffered a sharp decline, possibly because of a prolonged drought. During the reign of King Amenemhet I (1991–1962 B.C.E.), the Egyptian economy slowly recovered, which led to an era of rapid growth in trade with Syria, the Levant, and Mesopotamia.

Colored relief *Egyptian bakers are busy preparing bread cakes in this colored relief dating from the Fifth Dynasty (2500–2350 B.C.E.).*

CHAPTER 1
WHO'S WHO
An Alphabetical Listing of Characters in the Books of Genesis Through Deuteronomy

AARON
("lofty," "mountain of strength")
Eldest son of Amram and Jochebed, daughter of Levi (EXODUS 6:20). Aaron was born in Egypt three years before his brother Moses, and an unspecified number of years after his sister Miriam (EXODUS 2:1,4; 7:7). He married Elisheba, the daughter of Amminadab of the house of Judah, by whom he had four sons, Nadab and Abihu, Eleazar and Ithamar (I CHRONICLES 2:10). Aaron was sent by God to serve as the "mouthpiece" of Moses and speak on his behalf (EXODUS 4:14; 7:1-19). As such, he assisted Moses in all his interviews with Pharaoh. When the Israelites fought

A 20th-century British print depicts "Aaron Throwing Down the Rod That God Has Given Moses."

their first battle with Amalek in Rephidim, Moses stood on a hill overlooking the battle with the rod of God in his outstretched hand. Aaron and Hur, his sister's husband, held up Moses' wearied hands till Joshua and the chosen warriors of Israel gained victory. When Moses ascended Mount Sinai to receive the tablets of the Law, Aaron and his two sons, Nadab and Abihu, along with 70 of the elders of Israel, accompanied him part of the way (EXODUS 19:24; 24:9-11). Aaron then returned to the people, and yielding to their fear, made them a golden calf as an object of worship (EXODUS 32:4; PSALMS 106:19). When Moses came back to the camp, he sternly rebuked Aaron but interceded for him before God, who forgave him (DEUTERONOMY 9:20). Aaron and his sons were raised to the office of priest, with Aaron serving as high priest, though his sons Nadab and Abihu died (LEVITICUS CHAPTERS 8; 9). Soon after the Israelites reached Hazeroth, Aaron sided with Miriam in criticizing Moses for his relationship with an Ethiopian woman. God sided with Moses and punished Miriam with leprosy (NUMBERS CHAPTER 12). Aaron never lived to see the Promised Land; he died on Mount Hor at age 123.

ABEL
("breath," "emptiness," "vanity")
Second son of Adam and Eve, a shepherd, who was killed by his brother Cain, a farmer (GENESIS 4:1-16). One day, each of the brothers offered up to God the first fruits of their labors. Cain offered the fruits of the field; Abel, as a shepherd, the firstlings of his flock. God accepted Abel's offering, but "unto Cain and his offering he had not respect." Cain then became angry with his brother and killed him (GENESIS 4:3-9). There are several references to Abel in the New Testament. Jesus refers to him as "righteous" (MATTHEW 23:35). "The blood of sprinkling"

Johann Heinrich Roos (1631–1685) painted this canvas of "Abraham and Sarah before Abimelech" in 1681.

is said to speak "better things than that of Abel," comparing the sacrifice offered by Christ and that offered by Abel (HEBREWS 12:24).

ABIDA (OR ABI'DAH)
("father of knowledge or judgment")
One of the five sons of Midian, who was the son of Abraham by Keturah and the chief of an Arab tribe (I CHRONICLES 1:33).

ABIDAN
("father of the judge")
Son of Gideoni, leader of the tribe of Benjamin (NUMBERS 2:22; 10:24). He was chosen to represent his tribe at the census in the wilderness of Sinai (NUMBERS 1:11).

ABIHU
("worshipper of God")
Second son of Aaron by Elisheba (EXODUS 6:23; NUMBERS 3:2; 26:60; I CHRONICLES 6:3). Along with his three brothers, he was consecrated to the priest's office (EXODUS 28:1). Together with his elder brother Nadab, he was consumed by fire from heaven (LEVITICUS 10:1-2).

ABIMELECH
("father of the king")

1. Philistine king of Gerar in the time of Abraham (GENESIS 20:1-18). In an echo of the "wife-sister" confusion that prompted Pharaoh to take Sarah as his concubine (GENESIS 12:10-20), Abimelech also took Sarah, but later restored her to her husband, Abraham. As a mark of respect, he offered Abraham a settlement, while rebuking him for pretending that Sarah was only his sister. Abimelech later visited Abraham and entered into a league of peace and friendship with him (GENESIS 21:22-34).

2. A king of Gerar in the time of Isaac, of whom a similar narrative is recorded in relation to Rebekah (GENESIS 26:1-22).

3. Son of Gideon (JUDGES 9:1), proclaimed king after his father's death (JUDGES 8:33–9:6). He murdered his 70 brothers before being struck on his head by a stone, thrown by a woman from the wall above. Rather than die by the hands of a woman, he ordered his armor bearer to kill him with his sword (JUDGES 9:50-57).

4. The son of Abiathar and high priest in the time of David (I CHRONICLES 18:16).

ABIRAM
("proud")

1. A Reubenite, son of Eliab, who with Korah, a Levite, organized a conspiracy against Moses and Aaron. He and all the conspirators, with their families and possessions (except the children of Korah), were swallowed up by an earthquake (NUMBERS 16:1-27; 26:9; PSALMS 106:17).

2. Eldest son of Hiel, the Bethelite, who died when his father laid the foundations of Jericho (I KINGS 16:34), thus fulfilling the curse of Joshua (JOSHUA 6:26).

ABRAHAM
("father of multitude")

Originally Abram, later named Abraham. Son of Terah, and founder of the Hebrew nation. Abram, at 75, with his wife, Sarai (later Sarah), and nephew Lot, moved to Canaan. He was directed by divine command that he should become the founder of a great nation, and that all the families of the earth should be blessed in him (GENESIS

12:5-6). In Egypt, Abram tried to hide Sarai by representing her as his sister, but her beauty was reported to the king and she was taken into the royal harem. The deception was discovered and the pharaoh dismissed Abram from the country (GENESIS 12:10-20). He left Egypt and pitched his tent among the groves of Mamre (GENESIS 13:1). Here, the promise was repeated that his descendants should become a mighty nation (GENESIS 15:1). Sarah was still barren, however. After taking Hagar as his concubine, Abraham's son Ishmael was born (GENESIS 16:1). Three "men" (i.e., angels) then met with

Flemish artist Jan Provoost (ca 1462–1529) painted this panel of "Abraham, Sarah, and the Angel" around 1520.

Abraham and foretold the birth of Isaac. Abraham accompanied them to Sodom and tried, in vain, to avert the vengeance threatened on the cities of the plain (GENESIS 18:17-33). During his temporary residence among the Philistines in Gerar, his son Isaac was born. Ishmael and his mother were driven out (GENESIS 21:10). Years later, Abraham was ordered by God to sacrifice Isaac. The sacrifice was preempted by an angel of God, and Abraham and his son returned to Beersheba (GENESIS 22:1), followed by a return to Hebron (GENESIS 23:2). With his wife, Keturah, Abraham had another six children: Zimran, Jokshan, Medan, Midian, Ishbok,

and Shuah, who became the ancestors of nomadic tribes inhabiting the countries south and southeast of Palestine. At age 175, he died and was laid beside Sarah in the tomb of Machpelah (GENESIS 25:7-10).

ACHBOR
("gnawing of a mouse")

1. An Edomite king (GENESIS 36:38; I CHRONICLES 1:49).

2. One of Josiah's officers sent to the prophetess Huldah to inquire about the newly discovered Book of the Law (II KINGS 22:12-14). He is also called Abdon (II CHRONICLES 34:20).

ADAH
("ornament, beauty")

1. The first of the two wives of Lamech, who bore him Jabal and Jubal (GENESIS 4:19).

2. A Hittitess, one of the three wives of Esau, mother of Eliphaz (GENESIS 36:2,10,12,16). In Genesis 26:34, she is called Basemath.

ADAM
("man," "red earth")

The name in the Bible of the first man. The creation of man was on the sixth day. Adam was created (not born), a perfect man in body and spirit, but as innocent and completely inexperienced as a child. He was placed in a garden, which God had planted "eastward in Eden." Adam was permitted to eat the fruit from every tree in the garden but one, which was called "the tree of the knowledge of good and evil," to test Adam's obedience (GENESIS 2:8-9). While Adam was in the garden, beasts and fowls were brought to him to be named. After this, God put him in a deep sleep and took one of his ribs, which he fashioned into a woman: Eve (GENESIS 2:21-22). At this time, they were both described as being naked without the consciousness of shame. Eve was enticed by a serpent to eat the fruit of the forbidden tree and to give it to Adam. They became self-conscious and were aware that they were naked. God confronted Adam about this, but he passed the blame on Eve. "This woman whom you gave me," he said, "she gave it to me." God thereupon questioned Eve, who sought to pass the blame to the serpent (GENESIS 3:7). For this transgression, Adam and Eve were expelled from Eden. Shortly after their expulsion, Eve had their first child and called him Cain. Their other children included Abel and Seth (GENESIS 5:4).

ADBEEL
("offspring of God")
The third of the 12 sons of Ishmael (GENESIS 25:13; I CHRONICLES 1:29), and probably the progenitor of an Arab tribe.

"Samuel Killing Agag, King of the Amalekites" was painted by the Dutch artist Rombout van Troyen (ca 1605–1650).

AGAG
("flame")
1. A king of the Amalekites referred to by Balaam (NUMBERS 24:7).
2. King of the Amalekites (I SAMUEL 15:8-33), whom Saul spared contrary to God's will (EXODUS 17:14; 25:17).

AHIEZER
("brother of help")
1. Son of Ammishaddai, hereditary chieftain of the tribe of Dan (NUMBERS 1:12; 2:25; 7:66).
2. The Benjamite chief of a body of archers in the time of David (I CHRONICLES 12:3).

AIAH
("clamor")
1. Son of Zibeon, a descendant of Seir

and ancestor of one of the wives of Esau (I CHRONICLES 1:40), called Ajah in Genesis 36:24. He probably died before his father, as the succession fell to his brother Anah.
2. Father of Rizpah, the concubine of Saul (II SAMUEL 3:7; 21:8,10-11).

AMALEK
("dweller in a valley")
Son of Eliphaz by his concubine Timnah grandson of Esau, and chieftain of Edom (GENESIS 36:12,16; I CHRONICLES 1:36).

AMMIEL
("people of God")
1. One of the 12 spies sent by Moses to search the land of Canaan (NUMBERS 13:12). He was one of the 10 who perished by the plague for their unfavorable report (NUMBERS 14:37).
2. Father of Machir of Lo-debar, in whose house Mephibosheth resided (II SAMUEL 9:4-5; 17:27).
3. Father of Bathsheba, the wife of Uriah, and afterward of David (I CHRONICLES 3:5). He is called Eliam in II Samuel 11:3.
4. The sixth son of Obed-edom (I CHRONICLES 26:5), and one of the doorkeepers of the temple.

AMMIHUD
("people of praise")
1. An Ephraimite father of Elishama, the chief of the tribe at the time of the Exodus (NUMBERS 1:10; 2:18; 7:48; 7:53; 10:22; I CHRONICLES 1:1; 7:26) and, through him, ancestor of Joshua.
2. A Simeonite, father of Shemuel (NUMBERS 34:20).
3. Father of Pedahel, prince of the tribe of Naphtali (NUMBERS 34:28).
4. Father of Talmai king of Geshur (II SAMUEL 13:37).
5. A descendant of Pharez, son of Judah (I CHRONICLES 9:4).

AMRAM
("an exalted people," "kindred of the high")
1. Son of Kohath and the son of Levi. He married Jochebed, his father's sister. He was the father of Aaron, Miriam, and Moses (EXODUS 6:18-20; NUMBERS 3:19). He died in Egypt at the age of 137 (EXODUS 6:20). His

descendants were called Amramites (NUMBERS 3:27; I CHRONICLES 26:23).
2. One of the sons of Bani in the time of Ezra, who had married a foreign wife (EZRA 10:34).
3. Son of Dishon and descendant of Seir (I CHRONICLES 1:41).
4. Head of one of the branches of Levites (NUMBERS 3:19,27; I CHRONICLES 26:23).

AMRAPHEL
("keeper of the gods," "one that speaks of secrets")
1. A Hamite king of Shinar or Babylonia who joined the victorious incursion of the Elamite Chedorlaomer against the kings of Sodom and Gomorrah (GENESIS 14:1).
2. King of Shinar (GENESIS 14:1,9).

ANAH
("one who answers," "afflicted")
1. Son of Zibeon and father of Oholibamah, one of Esau's wives (GENESIS 36:2,14,25). He is supposed to have discovered the "hot springs" in the desert as he fed the asses of Zibeon, his father.
2. One of the sons of Seir, and head of an Idumean tribe, called a Horite (GENESIS 36:20,29; I CHRONICLES 1:38).

ANAK
("a collar," "long-necked")
1. Son of Arba and the father of the Anakim (JOSHUA 15:13; 21:11).
2. Father of three giants (JOSHUA 15:13-14; 21:11).

ANER
("boy")
A Canaanite chief who joined forces with those of Abraham in pursuit of Chedorlaomer (GENESIS 14:13,24).

ARAM
("high")
1. Son of Shem and a grandson of Nahor, ancestor of the Arameans (GENESIS 10:22; 22:21).
2. Son of Kemuel and descendant of Nahor (GENESIS 22:21).
3. Son of Shomer, an Asherite (I CHRONICLES 7:34).

ARD

("one that is descending")
The son of Bela and grandson of Benjamin (GENESIS 46:21; NUMBERS 26:38-40). In I Chronicles 8:3, he is called Addar.

ARIOCH

("venerable," "lionlike")
1. King of Ellasar, one of the allies of Chedorlaomer in his expedition against his rebellious tributaries (GENESIS 14:1).
2. Captain of Nebuchadnezzar's bodyguard (DANIEL 2:14).
3. King of the Elymaeans (JUDITH 1:6).

ARPACHSHAD

1. Son of Shem and ancestor of Eber (GENESIS 10:22,24; 11:10; I CHRONICLES 1:17-18; LUKE 3:36). He dwelt in Mesopotamia, and became, according to the Jewish historian Josephus, the progenitor of the Chaldeans.
2. King "who reigned over the Medes in Ecbatana" (JUDITH 1:1-4).

ASENATH

("gift of the sun-god," "peri," "misfortune")
Daughter of Potipherah and the wife of Joseph (GENESIS 41:45). She was the mother of Manasseh and Ephraim (GENESIS 41:50; 46:20).

ASHER

("happiness")
The eighth son of Jacob. His mother, Zilpah, was Leah's handmaid (GENESIS 30:13). Of the tribe founded by him, nothing is recorded beyond its holding a place in the list of the tribes (GENESIS 35:26; 46:17; EXODUS 1:4). It increased in numbers 29 percent during the 38 years of wanderings. The place of this tribe during the march through the desert was between Dan and Naphtali (NUMBERS 2:27).

ASHERAH

("straight")
Name of a Canaanite mother goddess. Her symbol was the stem of a tree deprived of its boughs, and rudely shaped into an image, planted in the ground. Such religious symbols ("groves") are frequently alluded to in Scripture (EXODUS 34:13; JUDGES 6:25; I KINGS 16:33; II KINGS 23:6). These images were also sometimes made of silver or of carved stone (II KINGS 21:7).

ASHKENAZ

("spreading fire")
One of the three sons of Gomer, and grandson of Japheth (GENESIS 10:3).

ASSHUR

("being straight")
The second son of Shem, grandson of Noah (GENESIS 10:22; I CHRONICLES 1:17). Asshur

This fourth-century terracotta figure found in Tunisia depicts the god Baal Hammon.

went from the land of Shinar and built Nineveh (GENESIS 10:11-12). Asshur was an ancestor of the Assyrians (NUMBERS 24:22,24; EZEKIEL 27:23).

BAAL

("Lord")
1. Name of the principal male god of the Phoenicians. It is found in several places in the plural Baalim (JUDGES 2:11; 10:10; I KINGS 18:18; JEREMIAH 2:23; HOSEA 2:17). Baal is also identified with Molech (JEREMIAH 19:5). The sun god, under the general title of Baal, or "lord," was the chief object of worship of the Canaanites. Each locality had its special Baal, and each Baal had a wife.
2. A Benjamite, son of Jehiel, the progenitor of the Gibeonites (I CHRONICLES 8:30; 9:36).
3. A Reubenite (I CHRONICLES 5:5).
4. Son of Jehiel, and grandfather of Saul (I CHRONICLES 8:30; 9:36).

BAAL-HANAN

("Lord of grace")
A king of Edom, son of Achbor (GENESIS 36:38-39; I CHRONICLES 1:49-50). An overseer of "the olive trees and sycamore trees in the low plains" under David (I CHRONICLES 27:28).

BALAAM

("Lord of the people")
Son of Beor, a seer from Aram known for the effectiveness of his curses (NUMBERS 31:8). He resided at Pethor (DEUTERONOMY 23:4) and in Mesopotamia (NUMBERS 23:7), and he received a vision from God not to consort with Balak's emissaries. Indeed, when the Israelites were encamped on the plains of Moab, Balak sent for Balaam to curse them. Balaam did not fulfill Balak's wish. In a battle between Israel and the Midianites, Balaam was slain while fighting on the side of Balak (NUMBERS 31:8).

BALAK
("spoiler")

Son of Zippor, and king of the Moabites (NUMBERS 22:2,4). For fear of the Israelites, who were encamped near the confines of his territory, he hired Balaam to curse them, but this was in vain (JOSHUA 24:9).

BASEMATH/BASHEMATH
("sweet-smelling")

1. Daughter of Ishmael and the last of Esau's three wives (GENESIS 36:3-4,13). The four tribes of the Edomites originated from her son Reuel. She is also called Mahalath (GENESIS 28:9).

2. Daughter of Solomon, and wife of Ahimaaz (I KINGS 4:15).

BECHER
("firstborn")

Second son of Benjamin (GENESIS 46:21), who came down to Egypt with Jacob. It is probable that he married an Ephraimite heiress and that his descendants were part of the tribe of Ephraim (NUMBERS 26:35; I CHRONICLES 7:20-21). However, these children are not considered descendants of Benjamin (NUMBERS 26:38).

BEERI
("illustrious")

1. Father of Judith, one of the wives of Esau (GENESIS 26:34).

2. Father of the prophet Hosea (HOSEA 1:1).

BELA
("destruction," "a thing swallowed")

1. Eldest son of Benjamin (NUMBERS 26:38; GENESIS 46:21).

2. Son of Beor, who reigned over Edom in the city of Dinhabah, eight generations before Saul (GENESIS 36:31-33; I CHRONICLES 1:43).

3. Son of Azaz, a Reubenite (I CHRONICLES 5:8).

BENJAMIN
("son of my right hand")

The younger son of Jacob and Rachel (GENESIS 35:18). His birth took place at Ephrath, on the road between Bethel and Bethlehem. His mother died giving him birth, and with

A 20th-century British print depicts "Jacob Parting From Benjamin."

her last breath named him Ben-oni, "son of my pain," a name his father changed to Benjamin. When the tribe of Benjamin entered Canaan, more than 45,000 warriors were present, carrying the symbol of the wolf (GENESIS 49:27). This tribe was almost exterminated from civil war between 11 other tribes (JUDGES 20:20-21; 21:10). Saul, a Benjamite, was the first king of the Jews. A close alliance was formed between this tribe and Judah during the time of David (II SAMUEL 19:16-17), which continued after his death (I KINGS 11:13; 12:20). These two tribes formed the great body of the Jewish nation (EZRA 1:5; 10:9).

BERA
("son of evil")

King of Sodom at the time of the invasion of the four kings under Chedorlaomer (GENESIS 14:2,8,17,21).

BETHUEL
("house of God")

Son of Nahor by Milcah. He is also the father of Rebekah and nephew of Abraham (GENESIS 22:22,23; 24:15,24,47).

BEZALEL
("in the shadow of God")

Member of the tribe of Judah, the son of Uri, and grandson of Hur (EXODUS 31:2). A craftsman, he designed the artwork of the Tabernacle (EXODUS 31:2; 35:30). In this, he was assisted by Aholiab, an apprentice using metal, wood, stone, and textiles (EXODUS 36:1-2; 38:22).

BILHAH
("faltering," "bashful")

Rachel's handmaid, whom Laban gave to Rachel when she married Jacob (GENESIS 29:29). Because Rachel was childless, Jacob took Bilhah as a concubine; she then gave birth to Dan and Naphtali (GENESIS 30:3-8). Later, Reuben was cursed by his father for committing adultery with her (GENESIS 35:22; 49:4). He was deprived of his birthright, which was given to the sons of Joseph.

BILHAN
("modest")

1. A Horite chief dwelling in Mount Seir (GENESIS 36:27; I CHRONICLES 1:42).

2. A Benjamite, son of Jediael (I CHRONICLES 7:10).

BIRSHA
("son of wickedness")

King of Gomorrah whom Abraham supported in the invasion of Chedorlaomer (GENESIS 14:2).

BUKKI
("wasteful")

1. Son of Jogli, and leader of the tribe of Dan. Moses appointed him to apportion the land of Canaan among the tribes (NUMBERS 34:22).

2. Son of Abishua, and a descendant of Aaron (I CHRONICLES 6:5).

BUZ
("disrespect")

1. Son of Nahor and Milcah, brother of Huz, a descendant of Elihu, and ancestor of Buzites (GENESIS 22:21; JOB 32:2).

2. Father of Jahdo, and one of the chiefs of the tribe of Gad (I CHRONICLES 5:14).

CAIN
("a possession," "a spear")
Firstborn son of Adam and Eve (GENESIS 4:1), brother to Abel, he became a farmer. Abel, however, became a shepherd. In a fit of jealousy, provoked by the rejection of his own sacrifice and the acceptance of Abel's, he killed his brother, for which he was expelled. Though Cain was condemned to roam the world as an outlaw, he could not be harmed. "Whoever slays Cain," said the Lord, "vengeance shall be taken on him sevenfold."

In this sixth-century mosaic from the San Vitale in Ravenna, Cain presents the offerings from the field.

Consequently, "God put a mark on Cain, so that no one who came upon him would kill him" (GENESIS 4:15). Cain subsequently settled in the land of Nod. Here he built a city, which he named after his son Enoch.

CALEB
("a dog")
1. Also named Chelubai, one of three sons of Hezron from Judah's tribe (I CHRONICLES 2:9). The son of Jephunneh (NUMBERS 13:6; 32:12; JOSHUA 14:6,14). He was one of the men Moses sent to reconnoiter the land of Canaan.

2. A "son of Hur, the firstborn of Ephratah" (I CHRONICLES 2:50).

CANAAN
("low," "flat")
The fourth son of Ham (GENESIS 10:6; I CHRONICLES 1:8), the ancestor of the Phoenicians and of various nations before the Israelite conquest; the seacoast of Palestine, and generally the country westward of the Jordan (GENESIS 10:13; I CHRONICLES 1:13). The name "Canaan" is also used for the country itself.

CARMI
("vinedresser")
1. Son of Reuben, grandson of Jacob, and ancestor of the clan of the Carmites. He immigrated to Egypt as one of the Israelites (GENESIS 46:9).
2. Son of Judah, and grandson of Jacob (I CHRONICLES 4:1). He is also called Caleb (I CHRONICLES 2:18).
3. Son of Zimri, and the father of Achan (JOSHUA 7:1). After Achan transgressed against Joshua, Carmi and his family were taken to the valley of Achor, stoned, and burned to death (I CHRONICLES 2:7).

CHEDORLAOMER
("handful of sheaves")
King of Elam in the time of Abraham, who with three other chiefs made war upon the kings of Sodom, Gomorrah, Admah, Zeboim, and Zoar (GENESIS 14:17).

CHEMOSH
("subdue")
A god of the Moabites (NUMBERS 21:29). King Solomon built a shrine to Chemosh in Jerusalem, which was destroyed by King Josiah (II KINGS 23:13).

CHESED
("gain")
Son of Milcah, the wife of Nahor, Abraham's brother (GENESIS 22:22).

COZBI
("deceitful")
Daughter of Zur, a chief of the Midianites (NUMBERS 25:15,18).

CUSH
("black")
1. The eldest son of Ham, and the father of Nimrod (GENESIS 10:8; I CHRONICLES 1:10). Nimrod was a great Cushite chief. He conquered the Accadians, a Tauranian race, already settled in Mesopotamia, the Cushites mingling with the Accads, and so forming the Chaldean nation.
2. A Benjamite, mentioned in the title of Psalms 7. Cush was probably a follower of Saul who sought to ingratiate himself with David.

DAN
("a judge")
The fifth son of Jacob, his mother was Bilhah, Rachel's maid, who also gave birth to Naphtali (GENESIS 30:6). He later traveled to Egypt to procure corn during a time of great famine. Dan was the ancestor of the tribe of Dan (NUMBERS 2:25,31; 10:25).

DATHAN
("belonging to a fountain")
Son of Eliab and ruler of Reuben. Dathan and his brother Abiram joined Korah in his conspiracy against Moses and Aaron. Dathan, Abiram, Korah, and their followers were then swallowed up by an earthquake after Moses' speech (NUMBERS 16:1; 26:9; DEUTERONOMY 11:6; PSALMS 106:17).

DEDAN
("low ground")
1. Son of Raamah, and descendant of Noah (GENESIS 10:7).
2. Son of Jokshan, and grandson of Abraham and Keturah (I CHRONICLES 1:32).

DINAH
("judged," "vindicated," "acquitted")
Daughter of Jacob and Leah, and sister of Simeon and Levi (GENESIS 30:21). She was raped by Shechem, son of Hamor, the ruler of Shechem (GENESIS 34:2). Shechem asked

Hamor to speak to Jacob and offer Dinah's hand in marriage to Shechem (GENESIS 34:12). Upon Dinah's brother's demands, the proposal was accepted on the condition that every Shechemite, including Shechem and Hamor, be circumcised. On the third day following the operations, Simeon and Levi, brothers of Dinah, attacked the

"The Rape of Dinah" is a work of Italian painter Giuliano Bugiardini (1475–1554).

Shechemites, killing all the males. Afterward, she is mentioned among the rest of Jacob's family that went down into Egypt (GENESIS 46:8,15).

DISHON
("antelope")
1. Son of Seir the Horite, and ancestor of the clans that settled in the land of Edom (GENESIS 36:21).
2. Son of Anah, grandson of Seir the Horite, and brother of Oholibamah (GENESIS 36:25).

DUMAH
("silence")
Son of Ishmael, and grandson of Abraham and Hagar (GENESIS 25:14). A tribe that descended from him lived in a region in Arabia (I CHRONICLES 1:30).

EBER
("the region beyond")
1. Son of Salah, great grandson of Shem, and ancestor of Abraham (GENESIS 10:24; GENESIS 11:14; I CHRONICLES 1:19). In Luke 3:35, he is referred to as Heber. He was the head of a priestly clan when Joiakim was the high priest in the days of Nehemiah (NEHEMIAH 12:20).
2. Eldest of three sons of Elpaal, the Benjamite (I CHRONICLES 8:12).

ELAM
("hidden")
1. Son of Shem, and grandson of Noah (GENESIS 10:22).
2. Son of Shashak, and leader of the tribe of Benjamin who lived in Jerusalem (I CHRONICLES 8:24).
3. Son of Meshelemiah. He was one of the gatekeepers of the Tabernacle during the reign of King David (I CHRONICLES 26:3).
4. Ancestor of Israelites who returned with Zerubbabel from Babylonian exile (EZRA 2:7).
5. One of the leaders who signed Nehemiah's covenant (NEHEMIAH 10:14).
6. One of the priests who marched and sang in celebration of the rebuilt walls of Jerusalem during the time of Nehemiah (NEHEMIAH 12:42).

ELDAAH
("God of knowledge")
Son of Midian, and a grandson of Abraham and Keturah (GENESIS 25:4).

ELDAD
("love of God")
One of the 70 elders Moses appointed to prophesy (NUMBERS 11:26,27). Joshua complained to Moses and Moses replied, "Are you worried about me? I wish that the Lord would give his Spirit to all his people, and make all of them prophets!" (NUMBERS 11:24-30).

ELIDAD
("God's beloved")
Son of Chislon, and chief of the tribe of Benjamin. He was one of the men appointed to divide Canaan among the tribes (NUMBERS 34:21).

ELEAZAR
("God has helped," "help of God")
1. Third son of Aaron and Elisheba, and father of Phinehas (EXODUS 6:23,25). After the death of older brothers Nadab and Abihu (LEVITICUS 10:12; NUMBERS 3:4) and later his father Aaron, he was appointed high priest (NUMBERS 3:32). He took part with Moses in numbering the people (NUMBERS 26:3,4), assisting at the inauguration of Joshua, and distributing the land after the conquest (JOSHUA 14:1). The high priesthood remained in his family until it was restored to the family of Eleazar in the person of Zadok (I SAMUEL 2:35). He was buried in

English artist William Brassey Hole (1846–1917) painted "The Consecration of Eleazar as High Priest."

Canaan on a hill that belonged to his son Phinehas (Joshua 24:33).

2. Son of Abinadab. He served as a guard of the Ark of the Covenant while it was in his father's house (I Samuel 7:1-2).

3. Son of Dodo the Ahohite of the tribe of Benjamin. He was one of the three bravest men in David's army (I Chronicles 11:12).

4. Son of Mahli, and descendant of Merari (I Chronicles 23:21).

5. Son of Phinehas who helped Meremoth count and weigh the silver and gold utensils of the Temple (Ezra 8:33).

6. Priest led by Jezrahiah who took part in the feast of dedication under Nehemiah (Nehemiah 12:42).

7. Son of Eliud, and father of Matthan in the genealogy of Jesus (Matthew 1:15).

ELIAB
("to whom God is father")
1. Son of Pallu, and father of Nemuel, Dathan, and Abiram (Numbers 16:1,12; 26:8,9; Deuteronomy 11:6).

2. Son of Helon, and ruler of the tribe of Zebulun in the days of Moses (Numbers 1:9; 2:7).

3. Son of Jesse, and eldest brother of David (I Samuel 16:6). He disapproved of David fighting Goliath (I Samuel 17:28). He was appointed to be leader of the tribe of Judah (I Samuel 16:6).

4. A Gadite who joined David in hiding from Saul (I Chronicles 12:9).

5. Son of Nahath, and ancestor of Samuel (I Chronicles 6:27). He was also called Elihu and Eliel (I Samuel 1:1; I Chronicles 6:34).

6. A Levite porter who sang and played musical instruments in front of the Ark of the Covenant during the reign of David (I Chronicles 15:18,20; 16:15).

ELIEZER
("God helps")
1. Abraham's steward (Genesis 15:2-3). Abraham sent Eliezer to Nahor to find a wife for his son Isaac. Upon arrival, Eliezer met Rebekah who offered water to him and his camels. Eliezer then asked Rebekah's father, Bethuel, for consent to take Rebekah to be Isaac's wife. He agreed and Rebekah

was taken to Isaac, who accepted her as his spouse (Genesis 24:67).

2. Second son of Moses and Zipporah, brother of Gershom, and father of Rehabiah (Exodus 18:4).

3. Son of Becher, and grandson of Benjamin (I Chronicles 7:8).

4. Priest who blew the trumpet before the Ark when it was brought to Jerusalem (I Chronicles 15:24).

5. Son of Zichri, and ruler of Reuben during the reign of David (I Chronicles 27:16).

"Eliezer of Damascus" was painted by Scottish artist William Dyce (1806–1864) in 1860.

6. Son of Dodavahu. He prophesied that King Jehoshaphat's ships would be broken, and he would not be able to reach Tarshish due to his alliance with King Ahaziah (I Chronicles 20:37).

7. Son of Jozadak. He was a priest who divorced his foreign wife (Ezra 8:16; 10:18, 23, 31).

8. Son of Jorim and father of Jose, in the genealogy of Jesus (Luke 3:29).

ELISHAMA
("whom God hears")
1. A prince of Benjamin and a grandfather of Joshua (Numbers 1:10; I Chronicles 7:26).

2. Son of David (II Samuel 5:16).

3. Another son of David (I Chronicles 3:6,8; 14:7).

4. A priest sent by Jehoshaphat to teach the people the Law (II Chronicles 17:8).

5. A descendant of Judah (I Chronicles 2:41).

6. A secretary to King Jehoiakim (Jeremiah 36:12).

7. Father of Nethaniah and grandfather of Ishmael (II Kings 25:25; Jeremiah 41:1).

8. A priest in the time of Jehoshaphat (II Chronicles 17:8) (912 b.c.e.).

ELISHEBA
("God is her oath," "God will restore")
Daughter of Amminadab of Judah, sister of Nahshon, wife of Aaron the high priest, and mother of Nadab, Abihu, Eleazar, and Ithamar (Exodus 6:23).

ELIZAPHAN
("whom God protects")
1. A Levite who was the son of Uzziel. He was chief of the house of the Kohathites at the time of the census in the wilderness of Sinai (Exodus 6:22; Leviticus 10:4; Numbers 3:30; I Chronicles 15:8) (1491 b.c.e.).

2. Prince of the tribe of Zebulun (Numbers 34:25).

ELIZUR
("God is my strength; my rock; rock of God")
Son of Shedeur of Reuben. He commanded his tribe's army into the wilderness (Numbers 1:5; 10:18).

ELKANAH
("God-created," "the zeal of God," "God provided")
1. Second son of Korah the Levite, who led the rebellion against Moses (Exodus 6:24). Elkanah is also referred to as Korah's grandson (I Chronicles 6:23).

2. Son of Jeroham of Ephraim, father of Samuel, husband of Hannah and Peninnah, and descendant of Levi and Heman (I Samuel 1:1; I Chronicles 6:27,34).

3. Son of Assir, a descendant of Kohath, and grandson of Korah (I Chronicles 6:23).

4. Son of Mahath, father of Zophai, descendant of Kohath, and ancestor of Judge Samuel (I Chronicles 6:35-36).

5. Father of Amasai, and son of Joel (I Chronicles 6:35).

6. Father of Asa, and grandfather of Berechiah (I CHRONICLE 9:16).

7. A Korhite who deserted King Saul's army and joined David at Ziklag (I CHRONICLES 12:6).

8. A doorkeeper of the Ark during the reign of David (I CHRONICLE 15:23).

9. A king Ahaz official killed by Zichri during a war between Judah and Israel (II CHRONICLES 28:7).

ELON
("oak," "grove," "strong")

1. A Hittite whose daughter, Basemath, was one of Esau's wives (GENESIS 26:34).

2. One of the sons of Zebulun (GENESIS 46:14; NUMBERS 26:26) and the founder of the tribe of the Elonites (1695 B.C.E.).

3. The 11th of the Hebrew judges. He held office for ten years (JUDGES 12:11,12).

ENOCH
("dedicated," "disciplined," "initiated")

1. Eldest son of Cain (GENESIS 4:17).

2. Son of Jared, father of Methuselah (GENESIS 5:21; LUKE 3:37). Founded the city "Enoch," east of Eden, in the land of Nod—the first city mentioned in the Bible.

EPHAH
("weary")

1. One of the five sons of Midian and the grandson of Abraham (GENESIS 25:4; I CHRONICLES 1:33; ISAIAH 60:6).

2. Caleb's concubine (I CHRONICLES 2:46).

3. Son of Jahdai. His brothers were Regem, Jotham, Gesham, Pelet, and Shaaph (I CHRONICLES 2:47). The city of Ephah, famous for its dromedaries (camels), is named after him (ISAIAH 60:6, 7; JUDGES 6:5).

EPHER
("calf")

1. Second son of Midian, who was Abraham's son by Keturah (GENESIS 25:4; I CHRONICLES 1:33) (1820 B.C.E.).

2. Son of Ezrah, who was a descendant of Judah. He was the brother of Jether, Jalon, and Mered (I CHRONICLES 4:17).

3. A chief of Manasseh who was a mighty warrior and leader of his clan (I CHRONICLES 5:24).

EPHRAIM
("double fruitfulness")

Second son of Joseph by his wife Asenath, born in Egypt (GENESIS 41:52; 46:20). He was chosen by Jacob to receive his blessing over his elder brother, Manasseh (GENESIS 50:23).

EPHRON
("fawnlike")

Son of Zohar, a Hittite, from whom Abraham bought the field and cave of Machpelah (GENESIS 23:8-17; 25:9; 49:29-30; 50:13).

ESAU
("hairy")

Eldest twinborn son of Isaac and Rebekah, brother of Jacob (GENESIS 25:25). A rugged huntsman, in contrast to his agrarian brother, he was driven by hunger to sell his birthright to Jacob for food (GENESIS 25:30-31). Later on, he also lost his

Lucas Cranach the Elder (1472–1553) painted this panel of Eve and the apple.

father's covenant blessing to Jacob through his own mother's trickery (GENESIS 27:1). These events set up an enmity between the two brothers that continued on through the tribes they led, Esau's Edomites and Jacob's Israelites (GENESIS 25:22-23).

EVE
("life," "living")

The first woman, created by God as a companion for Adam, and crafted from Adam's rib, or side (GENESIS 2:21-22). Tempted by a serpent in the Garden of Eden, she broke God's commandment by eating the forbidden fruit and sharing it with her husband. "And then," says Genesis, "the eyes of both of them were opened, and they knew that they were naked" (GENESIS 3:7). To cover their shame, they sewed fig leaves together as garments. For this transgression, Adam and Eve were evicted from Paradise. God told Eve, "I will greatly multiply your sorrow and your conception; in pain you shall bring forth children" (GENESIS 3:16). She is the mother of Cain, Abel, and Seth, among others.

EZER
("treasure")

1. One of the sons of Seir, the native princes, "dukes," of Mount Hor (GENESIS 36:21,27).

2. A son of Ephraim, who was slain by the aboriginal inhabitants of Gath (I CHRONICLES 7:21).

3. A priest who assisted in the dedication of the walls of Jerusalem under Nehemiah (NEHEMIAH 12:42).

4. Father of Hushah of the sons of Hur (I CHRONICLES 4:4).

5. One of the Gadite chiefs who fought with David (I CHRONICLES 12:8-9).

6. One who aided in repairing the wall at Jerusalem; a Levite (NEHEMIAH 3:19).

GADDI
("fortunate")

Son of Susi and the representative of the tribe of Manasseh among the 12 "spies" sent by Moses to spy on the land (NUMBERS 13:11).

GADDIEL
("fortune of God")

The representative of the tribe of Zebulun among the 12 spies (NUMBERS 13:10).

"The Apparition of Gamaliel to the Priest Lucien" was painted by Austrian artist Michael Pacher (1435–1498).

GAHAM

A son of Reumah, Nahor's concubine; brother to Tebah, Tahash, and Maacah, and nephew to Abraham (GENESIS 22:24).

GAMALIEL

("reward of God")

1. A chief of the tribe of Manasseh at the census at Sinai (NUMBERS 1:10; 2:20; NUMBERS 7:54,59).

2. The son of rabbi Simeon, and grandson of the famous rabbi Hillel. He was a Pharisee, and therefore an opponent of the Sadducee party. Gamaliel was noted for his learning, and served as president of the Sanhedrin during the reigns of Tiberius, Caligula, and Claudius. When the Apostles were brought before the council, charged with preaching the resurrection of Jesus, Gamaliel counseled moderation. If their work or counsel was of man, he said, it would come to nothing; but if it was of God, they could not destroy it, lest they should be "found fighting against God" (ACTS 5:34-40). Paul is believed to have been one of his disciples (ACTS 22:3). Gamaliel reportedly died about 18 years before the destruction of Jerusalem.

GERA

("grain")

1. The son of Bela and grandson of Benjamin (I CHRONICLES 8:3, 5, 7).

2. The father of Ehud the Judge (JUDGES 3:15).

3. The father of Shimei, who grossly abused David (II SAMUEL 16:5; 19:16, 18).

GERSHOM

("a stranger," "exile")

1. The eldest son of Levi (I CHRONICLES 6:16,17,20,43,62,71; 15:7), also known as "Gershon."

2. The elder of the two sons of Moses by Zipporah, born in Midian (EXODUS 2:22; 18:3). Moses gave him the name of Gershom for he said, "I have been a stranger in a strange land" (EXODUS 2:22). On his way to Egypt with his family, Moses suffered a severe illness (EXODUS 4:24-26). Zipporah, his wife, believed the reason was that he didn't circumcise his son. She took a "sharp stone" and circumcised Gershom.

3. A descendant of Phinehas who returned with Ezra from Babylon (EZRA 8:2).

4. The son of Manasseh (JUDGES 18:30).

GERSHON

("exile")

Also known as Gershom, Gershon was the eldest of the three sons of Levi, born before the descent of Jacob's family into Egypt (GENESIS 46:11; EXODUS 6:16). During the Exodus, his Levite descendants were responsible for the Tabernacle.

GETHER

One of the four sons of Aram and a grandson of Shem (GENESIS 10:23; I CHRONICLES 1:17).

GEUEL

("majesty of God")

Son of Machi and a leader from the tribe of Gad. He was sent to explore the land of Canaan (NUMBERS 13:15).

GIDEONI

("hewer")

Father of Abidan who was chosen by Moses to lead the tribe of Benjamin (NUMBER 1:11; 2:22; 7:60).

GILEAD

("hilly")

1. Son of Machir and grandson of Manasseh who was the ancestor of the clan of the Gileadites (NUMBERS 26:29).

2. The father of the Judge Jephthah, who was born from his relationship with a prostitute (JUDGES 11:1). After Gilead died, the sons that he had with his legitimate wife expelled Jephthah from their ancestral house, because they were afraid that he would try to share their inheritance.

3. Son of Michael, who was the father of Jaroah. His descendants lived in the region of Gilead, which was on the eastern side of the Jordan River (I CHRONICLES 5:14).

GOMER

("complete," "perfect")

1. The daughter of Diblaim who became the wife of Hosea (HOSEA 1:3).

2. The eldest son of Japheth and father of Ashkenaz, Diphath, and Togarmah (GENESIS 10:2,3). He is regarded as the legendary ancestor of the Celtae and the Cimmerii, who in early times settled to the north of the Black Sea, and gave their name to the Crimea, the ancient Chersonesus Taurica. In the seventh century B.C.E., they were driven out by the Scythians. They subsequently reappear in the times of the Romans as the Cimbri of the north and west of Europe.

GUNI

("painted")

1. A son of Naphtali (GENESIS 46:24; I CHRONICLES 7:13) and founder of the family of the Gunites (NUMBERS 26:48).

2. Leader of the tribe of Gad and father of Abdiel (I CHRONICLES 5:15).

HADAD (ALSO HADAR)

("sharp," "mighty")

1. Sixth son of Ishmael (GENESIS 25:15; I CHRONICLES 1:30).

2. An Edomite king who defeated the Midianites (GENESIS 36:35; I CHRONICLES 1:46).

3. Another Edomite king (I CHRONICLES 1:50-51), also called Hadar (GENESIS 36:39; I CHRONICLES 1:51).

4. One of "the king's seed in Edom." He fled into Egypt, where he was raised at Pharaoh's court and married the sister of the Pharaoh's wife. He later became one of Solomon's adversaries (I KINGS 11:14-22).

5. Name of a Syrian god.

HADORAM

1. Fifth son of Joktan, founder of an Arab tribe (GENESIS 10:27; I CHRONICLES 1:21).

2. Son of Tou, king of Hamath. He was sent by his father to congratulate David on his victory over Hadadezer, king of Syria (I CHRONICLES 18:10; II SAMUEL 8:10).

"Hagar and the Angel" is the work of Italian artist Giuseppe Bottani (1717–1784).

3. Also called Adoram (II SAMUEL 20:24) and Adoniram (I KINGS 4:6). He oversaw a levy, and was stoned to death during the ensuing revolt (II CHRONICLES 10:18).

HAGAR
("flight")
An Egyptian slave woman and Sarah's handmaid (GENESIS 16:1; 21:9-10), whom she gave to Abraham as a surrogate wife (GENESIS 16:2). When Hagar became pregnant, she fled from the cruelty of Sarah and planned to return to her relatives in Egypt. She reached the place she called Beer-lahai-roi ("well of the visible God") or Beersheba, where an angel of God urged her to return to Sarah. She complied and gave birth to her son Ishmael, remaining with Sarah until after the birth of Isaac. Anxious to settle the issue of birthright, Sarah then insisted that Hagar and Ishmael be dismissed. Reluctantly, Abraham sent

them away (GENESIS 21:14). They wandered out into the wilderness near Paran, where Ishmael, exhausted and faint from thirst, was about to die. Hagar "lifted up her voice and wept," and the angel of God, as before, appeared to her and told her not to fear. Hagar then saw a well nearby (GENESIS 21:18-19). Hagar and Ishmael remained in Paran, and when he became of age, Hagar sent for a young woman from Egypt to be his wife.

HAM
("hot," "sunburned")
One of the three sons of Noah (GENESIS 5:32). One day, Ham saw his father lying drunk and naked and told his brothers, Shem and Japheth. These brothers then took a garment and covered their father. When Noah awoke, he blessed Shem and Japheth but cursed Ham. Ham had four sons, who became the legendary progenitors of the nations of Egypt, Canaan, Cush, and Put (PSALMS 78:51; 105:23; 106:22). Noah's curse on Ham was fulfilled when the Hebrews slew the Canaanites (GENESIS 10:6).

HAMOR
("ass")
A Hivite tribal chief from whom Jacob purchased the plot in which Joseph would later be buried (GENESIS 33:19). He is called "Emmor" in Acts 7:16. His son Shechem founded the city of that name, which Simeon and Levi destroyed because of his crime against Dinah, Jacob's daughter (GENESIS 34:20).

HAMUL
("pitied")
The younger son of Perez, who was the son of Judah and Tamar (GENESIS 46:12; I CHRONICLES 2:5). His descendants are called Hamulites (NUMBERS 26:21).

HANOCH
("God's follower")
1. Son of Midian and a grandson of Abraham and Keturah (GENESIS 25:4).

2. The eldest son of Reuben, who went to Egypt when Jacob traveled there as well (GENESIS 46:9; EXODUS 6:14).

HARAN
("mountaineer")
1. The eldest and third son of Terah, brother of Abraham and Nahor, he was the father of Lot, Milcah, and Iscah. He died in Ur of the Chaldees (GENESIS 11:27).

2. Son of Caleb of Judah and his concubine Ephah (I CHRONICLES 2:46).

3. Son of Shimei, and a Gershonite Levite during the reign of King David (I CHRONICLES 23:9).

HAVILAH
("stretch of sand")
1. Son of Cush, grandson of Ham (GENESIS 10:7; I CHRONICLES 1:19).

2. Son of Joktan, a descendant of Shem (GENESIS 10:29; I CHRONICLES 1:23).

HEBER
("alliance")
1. Son of Beriah and grandson of Asher (GENESIS 46:17; I CHRONICLES 7:31,32).

2. A Kenite (JUDGES 4:11,17; 5:24) and descendant of Hobab, or Jethro. His wife Jael received Sisera into her tent and killed him (JUDGES 4:11-21; 5:24).

3. Descendant of Ezrah, father of Soco (I CHRONICLES 4:18).

4. Son of Elpaal, leader of the tribe of Benjamin, living in Jerusalem (I CHRONICLES 8:17).

HELON
("strong")
Father of Eliab of the Zebulun tribe (NUMBERS 1:9; 2:7).

HEMAN
("raging," "faithful")
1. Son of Lotan, brother of Hori, nephew of Timna, and grandson of Seir the Horite. He was the leader of a clan of Horites that lived in Edom, also called Homam (GENESIS 36:22; I CHRONICLES 1:39).

2. Son of Mahol. Heman, his brothers Chalcol and Darda, and Ethan the Ezrahite were wise and only surpassed by King Solomon (I KINGS 4:31).

3. Son of Zerah. He was a leader in the tribe of Judah (I CHRONICLES 2:6).

4. Son of Joel, of the clan of the Kohathites. He was one of the Levites appointed by King

David to be in charge of the singers in the house of God (I Chronicles 6:33).

5. Grandson of Samuel (I Chronicles 6:33; 15:17).

HEPHER

("pit," "a well," or "stream")

1. Son of Gilead, descendant of Manassah, and ancestor of the clan of the Hepherites (Numbers 26:32).

2. Son of Ashhur and Naarah (I Chronicles 4:6).

3. Known as Hepher the Mercherathite. He was one of "the 30," an elite group in King David's army (I Chronicles 11:36).

HOBAB

("beloved")

Brother-in-law to Moses (Numbers 10:29), or alternative name for Jethro, Moses' father-in-law (Judges 4:11).

HUL

("circle")

Son of Aram and grandson of Shem (Genesis 10:23).

British artist Sir John Everett Millais (1829–1896) painted this depiction of Moses surveying the battle with the Amalekites together with Aaron and Hur.

HUR

("noble")

1. Son of Caleb and Ephrath of the tribe of Judah, father of Uri, and grandfather of Bezaleel (Exodus 31:2).

2. Husband of Miriam, Moses' sister (Exodus 17:10-12). During the battle with the Amalekites, Hur and Aaron held up Moses' hands until sundown, so that the Israelites could triumph. He and Aaron were placed in charge of the Israelites while Moses dwelled on Sinai (Exodus 24:14).

3. One of the five kings of the Midian who were defeated by the Israelites under command of Phinehas (Numbers 31:8).

4. Father of Rephaiah, ruler of part of Jerusalem who helped rebuild the walls of Jerusalem (Nehemiah 3:9).

HUSHIM

("haste")

1. Son of Dan and grandson of Jacob (Genesis 46:23), also known as "Shuham" (Numbers 26:42).

2. Son of Aher, and grandson of Benjamin (I Chronicles 7:12).

3. One of Shaharaim's wives in the tribe of Benjamin, and mother of Abitub and Elpaal (I Chronicles 8:8-11).

I

IGAL

("redeem")

1. Son of Joseph of the Issachar tribe. One of the spies sent to Canaan (Numbers 13:7).

2. Nathan's son and one of David's warriors (II Samuel 23:36).

IRAD

("fugitive," "runner")

Son of Enoch, grandson of Cain, and father of Mehujael (Genesis 4:18).

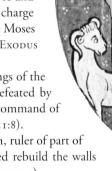

A 13th-century miniature depicts the sacrifice of Isaac.

ISAAC

("he laughs")

Son of Abraham and his wife, Sarah. After Abraham's son by his concubine, Hagar, had been born and given the name of Ishmael, God told Abraham and Sarah that they would have a son together as well. Both Abraham and Sarah laughed, wondering how a child could be born to a couple in their late 90s—which is why, when Isaac was indeed born, Sarah named him Yishaq, which means "he who laughs." When Isaac had grown up to be a boy, God decided to put Abraham to a test. He told Abraham to sacrifice Isaac as a burnt offering (Genesis 22:2). Abraham complied with a heavy heart, but just as he was about to strike his son with a knife, an angel of the Lord stopped him. Abraham offered a ram instead. Abraham then sent a servant to his clan living in Haran to find a suitable bride for Isaac. This was Rebekah, a very beautiful young woman who became Isaac's wife (Genesis 24:67). A famine caused the young couple to move to Egypt, but they came no farther than Gerar, ruled by King Abimelech. They settled in the area and increased their herds, but tension with local shepherds forced them to move to a nearby valley where Isaac's servants eventually found water. Isaac called it "Shibah." "Therefore," says Genesis, "the name of the city is Beer-sheba to this day" (GENESIS 26:33). Isaac and Rebekah had two sons, Esau and Jacob. Esau was masculine and became a hunter, whereas Jacob was a gentle lad more comfortable with his father's flocks. Whereas Isaac loved Esau the most ("because he was fond of game"), Rebekah's favorite was Jacob (GENESIS 25:28). Though Esau was the elder, Rebekah wanted Jacob to inherit the birthright, or *bekorah,* the rights of the firstborn son to their father's heritage. While Esau was away in the fields, she covered Jacob in Esau's coat and had Jacob

Italian artist Giambattista Tiepolo (1696–1770) created this painting of Hagar and Ishmael with the angel around 1732.

bring his father a favorite stew, leading the nearly blind Isaac to think that it was Esau. Isaac blessed Jacob, thus transferring God's covenant to Jacob rather than Esau (GENESIS 27:27-29). Thus, God's prophecy was fulfilled that "the elder shall serve the younger" (GENESIS 25:23).

ISHBAK
("leaving," "he will leave")
Son of Abraham and Keturah (GENESIS 25:2).

ISHMAEL
("God hears")
Son of Abraham by Hagar, Sarah's Egyptian handmaiden. Sarah gave Hagar to her husband, Abraham, because she herself was barren. When Hagar became pregnant, she fled from the cruelty of Sarah and planned to return to her relatives in Egypt. At a place called Beer-lahai-roi ("well of the visible God") or Beersheba, an angel of God urged her to return to Sarah. "You shall call him Ishmael," the angel spoke, "for the Lord has given heed to your affliction" (GENESIS 16:11). "Ishmael" is a contraction of *El* (God) and *shama'* ("hears"), meaning "God hears (me)." Hagar complied, returned to Abraham's camp and in due course gave birth to Ishmael, remaining with Sarah until after the birth of Isaac. Sarah then insisted that Hagar and Ishmael be dismissed. Reluctantly, Abraham sent them away (GENESIS 21:14). They wandered out into the wilderness near Paran, where Ishmael, exhausted and faint from thirst, was about to die. Hagar "lifted up her voice and wept," and the angel of God, as before, appeared to her and told her not to fear. Hagar then saw a well nearby (GENESIS 21:18-19). Hagar and Ishmael remained in Paran, where Ishmael became a skilled archer. When he came of age, Hagar sent for a young woman from Egypt to be his wife. Ishmael then had 12 sons who each would become the progenitor of an Arab nation, in fulfillment of the angel's prophecy that God would "so greatly multiply your offspring that they cannot be counted for multitude" (GENESIS 16:10-12). Indeed, Islam venerates Ishmael as its spiritual forefather; according to the Qur'an, Ishmael and Abraham built (or restored) the shrine of the Ka'bah in Mecca (QUR'AN 2:125).

ISRAEL
("prevails with God")
The name given to Jacob by a man who blessed him after wrestling with him, citing Jacob had fought with God and men, and he prevailed (GENESIS 32:28). Israel is the name given to Jacob's descendants.

ISSACHAR
("hired," "he will bring a reward")

Son of Leah and Jacob. Issachar was among the 70 Israelites who immigrated to Egypt. Eventually, his tribe settled in Jezreel until it was exiled by the Assyrians, and became one of the "ten lost tribes" (GENESIS 30:18).

IZHAR
("oil")
Son of Kohath, the grandson of Levi. Izhar was the uncle of Aaron and Moses, and father of Korah (EXODUS 6:18,21; NUMBERS 3:19; 16:1; I CHRONICLES 6:2,18).

JACHIN
("firm")
1. Fourth son of Simeon (GENESIS 46:10), called also Jarib (I CHRONICLES 4:24).
2. Head of one of the courses (the 21st) of priests (I CHRONICLES 24:17).
3. One of the priests who returned from the exile (I CHRONICLES 9:10).

JABAL
("stream")
Son of Lamech and Adah, brother of Jubal, and descendant of Cain (GENESIS 4:20).

JACOB
("supplanted")
Second son of Isaac and Rebekah. Jacob's brother Esau was a strong, masculine hunter, whereas Jacob was a gentle lad more comfortable with his father's flocks. Isaac loved Esau the most ("because he was fond of game"), but Jacob was Rebekah's favorite (GENESIS 25:28). Though Esau was the elder, Rebekah wanted Jacob to inherit the birthright, or *bekorah,* the rights of the firstborn son to their father's heritage. While Esau was away in the fields, she covered Jacob in Esau's coat and had Jacob bring his father a favorite stew, leading the nearly blind Isaac to think that it was Esau. Isaac blessed Jacob, thus transferring God's covenant to Jacob rather than Esau (GENESIS 27:27-29). Thus, God's prophecy was fulfilled that "the elder shall serve the

An anonymous artist from the 15th-century French School painted this panel of "Jacob's Ladder" around 1490.

younger" (GENESIS 25:23). To flee Esau's wrath, Jacob traveled north to his mother's clan in Haran. One night, he dreamed of a ladder going up into heaven. At the top stood God, reaffirming his covenant with Abraham that now would pass on to Jacob: "The land on which you lie I will give to you and to your offspring" (GENESIS 28:13). Jacob continued on to Haran, where he fell in love with the "beautiful and lovely" Rachel, daughter of his cousin Laban (GENESIS 29:17). Laban asked a steep price for Rachel's hand in marriage: Jacob would first have to work for seven years, tending Laban's flocks. When that time was fulfilled, Laban secretly slipped his oldest daughter Leah in Jacob's tent to spend the wedding night. Jacob had to work another seven years before he was finally able to marry his beloved Rachel. Jacob returned to Canaan with his wives and handmaidens, who also served as Jacob's concubines. By this time, these women had borne him 11 sons and one daughter.

When he came to the Jabbok River, Jacob met a stranger who challenged him to a struggle. At long last, the stranger—an angel of the Lord, or perhaps God himself—relented, declaring that henceforth Jacob would be known as Israel ("he who prevails with God") (GENESIS 31:28). Just as Jacob had struggled with God, so too would the nation of Israel wrestle for centuries with its obedience to the Lord. Jacob decided to call the place "Peniel" ("God's face"), saying, "I have seen God face to face" (GENESIS 31:30). Jacob settled near Shechem in Canaan, where his daughter Dinah was raped by Shechem, the son of the local ruler named Hamor. Hamor suggested the two should marry. Jacob agreed on the condition that the local population be circumcised. But Jacob's sons were incensed by the rape. While all males were still recovering from the circumcision, two of Jacob's sons—Simeon and Levi—entered the city and killed all the males by the sword (GENESIS 34:26). Rachel, who previously had given Jacob a son named Joseph, gave birth to a second child named Benjamin, but she died in childbirth.

Her death allowed Jacob's other sons to openly vent their resentment of Jacob's favoritism toward Joseph. They resolved to do away with him, and sold him to a passing caravan of traders. Joseph was taken to Egypt, where he eventually rose to the position of grand vizier. Jacob and all his sons were invited to settle in Egypt as well, in a region called Goshen (GENESIS 47:11). With their settlement in Egypt, the story of Genesis comes to a close.

JALAM
("young")
Son of Esau and Oholibamah, who later became a chieftain of a desert tribe in Edom (GENESIS 36:5,14,18; I CHRONICLES 1:35).

JAMIN
("right hand")
1. Second son of Simeon (GENESIS 46:10; EXODUS 6:15; I CHRONICLES 4:24), and founder of the family of the Jaminites (NUMBERS 26:12).

2. A man of Judah, second son of Ram the Jerahmeelite (I CHRONICLES 2:27).
3. One of the Levites who expounded the Law to the people (NEHEMIAH 8:7)
4. Descendant of Hezron (I CHRONICLES 2:27).

JAPHETH
("wide spreading")
One of the sons of Noah, mentioned last in order (GENESIS 5:32; 6:10; 7:13). He and his wife were two of the eight people saved in the ark (I PETER 3:20). He was the progenitor of many tribes inhabiting the east of Europe and the north of Asia (GENESIS 10:2-5). After the flood, the earth was repeopled by the descendants of Noah, "the sons of Japheth" (GENESIS 10:2), "the sons of Ham" (GENESIS 10:6), and "the sons of Shem" (GENESIS 10:22).

JESHURUN
("the upright people")
A poetical name for the people of Israel, used in token of affection (DEUTERONOMY 32:15; 33:5,26; ISAIAH 44:2).

Dutch artist Jan Victors (1619–1676) painted this canvas of "Moses Taking His Leave From Jethro the Priest" around 1635.

JETHRO
("excellence")
Priest of the Kenite tribe in the Midian. When Moses fled to the desert, he met a group of girls near a well in Sinai who were being harassed by shepherds. Moses

intervened, and in gratitude he was invited to dine with the girls' father, Jethro. Moses married one of his daughters, Zipporah, who presented him with a son named Gershom (EXODUS 2:22). Genesis intimates that Jethro was not a pagan priest, but one who worshipped Abraham's God, possibly because his tribe traced its ancestry to Abraham and his second wife, Keturah. "Now I know that the Lord is greater than all gods," he said when Moses delivered his people from Egypt (EXODUS 18:11), perhaps referring to the period in Syria-Canaan when *El* was worshipped among many other gods. Jethro then advised Moses to create a proper organization. "You must teach them ordinances and laws," he said. "Moreover, you must select out of all these people able men, who worship God, men of truth . . . to rule over them as officers and judges" (EXODUS 18:20-21). The Book of Numbers suggests that Jethro, now called Hobab, then served as a guide for the Israelites, to lead them out of Sinai and into the Promised Land.

JETUR
("an enclosure")
One of the 12 sons of Ishmael. He was the grandson of Abraham and his Egyptian concubine, Hagar. Jetur's sister Mahalath married Esau who was Isaac's son (GENESIS 25:15).

JEUSH
("assembler")
1. Oldest of Esau's three sons by Oholibamah (GENESIS 36:5,14,18; I CHRONICLES 1:35).
2. Son of Bilhan, grandson of Benjamin (I CHRONICLES 7:10).
3. A Levite who was one of the sons of Shimei (I CHRONICLES 23:10-11).
4. One of the three sons of Rehoboam who was the king of Judah (II CHRONICLES 11:19).

JIDLAPH
("weeping")
Son of Abraham's brother Nahor (GENESIS 22:22).

JOBAB
("a desert")
1. Last son of Joktan (GENESIS 10:29; I CHRONICLES 1:23).

2. One of the kings of Edom and the son of Zerah or Bozrah (GENESIS 3:34; I CHRONICLES 1:44-45).
3. King of Madon; one of the northern chieftains who attempted to oppose Joshua's conquest and was routed by him at Meron (JOSHUA 11:1).
4. Head of a Benjamite house (I CHRONICLES 8:9).
5. Name of two Benjamites of whom little is known (I CHRONICLES 8:9,18).

JOCHEBED
("whose glory is God")
The Egyptian-born daughter of Levi who married her nephew, Amram. She was the mother of Miriam, Moses, and Aaron (EXODUS 2:1; 6:20; NUMBERS 26:59). Her youngest son Moses was born at a time when the pharaoh had given orders to kill every newly born Israelite male baby. Jochebed hid Moses for three months and when she could no longer hide him, she put him in a basket and placed it on the bank of the Nile. The pharaoh's daughter discovered the baby when she went down to the river to bathe. The pharaoh's daughter believed the baby to be a Hebrew child and hired Jochebed to nurse Moses after Miriam, Moses' sister, recommended her (EXODUS 2:1-9).

JOKSHAN
("snarer")
Second son of Abraham and Keturah (GENESIS 25:2,3; I CHRONICLES 1:32).

JOKTAN
("little")
Second of the two sons of Eber (GENESIS 10:25; I CHRONICLES 1:19). There is an Arab tradition that Joktan (Arab: *Kahtan*) was the progenitor of tribes in central and southern Arabia.

JOSEPH
("increase")
The elder of Jacob and Rachel's two sons, and the 11th of 12 of Jacob's sons (GENESIS 30:23-24). His father loved him most of all his brothers, and gave him a garment of "many colors" or "long sleeves" (GENESIS 37:3), making his brothers jealous (GENESIS

37:4,11). While tending to their flocks, his brothers plotted to do away with him. They captured Joseph, but Reuben persuaded his brothers to hold him in a cistern; they then sold Joseph to a caravan of merchants passing by. To convince Jacob that his favorite son had been killed, the brothers smeared goat's blood on his garment (GENESIS 37:12-36). Joseph prospered as the personal servant to Potiphar, but was falsely accused

French artist James Tissot (1836–1902) created this watercolor of "Joseph and His Brethren Welcomed by Pharaoh" around 1900.

of raping his wife (GENESIS 39:1-20). These accusations led to Joseph's imprisonment for two years. The "chief of the cupbearers" and the "chief of the bakers" of Pharaoh's household were also imprisoned (GENESIS 40:2). Joseph interpreted the dreams of these prisoners. Pharaoh then had a dream, which was interpreted by Joseph as a sign of seven years of plentiful food and seven years of famine. As vizier, Joseph was put in charge of storing up food for this future famine (GENESIS 41:46), and he assumed the Egyptian name Zaphnath-Paaneah. His wife, Asenath, gave birth to their two children,

Manasseh and Ephraim. When the seven years of famine did arrive, Joseph's brothers came to Egypt to acquire food, but they did not recognize the vizier. Joseph did recognize them and accused them of being spies, sending them back to Canaan to retrieve another brother, Benjamin, to prove their truthfulness. The brothers told Jacob what had happened, and returned to Egypt with Benjamin. They were warmly welcomed into Joseph's house, but before they returned to Canaan, Joseph planted a silver cup in Benjamin's belongings. As soon as this cup was found, Benjamin was arrested and ordered to remain in Egypt as Joseph's slave. When Judah begged he be enslaved instead of Benjamin, Joseph broke down into tears. He confessed his true identity to his brothers and invited them and his father to live with him in Egypt. A caravan with Jacob and his entire household moved from Canaan to Goshen. When Jacob arrived, he embraced Joseph, his son he had not seen for 22 years (GENESIS 45:1-28; 46:1-34). Joseph lived until he was 110 years old, and made his family promise to take his remains with them when they left Egypt. During the Exodus, Moses took Joseph's remains and buried them in Shechem (EXODUS 13:19).

JUBAL
("jubilee," "music")
Lamech's second son by Adah, of the line of Cain. He was the inventor of "the harp" (Hebrew *kinnor,* properly "lyre") and "the organ" (Hebrew *'ugab,* properly "mouth organ" or "Pan's pipe") (GENESIS 4:21).

JUDAH
("praise")
Fourth son of Jacob and Leah (GENESIS 29:35). Judah helped spare Joseph's life when the other brothers wanted to murder him (GENESIS 37:26-27). He also took an active lead in family affairs (GENESIS 43:3-10; 44:14,16-34, 46:28; I CHRONICLES 5:2). After Joseph was sold into slavery, Judah moved to Adullam, where he married Shuah of Canaan. After his wife died, he returned to his father's house, and moved with the family to Egypt (GENESIS 49:8-12).

Italian artist Cristofano Allori (1577–1621) painted this depiction of Judith around 1599.

JUDITH
("Jewess")
Daughter of Beeri the Hittite, and one of Esau's wives (GENESIS 26:34), elsewhere called Oholibamah (GENESIS 36:2-14).

KEDAR
("dark-skinned")
Second son of Ishmael, grandson of Abraham (GENESIS 25:13; I CHRONICLES 1:29), and progenitor of an Arab tribe known as the Kedarites (JEREMIAH 49:28-29).

KEDEMAH
("eastward")
The last of Ishmael's 12 sons and a desert chieftain (GENESIS 25:15).

KEMUEL
("raised by God")
1. Third son of Nahor and Milcah, and father of Aram (GENESIS 22:21).
2. Son of Shiptan, and prince of the tribe of Ephraim. One of 12 men appointed by Moses to divide Canaan (NUMBERS 34:24).
3. A Levite, father of Hashabiah, and prince during the reign of David (I CHRONICLES 27:17).

KENAN
("owner")
Kenan or Cainan was the son of Enos, and the grandson of Seth. His first son Mahalalel was born when Kenan was 70 years old. He had other sons and daughters before his death at 910 years old (GENESIS 5:9-14).

KETURAH
("incense")
Abraham's wife after the death of his previous wife, Sarah (GENESIS 25:1-6), who had six sons by him (I CHRONICLES 1:32).

KOHATH
("assembly")
Second son of three sons of Levi, and father of Amram (GENESIS 46:11). He came to Egypt with Jacob and Levi, and lived until the age of 133 (EXODUS 6:18). Kohath was the head of a Levite family, which served the Tabernacle in the desert, and later served in the Temple in Jerusalem (NUMBERS 3:17; JOSHUA 21:4-42).

KORAH
("baldness")
1. Third son of Esau and Oholibamah, who became the leader of Edom. He was born in Canaan before Esau migrated to Mount Seir (GENESIS 36:5-9,14).
2. Son of Eliphaz, grandson of Esau (GENESIS 36:16).
3. Son of Hebron, a leader of the tribe of Judah (I CHRONICLES 2:43).
4. A Levite, son of Izhar, and brother of Amram, the father of Moses and Aaron (EXODUS 6:21). Along with members of the Reuben tribe and 250 other leaders, Korah rebelled against Moses and Aaron. The rebellion conspiracy ended in the death of Korah as well as all other rebels by fire and in an earthquake (NUMBERS 16:1-3,35; 26:9-11). Others on Korah's side suffered from a plague, "an atonement for the people" (NUMBERS 16:47).

LABAN
("white")
Son of Bethuel, brother of Rebekah and

father of Leah and Rachel. He lived at Haran, in Mesopotamia. When Abraham moved to Canaan, he met with Laban. Laban betrothed his sister Rebekah to her cousin Isaac (GENESIS 24:10,29-60, 27:43; 29:5). Jacob married Rachel and Leah, daughters of Laban, and stayed with him for 20 years.

"Lot and His Daughters" is a canvas that dates from ca 1650 by Italian artist Guercino (1591–1666).

LAMECH
("powerful")

1. Fifth descendant from Cain, and the first to violate the primeval ordinance of marriage (GENESIS 4:18-24). His speech to his two wives, Adah and Zillah (GENESIS 4:23,24), called "Lamech's sword-song," is perhaps the first example of antediluvian poetry. He had three sons: Jabal, Jubal, and Tubal-cain.

2. Father of Noah (GENESIS 5:29), the seventh in descent from Seth, only son of Methuselah.

LEAH
("gazelle")

Eldest daughter of Laban who was the first to marry Jacob, followed by her sister Rachel (GENESIS 29:16). Leah had seven children: Reuben, Simeon, Levi, Judah, Issachar, Zebulun, and Dinah, before Rachel had her child. Leah died some time after Jacob and was buried in the family grave in Machpelah, near Hebron (GENESIS 49:31).

LETUSHIM
("hammered")

Son of Dedan and great-grandson of Abraham and Keturah (GENESIS 25:3).

LEUMMIM
("peoples," "nations")

Son of Dedan and great-grandson of Abraham and Keturah, and head of an Arabian tribe (GENESIS 25:3).

LEVI
("adhesion," "joined")

1. Third son of Jacob by his wife, Leah, born in Haran. The origin of the name is derived from *lavah,* "to adhere" (GENESIS 29:34). Together with his brother Simeon, Levi took part in the reprisals after the rape of his sister Dinah (GENESIS 34:25-31). He and his three sons, Gershon, Kohath, and Merari, went down with Jacob into Egypt (EXODUS 6:16). Through Gershon and Merari, he founded the line of Temple servants called Levites.

2. Father of Matthat, and son of Simeon, the ancestors of Christ (LUKE 3:29).

LOT
("a covering," "veil")

Son of Haran, and nephew of Abraham (GENESIS 11:27). On the death of his father, he was left in charge of his grandfather Terah, after whose death he accompanied his uncle Abraham into Canaan, thence into Egypt and back again to Canaan (GENESIS 12:5, 13:1). After this, Lot separated from Abraham and settled in Sodom (13:11-12). There, his righteous soul was "vexed" from day to day (II PETER 2:7). He was taken captive by King Chedorlaomer of Elam, but was rescued by Abraham (GENESIS CHAPTER 14). When the judgment of God descended on the sinful cities of Sodom and Gomorrah (GENESIS 19:1-20), Lot's family was delivered, but as they were fleeing, his wife "looked back and became a pillar of salt." Lot and his daughters sought refuge first in Zoar, and then, fearing to remain there longer, retired to a cave in the neighboring

mountains (GENESIS 19:30). Lot's daughters, meanwhile, were bereft of menfolk and despaired of ever being able to bear children. They lay with their father, after they had served him wine until he passed out. Both daughters conceived and gave birth to a son: Moab, the ancestor of the Moabites; and Ben-ammi, "the ancestor of the Ammonites to this day" (GENESIS 19:37-38). Lot has been connected with the tribe referred to on Egyptian monuments as Rotanu or Lotanu.

MACHIR
("sold")

1. Manasseh's oldest son (JOSHUA 17:1), or probably his only son (I CHRONICLES 7:14,15). His descendants are referred to as Machirites, being the offspring of Gilead (NUMBERS 26:29). They settled in land taken from the Amorites (NUMBERS 32:39,40; DEUTERONOMY 3:15) by a special enactment (GENESIS 50:23; NUMBERS 36:1-3; JOSHUA 17:3,4). He is also mentioned as the representative of the tribe of Manasseh east of Jordan (JUDGES 5:14).

2. A descendant of Machir, residing at Lo-debar, where he cared for Jonathan's son Mephibosheth until he was taken under the care of David (II SAMUEL 9:4), and where he afterward gave shelter to David himself when he was a fugitive (II SAMUEL 17:27).

MAGDIEL
("God's choice gift")

Edomite tribal leader who descended from Esau (GENESIS 36:43; I CHRONICLES 1:54).

MAHALATH
("a lyre")

1. Daughter of Ishmael, and third wife of Esau (GENESIS 28:9), also called Basemath (GENESIS 36:3).

2. Daughter of Jerimoth, who was one of David's sons. She was one of the wives of King Rehoboam of Judah (II CHRONICLES 11:18).

MAMRE

("manliness")

An Amorite chieftain in alliance with Abraham (GENESIS 14:13,24). He gave his name to the place near Hebron where Abraham dwelt (GENESIS 23:17,19; 35:27), translated as the "plain of Mamre" or alternatively "the oaks [or 'terebinths'] of Mamre." The site of Mamre has been identified with Ballatet Selta, i.e., "the oak of rest," where there is a tree called "Abraham's oak," about a mile and a half west of Hebron.

MANAHATH

Second son of Shobal, grandson of Seir the Horite (GENESIS 36:23; I CHRONICLES 1:40).

MANASSEH

("forgetting")

Elder of the two sons of Joseph by his Egyptian wife, Asenath. He and his brother Ephraim were afterward adopted by Jacob as his own sons (GENESIS 48:1). In a parallel of Isaac's blessing of Jacob instead of Esau, Joseph brought his two sons to his father Jacob so that they would receive his blessing. Jacob placed his hand on the younger son Ephraim rather than the older Manasseh, saying that Ephraim's descendants would be more important. During the Exodus, the tribe of Manasseh was encamped on the west side of the Tabernacle. According to the census taken at Sinai, this tribe then numbered 32,200 (NUMBERS 1:10,35; 2:20,21). Forty years afterward, its numbers had increased to 52,700 (NUMBERS 26:34,37), and it was at this time the most distinguished of all the tribes.

MASSA

("a lifting up," "gift")

1. Son of Ishmael, and founder of an Arabian tribe (GENESIS 25:14).
2. A nomad tribe inhabiting the Arabian Desert toward Babylonia.

MEDAD

("measure")

One of the elders nominated to assist Moses in the government of the people. He and Eldad "prophesied in the camp" (NUMBERS 11:24-29).

MEDAN

("contention")

Son of Abraham and Keturah (GENESIS 25:2; I CHRONICLES 1:32).

MEHETABEL

1. Daughter of Matred, who was the wife of Hadad (or Hadar), one of the kings of Edom (GENESIS 36:39).
2. Father of Shemaiah, a false prophet in the time of Nehemiah (NEHEMIAH 6:10).

MELCHIZEDEK

("king of righteousness")

The king of Salem (GENESIS 14:18-20), which possibly refers to Jerusalem. When Abraham returned from rescuing Lot from four kings, Melchizedek welcomed him back. Psalm 110 extols Melchizedek as an ideal priestly king (PSALM 110:4).

METHUSELAH

("man of the dart")

Son of Enoch, father of Lamech and grandfather of Noah. The oldest man in the Bible,

An artist from the 17th-century French School created this "Meeting Between Abraham and Melchizedek."

he died at the age of 969 years, in the year of the Flood (GENESIS 5:21-27; I CHRONICLES 1:3).

MIBSAM

("fragrance")

One of Ishmael's 12 sons, and head of an Arab tribe (GENESIS 25:13).

MIDIAN

("strife")

Fourth son of Abraham by Keturah, and the progenitor of the Midianites (GENESIS 25:2-4).

MILCAH

("queen")

1. Wife of Abraham's brother Nahor. Her son Bethuel was the father of Rebekah, who became the wife of Isaac (GENESIS 11:29; 22:20; 24:15).
2. One of the five daughters of Zelophehad (NUMBERS 26:33; 27:1; JOSHUA 17:3).

MIRIAM

("bitterness")

Daughter of Amram and Jochebed, sister of Moses, and eldest child in the family. When Pharaoh's daughter found the baby Moses in the basket of pitch, it was Miriam who told the princess that she could find a wet nurse, thus allowing her mother to continue to care for her own child. Called "the prophetess" (EXODUS 15:20), she led the women in a song of triumph after the passage of the Red Sea. She and Aaron criticized Moses for his marriage to an Ethiopian woman, for which she was struck with leprosy. Moses intervened for her recovery. Miriam died and was buried at Kadesh, toward the end of the wanderings in the wilderness (NUMBERS 20:1).

MISHAEL
("who is like God")
Eldest of the three sons of Uzziel, the uncle of Aaron and Moses (EXODUS 6:22).

MISHMA
("hearing")
1. One of the sons of Ishmael (GENESIS 25:14), and founder of an Arab tribe.
2. Son of Mibsam and father of Hammuel, of the tribe of Simeon (I CHRONICLES 4:25).

MOAB
("of his father")
Moab was the son of Lot's eldest daughter as a result of her incestuous relations with her father. He is the progenitor of the Moabites (GENESIS 19:37).

MOLECH OR MOLOCH
("king")
Principal deity of the Ammonites, worshipped as a "fire god," common to many Canaanite, Syrian, and Arab tribes. Molech was particularly infamous for child sacrifice. Despite many injunctions in the Book of Leviticus, Molech continued to be worshipped during and after the monarchy, when even Solomon allowed altars to be built for him (LEVITICUS 18:21). Josiah later eradicated Molech sites (I KINGS 11:5; II KINGS 23:10; ISAIAH 30:33).

MOSES
("drawn forth")
Moses is the quintessential character of Hebrew Scripture: the prophet who led the Jewish people out of bondage in Egypt, gave the nation of Israel its laws, and brought them to the Promised Land. Moses was born in Egypt to Amram and Jochebed, during a time when Pharaoh (possibly Seti I) was trying to reduce and drive out the Jewish population (EXODUS 2:1-4; 6:20). Among his harsh edicts, Pharaoh required that all Jewish male babies be cast into the Nile River. Moses' mother then built a basket made of bulrushes and set it afloat, with the baby

inside, on the riverbank where Pharaoh's daughter bathed each day (EXODUS 2:3). As she had hoped, Pharaoh's daughter rescued and adopted the child, but was persuaded to allow Jochebed to act as his wet nurse, thus keeping her near Moses during his upbringing and making him aware of his true heritage (EXODUS 1:13,14). Moses spent

A basalt relief from Shihan, Jordan, carved between 1200 and 800 B.C.E., is believed to depict a Moabite god.

the next 20 years in luxury, but by the time he reached about 40, he could no longer ignore the plight of the Hebrew people in Egypt. After seeing an Egyptian taskmaster abuse a Hebrew, Moses killed the perpetrator and then had to flee Egypt to avoid the wrath of Pharaoh (EXODUS 2:11-22). He spent the next 40 years living in Midian, near the Sinai Peninsula, having married the daughter of Jethro, a priest. While walking in the wilderness, he saw a burning bush, through which God spoke to him and ordered him to return to Egypt to lead his people to freedom (EXODUS 3:7-10).

With his brother Aaron, he entreated Pharaoh to set the Israelites free. When the Egyptian king refused, Moses unleashed a series of plagues, the final and worst being the slaughter of the firstborn males for all families but the Israelites (EXODUS CHAPTERS 7–12). Securing the freedom of the Israelites, he led them across the wilderness, wandering for 40 years toward the Promised Land (EXODUS CHAPTER 16). At God's command, Moses climbed Mount Sinai to receive the Ten Commandments, which would serve as the basis for the Law governing the nation of Israel. Upon granting their release, however, Pharaoh had a change of heart and decided to recapture the Israelites. The two groups met up at the Red Sea, which Moses parted to allow his people to cross to safety, and then collapsed upon the Egyptian army as they followed in pursuit (EXODUS CHAPTER 14). The final Israelite encampment was on the Moab plains, where Moses provided his final counsel to the elders, then blessed all his people (DEUTERONOMY 1:1-4; 5:1–26:19; 27:11–30:20). Before he died, Moses ascended Mount Nebo, where God showed him all the lands that would become the homeland of the tribes of Israel. He himself, however, was destined to never cross the river Jordan into Canaan with his people (NUMBERS 27:12-14). He died at the age of 120 in a Moab valley (DEUTERONOMY 31:2).

NAAMAH
("loveliness," "beautiful")
Daughter of Lamech and Zillah (GENESIS 4:22), she is one of only four women whose names are associated with the period before the Great Flood.

NADAB
("liberal")
1. Eldest of Aaron's four sons (EXODUS 6:23; NUMBERS 3:2). He, his brothers, and his father were consecrated as priests of Jehovah

(Exodus 28:1). He perished with Abihu for offering strange fire on the altar of burnt offering (Leviticus 10:1-2; Numbers 3:4; 26:60).

2. King Jeroboam's son, whom he succeeded to the throne of Israel (I Kings 15:25-31).

3. One of the sons of Shammai in the tribe of Judah (I Chronicles 2:28,30).

4. Son of Gibeon in the tribe of Benjamin (I Chronicles 8:30; 9:36).

5. Son and successor of Jeroboam, the king of Israel (I Kings 14:20), slain by Baasha when a conspiracy broke out in his army (I Kings 15:25-28). The whole house of Nadab was then put to death (I Kings 15:29).

NAHATH
("rest")

1. One of the leaders of Edom, eldest of the four sons of Reuel, son of Esau (Genesis 36:13,17; I Chronicles 1:37).

2. A Kohathite Levite, son of Zophai (I Chronicles 6:26).

3. A Levite in the reign of Hezekiah, one of the overseers of the sacred offerings of the Temple (II Chronicles 31:13).

NAHOR
("snorting")

1. The son of Serug and father of Terah, who was the father of Abraham (Genesis 11:22-25; Luke 3:34).

2. Son of Terah, and elder brother of Abraham and Haran (Genesis 11:26-27; Joshua 24:2). He married Milcah, the daughter of his brother Haran, and remained in the land of his nativity on the east of the river Euphrates (Genesis 11:27-32).

NAHSHON
("enchanter")

A sorcerer, the son of Amminadab, and a prince of Judah at the time of the first numbering of the tribes in the wilderness (Exodus 6:23).

NAPHISH
("refresher")

One of the sons of Ishmael (Genesis 25:15; I Chronicles 1:31), and father of an Arab tribe.

This 14th-century stained glass window from Wells Cathedral in the United Kingdom displays a portrait of Naphtali.

NAPHTALI
("wrestling")

Fifth son of Jacob; his second child by Bilhah, Rachel's slave (Genesis 30:8). When Jacob went down to Egypt, Naphtali had four sons (Genesis 46:24). During the march through the wilderness, the tribe of Naphtali occupied a position to the north of the sacred tent with Dan and Asher (Numbers 2:25-31). In the apportionment of the land, the lot of Naphtali was enclosed by Asher on the west, Zebulun on the south, and Transjordanian Manasseh on the east.

NAPHTUHIM
("border people")

A Mizraite nation or tribe, mentioned only in the account of the descendants of Noah (Genesis 10:13; I Chronicles 1:11).

NEBAIOTH
("height")

1. Ishmael's eldest son (Genesis 25:13), and leader of an Israelite tribe. His sister Mahalath was one of Esau's wives (Genesis 28:9; 36:3).

2. The name of the Ishmaelite tribe descended from Nebaioth (Genesis 25:13,18). The "rams of Nebaioth" (Isaiah 60:7) were gifts that these wandering tribes would consecrate to God.

NEMUEL
("day of God")

1. A Reubenite, son of Eliab and eldest brother of Dathan and Abiram (Numbers 26:9).

2. Eldest son of Simeon's five sons called Jemuel (Numbers 26:12; I Chronicles 4:24). He is also called Jeruel (Genesis 46:10).

NETHANEL
("God has given")

1. A chief of Issachar (Numbers 1:8; 2:5; 7:18,23; 10:15).

2. Fourth son of Jesse (I Chronicles 2:14).

3. A trumpet blower before the Ark that was brought up from the house of Obed-edom (I Chronicles 15:24).

4. A Levite scribe; the father of Shemaiah (I Chronicles 24:6).

5. Fifth son of Obed-edom (I Chronicles 26:4).

6. One of the princes whom Jehoshaphat sent to teach in the cities of Judah (II Chronicles 17:7).

7. A Levite who gave cattle for Josiah's Passover (II Chronicles 35:9).

8. One of the priests who married foreign wives (Ezra 10:22).

NIMROD
("rebellion," "the valiant")

Nimrod was "the first on earth to become a mighty warrior . . . a mighty hunter before the Lord," says Genesis, though his actual deeds are not described (Genesis 10:8-9). Nimrod founded a kingdom in the land of Shinar; the prophet Micah would later associate this with the empire of Assyria (Micah 5:6). Nimrod went on to establish the cities of Babel, Erech, and Accad. Erech is usually identified as the Sumerian city of Uruk, whereas Accad is associated with a city known as Agade, later called Akkad, the capital of the Akkadian Empire.

NOAH
("rest")

1. Grandson of Methuselah and the son of Lamech (Genesis 5:25-29). Noah is regarded as the connecting link between the old and the new world and the second great progenitor of the human family. He lived 500 years, and bore three sons, Shem, Ham, and Japheth (Genesis 5:32). He was a "just man and perfect in his generation," and "walked with God" (Ezekiel 14:14,20). The story of

Noah begins with the descendants of Cain and Seth who began to intermarry, and bred a race distinguished for their ungodliness. Men became more and more corrupt, so that God determined to sweep the earth of its wicked population (GENESIS 6:7). But God entered into a covenant with Noah,

An anonymous artist created this mosaic of Noah in the Basilica di San Marco in Venice, Italy, around 1200.

promising to deliver him from the threatened deluge (GENESIS 6:18). He was ordered to build an ark to save himself and his house (GENESIS 6:14-16); while the ark was being built, 120 years elapsed (GENESIS 6:3), during which Noah regularly testified against the wickedness of that generation (I PETER 3:18-20; II PETER 2:5). When the ark of "gopher-wood" was completed, the living creatures to be preserved entered into it, Noah and his wife and sons and daughters-in-law then entered and the "Lord shut him in" (GENESIS 7:16). The ark floated on the waters for 150 days, and then rested on the mountains of Ararat (GENESIS 8:3-4). Upon leaving the ark, Noah's first act was to build an altar and offer a sacrifice to God for granting him possession of the earth (GENESIS 8:21–9:17).
2. One of the five daughters of Zelophehad (NUMBERS 26:33; 27:1; 36:11; JOSHUA 17:3).

NUN
("fish")
Father of Joshua (EXODUS 33:11). His genealogical descent from Ephraim is recorded in I Chronicles 7:1.

OCHRAN
("trouble")
Father of Pagiel, the prince of the tribe of Asher (NUMBERS 1:13; 2:27; 7:72,77; 10:26).

OG
("gigantic," "round")
King of Bashan, east of the Sea of Galilee. He fought against Moses and was defeated by the Israelites in Edrei (NUMBERS 21:32-35; DEUTERONOMY 1:4). The kingdom was divided among the tribes of Reuben and Gad, and half the tribe of Manasseh (DEUTERONOMY 3:1-13). His large iron bedstead or tomb was on display in Rabbath-Ammon, capital of Ammon (DEUTERONOMY 1:4; 3:1-13; 4:47; 29:7; 31:4).

OHOLIBAMAH
("tent of the high place")
1. Daughter of Anah the Hivite, and wife of Esau (GENESIS 36:2,5).
2. Edomite chief (GENESIS 36:41; I CHRONICLES 1:52).

ONAM
("vigorous")
Son of Shobal, grandson of Seir the Horite (GENESIS 36:23; I CHRONICLES 1:40).

ONAN
("strong")
Second son of Judah and a Canaanite woman, daughter of Shuah (GENESIS 38:4). He married his brother's widow, Tamar.

PALTI
("deliverance")
1. Son of Raphu, he was one of the 12 sent out to reconnoiter the Promised Land (NUMBERS 13:9).
2. Son of Laish from Gallim. He married

Michal, King Saul's daughter, after Saul drove away her husband David. When David became king, he took Michal back from Palti, who wept at her departure (I SAMUEL 25:44; II SAMUEL 3:15).

PELEG
("divided")
Son of Eber, brother of Joktan, father of Reu, and descendant of Noah and Shem (GENESIS 10:25).

PEREZ
("breach")
Son of Judah and Judah's daughter-in-law, Tamar. At birth, the hand of his twin brother Zerah burst out, and the midwife put a scarlet thread around his wrist (I CHRONICLES 27:3). He is also known as Phares and Pharez (MATTHEW 1:3; GENESIS 38:29).

PHINEHAS
("mouth of a serpent")
1. Son of high priest Eleazar, father of Abishua, and grandson of Aaron. After Phinehas killed Zimri and Cozbi for immoral behavior, God lifted the plague and created a covenant with Phinehas that he and his descendants would become priests. He led the army against the Midianites and won. High priest Phinehas then crossed into Jordan to investigate an altar there, and was told it was to worship God (EXODUS 6:25).
2. Son of high priest Eli, and brother of Hophni. God punished their descendants by no longer proclaiming them as a priestly family. Phinehas died in battle. The news of his death sent his wife into premature labor, and she died. Their son, Ichabod, lived (I SAMUEL 1:3).
3. Father of Eleazar (EZRA 8:33).

PILDASH
("flame of fire")
One of the eight sons of Milcah and Nahor, Abraham's brother (GENESIS 22:22).

POTIPHAR
("dedicated to Ra")
Official in the court of Pharaoh, and captain of his guard. He bought Joseph from the Midianites, who thereupon became a loyal

"Joseph and Potiphar's Wife" was created by Spanish artist Juan Urruchi (1829–1892) around 1852.

and efficient servant, and overseer of his household. Potiphar's wife tried to seduce Joseph, but he resisted. She falsely accused him of trying to rape her, and he was sent to prison (GENESIS 37:36).

POTIPHERAH
("dedicated to the sun")
An Egyptian priest of On. He is the father of Asenath, whom Pharaoh gave to Joseph as a wife (GENESIS 41:45).

PUAH
("splendid")
One of the two midwives who feared God, and disobeyed Pharaoh's orders to kill male Israelite babies (EXODUS 1:15-21).

RACHEL
("ewe")
Daughter of Laban, wife of Jacob, and mother of Joseph and Benjamin (GENESIS 29:6). Rachel was the love of Jacob's life. He was forced to marry Rachel's sister, Leah, before he could marry Rachel. Eventually, Jacob left Paddan-aram with his wives and

servants. Rachel died giving birth to Benjamin during their journey, and was buried in Ephrath (GENESIS 29:6).

REBA
("fourth")
One of the five kings of the Midianites who was slain by the children of Israel when Balaam fell (NUMBERS 31:8; JOSHUA 13:21) (1450 B.C.E.).

REBEKAH OR REBECCA
("joined together")
Daughter of Bethuel (GENESIS 22:23) and sister of Laban who was married to Isaac (GENESIS 24:1). For 19 years, she was childless, until Isaac prayed to God and she conceived of twins, Esau and Jacob, though the children struggled within her. God explained to her that there are "two nations in your womb, and two peoples born of you shall be divided" (GENESIS 25:23). Jacob was her favorite child (GENESIS 25:19-28), and she soon began to plot how Jacob could inherit the birthright—*bekorah,* the rights of the

"Rebecca Delights in Bracelet" from 1862 is the work of Italian artist Ignazio Affani (1828–1889).

firstborn son to their father's heritage—even though he was their second-born. She directed the conceit by which her husband blessed Jacob instead of Esau, and then

promptly sent Jacob away to Haran to her own clan (GENESIS 29:12). She probably died during Jacob's sojourn in Haran.

REKEM
("embroidered")
1. One of the five Midianite kings who was slain by the Israelites (NUMBERS 31:8; JOSHUA 13:21).
2. One of the four sons of Hebron and the father of Shammai (I CHRONICLES 2:43-44).

REUBEN
("behold the son")
Jacob's firstborn son with Leah (GENESIS 29:32). Leah named her son Reuben in hopes that Jacob would love her. Though Reuben was the eldest brother, he was not very bright and the leadership of the family passed to his younger brother Judah. Reuben and his brothers were jealous of their younger brother Joseph because he was their father's favorite. They conspired to kill him. It was Reuben, however, who convinced his brothers not to hurt him but to merely put him into a pit (GENESIS 37:21-30; 42:22). Judah then suggested that they sell him to a passing caravan as a slave. When their father was dying, Jacob took away Reuben's birthright for having an adulterous relationship with Jacob's concubine Bilhah (GENESIS 35:22; 49:4; I CHRONICLES 5:1).

REUEL
("friend of God")
Alternate name for Jethro, the father-in-law of Moses (EXODUS 2:18).

REUMAH
("elevated")
The concubine of Abraham's brother, Nahor (GENESIS 22:4).

SARAH
("princess")
1. The wife and half sister of Abraham and the mother of Isaac (GENESIS 20:12). Her name is

first introduced in Genesis 11:29 as Sarai. The change of her name from "Sarai," "my princess" (i.e., Abraham's), to "Sarah," "princess" (for all the race), was made at the same time that Abrams's name was changed to Abraham. Because Sarah was barren, the question of who would succeed Abraham as head of the clan was urgent. According to Mesopotamian custom, Sarah selected a slave girl named Hagar, and told her to lie with Abraham so as to procure a son. Hagar conceived and promptly looked down on Sarah with contempt. Sarah retaliated by forcing the young girl to run away into the desert. An angel found Hagar at an oasis near Shur and persuaded her to return to Abraham and Sarah. Sarah herself then received a prophecy that she, too, would bear a child. She laughed, saying, "After I have grown old, and my husband is old" she said, "shall I have pleasure?" God replied, "Is anything too wonderful for the Lord?" (GENESIS 18:12,14). But she did bear a son and named him Isaac (or *Yishaq*), which means "he who laughs." Concerned about which of Abraham's sons would inherit his birthright, Sarah urged her husband to "cast out this slave woman with her son." Abraham, advanced in age, could not resist his wife's entreaties. He gave Hagar and Ishmael some bread and a "skin of water," and sent her on her way (GENESIS 12:10). According to Genesis, Sarah died at Hebron at the age of 127 years, 28 years before her husband, and was buried by him in the cave (1860 B.C.E.).

2. Daughter of Asher (NUMBERS 26:46).

SETH
("substitute," "founder")
Third son of Adam and Eve, born after the death of Abel (GENESIS 4:25; 5:3). According to Genesis, Adam was 130 years old when Seth was born. Seth then became the father of Enosh and a long line of descendants; many of these names are similar to the genealogy ascribed by Genesis to Cain's son Enoch. One of these descendants was Noah, son of Lamech.

"Abraham and Sarah at the Court of the Pharaohs" was painted around 1875 by Italian artist Giovanni Muzzioli (1854–1894).

SHAUL
("asked")
1. Son of Simeon by a Canaanite woman and a grandson of Jacob (GENESIS 48:10; EXODUS 6:15; NUMBERS 26:13; I CHRONICLES 4:24).
2. An ancient king of Edom (I CHRONICLES 1:48-49).
3. Son of Uzziah who was a descendant of Kohath (I CHRONICLES 6:24).

SHEBA
("oath")
1. Son of Joktan, a descendant of Noah through Shem, Noah's second son (GENESIS 10:28).
2. Son of Jokshan and grandson of Abraham and Keturah (GENESIS 25:3).
3. Son of Bichri, a Benjamite (II SAMUEL 20:1-22), who rebelled against King David after the defeat of Absalom. Sheba traversed the whole of Palestine with Joab to the fortress Abel Beth-maachah, where Sheba was beheaded (II SAMUEL 20:3-22).
4. Leader of the tribe of Gad who lived in the land of Bashan (I CHRONICLES 5:13).

SHECHEM
("back," "shoulder")
1. Son of Hamor the Hivite who seduced Jacob's daughter. He was killed by Jacob's sons (GENESIS 33:19,34; JOSHUA 24:32; JUDGES 9:28).

2. Ancestor of the Shechemites (NUMBERS 26:31; JOSHUA 17:2).
3. Son of Shemidah, a descendant of Manasseh living in Gilead east of the Jordan (I CHRONICLES 7:19).

SHELOMITH
("peace")
1. Daughter of Dibri of the Dan tribe. Her son, the child of an Egyptian, got into a fight with an Israelite and was stoned to death as punishment (LEVITICUS 24:11).
2. Daughter of Zerubbabel, from the family of Judah (I CHRONICLES 3:19).

SHEM
("name")
Eldest son of Noah (GENESIS 5:32; 6:10). After the flood, he and his family received the blessing of God, and entered into the covenant (GENESIS 9:1). Much of the area of Syria, Assyria, Persia, and the Arabian Peninsula is inhabited by his descendants (GENESIS 11:10-26; I CHRONICLES 1:24-27).

SHEMEBER
("soaring")
The king of Zeboiim and ally of the king of Sodom, who was attacked by Chedorlaomer. He was later rescued by Abraham (GENESIS 14:2).

SHESHAI
("princely")
One of Anak's three sons (NUMBERS 13:22). Sheshai and his brothers were killed when the tribe of Judah attacked Hebron (JOSHUA 15:14; JUDGES 1:10).

SHIMEI
("famous")
1. Son of Gog, a Reubenite (I CHRONICLES 5:4).
2. Son of Gershom, and grandson of Levi (NUMBERS 3:18; I CHRONICLES 6:17,29). His descendants served the Tabernacle in Jerusalem (EXODUS 6:17).
3. Son of Zaccur, leader of the tribe of Simeon (I CHRONICLES 4:26).
4. Son of Libni, from the tribe of Levi (I CHRONICLES 6:29).

5. Son of Jahath, grandson of Gershom, he was the father of Zimmah (I CHRONICLES 6:42).

6. Leader of a tribe of Benjamin (I CHRONICLES 8:21).

7. A Benjamite of the house of Saul. He cursed and stoned David when he fled from Jerusalem during the rebellion of Absalom (II SAMUEL 16:5-13). After Absalom's defeat, he brought a thousand Benjamite tribesmen to apologize (II SAMUEL 19:18). David forgave him, but on his deathbed, he instructed Solomon to kill him. When Shimei violated his word by leaving Jerusalem and going to Gath to recover two of his servants, Solomon had him put to death (I KINGS 2:8-9).

8. One of David's mighty men who refused to acknowledge Adonijah as David's successor (I KINGS 1:8).

9. Son of Ela, and one of the 12 officers responsible for King Solomon's royal household (I KINGS 4:18).

10. Official of King David responsible for the king's vineyards (I CHRONICLES 27:27).

11. Levite who sanctified himself and cleansed the Temple on orders of Hezekiah (II CHRONICLES 29:14).

12. Brother of Conaniah, leader of the Levites in charge of Temple offerings (II CHRONICLES 31:12).

13. Son of Pedaiah, who led the exiles from Babylon to Judah (I CHRONICLES 3:19).

14. Levite who divorced his non-Jewish wife following Ezra's call (EZRA 10:23).

15. Hashumite who divorced his non-Jewish wife following Ezra's call (EZRA 10:33).

16. Descendant of Binnui who divorced his non-Jewish wife following Ezra's call (EZRA 10:38).

17. Son of Kish, father of Jair. His grandson Mordecai preempted a plan to kill all Jews in the Persian realm (ESTHER 2:5).

SHIMEON
("one who hears")
Descendant of Harim, who divorced his non-Jewish wife following Ezra's call (EZRA 10:31).

SHIPHRAH
("brightness")
One of the two midwives who disobeyed Pharaoh's orders to kill male Israelite babies (EXODUS 1:15-21).

SHUA
("wealth")
1. Daughter of a Canaanite and wife of Judah (I CHRONICLES 2:3).

2. Daughter of Heber (I CHRONICLES 7:32).

SIHON
("tempestuous")
King who ruled over the land of the Amorites and refused to let Israelites travel through. The Israelites defeated Sihon and his army, taking possession of the land (NUMBERS 21:21-30; DEUTERONOMY 2:24-37).

SIMEON
("God has heard")
1. Second son of Jacob and Leah (GENESIS 29:33). His sister Dinah was raped by Shechem, son of Hamor, who then asked Jacob to marry the two. Jacob and his sons demanded that Shechem, Hamor, and the men of their city be circumcised in exchange for their sister's hand in marriage. In the men's weakened state, Simeon and Levi killed all the men as revenge for their sister's honor (GENESIS 34:25-26). During his

brother Joseph's reign in Egypt, Simeon was detained in Egypt as a hostage during the famine. On his deathbed, Jacob blessed all his sons but remembered the bloody reprisals against Hamor's people by Simeon and Levi. "Weapons of violence are their swords," Jacob said. "I will divide them in Jacob and scatter them in Israel" (GENESIS 49:5,7).

2. A "righteous and devout" man who visited the Temple when the child Jesus was being presented by Joseph and Mary, and offering thanks and praise said, "This child is destined for the falling and the rising of many in Israel" (LUKE 2:29-35).

TAHASH
("porpoise")
Son of Abraham's brother Nahor and his concubine Reumah, who would later become the founder of an Aramean tribe (GENESIS 22:24).

TALMAI
("bold")
One of the three sons of Anakim, who were slain by men from Judah under Caleb's rule (NUMBERS 13:22; JOSHUA 15:14; JUDGES 1:10).

TAMAR
("palm")
1. Woman married to Er, the eldest son of Judah (GENESIS 38:6). After her husband's death, she married his brother Onan. When Onan also died, Judah refused to give her his third son Shelah in marriage. Tamar took revenge by sleeping with Judah in the guise of a prostitute, bearing him two sons, Perez and Zerah (GENESIS 38:6, 13-30; RUTH 4:12; I CHRONICLES 2:4).

2. Daughter of King David by his wife, Maacah, and sister of Absalom. She was raped by her

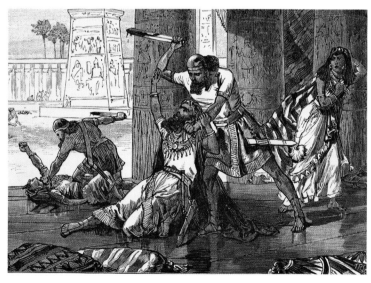

A 19th-century British lithograph, entitled "The Massacre of the Hivites by Simeon and Levi," depicts Simeon's revenge on Shechem and the men in his city.

half brother Ammon. Two years later, Absalom killed Ammon in revenge during a feast (II SAMUEL 13; I CHRONICLES 3:9).

3. Daughter of Absalom and granddaughter of King David (II SAMUEL 14:27).

"Judah and Tamar" is the work of French artist Horace Vernet (1789–1863), painted around 1840.

TARSHISH
("gold-colored stone")

1. One of the sons of Javan, great-grandson of Noah, and legendary founder of Tarshish (GENESIS 10:4; I CHRONICLES 1:7). Some believe this place was located on the Indian coast, given that "ships of Tarshish" sailed from Ezion-geber, on the Red Sea (I KINGS 9:26; 22:48; II CHRONICLES 9:21). Others argue that it refers to Carthage. Tarshish is also the name of a Phoenician port in Spain between the two mouths of the Guadalquivir. It was to this port that Jonah's ship was bound to sail from Joppa.

2. Son of Bilhan, a leader of the Benjamite tribe (I CHRONICLES 7:10).

3. One of seven princes from Media and Persia who joined King Ahasuerus at his table (ESTHER 1:14).

TEBAH
("slaughter")

Son of Abraham's brother Nahor by his concubine Reumah. He became the legendary founder of an Aramean clan (GENESIS 22:24).

TEMA
("desert")

One of the sons of Ishmael, and founder of a desert clan called Tema (GENESIS 25:15; I CHRONICLES 1:30; JOB 6:19; ISAIAH 21:14; JEREMIAH 25:23). This tribe lived at Tema, possibly today's Teyma, located some 250 miles southeast of Edom, on the route between Damascus and Mecca.

TEMAN
("south")

Son of Eliphaz and grandson of Esau, one of the leaders of Edom (GENESIS 36:11,15,42). Teman is also known as a place in southern Idumea, noted for the wisdom of its inhabitants (AMOS 1:12; OBADIAH 1:8; JEREMIAH 49:7; EZEKIEL 25:13).

TERAH
("the wanderer")

Father of Haran, Nahor, and Abram (GENESIS 11:26). Haran died before his father, but Abram and Nahor survived. Terah left his native city of "Ur of the Chaldees" and moved his sons and their wives, as well as Haran's son Lot, to the city of Haran in northern Mesopotamia. Here he spent the remainder of his days, and died at the age of 205 years (GENESIS 11:24-32; JOSHUA 24:2).

TIDAL

King of Goiim, meaning "nations," possibly the country of Gutium, east of Tigris and north of Elam (GENESIS 14:1-9).

TIMNA
("a portion")

1. Concubine of Esau's son Eliphaz. She bore him a son named Amalek (GENESIS 36:12).

2. Son of Eliphaz, grandson of Esau (I CHRONICLES 1:36).

3. Daughter of Seir, chieftain of the Edomites (GENESIS 36:22; I CHRONICLES 1:39).

4. A leader of Edom (GENESIS 36:40; I CHRONICLES 1:51).

URI
("fire")

Son of Hur of the tribe of Judah, father of Bezabel (EXODUS 31:2; 35:30).

UZ
("fertile land")

1. Son of Aram, and grandson of Shem (GENESIS 10:23; I CHRONICLES 1:17).

2. Eldest son of Nahor, Abraham's brother (GENESIS 22:21).

3. Son of Dishan, and one of the Horite leaders in the land of Edom (GENESIS 36:28).

ZAAVAN
("terror")

Son of Ezer and leader of Edom (GENESIS 36:27); called also Zavan (I CHRONICLES 1:42).

ZACCUR
("mindful")

1. Father of Shammua, who was one of the spies sent out by Moses (NUMBERS 13:4).

2. A Merarite Levite who ministered in the Tabernacle (I CHRONICLES 24:27).

3. Son of Hammuel and leader of the tribe of Simeon (I CHRONICLES 4:26).

4. Son of Asaph, and chief of one of the groups of singers as arranged by David, an ancestor of Zechariah (I CHRONICLES 25:2,10).

5. Descendant from Bigvai who returned with the exiles from Babylon to Judah (EZRA 8:14).

6. Son of Imri who helped rebuild the walls of Jerusalem (NEHEMIAH 3:2).

7. A Levite who signed the covenant during the time of Nehemiah (NEHEMIAH 10:12).
8. Son of Mattaniah, father of Hanan, who distributed tithes (NEHEMIAH 13:13).

ZAPHENATH-PANEAH
("the one who furnishes the nourishment of life")
Name given to Joseph by the Egyptian king upon his appointment of vizier (GENESIS 41:45).

ZEBULUN
("dwelling")
Zebulun was the tenth son of Jacob, the sixth borne to him by Leah in Haran. He was first among the five brethren presented to Pharaoh by Joseph, when his family and the Israelites arrived in Egypt (GENESIS 47:2). Zebulun had three sons—Sered, Elon, and Jahleel—who were born in Canaan, and became the ancestors of the three main divisions of the tribe (GENESIS 46:14).

ZELOPHEHAD
("protector from fear")
Leader of a Manassite tribe who died without a male heir. His daughters successfully pleaded with Moses to allow them to inherit. This resulted in a law, which dictated that for any man who died without sons, the inheritance would pass to his daughters (NUMBERS 26:33; 27:1,7; 36:2,6,10,11; JOSHUA 17:3; I CHRONICLES 7:15).

ZEPHI
("gaze")
Son of Eliphaz, grandson of Esau, and one of the chiefs of the Edomites (GENESIS 36:15).

ZERAH
("God's shine")
1. Son of Reuel and grandson of Esau, Zerah was a leader of the Edomites (GENESIS 36:17).
2. One of the twin sons born to Judah and Tamar (GENESIS 38:28-30).
3. Son of Simeon, and grandson of Jacob (GENESIS 46:10).
4. Father of Jobab, king of Edom (GENESIS 36:33; I CHRONICLES 1:44).
5. Son of Iddo, and a descendant of Levi's son Gershom (I CHRONICLES 6:21).
6. Son of Adaiah the Levite (I CHRONICLES 6:41).
7. An Ethiopian who invaded the kingdom of Judah with the largest army recorded in the Bible (II CHRONICLES 14:9-15). He was defeated by Asa, the third king of Judah.

ZICHRI
("memorable")
Son of Ishar, and grandson of Kohath (EXODUS 6:21).

A cloisonné work by Nicholas of Verdun (ca 1130–1205) depicts Moses and his wife, Zipporah, and their sons on their return from Egypt.

ZILPAH
("a dropping")
A Syrian woman given by Laban to his daughter Leah as a handmaid (GENESIS 29:24), and by Leah to Jacob as a concubine. She was the mother of Gad and Asher (GENESIS 30:9-13; 35:26; 37:2; 46:18).

ZIMRAN
("celebrated")
Eldest son of Abraham by Keturah (GENESIS 25:2; I CHRONICLES 1:32).

ZIMRI
("singer")
1. Son of Salu, a Simeonite chieftain, slain by Phinehas for bringing the Midianite princess, Cozbi, into his tent (NUMBERS 25:6-15).
2. A commander of Israel who ruled briefly in the Northern Kingdom after he killed King Elah in 885 B.C.E. He was eventually overthrown by Omri (I KINGS 16:9-20).
3. Son of Jehoaddah, of the Benjamin tribe, and a descendant of King Saul (I CHRONICLES 8:36; 9:42).

ZIPPORAH
("beauty")
One of the seven daughters of Jethro, the priest of Midian. She became the wife of Moses and mother of his two sons Gershom and Eliezer. On his way to Egypt with his family, Moses suffered a severe illness (EXODUS 4:24-26). Zipporah believed the reason was that he hadn't circumcised his son. She took a "sharp stone" and circumcised Gershom (EXODUS 2:21; 4:25; 18:2).

ZOHAR
("white")
Father of Ephron the Hittite from whom Abraham purchased the field with the cave of Machpelah (GENESIS 23:8; 25:9).

ZUAR
("little")
Father of Nethanel, the chief of the tribe of Issachar, at the time of the Exodus (NUMBERS 1:8; 2:5; 7:18,23; 10:15).

ZUR
("rock")
Father of Cozbi, and one of the five princes of Midian who were slain by the Israelites when Balaam fell (NUMBERS 25:15; 31:8).

FROM JOSHUA TO KINGS

So Joshua defeated the whole land,
the hill country and the Negeb
and the lowland and the slopes,
and all their kings;
he left no one remaining,
but utterly destroyed all that breathed,
as the Lord God of Israel
commanded.

JOSHUA 10:40

Flemish painter Peter Paul Rubens (1577–1640) painted this
evocative depiction of "Solomon's Judgment" around 1617.

THE SETTLEMENT TO THE FALL OF JERUSALEM

Who Wrote the Books of the Prophets?

THE EPIC SAGA OF ISRAEL'S MONARCHY, FROM THE ENTRY into the Promised Land to the capture of Jerusalem in 586 B.C.E., is the subject of the Bible collection known as the *Nevi'im,* or "Books of the Prophets." With these books, which also appear—though in a different order—in the Christian Old Testament, we enter into a period that is increasingly attested by archaeological discovery.

The story takes us from the Israelite settlement in Canaan to the division of the land among the 12 tribes, and the subsequent history of the monarchies of Israel and Judah. The first two books, known as Joshua and Judges, describe the Israelite conquest, although modern research has revealed that the Israelite "invasion" was probably less violent and abrupt than the Book of Joshua suggests. Archaeological discoveries point to a more gradual infiltration of Canaan, with most of the military activity confined to contested areas of agricultural importance, such as the rich plantations of Jericho or the fertile valley of the Jezreel, whose location guarding an important pass made it militarily significant as well.

Judges then relates the subsequent struggle of the Hebrew settlers against surrounding Canaanite communities as well as foreign invaders. One of these, the Philistines, came close to bringing the young Israelite commonwealth to its knees. It was this common threat that persuaded the tribes to appoint a series of tribal commanders—called Judges—that paved the way for the birth of Israel's monarchy.

The Books of Samuel and Kings continue with the unification of the tribes under one king, culminating in the reigns of David and Solomon. In the centuries to come, this glorious era would acquire almost mythical proportions, particularly during the time of foreign occupation. For as soon as Solomon rested in his tomb, his

British artist John Martin (1789–1854) depicts "Joshua Commanding the Sun to Stand Still" during battle in Gibeon. Martin made the painting in 1816.

storied empire, if it had existed, disintegrated along tribal fault lines. Thus weakened, the warring monarchies of the North and South, of Israel and Judah, were easy prey for the growing aggression from Assyria.

The Books of the Prophets (including Isaiah, Jeremiah, Ezekiel, and the Twelve Minor Prophets) argue that the fall of these monarchies was due to the Hebrew proclivity for pagan cults. Indeed, archaeologists have found evidence of pagan shrines that existed well into the sixth century B.C.E. It was Israel's misfortune to be placed at the crossroads of the great caravan routes of Antiquity, which brought often exotic and sensuous cultic practices. That same geographical position made ancient Israel inevitably the battleground in the proxy wars between Egypt and neo-Assyria/neo-Babylonia. Economically exhausted, torn by internecine strife, the Jewish kingdoms thus succumbed to the militarism from the east—ultimately leading to the era of the Babylonian captivity.

A majority of scholars have embraced the idea, first proposed by German scholar Martin Noth, that the Book of Joshua as well as the Books of Judges, Samuel, and Kings were composed as a group that also included the Book of Deuteronomy (the last of the "Five Books of Moses"), which emphasize the paramount importance of covenant Law. Taken together, scholars refer to this oeuvre as the "Deuteronomist history"; its predominant theme is that whenever Israel faltered in its observance of the Laws of Moses, the nation was inevitably afflicted by disaster or invasion. Recent research, pioneered by American scholar Frank Moore Cross, suggests that the Deuteronomist collection was compiled during and after the reign of King Josiah in the seventh century B.C.E., probably based on both oral and written traditions that were circulating about the history of ancient Israel.

LEADING FIGURES IN THE BOOKS OF
JOSHUA THROUGH KINGS

JOSHUA

Joshua is the principal protagonist of the story of the great settlement. His name, which means "God saves," summarizes the essential message of the Book of Joshua. A member of the Ephraim tribe, Joshua first caught Moses' eye during the battle against the Amalekites at the great oasis at Rephidim, which brought him a promotion as Moses' assistant or "servant" (EXODUS 24:13). He acquitted himself well during the journey to Mount Sinai (EXODUS 24:13), and formed part of the "reconnaissance team" that entered Canaan by stealth, reporting that the land "flows with milk and honey," but that its cities were stoutly defended (NUMBERS 13:28; 14:7-8).

The choice of Joshua as his successor probably reflected Moses' realization that the new leader of the Israelites had to be a military commander, rather than a figure of spiritual charisma. As a group of desert tribes, the Hebrews did not possess any of the modern weaponry that was revolutionizing warfare at the dawn of the Iron Age: the composite bow, the battering ram, and the war chariots deployed by Egyptians, Canaanites, Philistines, and later, Assyrians. They needed to compensate for that deficiency with military cunning and strategic acumen.

To make matters worse, the access road to Canaan was straddled by Jericho, an ancient city renowned for its massive walls. For six

This 19th-century print depicts "Joshua Commanding the Sun" not to set so he could finish battle in daylight.

days, Joshua and his troops marched around the walls of the city, carrying the Ark of the Covenant, while priests blasted away on their horns. On the seventh day, the priests gave one last and shattering blast, while the Israelites screamed at the top of their lungs. The walls collapsed, the Israelite warriors rushed in, and virtually all of Jericho was burned to the ground (JOSHUA 6:21).

During excavations in the 1950s, British archaeologist Kathleen Kenyon did indeed discover some of Jericho's massive, six-foot-thick walls, but she determined that these had been built in the Neolithic era (8000–6000 B.C.E.), thousands of years before the putative Israelite settlement. In the centuries to follow, the city would rebuild its ramparts from time to time, but these were modest walls of packed mud—nothing that would deter an army.

Next, Joshua focused his "conquest" on the hill country, knowing that the deep and lush valleys beyond the Judean Hills would be fiercely defended. He used a ruse to capture the city of Ai, tentatively identified with Khirbet el-Magatir some 12 miles north of Jerusalem, and left it "a heap of ruins" (JOSHUA 8:27-28; the name "Ai" means "ruin"). This feat caught the attention of the Canaanites. The king of Jerusalem, **Adoni-zedek**, rallied the forces from all the principal cities in the area, including Lachish and Hebron. According to the Bible, his army was routed in the valley of Aijalon, after God came to Joshua's

ca 1285 B.C.E.	ca 1279 B.C.E.	ca 1250 B.C.E.	ca 1240 B.C.E.
King Adadnirari I founds Assyrian Empire	Ramses II assumes throne in Egypt	Egyptians build a canal from the Nile to the Red Sea	Semitic workers migrate back to Canaan—putative date of the Exodus

aid by battering the enemy with stones from heaven (JOSHUA 10:11). Now the foothills lay wide open, so Joshua took the townships of Azekah, Makkedah, Libnah, Lachish, Eglon, Hebron, and Debir.

The Hebrew commander then swung north, where King **Jabin** of Hazor had also created a defensive coalition, this time consisting of all the northern kingdoms in Canaan (JOSHUA 11:1-3). Joshua was able to defeat the northern alliance, however, and burned Hazor "to the ground with fire" (JOSHUA 11:10-11).

Once most of the Canaanite kingdoms were pacified—at least for the time being—Joshua devoted himself to dividing the newly conquered lands among the 12 tribes, including "the hill country and all the Negeb . . . as far as Baal-gad in the valley of Lebanon below Mount Hermon" (JOSHUA 11:16-17). The division was made by drawing lots.

As Joshua lay on his deathbed, he received a pledge from all the tribes that they would continue to honor God and the Law, rather than any of the native Canaanite deities. Having been assured that they would do so, Joshua died at age 110 and was buried in the town given to him, Timnath-serah, close to Shechem (JOSHUA 24:30).

EHUD THE BENJAMITE

The sense of peace imposed by Joshua's supposed victories proved illusory, however. Soon, the tribes faced renewed hostilities—not only with the Canaanites but also with a new opponent, the Philistines. The upheaval of these early settlement years is the subject of the Book of Judges. According to the underlying Deuteronomist theme of this book, Israel's foes were in reality sent by God to punish the tribes for their transgressions and disobedience to the Law. But to sustain the Hebrews in their trials, God also raised up military commanders from among the tribes—"Judges" in biblical parlance—who possessed the necessary tactical acumen to defeat these enemy attacks and safeguard Israel's future. Nevertheless, though these "Judges" were effective leaders, their allegiance was principally

The Lord said to Joshua: "This day I will begin to exalt you in the sight of all Israel, so that they may know that I will be with you as I was with Moses."

JOSHUA 3:7

THE WORLD IN 1200 B.C.E.

The traditional dating of the settlement in Canaan, around the beginning of the 12th century B.C.E., coincides with important changes in the Levant. Chief among these was the gradual replacement of copper and bronze implements with items made of iron. Previously, iron had only been available in small quantities, used by major powers such as Egypt. With the discovery of iron in the northern hills of Hittite country (now Turkey), however, the metal became a plentiful commodity, not in the least because Phoenicians distributed it across their extensive trade network. This in turn encouraged a rapid development in smelting and blacksmithing techniques, which produced a wide variety of iron objects for cooking, leisure, or war. Scholars therefore describe the period of between 1200 and 1000 B.C.E. as the first Iron Age (Iron Age I), following the Bronze Age.

Politically, the 12th century saw the beginning of Egypt's decline. Up to this point, Egypt had served as the dominant cultural and economic power in the stories of the Bible; but this was about to change. Egypt's decline had several factors, including the failure of successive harvests and the inability of the royal house to sustain its possessions in Syria-Canaan by military means. This probably led to a mass emigration of Egypt's foreign workers to their native countries, which some scholars believe is the backdrop of the Exodus story. It also explains why the Israelite settlement of Canaan did not invite a military response from Egypt, which in preceding centuries would very likely have been the case. ■

This Achaean-type sword with ivory handle, dated to the Early Iron Age (1200–1000 B.C.E.), was discovered in Mycenae, Greece.

to the tribe they were sworn to defend. A "unified" supreme commander lay still far in the future.

One of these tribal commanders was **Ehud** from the Benjamin tribe, which lived along the Jordan and was therefore the first to be attacked by the king of Moab, named **Eglon**. Having joined forces with Amalek and Ammon, the Moabites took much of the Jordan Valley, including Jericho, until Ehud assassinated the Moabite king with his two-edged dagger, and his forces were driven back across the Jordan (JUDGES 3:12-30).

ca 1207 B.C.E. "Victory slab" of Pharaoh Merneptah, which mentions "Israel"	ca 1230 B.C.E. Israelites destroy Hazor	ca 1207 B.C.E. Assyria defeats Babylon	ca 1200 B.C.E. Mesopotamian artisans craft iron tools

1 Jericho This massive tower and surrounding fortifications in ancient Jericho date from the Middle Bronze Age IIA and IIB (1950–1550 B.C.E.).

2 Gibeon The landscape near Gibeon as it appears today. This is where, according to the Bible, Joshua attacked an army of Amorites and routed the enemy.

3 Hazor The Canaanite temple complex of Hazor is believed to have been destroyed in the 13th century B.C.E. during the Israelite settlement in Canaan.

4 Negev According to the Bible, Joshua penetrated as deep as the Negev, where today a shepherd tends his flocks.

JOSHUA AND THE CONQUEST OF CANAAN

MAP KEY

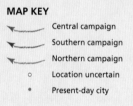

Central campaign

Southern campaign

Northern campaign

○ Location uncertain

● Present-day city

0		20		40	kilometers

| 0 | | 20 | | 40 | miles |

Present-day drainage, coastlines, and country boundaries are represented. Modern names appear in parentheses.

THE GREAT SEA

(MEDITERRANEAN SEA)

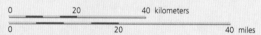

E G Y P T

Sidon
(Saïda)

Damascus

A R A M

2,814 m
9,232 ft
Mt. Hermon

L E B A N O N

S Y R I A

Tyre
(Soûr)

P H O E N I C I A

B A S H A N

Joshua attacked and defeated the combined
armies of several northern Canaanite cities.
The victors chased the fleeing forces
northward into the region of Sidon.
(Joshua 11:7–8)

Dan
(Tel Dan)

Kedesh
(Tel Qedesh)

Hazor (Tel Hazor)
❸

Hazor, the main Canaanite city of
the north, was taken and burned.
(Joshua 11:11)

Achzib
(Tel Akhziv)

Merom

Acco
('Akko)
○ **Achshaph**
(KafrYasīf)

Bay of Acco
(Bay of Haifa)

Sea of
Kinnereth
(Sea of
Galilee)

Ashtaroth

Madon ○

Hammath
(Hammat)

Mt. Carmel
546 m ▲
1,791 ft

Shimron
Meron
(Semunieh)

Mt. Tabor
588 m
1,929 ft ▲

Jabneel

Joshua continued attacking and taking
the rest of the Canaanite cities that had
sent their armies to fight at Merom.
(Joshua 11:12)

Jokneam
(Yoqne'am)

Shunem
(Sūlam)

Endor
('En Dor)

Edrei
(Dar'ā)

Dor ○

Megiddo
(Tel Megiddo)

Valley of Jezreel

Ta'anach
(Ta'annuk)

En-gannim
(Janīn)

Beth Shan
(Bet She'an)

Ramoth-gilead
(Khirbat ar
Rumaythah)

Dothan
(Khirbat al Ḥufayrah)

○ **Jabesh-gilead**

West Bank

Joshua brought all the tribes
together to renew the covenant
with the Lord, and remind the
people to stay faithful.
(Joshua 24:1–27)

G I L E A D

Mt. Ebal
940 m
3,084 ft ▲

Tirzah
(Tallūza)

Succoth (Dayr 'Allā)

Penuel

The inheritance of Joshua
where he was buried.
(Joshua 24:30)

Mt. Gerizim ▲
881 m
2,890 ft

Shechem
(Nablus)

Joppa
(Tel Aviv-Yafo)

Yarqon

Aphek
(Tel Afeq)

Shiloh
(Khirbat Saylūn)

After an initial defeat, the
Hebrews took Ai with a
well planned ambush.
(Joshua 7–8)

The Hebrews crossed the Jordan
and established their first
permanent camp in Canaan.
(Joshua 4:19)

A M M O N

Joshua, after a forced march from
Gilgal, attacked an army of Amorites in
defense of the allied city of Gibeon.
The battle became a rout and the
Hebrews pursued the remaining force.
(Joshua 10:9–10)

Timnath-serah

B E N J A M I N

Bethel **Ai** (Khirbat at Tall)

Ambushing
Force

Main Force

Gilgal

Rabbah
(Amman)

Joshua sent spies to evaluate
the land, especially Jericho, a
key Canaanite city.
(Joshua 2:1)

One of the five city-states of the
Philistines. Others were Ashkelon,
Ekron, Gath, and Gaza.

Upper Beth-horon
(Bayt 'Ūr al Fawqā)

Gezer
(Tel Gezer)

Gibeon
(Al Jīb) ❷

Jericho
(Tall as-Sulṭān)

Jericho
(Arīḥā)

Abel-shittim

❶

Heshbon
(Ḥisbān)

Ekron
(Tel Miqne)

Ashdod
(Tel Ashdod)

Beth Shemesh
(Tel Bet Shemesh)

Jerusalem

Mt. Nebo
802 m
2,631 ft ▲

Medeba
(Mādabā)

Ashkelon
(Tel Ashkelon)
● *Ashqelon*

Jarmuth
(Tel Yarmut)

Bethlehem

Gath
(Tel Zafit)

Adullam
(Horbat 'Adullam)

P H I L I S T I A

Lachish
(Tel Lakhish)

Beth-zur
(Khirbat
Ṭubayqah)

Wilderness of Judah

Salt
Sea
(Dead
Sea)

Jericho was taken after the
walls collapsed before the Ark
of the Covenant, opening the
way into all Canaan.
(Joshua 6:20)

Dibon
(Dhībān)

Gaza Strip

Makkedah

Tappuah
(Tuffuh)

Hebron

Eglon

Debir

Eshtemoa
(As Samū')

En-gedi
(Tell el Jurn)

Aroer
('Arā'ir)

Arnon
(Wadi
el Mujib)

Gaza

Libnah
(Qiryat Gat)

S H E P H E L A H

Gerar (Tel Gerar)

The defeated Amorite kings hid
themselves in a cave. Joshua trapped
then executed them.
(Joshua 10:26)

'Arad
(Tel Arad)

M O A B

Sharuhen
(Tel Sharuhen)

Beersheba
(Be'ér Sheva')

○ 'Arad

Besor

After he took the key cities, Joshua
captured several more in the Negev. He
then returned to the camp at Gilgal.
(Joshua 10:41–43)

N E G E V
❹

Zered (Ḥasā)

J O R D A N

E S D R A E L O N

P L A I N   O F   S H A R O N

Kishon
(Qishon)

Jordan

Yarmuk

Jabbok
(Zarqa)

Sorek
(Sarar)

At that time Deborah, a prophetess, wife of Lappidoth, was judging Israel. She used to sit under the palm of Deborah between Ramah and Bethel in the hill country of Ephraim; and the Israelites came up to her for judgment.

JUDGES 4:4-5

DEBORAH

Elsewhere in the land, the Canaanites still controlled the fertile valleys and plains that produced most of the region's agriculture. The Hebrew tribes "could not drive out the inhabitants of the plain," says the Bible, "because they had chariots of iron"—the Iron Age version of tanks (JUDGES 1:19). Flexing their military superiority, some Canaanite leaders, such as King Jabin of Hazor, even forced the adjoining Israelite tribes to pay tribute (JUDGES 4:1-3). One woman, a prophetess named **Deborah** from the tribe of Issachar, found this situation intolerable. As the first and only female "Judge" in the Book of Judges, she was determined to establish Israelite power in the Jezreel Valley once and for all.

Deborah realized that no single tribe could defeat the enemy. She therefore organized a *levée en masse* among all the Hebrews.

Some tribes, including Ephraim, Benjamin, and East Manasseh, gladly sent their militias, but others turned a blind eye; they were ruthlessly denounced as lacking bravery, and for tarrying "among the sheepfolds" (JUDGES 5:16). Deborah's forces, led by her commander **Barak**, then rode out to face the Canaanite army at Mount Tabor.

The opposing forces were led by a general named **Sisera**. As soon as Sisera's 900 chariots were given the order to advance, God unleashed a rainstorm that flooded the Jezreel Valley and stranded the chariots in the mud. Barak's militia made short work of them. Deborah commemorated the victory in a rousing song: "Hear, O kings; give ear, O princes; to the Lord I will sing, I will make melody to the Lord, the God of Israel" (JUDGES 5:3).

THE CONQUEST OF CANAAN

The Bible describes the Israelite conquest as a series of fierce battles, which left many of the local towns destroyed. Modern biblical archaeology, however, has not been able to corroborate this narrative. Many of the locations described in the Book of Joshua (such as Jericho, Ai, and Bethel) have no remains of violent destruction in this period, though there is plenty of debris from a later period, which scholars have identified with the Philistine conquest. Only in Hazor, Israeli archaeologist Yigael Yadin found evidence of a major fire that destroyed the royal palace of "King Ibni-Addu"—possibly the biblical "King Jabin." Using pottery sherds found in this stratum, Yadin was able to date the destruction to the late 13th or early 12th century B.C.E.—right at the putative beginning

Hazor is perhaps the only ancient settlement in Israel today that bears evidence of destruction during the early 13th century B.C.E., the presumed period of the Israelite settlement in Canaan.

of the "conquest." Other scholars continue to challenge Yadin's assumptions.

However, archaeologists *have* found unmistakable evidence of a major immigration wave in Canaan at the beginning of the Iron Age. In one region, excavators found that its Late Bronze Age sites more than tripled in the Early Iron Age. Many of these new settlements were different from their Canaanite neighbors as witnessed by an absence of pig bones (pork being forbidden in the Mosaic Laws); the presence of large plastered cisterns to catch rainfall; and tall clay *pithoi*, or jars, used to store olive oil or wine. The "conquest" was therefore probably a period of gradual infiltration, which only occasionally resulted in clashes with existing Canaanite towns and clans. ■

ca 1200 B.C.E.	ca 1200 B.C.E.	ca 1200 B.C.E.	ca 1187 B.C.E.
Putative date of the Trojan War in Anatolia (northern Turkey)	First bell cast in bronze in China	Four-pillared house appears in Canaan	Reign of Ramses III begins in Egypt

GIDEON

Soon, however, another danger emerged farther south. Here, Hebrew territory had also become prone to raids by foreign bands, including the Midianites. While this predominantly Arab tribe traced its ancestry to Abraham and his second wife, Keturah, and Moses had once dwelled in the Midian together with Zipporah and Jethro the priest, the Midianites were hostile to Israelite settlement.

This is when a man named **Gideon**, from the tribe of Manasseh, was chosen by an angel to serve as the next Judge. Gideon was skeptical and asked for a sign from God. The angel told him to prepare a sacrifice, which Gideon placed on a rock. A fire then erupted from the rock and consumed the sacrifice. Thus assured of a divine mandate, Gideon assumed his responsibility as a military leader. He first destroyed a nearby altar to Baal, a popular deity among both Canaanites and Midianites, and then gathered an army of recruits from Asher, Manasseh, Zebulun, and Naphtali. As the Midianite forces lay in camp near Endor, Gideon staged a daring nighttime raid that sent the Arab invaders packing across the Jordan and into the desert (JUDGES 7:20-22). So successful was Gideon's leadership that the tribes clamored for him to be crowned king. Gideon refused, saying that only God should rule as king. The time of a unified monarchy was not yet at hand (JUDGES 8:22-23).

Several "Judges" followed after Gideon, including **Tola**, son of **Puah** from the Issachar tribe; **Jair**, another man from Manasseh; **Jephthah**, the son of **Gilead**, who tragically was forced to kill his daughter after having made a rash vow; **Ibzan**, who hailed from Bethlehem (possibly the same village that would soon play a major role in Israel's history); **Elon**, from the tribe of Zebulun; and **Abdon**, who came from Ephraim. But none was as powerful or charismatic as **Samson** from the tribe of Dan.

SAMSON

Of all the Hebrew tribes in Canaan, Dan held the most precarious position, clinging to a narrow strip of land in the Shephelah, between the Judean highlands and the

Dutch artist Rembrandt van Rijn (1606–1669) painted this portrait of Samson and Delilah in 1636.

THE PHILISTINES

During the 12th century B.C.E., the Levant was convulsed by the movement of migratory peoples of possibly Aegean or Anatolian origins. Ugaritic texts refer to them as the *Shiqalaya*, while Egyptian records describe them as "Sea Peoples." A subgroup of these Sea Peoples, called *Peleset*, attacked Canaan and then Egypt, where they were narrowly defeated by Ramses III. Ashkelon, Ekron, Ashdod, Gaza, and Gath were turned into a confederacy known as *Philistia*, from which the word "Philistines" is derived (as well as the later Greek word "Palestine"). The Philistines emerged as the most dangerous enemy of the newly settled Israelite tribes, in part because of their superior military organization, centralized command structure, and heavy armament, including the iron chariot. The Philistine threat forced the tribes to coalesce around a supreme commander of their own, beginning with Saul, thus laying the foundation of Israel's monarchy. ■

coastal region, which had been occupied by another group of invaders: the Philistines. Many of the Danite families had been forced to flee and settle in the far northern highlands. One of these was a man named **Manoah**, who lived with his wife in the village of Zorah. They were childless, but one day an angel appeared to the wife, saying that she would give birth to a "Nazarite," a person consecrated to God, who will "deliver Israel from the hand of the Philistines" (JUDGES 13:5). The boy was named **Samson** and grew up to be a man of almost superhuman strength.

Once, while visiting a Philistine girl from the village of Timnah (which some archaeologists have identified with Tell Batash near Beth-Shemesh), he came across a lion and killed it with his bare hands. Samson decided to marry the girl, despite his parents' misgivings about their son marrying outside his tribe, let alone a daughter of the hated Philistines. Samson persisted and staged a great wedding feast, but a dispute broke out with some of his Philistine guests over a riddle. Enraged, Samson killed 30 Philistines in the nearby town of Ashkelon (JUDGES 14:19).

ca 1180 B.C.E.	ca 1150 B.C.E.	ca 1140 B.C.E.	ca 1125 B.C.E.
Sea Peoples' invasion of Egypt is repulsed	Philistines consolidate their territory in Canaan	First Phoenician colony in Africa at Utica	Israelites and Canaanites clash near Megiddo

Dutch artist Jan Steen (ca 1625–1679) painted this depiction of "Amnon and Tamar" around 1670. Tamar, daughter of King David and sister of Absalom, was raped by her half brother Amnon. Two years later, Absalom killed Amnon in revenge.

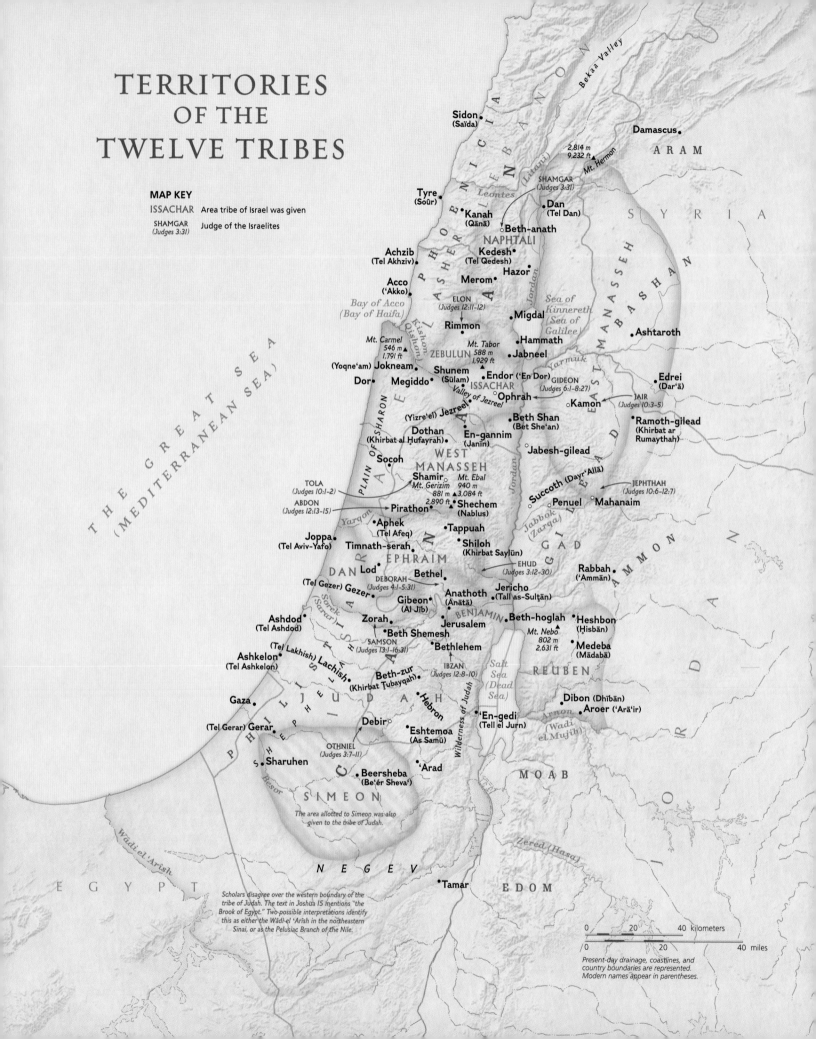

His longing for his bride drove him back to Timnah, only to be told that she had been married to a Philistine—his best man, no less. Samson took his revenge by capturing 300 foxes, tying their tails together and placing flaming torches in the knot, and chasing them across the nearby fields to destroy the Philistine harvest (JUDGES 15:4-5). A large Philistine force was dispatched to capture Samson, but he killed a thousand of them with the jawbone of an ass.

But Samson's weakness for beautiful Philistine women soon drove him into the arms of another lady. Her name was **Delilah**. When news of the affair spread, the Philistines offered Delilah a large sum of money if she could discover the source of Samson's great strength. Samson, suspecting what was afoot, fed her several false leads, frustrating Philistine attempts to capture him.

At long last, Delilah exploded. "You have mocked me three times now and have not told me what makes your strength so great," she cried indignantly. Samson confessed that he would lose his strength "if my head were shaved" (JUDGES 16:15-17). While he slept, the faithless Delilah brought in a Philistine who cut Samson's hair, draining his strength. The Philistines took him

MUSIC IN THE BIBLE

The first biblical reference to music appears in Genesis, which refers to Jubal, a descendant of Cain, who is credited with the "invention" of music as the "ancestor of all those who play the lyre and pipe" (GENESIS 4:20-21). Deborah, the female judge, celebrated her victory over King Jabin with a song of victory. David secured a place at Saul's court because of his skill with the lyre, and as a composer of songs. David is also credited with composing some of the Psalms (*Tehillim,* or "Praises" in Hebrew), a collection of hymns, poems, and prayers developed over many centuries of Israel's history. Some have musical notations, but their proper application is uncertain. Other biblical references suggest that music, particularly vocals, played an important role in daily life. An important liturgical instrument was the *shofar* ("ram's horn") used at religious festivals, and long-necked trumpets used during ceremonies in the Temple. ∎

prisoner, gouged out his eyes, and forced him to work as a draft animal, turning a mill in a Gaza prison.

While in captivity, Samson's hair gradually grew back. One day, the Philistines held a great ceremony in their temple, which was devoted to the god Dagon. The assembly clamored to see Samson, and so the prisoner was brought out and tied between two pillars. As the crowd around him jeered, Samson prayed to God for a restoration of his powers, "only this once." God granted his request; Samson pushed the pillars and brought down the temple roof, killing all those inside (JUDGES 16:30). He was buried in the tomb of his father, Manoah, near the village of Zorah.

RUTH

The story of **Ruth**, described in the Book of Ruth (one of the few books in the Bible named after a woman) is set in the same time period. A famine struck the land, forcing a man named **Elimelech** to leave his hometown of Bethlehem and take his wife, **Naomi,** and sons **Mahlon** and **Chilion** to the country of the Moabites. Elimelech died, whereupon Mahlon and

This Philistine anthropoid, or human-shaped, coffin from Tel Rehov dates from the Iron Age II (1000–800 B.C.E.).

THE 12 TRIBES

According to the Bible, the 12 tribes of Israel were founded by the sons (and grandsons) of Jacob by his two wives and concubines—in order of birth: **Reuben, Simeon, Levi, Judah, Dan, Naphtali, Gad, Asher, Issachar, Zebulun, Joseph,** and **Benjamin.** Joseph did not found a tribe, but his two sons—**Manasseh** and **Ephraim**—did. Each of these "tribes," which included manifold clans and families, would develop a unique cultural identity, yet still retain a sense of kinship with others in their shared allegiance to God and his Law. The Book of Joshua tells us that once Canaan was pacified, Joshua set about partitioning the land among these tribes. Striving for fairness was difficult, because

the available land ranged from fertile grasslands to dry hills, which is why Joshua settled the matter by lot. So, for example, was the tribe of Manasseh split between east and west of the river Jordan (JOSHUA 13:15-28), while the Simeon tribe went south into the desert, and Galilee in the north was occupied by Asher, Zebulun, and Naphtali. Issachar drew the fertile region adjoining the Jezreel. Judah, by contrast, was given the dry region south of Jerusalem (JOSHUA CHAPTER 15), while Benjamin's tribe received the hill country north of Jerusalem (JOSHUA 18:11-28). The desirable coastal plain was given to the tribe of Dan (JOSHUA 19:40-48), but Simeon's tribe had to settle with the Negev

around Beersheba (JOSHUA 19:1-9). The tribe of Levi was not given any particular region; they were scattered over Israelite-held territory, there to serve the worship of God. ∎

ca 1124 B.C.E.	ca 1120 B.C.E..	ca 1103 B.C.E.	ca 1100 B.C.E.
Nebuchadnezzar captures Babylon	"Dark Age" of Greece begins	Phoenicians develop alphabetic script	First Chinese dictionary is created

CHAPTER 2: FROM JOSHUA TO KINGS 93

THE LOST ARK

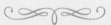

The gold-plated chest that contained the stone tablets handed by God to Moses plays an important role in Israel's early saga. The Book of Joshua reports that the riverbed of the Jordan River ran dry as soon as the feet of the priests carrying the Ark touched the water when crossing (JOSHUA 3:15-16). During the siege of Jericho, priests carried the Ark around the walls of the city while others blew on their horns, until the walls collapsed on the seventh day.

The Ark was installed in the shrine of Shiloh (I SAMUEL 3:3), but after the Philistines defeated the Hebrew army at Ebenezer, it was rushed to the battlefield to bolster the Israelite ranks. The Philistines then captured the Ark and placed it in the temple of Dagon in Ashdod, but God took revenge by toppling Dagon's cult statue and by inflicting disease wherever the Ark was carried. Finally, the Ark was returned to the Israelites near Beth-shemesh (I SAMUEL 6:1-12) and was installed in the village of Kiriath-jearim, "in the house of Abinadab on the hill" (I SAMUEL 7:1). There it remained until David carried the Ark to a tabernacle (a tentlike shrine) in the newly conquered city of Jerusalem, and ultimately placed it in the Holy of Holies, the inner sanctum of Solomon's Temple. In 586 B.C.E., Jerusalem was captured by the neo-Babylonian King Nebuchadnezzar. Most scholars assume that the Ark was destroyed in the process. ∎

French artist James Tissot (1836–1902) created this impression of the Ark of the Covenant around 1900.

Then all the elders of Israel gathered together and came to Samuel at Ramah, and said to him, "You are old and your sons do not follow in your ways; appoint for us, then, a king to govern us, like other nations."

1 SAMUEL 8:4-5

Chilion both married local women. Mahlon chose a young woman named Ruth, but he also died shortly thereafter. Heartbroken, Naomi prepared to move back to Bethlehem and told Ruth to return to her own family. Ruth decided to stay with her, saying, "Where you go, I will go" (RUTH 1:16).

In Bethlehem, Ruth sustained herself and her mother-in-law by gleaning kernels from the barley harvest. One day, she met the owner of a field named **Boaz**, who received her kindly. Naomi urged Ruth to return to Boaz at night and "uncover his feet"—an invitation to have relations with her. In response, Boaz promised to take care of her, a symbolic acceptance of marriage (RUTH 3:11). After they married, Ruth bore Boaz a son named **Obed**, the future father of **Jesse**, who would become the father of King **David**. Thus, Ruth was David's great-grandmother, and is listed as such in the Book of Ruth and in the Gospels of Luke and Matthew.

SAMUEL

Despite Samson's heroic example, the Philistines continued to expand their control of the land. Philistine pottery and other artifacts have been found as far as Megiddo and Beth She'an in the north and the Transjordan in the east. At the same time, Israelite settlements in the highlands and other outlying regions continued to grow; archaeologists estimate that during the 11th century B.C.E., the Hebrew population grew from 45,000 to around 150,000. A great clash between the growing Israelite and Philistine powers was inevitable.

Around this time, according to the Book of Samuel, a woman named **Hannah** from the hill country of Ephraim made a pilgrimage to the ancient shrine at Shiloh, praying to God for a son, and promising him that she would raise the newborn to serve God (SAMUEL 1:11). Her wish was granted, and she named her son *Shmu'el*,

ca 1100 B.C.E.	ca 1100 B.C.E.	ca 1075 B.C.E.	ca 1050 B.C.E.
Dorians capture Mycenaean kingdom	Shang dynasty in China is overthrown by the Zhou	Egyptian New Kingdom ends	The Chou produce the first compass

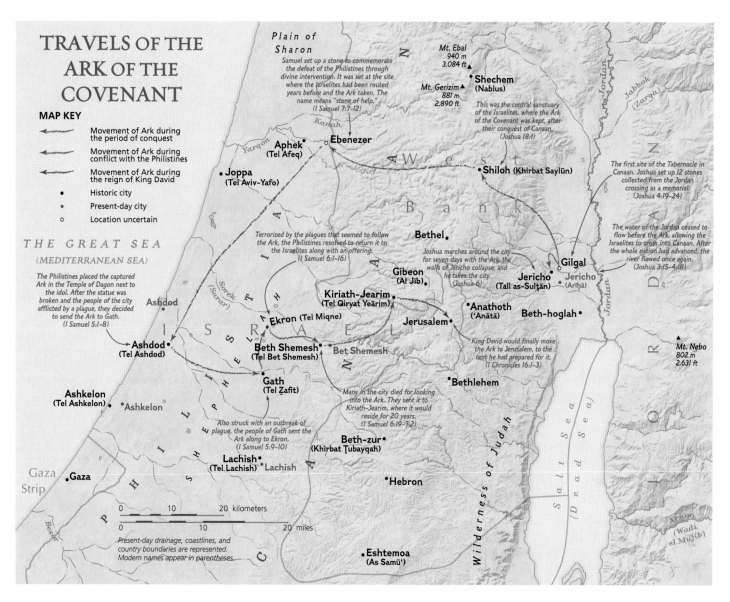

TRAVELS OF THE ARK OF THE COVENANT

MAP KEY

← ← ← Movement of Ark during the period of conquest

← ← ← Movement of Ark during conflict with the Philistines

← ← ← Movement of Ark during the reign of King David

● Historic city

• Present-day city

○ Location uncertain

THE GREAT SEA
(MEDITERRANEAN SEA)

The Philistines placed the captured Ark in the Temple of Dagon next to the idol. After the statue was broken and the people of the city afflicted by a plague, they decided to send the Ark to Gath. (1 Samuel 5:1-8)

Plain of Sharon
Samuel set up a stone to commemorate the defeat of the Philistines through divine intervention. It was set at the site where the Israelites had been routed years before and the Ark taken. The name means "stone of help." (1 Samuel 7:7-12)

Mt. Ebal
940 m
3,084 ft ▲

Mt. Gerizim ▲
881 m
2,890 ft

Shechem
(Nablus)

This was the central sanctuary of the Israelites, where the Ark of the Covenant was kept, after their conquest of Canaan. (Joshua 18:1)

Kanah

Yarqon

Aphek
(Tel Afeq)

Ebenezer

• **Joppa**
(Tel Aviv-Yafo)

Shiloh (Khirbat Saylūn)

The first site of the Tabernacle in Canaan. Joshua set up 12 stones collected from the Jordan crossing as a memorial. (Joshua 4:19-24)

Bethel ●

Terrorized by the plagues that seemed to follow the Ark, the Philistines resolved to return it to the Israelites along with an offering. (1 Samuel 6:1-16)

The water of the Jordan ceased to flow before the Ark, allowing the Israelites to cross into Canaan. After the whole nation had advanced, the river flowed once again. (Joshua 3:15-4:18)

Sorek (Sarar)

Gibeon
(Al Jīb) ●

Joshua marches around the city for seven days with the Ark, the walls of Jericho collapse, and he takes the city. (Joshua 6)

Gilgal ○

Jericho
(Tall as-Sulṭān) ●

Jericho
(Arīḥā)

Ashdod

Kiriath-Jearim
(Tel Qiryat Yeārim) ●

Ekron (Tel Miqne)

Anathoth
('Anātā) ●

Beth-hoglah •

Ashdod ●
(Tel Ashdod)

Beth Shemesh ●
(Tel Bet Shemesh)

Bet Shemesh

Jerusalem ●

King David would finally move the Ark to Jerusalem, to the tent he had prepared for it. (1 Chronicles 16:1-3)

Mt. Nebo
802 m
2,631 ft ▲

Ashkelon
(Tel Ashkelon) ●

• Ashkelon

Gath
(Tel Zafit) ●

Many in the city died for looking into the Ark. They sent it to Kiriath-Jearim, where it would reside for 20 years. (1 Samuel 6:19-7:2)

• **Bethlehem**

Also struck with an outbreak of plague, the people of Gath sent the Ark along to Ekron. (1 Samuel 5:9-10)

Beth-zur •
(Khirbat Ṭubayqah)

Gaza • **Gaza**
Strip

Lachish ●
(Tel Lachish) • Lachish

• **Hebron**

Wilderness of Judah

Salt Sea
(Dead Sea)

| 0 | 10 | 20 kilometers |

| 0 | 10 | 20 miles |

Present-day drainage, coastlines, and country boundaries are represented. Modern names appear in parentheses.

• **Eshtemoa**
(As Samū')

Arnon (Wadi el Mujib)

"God heard [me]." Thus begins the story of the first major prophet in the land of Israel, Samuel.

Samuel was serving God at the shrine of Shiloh when the Philistines launched their long-anticipated assault on the Israelites near the city of Aphek. The Hebrew defenses crumbled, and the Philistines were able to capture the Ark of the Covenant, which had been placed in the center of the Israelite camp in the hope of warding off defeat. But God intervened; every Philistine city in which the Ark was placed as war booty was promptly struck by the plague. Exasperated, the Philistines put the Ark on a cart pulled by cows, which took it to the Hebrew settlement of Beth-shemesh (1 SAMUEL 6:1-12).

What made the Philistines so successful in battle was their military discipline and unified command structure. Israel's forces, by contrast, were a quarrelsome lot in which each tribe prized its independence. In due course, as the Book of Samuel states, the tribes realized that in order to defeat the Philistines, they had to act in unison. They approached Samuel and asked that he appoint a king or a supreme commander—the word Samuel uses, *melekh,* can mean both—so that "we can be also like other nations, and that our king may . . . fight our battles" (1 SAMUEL 8:19-20).

Samuel was reluctant to do so. Indeed, scholars believe that there are several different sources at work in the first Book of Samuel.

ca 1027 B.C.E.	ca 1025 B.C.E.	ca 1010 B.C.E.	ca 1000 B.C.E.
Shang dynasty is replaced by the Chou	Samuel anoints Saul as king of Israel	Hebrew alphabet emerges from earlier Semitic scripts	Beginning of Iron Age II

One "monarchic" source insists that the creation of Israel's monarchy was the inevitable will of YHWH, while another strand clearly advocates the opposite view, arguing that the choice of kingship was imposed by tribal elders on Samuel against his will (I SAMUEL 8:4-6). "[A king] will take the best of your fields," this version warns. "He will take your male and female slaves, and the best of your cattle and donkeys, and put them to his work" (I SAMUEL 8:14-16).

SAUL

According to the monarchic strand, however, God did charge Samuel to anoint a young man from the tribe of Benjamin as the "ruler over my people Israel" (I SAMUEL 9:16). His name was **Saul**, and it was not a moment too soon. **Nahash**, the king of Ammon, had launched an invasion of Israelite territory in the north, and captured the city of Jabesh-gilead, just east of the Jordan. Saul mobilized all the tribal militias and attacked the Ammonites at dawn, taking their forces by surprise and scattering them (I SAMUEL 11:11).

Exploiting the momentum of this victory, Saul then turned his army against the Philistines and steadily evicted them from the highlands. But Saul failed to achieve a decisive victory. Despite Hebrew triumphs at the battle of Bozez and Michmash, the conflict evolved into a protracted war of attrition that neither side could afford. This may be the reason why the Deuteronomist redactor of the Books of Samuel depicts Saul as a conflicted and even unstable character. "There was hard fighting against the Philistines all the days of Saul," says the book (I SAMUEL 14:52). Even though Saul did win against other enemy forces, including the Amalekites, he failed in his mission to defeat the greatest threat to the nation of Israel. "I regret that I made Saul king," said the Lord in the first Book of Samuel; "he has not carried out my commands" (I SAMUEL 15:11).

Italian artist Andrea del Castagno (ca 1419–1457) completed this shield with David and the head of Goliath at his feet around 1455.

This is when another promising young man appears on the scene. God had sent Samuel to **Jesse** the Bethlehemite to search for a new leader, "a king among his sons" (I SAMUEL 16:1). His choice fell upon Jesse's youngest son David, a humble shepherd who was nevertheless blessed with exceptional musical skills. Whenever Saul found himself vexed by an "evil spirit" sent by God, David's harp playing soothed him. Saul appointed David as his armor bearer.

Soon thereafter, another major Philistine battle loomed. The Hebrew and Philistine armies were moving toward each other "between Socoh and Azekah, in Ephesdammim," possibly located near today's Khirbet 'Abbad, west of Bethlehem (I SAMUEL 17:1). This time, the Philistines fielded a fearsome new weapon: a giant named **Goliath**, carrying a huge bronze spear (I SAMUEL 17:5-7). The Israelites were frozen in fear—except young David. Armed with only a sling, he picked a stone from a riverbed and slung it at Goliath's head. David's aim was true; the stone struck the giant and killed him, prompting the Philistines to flee. The Israelites were jubilant. Saul was compelled to place young David at the head of his army (I SAMUEL 18:5).

Even though David then married Saul's daughter **Michal** and became a close friend of Saul's son **Jonathan**, an intense rivalry developed between the young new general and the king. Saul even began to plot to kill him. David had little choice but to flee to enemy territory, the Philistine-held coastal plains. Saul forced his daughter Michal to marry another man, whereupon David took a woman named **Ahinoam**, a local woman from the Jezreel.

The country was once again torn by war. Philistine forces were massing at Mount Gilboa, and Saul and his sons, all serving as commanders in his army, rushed to meet them. But God had turned against Saul,

ca 1000 B.C.E.	ca 995 B.C.E.	ca 994 B.C.E.	ca 985 B.C.E.
Villanova culture in Italy	Phoenicians establish colonies in Mediterranean	Teutonic tribes move west toward the Rhine	Phoenicians introduce purple dyes

and the Israelite ranks were decimated. All of Saul's sons fell to Philistine swords, including his heir, Jonathan. Badly wounded himself, Saul ordered his armor bearer to finish him off, but the man refused. Saul then fell upon his own sword (I SAMUEL 31:1-7). His corpse, and those of his sons, were dragged by the Philistines to the walls of Beth She'an and hung from the walls. The story of the Israelites in the Promised Land had reached its nadir.

ABNER

"How the mighty have fallen!" David exclaimed in despair when hearing of Saul's defeat (II SAMUEL 1:19-20). Indeed, the situation was dire. With Israel's army, now led by Saul's uncle **Abner**, in headlong retreat, the Philistines were flooding over the Hebrew highlands. Abner, anxious to retain Israelite unity, designated Saul's only surviving son **Ishbaal** (known in later traditions as "Ishbosheth," or "man of shame") as the new king. Ishbaal's elevation was supported by the northern tribes, but ominously, not by the south. The southern elders went instead to Hebron, David's military base, and in due course anointed him king "over the house of Judah" (II SAMUEL 2:4).

Now, there were two rival kings. A civil war loomed between the Hebrew north and south, just when Philistine power was at its zenith. But then a dispute broke out between Abner and King Ishbaal. Abner had taken a fancy to one of Saul's concubines, **Rizpah**, and planned to marry her. If he did, he would become the guardian of Rizpah's children who were the heirs of the late king—a direct challenge to Ishbaal's legitimacy. Ishbaal lashed out at Abner, at which the general promptly switched his allegiance to David, promising to "bring all Israel over to you" (II SAMUEL 3:12). David welcomed him, but on one condition: that he would be reunited with his first wife, Michal. Their reunion would heal the rift between the house of David and Saul, and seal the restoration of a unified nation. Abner agreed.

Mount Gilboa is the place where, according to the first Book of Samuel, Saul and his sons met their death during the battle with the Philistines.

LOVE AND SEX IN THE BIBLE

Despite the Law's prohibition against adultery and incest, the biblical stories are filled with tales of lust. Jacob's daughter Dinah was raped by the son of King Hamor; King David seduced a married woman named Bathsheba, while his daughter was sexually abused by her half brother Amnon. Polygamy was common, given the high infant mortality rate and the short life expectancy of women, generally around 40 years. In ancient Israel, moreover, sex often served a cultic function. Canaanite farmers (or their wives) visited the shrines of fertility idols such as the Phoenician *Astarte,* to mate with temple prostitutes in the hope of securing a good harvest (I KINGS 15:12). Astarte (not to be confused with *Asherah*) was also revered as the goddess of sexual love. By contrast, Asherah was an Akkadian mother goddess. Some scholars have argued that during the monarchical period, she was sometimes revered as YHWH's consort and worshipped as "Queen of Heaven," which may explain the persistence of her cult. ■

Ishbaal, now devoid of support, was murdered by his own court. Abner himself did not survive either; he was killed by David's top commander, **Joab**, who thought Abner had come to spy on David's order of battle. David was horrified, but kept Joab in his service, knowing that his military skills were without equal.

The northern tribes had little choice but to go to Hebron and pledge their submission to David as their new king. Although it is difficult to pinpoint a particular date in this early stage of Israel's history, some scholars believe this took place near the end of the 11th century, around 1010 B.C.E.

DAVID

Thus began the reign of King David, which in the centuries to come would gain mythic proportions and serve as a beacon of messianic hope in troubled times. Nevertheless, at that moment, the Hebrew strategic situation was still highly disadvantageous, with the Philistines controlling major swaths of Hebrew land. Surprisingly, David chose to ignore the Philistines for the moment and instead marched on the city of the Jebusites, known as Jerusalem (II SAMUEL 5:6).

ca 980 B.C.E.	ca 980–930 B.C.E.	ca 978–960 B.C.E.	ca 960 B.C.E.
King David conquers Jesubite city of Jerusalem	Unified kingdom of Israel	Reign of King Siamun of Egypt	Solomon succeeds David

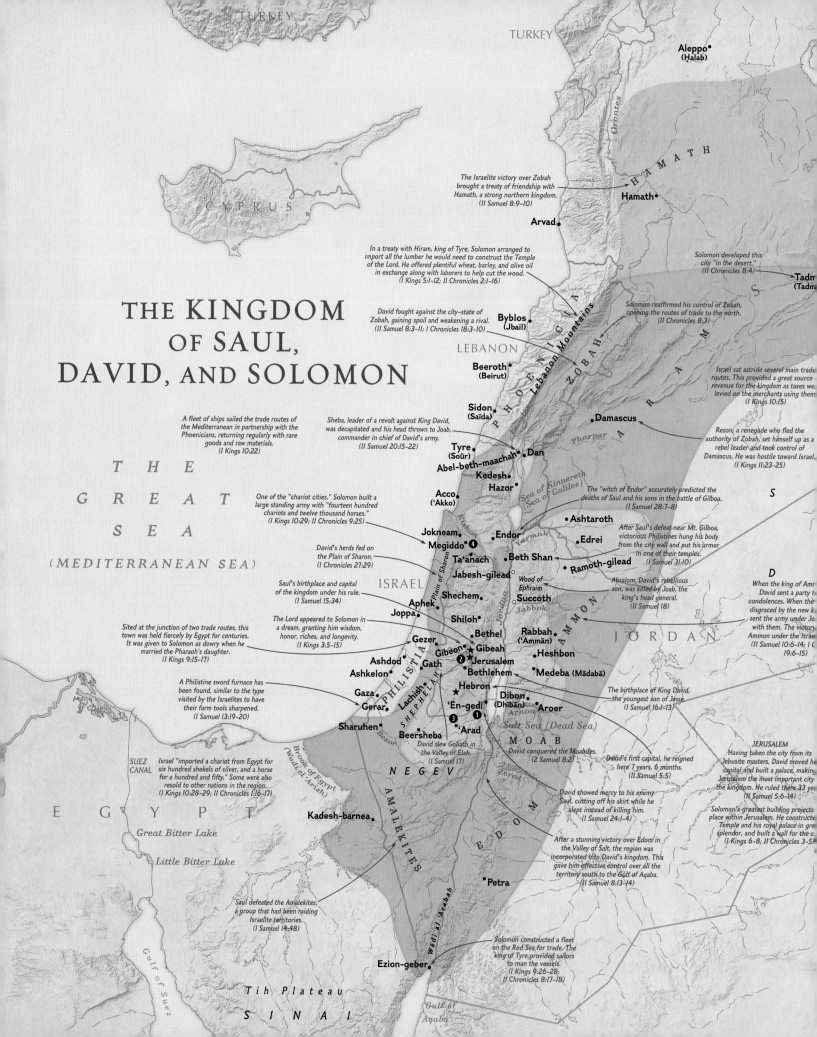

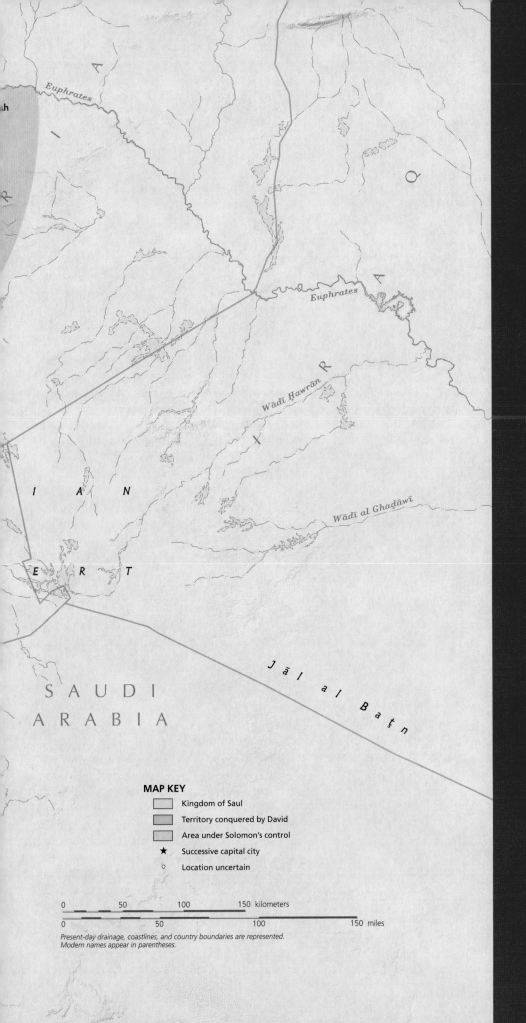

SAUDI
ARABIA

Euphrates

Euphrates

Wādī Ḥawrān

Wādī al Ghaḍāwī

Jāl al Baṭn

MAP KEY

- Kingdom of Saul
- Territory conquered by David
- Area under Solomon's control
- ★ Successive capital city
- ○ Location uncertain

0   50   100   150 kilometers
0   50   100   150 miles

Present-day drainage, coastlines, and country boundaries are represented.
Modern names appear in parentheses.

1 Ein Gedi According to I Samuel 24:1-2, David found refuge in this lush oasis from King Saul and his "three thousand chosen men."

2 Jerusalem David captured the hill of a Jesubite stronghold known as Jerusalem, and made it the new capital of his unified kingdom.

3 Arad In this city, one of the southernmost outposts of the new kingdom, both David and Solomon built a citadel, which featured a recently excavated sanctuary.

4 Megiddo This ancient Canaanite fortress guarded the Jezreel Valley, though the stables and stone troughs depicted here were probably built by King Ahab (874–853 B.C.E.).

99

So all the elders of Israel came to the king at Hebron; and King David made a covenant with them at Hebron before the Lord, and they anointed David king over Israel.

II SAMUEL 5:3

David wanted to anchor the newly unified nation with a proper capital and a national shrine of YHWH worship. But the place had to be on neutral territory, lest David be accused of favoritism toward any one tribe.

In that respect, the city of Jerusalem was an excellent choice. It was located on the boundary between Judah and the northern tribes, and was easily defended because it sat on a hill surrounded by valleys. What's more, it enjoyed its own source of fresh water, the spring of Gihon. The only problem was that Jerusalem was not his, but the capital of the Jebusites. David intended to change this.

He captured the city through stealth, sending his soldiers up "the water shaft," quite possibly a tunnel that connected the spring of Gihon with the citadel (II SAMUEL 5:8). No bloodbath ensued; the Jebusites capitulated and continued to live in peace with their new Israelite masters. Alarmed, the Philistines then marched on Jerusalem to crush David before he became too powerful. With God's help, says the second Book of Samuel, David was able to defeat the Philistines, not once but twice, pushing them back to their original homesteads along the coast. Eventually, all of the regions in Canaan, including the Jezreel Valley, the Shephelah, the Galilee, and the stronghold of Beth She'an, came under David's control.

Now, at last, the king could turn his attention to building a state, ruled from a proper Israelite capital. He built an elaborate palace in Jerusalem, in a location known as the "City of David," using architects and artisans from Lebanon who brought precious cedar wood. He also pitched the Tabernacle on the top of the mount, previously used by the Jebusites as a threshing floor, to house the Ark of the Covenant. This was obviously not a satisfactory solution, and the king complained to Nathan—the first of a line of prophets who would advise, and

This "David" by Renaissance artist Donatello (1386–1466) is the first freestanding bronze sculpture since Antiquity.

often chastise, the kings of Israel—how "I am living in a house of cedar, but the ark of God stays in a tent" (II SAMUEL 7:2). Nathan then received an oracle from God, assuring David that "the Lord will make you a house"—a Davidic dynasty—but that it would be up to his offspring (in this case, Solomon) to "build a house for my name" (II SAMUEL 7:11-13).

According to the Books of Samuel and the subsequent Books of Kings, David then expanded his territory until Israel had become the dominant state in the Levant, absorbing the nations of Ammon, Moab, and Edom that had vexed the Israelites in years past. Modern research has questioned this claim, and many scholars believe that some of the legendary material surrounding David served to exalt him as an ideal king, as successful in peace as in war, beloved by God as well as his people. Indeed, David's greatest achievement (and that of his son Solomon) is not the extent of their putative realm, but the fusion of the quarrelsome tribes into one nation. Some scholars have even questioned whether David is a historical figure, though the discovery of a stela from Tel Dan with the inscription *bytdwd* (which may mean "House of David") would argue otherwise.

ABSALOM

Notwithstanding David's political achievements, his family life was filled with conflict and tragedy. One reason was that David felt compelled to take a wife from different tribes or subject nations, like a Babylonian satrap. With rivalry between his various sons (and their mothers) running rampant, the strength of family—backbone of the Israelite patriarchal tradition—was torn asunder.

A case in point was David's offspring by his wife **Maacah**, daughter of the king of Geshur; they had a son named **Absalom**

ca 950 B.C.E.	ca 945 B.C.E.	ca 931 B.C.E.	ca 931-910 B.C.E.
Darius builds new canal from the Nile to the Red Sea	Pharaoh Shoshenq I founds 22nd Dynasty	Solomon's kingdom splits into two	Reign of King Jeroboam I of Northern Kingdom of Israel

and a daughter named **Tamar**. One day, Tamar was raped by her half brother **Amnon**, David's firstborn son by his wife **Ahinoam**. David was furious, but he loved Amnon too much to inflict the punishment he deserved (II Samuel 13:21). Tamar's brother Absalom then took matters in his own hands by killing Amnon during a sheepshearing festival—an act that forced him to go into hiding to escape David's wrath.

This had tragic consequences, for Absalom soon began to foment a rebellion in David's former base of Hebron with the support of

Florentine artist Francesco di Stefano Pesellino (1422–1457) created this depiction of the "Death of Absalom." King David's General Joab used three spears to kill Absalom.

one of the king's counselors, **Ahithophel**. The revolt gained such a following that it was David's turn to go into hiding, until his forces were able to rout the rebels. Defeated, Absalom fled the field on his horse with David's General **Joab** in hot pursuit, but his hair got tangled in the branches of an oak tree. He was lifted from his horse and hung there until Joab killed him. Despite all the trouble his son had caused him, David grieved deeply upon hearing the news, crying, "O my son Absalom, my son, my son Absalom! Would that I had died instead of you!" (II Samuel 18:33).

ca 931–913 B.C.E.	ca 928 B.C.E.	ca 913–911 B.C.E.	ca 911–870 B.C.E.
Reign of King Rehoboam of Judah	Shoshenq I invades Judah and Israel	Reign of King Abijah of Judah	Reign of King Asa of Judah

BATHSHEBA

David further compromised his reputation by pursuing the beautiful Bathsheba, whom he had seen bathing at night. Bathsheba, however, was married to Uriah, one of David's top commanders, then serving under Joab. Undaunted, David began an affair with the young woman until one day, she found out she was pregnant. David quickly summoned Uriah back from the field, so as to make it plausible that he had fathered Bathsheba's child, but that plot failed. David then decided to get rid of Uriah by ordering Joab to place him at the very front of the planned assault against the Ammonites, where he was certain to be killed—and he was. As soon as Bathsheba finished her time of mourning, David married her and she bore his son. But the prophet Nathan sternly rebuked David for his evil scheming because it had "displeased the Lord," and indeed, the baby died (II SAMUEL 11:27). David then repented before God, and in return was promised that Bathsheba would bear him a second son. His name was Solomon. David loved Bathsheba

Then David consoled his wife Bathsheba, and went to her, and lay with her; and she bore a son, and he named him Solomon.

II SAMUEL 12:24

deeply, but soon she too began to plot her son's future against his rivals at court. As David grew older and feeble, Bathsheba extracted David's promise that their son Solomon would succeed him. But other parties were one step ahead of her.

ADONIJAH

One night, as an ailing David lay in bed, Bathsheba slipped into his room and—prodded by Nathan—warned him that **Adonijah**, David's son by his wife **Haggith**, was planning to seize power and have himself crowned. This account is provided by the next set of books in the Bible, that of Kings, which provide a comprehensive history of Israel's monarchical period (I KINGS 1:11-27).

Adonijah certainly had a legitimate claim on the throne; he was David's oldest son, and his ascendancy was supported by Joab, David's ablest general, as well as one of the high priests attending the Tabernacle, named **Abiathar**. So confident was Adonijah of his impending anointment that he decided to throw a big celebration party at the springs of En-rogel, in the Kidron Valley, to which all of his brothers were invited—except Solomon.

David moved quickly to preempt Adonijah's coup. He ordered that Solomon be taken to the Gihon Spring and be anointed as king by Zadok the priest (I KINGS 1:34). Shortly thereafter, the old king died—on Shavuot, as legend has it, which is why to this day, many Jewish pilgrims visit the tomb of David, located just outside of the Zion Gate, during this festival.

Needless to say, Adonijah was furious to be deprived of his throne. He knew he had broad support among the northern tribes, who felt that the Davidic monarchy had become too powerful and was usurping tribal autonomy. As soon as Solomon was announced

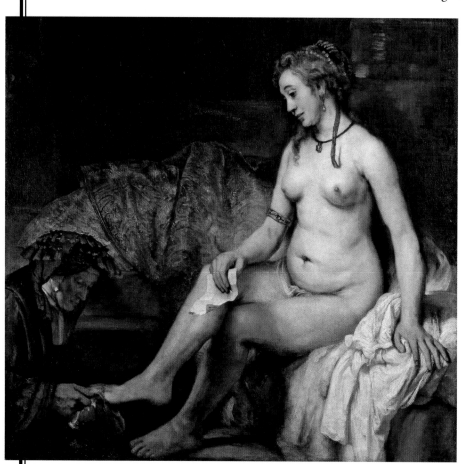

Dutch artist Rembrandt van Rijn (1606–1669) painted this portrait of "Bathsheba at Her Bath" in 1654.

| ca 909–866 B.C.E. | ca 900 B.C.E. | ca 900 B.C.E. | ca 885–874 B.C.E. |
| Reign of King Baasha of Northern Kingdom of Israel | Assyria is dominant power in Mesopotamia | Kingdom of Kush breaks away from Egypt | Reign of King Omri of Northern Kingdom of Israel |

In a colored woodcut from the 15th-century Nuremberg Bible, Bathsheba asks Solomon whether Adonijah can marry Abishag.

with whom he struck an alliance. One of these foreign wives was an Egyptian princess, daughter of Pharaoh (I KINGS 11:1); her father was probably Siamun of the 21st Dynasty (ca 978–959 B.C.E.). In centuries past, it was Pharaoh who married daughters from foreign potentates. The fact that the situation was now reversed vividly illustrates the decline of Egyptian power in the region.

Apparently, Solomon also found time to adjudicate civil cases, such as the one where two prostitutes were fighting over a baby, each claiming it was hers. Solomon said, "Bring me a sword," and ordered the child cut in two, with each woman receiving half of the body. Shocked, one of the mothers said, "Please, my lord, give her the living boy!" (I KINGS 3:26). Solomon knew that the true mother had spoken, for no woman could see her own child killed. The king also composed "three thousand proverbs" and "over a thousand songs," and could speak with authority about a vast range of subjects, from cedar wood and hyssop to different species of animals and birds (I KINGS 4:33).

as David's successor, Adonijah began to plot against him. His first move seemed innocuous. He asked Bathsheba to petition the new king on his behalf, so that he could marry a young woman named **Abishag**. As it happened, Abishag had been David's nursemaid and confidante in the king's final days. Solomon saw right through this thinly veiled attempt at sedition: To marry the concubine of the former king was tantamount to claiming a right to succeed. Why not "ask for him the kingdom as well," he mused sarcastically (I KINGS 2:22). Adonijah's petition gave Solomon the pretext he needed to get rid of his dangerous rival. Adonijah was put to death. Other prominent figures of the Adonijah party, including Abiathar and even General Joab, were either banished or put to the sword.

SOLOMON

No king in the stories of the Bible so speaks to our imagination as King Solomon. His reign was crowned with glory. He was rich and powerful, and he was wise, a quality bestowed upon him by God. In a dream, God had asked him what he wanted most, and Solomon replied, "an understanding mind to govern your people, able to discern between good and evil" (I KINGS 3:9).

Solomon used his wisdom to create a modern administrative apparatus, dividing his realm into 12 districts that deliberately cut across tribal boundaries so as to further centralize power in Jerusalem. To pacify tribal sensibilities, he continued his father's policy of marrying wives from many tribes, as well as from those nations

The Bible depicts Solomon's reign as an era of unprecedented prosperity, and indeed there is evidence that the Levant was experiencing strong economic growth. The havoc of the Philistine invasion was a distant memory, and even the Philistines themselves were now deeply engaged in regional trade. Much of the maritime trade was carried by a new type of cargo vessel, designed by the Phoenicians, Canaanites who had been displaced by the Philistines to the coastal areas of what is today Lebanon, which used a flat bilge and low draft to navigate the coastal sea lanes and inland rivers. At the same time, the domesticated camel became the mainstay of long-distance travel across the Arabian and Sinai Deserts, replacing the donkey. The biblical narrative even suggests that Solomon went to fill his coffers with the rich gold ores of Ophir, located on the eastern coast of Africa.

As wealth poured into his treasury, Solomon fulfilled God's promise to David: to build a true sanctuary to house the Ark of the Covenant, large enough to also accommodate the priests charged with supervising the Mosaic sacrificial rites. To do so, he instigated a "donation drive" among his populace, which netted 5,000 gold and 10,000 silver talents (roughly $100 million in today's currency).

When this massive project was finished, a new citadel of white and gold had risen over Jerusalem. In addition to the Temple sanctuary

ca 883–859 B.C.E.	ca 875 B.C.E.	ca 875 B.C.E.	ca 874–853 B.C.E.
Reign of Ashurnasirpal II of Assyria	Symbol in India is first reference to the number zero	Chinese begin to use natural gas	Reign of King Ahab of Northern Kingdom of Israel

SOLOMON'S TEMPLE

The Temple built by Solomon on Temple Mount in Jerusalem conforms to the archetype of a *megaron* used throughout the Mediterranean and the Near East. Similar designs have been found in Hazor and in the sanctuary of Arad. A pillared *ulam,* or portal, led to a tall nave surrounded on three sides by administrative offices and storage rooms. At the end of the nave, or *hekal,* was an inner sanctuary known as the Holy of Holies, where the Ark of the Covenant was placed. The exterior was adorned with "carved engravings of cherubim, palm trees, and open flowers" (I KINGS 6:29).

Measuring some 120 feet in length and 55 feet in width, the Temple was fronted by a spacious courtyard that contained a sacrificial altar and a bronze vessel, known as the "Sea of Bronze." This vessel rested on 12 bronze oxen, each group of three facing the four points of the compass.

During its roughly 400-year history, the Temple was repeatedly plundered, first by Pharaoh Shishak or Shoshenq (I KINGS 14:25-26), followed by a vengeful King Jehoash of the Northern Kingdom (II KINGS 14:14). It was then ransacked by King Ahaz of Judah in order to gather the ransom needed to placate the Assyrian King Tiglath-pileser (II KINGS 16:8), and finally by the Babylonian King Nebuchadnezzar in 598 B.C.E. (II KINGS 24:13) during his sack of Jerusalem. It is therefore unclear how much of Solomon's original treasure and decoration still existed when the Temple was finally destroyed by Nebuchadnezzar in 586 B.C.E. (II KINGS 24:25). ■

This lavish illustration of "The Visit of the Queen of Sheba to King Solomon" was painted by Sir Edward John Poynter (1836–1919) in the early 1900s.

ca 870–848 B.C.E.	ca 853 B.C.E.	ca 853–852 B.C.E.	ca 852–841 B.C.E.
Reign of King Jehoshaphat of Judah; ministry of prophet Elijah	Israel, Tyre, and Syria clash with Assyrians in Qarqar	Reign of King Ahaziah of Northern Kingdom of Israel	Reign of King Jehoram of Northern Kingdom of Israel

proper, there were residential buildings for Solomon's staff, servants, and his extensive harem, although Pharaoh's daughter was housed in a separate pavilion for her private use (I Kings 7:8). At the same time, Solomon built a ring of strongholds to protect his kingdom, with fortresses in Megiddo, Hazor, and Gezer, although the remains of Solomon's so-called "stables" at Megiddo have now been shown to date to a later era.

Solomon's good fortune could not last; the prosperity of his kingdom would soon invite invasions by envious kings, including King **Hadad** of Edom and a chieftain named **Rezon**, who led a band of marauders that took control of Damascus (I Kings 11:14,23). The Deuteronomist editors portray these setbacks as God's punishment, for as Solomon grew older, he tolerated the growing popularity of pagan deities introduced by his foreign-born wives (I Kings 11:4). The prophet **Ahijah** was so incensed by this pagan worship that he encouraged one of Solomon's ministers, **Jeroboam**, to plot Solomon's overthrow. The conspiracy was discovered, however, and Jeroboam was sentenced to death—though not before he was allowed to escape to Egypt, where he continued his plotting with the support of **King Shishak** (I Kings 11:40), arguably Pharaoh Shoshenq I (945–925 B.C.E.). But Solomon's kingdom was doomed. As soon as the old king died and was laid to rest, tribal support for a unified Israel began to crumble.

One of the four plaques in this imperial crown, which was used in the coronation of King Otto I (912–973), shows King Solomon as the symbol of wisdom.

REHOBOAM

Solomon was succeeded by **Rehoboam**, his 41-year-old son by an Ammonite woman named **Naamah**. But Rehoboam, who ruled from around 931 to 913 B.C.E., was not up to the task. No sooner did he travel to the north to receive their renewed pledge of allegiance than the northern chieftains hit him with a list of grievances. Solomon's wealth had been built on the backs of their taxes, their fruits of the field, and their hard labor; now they wanted that heavy yoke lifted. "Lighten the hard service of your father . . . and we will

serve you," the elders stated (I Kings 12:4). A more adept politician might have salvaged the situation through careful negotiation, but Rehoboam was not that man. Brushing aside their conditions, he told them that he would "add to your yoke," and warned that "My father disciplined you with whips, but I will discipline you with scorpions" (I Kings 12:14).

This was music to the ears of Jeroboam, who had slipped back into Israel after Solomon's passing. Rehoboam had given the northern tribes exactly the excuse they needed to formally secede from Jerusalem. The elders then formed their own kingdom, the Northern Kingdom, which they defiantly called Israel, so as to rob the south of its legitimacy. Jeroboam was anointed as their new king (931–910 B.C.E.).

Rehoboam fled back to Jerusalem to take charge of a kingdom that had now shrunk to the territory of Judah and Benjamin, known henceforth as "the kingdom of Judah."

Thus ended the unified kingdom of David and Solomon.

Jeroboam's sojourn as a political refugee in Egypt cast a long shadow, however. Intrigued by Jeroboam's stories of turmoil in the Hebrew land, Pharaoh Shoshenq I decided to attack the new kingdom of Judah around 918 B.C.E., and laid siege to Jerusalem. Rehoboam had no choice but to pay the Egyptian king a hefty ransom, consisting of "the treasures of the house of the Lord and the treasures of the king's house; he took everything" (I Kings 14:25-26).

Impoverished, the king of Judah nevertheless continued to maintain a lavish court of 18 wives, 60 concubines, 28 sons, and 60 daughters. He died after a reign of 17 years, and his crown passed to his son **Abijah** by his favorite wife **Maacah** (I Kings 11:43).

JEROBOAM

King Jeroboam, meanwhile, set about to reorganize the Northern Kingdom as a modern state in much the same way as his former

ca 850 B.C.E.	ca 848–841 B.C.E.	ca 841–814 B.C.E.	ca 841–835 B.C.E.
Greek city-states coalesce, ending "Dark Age"	Reign of King Jehoram of Judah; ministry of prophet Elisha	Reign of King Jehu of Northern Kingdom of Israel	Reign of Queen Athalia of Judah

CHAPTER 2: FROM JOSHUA TO KINGS **105**

THE LINEAGE OF
KINGS

KINGS OF THE NORTHERN KINGDOM OF ISRAEL	KINGS OF THE SOUTHERN KINGDOM OF JUDAH
JEROBOAM I ca 931-910 B.C.E.	REHOBOAM ca 931-913 B.C.E.
NADAB ca 910-909 B.C.E.	ABIJAH ca 913-911 B.C.E.
BAASHA ca 909-886 B.C.E.	ASA ca 911-870 B.C.E.
ELAH ca 886-885 B.C.E.	JEHOSHAPHAT ca 870-848 B.C.E.
ZIMRI ca 885 B.C.E.	JEHORAM ca 848-841 B.C.E.
OMRI ca 885-874 B.C.E.	AHAZIA ca 841 B.C.E.
AHAB ca 874-853 B.C.E.	ATHALIA ca 841-835 B.C.E.
AHAZIAH ca 853-852 B.C.E.	JEHOASH ca 835-796 B.C.E.
JEHORAM ca 852-841 B.C.E.	AMAZIAH ca 796-781 B.C.E.
JEHU ca 841-814 B.C.E.	UZZIAH ca 781-740 B.C.E.
JEHOAHAZ ca 814-798 B.C.E.	JOTHAM ca 740-736 B.C.E.
JEHOASH ca 798-783 B.C.E.	AHAZ ca 736-716 B.C.E.
JEROBOAM II ca 783-743 B.C.E.	HEZEKIAH ca 716-687 B.C.E.
ZECHARIAH ca 743 B.C.E.	MANASSEH ca 687-642 B.C.E.
SHALBUM ca 743 B.C.E.	AMON ca 642-640 B.C.E.
MENAHEM ca 743-738 B.C.E.	JOSIAH ca 640-609 B.C.E.
PEKAHIAH ca 738-737 B.C.E.	JEHOAHAZ ca 609 B.C.E.
PEKAH ca 737-732 B.C.E.	JEHOAIKIM ca 609-598 B.C.E.
HOSHEA ca 732-721 B.C.E.	JEHOIACHIN ca 598 B.C.E.
	ZEDEKIAH ca 598-587 B.C.E.

So [Jeroboam] took counsel, and made two calves of gold. He said to the people, "You have gone up to Jerusalem long enough. Here are your gods, O Israel, who brought you up out of the land of Egypt."

1 KINGS 12:28

employer, King Solomon, had done. Given that the North controlled the Jezreel and the fertile valleys of Galilee, its economy and agricultural output were far greater than the South. Jeroboam also created rival shrines to God in the former cult centers of Bethel and Dan, and commissioned golden calves—the traditional symbol of *El*—to be placed in them. The Deuteronomist narrator of the Books of Kings depicts this idolatry as "a sin" (I KINGS 12:30), even though Bethel was a much older YHWH shrine than the Jebusite mount of Jerusalem, going back to the days when Jacob built an altar after his vision of a ladder reaching into heaven.

When Pharaoh Shoshenq, Jeroboam's former protector, invaded Judah, Jeroboam hoped that the Egyptian king would satisfy himself with the Southern Kingdom, but those hopes were dashed. The Egyptian king continued north and raided most of Israel's principal cities, including the stronghold of *Ma-ke-thu,* or Megiddo. Archaeologists have found fragments of a victory inscription at Megiddo, dedicated to Shoshenq's triumph. Upon his return to Egypt, the king's "victory" was further celebrated in the famous "Bubastite Portal" of the Ramesside temple in Karnak. But Egypt's revival under Shoshenq was brief. Its power continued to wane in favor of the emerging Assyrian Empire in Mesopotamia.

ABIJAH

The North had barely recovered from the Egyptian incursion when the new king of Judah, Rehoboam's son **Abijah** (ca 913–911 B.C.E.), staged an attack on Israel with the aim of reunifying the two kingdoms. Even though Judah's army of 400,000 men was vastly inferior to Jeroboam's 800,000 soldiers, Abijah was able to rout his enemy and capture several townships on the frontier between the two kingdoms (I KINGS 15:1-8). But Abijah's reign was cut short by his untimely death, and he was succeeded by his son **Asa** (911–870 B.C.E.).

ca 835–796 B.C.E.
Reign of King Joash of Judah

ca 823 B.C.E.
Assyrian astronomers record
first solar eclipse

One year later, his northern foe King Jeroboam died as well. He was succeeded by his son **Nadab** (ca 910–909 B.C.E.), who was assassinated after having sat on his throne for only one year, during a coup staged by an Issachar commander named **Baasha** (ca 909–886 B.C.E.). For good measure, Baasha then murdered all of the remaining members of Jeroboam's family (I KINGS 15:16-22).

OMRI

This 16th-century woodcut of King Omri appears in Guillaume Rouillé's Promptuarii Iconum Insigniorum, *a compilation of portrait types of Antiquity.*

With multiple usurpers vying for the throne, the Northern Kingdom entered a period of volatility that only ended with **Omri's** reign (ca 885–874 B.C.E.). Omri was a general who had commanded the forces during one of its periodic campaigns against the Philistines. He was put on the throne by popular acclaim, after news spread that their new king, **Zimri**, had murdered his predecessor, **King Elah** (ca 886–885 B.C.E.). Worse, the king of "Aram-Damascus," Syria, then sought to exploit Israel's instability and invaded the kingdom.

To face this threat, Omri first ended the long-running state of war between Israel and Judah by striking a pact with King Asa, thus ending a half century of enmity between the two Hebrew realms. He then signed a treaty with **King Ithobaal** (or "Ethbaal") of Sidon on the Phoenician coast. The alliance was sealed with the marriage of Omri's son, **Ahab**, to **Jezebel**, daughter of Ithobaal—a union that would have considerable consequences for the future. His eastern and southern flanks thus secure, Omri lashed out at Syria, evicting its forces while conquering some territory in the bargain.

With the political situation secure, Omri directed his attention to building a new capital of the North. Previously, Shechem and Tirzah had served as the residence of the northern court, but Omri wanted a proper city that could rival Jerusalem. He settled on a hill near Ephraim, which he called "Samaria," after the owner of the hill whose name was Shemer (I KINGS 16:24). Because Phoenicia was the leading culture at the time, Omri recruited Phoenician artisans to adorn his palace with ivory and precious metals. Later, the prophet Amos would condemn Israel's "ivory houses" and those who slept on "beds of ivory" (AMOS 6:4).

By all accounts, Omri's rule restored Israel's position in the region. His prominence is attested by a stela from Moab, now in the Louvre, which states that "Omri humbled Moab for many years,"

FAMOUS KINGS AND QUEENS

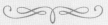

The stories of the Bible are filled with kings, from pharaohs to sheikhs and chieftains. Some of the royal figures mentioned in the Bible stories are known to us from other sources as well. Several of the Egyptian kings, for example, can tentatively be associated with known historical figures. The king who married his daughter to Solomon is probably the Pharaoh Siamun (ca 978–959 B.C.E.), who was forced to move his court to a new capital named Tanis, which used the remnants of cities built by Israelite slaves. Likewise, "Pharaoh Neco" who fought King Josiah at Megiddo (II KINGS 23:29) is probably King Necho II (610–595 B.C.E.). In addition, the Assyrian despots who vexed the kingdoms of Israel are also well attested.

Although queens are rare in the biblical account, there are two exceptions. One is Queen Athaliah, possibly a granddaughter of Omri who was the consort of King Jehoram and mother of King Ahaziah (II KINGS 11:1). She ruled after her son's death from ca 841 to 835 B.C.E., but stained her reign by purging all throne pretenders in her family. One grandson, Jehoash, escaped the purge and was installed as king in 835 B.C.E. Another famous female monarch is the Queen of Sheba. Intrigued by Solomon's fame, she traveled to Jerusalem "to test him with hard questions" (I KINGS 10:1). Though there is no historical record of this queen, scholars have identified Sheba with the kingdom of Saba, a region in southwest Arabia today occupied by Yemen. ■

This statuette depicts King Necho (610–595 B.C.E.) of the 26th Dynasty (664–525 B.C.E.).

while Assyrian sources would refer to Israel as "the House house of Omri" for many years to come. The Moab stone is probably the first attestation of a king of Israel in nonbiblical sources.

Omri's description in the Book of Kings, arguably edited by a pro-Judah redactor, is far less kind. "Omri did what was evil in the sight of the Lord," the book states; "he did more evil than all who were before him," although these transgressions are not further specified (I KINGS 16:25).

An anonymous Swedish artist painted this portrait of King Asa in the 17th century.

ASA

Not much is known of King Asa, who reigned in Judah during this period, and most of our information does not come from the Books of Kings but from the Books of Chronicles (see From Chronicles to Maccabees). One thing we do know is that his reign was 41 years, a very long rule by Israel's standards (I KINGS 15:10). Asa fortified the towns of Geba and Mizpah to deter any new aggression from the Northern Kingdom, thus creating an actual frontier between the two kingdoms that remained in place for quite some time. Judah was then invaded from the south by an Ethiopian force led by Zerah the Cushite, but this incursion was successfully repelled. In Jerusalem proper, Asa banned all pagan idolatry that still lingered from the days of Solomon, and focused all national worship on the Temple (I KINGS 15:12). He even went as far as to condemn all pagan believers to death. For this, he received high praise in the Bible, because "Asa did what was good and right in the eyes of the Lord his God" (I KINGS 15:11; II CHRONICLES 14:2).

AHAB

Meanwhile, up north, work on the new acropolis of Samaria was in full swing when Omri suddenly died. He was succeeded by his son Ahab (ca 874–853 B.C.E.) and his Phoenician wife, Jezebel. Politically, Ahab seemed as gifted as his father; he honored the peace treaty with Judah, contained the ambitions of his nettlesome neighbor Syria, and actively spurred the growth of trade with other, less militant regions, such as Phoenicia.

Unfortunately, as more Phoenician artisans arrived to help build his palace in Samaria, so too rose the popularity of pagan deities, including the Phoenician god **Baal** ("lord" or "master"). Baal appears in Mesopotamian and Ugaritic texts as the god of storm, rain, and dew, which made him critical to the success of the harvest—reason why some Israelite farmers may have wanted to placate the god in addition to their worship of YHWH.

Ahab felt powerless to stem this influx of paganism, possibly because his Phoenician queen Jezebel was a fervent devotee herself. Indeed, the king went as far as to erect "an altar for Baal in the house of Baal" himself (I KINGS 16:32), which in the eyes of those in the South further underscored the perfidy of the Northern Kingdom. Modern scholars, however, speculate that Ahab merely sought to accommodate the religious needs of his foreign workers, while himself remaining true to YHWH.

ELIJAH

Whatever the case may be, the growing prominence of Baal in and around Samaria provoked the ire of the prophet **Elijah**, who lived in Gilead across the Jordan River. The prophet warned that because of the king's tolerance of foreign gods, "there shall be neither dew nor rain these years, except by my word" (I KINGS 17:1)—a swipe at the Baal deity itself, who was revered as the god of rain and dew. For Israel, whose economy was almost entirely based on agriculture, this was a devastating prophecy. Fearing for Elijah's safety, God ordered the prophet to flee back to the Transjordan, and eventually found shelter in the house of a widow in Zarephath. In what some Christian

Ahab did more to provoke the anger of the Lord, the God of Israel, than had all the kings of Israel who were before him.

I KINGS 16:33

ca 783–743 B.C.E.	ca 781–740 B.C.E.	ca 776 B.C.E.	ca 771 B.C.E.
Reign of King Jeroboam II of Northern Kingdom of Israel	Reign of King Uzziah of Judah; ministry of Amos and Hosea	First Olympic Games held in Greece	Zhou dynasty in China moves capital east to Luoyang

scholars believe is a foreshadowing of the multiplication of loaves and fish by Jesus, Elijah then used a small flask of meal and olive oil to sustain the widow's family and himself for many months (I KINGS 17:8-16). Later, Elijah's protégé, the prophet **Elisha**, would perform a similar miracle when he fed a hundred people from a sack of 20 loaves and fresh ears of grain (II KINGS 4:42-44).

In the meantime, the drought plunged Israel in a prolonged three-year famine. God sent Elijah back to Samaria to deal with the crisis and to eradicate the Baal cult once and for all. This cult had by now grown to 450 prophets, as well as 400 prophets of Baal's consort Asherah, all of whom were welcomed "at Jezebel's table" (I KINGS 18:19). Elijah challenged this host of pagan priests to a test. They would each slaughter a bull and place the meat on a pyre of firewood. Whichever deity ignited the sacrifice with a lightning strike would be recognized as the true god.

After Baal's priests had sung and danced all day in vain, it was Elijah's turn. He drenched his sacrifice with water—making it more difficult for the wood to ignite. As soon as he was done, fire rained from the sky, setting the pyre aflame. The crowd fell to the ground and said, "The Lord indeed is God" (I KINGS 18:38-39). All of the Baal priests were

put to death. Shortly thereafter, the Lord opened the skies and rains poured forth, ending the drought. Jezebel was furious.

Some time thereafter, Ahab became upset when he learned that the owner of a superb vineyard abutting his palace in the Jezreel, a man named Naboth, was not willing to sell the property. Queen Jezebel then arranged for Naboth to be arrested on a trumped-up blasphemy charge, and the vineyard owner was stoned to death. His property thus fell to the crown.

Shocked by this blatant crime, Elijah pronounced a curse on Ahab and his house. His prophecy was fulfilled: Ahab would be killed during another campaign against his old Syrian foe, while his son **Ahaziah** (ca 853–852 B.C.E.) would die after a fall from his window. Ahab's second son **Jehoram** was then ousted from the throne in a bloody coup by a commander named **Jehu**, reportedly with Elijah's assistance, while Queen Jezebel was thrown to her death and set upon by dogs (II KINGS 9:34; 10:9).

"Elisha Raising the Son of the Shunamite" is an 1881 canvas by British painter Sir Frederic Leighton (1830–1896).

ELISHA

After Elijah was taken to heaven in a fiery chariot, the prophet Elisha donned his mantle and continued in

| ca 765 B.C.E. | ca 763 B.C.E. | ca 753 B.C.E. | ca 750 B.C.E. |
| Birth date of Prophet Isaiah | Babylonian astronomers record solar eclipse | Traditional founding date of Rome | Composition of Homer's Iliad and Odyssey |

CHAPTER 2: FROM JOSHUA TO KINGS **109**

THE KINGDOMS OF ISRAEL AND JUDAH

MAP KEY

☐ Kingdom of Israel

▨ Kingdom of Judah

★ Successive capital city

○ Location uncertain

■ Royal sanctuary of Israel

Note: The boundaries of Israel and Judah changed repeatedly throughout their history.

Elijah hid from Ahab in the care of a widow. The Lord miraculously provided an unending supply of flour and oil, and raised the woman's son from the dead. (I Kings 17:7-24)

The capital of Aram. Ahab defeated Ben-hadad their king, forcing a treaty. (I Kings 20:1-34)

The Kingdom of Israel's second sanctuary was set up in Dan. (I Kings 12:29-30)

In a contest between Elijah and the prophets of Baal, fire of the Lord fell from the sky, consuming Elijah's sacrifice. The servants of Baal were killed in the Kishon Valley. (I Kings 18:16-40)

Elisha raised the son of his caretaker from the dead. (II Kings 4:8-37)

Hit by a randomly shot arrow in battle, King Ahab died here fighting the Arameans. (I Kings 22:29-40)

THE GREAT SEA

(MEDITERRANEAN SEA)

Omri founded this city as Israel's third capital. (I Kings 16:24)

Birthplace of the prophet Elisha.

Israel's second capital.

Jonah departed for Tarshish and was swallowed by a great fish. (Jonah 1:3,17)

Jeroboam, the first ruler of the Northern Kingdom of Israel, chose Shechem as his capital. He had been an exiled district governor under Solomon. (I Kings 12:25)

The royal sanctuary of Israel was constructed in about 920 B.C.E. to rival the temple in Jerusalem. (I Kings 12:28-33)

Elisha healed the water supply of the city. (II Kings 2:19-22)

Birthplace of the prophet Jeremiah.

Birthplace of the prophet Micah.

Birthplace of the prophet Amos.

Onetime capital of the Moabites, whose King Mesha about 835 B.C.E. had the Moabite Stone carved as a record of his battles against the Israelites. (II Kings 3)

PROPHETS IN JERUSALEM
Many of the Old Testament prophets ministered primarily in Jerusalem. They include: Ahaziah, Gad, Haggai, Hananiah, Isaiah, Jehaziel, Jeremiah, Joel, Malachi, Micah, Nathan, Shemaiah, Zechariah, and Zephaniah.

During the rule of King Jehoram, Edom rebelled and cast off the rule of Judah, setting up its own monarchy. (II Chronicles 21:8-10)

Obadiah prophesied against the Edomites.

Present-day drainage, coastlines, and country boundaries are represented. Modern names appear in parentheses.

Sidon (Saïda)
Zarephath (Aş Şarafand)
Damascus
Tyre (Soûr)
Kanah (Qānā)
Dan (Tel Dan)
Kedesh (Tel Qedesh)
Achzib (Tel Akhziv)
Hazor
Merom
Acco ('Akko)
Gath-hepher (Mash-had)
Migdal
Ashtaroth
Mt. Carmel 546 m 1,791 ft
Hammath
Mt. Tabor 588 m 1,929 ft
Dor
Megiddo
Shunem (Sūlam)
Edrei (Dar'ā)
Beth Shan (Bet She'an)
Ramoth-gilead (Khirbat ar Rumaythah)
(Yizre'el) Jezreel
(Janīn) En-gannim
Jabesh-gilead
Tishbe
Abel-meholah
(Tallūza) Tirzah
Succoth (Dayr 'Allā)
Gerasa (Jarash)
Samaria (Shomron)
Mt. Ebal 940
Penuel
Mt. Gerizim 881
Shechem (Nablus)
Joppa (Tel Aviv-Yafo)
Aphek (Tel Afeq)
Shiloh (Khirbat Saylūn)
Rabbah ('Ammān)
(Tel Gezer) Gezer
Aijalon (Yālū)
Bethel
Jericho (Tall as-Sulţān)
Heshbon (Hisbān)
Gibeon (Al Jīb)
Anathoth ('Anāta)
Ashdod (Tel Ashdod)
Zorah
Jerusalem
Beth-hoglah
Gath (Tel Zafit)
Beth Shemesh
Mt. Nebo 802 m 2,631 ft
Medeba (Mādabā)
Ashkelon (Tel Ashkelon)
Mareshah
Bethlehem
Moresheth-gath
Tekoa (Tuqū')
Beth-zur (Khirbat Ţubayqah)
Gaza
Lachish (Tel Lakhish)
Hebron
Dibon (Dhībān)
(Tel Gerar) Gerar
Aroer ('Arā'ir)
Eshtemoa (As Samū)
'En-gedi (Tell el Jurn)
Sharuhen (Tel Sharuhen)
'Arad (Tel 'Arad)
Beersheba (Be'ér Sheva')
Kir-hareseth (Al Karak)
Tamar
Kadesh-barnea
Petra

PHOENICIA
Leontes
LEBANON
Bekaa Valley
2,814 m 9,232 ft Mt. Hermon
ARAM
SYRIA
Bay of Acco (Bay of Haifa)
Kishon Qishon
Sea of Kinnereth (Sea of Galilee)
Jordan
Yarmuk
Valley of Jezreel
PLAIN OF SHARON
GILEAD
Jabbok (Zarqa)
AMMON
Yarqon
Sorek (Sarar)
Besor
PHILISTIA
SHEPHELAH
Salt Sea (Dead Sea)
Arnon (Wadi el Mujib)
NEGEV
MOAB
Brook of Egypt (Wadi el Arish)
EGYPT
EDOM
Zered (Hasa)

0   20   40 kilometers
0   20   40 mi

JEHU'S AND AHAB'S TRIBUTE

In 1861, a large stela was uncovered near the city of Kurkh in southeast Turkey. The stone, dated around 853 B.C.E., contains a profile of King Shalmaneser III, surrounded by the symbols of the familiar Assyrian divinities—Ashur, Ishtar, Anu, and Sin. The stone contains 102 lines of tightly spaced cuneiform script—one of the first historical attestations of the kingdoms of Israel.

Determined to subjugate the Levant, King Shalmaneser III faced a coalition of Israelites, Phoenicians, Syrians, and Egyptians. The stone lists the complete allied order of battle, including Israel's forces, which numbered "2,000 chariots and 10,000 horses under the command of Ahab, the Israelite." The figures are probably inflated to make Shalmaneser's victory appear even more glorious.

King Jehu of Israel prostrates before King Shalmaneser III of Assyria in a detail from the black stela of Shalmaneser III.

King Jehu also appears in a large black obelisk dated to 841 B.C.E., which in 1846 was uncovered near the ancient city of Nimrud by British diplomat-archaeologist A. H. Layard. The obelisk shows Shalmaneser and his winged patron god Ashur receiving tribute from a king. The inscription reads: "Tribute of Jehu the Israelite." The name is spelled *ia-ú-a mar hu-um-ri-i*, which literally means "Jehu, son of Omri." King Jehu was not the son of Omri, for Jehu had usurped the throne from Omri's descendant Jehoram. However, Assyrian texts often referred to Israel as *bit humri*—the "house of Omri." Arguably, the legend of this king had so impressed Assyrian scribes that his dynasty became synonymous with the Northern Kingdom. ∎

his footsteps, serving God while fighting the pernicious influence of pagan gods at every turn. He even revived the dead child of a woman from the village of Shunem, just as his mentor Elijah had once brought the son of the widow from Zarephath back to life (II KINGS 4:34).

Elisha continued his career as a prophet in the North during the successive reigns of Jehoram, Jehu, **Jehoahaz**, and **Joash**. His fame became so widespread that a Syrian army commander by the name of **Naaman** approached Elisha after contracting leprosy—much to the distress of King Jehoram, who suspected the Syrians of plotting an attack. Elisha told Naaman to bathe himself seven times in the Jordan. Naaman did so and was cured. The Syrian then pledged himself to the worship of YHWH and offered Elisha many riches as a reward. The prophet refused, but Elisha's servant **Gehazi** had other thoughts. He hurried after Naaman and extracted two talents of silver as well as clothing, promising to offer them to a group of needy prophets. Elisha found out about this deception, and Gehazi was struck with the leprosy from which Naaman was cured (II KINGS 5:20-27).

JEHU

The constant warring between the Northern Kingdom and Syria was soon overshadowed by a greater threat, the rising Assyrian Empire in the east. This great conflict is described in the second Book of Kings.

Long before the settlement in the Promised Land, Assyria has steadily expanded its territory, from Carchemish in the west to Ashur (its capital city) in the east. During the reign of Omri, the Assyrian King Ashurnasirpal II (ca 883–859 B.C.E.) then took control of all Mesopotamia, from Haran (in today's southern Turkey) to the Persian Gulf. All conquered peoples were forced to pay a heavy annual tribute, which Ashurnasirpal used to build temples to the god Ashur, who invariably appears in all depictions of Assyrian kings.

Ashurnasirpal's son Shalmaneser III (859–824 B.C.E.) continued his father's work by setting his sights on the lands farther down south. This threat convinced the regional powers—Syria, Phoenicia, the Northern Kingdom, Judah, and Egypt—to set aside their old rivalry and create a defensive alliance—the first such coalition in history. It was to no avail. The alliance was defeated, and the Northern Kingdom of Israel, ruled by King Jehu (ca 841–814 B.C.E.), became a vassal state.

Nevertheless, it retained considerable freedom of action, because Shalmaneser's successors were more interested in their internal affairs that in the conduct of their nominal vassal subjects. Consequently, the northern coalition crumbled and King Jehu and his successors found themselves once again fighting their old foe Syria, specifically **King Hazael** of Aram-Damascus, who brazenly

Prophet Hosea is depicted by Ghe-rardo Starnina, who was known as the "Master of the Bambino Vispo" (ca 1360–ca 1413). A group of unsigned paintings was grouped under this name.

captured Israel's possessions east of the Jordan. The war with Syria continued for so long that Jehu's son and successor, **Jehoahaz**, saw his army reduced to a mere ten chariots and 10,000 foot soldiers (II KINGS 13:7).

JEROBOAM II

But then, Israel experienced a dramatic change in fortune under the energetic **King Jeroboam II** (ca 786–746 B.C.E.). Even though the Books of Kings only devote seven verses to his reign and criticize him for doing "what was evil in the sight of the Lord," it does grudgingly admit that Jeroboam was able to restore much of the northern territory it once held in the time of Solomon, from the border with Lebanon to the "Sea of the Arabah," which probably refers to the Dead Sea (II KINGS 14:24-25). The fierce clashes between Jeroboam and his northern neighbors, particularly Syria, are detailed in the book of the most important prophet in this period, a man named **Amos** (AMOS 1:3-5).

AMOS

As a result of its conquests, Israel enjoyed a period of renewed prosperity, which was soon reflected in the lavish lifestyle of those who benefitted the most—the landowners and the merchants. The growing gap between rich and poor became the focus of Amos's ministry. Amos, a sheep farmer from Tekoa (a village six miles south of Bethlehem in Judah), denounced the aggregation of land at the expense of local farmers, which threatened the social cohesion of the nation. God's punishment, Amos foretold, would be swift; "Woe . . . to those who feel secure on the mountain of Samaria," he said, accurately anticipating the future Assyrian invasion (AMOS 6:1). Amos's condemnation of the exploitation of disenfranchised

ca 736–716 B.C.E.	ca 732–724 B.C.E.	ca 732–627 B.C.E.	ca 730 B.C.E.
Reign of King Ahaz of Judah; ministry of the prophet Micah	Reign of King Hoshea of Northern Kingdom of Israel	Judah is vassal state of Assyria	Nubians conquer and rule Egypt until Assyrian invasion

Fallen, no more to rise, is maiden Israel;
forsaken on her land, with no
one to raise her up.

AMOS 5:2

peasants by landowning elites, and his advocacy of a new, more spiritual Judaism would find a particular resonance, 700 years later, in the ministry of Jesus.

Israel was not the only target of his wrath. The southern kingdom of Judah, Amos warned, would likewise feel God's punishment "because they have rejected the Law of the Lord" and were more intent on accumulating wealth, selling "the righteous for silver, and the needy for a pair of sandals" (AMOS 2:4,6).

Amos's criticism of Israel's social injustice was taken up by the prophet **Micah**, who was active "in the days of Kings Jotham, Ahaz, and Hezekiah of Judah," hence from 742 to 687 B.C.E. (MICAH 1:1). Micah came from Moresheth-gath in the Shephelah and spent most of his time arguing the plight of the poor in front of officials in Jerusalem. Like Amos, Micah believed that the kingdom's social ills violated the fundamental foundation of the Mosaic Law.

HOSEA

The prosperity of Jeroboam's reign was short-lived. Soon after the king died around 743 B.C.E., the country entered a precipitous decline. The reason was, once again, political turmoil: No less than four kings ruled and died (often by assassination) in the two years after Jeroboam's death: **Zechariah**, **Shallum**, **Menahem**, and **Pekahiah**.

The prophet **Hosea**, whose career spanned from ca 750 to 722 B.C.E., vigorously denounced the reemergence of polytheism that accompanied these turbulent times, as people flocked to pagan deities for succor, including the worship of Baal. In response, the prophet compared Israel to a "whore," rather than God's "wife." "I will punish her for the festival days of the

This portrait in profile of King Tiglath-pileser III from ca 728 B.C.E. was found in the Central Palace of Nimrud.

Baals," God warns in one of Hosea's verses, "when she offered incense to them . . . and forgot me" (HOSEA 2:13). Perhaps the analogy of a spouse and whore was inspired by Hosea's own turbulent life; he denounced his wife, Gomer, as a "wife of whoredom" (HOSEA 1:2). After she bore him three children—**Jezreel**, **Lo-ammi** ("not of my people"), and **Lo-ruhamah** ("not pitied"), names that suggest Hosea's bitterness toward his wife—the prophet declared that "she is not my wife, and I am not her husband" (HOSEA 2:2).

Elsewhere, however, Hosea pleaded with his audience to return to the precepts of the Law, not mere observance of rituals, but true faith in God. His famous words—"I desire mercy and not sacrifice, and the knowledge of God rather than burnt offerings" (HOSEA 6:6)—would later inspire Yohanan ben Zakkai in the foundation of Rabbinic Judaism, after the destruction of the Temple in 70 C.E.

PEKAH

God's revenge on Israel was indeed not long in coming. In Assyria, a new king had ascended the throne, **Tiglath-pileser III** (ca 745–727 B.C.E.). Known as "Pul" in the Bible, Tiglath-pileser was determined to reassert Assyrian control over Shalmaneser's former vassal states, and to integrate them in an empire from the Tigris to the Nile.

As a first step, he forced Israel's **King Menahem** (ca 743–738 B.C.E.) to pay a huge tribute amounting to one thousand talents—a sum that the king was only able to raise by imposing crushing taxes on the wealthy (II KINGS 15:19-20). The tax burden may have led to the assassination of Menahem's successor, his son **Pekahiah** (ca 738–737 B.C.E.), during a coup led by an army officer named **Pekah** (ca 737–732 B.C.E.).

Pekah understood that Tiglath-pileser would become Israel's greatest threat, and worked hard to restore the old anti-Assyrian coalition, combining Israel and Syria with the city-states of Ashkelon and Tyre.

His moves were observed with alarm by the king of Judah at that time, **King Ahaz** (736–716 B.C.E.). He interpreted King Pekah's alliance as an attempt by the North to encircle Judah and

ca 720 B.C.E. Chinese astronomers record solar eclipse	ca 721 B.C.E. Rump state of Samaria falls to Sargon II	ca 716–687 B.C.E. Reign of King Hezekiah of Judah	ca 700 B.C.E. Creation of large mounds in Ohio for burial and worship

1 Qarqar A record of the pivotal Battle of Qarqar in 853 is contained in this limestone monument of Shalmaneser III.

2 Nimrud Royal attendants guard the chariot of Tiglath-pileser III in this Assyrian relief from ca 728 from the Central Palace of Nimrud.

3 Nineveh Assyrian soldiers parade their prisoners before King Sennacherib in this relief from the South-West Palace of Nineveh, ca 700 B.C.E.

4 Babylon This lion of glazed brick from the early sixth century B.C.E. once guarded the Processional Way of Babylon, leading to the temple of Marduk.

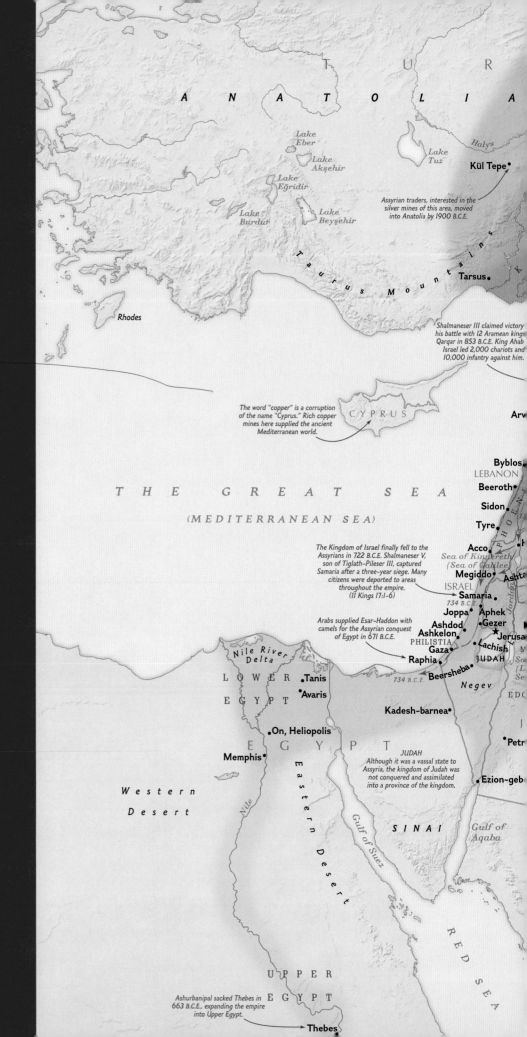

ANATOLIA

TUR

Lake Eber

Lake Akşehir

Lake Tuz

Halys

Kül Tepe

Lake Eğridir

Lake Beyşehir

Assyrian traders, interested in the silver mines of this area, moved into Anatolia by 1900 B.C.E.

Lake Burdur

Taurus Mountains

K

Tarsus

Rhodes

Shalmaneser III claimed victory his battle with 12 Aramean kings Qarqar in 853 B.C.E. King Ahab Israel led 2,000 chariots and 10,000 infantry against him.

The word "copper" is a corruption of the name "Cyprus." Rich copper mines here supplied the ancient Mediterranean world.

CYPRUS

Arv

Byblos

LEBANON

Beeroth

THE GREAT SEA

(MEDITERRANEAN SEA)

Sidon

Tyre

PHOE

Acco

Sea of Kinnereth (Sea of Galilee)

The Kingdom of Israel finally fell to the Assyrians in 722 B.C.E. Shalmaneser V, son of Tiglath-Pileser III, captured Samaria after a three-year siege. Many citizens were deported to areas throughout the empire. (II Kings 17:1-6)

Megiddo

Ashta

ISRAEL

Samaria

734 B.C.E.

Joppa

Aphek

Gezer

Jerusa

Ashdod

Arabs supplied Esar-Haddon with camels for the Assyrian conquest of Egypt in 671 B.C.E.

Ashkelon

Lachish

PHILISTIA

Gaza

JUDAH

Raphia

Beersheba

Nile River Delta

734 B.C.E.

Negev

LOWER

Tanis

EDO

EGYPT

Avaris

Kadesh-barnea

Petr

On, Heliopolis

JUDAH

Although it was a vassal state to Assyria, the kingdom of Judah was not conquered and assimilated into a province of the kingdom.

Memphis

EGYPT

Ezion-geb

Western Desert

Eastern Desert

Gulf of Suez

SINAI

Gulf of Aqaba

Nile

RED SEA

UPPER

EGYPT

Ashurbanipal sacked Thebes in 663 B.C.E., expanding the empire into Upper Egypt.

Thebes

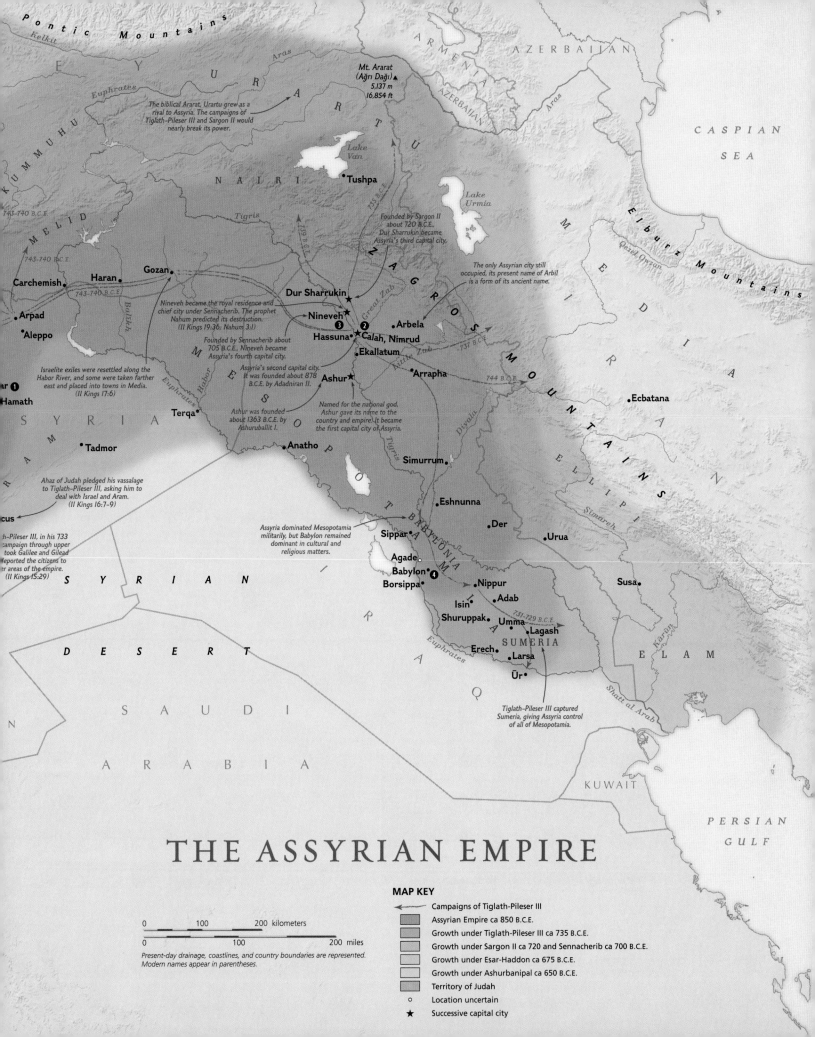

Pontic Mountains

Kelkit

AZERBAIJAN

CASPIAN SEA

Mt. Ararat
(Ağrı Dağı) ▲
5,137 m
16,854 ft

The biblical Ararat, Urartu grew as a rival to Assyria. The campaigns of Tiglath-Pileser III and Sargon II would nearly break its power.

Aras

ARMENIA

AZERBAIJAN

Euphrates

U R A R T U

N A I R I

Lake Van

• **Tushpa**

Lake Urmia

M E D I A

Founded by Sargon II about 720 B.C.E., Dur Sharrukin became Assyria's third capital city.

Eiburz Mountains

Qezel Owzan

• **Carchemish**
• **Haran**
• **Gozan**

Dur Sharrukin ★

The only Assyrian city still occupied, its present name of Arbil is a form of its ancient name.

743-740 B.C.E.

MELID

KUMMUHU

• **Arpad**

• **Aleppo**

743-740 B.C.E.

Nineveh became the royal residence and chief city under Sennacherib. The prophet Nahum predicted its destruction.
(II Kings 19:36; Nahum 3:1)

➌ • **Nineveh**

Hassuna •

❷ ★ **Calah, Nimrud**

• **Arbela**

Great Zab

Z A G R O S

M O U N T A I N S

• **Ecbatana**

Israelite exiles were resettled along the Habor River, and some were taken farther east and placed into towns in Media.
(II Kings 17:6)

➊
Hamath

Ekallatum •

Founded by Sennacherib about 705 B.C.E., Nineveh became Assyria's fourth capital city.

Assyria's second capital city. It was founded about 878 B.C.E. by Adadniran II.

Ashur ★

• **Arrapha**

744 B.C.E.

E L L I P I

S Y R I A

Terqa •

Habor

M E S O P O T A M I A

Named for the national god, Ashur gave its name to the country and empire. It became the first capital city of Assyria.

Ashur was founded about 1363 B.C.E. by Ashuruballit I.

Euphrates

• **Tadmor**

• **Anatho**

Tigris

• **Simurrum**

Diyala

Sundreh

Ahaz of Judah pledged his vassalage to Tiglath-Pileser III, asking him to deal with Israel and Aram.
(II Kings 16:7-9)

—cus

• **Eshnunna**

• **Der**

• **Urua**

...-Pileser III, in his 733
...campaign through upper
...took Galilee and Gilead
...eported the citizens to
...r areas of the empire.
(II Kings 15:29)

S Y R I A N

Sippar •

B A B Y L O N I A

Assyria dominated Mesopotamia militarily, but Babylon remained dominant in cultural and religious matters.

• **Susa**

Agade •

Babylon • ❹

Borsippa •

• **Nippur**

• **Adab**

E L A M

Karun

D E S E R T

Isin •

• **Umma**

731-729 B.C.E.

Shuruppak •

S U M E R I A

• **Lagash**

Erech •

• **Larsa**

S A U D I

A R A B I A

Ur •

Euphrates

Tiglath-Pileser III captured Sumeria, giving Assyria control of all of Mesopotamia.

Shatt al Arab

KUWAIT

PERSIAN
GULF

THE ASSYRIAN EMPIRE

MAP KEY

← **Campaigns of Tiglath-Pileser III**

▭ **Assyrian Empire ca 850 B.C.E.**

▭ **Growth under Tiglath-Pileser III ca 735 B.C.E.**

▭ **Growth under Sargon II ca 720 and Sennacherib ca 700 B.C.E.**

▭ **Growth under Esar-Haddon ca 675 B.C.E.**

▭ **Growth under Ashurbanipal ca 650 B.C.E.**

▭ **Territory of Judah**

○ **Location uncertain**

★ **Successive capital city**

| 0 | 100 | 200 kilometers |

| 0 | 100 | 200 miles |

Present-day drainage, coastlines, and country boundaries are represented. Modern names appear in parentheses.

The king of Assyria found treachery in Hosea; for he had sent messengers to King So of Egypt, and offered no tribute to the king of Assyria.

II KINGS 17:4

ultimately conquer it. In response, Ahaz took a fateful step: He brokered an alliance between Judah and Tiglath-pileser himself.

TIGLATH-PILESER

Delighted by the unexpected support of Judah, the Assyrian king brought his forces to bear and dealt a crushing defeat to Pekah's coalition. Now, the Northern Kingdom of Israel lay defenseless as Tiglath-pileser's Assyrian steamroller moved in high gear. The Assyrian king took "Kedesh, Hazor, Gilead, and Galilee, [and] all the land of Naphtali, and he carried the people captive to Assyria" (II KINGS 15:29). The first deportation of the Hebrew nation had begun.

The kingdom of Israel ceased to exist. Its lands were subsumed in the Assyrian provinces of Dor, Megiddo, Gilead, and Karnaim. Only the region around Samaria was given a measure of autonomy, after Pekah was assassinated by **Hoshea** (ca 732–724 B.C.E.), perhaps with the support of the Assyrians. Pleased with the results, Tiglath-pileser returned north and focused his energies on suppressing Babylonia, which succumbed in 729 B.C.E. The king died two years later.

HOSHEA

Hoshea had begun his tenuous reign as a faithful vassal, but the death of Tiglath-pileser gave him second thoughts. He began to dream of restoring Israel's former might. Even though overtly he still paid his tribute to Assyria (II KINGS 17:3), the king began to discuss the idea of a revolt with the king of Egypt, "**King So**," who is probably Osorkon IV (775–750 B.C.E.).

Emboldened by Pharaoh's support, Hoshea stopped paying tribute altogether. This was bound to provoke Tiglath-pileser's successor, **Shalmaneser V**, to action, and he did not fail to do so. Shalmaneser vowed to destroy Samaria once and for all (II KINGS 17:5), but in a leisurely fashion. A lengthy siege followed—so long, in fact, that Shalmaneser died and was succeeded by **Sargon II** (721–705 B.C.E.). A far more aggressive personality, Sargon decided to simply storm the Samarian citadel. Hoshea's defenses crumbled under the Assyrian onslaught, and the Israelites surrendered.

Now, a second deportation began as Sargon II "carried the Israelites away to Assyria . . . (and) . . . placed them in Halah, on Habor, by the river of Gozan, and in the cities of the Medes" (II KINGS 17:6). According to Assyrian records, some 27,000 Israelites were deported. King Hoshea was imprisoned, but his ultimate fate is uncertain; most scholars assumed he was put to death on Sargon's orders.

UZZIAH

Naturally, the southern kingdom of Judah observed these developments with alarm. Apart from Ahaz's flirtations with Tiglath-pileser, Judah had remained relatively isolated from the turmoil up north.

Dutch artist Rembrandt van Rijn (1606–1669) painted this portrait of "King Uzziah Stricken with Leprosy" in 1635.

ca 700 B.C.E.	ca 700 B.C.E.	ca 687–642 B.C.E.	ca 650 B.C.E.
Introduction of standard coinage in Lydia	Emergence of early Hinduism in India	Reign of King Manasseh of Judah	Babylon is largest city in the world, covering 25,000 acres

The Books of Chronicles suggest that **King Uzziah** (ca 783–742 B.C.E.) was even able to expand Judah's territory to the port of Elath (today's Eilat) at the expense of Edom, and that Judah next extended westward to Yabneh and Ashdod on the Mediterranean Sea (II CHRONICLES 26:2,6). Thus enlarged, Judah's economy had grown. The harvests of the Shephelah were bountiful, with "farmers and vinedressers in the hills and in the fertile lands" (II CHRONICLES 26:10).

Uzziah himself, however, was struck with leprosy, which Chronicles interprets as punishment for his act of burning incense on the Temple altar—a rite only reserved for priests. For the remaining 11 years of his life, he ruled jointly with his son **Jotham**, who ascended the throne after Uzziah's death around 742 B.C.E. A tablet now in the Israel Museum, known as the Uzziah Tablet, may be the tombstone of the king's grave, dating to the first century B.C.E., when his remains were reinterred.

AHAZ

Unlike Israel, **King Ahaz** of Judah—who succeeded Jotham around 736—pursued a realpolitik with regard to the Assyrian Empire. As we saw, he refused to join the northern alliance against Tiglath-pileser. This incurred the wrath of both King Pekah of Israel and King Rezin of Syria, who jointly launched a punitive expedition against Judah. In response, Ahaz sought Assyria's protection, thus becoming an Assyrian vassal state by default. The tribute Ahaz paid faithfully was recorded in Assyrian annals.

At the same time, Ahaz succumbed to the pagan practices of Moloch, a bull-headed idol with origins in Ammon in the Transjordan, which required parents to sacrifice a child by fire. The purpose of such a horrific act was usually to promote fertility or a bountiful harvest. Even Ahaz himself "made his son pass through fire," says the Bible in reference to this abominable practice (II KINGS 16:3).

In the meantime, Tiglath-pileser had come to Ahaz's rescue by investing Damascus and killing King Rezin (II KINGS 16:9). Ahaz dutifully traveled to Damascus to meet the Assyrian king personally and offer his gratitude. While there, he saw an altar that so impressed him that he sent a model to the high priest in Jerusalem, **Uriah**, with instructions that it should replace the existing altar in the Temple. The king died in 716 B.C.E. and was succeeded by his son **Hezekiah** (716–687 B.C.E.). In the 1990s, a *bulla*—a stone seal used to keep letters and bags tamper-proof—began to circulate on the antiquities market, with some of the original twine string still intact. An inscription states "Belonging to Ahaz (son of) Yehotam, King of Judah." If genuine, the seal is a strong attestation of Ahaz's reign, although in recent years, the authenticity of this artifact has been called into question.

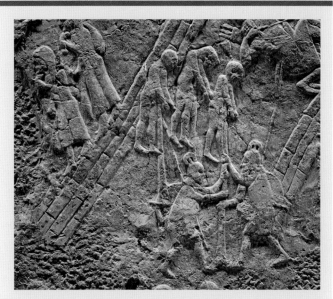

In this relief from Sennacherib's palace at Nineveh of around 701 B.C.E., Assyrian soldiers impale prisoners captured in Lachish on stakes.

THE SIEGE OF LACHISH

I n his prism stone, the Assyrian King Sennacherib boasts that he "laid siege to 46 of [King Hezekiah's] strong cities . . . and conquered them by means of well-stamped earth ramps and battering rams." One of these "strong cities" was the Judean city of Lachish, just 30 miles southwest of Jerusalem.

The terrible siege of Lachish is vividly illustrated by wall reliefs from Sennacherib's palace in Nineveh. The panels feature the redoubtable Assyrian armored ram on wheels, the tank of antiquity, battering the city's walls. Another panel shows the male defenders being stripped and bound by Assyrian soldiers, before being forcibly impaled on stakes. These stakes are then raised and planted along the main road—leaving the victims to die a slow and agonizing death. A last panel shows the tearful women and children, grieving for their menfolk. Assyrian soldiers whip them in line and force them to march toward the north. Some of the women struggle under the weight of braziers, incense stands, and other loot that their tormentors force them to carry.

Ironically, King Hezekiah may have been under the impression that Lachish's defenders were holding firm. Excavators have found several *ostraca*, or inscribed pottery sherds, used to transmit military signals. One of these pieces states hopefully: "May YHWH cause my lord to hear news of peace, even now, even now . . ." Soon, however, Hezekiah learned of the true fate of Lachish. With his forts gone, the king realized that nothing stood between Sennacherib and Jerusalem itself. ■

ca 640–609 B.C.E.	ca 622 B.C.E.	ca 612 B.C.E.	ca 609 B.C.E.
Reign of King Josiah of Judah; ministry of the prophet Nahum	High priest Hilkiah discovers Book of the Law	Medes and Babylonians sack Nineveh	Pharaoh Necho II defeats Josiah at Megiddo

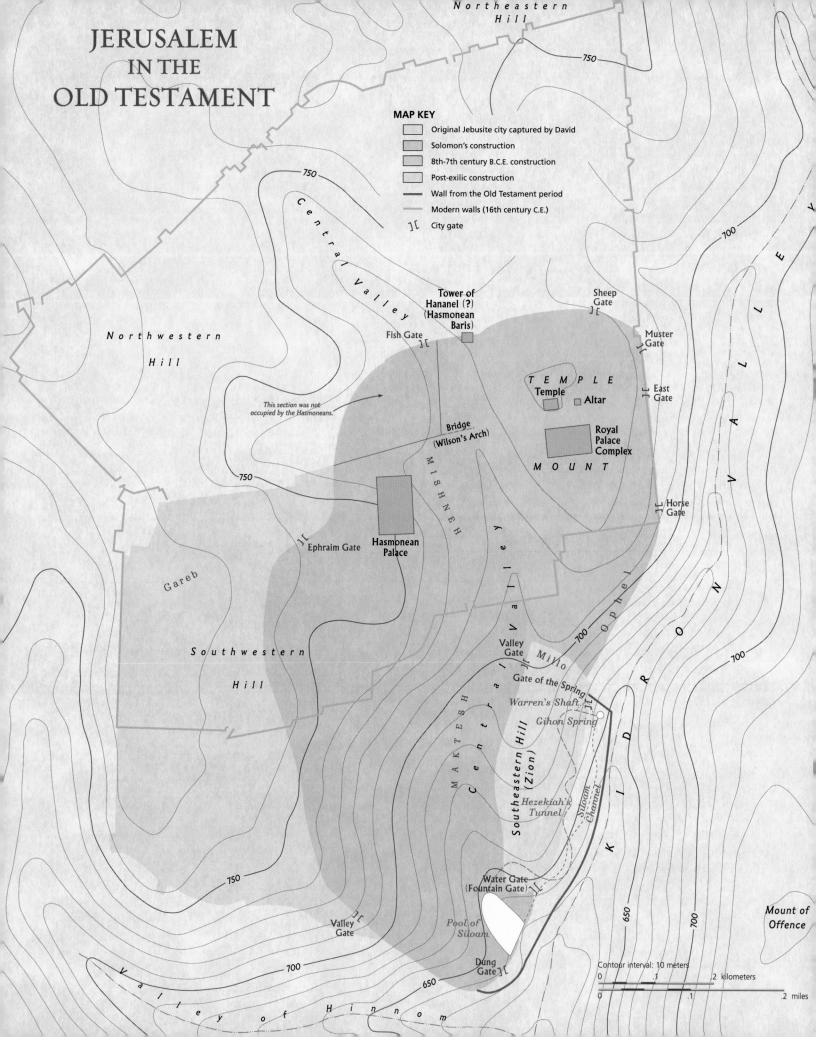

JERUSALEM IN THE OLD TESTAMENT

MAP KEY

- Original Jebusite city captured by David
- Solomon's construction
- 8th-7th century B.C.E. construction
- Post-exilic construction
- Wall from the Old Testament period
- Modern walls (16th century C.E.)
- City gate

Northeastern Hill

Central Valley

Tower of Hananel (?) (Hasmonean Baris)

Sheep Gate

Fish Gate

Muster Gate

Northwestern Hill

T E M P L E
Temple ◻ Altar

East Gate

This section was not occupied by the Hasmoneans.

Bridge (Wilson's Arch)

Royal Palace Complex

M O U N T

MISHNEH

Ephraim Gate

Hasmonean Palace

Horse Gate

Gareb

Southwestern Hill

Valley Gate

Millo

Ophel

Gate of the Spring

Warren's Shaft

Gihon Spring

Central Valley

M A K T E S H

Southeastern Hill (Zion)

Hezekiah's Tunnel

Siloam Channel

K I D R O N   V A L L E Y

Valley Gate

Water Gate (Fountain Gate)

Pool of Siloam

Mount of Offence

Dung Gate

Valley of Hinnom

Contour interval: 10 meters

0   .1   .2 kilometers

0   .1   .2 miles

HEZEKIAH

King Hezekiah earns praise in the Book of Kings, because he moved to destroy the idolatrous shrines that had been allowed to flourish under King Ahaz. "There was no one like him among all the kings of Judah after him, or among those who were before him" (II KINGS 18:4-5). Hezekiah then focused his energies on restoring Judah's economy, which had suffered badly as a result of Assyria's conquest of the north.

Nevertheless, Hezekiah could not resist engaging in the same political brinkmanship as his father. Just as Hoshea had done, he began to solicit Egypt's help in a possible revolt against Assyria. He even went as far as suspending tribute payments, which was bound to invite Assyrian retaliation. In preparation for this coming war, Hezekiah fortified Jerusalem's walls and either built or restored the shaft (sometimes referred to as "Hezekiah's Tunnel") that gave the city direct access to the spring of Gihon, its principal source of water.

ISAIAH

These initiatives were a source of deep concern for prophet **Isaiah** or *Yeshayáhu*, whose name means "salvation is the Lord." Isaiah was firmly committed to preserving the Davidic dynasty and the Temple of Jerusalem as God's throne on earth. More than a mere prophet, Isaiah served as royal counselor for many kings, beginning with the last years of King Uzziah's reign. During the dark days when Israel's King Pekah and Syria's King Rezin invaded Judah, it was Isaiah who had advised King Ahaz to "take heed, be quiet, do not fear, and do not let your heart be faint" (ISAIAH 7:4). To indicate the short period in which these kings would be driven away, the prophet said, "The young woman is with child and shall bear a son, and shall name him Emmanuel . . . before the child knows how to refuse the evil and choose the good, the land before whose two kings you are in dread will be deserted" (ISAIAH 7:14,16). The Gospel of Matthew uses this verse as foretelling of Jesus as the Messiah (MATTHEW 1:23).

It was during Hezekiah's rule that Isaiah rose to full prominence. Knowing the futility of confronting Assyria's might, the prophet denounced those who "go down to Egypt without asking for my council, to

The prophet Isaiah is depicted here in a sixth-century mosaic from the San Vitale in Ravenna, Italy.

Look, the young woman is with child and shall bear a son, and shall name him Emmanuel.

ISAIAH 7:14

take refuge in the protection of Pharaoh," for such an overture would bring "neither help nor profit, but shame and grace" (ISAIAH 30:2,5).

He was proven correct; around 701 B.C.E., the new Assyrian **King Sennacherib** (704–681 B.C.E.) led a powerful invasion force to suppress Judah's revolt. The prism stone of Sennacherib, which details the king's triumphs, states that "as for Hezekiah (*ha-za-qi-a-u*), he did not submit to my yoke." The Assyrian juggernaut, propelled by scores of chariots, rams, and siege engines, proved unstoppable. "King Sennacherib of Assyria came up against all the fortified cities of Judah and captured them," the second Book of Kings notes regretfully (II KINGS 18:13).

Chastened, Hezekiah rushed to appease the Assyrian king. He ransacked the Temple to come up with a ransom, and gave Sennacherib "all the silver that was found in the house of the Lord" (II KINGS 18:15). But Sennacherib wasn't interested in money; he wanted Jerusalem itself.

In panic, Hezekiah turned to Isaiah. What should he do? Do nothing, replied Isaiah; "by the way that he came, by the same he shall return; he shall not come into this city" (II KINGS 19:33). And indeed, Sennacherib's siege of Jerusalem failed.

The reason for this failure has never been convincingly established. The second Book of Kings explains that "the angel of the Lord set out and struck down" 185,000 soldiers in the Assyrian camp (II KINGS 19:35). Scholars have interpreted this as an indication that Sennacherib's soldiers must have contracted some kind of disease. Whatever the case may be, the siege was lifted, and Sennacherib returned to Assyria. But Judah lay in ruins, with much of the country now under Assyrian control.

---

ca 609–598 B.C.E.
Reign of King Jehoiakim of Judah; ministry of the prophet Habakkuk

ca 605 B.C.E.
Babylonians defeat Egyptians and Assyrians at Carchemish

ca 604 B.C.E.
Lao-tzu, founder of Taoism, is born during Zhou dynasty

ca 600 B.C.E.
Phoenicians sail around Africa

THE PROPHETS

The collection known as "The Prophets" *(Nevi'im)* in Hebrew Scripture distinguishes between the so-called "Former Prophets" (the narrative Books of Joshua, Judges, Samuel, and Kings) and the individual books of the so-called "Latter Prophets," who were active in the period of the divided monarchy. These are the Books of **Isaiah**, **Jeremiah**, **Ezekiel**, as well as the "Minor Prophets"—12 prophets who worked in both the Northern Kingdom and the Southern Kingdom. Ezekiel's ministry spanned from 593 to 571 B.C.E., during the years of Assyrian invasion, which culminated in his captivity in Nippur; his work will be discussed in Chapter 3.

As noted in this chapter, **Hosea** prophesied in the North, whereas **Amos** worked in that same period in Judah. **Jonah**, whose book describes God's command to prophesy to the "wicked" people of Nineveh, may have been their contemporary. **Micah** worked in the latter part in the eighth century around Jerusalem, which coincided with the early activity of Isaiah. Seventh-century prophets include **Nahum**, who rejoiced in the fall of the Assyrian Empire; **Zephaniah**, who worked in Judah during the reign of Josiah; and **Habakkuk**, whose oracles dealt with the fate of Babylonia during the kingship of Jehoiakim. **Obadiah**'s short book suggests he lived in Judah after the fall of Jerusalem, while **Haggai** and **Zechariah** both urged the people of Judah to complete the rebuilding of the Temple after the Babylonian captivity. The fifth century saw the prophecy of **Joel**, whose oracles include a memorable vision of locusts swarming over Judah, heralding the "day of the Lord"; and that of **Malachi**, the last of the Twelve, who urged a faithful observance of the Covenant Law, possibly coinciding with **Nehemiah**'s activity in Jerusalem. ∎

This portrait of the prophet Amos was painted in 1535 by Spanish artist Juan de Borgona (ca 1470–ca 1535).

ca 600 B.C.E.	ca 598–587 B.C.E.	ca 595 B.C.E.	ca 594 B.C.E.
Widespread use of sundials in China	Reign of King Zedekiah of Judah	Road is built across the isthmus of Corinth to transport ships	Solon creates democratic government in Athens

MANASSEH

According to the Bible, Hezekiah's successor **Manasseh** (ca 687–642 B.C.E.) then presided over a wholesale return to pagan idolatry, which was even more pervasive because of Manasseh's long reign: some 45 years (II KINGS 21:3). Despite the critical treatment in the Books of Kings, however, modern scholarship has determined that Manasseh energetically strove to restore Judah's ravaged agricultural economy, possibly striking favorable trading pacts with the Assyrian regime. This in turn may have motivated his tolerance of pagan cults—not only practices from the time of his grandfather Ahaz, but also those that may have been imported from Assyria. In the eyes of the Deuteronomist narrators of the Books of Kings, this is why Manasseh is ultimately to blame for the fall of Jerusalem, just as Ahab, Jeroboam II, and other idolatrous kings of the North were responsible for the destruction of Samaria.

JOSIAH

Before that cataclysm came to pass, however, Judah would experience one last renaissance during the reign of **King Josiah** (640–609 B.C.E.), son of **King Amon** (642–640 B.C.E.) and grandson of King Manasseh. Josiah initiated a vast purge of all pagan influences and presided over a comprehensive restoration of ritual and legal practices related to the worship of YHWH. Many modern scholars accept that the composition of Hebrew Scripture of all known books at that time, and particularly the Deuteronomist history of Deuteronomy through the Books of Kings, came about during his reign. Some authors even speak of Josiah's rule as the era of Deuteronomic reform.

Josiah's ability to "reset" his kingdom to faithful observance of the Mosaic Law was due in no small part to his foreign policy achievements. Upon the death of the Assyrian King Ashurbanipal in 627 B.C.E., the Assyrian Empire had begun to crumble. More and more vassal states slipped from Assyria's grasp. Josiah skillfully exploited this power vacuum and gradually expanded Judah's territory, even recovering some of the northern regions that were ruled as Assyrian provinces.

The second Book of Kings suggests that the program to collect and document the

This mosaic of the prophet Jeremiah was created for the sixth-century Basilica of San Vitale in Ravenna, Italy.

various books of Hebrew Scripture was prompted by a major discovery: During a search of the Temple archives in 622 B.C.E., the high priest **Hilkiah** found an ancient scroll that contained "the Book of the Law" (II KINGS 22:8). Many scholars believe that this was the Book of Deuteronomy. Impressed with this scroll, Josiah resolved that whatever remained of ancient Jewish Scripture needed to be identified, documented, and placed in a comprehensive canon. Thus began the composition of the Torah, the Five Books of Moses (Genesis through Deuteronomy), based on the fragmentary sources that had survived up to that point. Many scholars also accept that this was the time when the "Deuteronomist history" of Joshua, Judges, Samuel, and Kings was composed, heavily influenced by the Davidic ideal of a divinely anointed dynasty of Judah, of which Josiah's rule was naturally seen as the ultimate heir.

JEREMIAH

Josiah's reign coincides with the work of Israel's next great prophet, **Jeremiah**. Jeremiah was the son of a priest named Hilkiah (no relation to the high priest, we assume) from the village of Anathoth, located three miles north of Jerusalem. Like Isaiah, he was driven by the need to inspire greater faith in God among his listeners, but like Amos,

CAMELS—OR MULES

The Book of Genesis relates how the Ishmaelite merchants carrying Joseph to Egypt traveled in a caravan of "camels" *(gamel)* (GENESIS 37:25). To the scribes who compiled the Pentateuch, probably during the reign of King Josiah in the seventh century B.C.E., the idea of traveling across the desert on anything other than a camel would have been inconceivable, because only camels could travel without water for up to two weeks. But archeological evidence has conclusively shown that camels were not domesticated in the Near East until around 1200 B.C.E. Indeed, camels only become a common motif on Assyrian reliefs in the late eighth and early seventh centuries B.C.E., mere decades before the compilation of the Bible. Before then, donkeys and mules were the preferred beasts of burden; the Bible has more than 20 references to mules, attesting to their prominence. The return caravan that brought the exiles back from Babylon, for example, numbered no less than 245 mules (EZRA 2:66). ■

ca 590 B.C.E.	ca 587 B.C.E.	ca 580 B.C.E.	ca 560 B.C.E.
Anacharis the Scythian invents the anchor	Nebuchadnezzar captures Jerusalem and destroys the Temple	The Greek mathematician Pythagoras is born on Samos	Golden era of Greek drama begins

If you truly act justly one with another, if you do not oppress the alien, the orphan, and the widow, or shed innocent blood . . . then I will dwell with you in this place.

JEREMIAH 7:5-7

The casemate portal of Megiddo has been dated by archaeologist Yigael Yadin to the time of Solomon—though recent studies date it much later in Israel's history.

he was also deeply engaged with the growing social underclass of Hebrew society—the have-nots who did not materially benefit from Josiah's great revival. As a result, Jeremiah's relationship with Josiah was ambivalent, and would remain so through the end of Judah's royal dynasty.

Naturally, Jeremiah wholeheartedly rejoiced in Josiah's campaign to root out polytheism and pagan ritual, but he observed the king's political ambition with the same apprehension that Isaiah had followed the brinkmanship of Josiah's predecessor, King Hezekiah. Above all, he poured scorn on those who "amass wealth unjustly; in mid-life it will leave them, and at their end they will prove to be fools" (JEREMIAH 17:11). But in the same sermon, documented by his faithful scribe Baruch, Jeremiah seems to echo Hosea's verse "I desire . . . the knowledge of God rather than burnt offerings" (HOSEA 6:6). "I the Lord test the mind and search the heart," the sermon says, "to give to all according to their ways, according to the fruit of their doings" (JEREMIAH 17:10).

Jeremiah therefore did not share the king's enthusiasm about the newly discovered biblical scrolls and their sacrificial ritual; he was more interested in genuine spirituality. "How can you say, 'We are

wise, and the Law of the Lord is with us,'" Jeremiah writes elsewhere, "when in fact, the false pen of the scribes have made it into a lie?" (JEREMIAH 8:8).

Jeremiah was also concerned about Josiah's political moves, and not without reason. When the kingdoms of the Medes and the Babylonians seceded from the Assyrian Empire, precipitating a civil war, the Egyptian King Psammetichus I (664–610 B.C.E.) rather surprisingly chose the side of the Assyrian king. Psammetichus's motives are unclear, though the king was certainly concerned about safeguarding the caravan routes from Egypt to Carchemish that were his nation's lifeline.

Psammetichus died in 610 and was succeeded by **Necho** II (610–595 B.C.E.). The new Egyptian king took things a step further, and actually sent troops to help the hard-pressed Assyrian forces on the Euphrates River. Inevitably, his army had to march through Josiah's kingdom to get there. Josiah, who had chosen the side of the Median-Babylonian rebels, impulsively decided to stop them. He met Necho's forces at Megiddo—a battle that ended in Judah's defeat. Josiah succumbed to his injuries sustained in combat (II KINGS 23:29-30). Worse, Judah now became a vassal state of Egypt. The Josian renaissance had come to an end.

JEHOIAKIM

Josiah was succeeded by his son **Jehoahaz**, but this was not to Pharaoh's liking. As Judah's new overlord, Necho peremptorily ordered Jehoahaz deposed. He was replaced by Josiah's other son, the more pliable **Jehoiakim** (609–598 B.C.E.), to rule as Egypt's puppet king. Jehoahaz was taken to Egypt and died in captivity.

Jehoiakim did not share his father's enthusiasm for religious reform. Before long, pagan practices were once again being performed in the valley of Hinnom, where the odious Moloch shrine once stood (JEREMIAH 19:2-5). This may explain why a few months after Jehoiakim's accession, Jeremiah stood in the Temple courtyard and delivered his famous Temple sermon. He urged his audience to return to repentance, and to observe the true tenets of God's Covenant—social justice, compassion, and genuine faith in God. "In the day that I brought your ancestors out of the land of Egypt, I did not

ca 560 B.C.E.	ca 559 B.C.E.	ca 558 B.C.E.	ca 552 B.C.E.
Putative birth date of Siddhartha Gautama, known as the Buddha	Beginning of the reign of King Cyrus II of Anshan	Putative start date of the ministry of Zoroaster in Persia	Confucius is born in Zou, China

speak to them or command them concerning burnt offerings," Jeremiah roared, "but this command I gave them, 'Obey my voice, and I will be your God, and you shall be my people'" (JEREMIAH 7:22-23).

Jehoiakim had little patience for meddlesome prophets, certainly those who, like Jeremiah, liked to involve themselves with foreign policy. Already, Jehoiakim had another prophet named **Uriah** put to death for making provocative statements. But Jeremiah was popular, and he had friends at court, including **Ahikam**, son of Josiah's leading biblical scholar. Thus, the prophet got off with a proper beating and a night in the Temple stockade—such on the orders of **Pashhur**, the chief officer in charge of the Temple guards (JEREMIAH 20:2). Jeremiah was unrepentant. Forbidden to enter the Temple precinct, he simply sent his scribe and devoted follower, Baruch, to the Temple to preach on his behalf.

Meanwhile, Jehoiakim decided to plunge headlong into the power politics of the region, just as his predecessors had done. When the Median-Babylonian coalition dealt a stinging defeat to the Assyrian and Egyptian armies at Carchemish, Jehoiakim rushed to pay tribute to the new superpower, neo-Babylonia. As it turned out, the Babylonian **King Nebuchadnezzar** (604–562 B.C.E.) had every intention of restoring the former Assyrian Empire, albeit under Babylonian sway, and accepted Jehoiakim's tribute as merely his due. Frustrated in his efforts to curry special favor, Jehoiakim switched back to the Egyptian camp, and tried to form an anti-Babylonian alliance that would include Moab, Tyre, Sidon, and Edom.

Jeremiah warned the king that this course of action was bound to end in catastrophe. Judah needed to repent, abolish all pagan worship, and abstain from any provocative policies, if the area was to be saved from Babylonian retaliation. If the people and their king refused, Jeremiah said, the whole land "shall become a ruin and a waste, and these nations shall serve the king of Babylon seventy years" (JEREMIAH 25:9-11). His prophecy was fulfilled when in 598 B.C.E., after Jehoiakim had been succeeded by his son **Jehoiachin,** Nebuchadnezzar gathered his forces and marched down to Jerusalem.

ZEDEKIAH

As soon as the terrifying Babylonian war machines appeared before Jerusalem, Jehoiachin capitulated to Nebuchadnezzar. The young king and his family were dispatched to Babylon, and Judah was burdened with crushing reparation payments. Jehoiachin's uncle,

Zedekiah, was placed on the throne and told to do Nebuchadnezzar's bidding. For nine years, this is what Zedekiah appeared to be doing. But behind the scenes, he too began to plot with the Egyptian king, in this case, King Apries (589–570 B.C.E.). By 589 B.C.E., Judah was once again in open rebellion against Babylon.

Incensed, Nebuchadnezzar marched his army down to Judah once more. But Jerusalem enjoyed a temporary reprieve when Zedekiah's ally, Pharaoh Apries, attacked a Babylonian frontier garrison, which forced Nebuchadnezzar to divert his army. As soon as Apries was defeated, however, the Babylonian king turned on Jerusalem, determined to give no quarter. A breach in the walls was made, and Babylonian footmen and archers poured into the city (JEREMIAH 39:1-2). Thousands were slaughtered or sent off into captivity, but Jeremiah was spared. Nebuchadnezzar had been told about the prophet's efforts to restrain Zedekiah, and let him live. But Judah was no more, and its survivors now sat and wept by the rivers of Babylon.

This evocative portrait of "Jeremiah Lamenting the Destruction of Jerusalem" was painted by Dutch artist Rembrandt van Rijn (1606–1669) in 1630.

ca 550 B.C.E.	ca 546 B.C.E.	ca 539 B.C.E.	ca 539 B.C.E.
Athens begins its cultural domination of the region, known as Hellenism	Cyrus II defeats King Croesus, last monarch of the Median Empire	Cyrus the Great captures Babylon	Cyrus establishes the Achaemenid Empire

CHAPTER 2: FROM JOSHUA TO KINGS **123**

Nineveh relief *King Ashurbanipal attacks a lion with his spear in this relief from Nineveh from around 645* B.C.E.

Golden earrings *These Greek gold earrings from the seventh century* B.C.E. *betray an influence from Persian designs.*

Petal bowl *This magnificent silver bowl from Anatolia—today's Turkey—in the shape of a petal dates from the eighth or seventh century* B.C.E.

Bronze guard *This bronze* mitra *guard, meant to protect the lower abdomen, was found on Crete and dated to the seventh century* B.C.E.

Gold death mask *This is one of five gold death masks discovered by Heinrich Schliemann in Mycenae and dated to the 12th century* B.C.E., *though recent research suggests the masks may be older.*

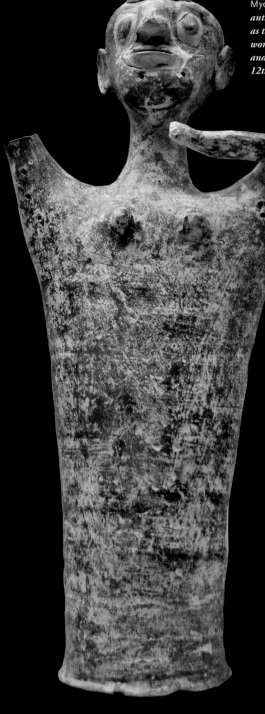

Mycenaean vessel *Several anthropomorphic vases such as this vessel in the shape of a woman were found in Mycenae and dated to the 12th century B.C.E.*

Terra-cotta tilework *This glazed terra-cotta tile is a rare polychrome depiction of an Assyrian king and his attendants from around 850 B.C.E.*

TREASURES OF THE IRON AGE (1200–600 B.C.E.)

Most scholars agree that the first appearance of distinctly Israelite settlements in Canaan probably took place in the Early Iron Age (1200–1000 B.C.E.). Archaeologists have determined that in the span of only two hundred years, the population in northern Canaan increased from 39 inhabited sites to 116 hamlets and villages. This population growth, here and elsewhere, was aided by the advent of quantities of farming tools and other implements made of iron throughout the Near East—hence the name "Iron Age." Iron was mined in the northern hills of Hittite country, now Turkey, and traded throughout the region by the Phoenicians. The new prosperity made possible by iron tools is reflected in artifacts and ornaments produced throughout the Mediterranean basin, from the Levant to Greece.

At the same time, evidence of a language that could be tentatively identified as ancient (or "Old") Hebrew began to emerge in Canaan. This coincided with the development of the first truly alphabetic script, known as the Phoenician alphabet. Old Hebrew continued to evolve as a separate branch of the Phoenician alphabet until it became a clearly distinct script by the seventh century—the time when, scholars believe, the Torah (or the Five Books of Moses) was first composed in its current form.

Phoenician arrowhead
This "arrowhead of Ada," written in the Phoenician alphabet and dating from the 11th century B.C.E., is perhaps one of the first examples of early Hebrew.

CHAPTER 2
WHO'S WHO
An Alphabetical Listing of Characters in the Books of Joshua Through Kings

ABDEEL
("vapor")
The father of Shelemiah (JEREMIAH 36:26).

ABDON
("servile")
1. The son of Hillel, the tenth Judge of Israel (JUDGES 12:13-15).
2. Firstborn of Gibeon of the tribe of Benjamin (I CHRONICLES 8:30; 9:36).
3. Son of Micah, one of those whom Josiah sent to the prophetess Huldah to ascertain the meaning of the recently discovered Book of the Law (II CHRONICLES 34:20). He is called Achbor in II Kings 22:12.
4. One of the "sons" of Shashak (I CHRONICLES 8:25).

ABI
Mother of King Hezekiah (II KINGS 18:2).

ABIATHAR
("father of abundance")
Son of Ahimelech the high priest. He was the tenth high priest, and the fourth in descent from Eli. When his father was slain with the priests of Nob, he escaped and joined David (I SAMUEL 22:20-23; 23:6). When David ascended the throne of Judah, Abiathar was appointed high priest (I CHRONICLES 15:11; I KINGS 2:26) and became the "king's companion" (I CHRONICLES 27:34). Abiathar was deposed and banished to his home by Solomon, because he took part in the attempt to raise Adonijah to the throne. Zadok then became the high priest.

ABIEZER
("father of help, helpful")
1. Eldest son of Gilead, and descendant

of Manasseh (JOSHUA 17:2; I CHRONICLES 7:18). He was the ancestor of the great Judge Gideon. Abiezer was called Jeezer in the Book of Numbers (NUMBERS 26:30).
2. One of "the 30," an elite group of warriors in David's army (II SAMUEL 23:27).

ABIGAIL
("father of joy")
1. Beautiful wife of Nabal, a wealthy owner of goats and sheep. When David's messengers were slighted by Nabal, Abigail supplied David and his followers with provisions to appease his anger. Shortly after Nabal died, David sent for Abigail and married her (I SAMUEL 25:14). He had a son by her

Spanish artist Juan Antonio de Frías y Escalante (1633–1669) painted this canvas of "David and Abigail" in 1667.

called Chileab (II SAMUEL 3:3); according to Chronicles, he was called Daniel (I CHRONICLES 3:1).
2. Sister of David, married to Jether the Ishmaelite, and mother, by him, of Amasa (I CHRONICLES 2:17). In II Samuel 17:25, Abigail's father is called Nahash, indicating that she had the same mother as David but not the same father.

ABIMELECH
("father of the king")
1. Philistine king of Gerar in the time of Abraham (GENESIS 20:1-18). In an echo of the "wife-sister" confusion that prompted Pharaoh to take Sarah as his concubine (GENESIS 12:10-20), Abimelech also took Sarah, but later restored her to her husband, Abraham. As a mark of respect, he offered Abraham a settlement while rebuking him for pretending that Sarah was only his sister. Abimelech later visited Abraham and entered into a league of peace and friendship with him (GENESIS 21:22-34).
2. King of Gerar in the time of Isaac, of whom a similar narrative is recorded in relation to Rebekah (GENESIS 26:1-22).
3. Son of Gideon (JUDGES 9:1) who was proclaimed king after his father's death (JUDGES 8:33–9:6). He murdered his 70 brothers before being struck on his head by a stone, thrown by a woman from the wall above. Rather than die by the hands of a woman, he ordered his armor bearer to kill him with his sword (JUDGES 9:50-57).
4. Son of Abiathar, and high priest in the time of David (I CHRONICLES 18:16).

ABINADAB
("father of nobleness")
1. Abinadab's house held the Ark of the Covenant after it was brought back from the land of the Philistines for 20 years until David removed it (I SAMUEL 7:1-2; I CHRONICLES 13:7).
2. Second of the eight sons of Jesse (I SAMUEL 16:8). He was with Saul in the campaign against the Philistines (I SAMUEL 17:13).
3. One of Saul's sons, who persisted with his father in the battle of Gilboa (I SAMUEL 31:2; I CHRONICLES 10:2).
4. One of Solomon's officers, who "provided victuals for the king and his household." He presided over the district of Dor (I KINGS 4:11).

ABISHAG

A beautiful young woman of Shunem chosen to minister to David in his old age. She became his concubine (I Kings 1:3-4,15). After David's death, Adonijah persuaded Bathsheba, Solomon's mother, to ask the king's permission for him to marry Abishag. Solomon suspected that this request was part of a plan to take the throne and had Abishag killed (I Kings 2:17-25).

ABISHAI
("father of a gift")
Eldest son of Zeruiah, David's sister, and the brother of Joab and Asahel (II Samuel 2:18; I Chronicles 2:16). Abishai was the only one who accompanied David to the camp of Saul and took the spear from Saul's holster (I Samuel 26:5-12). He commanded one of David's three divisions in the battle with Absalom (II Samuel 18:2,5,12), and killed the Philistine

French painter James Tissot (1836–1902) created this depiction of "David and Abishag" ca 1900.

giant Ishbi-benob (II Samuel 21:15-17). He was the chief of the second rank of the three "mighties" (II Samuel 23:18-19; I Chronicles 11:20-21), and on one occasion withstood 300 men, and slew them with his own spear (II Samuel 23:18).

ABITAL
("fresh," "dew")
David's fifth wife (II Samuel 3:4).

ABNER
("father of light")
1. Son of Ner, who was the brother of Kish (I Chronicles 9:36) and Saul's first cousin. Saul made him commander-in-chief of his army (I Samuel 14:51; 17:57; 26:5-14). After the death of Saul, David was proclaimed king of Judah; Abner later proclaimed Ishbaal, Saul's son, king of Israel. War broke out between the two rival kings, with the men of Israel choosing Abner's side and the men of Judah rallying to Joab (I Chronicles 2:16). Abner married Rizpah, Saul's concubine, which Ishbaal interpreted as an attempt to usurp the throne. Abner then opened negotiations with David and was favorably received, but then was enticed back by Joab, and murdered by him and his brother Abishai in retaliation for the death of Asahel. David buried Abner with full honors (II Samuel 3:33-34).
2. Father of Jaasiel, chief of the Benjamites in David's reign (I Chronicles 27:21), possibly the same as the preceding.

ABSALOM
("father of peace," "peaceful")
Son of King David and Maacah (II Samuel 3:3). Absalom killed his older half brother, Amnon, after he raped his sister Tamar. He fled to Geshur for protection, and stayed for three years. King David's army commander, Joab, sent for Absalom to come back to Jerusalem. He returned, but was not admitted to see his father for two years. In his ambition for David's throne, he went to Hebron to declare himself king with the support of one of the king's counselors, Ahithophel. Absalom raised

"The Death of Absalom" was painted by English artist William Brassey Hole (1846–1917).

an army to oust David, but was defeated himself. He tried to flee, but his hair was caught in an oak tree where Joab killed him, against David's command. David mourned Absalom's death. David grieved deeply upon hearing the news, crying "O my son Absalom, my son, my son Absalom! Would that I had died instead of you!" (II Samuel 18:33).

ACHAN
("troublesome")
Son of Carmi. Achan stole forbidden gold, silver, and Babylonian garments, and buried them under his tent. After the Israelites were defeated by Ai, Joshua ordered the 12 tribes and lots to be searched, and thus found Achan's stolen property. Achan, his family, and all of his possessions were taken to Achor, where he and his family were stoned to death, buried, and covered with stones (Joshua 7:1-26). He is also known as Achar (I Chronicles 2:7).

ACHISH
("angry")
Son of Maoch, and king of Gath, the city where David fled, while escaping from Saul's persecution (I Samuel 21:10). King Achish made David his bodyguard when Gath went to war with Israel. However, David

was eventually sent back at the request of Philistine leaders.

ACHSAH
("anklet")

Only daughter of Caleb, who was promised in marriage to any man who conquered the city of Debir. With his victory, Othniel, her father's younger brother, was given her hand in marriage (JOSHUA 15:15-19; JUDGES 1:11-15).

ADONI-BEZEK
("king of Bezek")

King of Bezek, a city in Canaan. He was defeated by the army of Judah and, while a prisoner in Jerusalem, had his thumbs and large toes cut off, eventually dying there (JUDGES 1:3-7).

British artist Clive Uptton (1911–2006) created this portrait of "Adonijah."

ADONI-ZEDEK
("lord of justice")

King of Jerusalem who, along with five other Canaanite kings, attacked the city of Gibeon. Joshua fought them and won. The kings fled and hid in a cave in Makkedah. When they were found, they were taken out, humiliated, and hung. Their bodies were thrown in the Makkedah Cave, and covered by large stones (JOSHUA 10:18).

ADONIJAH
("my Lord is Jehovah")

1. Son of David and Haggith. Adonijah

prepared to proclaim himself king, whereupon Nathan and Bathsheba convinced a dying King David that he should proclaim his young son, Solomon, instead. After King David died, Adonijah made a second attempt to regain the throne, but was killed (II SAMUEL 3:4).

2. A Levite, who was sent by King Jehoshaphat to teach the Book of the Law in Judah (II CHRONICLES 17:8).

3. One of the leaders of Judah who signed Nehemiah's agreement to separate themselves from the foreigners living in the land, to refrain from intermarrying with them, and to dedicate their firstborn to God (NEHEMIAH 10:16).

ADONIRAM
("my God is most high")

Son of Abda, and court official during the reigns of David, Solomon, and Rehoboam in charge of levying forced labor. He was stoned to death by the people of Israel (I KINGS 4:6). He was also known as Adoram (II SAMUEL 20:24; I KINGS 12:18) and Hadoram (II CHRONICLES 10:18).

ADRAMMELECH
("splendor of the king")

1. The name of an idol introduced into Samaria by the people of Sepharvaim (II KINGS 17:31). He was worshipped with rites similar to those of Molech, including child sacrifice.

2. Seventh-century man who with his brother Sharezer killed their father, the Assyrian King Sennacherib, after the suspension of the Assyrian siege of Jerusalem. The brothers then escaped into Armenia (II KINGS 19:37; II CHRONICLES 32:21; ISAIAH 37:38).

ADRIEL
("flock of God")

Son of Barzillai the Meholathite, and husband of Merab, the daughter of King Saul (I SAMUEL 18:19). His five sons were hanged by order of King David (II SAMUEL 21:8-9).

AGAG
("flame")

King of Amalekites. King Saul spared Agag's life after defeating him, but Samuel

The artist Mary L. Gow (1851–1929) created this illustration of "Elijah Rebuking Ahab."

demanded justice, killed Agag, and cut him into pieces (I SAMUEL 15:8-33).

AHAB
("father's brother")

1. Son of Omri, husband of Jezebel, and seventh king of Israel. Persuaded by his wife, Ahab erected a statue to worship Baal. Elijah voiced his opposition, but was forced to flee after Ahab sought to kill him. Ahab honored Omri's peace treaty with Judah, contained the ambitions of his nettlesome neighbor Syria (specifically, King Ben-hadad of Aram-Damascus), and actively spurred the growth of trade with other, less militant regions, such as Phoenicia. After three years of peace, Ahab renewed hostilities with Syria (I KINGS 22:3) by assaulting the city of Ramoth-gilead, although the prophet Micaiah warned him that he would not succeed, and that the 400 false prophets who encouraged him were only leading him to his ruin. Micaiah was imprisoned for trying to dissuade Ahab from his purpose. Ahab went into the battle disguised, so that he would escape the notice of

his enemies, but an arrow struck him, and though he stayed up in his chariot, he died toward evening, thus fulfilling a prophecy by Elijah (I KINGS 21:19).

2. Son of Maaseiah. Ahab and Maaseiah were false prophets who lived in Babylon during the days of Jeremiah. Jeremiah accused them of various crimes, and predicted they would die by fire by Nebuchadnezzar (JEREMIAH 29:29).

AHAZ
("possesser")
Son of Micah, father of Jehoadah, and descendant of King Saul (I CHRONICLES 8:35).

AHAZIAH
("held by God")
1. Son and successor of Ahab as eighth king of Israel. During his reign, the Moabites revolted from his authority (II KINGS 3:5-7). He united with Jehoshaphat in an attempt to revive maritime trade by the Red Sea, which proved a failure (II CHRONICLES 20:35-37). His messengers, sent to consult the god of Ekron to see about his recovery from a fall from the roof gallery of his palace, were met on the way by Elijah, who sent them back to tell the king that he would never rise from his bed (I KINGS 22:51; II KINGS 1:18).

2. Son of Joram, or Jehoram, and sixth king of Judah. He was called Jehoahaz (II CHRONICLES 21:17; 25:23) and Ahaziah (II CHRONICLES 22:6). He joined his uncle Jehoram, king of Israel, in an expedition against Hazael, the king of Damascus, but was wounded at the pass of Gur when he attempted to escape. He had just enough strength to reach Megiddo, where he died, having reigned for only one year (II KINGS 9:22-28). Because he was childless, he was succeeded by his brother Jehoram (II KINGS 3:1).

AHIJAH
("friend of God")
1. Son of Ahitub (I SAMUEL 14:3,18), grandson of Phinehas, and great-grandson of Eli. Ichabod's brother who was probably the same as Ahimelech, who was high priest at Nob in the reign of Saul (I SAMUEL 22:11). Some believe that Ahimelech was the brother of Ahijah, and that they both officiated as high priests, Ahijah at Gibeah or Kiriath-jearim, and Ahimelech at Nob.

2. One of the sons of Bela (I CHRONICLES 8:7). In the King James Bible he is called Ahiah.

3. One of the five sons of Jerahmeel who was great-grandson of Judah (I CHRONICLES 2:25).

4. A Pelonite who was one of David's brave warriors (I CHRONICLES 11:36) and was also called Eliam (II SAMUEL 23:34).

5. A Levite who was in charge of the sacred treasury in the Temple during the reign of King David (I CHRONICLES 26:20).

6. One of Solomon's secretaries (I KINGS 4:3).

7. A prophet of Shiloh (I KINGS 11:29; 14:2) called the "Shilonite" in the days of Rehoboam. Two of his remarkable prophecies are announcing the rending of the ten tribes from Solomon (I KINGS 11:31-39) and telling Jeroboam's wife that God would bring evil upon Jeroboam's dynasty and that his son Abijah would die because Jeroboam had worshipped idols (I KINGS 14:6-16).

AHIMAAZ
("brother of anger")
1. Son of Zadok, the high priest in David's reign (II SAMUEL 15:36; 17:17-20; 18:19-33; I CHRONICLES 6:8-9,53). He was famous for his speed on foot. During Absalom's rebellion, he informed David that Ahithophel had advised an immediate attack upon David and his followers (II SAMUEL 15:24-37; 17:15-22). Shortly afterward, he was the first to bring to the king the good news of Absalom's defeat (II SAMUEL 18:19-33).

2. Father-in-law of King Saul (I SAMUEL 14:50) (before 1093 B.C.E.).

3. Solomon's son-in-law (I KINGS 4:15) (after 1014 B.C.E.).

4. Father of Ahinoam, who was the wife of Saul (I SAMUEL 14:50).

AHIMELECH
("brother of the king")
1. Son of Ahitub (I SAMUEL 22:11-12) and high priest of the Nob sanctuary in the days of Saul. He was the father of Abiathar (I SAMUEL 22:20-23). When David arrived at the Nob shrine, destitute and without weapons, he gave David some of the hallowed bread to eat, as well as the sword of Goliath (I SAMUEL 21; MARK 2:26). Saul then ordered that Ahimelech, along with the other priests that stood beside him, be put to death for being disloyal. They were executed by Doeg the Edomite in the cruelest manner (I SAMUEL 22:9-23).

2. A Hittite and friend of David (I SAMUEL 26:6).

3. Also called Abimelech (I CHRONICLES 18:16), who is probably the same as Ahijah (I SAMUEL 14:3,18).

"Ahimelech Giving the Sword of Goliath to David" was painted by Dutch painter Aert de Gelder around 1680.

AHINOAM
("brother of grace")
1. Daughter of Ahimaaz, and wife of Saul (I SAMUEL 14:50).

2. A woman from the Jezreel, the first wife of David (I SAMUEL 25:43; 27:3). Ahinoam lived with him and his other wife Abigail at the court of Achish (I SAMUEL 27:3). She was taken prisoner by the Amalekites when they plundered Ziklag (I SAMUEL 30:5), but rescued by David (I SAMUEL 30:18). She was the mother of Amnon (II SAMUEL 3:2).

AHISHAR
("brother of song")
An officer who was the controller of Solomon's household (I KINGS 4:6).

AHITHOPHEL
("God is my brother")
A native of Giloh who was one of King David's top advisers. His wisdom was highly

esteemed (II SAMUEL 16:23) (1055–1023 B.C.E.). Ahithophel joined Absalom's conspiracy against David, and persuaded Absalom to take possession of the royal harem (II SAMUEL 16:21). He also recommended an immediate pursuit of David. When Ahithophel saw that his influence had waned, he left Absalom's camp and returned to Giloh where he "put his household in order and hanged himself" (II SAMUEL 17:1-23). He was buried in the tomb of his fathers.

AHITUB
("brother of goodness")
1. Son of Phinehas and the brother of Ichabod. His father was killed in a battle with the Philistines. When his grandfather, Eli, heard

"The Feast of Absalom," during which Absalom killed his half brother Amnon, was painted by Italian artist Mattia Preti (1613–1699).

that Phinehas was killed, he fell and broke his neck. After his grandfather's death, Ahitub succeeded to the office of high priest and was succeeded by his son Ahijah (I SAMUEL 14:3; 22:9,11-12,20).
2. Father of Zadok, who was made high priest by Saul after murdering the family of Ahimelech (I CHRONICLES 6:7-8; II SAMUEL 8:17).

AMASA
("a burden")
1. Son of Ithra and Abigail, who was a sister of King David (I CHRONICLES 2:17; II SAMUEL 17:25). He joined in Absalom's rebellion, was appointed commander-in-chief, and suffered defeat by Joab (II SAMUEL 18:6). Because

David was upset with Joab for killing Absalom, he forgave Amasa and appointed him Joab's successor (II SAMUEL 19:13). Amasa was then put to death by Joab because Joab considered him a dangerous rival (II SAMUEL 20:4-12).
2. A son of Hadlai and chief of Ephraim in the reign of Ahaz (II CHRONICLES 28:12).

AMAZIAH
("strength of God")
1. Amaziah was the eighth king of Judah after the partition of the united monarchy. He was the son of Jehoaddan and King Joash (II KINGS 12:21). Amaziah took over the throne when he was 25 years old, after court officials murdered his father. Once in power, he killed the conspirators and reigned for 29 years, until he too was felled by assassins. His 16-year-old son, Azariah or Uzziah, succeeded him to the throne.
2. Amaziah, the son of Hilkiah, a descendant of Merari (I CHRONICLES 6:45). King David appointed his descendant Ethan to look after the singers in the House of the Lord.
3. A priest of the royal sanctuary at Bethel (AMOS 7:10). He accused the prophet Prophet Amos of conspiring against King Jeroboam II of Israel. Amaziah told the prophet to leave the land of Judah and to never return to Bethel.

AMITTAI
("truthful")
Father of the prophet Jonah (II KINGS 14:25).

AMNON
("faithful")
1. Eldest son of David by Ahinoam of Jezreel (I CHRONICLES 3:1; II SAMUEL 3:2). Absalom killed Amnon in revenge for raping his sister Tamar (II SAMUEL 13:28-29).
2. One of the sons of Shimon, of Ezra's children (I CHRONICLES 4:20).

AMON
("faithful")
1. Governor of Samaria during the reign of Ahab. He cared for the prophet Micaiah while Micaiah was imprisoned (I KINGS 22:26; II CHRONICLES 18:25).
2. Son of Manasseh, and 14th king of Judah.

He restored idolatry, which his father had removed (ZEPHANIAH 1:4; 3:4,11), and was assassinated by his own servants (II KINGS 21:18-26; II CHRONICLES 33:20-25).
3. An Egyptian god, usually depicted with a human body and the head of a ram (JEREMIAH 46:25). Amon is identified with Ra, the sun god of Heliopolis (NEHEMIAH 7:59).

AMOS
("burden")
One of the 12 "minor prophets." He was a herdsman from Tekoa, a town about 12 miles southeast of Bethlehem; Isaiah and Hosea were his contemporaries (AMOS 1:1; 7:14-15; ZECHARIAH 14:5). During Jeroboam II's reign, the kingdom of Israel prospered; however, Amos denounced the aggregation of land at the expense of local farmers, which threatened the social cohesion of the nation. Amos was the first prophet to present God as a universal God of all people, not just Israel. As a corollary, Amos believed God could not be assuaged through the Jewish rite of sacrifice, but through acts of faith and compassion. "I despise your festivals," he wrote, "and I take no delight in your solemn assemblies" (AMOS 5:21). Amos's condemnation of the exploitation of disenfranchised peasants by landowning elites, and his advocacy of a new, more spiritual Judaism, would find a particular resonance, 700 years later, in the ministry of Jesus.

AMOZ
("strong")
Father of the prophet Isaiah, and—according to rabbinical tradition—brother of Amaziah, king of Judah (II KINGS 19:2; 19:20; 20:1; ISAIAH 1:1; 2:1). He may have been the "man of God" spoken of in II Chronicles 25:7-8.

ARAUNAH
("ark")
A Jebusite who dwelt in Jerusalem before it was taken by the Israelites, and was also known as Ornan (I CHRONICLES 21:15). David was sent by the king to build an altar near Araunah's threshing floor on Mount Moriah. Araunah offered it to David as a free gift, with oxen and tools, but the king insisted on paying (II SAMUEL 24:24;

I Chronicles 21:24-25). The altar was built on the same plot of land on which Solomon would later build the Temple (II Samuel 24:16; II Chronicles 3:1).

ARMONI

First of two sons of Saul and Rizpah. He was delivered to the Gibeonites by David, and subsequently hanged (II Samuel 21:8-9).

ASA
("physician")

Son of Abijah, grandson of Rehoboam, and the third king of Judah. He maintained worship of YHWH and got rid of all other idolatry (I Kings 15:8-14). In return, God gave him rest and prosperity. In his old age, he "sought not to God, but to the physicians" (Jeremiah 17:5). He died in the 41st year of his reign, honored by his people, and was succeeded by his son Jehoshaphat (II Chronicles 16:1-13).

This Canaanite figurine of Ashtoreth, goddess of fertility, is dated to between 999 and 600 B.C.E.

ASAHEL
("made by God")

Youngest son of Zeruiah, David's sister. While fighting Isbaal at Gibeon in the army of his brother Joab, Abner killed him in battle (II Samuel 2:18-19). He was one of David's "30 mighty men" (II Samuel 23:24; I Chronicles 11:26).

ASHHUR OR ASHUR
("black")

1. The son of Hezron and Abijah. He had two wives, both of whom bore him children. His title, "Father of Tekoa," may suggest he founded the city where the prophet Amos was born (I Chronicles 2:24; 4:5).
2. Son of Shem, and traditionally considered the ancestor of the Assyrians (I Chronicles 1:17; Genesis 10:22).

ASHIMA

A god of the Hamathite colonists in Samaria (II Kings 17:30), believed by some to be identical with Pan of the Greeks.

ASHTORETH OR ASHTAROTH
("Phoenician goddess")

Ashtaroth is the plural Hebrew word for "Astarte," a Canaanite moon goddess and one of several female deities associated with fertility. She is frequently associated with Baal, the sun god and the chief male deity (Judges 10:6; I Samuel 7:4; 12:10). The Philistines built a temple for her during the reign of Saul (I Samuel 31:10), and Solomon built a shrine to worship Ashtoreth (I Kings 11:33). Ashtaroth was usually represented naked, underlying her role as a goddess of fertility.

ATHALIAH
("whom God afflicts")

Daughter of Ahab and Jezebel, and the wife of Jehoram, king of Judah (II Kings 8:18). When her husband and son Ahaziah died, she took over the throne and reigned as the sole queen in the period of the divided monarchy. She killed all of Ahaziah's children except Joash, the youngest (II Kings 11:1-2). After a six-year reign, she was killed (II Kings 11:20; II Chronicles 21:6; 22:10-12; 23:15). Josiah was then crowned king.

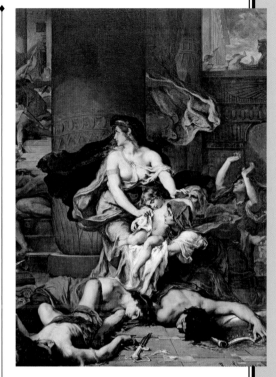

Henri Leopold Levy (1840–1904) painted "Joash Saved From the Massacre of the Royal Family" in 1867. Athaliah killed all of Ahaziah's children except for Joash.

AZZUR
("helper")

1. Father of Hananiah, a prophet who falsely foretold that the exile of leaders to Judah would end shortly (Jeremiah 28:1).
2. Father of Jaazaniah, who said that Jerusalem would not be destroyed (Ezekiel 11:1).
3. Leader of Judah who signed the covenant with YHWH upon returning from Babylon (Nehemiah 10:17).

BAALIS
("rejoicing")

King of the Ammonites during Babylonian captivity (Jeremiah 40:14). He sent Ishmael to kill Gedaliah, governor of Judah.

BAANA
("son of God")

1. Son of Ahilud, Solomon's commissariat

officer in Jezreel and north of the Jordan Valley (I KINGS 4:12).

2. Son of Hushai, another of Solomon's purveyors (I KINGS 4:16).

3. Father of Zadok, who assisted in rebuilding the walls of Jerusalem under Nehemiah (NEHEMIAH 3:4).

BAANAH
("son of God")

1. Son of Rimmon, a Benjamite, who with his brother Rechab murdered Ishbaal (or Ishbosheth) and was then killed by David; their mutilated bodies were hung up over the pool at Hebron (II SAMUEL 4:2-9).

2. A Netophathite, father of Heled, one of David's mighty men (II SAMUEL 23:29; I CHRONICLES 11:30).

3. Baanah or Baana, son of Hushai, Solomon's officer in Asher (I KINGS 4:16).

4. One of the men who accompanied Zerubbabel on his return from exile (EZRA 2:2; NEHEMIAH 7:7).

BAASHA
("he that seeks")

Third sovereign of Israel during the divided monarchy, and founder of its second dynasty. Baasha was the son of Ahijah of the tribe of

The canvas "Barak and Deborah" was painted by Italian artist Francesco Solimena (1657–1747).

Issachar and conspired against King Nadab (I KINGS 15:27), whom he killed along with his family (I KINGS 16:2). During the 13th year of his reign, he declared war on King Asa, but was defeated by the unexpected alliance of Asa with Ben-hadad I of Aram-Damascus. Baasha died in the 24th year of his reign, and was buried in his capital of Tirzah (I KINGS 15-16:6; II CHRONICLES 16:1-6).

BARAK
("lightning")

Son of Abinoam of Kedesh in the Naphtali region (JUDGES 4:6). Chosen by the prophetess Deborah, he made war against King Jabin's general Sisera, defeating the Canaanite army.

BARUCH
("blessed")

1. Son of Neriah, the friend and attendant of Jeremiah (JEREMIAH 36:10). He was accused of influencing Jeremiah in favor of the Assyrians (JEREMIAH 43:3), and was imprisoned until the capture of Jerusalem in 586 B.C.E. He remained with Jeremiah at Mizpeh, but later went to Egypt (JEREMIAH 43:6).

2. Son of Zabbai, who assisted Nehemiah in rebuilding the walls of Jerusalem (NEHEMIAH 3:20).

3. A priest who signed the covenant with Nehemiah (NEHEMIAH 10:6).

4. Son of Col-hozeh, a descendant of Perez or Pharez, the son of Judah (NEHEMIAH 11:5).

BATHSHEBA
("daughter of the oath")

Also known as Bath-shua in (I CHRONICLES 3:5), the daughter of Eliam and wife of Uriah the Hittite (II SAMUEL 11:3). David began an affair with her until she found out she was pregnant. David then decided to get rid of Uriah by ordering Joab to place him at the very front of the planned assault against the Ammonites, where he was certain to be killed, as he was. As soon as Bathsheba finished her time of mourning, David married her and she bore his son. This child died in infancy, but their second child, Solomon, grew up to be king. She had three other children: Shimea, Shobab, and Nathan (MATTHEW 1:6).

Dutch painter Nicolaes Verkolje (1673–1746) created "The Toilet of Bathsheba" in 1710.

BEL
("Lord")

The Aramaic form of Baal, the name of the principal male god of the Phoenicians (ISAIAH 46:1; JEREMIAH 50:2; 51:44). It is found in several places in the plural Baalim (JUDGES 2:11; 10:10; I KINGS 18:18; JEREMIAH 2:23; HOSEA 2:17). Baal is also identified with Molech (JEREMIAH 19:5). The sun god, under the general title of Baal, or "lord," was the chief object of worship of the Canaanites. Each locality had its special Baal, and each Baal had a wife.

BEN-ABINADAB

Son of Abinadab, he was one of Solomon's officers responsible for supplying the provisions of the king's household (I KINGS 4:11).

BENAIAH
("God has built")

1. Son of Jehoiada the chief priest (I CHRONICLES 27:5), of the tribe of Levi, though a native of Kabzeel (II SAMUEL 23:20). One of King David's most distinguished military commanders (I CHRONICLES 11:25), Benaiah remained faithful to Solomon during Adonijah's attempt to seize the crown (I KINGS 1:8-10,32,38,44). He then replaced Joab as commander-in-chief of the army (I KINGS 2:35; 4:4).

2. Benaiah the Pirathonite, one of King David's "30" (II SAMUEL 23:30; I CHRONICLES 11:31), and the captain during the 11th month of each year (I CHRONICLES 27:14).

3. A Levite in the time of David (I CHRONICLES 15:18,20; 16:5).

4. A priest in the time of David, appointed to blow the trumpet before the Ark of the Covenant (I CHRONICLES 15:24; 16:6).

5. Father of Jehoiada and a counselor of King David (I CHRONICLES 27:34).

6. A Levite of the sons of Asaph (II CHRONICLES 20:14).

7. A Levite in the time of Hezekiah (II CHRONICLES 31:13).

8. One of the "princes" of the families of Simeon (I CHRONICLES 4:36.)

9. Four laymen in the time of Ezra (EZRA 10:25,30,35,43).

10. The father of Pelatiah (EZEKIEL 11:1,13).

BEN-HADAD
("son of Hadad")
1. King of Syria with whom King Asa of Judah invaded Israel (I KINGS 15:18).

2. Son of the preceding, also king of Syria. He was murdered by Hazael, who succeeded him (II KINGS 8:7-15).

3. King of Damascus and successor of his father, Hazael, on the throne of Syria (II KINGS 13:3-4).

BEN-HESED
("son of mercy")
One of Solomon's officers responsible for supplying the provisions of the king's household (I KINGS 4:10).

BEN-HUR
("son of Hur")
One of Solomon's officers responsible for supplying the provisions of the king's household (I KINGS 4:8).

BUZI
1. Second son of Nahor, brother of Abraham,

his descendants formed an Arabian desert tribe (GENESIS 22:21).

2. Father of the prophet Ezekiel (EZEKIEL 1:3).

CALCOL
("sustenance")
1. Son of Zerah and leader of the tribe of Judah (I CHRONICLES 2:6).

2. Son of Mahol. Calcol and his two brothers, Heman and Darda, were cited for their wisdom, which was only surpassed by King Solomon (I KINGS 4:31).

CHILEAB
David's second son by Abigail (II SAMUEL 3:3), also known as Daniel (I CHRONICLES 3:1).

CUSHAN-RISHATHAIM
Also known as Cushan or Cush, a king of Mesopotamia. He oppressed the Israelites and forced them to pay heavy tribute for eight years until Othniel broke his hold (JUDGES 3:8).

DAGON
("grain")
Principal Philistine deity with the body of a fish, and the head and hands of a man. Temples were built to him at Gaza (JUDGES 16:23), Ashdod (I SAMUEL 5:5), and Beth-shean.

DARDA
("thistle")
Son of Mahol. Darda and his two brothers, Heman and Calcol, were famous for their wisdom, only surpassed by King Solomon (I KINGS 4:31).

DEBIR
("oracle")
King of Eglon and one of the five kings hanged by Joshua (JOSHUA 10:3,23).

DEBORAH
("a bee")
A prophetess and Judge from the tribe of Issachar, who led the battle against the Canaanite army of King Jabin from Mount Tabor, leading to a decisive victory for the Hebrew army (JUDGES 4:6,14; 5:7). Deborah commemorated the victory in a rousing song: "Hear, O kings; give ear, O princes; to the Lord I will sing, I will make melody to the Lord, the God of Israel" (JUDGES 5:3).

DELAIAH
("freed by God")
1. A priest in the time of David and leader of the 23rd course of priests (I CHRONICLES 24:18). The "children of Delaiah" were among the people of uncertain pedigree who returned to Judah from Babylon with

French artist Charles Landelle (1821–1908) painted this portrait of Deborah, wife of Isaac.

Zerubbabel (Ezra 2:60; Nehemiah 7:62).
2. Son of Mehetabel and the father of Shemaiah (Nehemiah 6:10).
3. Son of Shemaiah, who was one of the "princes" at the court of Jehoiakim (Jeremiah 36:12,25).

DELILAH
("languishing")
Philistine courtesan and the mistress of Samson, who was bribed by the Philistines to trick Samson, a Judge of Israel, into revealing the source of his extraordinary powers. While he slept with his head on her lap, a coconspirator cut seven locks of hair from Samson's head, robbing him of his power (Judges 16:4-18).

Artist Michelangelo Merisi da Caravaggio (1571–1610) created this impression of "Samson and Delilah."

DODO
("loving")
1. A man from Bethlehem who was the father of Elhanan, one of David's 30 captains (II Samuel 23:24; I Chronicles 11:26).
2. Dodo the Ahohite, who was the father of Eleazar, one of King David's three chief officers (II Samuel 23:9; I Chronicles 11:12).
3. Descendant of Issachar (Judges 10:1).

DOEG
("fearful")
Man from Edom and chief herdsman of Saul's flocks (I Samuel 21:7). He was at Nob when Ahimelech gave David the sword of Goliath. The priests of Nob had helped David, which infuriated King Saul. He ordered Doeg to kill the priests, and so he slew 85 of them (I Samuel 21:7).

EBED-MELECH
("servant of the king")
An Ethiopian eunuch who served King Zedekiah. He was a friend and protector of the prophet Jeremiah, and interceded with the king on Jeremiah's behalf (Jeremiah 38:7-13).

EGLAH
("a heifer")
One of David's wives during his stay in Hebron and the mother of Ithream (II Samuel 3:5; I Chronicles 3:3).

EGLON
("calf-like")
Chieftain of one of the Moabite tribes who captured Jericho, making the city his capital and subjugating the Israelites for 18 years. He was killed by Ehud (Judges 3:12-14).

EHUD
("God of praise")
1. Son of Bilhan, and great-grandson of Benjamin (I Chronicles 7:10).
2. Son of Gera, of the tribe of Benjamin, and second Judge of Israel who killed the Moab King Eglon after Eglon had subjected the Israelites to 18 years of suppression (Judges 3:15).

ELAH
("oak")
1. One of the Edomite chiefs of Mount Seir, descended from Esau (Genesis 36:41).
2. Second son of Caleb, grandson of Jephunneh (I Chronicles 4:15).
3. Father of Shimei (I Kings 4:18).
4. Son and successor of Baasha, king of Israel, and the last king of this lineage (I Kings 16:8-10). He was killed while drunk by one of his captains, Zimri, fulfilling a prophecy by Jehu (I Kings 16:1-14).
5. A Benjamite chief and son of Uzzi (I Chronicles 9:8).
6. Father of Hoshea, the last king of Israel (I Chronicles 1:52; 4:15; 9:8).

ELASAH
("whom God made")
1. Son of Pashhur, a priest who married a Gentile woman (Ezra 10:22).
2. Son of Helez, also called Eleasah; one of the descendants of Judah of the family of Hezron (I Chronicles 2:39).
3. Descendant of King Saul (I Chronicles 8:37; 9:43).
4. Son of Shaphan, one of two men who were sent on a mission by King Zedekiah to Nebuchadnezzar, and brought Jeremiah's letter to captives in Babylon (Jeremiah 29:3).

ELI
("ascension")
High priest at the shrine of Shiloh, a descendant of Aaron through Ithamar, the youngest of his two surviving sons (Leviticus 10:1-2,12). It was Eli who told Hannah that she would bear a son, the future prophet Samuel (I Samuel 1:14). Eli was punished when his sons profaned the priesthood (I Samuel 2:22-25). Notwithstanding this, Eli is marked by eminent piety, as shown by his meek submission to the divine judgment (I Samuel 3:18) and his supreme regard for the Ark of God. He died at 98 years old (I Samuel 4:18) from a fall from his throne when he heard that the Ark of the Covenant had been taken in battle by the Philistines, at which his sons Hophni and Phinehas were also slain (I Samuel 4:18).

ELIJAH
("my God is YHWH")
One of the leading Hebrew prophets. He is introduced in the first Book of Kings 17:1 as delivering a message from God to Ahab. He then retired, at God's command, to a hiding place where he was fed by ravens. When the brook there dried up, God sent him to Zarephath's widow. Her son died, but was restored to life by Elijah (I Kings 17:17-24). A famine prevailed in the land. King Ahab accused Elijah of being the cause

"Elijah Visited by an Angel" from the Altarpiece of the Last Supper, 1464–1468, was painted by Dirck Bouts (ca 1415–1475).

of it, whereupon it was agreed that sacrifices would be offered to determine whether Baal or YHWH was the true God. When Elijah's sacrifice was struck by lightning from above, the people fell down crying, "The Lord, he is the God." Elijah then ordered all of the prophets of Baal killed, which was followed by rain, in answer to his prayer. King Ahab's consort, Queen Jezebel however was angered at the fate of her priests and threatened to kill Elijah (I KINGS 19:1-13). The prophet was forced to flee into the wilderness, where he sat down in despair under a juniper tree. As he slept an angel touched him, and said, "Arise and eat; because the journey is too great for thee." He awoke to bread and water and continued on for 40 days and nights to Horeb, where he took up in a cave. There, God appeared and bade him to return to Damascus. Hazael would become king over Syria, and Jehu would be the new king of Israel (I KINGS 19:13-21). Six years later, he also warned Ahab and Jezebel of their inevitable deaths (I KINGS 21:19-24; 22:38). Elijah then went to Gilgal where his protégé and successor, Elisha, lived. At the borders of Gilead, while they were talking, they were

suddenly separated by a chariot and horses of fire, and "Elijah went up by a whirlwind into heaven." Elisha received his mantle, which fell as Elijah ascended.

ELIPHELET
("God of deliverance")
1. Son of David, born to him after his establishment in Jerusalem (I CHRONICLES 3:6).
2. Another son of David belonging to the Jerusalem family; the last of his sons (I CHRONICLES 3:8).
3. One of the 30 distinguished warriors of David's guard (II SAMUEL 23:34).
4. Son of Eshek, a descendant of King Saul through Jonathan (I CHRONICLES 8:39).
5. One of the leaders of the Bene-Adonikam who returned from Babylon with Ezra (EZRA 8:13).
6. A man of the Bene-Hushum who married a foreign wife (EZRA 10:33).

ELISHA
("God is salvation")
Son of Shaphat of Abel-meholah, who became the attendant and disciple of Elijah (I KINGS 19:16-19). One of the three commands given to Elijah was to anoint Elisha as his successor. He found the young man at his home, plowing his field, and adopted him as a son and protégé, ultimately endowing him with the prophetical office. After Elijah's departure, Elisha returned to Jericho,

and healed the spring there by casting salt into it (II KINGS 2:21). He then predicted rain when the army of Jehoram was faint from thirst (II KINGS 3:9-20), multiplied the poor widow's cruse of oil (II KINGS 4:1-7), restored the son of the woman of Shunem to life (II KINGS 4:18-37), multiplied 20 loaves of bread into a supply for a hundred men (II KINGS 4:42-44), cured Naaman of his leprosy (II KINGS 5:1-27), punished Gehazi for his falsehood and covetousness, recovered a borrowed axe lost in the waters of Jordan (II KINGS 6:1-7), and prophesied the relief that would come to the people suffering from the siege of Samaria by the Syrian king (II KINGS 6:24–7:2). At Damascus, Elisha carried out Elijah's command to anoint Hazael king over Syria (II KINGS 8:7-15), and thereafter, he ordered the anointing of Jehu, the son of Jehoshaphat, as king of Israel instead of Ahab. Elisha possessed "a double portion" of Elijah's spirit (II KINGS 2:9) and held the office of "prophet in Israel" for approximately 60 years (II KINGS 5:8). He died in his own house (II KINGS 13:14-19), but even in his tomb he had the power to restore the dead to life (II KINGS 13:21).

ELNATHAN
("God hath given")
1. Inhabitant of Jerusalem who was the father of Nehushta, the mother of King Jehoiachin (II KINGS 24:8; JEREMIAH 26:22; 36:12,25).

Pieter Fransz Grebber (ca 1600–1653) painted "The Prophet Elisha Rejecting Gifts from Naaman" in 1637.

2. Son of Achbor who was sent by King Jehoiakim to Egypt to capture the prophet Uriah, who had predicted doom. When Elnathan brought Uriah to Judah, the prophet was killed by the king (JEREMIAH 26:22). Elnathan, along with Delaiah and Gemariah, then tried to convince King Jehoiakim not to burn the roll on which Baruch had written Jeremiah's oracles.

3. Name of three Levites in the time of Ezra (EZRA 8:16).

ESAR-HADDON
("Asshur has given a brother")

One of the greatest kings of Assyria, Esarhaddon was the son of Sennacherib (II KINGS 19:37) and the grandson of Sargon II, who succeeded Shalmaneser. He appears to have been one of the most powerful of the Assyrian monarchs and expanded his empire by the occupation of Lower Egypt. During his 13-year reign, Manasseh, king of Judah, was apparently brought before him to pay tribute (II CHRONICLES 33:11). He is distinguished as a builder of great works; besides his palace at Babylon, he built at least three others and 30 temples.

EVIL-MERODACH
("man of Merodach")

Successor to Nebuchadnezzar. As king, he released Jehoiachin from prison, treated him as a guest, and gave him an allowance for the rest of his life (II KINGS 25:27). He was succeeded by his assassin, Neriglissar.

GAD
("fortune")

1. Jacob's seventh son, the firstborn of Zilpah, Leah's maid (GENESIS 30:11-13; 46:16,18). With his brothers, he was involved in the selling of his brother Joseph as a slave in Egypt.

2. "The seer" or "the king's seer" (I CHRONICLES 29:29; II CHRONICLES 29:25) who joined David when he was old (I SAMUEL 22:5). He reappears in connection with the punishment of pestilence inflicted for David's taking a census (II SAMUEL 24:11-19; I CHRONICLES 21:9-19). Gad wrote a book on the acts of David (I CHRONICLES 29:29) and assisted in the arrangements for the musical service of the "House of God" (II CHRONICLES 29:25).

GEDALIAH
("God is my greatness")

1. Son of Jeduthun (I CHRONICLES 25:3,9).

2. Grandfather of the prophet Zephaniah, and the father of Cushi (ZEPHANIAH 1:1).

3. Son of Pashhur, and one of the Jewish nobles who conspired against Jeremiah (JEREMIAH 38:1).

4. Son of Ahikam (Jeremiah's protector) (JEREMIAH 26:24), and grandson of Shaphan, the

This 13th-century French stained glass window depicts "Gideon's Fleece."

secretary of King Josiah. After the destruction of Jerusalem, Nebuchadnezzar left him to govern at Mizpah (II KINGS 25:22; JEREMIAH 40:5; 52:16). Joined there by the prophet Jeremiah, Mizpah became a refuge for many Hebrews (JEREMIAH 40:6,11). He was murdered by Ishmael.

GEHAZI
("valley of vision")

Trusted manservant of Elisha (II KINGS 4:31; 5:25; 8:4-5), who appears in connection with the story of the woman of Shunem (II KINGS 4:14,31) and of Naaman the Syrian. Gehazi fraudulently obtained money and garments from Naaman, was cursed with incurable leprosy, and was dismissed from the prophet's service (II KINGS 5:1). He afterward appeared before King Joram, to whom he recounted the great deeds of his master (II KINGS 8:1-6).

GEMARIAH
("God has made perfect")

1. Son of high priest Hilkiah. He was sent by King Zedekiah to Nebuchadnezzar, and brought a letter of comfort from Jeremiah to Jewish captives (JEREMIAH 29:3).

2. Son of Shaphan the scribe, and one of the Levites living in the Temple (JEREMIAH 36:10).

GIDEON
("hewer")

Son of Joash, from the tribe of Manasseh, Gideon was chosen by an angel to serve as the fifth Judge of the Israelite tribes. He first destroyed a nearby altar to Baal, a popular deity among both Canaanites and Midianites, and then gathered an army of recruits from Asher, Manasseh, Zebulun, and Naphtali. As the Midianite forces lay in camp near Endor, Gideon staged a daring nighttime raid that sent the Arab invaders packing across the Jordan and into the desert (JUDGES 7:20-22). Two kings, Zalmunna and Zebah, fled, but were eventually captured and killed by Gideon. So successful was Gideon's leadership that the tribes clamored for him to be crowned king. Gideon refused, saying that only God should rule as king. The time of a unified monarchy was not yet at hand (JUDGES 8:22-23). Gideon died as an old man with 70 sons.

GINATH
("garden")

Father of Tibni, who fought Omri for the throne of Israel (I KINGS 16:21).

GOG

Chief prince of Meshech and Tubal. God

"David Victorious Over Goliath," ca 1600, was painted by Michelangelo Merisi da Caravaggio (1571–1610).

instructed Ezekiel to prophesy that Gog would lead an alliance against Israel and would be utterly destroyed in battle (EZEKIEL 38:2).

GOLIATH
("great")

A ten-foot-tall giant from Gath, who challenged the Israelites to battle. David accepted the challenge, and used a stone from a sling to hit Goliath in the forehead, killing him. David then cut off his head with Goliath's own sword, and took it back to Jerusalem (I SAMUEL 17:4).

GOMER
("ember")

Daughter of Diblaim, and Hosea's unfaithful wife (HOSEA 1:3).

HABAKKUK
("basil plant")

One of the 12 "minor prophets" who lived in Jerusalem near the end of the kingdom of Judah. He warned his contemporaries that the wicked would eventually fail, while the righteous would live by their faith. Habakkuk anticipated the Babylonian invasion in an oracle, which details the suffering to be inflicted on the people of Judah (HABAKKUK 2:12). Nevertheless, near the end of his short book, the prophet speaks of the Lord's glory as the source of future salvation (HABAKKUK 3:19).

HADAD
("sharp")

1. Son of Ishmael, and grandson of Abraham (GENESIS 25:15; I CHRONICLES 1:30).
2. Son of Bedad, who reigned as king of Edom and defeated the Midianites (GENESIS 36:35).
3. A royal prince of Edom who escaped David and Joab's conquest of the Edomite kingdom. He was raised in Egypt and married the queen's sister. When both David and Joab were dead, he returned to his native kingdom and conducted multiple raids against Israel (I KINGS 11:14-22).

HADADEZER
("Hadad is help")

Son of Rehob and king of Zobah. He attacked King David numerous times, always ending in defeat (II SAMUEL 8:3).

HAGGITH
("festive")

One of David's wives and the mother of Adonijah (II SAMUEL 3:4; I KINGS 1:5,11; 2:13; I CHRONICLES 3:2).

HAMUTAL
("protection")

Daughter of Jeremiah of Libnah and wife of King Josiah. Her sons Jehoahaz and Zedekiah also went on to reign as kings (II KINGS 23:31; 24:18; JEREMIAH 52:1).

HANAMEEL OR HANAMEL
("God has favored")

Son of Shallum and cousin of Jeremiah. He sold the field he possessed in Anathoth to Jeremiah before the siege of Jerusalem (JEREMIAH 32:6-12).

HANANIAH
("the Lord is gracious")

1. Son of Shashak and leader of the tribe of Benjamin (I CHRONICLES 8:24).
2. Son of King David's musician Heman, who performed music during Tabernacle services; Hananiah played during the 16th turn of service (I CHRONICLES 25:4,23).
3. Army commander of Uzziah, king of Judah (II CHRONICLES 26:11).
4. Son of Azzur and prophet from Gibeon. He appeared before King Zedekiah and proclaimed that the Lord had broken the yoke of the king of Babylon; to illustrate his point, he destroyed the yoke that Jeremiah was wearing (JEREMIAH 28:11). Jeremiah disagreed with him, and presaged that Hananiah would be dead within a year; indeed, he died two months later.
5. Father of Zedekiah, a leader of Judah to whom Jeremiah's oracle was read (JEREMIAH 36:12).
6. Grandfather of Irijah, an army captain who arrested Jeremiah on the charge of having defected to the Babylonians (JEREMIAH 37:13).
7. Son of Zerubbabel, who led the Israelites from exile to Judah (I CHRONICLES 3:19).
8. Descendant of Bebai, who divorced his non-Jewish wife during Ezra's time (EZRA 10:28).
9. Son of a perfumer, who was one of the men who repaired the wall of Jerusalem during the days of Nehemiah (NEHEMIAH 3:8).
10. Son of Shelemiah, who was one of the men who repaired the wall of Jerusalem during the days of Nehemiah (NEHEMIAH 3:30).
11. Governor of the king's palace in Jerusalem during the time of Nehemiah, who was responsible for the city's gates (NEHEMIAH 7:2).
12. One of the leaders of Judah who signed the covenant during the time of Nehemiah (NEHEMIAH 10:23).

HANNAH
("grace," "merciful")

One of two wives of Elkanah who hailed from the hill country of Ephraim, and lived in the town of Ramathaim-zophim (I SAMUEL 1:1). Hannah made a pilgrimage to the ancient shrine at Shiloh, praying to God for a son, and promising him that she would raise the newborn to serve God (I SAMUEL 1:11). Her wish was granted, and she named her son Shmu'el, "God heard [me]." When Samuel was weaned, she brought him to Shiloh and left him with the priest Eli, so he could bring him up. Every year, Hannah made a coat for Samuel and brought it to him during the family's annual pilgrimages to Shiloh. During these pilgrimages, Eli would bless her and grant her more children; thus, Elkanah and Hannah had three more sons and two daughters. Samuel grew up to be a prophet, the last and greatest of the Judges, and the anointer of King Saul and King David.

"The Infant Samuel Brought by Hannah to Eli" is the work of Dutch artist Gerbrand van den Eeckhout (1621–1674) from 1664.

HANUN
("gracious")
1. Son of Nahash (II SAMUEL 10:1-2; I CHRONICLES 19:1-2) and king of Ammon, who dishonored the ambassadors of David (II SAMUEL 10:4) and involved the Ammonites in a disastrous war (II SAMUEL 12:31; I CHRONICLES 19:6).
2. A man who, along with the people of Zanoah, repaired the ravine gate in the wall of Jerusalem (NEHEMIAH 3:13).
3. Sixth son of Zalaph, who also assisted in the repair of the wall, apparently on the east side (NEHEMIAH 3:30).

HAZAEL
("whom God sees")
King of Damascus. Prior to his appointment, he was a highly placed official at the court of King Ben-hadad and was sent by his master to Elisha to inquire if the king would recover from an illness. Elisha told Hazael that he would become king and inflict great suffering onto the Israelites. Elisha's response led to the murder of Ben-hadad by Hazael, who then took over the throne (II KINGS 8:7-15). He was soon engaged in war with the kings of Judah and Israel for the possession of the city of Ramoth-gilead (II KINGS 8:28). Toward the end of the reign of King Jehu, Hazael led the Syrians against the Israelites, whom he "smote in all their coasts" (II KINGS 10:32), thus accomplishing Elisha's prophecy. Near the close of his reign, he prepared to attack Jerusalem (II CHRONICLES 24:24) when Joash bribed him to retire (II KINGS 12:18).

HEBER
("alliance")
1. Son of Beriah and grandson of Asher (GENESIS 46:17; I CHRONICLES 7:31-32).
2. Member of the Kenite tribe (JUDGES 4:11,17; 5:24) and a descendant of Hobab. His wife, Jael, received Sisera, the commander of the army of King Jabin of Hazor, into her tent and killed him while he was sleeping.
3. Son of Elpaal, and a Benjamite who was the leader of a clan that lived in Jerusalem (I CHRONICLES 8:17,22).
4. Head of a family in the tribe of Gad, who lived in the land of Bashan (I CHRONICLES 5:13).
5. A husband of Jael (JUDGES 4:11,17,21; JUDGES 5:24).
6. Son of Ezra (I CHRONICLES 4:18).
7. Son of Sala and an ancestor of Abraham, David, and Jesus (LUKE 3:35).
8. Descendant of Judah and the son of Jehudijah (I CHRONICLES 4:18).
9. Father of Socho (I CHRONICLES 4:18).

HEPHZIBAH
("my delight is in her")
1. Queen and consort of King Hezekiah, and mother of King Manasseh (II KINGS 21:1).
2. Symbolical name of Zion, to illustrate the Lord's favor toward her (ISAIAH 62:4).

HEZEKIAH
("the might of God")
1. The 13th king of Judah, and son of King Ahaz of Judah and Abijah. He ascended the throne at the age of 25 when Judah had been reduced to mere vassal status under Assyria. His first act was to purge, repair, and reopen the Temple, and to destroy all other shrines. Hezekiah then invited all the people, even those from occupied Israel in the north, to a Passover feast, which continued for 14 days (II CHRONICLES 29:30,31). Hezekiah refused to pay tribute to Assyria, forged an alliance with Egypt, and steadily reconquered many of the cities that his father had lost (II CHRONICLES 28:18; II KINGS 18:7). Naturally, war with Assyria was inevitable, and Hezekiah used every available means to strengthen the city and his kingdom (II KINGS 20:20). He also either built or restored the shaft that gave the city direct access to the spring of Gihon, its principal source of water, and built a tunnel in anticipation of an Assyrian attack (sometimes referred to as "Hezekiah's Tunnel") to divert water from the spring to inside the city's walls. Hezekiah's brinkmanship was sharply criticized by the prophet Isaiah, who had up to this point been a staunch supporter of the king. It was to no avail; the new Assyrian King Sennacherib (704–681 B.C.E.) invaded the kingdom, "came up against all the fortified cities of Judah and captured them" (II KINGS 18:13). Hezekiah rushed to appease the Assyrian king with a bribe, using the silver and gold from the Temple, but Sennacherib was not to be dissuaded. Nevertheless, the siege of Jerusalem was mysteriously lifted. Hezekiah was succeeded by his son Manasseh. "There was no one like him among all the kings of Judah after him, or among those who were before him" (II KINGS 18:4-5).
2. Son of Neariah and one of the descendants of the royal family of Judah, who was taken to captivity in Babylon (I CHRONICLES 3:23).
3. Ancestor of a group of men who returned with Zerubbabel from the Babylonian exile (EZRA 2:16).

"The Healing of Hezekiah" is a tenth-century miniature from the Psalter of Paris manuscript.

HIEL
("God lives")

During the reign of King Ahab, Hiel of Bethel rebuilt the city of Jericho. His sons Abiram and Segub died as a result of the reconstruction, which fulfilled Joshua's curse (JOSHUA 6:26).

HILLEL
("praise")

Native of Pirathon in Mount Ephraim. Hillel's son Abdon was one of the Judges of Israel (JUDGES 12:13,15).

HIRAM
("my brother is exalted")

1. King of Tyre and a close ally of King David and King Solomon, who sent workmen and materials to Jerusalem (II SAMUEL 5:11; I CHRONICLES 14:1) to build a palace for David (I KINGS 5:1) and a temple for Solomon (I KINGS 5:11-12). Both King David and King Solomon also used Hiram's ships to import precious items from Ophir and Tarshish.
2. Hiram was the name of a man of mixed race who served as the principal architect and engineer sent by King Hiram to Solomon (I KINGS 7:13,40).

HOPHNI
("pugilist")

Son of Eli the Shiloh priest. Hophni and his brother Phinehas ("brazen mouth") were wicked and corrupt. Their brutal and scandalous ways filled the people with disgust and indignation (I SAMUEL 2:12-17,22). Hophni's father was charged with honoring his sons more than he honored God. His punishment was that both of his sons would die on the same day, his descendants would no longer be heads of the priestly family, and his survivors would end up begging for food and money (I SAMUEL 1:3). During the battle with the Philistines at Aphek, the Ark of the Covenant that Hophni and Phinehas accompanied was captured, more than 30,000 men were killed, and Hophni and Phinehas lost their lives (I SAMUEL 4:10,11). Eli was 98 years old when his sons were killed. Upon hearing the news, he fell off his chair and broke his neck.

HOPHRA

King of Egypt (589–570 B.C.E.) and ally of Zedekiah, king of Judah (JEREMIAH 37:5; 44:30; EZEKIEL 29:6,7). Called Apries by the Greek historian Herodotus, Hophra was defeated by Nebuchadnezzar, who had to temporarily lift the siege of Jerusalem to suppress the Egyptian rebellion.

HORAM
("hill")

King of Gezer who came to the aid of the town of Lachish when it was attacked by Joshua (JOSHUA 10:33).

HOSEA
("salvation")

Son of Beeri, and one of the minor prophets. The prophetic career of Hosea spanned from ca 750 to 722 B.C.E., during which he vigorously denounced the reemergence of polytheism. Hosea is remembered for his insistence that God does not demand mere observance of ritual, but true faith and compassion. His famous words "I desire mercy and not sacrifice, and the knowledge of God rather than burnt offerings" (HOSEA 6:6) would later inspire Yohanan ben Zakkai in the foundation of Rabbinic Judaism, after the destruction of the Temple in 70 C.E. When the kings of Israel flirted with alliances against the great powers, Hosea warned the oft-repeated words that "they sow the wind, and they shall reap the whirlwind" (HOSEA 8:7). The prophet also denounced the people who flocked to pagan deities for succor, and compared Israel to a "whore," rather than God's "wife." "I will punish her for the festival days of the Baals," God warns in one of Hosea's verses, "when she offered incense to them . . . and forgot me" (HOSEA 2:13). Perhaps the analogy of a spouse and whore was inspired by Hosea's own turbulent life; he denounced his wife, Gomer, as a "wife of

This detail of Hosea appears in "The Prophet Jeremiah, the Flight Into Egypt and the Prophet Hosea," painted by Duccio di Buoninsegna (ca 1260–1319).

whoredom" (HOSEA 1:2). After she bore him three children, Hosea declared that "she is not my wife, and I am not her husband" (HOSEA 2:2).

HOSHEA
("salvation")

1. Original name of the son of Nun, and later called Joshua (NUMBERS 13:8,16; DEUTERONOMY 32:44).
2. Leader of the tribe of Ephraim during King David's reign (I CHRONICLES 27:20).
3. Last king of Israel (ca 732–724 B.C.E.), who conspired against and killed his predecessor, Pekah (ISAIAH 7:16; II KINGS 17:1-2). He then plotted a revolt against Assyria with the king of Egypt, "King So," who is probably Osorkon IV (775–750 B.C.E.). Shalmaneser retaliated by vowing to destroy Samaria once and for all (II KINGS 17:5), but it was King Sargon II (721–705 B.C.E.) who stormed the citadel of Samaria and dispersed the tribes beyond the Euphrates (II KINGS 17:5-6; 18:9-12). According to Assyrian records, some 27,000 Israelites were deported. King Hoshea was imprisoned, but his ultimate fate is uncertain; most scholars assumed he was put to death on Sargon's orders.

HULDAH
("weasel")

A prophetess and wife of Shallum, the keeper of King Josiah's wardrobe (II KINGS 22:14-20; II CHRONICLES 34:22-28). She resided in Mishneh, a suburb between the inner and the outer wall of Jerusalem. She is one of three female prophetesses; the others are Miriam (EXODUS 15:20) and Deborah (JUDGES 4:4).

HUSHAI
("my brother's gift")

When King David fled from Jerusalem to escape Absalom's rebellion, he met Hushai at the summit of Olivet. Hushai was sent back to Jerusalem to defeat Ahithophel, who had joined Absalom (II SAMUEL 15:32,37; 16:16-18). He then persuaded Absalom to refrain from pursuing David. This delay allowed David to regroup, rally his army, and ultimately defeat Absalom.

I

IBHAR
("chosen")

One of David's sons born in Jerusalem (II SAMUEL 5:15; I CHRONICLES 3:6; 14:6).

IBZAN
("illustrious")

A native of Bethlehem, the tenth Judge of Israel who served for seven years after Jephthah (JUDGES 12:8,10).

ICHABOD
("inglorious")

Son of Phinehas and grandson of Eli. While Phinehas's wife was pregnant with Ichabod, the Ark of the Covenant was captured. She also learned her husband and father-in-law were dead, and at that moment, she gave birth to Ichabod and died soon after, saying "The glory is departed from Israel" (I SAMUEL 4:19-22).

This portrait of Isaiah was painted by Jean-Louis Ernest Meissonier (1815–1891) around 1838.

IMMANUEL
("God is with us")

The symbolic name given by the prophet Isaiah to a child to be born unto the royal family of Judah (ISAIAH 7:14); the verse was later invoked by the evangelist Matthew to the birth of Jesus (MATTHEW 1:23).

IRA
("wakeful")

1. A Tekoite, one of King David's 30 warriors (II SAMUEL 23:26).
2. An Ithrite, one of King David's 30 warriors (II SAMUEL 23:38).
3. A Jairite and priest of King David (II SAMUEL 8:18; I CHRONICLES 18:17).

IRIJAH
("God sees")

Son of Shelemiah and grandson of Hananiah. A captain during the reign of King Zedekiah of Judah, Irijah falsely accused Jeremiah for treason in Jerusalem (JEREMIAH 37:13).

ISAIAH
("the salvation of God")

Son of Amoz and, according to religious tradition, the author of the biblical book that bears his name. Isaiah is considered one of the greatest of all the Hebrew prophets. He lived in Jerusalem and had two sons with a woman whom he called "the prophetess" (ISAIAH 8:3). More than a mere prophet, Isaiah served as royal counselor for many kings, beginning with the last years of King Uzziah's reign, and followed by the rule of Jotham, Ahaz, and Hezekiah (ISAIAH 1:1). Isaiah was firmly committed to preserving the Davidic dynasty and the Temple of Jerusalem as God's throne on earth. During the dark days when Israel's King Pekah and Syria's King Rezim invaded Judah, it was Isaiah who had advised King Ahaz to "take heed, be quiet, do not fear, and do not let your heart be faint" (ISAIAH 7:4). Isaiah rose to full prominence during Hezekiah's rule. Knowing the futility of confronting Assyria's might, the prophet denounced those who "go down to Egypt without asking for my council, to take refuge in the protection of Pharaoh," for such an overture would bring "neither help nor profit, but shame and grace" (ISAIAH 30:2,5). He was proven correct; around 701 B.C.E., the new Assyrian King Sennacherib led a powerful invasion force to suppress Judah's revolt. In panic, Hezekiah turned to Isaiah. What should he do? Do nothing, replied Isaiah; "by the way that he came, by the same he shall return; he shall not come into this city" (II KINGS 19:33). And indeed, Sennacherib's siege of Jerusalem failed. Isaiah lived until the 14th year of Hezekiah, and in all likelihood outlived that monarch; therefore, Isaiah may have prophesied at least 64 years.

ISHBAAL OR ISHBOSHETH
("man of shame")
Youngest of Saul's four sons, and his successor after his father and three brothers fell at the battle of Gilboa (I CHRONICLES 8:33; 9:39). Ishbaal's elevation was supported by the northern tribes, but ominously, not by the South. The southern elders went instead to Hebron, David's military base, and in due course anointed David king "over the house of Judah" (II SAMUEL 2:4). Ishbaal ruled for two years from his capital of Mahanaim, on the east of Jordan (II SAMUEL 2:9). After a troubled and uncertain reign, he was murdered by his guard, who stabbed him while he was asleep (II SAMUEL 4:5-7).

ISHVI
("quiet")
1. Second of Saul and Ahinoam's sons (I SAMUEL 14:49). Also spelled "Ishui."
2. Third of Asher's sons (GENESIS 46:17; I CHRONICLES 7:30), and founder of the Ishvites (NUMBERS 26:44).

ITTAI
("near")
1. A Benjamite, one of David's 30 heroes (II SAMUEL 23:29).
2. A native of Gath, a Philistine, who commanded one-third of King David's army in the battle that defeated forces of Absalom (II SAMUEL 15:19-22). In the first Book of Chronicles, he is called Ithai (I CHRONICLES 11:31).

JAAZANIAH
("may God hear")
1. One of the captains who accompanied Hohanan ben-Kareah to pay his respects to Gedaliah at Mizpah (II KINGS 25:23), and afterward assisted in recovering Ishmael's prey from his clutches.
2. Son of Shaphan (EZEKIEL 8:11).
3. Son of Azzur; one of the princes of the people against whom Ezekiel was directed to prophesy (EZEKIEL 11:1).

A miniature illustration from around 1200 depicts scenes of King Saul's death and the recovery of his body from the walls of Beth-She'an.

4. A Rechabite, son of Jeremiah (JEREMIAH 35:3).
5. A Maacathite (II KINGS 25:23; JEREMIAH 40:8; 42:1). He is also called Azariah (JEREMIAH 43:2).

JABESH
("dry")
Father of Shallum (II KINGS 15:10,13-14), who usurped the throne of Israel on the death of Zechariah.

JABIN
("discerner," "the wise")
1. King of Hazor, who organized a confederacy of the northern princes against the Israelites (JOSHUA 11:1-3). During the ensuing wars, Joshua attacked Jabin and burned his city (JOSHUA 11:1-14).
2. A king of Hazor, called "the king of Canaan," who oppressed the Israelites 160 years after Joshua's death (JUDGES 5:6-11). The king was eventually defeated by Deborah and Barak (JUDGES 5:31).

JAEL
("deer")
Wife of Heber the Kenite (JUDGES 4:17-22). The captain of Jabin's army, Sisera, had sought refuge with the tribe of Heber after the Canaanites were defeated by Barak. Jael killed him in her tent by hammering a nail in his head (JUDGES 5:27).

JAIR
("enlightener")
1. Son of Segub, who was brought up by his mother in Gilead (I CHRONICLES 2:22). He distinguished himself in an expedition against Bashan, and settled in the part of Argob on the borders of Gilead (NUMBERS 32:41; DEUTERONOMY 3:14; JOSHUA 13:30).
2. Eighth Judge of Israel, which he ruled for 22 years (JUDGES 10:3-5). He had 30 sons, who had possession of 30 of the 60 cities that formed the ancient Havoth-jair (I KINGS 4:13; I CHRONICLES 2:23).
3. A Benjamite, the father of Mordecai, Esther's uncle (ESTHER 2:5).
4. Father of Elhanan, who slew Lahmi, the brother of Goliath (I CHRONICLES 20:5).

JAPHIA
("splendid")
1. King of Lachish at the time of the conquest of Canaan by the Israelites (JOSHUA 10:3).

2. One of the sons of David born in Jerusalem (II SAMUEL 5:15; I CHRONICLES 3:7; 14:6).

JASHEN
("sleeping")
Also referred to as Hashem (I CHRONICLES 11:34), Jashen was father of several men who fought in King David's army (II SAMUEL 23:32).

JECOLIAH
("God is mighty")
Born in Jerusalem, the wife of King Amaziah, and mother of King Uzziah (II CHRONICLES 26:3).

JEDIDAH
("one beloved")
Queen of Amon and mother of King Josiah (II KINGS 22:1).

JEHOAHAZ
("God possessed")
1. Youngest son of Jehoram, king of Judah (II CHRONICLES 21:17; 22:1,6,8,9).
2. Son and successor of Jehu, king of Israel (II KINGS 10:35), who reigned for 17 years. The Syrians, under Hazael and Ben-hadad, prevailed over him, but were at length driven out of the land by his son Jehoash (II KINGS 13:1-9).
3. Josiah's third son, usually called Shallum (I CHRONICLES 3:15). He succeeded his father and reigned over Judah for three months until he was deposed by Pharaoh Necho (II KINGS 23:31,34). He became a prisoner of Egypt, where he died in captivity (II KINGS 23:33-34; JEREMIAH 22:10-12; II CHRONICLES 36:1-4).

JEHOIACHIN
("whom God has appointed")
King of Judah who succeeded his father, Jehoiakim, when he was only eight years of age, and reigned for one hundred days (II CHRONICLES 36:9). He is also called Jeconiah (JEREMIAH 24:1; 27:20). When the Babylonian army appeared before Jerusalem, Jehoiachin capitulated to Nebuchadnezzar. The young king and his family were dispatched to Babylon, and Judah was burdened with crushing reparation payments (II KINGS 24:12-16; JEREMIAH 52:28).

JEHOIADA
("God-known")
A high priest of Judah and the father of Benaiah, who was one of David's chief warriors (II SAMUEL 8:18; 20:23). He married Jehosheba, the daughter of King Jehoram (II CHRONICLES 22:11), and took an active part, with his wife, in first hiding and then aiding Jehoash in regaining the throne of Judah from Queen Athaliah (II KINGS 11:2; 12:2).

JEHOIAKIM (ELIAKIM)
("whom God sets up")
A king of Judah, son of Josiah and Zebidah. Josiah was originally succeeded by his son Jehoahaz, but this was not to Pharaoh Necho's liking. As Judah's new overlord, he ordered Jehoahaz deposed and replaced by

An early 20th-century British illustration depicts "Jehoiakim Burning the Roll."

Eliakim under the new name of Jehoiakim, because he was considered more pliable. Jehoahaz was taken to Egypt and died in captivity. When the Median-Babylonian coalition dealt a stinging defeat to the Assyrian and Egyptian armies at Carchemish, Jehoiakim rushed to pay tribute to the new superpower, neo-Babylonia (II KINGS 24:1,7). When this failed to get him any special favors, Jehoiakim switched back to

the Egyptian camp, and tried to form an anti-Babylonian alliance that would include Moab, Tyre, Sidon, and Edom. The Babylonian King Nebuchadnezzar gathered his forces and marched down to Jerusalem, but Jehoiakim died before he arrived, and was succeeded by his son Jehoiachin.

JEHORAM
("exalted")
1. A king of Israel, son of Ahab and Jezebel, and successor to his brother Ahaziah (II KINGS 1:17; 3:1). He subjected the Moabites, who had gained independence during his brother's reign.
2. A king of Judah, eldest son and successor of Jehoshaphat (II CHRONICLES 21:5,20; II KINGS 8:16). His wife was Athaliah, the daughter of Ahab and Jezebel. During his reign, the Edomites revolted, and the Philistines, Arabians, and Cushites invaded his kingdom (II KINGS 8:16-24; II CHRONICLES 21:5,20).
3. Son of Ahab (see Joram).
4. Son of Toi, king of Hamath, who was sent by his father to congratulate David on his victory over Hadadezer (II SAMUEL 8:10).
5. A Levite of the family of Gershom (I CHRONICLES 26:25).
6. A priest sent by Jehoshaphat to instruct the people in Judah (II CHRONICLES 17:8).

JEHOSHAPHAT
("whom God judges")
1. Son of Ahilud, who held the high-ranking office of recorder in David's court (II SAMUEL 8:16) as well as in Solomon's court (I KINGS 4:3,17).
2. A priest during David's time (I CHRONICLES 15:24).
3. One of David's bodyguards (I CHRONICLES 11:43).
4. Son of Parvah, and one of the 12 purveyors of King Solomon (I KINGS 4:17).
5. Son of Nimshi and father of King Jehu (II KINGS 9:2,14).
6. A king of Judah, son of Asa, who reigned for 25 years (I KINGS 15:24; II KINGS 8:16). He was a contemporary of Ahab, Ahaziah, and Jehoram, and is upheld as one of the best kings of Judah (I KINGS 15:24; 22:41; I CHRONICLES 3:10; II CHRONICLES 17:1).

For most of his reign, Judah was at peace with its neighbors, while the region recovered some of its erstwhile economic prosperity. Jehoshaphat even signed a peace treaty with the northern kingdom of Israel, and married his crown prince, Jehoram, to Athaliah, daughter of King Ahab. Years later, he fought jointly with Ahab's son and successor (who was also named Jehoram) against the king of Moab.

7. A priest who assisted in bringing the Ark of the Covenant from Obed-edom to Jerusalem (I Chronicles 15:24).

JEHOSHEBA
("God's oath")
Daughter of Jehoram, the king of Israel; she is also called Jehoshabeath in II Chronicles 22:11. Jehosheba was the only princess of the royal house who was married to a high priest, Jehoiada (II Chronicles 22:11).

JEHU
("God is he")
1. Son of Obed and a leader of a tribe of Judah (I Chronicles 2:38).
2. Benjamite soldier who switched allegiance from King Saul to King David (I Chronicles 12:3).
3. A prophet, son of Hanani, who prophesied the death of King Baasha of Israel (I Kings 16:1).
4. King of Israel, ca 841–814 B.C.E. (II Kings 9:2). After King Jehoram was wounded in a war against the Syrians and left the battlefield, leaving Jehu in command, the prophet Elisha initiated a rebellion against Jehoram and his mother, Jezebel. Jehu then killed Jehoram, and had Jezebel thrown from the palace window to her death. During Jehu's rule, the northern kingdom of Israel became an Assyrian vassal state; a large black obelisk found in 1846 shows Jehu bowing in tribute to King Shalmaneser. Jehu engaged in a long war of attrition against King Hazael of Aram-Damascus, who had captured Israel's possessions east of the Jordan. The war with Syria continued for so long that under Jehu's son and successor, Jehoahaz, Israel's army was reduced to a mere ten chariots and 10,000 foot soldiers (II Kings 13:7).

This 19th-century English engraving depicts King Jehu, leader of a tribe of Judah.

JEHUCAL (JUCAL)
("able")
Son of Shelemiah, and one of two people sent by King Zedekiah to Jeremiah, asking the prophet to pray for the kingdom during the final siege by Nebuchadnezzar (Jeremiah 37:3).

JEHUDI
("Judean")
Son of Nethaniah and an official in the court of Jehoiakim, who was ordered by the king to read Jeremiah's scroll to him (Jeremiah 36:14,21,23).

JEPHTHAH
("whom God sets free")
An illegitimate son of Gilead who was driven away from his inheritance by his half brothers (Judges 11:1-2). He settled in Tob, where he became a renowned officer, and was invited back to his native land. He freed Israel from the oppression of the Ammonites (Judges 11:1-33), but was compelled to sacrifice his only child for the victory. He was victorious in a war against the tribe of Ephraim, and served as a Judge of Israel for six years until his death (Judges 12:7).

JEREMIAH
("whom God has appointed")
1. One of the greatest prophets of Hebrew Scripture, Jeremiah was the son of a priest named Hilkiah from the village of Anathoth, located three miles north of Jerusalem. Like Isaiah, he was driven by the need to inspire greater faith in God among his listeners, but like Amos, he was also deeply engaged with the growing social underclass of Hebrew society. He poured scorn on those who "amass wealth unjustly; in mid-life it will leave them, and at their end they will prove to be fools" (Jeremiah 17:11). Jeremiah wholly supported King Josiah's campaign to root out polytheism and pagan ritual, but he observed the king's political ambition with the same apprehension that Isaiah had followed the brinkmanship of Josiah's predecessor, King Hezekiah. Indeed, Josiah's ill-advised alliance with Median-Babylonian rebels resulted in his death during the battle of Megiddo. Josiah's eventual successor, Jehoiakim, once again tolerated pagan sacrifices, which prompted Jeremiah to deliver his famous Temple sermon, "Obey my voice, and I will be your God, and you shall be

A detail from the Vatican's Sistine Chapel ceiling shows the prophet Jeremiah as painted by Michelangelo Buonarroti (1475–1564).

my people" (Jeremiah 7:22-23). Jeremiah later issued a warning from God that the Babylonians would soon attack: The whole land "shall become a ruin and a waste, and these nations shall serve the king of Babylon seventy years" (JEREMIAH 25:9-11). He was imprisoned and beaten for his efforts, but eventually released. He continued to warn of the Babylonian danger even as the new king of Judah, Zedekiah, plotted a revolt in alliance with the Egyptian king. In 587 B.C.E., after the Babylonian King Nebuchadnezzar conquered Jerusalem, thousands were slaughtered or sent off into captivity, but Jeremiah was spared. He left the city for Mizpah in Judea and continued to prophesy for many years, dying around the age of 90 years.

2. A Gadite/Benjamite, who joined David in the wilderness (I CHRONICLES 12:10).

3. One of the chiefs of the tribe of Manasseh on the east of Jordan (I CHRONICLES 5:24).

4. Father of Hamutal (II KINGS 23:31), the wife of Josiah.

Jean-Honoré Fragonard (1732–1806) painted "Jeroboam Sacrificing to the Golden Calf" in 1752.

JEROBOAM
("whose people are many")

1. Son of Nebat (I KINGS 11:26-39), and the first king of the Northern Kingdom of Israel, Jeroboam first worked for Solomon as the chief superintendent overseeing forced laborers. Encouraged by the prophet Ahijah, Jeroboam began to plot Solomon's overthrow. The conspiracy was discovered, however, and Jeroboam was sentenced to death—though not before he was allowed to escape to Egypt, where he continued his plotting with the support of "King Shishak" (I KINGS 11:40), arguably Pharaoh

Shoshenq I (945–925 B.C.E.). Upon Solomon's death, the ten tribes of the North revolted and invited Jeroboam to become their king (I KINGS 12:1-20). Jeroboam then set about to reorganize his new domain in much the same way as his former employer, King Solomon, had done. Given that the North controlled the Jezreel and the fertile valleys of Galilee, its economy and agricultural output was far greater that the South. Jeroboam also created rival shrines to God in the former cult centers of Bethel and Dan, and commissioned golden calves—the traditional symbol of El—to be placed in them. The Deuteronomist narrator of the Books of Kings depicts this idolatry as "a sin" (I KINGS 12:30), even though Bethel was a much older YHWH shrine than the Jebusite mount of Jerusalem, going back to the days when Jacob built an altar after his vision of a ladder reaching into heaven. When Pharaoh Shoshenq, Jeroboam's former protector, invaded Judah, Jeroboam hoped that the Egyptian king would satisfy himself with the southern kingdom, but those hopes were dashed. The Egyptian king continued north and raided most of Israel's principal cities, including the stronghold of Ma-ke-thu, or Megiddo. The North had barely recovered from the Egyptian incursion when the new king of Judah, Rehoboam's son Abijah (ca 913–911 B.C.E.), staged an attack on Israel and was able to capture several townships on the frontier between the two kingdoms (I KINGS 15:1-8). But Abijah's reign was cut short by his untimely death. One year later his northern foe, King Jeroboam, died as well. He was succeeded by his son Nadab (ca 910–909 B.C.E.), who was assassinated after only one year, during a coup staged by an Issachar commander named Baasha who also murdered all of the remaining members of Jeroboam's family (I KINGS 15:16-22).

2. Jeroboam II, the son and successor of Jehoash, was king of Israel (ca 786–746 B.C.E.), over which he ruled for 40 years (II KINGS 14:23). His reign was contemporary with those of Amaziah (II KINGS 14:23) and Uzziah (II KINGS 15:1), two kings of Judah, and was the most prosperous that Israel had known for some time. However, it was also characterized as a period of social iniquity

(AMOS 2:6-8; 4:1; 6:6; HOSEA 4:12-14). He was victorious over the Syrians (II KINGS 13:4; 14:26-27), and extended Israel to its former borders (II KINGS 14:25; AMOS 6:14).

JEROHAM
("God will have mercy")

1. Father of Elkanah and grandfather of the prophet Samuel (I SAMUEL 1:1; I CHRONICLES 6:27-34).

2. A Benjamite, the founder of a family of Bene-Jeroham (I CHRONICLES 8:27).

3. Father (or progenitor) of Ibneiah (I CHRONICLES 9:8).

4. A descendant of Aaron, son of Pashhur, and father of Adaiah (I CHRONICLES 9:12)

5. Jeroham of Gedor, who bore sons who joined David at Ziklag (I CHRONICLES 12:7).

6. A Danite, whose son (or descendant) Azarel was head of the Dan tribe during the reign of David (I CHRONICLES 27:22).

7. Father of Azariah, one of the "captains of hundreds," during the reign of Athaliah (II CHRONICLES 23:1).

JERUSHA
("inheritance")

Wife of King Uzziah, daughter of Zadok, and mother of King Jotham (II KINGS 15:33; II CHRONICLES 27:1).

JEZEBEL
("chaste")

Wife of Ahab, king of Israel. Jezebel was a Phoenician princess, daughter of the Phoenician King Ethbaal or Ithobaal. According to the first Book of Kings, she established Phoenician pagan worship at Ahab's court on a grand scale. At her table were no less than 450 prophets of Baal and 400 prophets of Baal's consort Asherah (I KINGS 16:31,21; 18:19). The prophets of YHWH were attacked by her orders and put to the sword (I KINGS 18:13; II KINGS 9:7). Possibly at her prompting, King Ahab went as far as to erect "an altar for Baal in the house of Baal" himself (I KINGS 16:32), which in the eyes of the Judah scribes further underscored the perfidy of the Northern Kingdom. Ahab then became upset when he learned that the owner of a vineyard abutting his palace, a man named Naboth, was not willing to sell the property. Queen Jezebel arranged for Naboth to be arrested on a trumped-up blasphemy charge, and the vineyard owner was stoned to death (I KINGS 21:7). His property thus fell to the crown. Shocked by this blatant crime, Elijah pronounced a curse on Ahab and his house. His prophecy was fulfilled: Ahab would be killed during another campaign against his old Syrian foe, while his son Ahaziah would die after a fall from his window. Ahab's second son Jehoram was then ousted from the throne in a bloody coup by a commander named Jehu, reportedly with Elijah's assistance, while Queen Jezebel was thrown to her death and set upon by dogs (II KINGS 9:34; 10:9). In the centuries to come, her name would become synonymous with a wicked woman (REVELATION 2:20).

JEZREEL
("God scatters," "seed of God")

1. A symbolic name given by Hosea to his oldest son, to describe a great slaughter such as had formerly taken place in the plain of Esdraelon or Jezreel (HOSEA 1:4-5).

2. A descendant of the father or founder of Etam, of the line of Judah (I CHRONICLES 4:3).

A 13th-century stained glass window from the St. Thomas Church in Strasbourg, France, depicts how "Joab Kills the General Amase."

JOAB
("whose father is God")

1. One of the three sons of Zeruiah, David's sister, and principal military commander during David's reign (II SAMUEL 2:13; 10:7; 11:1; I KINGS 11:15). His two brothers were Abishai and Asahel, the "swift of foot." Asahel was killed by Abner (II SAMUEL 2:13-32), after which Joab murdered Abner (II SAMUEL 3:22-27). Joab then led the assault on the Jesubite fortress of Mount Zion, and was raised to the rank of "prince of the king's army" (II SAMUEL 5:6-10; I CHRONICLES 27:34). His chief military achievements were against the allied forces of Syria and Ammon; against Edom (I KINGS 11:15-16); and against the Ammonites (II SAMUEL 10:7-19; 11:1,11). Nevertheless, his character is stained by the part he played in the murder of Uriah (II SAMUEL 11:14-25). After Joab killed David's rebellious son Absalom, David passed command of the army to Amasa, Joab's cousin (II SAMUEL 19:13; 20:1-13). In retaliation, Joab supported the claim of Adonijah as David's heir instead of Solomon. He was killed by Benaiah, on orders of Solomon at the altar where he had fled for refuge, and was buried in his own property in the "wilderness," probably in the northeast of Jerusalem (I KINGS 2:5, 28-34). Benaiah succeeded him as commander-in-chief of the army.

2. Son of Seraiah of the Judah tribe, and head of a family of artisans (I CHRONICLES 4:14).

This portrait of Jezebel was painted in 1896 by British artist John Byam Liston Shaw (1872–1919).

3. Head of a family descended from Pahath-moab, which returned from exile in Babylon (EZRA 2:6; 8:9).

JOASH
("given by God")

1. Son of Ahaziah, and eighth king of Judah. He was hidden for six years after his father's sister Jehoshabeath, the wife of Jehoiada the high priest, stole him from among the king's sons to escape the murderous hand of Athaliah. After a successful coup orchestrated by Jehoiada, he took the throne at age seven. While Jehoiada lived, his reign was prosperous but after the high priest's death, Joash was persuaded to revive the worship of Baal. After being rebuked for this by Zechariah, Jehoiada's son, Joash had him stoned to death. That year, King Hazael of Syria marched against Jerusalem, and demanded a high tribute as the price of his departure. Shortly after this, two of Joash's servants murdered him in his bed in the fortress of Millo. His reign lasted 40 years.

2. Father of Gideon, and a wealthy man among the Abiezrites (JUDGES 6:11).

3. Younger son of Ahab, who held a subordinate jurisdiction during his father's lifetime (I KINGS 22:26; II CHRONICLES 18:25).

4. Descendant of Shelah, the son of Judah (I CHRONICLES 4:22).

5. A Benjamite archer, son of Shemaah of Gibeah (I CHRONICLES 12:3), who joined David at Ziklag.

6. One of the officers of David's household (I CHRONICLES 27:28).

7. Son of Becher and head of a Benjamite house (I CHRONICLES 7:8).

JOEL
("to whom Lord is God")

1. Eldest son of the prophet Samuel (I SAMUEL 8:2; I CHRONICLES 6:33; 15:17) and father of Heman the singer.

2. A Simeonite chief (I CHRONICLES 4:35).

3. A descendant of Reuben (I CHRONICLES 5:4).

4. Chief of the Gadites, who dwelt in the land of Bashan (I CHRONICLES 5:12).

5. Son of Izrahiah, of the tribe of Issachar (I CHRONICLES 7:3).

6. Brother of Nathan of Zobah (I CHRONI-CLES 11:38), and one of David's guards.

7. Chief of the Gershomites in the reign of David (I CHRONICLES 15:7,11).

8. A Gershonite Levite during the reign of David, son of Jehiel, a descendant of Laadan and possibly the same as the preceding (I CHRONICLES 23:8; 26:22).

9. Son of Pedaiah, and a chief of the tribe of Manasseh west of Jordan during the reign of David (I CHRONICLES 27:20).

10. A Kohathite Levite in the reign of Hezekiah (II CHRONICLES 29:12).

11. One of the sons of Nebo, who returned with Ezra and had married a foreign wife (EZRA 10:43).

12. Son of Zichri, a Benjamite (NEHEMIAH 11:9).

JOHANAN
("gift or grace of God")

1. Son of Azariah and grandson of Ahimaaz the son of Zadok, and father of Azariah (I CHRONICLES 6:9-10).

2. Son of Elioenai, the son of Neariah, the son of Shemaiah, in the line of Zerubbabel's heirs (I CHRONICLES 3:24).

3. Son of Kareah, and one of the captains of the scattered army of Judah, who escaped in the final attack on Jerusalem by the Babylonians (II KINGS 25:23). They pledged their loyalty to Gedaliah, who had been appointed governor; after Gedaliah was assassinated by another officer named Ismael, Johanan pursued the assassin to Gibeon but was unable to take him (JEREMIAH 41:11-16). Fearing the vengeance of the Babylonians, Johanan and his officers then withdrew to Egypt, taking Jeremiah, his scribe Baruch, and Gedaliah's family with them.

4. Firstborn son of Josiah, king of Judah (I CHRONICLES 3:15).

5. A valiant Benjamite who joined David at Ziklag (I CHRONICLES 12:4).

6. One of the Gadite heroes who joined David in the desert of Judah (I CHRONICLES 12:12).

7. Father of Azariah, an Ephraimite in the time of Ahaz (II CHRONICLES 28:12).

8. Son of Hakkatan, and chief of the Bene-Azgad who returned with Ezra (EZRA 8:12).

9. Son of Eliashib, one of the chief Levites (EZRA 10:6; NEHEMIAH 12:23).

10. Son of Tobiah the Ammonite (NEHEMIAH 6:18).

JONADAB
("the Lord is bounteous")

1. Son of Shimeah and nephew of David (II SAMUEL 13:3). He befriended his cousin Amnon who raped Tamar (II SAMUEL 13:5-6).

2. Son of Rechab and founder of the Rechabites, an ascetic group, who supported Jehu's coup against King Ahab (II KINGS 10:15; JEREMIAH 35:6,10).

JONAH
("dove")

Son of Amittai of Gath-hepher, and a prophet of Israel who prophesied during the reign of Jeroboam II and predicted the restoration of the ancient boundaries of the kingdom (II KINGS 14:25-27). According to the Book of Jonah, God sent the prophet to Nineveh, then the capital of the Assyrian Empire, because "their wickedness has come before me" (JONAH 1:2). Jonah tried to evade this commission and fled to Tarshish. On his journey aboard a ship, God called down a great wind. In despair, the ship's crew threw Jonah overboard, believing

"Jonah and the Big Fish" is the subject of this early Byzantine sculpture from the early fourth century.

him to be the cause of the storm. He was swallowed by a large fish (a sea monster, possibly a whale) and stayed in the fish's belly for three days and nights, after which he was cast out on the shore. Jonah then obeyed God and went to Nineveh, where he proclaimed that the city would be destroyed in 40 days. Everyone from the king on down believed him, and observed a fast of repentance, thus averting the threatened judgment. The Book of Jonah, in sum, is an object lesson of God's forgiveness and mercy.

JONATHAN
("the gift of God")

1. Son or descendant of Gershom, the son of Moses, who became priest at the shrine of Dan, a role that continued in his family until the captivity (JUDGES 17:7-13; 18:30).

2. Eldest son of King Saul, and a friend of David first mentioned after his father's accession to the throne (I SAMUEL 13:2). Like his father, Jonathan was a man of great strength (II SAMUEL 1:23). Saul's growing depression, however, caused Jonathan to leave his father and to follow David instead (I SAMUEL 20:34). After an eventful career, primarily interwoven with that of David, he died on the field of Gilboa, along with his father and two brothers (I SAMUEL 31:2,8). At his death, David composed the famous elegy of "The Song of the Bow": "I am distressed for you, my brother Jonathan; very pleasant have you been to me; your love to me was wonderful, surpassing the love of women" (II SAMUEL 1:17-27). He left one son, Merib-baal or Mephibosheth (II SAMUEL 4:4; I CHRONICLES 8:34).

3. Son of the high priest Abiathar; a follower of David at the time of Absalom's rebellion, who later informed Adonijah that David had anointed Solomon as his successor (II SAMUEL 15:27,36).

4. Son of Shimei and David's nephew; also one of his chief warriors who slew a giant in Gath (II SAMUEL 21:21).

5. Son of Shammah the Hararite and a soldier in David's army who was renowned for his bravery (II SAMUEL 23:32).

6. A scribe in whose house Jeremiah was held prisoner (JEREMIAH 37:15,20).

7. Son of Kareah, and brother of Johanan (JEREMIAH 40:8).

8. Father of Ebed who returned from exile in Babylon with Ezra (EZRA 8:6).

9. A priest, the son of Asahel, who was with Ezra when he called on the men of Judah to divorce their non-Jewish wives (EZRA 10:15).

10. A chief priest of Judah in the last years of Nehemiah (NEHEMIAH 12:14).

11. Son of Joiada, and his successor in the high priesthood who returned from exile in Babylon (NEHEMIAH 12:11,22-23).

12. Father of Zechariah, a priest who blew the trumpet at the dedication of the wall (NEHEMIAH 12:35).

JORAM
("whom God has exalted")

1. Son of Toi, king of Hamath, who was sent to congratulate King David on his victory over the king of Zobah, bringing many precious gifts (II SAMUEL 8:10).

2. Son of King Ahab (II KINGS 8:16,25,28). See Jehoram.

3. Son of Jehoshaphat; a king of Judah (II KINGS 8:21,23-24; I CHRONICLES 3:11). See Jehoram.

4. A priest during the reign of Jehoshaphat (II CHRONICLES 17:8). See Jehoram.

5. A Levite, the grandfather of Shelomoth, who was in charge of all battle trophies and treasures captured by King David and dedicated to the Tabernacle (I CHRONICLES 26:25).

JOSHUA
("God is salvation")

The name "Joshua" is a variant of Hoshea, Oshea, Jehoshua, Jeshua, and Jesus.

1. Son of Nun, of the tribe of Ephraim, who is first mentioned in the battle against Amalek at Rephidim, when Moses chose him to lead the Israelites (EXODUS 17:9; I CHRONICLES 7:27). Soon afterward, he was one of the 12 sent to explore the land of Canaan, and one of two who gave an encouraging report of their journey (NUMBERS 13:17; 14:6). Moses was then told to give Joshua authority over the people (NUMBERS 27:18). Under the direction of God (JOSHUA 1:1), Joshua assumed command and crossed the

Artist Arthur A. Dixon (1872–1959) painted "Moses and Joshua Descending from the Mount."

Jordan, fortified a camp at Gilgal, circumcised the people, kept the Passover, and initiated the wars of conquest. Having subdued the Canaanites after hard fighting, Joshua—now stricken in years—divided the conquered lands among the 12 tribes, including "the hill country and all the Negeb . . . as far as Baal-gad in the valley of Lebanon below Mount Hermon" (JOSHUA 11:16-17). The division was made by drawing lots. Timnath-serah in Mount Ephraim was assigned as Joshua's own inheritance. After an interval of rest, Joshua convoked an assembly from all Israel. He delivered two solemn addresses, recorded in Joshua 23:24, and died at 110 years, to be buried in his own city, Timnath-serah, close to Shechem (JOSHUA 24:30).

2. An inhabitant of Beth-shemesh, where the Ark of the Covenant carried on a cart pulled by cows came to rest after it had been sent on its way by the Philistines (I SAMUEL 6:1-12).

3. A governor of the city who gave his name to a gate of Jerusalem (II KINGS 23:8).

4. Jeshua, the son of Jozadak (HAGGAI 1:14; 2:12; ZECHARIAH 3:1).

JOSIAH
("God healed")

King Josiah (640–609 B.C.E.) was the son of King Amon (642–640 B.C.E.) and grandson of King Manasseh. He began his reign after his father died when he was eight years old. Josiah initiated a vast purge of all pagan influences and presided over a comprehensive restoration of ritual and legal practices related to the worship of YHWH. During a search of the Temple archives in 622 B.C.E., the high priest Hilkiah found an ancient scroll that contained "the Book of the Law" (II KINGS 22:8). Many scholars believe that this was the Book of Deuteronomy. Impressed with this scroll, Josiah resolved that whatever remained of ancient Jewish Scripture had to be documented and placed in a comprehensive canon. Thus began the final composition of the Torah, the Five Books of Moses (Genesis through Deuteronomy), based on the fragmentary sources that had survived up to that point. When the kingdoms of the Medes and the Babylonians seceded from the Assyrian Empire, precipitating a civil war, Josiah chose the side of the rebellious kingdoms. Egyptian King Psammetichus I

"The Death of King Josiah at Megiddo" was painted by William Brassey Hole (1846–1917).

(664–610 B.C.E.), on the other hand, chose the side of the Assyrian king. Psammetichus died in 610 and was succeeded by Necho II (610–595 B.C.E.), who actually sent troops to help the hard-pressed Assyrian forces on the Euphrates River. His army had to march through Josiah's kingdom to get there, and

Josiah impulsively decided to stop them. He met Necho's forces at Megiddo, but was defeated. Josiah succumbed to his injuries sustained in combat (II KINGS 23:29-30).

JOTHAM
("God is perfect")
1. Son of Gideon. After his father died, his brother Abimelech hired assassins to kill his brothers. Jotham fled and escaped to Beer (JUDGES 9:5).
2. Son of King Uzziah and Jerushah, and the tenth king of Judah. He fortified Jerusalem, built fortresses, and forced Ammonites to pay tribute (II KINGS 15:5).

KAIWAN
A star god, mentioned in the following citation: "Truly, you will take up Sakkuth your king and Kaiwan your images, the star your God, which you made for yourselves" (AMOS 5:26).

KENAZ
1. Son of Eliphaz and grandson of Esau, and a king of Edom (GENESIS 36:11,15,42).
2. Brother of Caleb, son of Jephunneh, father of Othniel, and a leader of the Judah tribe (JOSHUA 15:17; JUDGES 1:13).
3. Son of Elah and grandson of Caleb, son of Jephunneh (I CHRONICLES 4:15).

KISH
("bow")
1. One of the ten sons of Jeiel, father of Gibeon (I CHRONICLES 8:30).
2. Father of King Saul and son of Abiel of the Benjamin tribe. When Kish lost his asses, Saul went looking for them and thus met the prophet Samuel, who anointed him (I SAMUEL 9:1,3; 10:11,21).

3. Son of Mahli, and descendant of Merari, the son of Levi. His sons married the daughters of his brother, Eleazar (I CHRONICLES OF 23:21).
4. Son of Abdi and one of the Levites who cleansed the Temple on King Hezekiah's orders (II CHRONICLES 29:12).
5. Ancestor of Mordecai, cousin of Queen Esther (ESTHER 2:5).

KOLAIAH
1. Leader of the Benjamin tribe whose descendant Sallu returned from exile to settle in Jerusalem (NEHEMIAH 11:7).
2. Father of Ahab, one of the false prophets who supported King Zedekiah's rebellion against Babylon (JEREMIAH 29:21).

KORE
1. Son of Ebiasaph and a descendant of Korah, whose son Shallum served in the Tabernacle (I CHRONICLES 9:19).

Musicians such as Kushaiah playing trumpets while David brings the Ark of the Covenant to Jerusalem are depicted in this illustration from the 13th-century Morgan Bible.

2. Son of Imnah the Levite, who was in charge of offerings in the Temple during King Hezekiah's reign (II CHRONICLES 31:14).

KOZ
("thorn")
Leader of the tribe of Judah (I CHRONICLES 4:8).

KUSHAIAH
("bow")
Son of Abdi, a descendant of Merari, and a musician who performed when King David brought the Ark of the Covenant to Jerusalem (I CHRONICLES 6:44; 15:17).

LAHMI
("warrior")
Brother of Goliath, the giant killed by David, Lahmi was a Philistine soldier who was killed in battle by Elhanan, son of Jair (I CHRONICLES 20:5).

LAISH
Father of Palti who married Michal, King Saul's daughter, after Saul drove away her husband David. When David became king, he took Michal back from Palti, who wept at her departure (I SAMUEL 25:44; II SAMUEL 3:15).

LAPPIDOTH
("torches")
Husband of Deborah, the Judge, prophetess, and leader of Israel (JUDGES 4:4).

LIBNI
("whiteness")
1. Son of Mahli, grandson of Merari, whose descendant Asaiah served in the Tabernacle during the reign of King David (I CHRONICLES 6:29).
2. A Levite and descendant of Gershon, who ministered in the Tabernacle (I CHRONICLES 6:17,20).

LO-AMMI
("not of my people")
Second son of the prophet Hosea by his wife Gomer. The name evokes God's rejection of Israel because of the nation's sins (HOSEA 1:9), and reflects Hosea's bitterness toward his wife, possibly because he doubted that

their child was his. After Gomer bore him another child, her third, Hosea declared that "she is not my wife, and I am not her husband" (HOSEA 2:2).

LO-RUHAMAH
("not pitied")
Daughter of the prophet Hosea by his wife Gomer. The name evokes God's refusal to intervene in Israel's conquest and deportation because of the nation's sins (HOSEA 1:9), and reflects Hosea's bitterness toward his wife, possibly because he doubted that their child was his.

MAACAH
1. Son of Abraham's Nahor by Reumah, his brother's concubine (GENESIS 22:24).
2. Concubine of Caleb, who bore him five sons; they would grow up to become leaders of Judah (I CHRONICLES 2:48).
3. Wife (or sister?) of Machir, the son of Manasseh (I CHRONICLES 7:15-16).
4. Wife of Jeiel, a leader of Benjamin (I CHRONICLES 8:29).
5. Father of Hanan, a soldier in King David's army renowned for his courage (I CHRONICLES 11:43).
6. Daughter of King Talmai of Geshur and wife of King David. She bore him a son named Absalom and a daughter named Tamar (II SAMUEL 3:3; I CHRONICLES 3:2).
7. Mother of King Asa of Judah, who was sent away from court because of her worship of Asherah (I KINGS 15:10).
8. Daughter of Abishalom and wife of King Rehoboam of Judah. She bore him a son named Abijah, his successor (I KINGS 15:2; II CHRONICLES 11:20-22).

MAASEIAH
("work of God")
1. One of the Levites whom King David appointed as porter at the gates of the Tabernacle (I CHRONICLES 15:18,20).
2. One of the five army commanders who, under instructions from the high priest

Jehoiada, proclaimed Joash as king of Judah (II CHRONICLES 23:1).
3. An officer of King Uzziah in charge of the king's army (II CHRONICLES 26:11).
4. Son of King Ahaz, who was killed by Zichri of the tribe of Ephraim during the invasion of Judah by the armies of Israel and Syria (II CHRONICLES 28:7).
5. Governor of Jerusalem during the reign of King Josiah (II CHRONICLES 34:8).
6. Father of the priest Zephaniah (JEREMIAH 21:1; 37:3).
7. Father of the prophet Zedekiah, whom Jeremiah accused of spreading lies (JEREMIAH 29:21).
8. Son of Shallum, a doorkeeper at the entrance to the Temple (JEREMIAH 32:12; 51:59).

MAHALATH
("harp")
1. Daughter of Ishmael and wife of Esau (GENESIS 28:9).
2. Daughter of Jerimoth and granddaughter

"Death of King Saul" and his sons, including his third son Malchishua, was painted by Elie Marcuse (1817–1902).

of King David who married King Rehoboam of Judah (II CHRONICLES 11:18).

MAHAZIOTH
("visions")
Son of Heman, a musician, who performed in the Tabernacle with his brothers under their father's direction (I CHRONICLES 25:4,30).

MAHER-SHALAL-HASH-BAZ
("booty and shame are imminent")
Son of the prophet Isaiah and a woman called the prophetess; the name symbolizes the feared destruction of Israel (ISAIAH 8:1).

MAHLI
("sick")
1. Son of Merari and grandson of Levi, whose descendants served in the Temple (I CHRONICLES 6:19,29; EZRA 8:18).
2. Son of Mushi whose descendants served in the Temple during King David's reign (I CHRONICLES 6:47; 23:23).

MAHSEIAH
("God is my refuge")
Grandfather of Jeremiah's scribe Baruch and of King Zedekiah's quartermaster Seraiah (JEREMIAH 32:12; 51:59).

MALCHIAH
("God is my king")
Son of Hammelech, who owned a dungeon in the court of the prison where Jeremiah was kept (JEREMIAH 38:6).

MALCHIJAH
("God is my king")
1. Son of Ethni, father of Baaseiah, and ancestor of Asaph, one of the Levites appointed by King David to be in charge of the singers in the House of God (I CHRONICLES 6:40).
2. A priest and father of Pashhur during the reign of King Zedekiah (I CHRONICLES 9:12; JEREMIAH 38:1).
3. A descendant of Parosh, who divorced his wife during the days of Ezra (EZRA 10:25).

4. A descendant of Harim, who divorced his wife during the days of Ezra (EZRA 10:31).

5. Son of Rechab, who repaired the Dung Gate of Jerusalem (NEHEMIAH 3:14).

6. Son of a goldsmith, who helped to repair the walls of Jerusalem, during the days of Nehemiah (NEHEMIAH 3:31).

7. A priest who stood next to Ezra when he read in the Book of the Law of God (NEHEMIAH 8:4).

8. Ancestor of the priest Adaiah who worked in the Temple during the days of Nehemiah (NEHEMIAH 11:12).

MALCHISHUA
("my king is salvation")

Third son of King Saul by his wife, Ahinoam. He fought with his father against the Philistines in the battle of Mount Gilboa and was killed along with his brothers, Jonathan and Abinadab (I CHRONICLES 8:33).

MANASSEH
("causing to forget")

1. Son of Joseph and his Egyptian wife, Asenath. Manasseh went with his father and brother, Ephraim, to see Jacob when he was dying. Jacob adopted the boys and blessed them (GENESIS 41:51). Both would become the progenitors of Hebrew tribes.

2. Fourteenth king of Judah (ca 687–642 B.C.E.). King Manasseh presided over a return to pagan idolatry, which was even more pervasive because of Manasseh's long reign of some 45 years (II KINGS 21:3). Although vilified in the Books of Kings, Manasseh energetically strove to restore Judah's ravaged agricultural economy, possibly striking favorable trading pacts with the Assyrian regime. According to the Books of Chronicles, Manasseh was deported to Babylon, but exonerated and allowed to return to Judah. He then purified the Temple. Assyrian records confirm that Manasseh was among several vassal kings who were ordered to give tribute to the king in Nineveh (II CHRONICLES 33:11-13).

3. Descendant of Pahath-moab who obeyed Ezra's edict and divorced his non-Jewish wife (EZRA 10:30).

4. Descendant of Hashum who obeyed Ezra's edict and divorced his non-Jewish wife (EZRA 10:33).

MANOAH
("rest")

Father of Samson and a native of the town of Zorah (JUDGES 13:2).

MAOCH

Father of Achish, king of Gath, where David sought refuge with his family while being pursued by King Saul (I SAMUEL 27:2; I KINGS 2:39).

MATTAN
("a gift")

1. The priest of Baal who was appointed by Queen Athaliah to minister to Baal in Jerusalem. He was slain by the people before his altar (II KINGS 11:18; II CHRONICLES 23:17).

2. Father of Shephatiah who threw Jeremiah into prison (JEREMIAH 38:1).

MATTANIAH

1. A Levite, son of Heman, one of King David's musicians and the leader of the

Ernest Wallcousins (1883–1976) painted "Merodach Sets Forth to Attack Tiamat," an illustration from Myths of Babylonia and Assyria *by Donald A. Makenzie, 1915.*

ninth turn of temple service (I CHRONICLES 25:4,16).

2. A Levite who assisted in purifying the Temple during the religious reformation of King Hezekiah (II CHRONICLES 29:13).

3. Original name of Zedekiah, the last of the kings of Judah (II KINGS 24:17). He was the third son of Josiah, who fell at Megiddo.

MELECH
("king")

Son of Micah and a descendant of Jonathan, the son of King Saul (I CHRONICLES 8:35).

MENAHEM
("comforter")

Sixteenth king of the Northern Kingdom of Israel. Formerly the governor of Tirzah, Menahem marched on Samaria and slew the usurper Shallum, then crowned himself king. When the king of Assyria invaded Israel, Menahem was successful in appeasing him by paying him a tribute of one thousand talents of silver, which he got by taxing the wealthy men in the kingdom. He was succeeded by his son Pekahiah (II KINGS 15:14-22).

MEPHIBOSHETH
("contender against shame")

1. Saul's son by his concubine, Rizpah, who was the daughter of Aiah. He and his brother Armoni were among the seven victims who were surrendered by David to the Gibeonites and subsequently executed, in the belief that such would avoid a famine (II SAMUEL 21:8).

2. Son of Jonathan and grandson of Saul, whose life seems to have been one of trial and discomfort. When his father and grandfather were killed on Mount Gilboa, he was a five-year-old infant. Fleeing for his life, he fell in an accident, which deprived him of the use of both feet for life (II SAMUEL 4:4). He was then raised by Machir ben-Ammiel. David later invited him to Jerusalem, and there he treated him and his son Micah with great kindness (I CHRONICLES 8:34).

MERAB
("increase")

Eldest daughter of King Saul and his wife, Ahinoam, Merab was promised to whomever would be able to kill Goliath (I SAMUEL 14:49). When David slew the giant and came to claim her, it transpired that Merab was already promised to Adriel. He was given Merab's younger sister Michal instead. After David became king, he exacted his revenge by handing over Merab's five sons to the Gibeonites to be executed, in the belief that such would avoid a famine (II SAMUEL 21:8).

MERODACH
("death")
A Babylonian idol (JEREMIAH 50:2).

MERODACH-BALADAN
King of Babylonia during the reign of Hezekiah. When he found out that the king of Judah was very ill, he sent messengers, bearing gifts, to wish him a speedy recovery. Pleased, King Hezekiah showed the messenger the Temple and palace treasures, whereupon the prophet Isaiah warned that one day the Babylonians would destroy Judah and claim these treasures. Merodach-baladan was toppled by King Sargon (II KINGS 20:12).

MESHA
("freed")
1. King of Moab who was a vassal of King Ahab. When Ahab fell at Ramoth-gilead, Mesha refused to pay tribute to his successor, King Jehoram. Jehoram then solicited the assistance of Jehoshaphat, his father's ally, in forcing the Moabites to their former condition. The Moabites were duly defeated, while King Mesha took refuge in his last stronghold. He made one attempt to break through with a mere 700 men, but was beaten back. In desperation, he then offered his firstborn son, his successor in the kingdom, as a burnt offering to Chemosh, the fire god of Moab. The Israelite forces then retreated (II KINGS 3:4).
2. Son of Shaharaim by his wife, Hodesh, who bore him in the land of Moab; he later became a leader of the tribe of Benjamin (I CHRONICLES 8:9).

MESHILLEMOTH
("repaid")
Father of Berechiah of the tribe of Ephraim,

who ordered the release of the Judah prisoners that they had captured in the war between King Ahaz of Judah and King Pekah of Israel (II CHRONICLES 28:12).

MIBHAR
("chosen")
Son of Hagri, Mibhar served in the army of King David with distinction (I CHRONICLES 11:38).

MICAH
("who is like God?")
1. A man of Mount Ephraim who took 1,100

This detail of the prophet Micah from the Ghent Altarpiece was painted by Hubert van Eyck (ca 1370–1426) and Jan van Eyck (1390–1441) in 1432.

shekels of silver from his mother. When his mother cursed whoever took the silver, Micah confessed. She told her son that God would bless him, and she had two idols made for him. Micah then consecrated one of his sons to serve as priest, until he met a young Levite and made him priest instead (JUDGES 17:1). When the army of Dan set out to conquer Laish, they stopped by Micah's house and took all of the idols, as well as the Levite. The name of Laish was changed to Dan (JUDGES 18:29).

2. Son of Merib-baal (Mephibosheth), a descendant of King Saul (I CHRONICLES 8:34, 35).
3. Eldest son of Uzziel and the brother of Amram, he served the Tabernacle during the reign of King David (I CHRONICLES 23:20).
4. Son of Shimei and the father of Reaiah, who became a leader of the tribe of Reuben (I CHRONICLES 5:5).
5. Micah "the Morasthite," so called to distinguish him from Micaiah, the son of Imlah (I KINGS 22:8), was a prophet of Judah and a contemporary of Isaiah (MICAH 1:1). Micah was active "in the days of Kings Jotham, Ahaz, and Hezekiah of Judah," hence from 742 to 687 B.C.E. (MICAH 1:1). He came from Moresheth-gath in the Shephelah and spent most of his time arguing the plight of the poor in front of officials in Jerusalem. Like Amos, Micah believed that the kingdom's social ills violated the fundamental foundation of the Mosaic Law; and like Hosea, he argued that God could not be assuaged with mere sacrifices, but demanded true faith. "Will the Lord be pleased with thousands of rams?" he asked rhetorically. "What does the Lord require of you but to do justice, and to love kindness, and to walk humbly with your God?" (MICAH 6:7,8). Micah was among the first to formulate the promise of a future Messianic deliverance, which would become a major theme of Judaism in the centuries to come.
6. Father of Abdon who was a leader of Judah and was dispatched by King Josiah to ask the prophetess Huldah about the fate of Judah (II CHRONICLES 34:20). He is called Micaiah in the second Book of Kings (II KINGS 22:12).

MICAIAH
("who is like God?")
1. Son of Imlah, a prophet in Samaria during the reign of King Ahab. Ahab had proposed to Jehoshaphat, king of Judah, that they should join forces to retake the town of Ramoth-gilead from Syria. Jehoshaphat and Ahab then sat on thrones while a steady line of prophets gave their prophecy on the outcome of the battle. All of Ahab's prophets approved of the expedition, but Jehoshaphat, still dissatisfied, asked if

there was no other prophet besides the hundreds who had appeared. Ahab admitted that there was one other, Micaiah, whom he had thrown in prison. Micaiah was sent for, and he promptly condemned the plan, and prophesied that it would end in disaster, as it did. Nothing further is known of this prophet (I KINGS 22:8-28).

2. A leader of Judah, who was sent by King Jehoshaphat to teach the Book of the Law in Judah (II CHRONICLES 17:7).

3. Son of Gemariah, a leader of Judah to whom Jeremiah's oracle was read (JEREMIAH 36:12).

MICHAL
("who is like God?")
David's wife and the younger of Saul and

This illustration of "Michal Playing the Harp" was painted by French artist Jean Pichore between 1502 and 1521.

Ahinoam's two daughters (I SAMUEL 14:49-50). King Saul was envious of David's successes as an officer, and sent him to battle against the Philistines. David was victorious and, instead of marrying Michal's older sister as he had been promised, he was given Michal instead. David continued to be successful and survive Saul's multiple attempts to have him killed; Michal even helped David escape during one of her father's attempts to kill him. While David lived as a fugitive, she was forced to marry Palti, the son of Laish (I SAMUEL 25:44). David and Michal were reunited after Saul's death, but the marriage had suffered from the years of living apart. When David brought the Ark of the Covenant to Jerusalem, Michal took offense to David's excessive celebration and died with hatred toward David (I CHRONICLES 15:29).

MIKNEIAH
("possessed by God")
A Levite who performed music when the Ark of the Covenant was brought up to Jerusalem on King David's orders (I CHRONICLES 15:18,21).

MISHMANNAH
("fat")
One of the soldiers from the tribe of Gad who defected from King Saul's army and joined David instead (I CHRONICLES 12:10).

MOLECH
("king")
Principal deity of the Ammonites, worshipped as a "fire god," common to many Canaanite, Syrian, and Arab tribes. Molech was particularly infamous for child sacrifice. Despite many injunctions in the Book of Leviticus, Molech continued to be worshipped during and after the monarchy, when even Solomon allowed altars to be built for him. Josiah later destroyed the Molech sites (I KINGS 11:7; II KINGS 23:10; ISAIAH 30:33).

NAAMAN
("pleasantness")
1. Syrian commander of the armies of Benhadad II during the reign of Jehoram, king of Israel. When he was infected with leprosy, his wife's slave told her of a prophet in Samaria named Elisha. Elisha told Naaman to bathe himself seven times in the Jordan. Naaman did so, and was cured. The Syrian then pledged himself to the worship of YHWH (II KINGS 5:14).

2. Son of Benjamin who came to Egypt with Jacob (GENESIS 46:21). In the first Book of Chronicles, Naaman is described as the grandson of Benjamin, the son of Bela (I CHRONICLES 8:4).

NABAL
("foolish")
A sheep and goatherder from Carmel in the Hebron hills who was married to Abigail. David's men approached him for provisions, because they were in hiding. Nabal took offense to this and refused. When David returned with his men to retaliate, he was met by Abigail, who offered an apology and gave him what he wanted. When she later told this story to Nabal, reminding him how close he came to being killed, Nabal had a heart attack and died ten days later (I SAMUEL 25:2,4,36).

NABOTH
("fruits")
Owner of a small vineyard in Jezreel (II KINGS 9:25-26). King Ahab wanted this plot of land but because Naboth had inherited it from his father, he refused. Queen Jezebel, Ahab's wife, then arranged for Naboth to be arrested on a trumped-up blasphemy charge, and the vineyard owner was stoned to death. His property thus fell to the crown. When Ahab walked in his new garden, Elijah pronounced doom upon him (I KINGS 21:17-24).

"Nahum Announcing the Destruction of Nineveh" is an illustration from the 15th-century French Bible of Jean XXII.

NACON
("prepared")
Owner of a threshing floor where the oxen carrying the Ark of the Covenant stumbled, and where Uzzah was killed (II SAMUEL 6:6). Also named Chidon (I CHRONICLES 13:9).

NAHARAI
Born in Beeroth, he was an armor bearer of Joab, and one of David's heroes (II SAMUEL 23:37).

NAHASH
("serpent")
1. King of the Ammonites during the reign of Saul, who besieged the city of Jabesh-gilead, forcing the frightened inhabitants to sue for terms. Nahash insisted that once the city surrendered, every man, woman, and child was to lose their right eye. In desperation, the elders of Jabesh sent runners to the neighboring tribes. One of these reached Gibeah, some 40 miles south of Jabesh, on the other side of the Jordan. Here lived "a handsome young man" named Saul, "who stood head and shoulders above anyone else" (I SAMUEL 9:2). Jabesh's predicament spurred him to action. He slaughtered two oxen and sent

their bloody remains throughout Israelite territory. The pieces of flesh were a reminder of the animal sacrifice that had sealed the tribes' mutual defense pact. Before long, all of the Israelite militia mobilized and dispatched their troops to Gibeah (I SAMUEL 11:7-9). Saul deployed the soldiers around the siege works of the Ammonites. A daring attack at dawn caught the opposing forces by surprise. "They cut down the Ammonites until the heat of day," says the Bible, "and those who survived were scattered, so that no two of them were left together" (I SAMUEL 11:11).
2. Another king of the Ammonites who was kind to David while he was wandering the land (II SAMUEL 10:2). When he died, David sent his sympathies to his son and successor, Hanun. This was seen as an insult, leading to a war against the Ammonites, with the Syrians as their allies. The Syrian army suffered great losses and hesitated to help the Ammonites again (II SAMUEL 10:19).

NAHUM
("comforted")
One of the "minor prophets" and a contemporary of Habakkuk, Zephaniah, and Jeremiah, who hailed from Elkosh. In the latter part of the seventh century B.C.E., the kingdoms of the Medes and the Babylonians, former vassals of Assyria, rose against Assyria, ultimately destroying its capital, Nineveh. The impending doom of Assyria figures prominently in the oracles of the prophet Nahum, who said that "Nineveh is like a pool whose waters run away" (NAHUM 2:8). For Judah, these must have been encouraging words, given that Assyria was still a major threat. But God's power was far greater, says Nahum; the Lord "is slow to anger but great in power" (NAHUM 1:3).

NATHAN
("giving")
1. Son of Attai, a descendant from Jerahmeel, and father of Zabad (I CHRONICLES 2:36).
2. A prophet during the reigns of David and Solomon (II CHRONICLES 9:29). King David complained to Nathan how "I am living in

a house of cedar, but the ark of God stays in a tent" (II SAMUEL 7:2). Nathan then received an oracle from God, assuring David that "the Lord will make you a house"—a Davidic dynasty—but that it would be up to his offspring (in this case, Solomon) to "build a house for my name" (II SAMUEL 7:11-13). After the king arranged the death of Uriah, the husband of his lover Bathsheba, Nathan sternly rebuked David for his evil scheming because it had "displeased the Lord." Indeed, when Bathsheba conceived, the baby died (II SAMUEL 11:27). David then repented before God, and in return was promised that Bathsheba would bear him a second son; his name was Solomon.
3. Son of King David and Bathsheba (II SAMUEL 5:14; I CHRONICLES 3:5).
4. Father of Igal, one of the members of David's elite guard, and the brother of Joel (II SAMUEL 23:36; I CHRONICLES 11:38).
5. A leader of Judah in Babylon, who was sent to ask Iddo to send Levites to Jerusalem so they could serve in the Temple (EZRA 8:16).
6. Descendant of Binnui who divorced his non-Jewish wife (EZRA 10:39).

"Israelites in Chains Before Nebuchadnezzar" is an illustration from the 13th-century Beatae Elisabeth Psalter.

NATHAN-MELECH
("the gift of the king")
An official at the court of Josiah (II KINGS 23:11).

NEBUCHADNEZZAR
("Nabu protects my boundary")

Nebuchadnezzar (604–562 B.C.E.) was a leading neo-Babylonian king. Son and successor of Nabopolassar, he married the daughter of Cyaxares, uniting the Median and Babylonian dynasties. He then conquered Egypt (II KINGS 24:7) and Jerusalem (II KINGS 24,25), exiling many Hebrews, including Daniel (DANIEL 1:1-2; JEREMIAH 27:19; 40:1). Three years later, King Jehoiakim of Judah rose up against him (II KINGS 24:1). Nebuchadnezzar then took Jerusalem in 598 B.C.E. Jehoiakim's son, King Jehoiachin, surrendered to Nebuchadnezzar, who appointed Zedekiah the new king of Jerusalem. Zedekiah also rebelled, which led to Nebuchadnezzar's destruction of Jerusalem and the Temple in 586. Zedekiah escaped but was captured as a prisoner near Jericho and taken to Nebuchadnezzar where his eyes were gouged out. Nebuchadnezzar then rebuilt Babylon into a city of grandeur (DANIEL 2:37), including a new palace complex of Babylon that featured the famous "Hanging Gardens." According to ancient tradition, the gardens were built by Nebuchadnezzar to surpass the legendary palaces of his Assyrian predecessors in Nineveh and Ashhur. The king died in 562 B.C.E. at the age of 84, after a 43-year reign.

NEBUZARADAN

High-ranking Babylonian commander of Nebuchadnezzar's guard who led the capture of Jerusalem, burned the Temple, and leveled the city walls. He released the prophet Jeremiah and installed Gedaliah as governor of the new vassal state of Judah (II KINGS 25:8-20; JEREMIAH 39:11; 40:2-5).

NECHO

Pharaoh Neco who fought King Josiah at Megiddo (II KINGS 23:29) is probably King Necho II of Egypt (610–595 B.C.E.). The Egyptian king succeeded Psammetichus I (664–610 B.C.E.) and continued his policy of supporting the Assyrian king against the Median-Babylonian rebellion, going as far as to send troops to help the hard-pressed Assyrian forces on the Euphrates River. Inevitably, his army had to march through Josiah's kingdom to get there. Josiah, who had chosen the side of the Median-Babylonian rebels, impulsively decided to stop them. He met Necho's forces at Megiddo—a battle that ended in Judah's defeat. Josiah succumbed to his injuries sustained in combat (II KINGS 23:29-30). Josiah was succeeded by his son Jehoahaz, but Necho

A 13th-century French stained glass window depicts the prophet Obadiah.

peremptorily ordered him deposed and replaced by Josiah's other son, the more pliable Jehoiakim (609–598 B.C.E.), to rule as Egypt's puppet king.

NEHUSHTA

("brazen")

Daughter of Elnathan of Jerusalem, wife of Jehoiakim and mother of Jehoiachin, king of Judah (II KINGS 24:8).

NERGAL

One of the chief gods of the Assyrians and Babylonians, Nergal was the god of war and hunting (II KINGS 17:30).

NETHANIAH

("given by God")

1. One of Asaph's sons, who was appointed by David as chief musician to lead the players in the Tabernacle (I CHRONICLES 25:2,12).
2. A Levite sent by Jehoshaphat to teach the Law to the people of Judah (II CHRONICLES 17:8).
3. Son of Shelemiah and father of Jehudi, the official who read aloud Jeremiah's prophecies (JEREMIAH 36:14).
4. Son of Elishama and a descendant of Judah's royal dynasty. His son, Ishmael, assassinated Gedaliah, the governor of Judah appointed by the Babylonians (II KINGS 25:23; JEREMIAH 40:8,14-16).

NIMSHI

Grandfather of Jehu, who commanded King Jehoram's army and ousted the king in a coup; in some verses, Jehu is also referred to as Nimshi's son (I KINGS 19:16; II KINGS 9:2; II CHRONICLES 22:7).

NISROCH

An idol of Nineveh. King Sennacherib of Assyria was visiting his temple when he was assassinated by his sons, Adrammelech and Shizrezer (II KINGS 19:37; ISAIAH 37:38). This idol is identified as an eagle-headed human figure, one of the most prominent on the Assyrian monuments.

NOGAH

("bright")

One of King David's sons, born in Jerusalem (I CHRONICLES 3:7; 14:6).

NUN

("fish")

Father of Joshua (JOSHUA 1:1).

OBADIAH
("servant of the Lord")

1. Son of Izrahiah, he and his five brothers were leaders of the tribe of Issachar (I Chronicles 7:3).

2. One of 11 commanders from the tribe of Gad who left King Saul and joined David at Ziklag (I Chronicles 12:9).

3. Father of Ishmaiah who was chief of the tribe of Zebulun in David's reign (I Chronicles 27:19).

4. An officer of high rank at the court of King Ahab. He was pious and faithful in God, and during Queen Jezebel's persecution of YHWH's priests, he hid a hundred priests in a cave (I Kings 18:3-16). Later, he took the prophet Elijah to King Ahab, even though the king had placed a price on his head (I Kings 18:3).

5. One of the six sons of Azel, a descendant of Saul (I Chronicles 8:33; 9:44).

6. One of the leaders of Judah who was sent by King Jehoshaphat to teach the Torah throughout Judah (II Chronicles 17:7).

7. A Levite and descendant from Merari who supervised the reconstruction of the Temple during the reign of King Josiah (II Chronicles 34:12).

8. A leader of the tribe of Judah, and member of the royal house of King David (I Chronicles 3:21).

9. A Levite, son of Shemaiah, a descendant from Jeduthun, and one of the first Levites to settle in Jerusalem after the Babylonian exile (I Chronicles 9:16; Nehemiah 12:25).

10. Son of Jehiel, of the sons of Joab, who came up in the second caravan with Ezra (Ezra 8:9).

11. A priest who signed the covenant with Nehemiah (Nehemiah 10:5).

12. A Levite who served as a porter of the Temple Gates during the time of Nehemiah (Nehemiah 12:25).

13. One of the minor prophets who ministered after the Babylonian exile. Obadiah's short book, the shortest in Hebrew Scripture, suggests he lived in Judah after the fall of Jerusalem. The first part of his book is a polemic against Edom, one of Judah's hostile neighbors, and the other projects a vision of Judah in control of its surrounding lands. It depicts a utopian Israel in command of its destiny, and blessed with the favor of the Lord: "Those who have been saved shall go up to Mount Zion to rule Mount Esau; and the kingdom shall be the Lord's" (Obadiah 1:21).

OBED
("servant")

1. Son of Boaz and Ruth, and grandfather of David (Ruth 4:17).

2. One of David's warriors noted for his bravery (I Chronicles 11:47).

3. Son of Shemaiah and one of the gatekeepers of the Temple (I Chronicles 26:7).

4. Son of Ephlal, grandson of Zabad, and father of Jehu (I Chronicles 2:37-38).

5. Father of Azariah, one of the captains who joined with the high priest Jehoiada in the coup against Athaliah (II Chronicles 23:1).

OBED-EDOM
("servant of Edom")

1. A Philistine from Gath. After the death of Uzzah, the Ark, which was being taken from the house of Abinadab in Gibeah to the city of David, was taken aside into Obed-edom's house, where it stayed for three months. The Ark was then taken by David to Jerusalem (II Samuel 6:12; I Chronicles 15:25).

2. Son of Jeduthun, who with his eight sons guarded the Ark and played musical instruments (I Chronicles 15:18,21; I Chronicles 26:4,8,15).

3. A servant in charge of the gold and silver treasures in the Temple (II Chronicles 25:24).

ODED
("restoring")

1. Father of the prophet Azariah who ministered to King Asa of Judah (II Chronicles 15:1).

2. A prophet in Samaria at the time of King Pekah's invasion of Judah, who intervened in Pekah's forceful deportation of captives from Judah to Samaria (II Chronicles 28:9).

This ninth-century B.C.E. Phoenician ivory, depicting a palm tree, was excavated in the palace of Omri in Samaria.

OMRI
("pupil")

1. One of the sons of Becher, the son of Benjamin (I Chronicles 7:8).

2. Son of Michael, and chief of the tribe of Issachar in the reign of David (I Chronicles 27:18).

3. Sixth king of the Northern Kingdom of Israel (ca 885–874 b.c.e.). Omri was a general who had commanded the Northern forces during one of their periodic campaigns against the Philistines. While engaged in the siege of Gibbethon, which had been occupied by the Philistines, news spread that Zimri had assassinated King Elah (ca 886–885 b.c.e.). As soon as the army heard of the assassination, they proclaimed Omri king. Omri broke up the siege of Gibbethon and attacked Tirzah, where Zimri was residing as the new king of Israel. The city was taken, and Zimri was killed. The opposition to Omri's rule was eventually suppressed (I Kings 16:15). Meanwhile, the king of "Aram-Damascus," Syria, tried to exploit Israel's instability and invaded the kingdom. To face this threat, Omri first ended the long-running state of war between Israel and Judah by striking a pact with King Asa. He then signed a treaty with King Ithobaal (or "Ethbaal") of Sidon on the Phoenician coast. The alliance was sealed with the marriage of Omri's son, Ahab, to Jezebel,

The illustrator Caroline Innis painted this watercolor of "Caleb, Achsah, and Othniel" in 1827.

daughter of Ittobaal. His eastern and southern flanks thus secure, Omri lashed out at Syria, evicting its forces while conquering territory in the bargain. Omri then directed his attention to building a new capital of the North in Samaria. Omri suddenly died in 874 and was succeeded by his son Ahab (ca 874–853 B.C.E.).
4. Son of Imri, father of Ammihud; his grandson was one of the first men of Judah to return from the Babylonian exile (I CHRONICLES 9:4).

OREB
("raven")
A prince of Midian, who after his defeat by Gideon, was slain along with Zeeb (JUDGES 7:20-25). Many of the Midianites perished along with him (PSALMS 83:9; ISAIAH 10:26).

OTHNIEL
("force of God")
Son of Kenaz and nephew of Caleb, Othniel was the first Judge of Israel after the death of Joshua (JOSHUA 15:16-17; JUDGES 1:13). He gained the hand of Achsah as a reward for his bravery in conquering the town of Kirjath-sepher. After Joshua's death, the Israelites fell under the control of Cushan-rishathaim, the king of Mesopotamia. Othniel rallied the Israelites against this foreign tyrant and liberated his people (JUDGES 3:8,9-11).

OZEM
1. Sixth son of Jesse and a brother of King David (I CHRONICLES 2:15).
2. Son of Jerahmeel, and a leader of Judah (I CHRONICLES 2:25).

PALTI
("delivered")
1. One of the spies from the tribe of Benjamin who was chosen by Moses to reconnoiter the Promised Land (NUMBERS 13:9).
2. Son of Laish who married King Saul's daughter Michal, the wife of David, after Saul broke with David and made him a fugitive. When David became king, he took Michal back from Palti, who wept at her departure (I SAMUEL 25:44; II SAMUEL 3:15).

PEDAIAH
("whom God redeems")
1. Father of Zebidah, who was the wife of King Josiah and mother of King Jehoiakim (II KINGS 23:36).
2. Father of Zerubbabel (I CHRONICLES 3:17-19).
3. Father of Joel, ruler of the half tribe of Manasseh (I CHRONICLES 27:20).
4. Son of Parosh who helped repair the walls of Jerusalem after the return from the Babylonian exile (NEHEMIAH 3:25).
5. Son of Kolaiah, father of Joed and ancestor of Sallu of the tribe of Benjamin who was among the first to settle in Judah after the return from the Babylonian exile (NEHEMIAH 11:7).
6. Leader who stood by Ezra as he read the Law to the people of Judah (NEHEMIAH 8:4).
7. One of four Levites charged by Nehemiah to distribute offerings (NEHEMIAH 13:13).

PEKAH
("open-eyed")
King of Israel (ca 737–732 B.C.E.), son of Remaliah, and a commander in the army of King Pekahiah of Israel. Pekah staged a coup against Pekahiah, whom he killed and succeeded on the throne (II KINGS 15:25). Pekah recognized that Tiglath-pileser would become Israel's greatest threat and restored the Anti-Assyrian Coalition, combining Israel and Syria with the city-states of Ashkelon and Tyre. His moves were observed with alarm by the king of Judah at that time, King Ahaz (736–716 B.C.E.). In response, Ahaz brokered an alliance between Judah and Tiglath-pileser himself. The Assyrian king then brought his forces to bear and dealt a crushing defeat to Pekah's coalition. Tiglath-pileser then took "Kedesh, Hazor, Gilead, and Galilee, [and] all the land of Naphtali, and he carried the people captive to Assyria" (II KINGS 15:29). The first deportation of the Hebrew nation had begun. Pekah was assassinated and succeeded by King Hoshea, who ruled as Assyria's vassal king.

PEKAHIAH
("God watches")
Son and successor of Menahem on the throne of Israel (ca 738–737 B.C.E.). He was murdered in Samaria by Pekah, a commander in his army (II KINGS 15:23-26), after a reign of two years.

PELATIAH
("deliverance of the Lord")
1. Son of Ishi during King Hezekiah's reign who led a detachment of Simeonites; the unit drove out the Amalekites (I CHRONICLES 4:42).
2. Son of Benaiah, and one of the two leaders who appeared in a vision by Ezekiel at the city gates, giving false counsel to Ezekiel (EZEKIEL 11:1-13).
3. Son of Hananiah and a grandson of Zerubbabel who led the return from exile in Babylon (I CHRONICLES 3:21).
4. A leader of Judah who signed the covenant with Nehemiah (NEHEMIAH 10:22).

PENINNAH
("pearl")
One of the two wives of Elkanah, the father of the prophet Samuel. Though Peninnah had given her husband several children, he favored his other wife, Hannah, who would give birth to Samuel (I SAMUEL 1:2,4).

PETHUEL
("vision of God")
Father of the prophet Joel (JOEL 1:1).

PIRAM
("wild ass")
Amorite king of Jarmuth, who joined with four other kings to attack the Gibeonites. He was defeated and put to death by Joshua (JOSHUA 10:3,23,26).

RAHAB
("broad," "large")
1. A prostitute who lived on the city walls of Jericho and aided Joshua and the Israelites in capturing the city (JOSHUA 2:1-7). She and her family were subsequently moved to safety (JOSHUA 6:17-25).
2. A poetic name for Egypt, signifying "fierceness, pride" (PSALMS 89:10; ISAIAH 51:9).

RECHAB
("horseman," "chariot")
1. One of the commanders of King Saul's son Ishbosheth who served under General Abner. When Abner died, Rechab and his brother Baanah recognized that Ishbosheth's claim on the throne was a lost cause, and decided to kill him so as to ingratiate themselves with David. Horrified, David ordered both men put to death, and ordered a proper burial for Ishbosheth (II SAMUEL 4:2,5-12).
2. Father of Jonadab, who supported Jehu's coup against King Ahab and the subsequent destruction of the Baal cult. Founder of the Rechabites movement, an ascetic group that abstained from drinking wine and lived in tents (II KINGS 10:15,33; I CHRONICLES 2:65; JEREMIAH 35:6-19).
3. Father of Malchiah, ruler of part of Beth-haccerem (NEHEMIAH 3:14).

REHOB
("width")
1. Father of Hadadezer, king of Zobah, who was killed by David in battle (II SAMUEL 8:3,12; NEHEMIAH 10:11).

2. Levite who returned from the Babylonian exile and signed the covenant during Nehemiah's time (NEHEMIAH 10:11).

REHOBOAM
("increase of the nation")
Solomon's successor on the throne, King Rehoboam (931 to 913 B.C.E.) was Solo-

"Rahab and the Spies" is an early 20th-century British illustration.

mon's only son by Naamah, an Ammonite princess (I KINGS 14:21; II CHRONICLES 12:13). He was acknowledged as the rightful heir to the throne, but the northern chieftains gave him a long list of grievances and demanded relief from the king. Solomon's wealth had been built on the backs of their taxes, their fruits of the field, and their hard labor; now they wanted that heavy yoke lifted. "Lighten the hard service of your father . . . and we will serve you," the elders stated (I KINGS 12:4). After three days, Rehoboam told them that he would not give in and instead "add to your yoke," warning that "My father disciplined you with whips, but I will discipline you with scorpions" (I KINGS 12:14). This led to a rupture of the kingdom; the northern tribes broke away, leaving Rehoboam only in charge of the southern state of Benjamin and Judah, with Jerusalem as its capital. The

northern ten tribes formed themselves into a separate kingdom, choosing Jeroboam as their king. Rehoboam wanted to declare war to win back the North, but he was dissuaded by the prophet Shemaiah (I KINGS 12:21-24; II CHRONICLES 11:1-4). Pharaoh Shoshenq I then decided to attack the new kingdom of Judah around 918 B.C.E. Rehoboam had no choice but to pay the Egyptian king a hefty ransom, consisting of "the treasures of the house of the Lord and the treasures of the king's house; he took everything" (I KINGS 14:25-26). Impoverished, the king of Judah nevertheless continued to maintain a lavish court of 18 wives, 60 concubines, 28 sons, and 60 daughters. He died after a reign of 17 years, and his crown passed to his son Abijah by his favorite wife, Maacah (I KINGS 11:43). The kingdom of Judah, under Rehoboam, sank deeper into moral and spiritual decay. "There was war between Rehoboam and Jeroboam all their days." At age 58, Rehoboam "slept with his fathers, and was buried with his fathers in the city of David" (I KINGS 14:31). He was succeeded by his son Abijah.

REPHAIAH
("healed by God")
1. Son of Tola, grandson of Issachar, and leader of a tribe of mighty warriors (I CHRONICLES 7:2).
2. Son of Ishi of the tribe of Simeon who commanded the 500 men who drove the Amalekites from Mount Seir (I CHRONICLES 4:42).
3. Descendant of King David and contemporary of Zerubbabel (I CHRONICLES 3:21).
4. Son of Hur, who ruled part of Jerusalem during Nehemiah's time and helped rebuild the walls of Jerusalem (NEHEMIAH 3:9).

REZIN
("firm")
1. King of Aram-Damascus who attacked King Ahaz of Judah in collusion with King Pekah of Israel. Though unsuccessful in his siege of Jerusalem, he "recovered Elath to Syria" (II KINGS 16:6). Ahaz turned to the Assyrian King Tiglath-pileser III for help, accepting Assyrian vassal status as the price. The Assyrian king then came to Ahaz's rescue

by investing Damascus and killing King Rezin (II KINGS 16:9).

2. Head of a family of Temple servants who returned with Zerubbabel from exile in Babylon (EZRA 2:48; NEHEMIAH 7:50).

REZON

Son of Eliada and commander of the army of Hadadezer, the king of Zobah. After Zobah was defeated by David, Rezon fled with a "band" of marauders. He eventually took Damascus and became king of Syria (I KINGS 11:23-25).

RIZPAH

("hot stone")

Daughter of Aiah, concubine to King Saul and mother of his sons Armoni and Mephibosheth (II SAMUEL 3:7; 21:8,10-11). After Saul's death, General Abner made moves to marry her, but was prevented from doing so by Saul's successor, Ishbosheth or Ishbaal. During David's reign, the people of Gibeon demanded that all of Saul's children be put to death so as to atone for a severe famine. David had no choice but to comply. Rizpah's children, as well as five grandsons by Saul's eldest daughter, were put to death. The moving story of the love with which she watched over the bodies of her two sons made Rizpah one of the most tragic figures in the Bible (II SAMUEL 21:8-11).

RUTH

("beloved")

Ruth was the Moabite wife of Mahlon, whose father Elimelech and mother Naomi had settled in the land of Moab because of a famine in their hometown of Bethlehem. On the death of both Elimelech and Mahlon, Naomi prepared to move back to Bethlehem and told Ruth to return to her own family. Ruth decided to stay with her, saying, "Where you go, I will go" (RUTH 1:16). In Bethlehem, Ruth sustained herself and her mother-in-law by gleaning kernels from the barley harvest. There she had a rich relative, Boaz, to whom Ruth was eventually married. She then became the mother of Obed, the grandfather of David. Ruth, a Gentile, is mentioned in Matthew's genealogy of Jesus (MATTHEW 1:5).

SAMSON

("like the sun")

Son of Manoah, Samson hailed from the tribe of Dan and was one of the Judges (JUDGES 13:3-5). Dan had been occupied by the Philistines, forcing many Hebrews to flee and settle in the highlands. Thus, Samson grew up in the village of Zorah. He met a Philistine girl from the village of Timnah and decided to marry her. He staged a great wedding feast, but a dispute over a riddle broke out with some of his Philistine guests. Enraged, Samson killed 30 Philistines in the nearby town of Ashkelon (JUDGES 14:19). His longing for his bride drove him back to Timnah, only to be told that she had been married to a Philistine—his best man. Samson took his revenge by capturing 300 foxes, tying their tails together and placing flaming torches in the knots, and chasing them across the nearby fields to destroy their harvest (JUDGES 15:4-5). A large Philistine force was dispatched to

Artus Quellinus the Elder (1609–1668) created this terra-cotta sculpture of "Samson and Delilah" around 1640.

capture Samson, but he killed a thousand of them with the jawbone of an ass. Samson's weakness for beautiful Philistine women soon drove him into the arms of a woman named Delilah. The Philistines offered Delilah a large sum of money if she could discover the source of Samson's great strength. Under pressure, Samson told her that he would lose his strength "if my head were shaved" (JUDGES 16:15-17). While he slept, the faithless Delilah brought in a Philistine who cut Samson's hair, draining his strength. The Philistines took him prisoner, gouged out his eyes, and forced him to work as a draft animal, turning a mill in a Gaza prison. While in captivity, Samson's hair gradually grew back. One day, the Philistines held a great ceremony in their temple, which was devoted to the god Dagon. Samson was brought out and tied between two pillars. As the crowd around him jeered, Samson prayed to God for a restoration of his powers, "only this once." God granted his request; Samson pushed the pillars and brought down the temple roof, killing all those inside (JUDGES 16:30). He was buried in the tomb of his father Manoah near the village of Zorah.

SAMUEL

("God heard")

Son of Elkanah and Hannah, Samuel was born at Ramathaimzophim, among the hills of Ephraim. Before his birth, he was dedicated by his mother to the office of a Nazarite; as a young child he was placed in the shrine at Shiloh and ministered there (SAMUEL 1:11,20, 23-28). While here, he received his first prophetic call

(I Samuel 3:1-18). Around this time, the Philistines launched their long-awaited assault on the Israelites near the city of Aphek. The Hebrew defenses crumbled, and the Philistines were able to capture the Ark of the Covenant. For 20 years after this fatal battle, the whole land lay under the oppression of the Philistines. During all these dreary years, Samuel was a spiritual power in the land, visiting the three chief sanctuaries to the west of Jordan—Bethel, Gilgal, and Mizpeh (I Samuel 7:16). The Israelite tribes realized

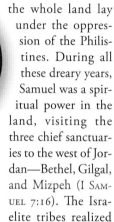

A seventh-century Byzantine silver plate from Constantinople shows David being anointed by Samuel.

that to defeat the Philistines, they had to act in unison. They approached Samuel and asked that he appoint a king or a supreme commander, so that "we can be also like other nations, and that our king may . . . fight our battles" (I Samuel 8:19-20). Samuel was reluctant to do so. "[A king] will take the best of your fields," he warned; "he will take your male and female slaves, and the best of your cattle and donkeys, and put them to his work" (I Samuel 8:14-16). God however charged Samuel to anoint a young man named Saul, from the tribe of Benjamin, as the "ruler over my people Israel" (I Samuel 9:16). Saul did win many battles against enemy forces, including the Amalekites, but he failed in his mission to defeat the greatest threat to the nation of Israel, the Philistines. "I regret that I made Saul king," said the Lord in the first Book of Samuel; "he has not carried out my commands" (I Samuel 15:11). This is when God sent Samuel to Jesse from Bethlehem to search for a new leader, "a king among his sons" (I Samuel 16:1). His choice fell upon Jesse's youngest son David, a humble shepherd who was nevertheless blessed with exceptional musical skills. When Samuel died, "all the Israelites were gathered together" from all parts of the country, and "buried him" within his own house (I Samuel 25:1).

SAPH

A giant in the Philistine army killed by a soldier in David's army (II Samuel 21:18). He is also called Sippai (I Chronicles 20:4).

SARGON
("lawful king")

One of the greatest of the Assyrian kings, Sargon II (721–705 b.c.e.) was the successor of Shalmaneser. He continued Shalmaneser's siege of Samaria and took the capital, after which he "carried the Israelites away to Assyria . . . (and) . . . placed them in Halah, on Habor, by the river of Gozan, and in the cities of the Medes" (II Kings 17:6). In their stead, Sargon moved various other subject peoples, mostly Babylonians and people from Aram-Damascus, into the settlements in Samaria. These included settlers from Babylon, from Cuthah (possibly Tell Ibrahim, northeast of Babylon), Avva (or Awa in eastern Babylonia), Hamath (a major Syrian trade city on the Orontes River), and Sepharvaim (possibly Shabarain in Aram-Damascus) (II Kings 17:24).

SAUL
("loaned")

1. First king of Israel, son of Kish, and of the tribe of Benjamin. He is noted for his strength (II Samuel 1:25), height, and attractiveness (I Samuel 9:2). He was likely born in Zelah in Benjamin (II Samuel 21:14). Saul met Samuel, who had been charged by God to anoint a young man from the tribe of Benjamin as the "ruler over my people Israel" while in search of a group of asses gone astray. Samuel poured the consecrated oil over Saul's head, and with a kiss announced to him that he was to be king (I Samuel 9:25; 10:1). Returning to Gibeah, Saul heard about the threat of Nahash, king of Ammon, against Jabesh-gilead and led an army to rescue Jabesh (I Samuel 11:1-15). In the second year of his reign, he formed an army to drive the Philistines back to their own country; he steadily evicted them from the highlands, but failed to achieve a decisive victory. Despite Hebrew triumphs at the battles of Bozez and Michmash, the conflict evolved into a protracted war of attrition. Meanwhile, Samuel had chosen David as the new future king of

Israel (I Samuel 16:1). Saul liked David's harp playing, and appointed the young man as his armor bearer. David slew the giant Goliath, which endeared him to the people and forced Saul to promote him. Even though David married Saul's then daughter Michal and became a close friend of Saul's son Jonathan, an intense rivalry developed between the young new general and the king. Saul even began to plot to kill him. David had little choice but to flee to enemy territory, the Philistine-held coastal plains. Saul forced his daughter Migdal to marry another man, whereupon David took a woman named Ahinoam, a local woman from the Jezreel. Meanwhile, Philistine forces were amassing at Mount Gilboa, and Saul and his sons, all serving as commanders in his army, rushed to meet them. But God had turned against Saul,

This eighth-century B.C.E. bas-relief of King Sargon II of Assyria was taken from Sargon's Palace at Khorsabad, Mesopotamia.

and the Israelite ranks were decimated. All of Saul's sons fell to Philistine swords, including his heir, Jonathan. Badly wounded himself, Saul ordered his armor bearer to finish him off, but the man refused. Saul then fell upon his own sword (I Samuel 31:1-7). His corpse, and those of his sons, were dragged by the Philistines to the walls of Beth She'an and hung from the walls.

2. Original Hebrew name of Paul, apostle to the Gentiles (Acts 7:58).

King Sennacherib watches on his throne as prisoners from Lachish are being executed in this relief from Nineveh, around 700 B.C.E.

SENNACHERIB

Son of Sargon, whom he succeeded on the throne of Assyria (704–681 B.C.E.). When King Hezekiah of Judah plotted a new rebellion against Assyria with help from Egypt, Sennacherib marched to Jerusalem and laid waste to Judah (II KINGS 18:17,19,37; II CHRONICLES 32:9-23; ISAIAH 36:2-22). "King Sennacherib of Assyria came up against all the fortified cities of Judah and captured them," the second Book of Kings notes (II KINGS 18:13). Hezekiah rushed to appease the Assyrian king. He ransacked the Temple to come up with a ransom, and gave Sennacherib "all the silver that was found in the house of the Lord" (II KINGS 18:15). Sennacherib wasn't interested in money; he wanted Jerusalem itself. But Sennacherib's siege of Jerusalem failed, because "the angel of the Lord set out and struck down" 185,000 soldiers in the Assyrian camp (II KINGS 19:35). Sennacherib withdrew and never renewed his attempt against Jerusalem. He was murdered by two of his sons, Adrammelech and Sharezer, and succeeded by another son, Esar-haddon.

SERAIAH
("warrior of God")

1. Secretary in the court of King David; his two sons also served King Solomon in that capacity (II SAMUEL 8:17).
2. Son of Azariah, and high priest of the Temple. After the destruction of Jerusalem, Seraiah was killed by the king of Babylon (II KINGS 25:18).
3. Officer of the Judean army who joined Gedaliah upon his appointment as governor of Judah (II KINGS 25:23).
4. Son of Kenaz, brother of Othniel of Judah, and the head of a family of craftsmen (I CHRONICLES 4:13).
5. Grandfather of Jehu who was a leader of the Simeon tribe (I CHRONICLES 4:35).
6. One of the men who seized Jeremiah and his scribe Baruch upon orders of King Jehoiakim (JEREMIAH 36:26).
7. Son of Neriah and official of King Zedekiah, Seraiah joined the king in exile in Babylon (JEREMIAH 51:59).
8. One of the men who returned with Zerubbabel from Babylonian exile (EZRA 2:2).
9. Son of Azariah, grandson of Hilkiah, descendant of Eleazar. His son was Ezra the scribe (EZRA 7:1).
10. Priest who signed Nehemiah's covenant (NEHEMIAH 10:2).
11. One of the priests who returned to Jerusalem after the Babylonian exile (I CHRONICLES 9:11).

SHALLUM
("reward")

1. Son of Shaul, father of Mibsam, and grandson of Simeon (I CHRONICLES 4:25).
2. Son of Sismai, and father of Jekamiah (I CHRONICLES 2:40).
3. Son of Kore, and descendant of Korah. Shallum was chosen to be in charge of the East Gate of the Tabernacle during the reign of King David (I CHRONICLES 9:17).
4. Fifteenth king of Israel who reigned for one month in 743 B.C.E. He gained the throne in a coup that overthrew King Zechariah, but was assassinated himself a month later by his successor Menahem (II KINGS 15:10-15).
5. Father of Jehizkiah, a leader of Ephraim who intervened for the prisoners of Judah captured by Israel's army during King Pekah's reign (II CHRONICLES 28:12).
6. Husband of Huldah the prophetess, son of Tikvah, and grandson of Harhas, who was the keeper of the royal wardrobe in the court of King Josiah (II KINGS 22:14).
7. King of Judah, after the partition of the United Monarchy (I CHRONICLES 3:15).
8. Son of Zadok, and father of Hilkiah, the high priest during King Josiah's reign (I CHRONICLES 6:12).
9. Father of Hanameel, and uncle of the prophet Jeremiah (JEREMIAH 32:7).
10. Father of Maaseiah who was the Temple gatekeeper during the reign of King Jehoiakim (JEREMIAH 35:4).
11. Temple gatekeeper who divorced his foreign wife in the time of Ezra (EZRA 10:24).
12. Son of Naphtali, and grandson of Jacob and Bilhah. He was one of the 70 Israelites who immigrated to Egypt (I CHRONICLES 7:13).

This Phoenician ivory plaque depicting a winged sphinx is dated to the ninth or eighth century B.C.E.

13. A descendant of Binhui who divorced his foreign wife in the time of Ezra (EZRA 10:42).
14. Son of Halohesh, who was the chief of half the district of Jerusalem. He helped to repair the walls in Jerusalem (NEHEMIAH 3:12).

SHALMANESER V

King of Assyria (727–721 B.C.E.), who attacked Samaria after King Hoshea of Israel stopped paying the yearly tribute. He vowed to destroy Samaria once and for all (II KINGS 17:5), but in a leisurely fashion. A lengthy siege followed—so long, in fact, that Shalmaneser died before it did result in Samaria's destruction under his successor, Sargon II.

SHAMGAR

("sword")
Son of Anath and third Judge of Israel after Ehud. He fought against the Philistines, and killed 600 men with an ox goad (JUDGES 3:31).

SHAMMAH

("ruin")
1. Son of Reuel, grandson of Esau and Basemath, and leader of Edom (GENESIS 36:13).
2. Son of Jesse and brother of David. He fought with his brothers Eliab and Abinadab in Saul's army against the Philistines (I SAMUEL 16:9). He was also known as Shimma, Shimea, and Shimeah (I CHRONICLES 2:13,20; II SAMUEL 13:3).
3. Son of Agee and one of David's three renowned soldiers, and a member of "the 30," an elite group in King David's army (II SAMUEL 23:11-12,25). He was also known as Shammoth and Shamhuth (I CHRONICLES 11:27-28).

SHAMMUA

("heard")
1. Son of Zaccur of Reuben. He was one of 12 men sent by Moses to scout Canaan (NUMBERS 13:4).
2. Son of King David, born while David was in Jerusalem (I CHRONICLES 14:4). He is also known as Shimea (II SAMUEL 5:14; I CHRONICLES 3:5).
3. Leader of a family of priests, descended from Bilgah, who served as chief priest of Judah toward the end of Nehemiah's lifetime (NEHEMIAH 12:18).

SHAPHAN

("rabbit")
1. Son of Azaliah and grandfather of Gehaliah who was the scribe of King Josiah (II KINGS 22:3). His son Ahikam saved the prophet Jeremiah from being executed by King Jehoiakim (II KINGS 22:3).
2. Father of Jaazaniah, a leader of Judah denounced by the prophet Ezekiel for sacrificing to idols near the Temple (EZEKIEL 8:11).

Konrad Witz (ca 1400–1446) painted "The Queen of Sheba before Solomon" around 1435–1437.

SHAREZER

("prince")
Son of Sennacherib who with his brother, Adrammelech, murdered their father, and then fled into the land of Armenia (II KINGS 19:37). His brother Esar-haddon ascended to the throne.

SHEAR-JASHUB

("a remnant shall return")
Son of prophet Isaiah whom God ordered to go with Isaiah to meet with King Ahaz of Judah (ISAIAH 7:3). His name refers to Isaiah's prophecy that even though Judah will be destroyed, a remnant would survive.

SHEBA

1. Son of Joktan, a descendant of Shem (GENESIS 10:28).
2. Son of Jokshan, and grandson of Abraham and Keturah (GENESIS 25:3).
3. A leader of the tribe of Gad, east of the Jordan (I CHRONICLES 5:13).
4. Queen of Sheba, a kingdom in southern Arabia, possibly the kingdom of Saba, which traded in spices with the other peoples of the ancient world. They were Semites, speaking one of the two main dialects of Himyaritic or South Arabic. The queen brought King Solomon gold, spices, and precious stones (I KINGS 10:1-13).
5. Son of Bichri, of the Benjamin tribe, who raised the standard of revolt against King David after the defeat of Absalom. With his followers, he proceeded northward. David ordered Joab to take all such troops as he could gather and pursue Sheba. Sheba then took refuge in Abel-Beth Maachah, a fortified town some miles north of Lake Merom. Joab besieged the city, but a woman reminded him of the town's loyalty to David. Joab agreed to lift the siege if the town would hand over Sheba. This they did, by cutting off his head and sending it to Joab (II SAMUEL 20).

SHEBNA

("may God sit")
Scribe and counselor to King Hezekiah. Shebna was sent with a delegation to negotiate with the invading Assyrians, but after negotiations failed, he went to the prophet Isaiah, who told them the Assyrian army would withdraw without taking Jerusalem (II KINGS 18:18). He was replaced by Eliakim, as Isaiah had foretold (ISAIAH 22:15-25).

SHELEMIAH

("whom God repays")
1. Son of Cushi and father of Nethaniah, his grandson Jehudi read Jeremiah's prophecies to King Jehoiakim (JEREMIAH 36:14).
2. Son of Abdeel and an officer of King Jehoiakim who was ordered to arrest Baruch and Jeremiah upon hearing the prophet's oracles (JEREMIAH 36:26) (604 B.C.E.).
3. Father of Jehucal who was sent by King Zedekiah to ask the prophet Jeremiah to pray for Judah during the Babylonian siege (JEREMIAH 37:3; 38:1).
4. Son of Hananiah and the father of Irijah, the captain who falsely accused Jeremiah of defecting to the Babylonians (JEREMIAH 37:13).

5. Name of two descendants of Binnui who divorced their non-Jewish wives (Ezra 10:39,41).

6. Father of Hananiah who helped repair the walls of Jerusalem (Nehemiah 3:30).

7. A priest of Judah who was made treasurer by Nehemiah in charge of the distribution of corn, wine, and oil (Nehemiah 13:13).

This terra-cotta plaque of a seated harpist from Mesopotamia is dated to the beginning of the second millennium B.C.E.

SHEMAIAH

("God has heard")

1. Father of Shimri who was an ancestor of Ziza. He was one of the leaders of the tribe of Simeon who went to the valley of Gedor looking for pasture for their flocks of sheep (I Chronicles 4:37).

2. The prophet Shemaiah lived during the reign of King Rehoboam, whom he wrote a book about (I Kings 12:22). When the king assembled a large army from the tribes of Judah and Benjamin to suppress the rebellious tribes of the North, Shemaiah advised him not to go to war. When Pharaoh Shishak invaded Judah, he told the king that God was punishing Judah for forsaking him. The king and his men agreed,

did not resist, and thus became a vassal kingdom of Egypt.

3. Leader of a family of Levites during the reign of King David, who participated in the ceremony of bringing the Ark of the Covenant to Jerusalem (I Chronicles 15:8).

4. Son of Nethanel, he was a scribe during the reign of King David (I Chronicles 24:6).

5. Firstborn son of Obed-edom who was a gatekeeper of the Tabernacle during the reign of King David (I Chronicles 26:4).

6. A Levite who was sent by King Jehoshaphat in the third year of his reign to teach the Laws of God in the cities of Judah (II Chronicles 17:8).

7. One of the Levites who obeyed the order of King Hezekiah of Judah to purify the Temple (II Chronicles 29:14).

8. A Levite who was charged with the distribution of offerings during the reign of King Hezekiah (II Chronicles 31:15).

9. One of the Levites during the reign of King Josiah who donated a large herd of cattle as Passover sacrifice (II Chronicles 35:9).

10. A leading priest of Judah who returned to Jerusalem with Zerubbabel from the Babylonian exile (Nehemiah 12:6).

11. Father of the prophet Urijah who hailed from Kiriath-jearim and was put to death by Jehoiakim for his prophecy of Jerusalem's destruction (Jeremiah 26:20).

12. A false prophet of Judah who was taken to exile by the Babylonians, and who told the priest Zephaniah that the exile would be short lived (Jeremiah 29:24).

13. Father of Delaiah, one of the leaders who reported Jeremiah's oracles to King Jehoiakim (Jeremiah 36:12).

14. Son of Shechaniah and a leader of the tribe of Judah. Shechaniah was a keeper of the East Gate of Jerusalem (I Chronicles 3:22).

15. Son of Hasshub and one of the first Levites to settle in Jerusalem after the Babylonian exile (I Chronicles 9:14).

16. Son of Joel and the father of Gog and an ancestor of Beerah. He was the leader of the tribe of Reuben who was taken captive by Tiglath-pileser, the king of Assyria (I Chronicles 5:4).

17. Son of Galal, a descendant of Jeduthun and the father of Obadiah, who was

responsible for the prayer of Thanksgiving in the Temple (I Chronicles 9:16).

18. Descendant of Adonikam who returned with Ezra to Jerusalem from the Babylonian exile (Ezra 8:13).

19. A priest and descendant of Harim, who divorced his non-Jewish wife (Ezra 10:21).

20. Son of Delaiah, who invited Nehemiah for a secret meeting in the Temple. Suspecting a trap, Nehemiah declined (Nehemiah 6:10).

21. One of the priests who signed Nehemiah's solemn agreement (Nehemiah 10:8).

22. One of the leaders of Judah who participated in the ceremonies dedicating the rebuilt walls of Jerusalem (Nehemiah 12:34).

23. Grandfather of Zechariah, one of the priests who blew a trumpet during the ceremonies dedicating the rebuilt walls of Jerusalem (Nehemiah 12:35).

24. A Levite who played a musical instrument during the ceremonies dedicating the rebuilt walls of Jerusalem (Nehemiah 12:36).

SHIMEI

("famous")

1. A Reubenite who lived in Aroer, east of the Jordan (I Chronicles 5:4).

2. Son of Gershon and the grandson of Levi, his descendants were Levites who ministered in the Tabernacle (Numbers 3:18; I Chronicles 6:17,29).

3. Son of Zaccur and a leader of the tribe of Simeon (I Chronicles 4:26-27).

4. A Levite and son of Libni, and a descendant of Merari (I Chronicles 6:29).

5. A Levite, son of Jahath and grandson of Gershon, he was the father of Zimmah and an ancestor of Asaph, one of King David's musicians (I Chronicles 6:42).

6. Leader of the tribe of Benjamin who lived in Jerusalem (I Chronicles 8:21).

7. Son of Gera and a Benjamite of the house of Saul, who threw stones at David as he passed through the town of Bahurim in his flight from Jerusalem during Absalom's rebellion (II Samuel 16:5-13). After the defeat of Absalom, Shimei humbly begged for forgiveness (II Samuel 19:16-23). David forgave him; but on his deathbed, he told Solomon to "bring his grey head down with blood to Sheol" (I Kings 2:9). When Shimei left on an unauthorized journey to Gath to retrieve two of his slaves that had run away, Solomon ordered Benaiah to kill him.

8. One of David's mighty men who refused to acknowledge Adonijah as David's successor (I KINGS 1:8).

9. Son of Ela and one of 12 officers charged with the royal household of King Solomon (I KINGS 4:18).

10. Officer of King David who was responsible for the king's vineyards (I CHRONICLES 27:27).

11. One of the Levites descended from Heman who gathered to purify the Temple during the reign of King Hezekiah of Judah (II CHRONICLES 29:14).

12. Brother and deputy of Conaniah, leader of the Levites who were responsible for the offerings at the Temple during the time of King Hezekiah (II CHRONICLES 31:12).

13. Son of Pedaiah of the tribe of Judah and the brother of Zerubbabel, who led the return from the Babylonian exile (I CHRONICLES 3:19).

14. A Levite, who divorced his non-Jewish wife during Ezra's time (EZRA 10:23).

15. Descendant of Hashum, who divorced his non-Jewish wife during Ezra's time (EZRA 10:33).

16. Descendant of Binnui, who divorced his non-Jewish wife during Ezra's time (EZRA 10:38).

17. Son of Kish of the tribe of Benjamin, father of Jair, and grandfather of Mordecai who stopped the plot of King Ahasuerus to kill all Jews in the Persian Empire (ESTHER 2:5)

The silver sarcophagus with a falcon head is believed to contain the remains of Pharaoh Shishak or Shoshenq I (ca 945–925 B.C.E.).

"The Death of Sisera" was painted by Palma Il Giovane (1548–1628).

SHISHAK

Pharaoh Shishak or Shoshenq (I KINGS 14:25-26), the king of Egypt and the first sovereign of the Bubastite 22nd Dynasty. At the beginning of his reign, he received the fugitive Jeroboam (I KINGS 11:40). It was probably at his instigation that Shishak then attacked King Rehoboam of Judah. He took away all the treasures of the Temple and the royal palace in Jerusalem. He also raided most of Israel's principal cities, including Megiddo; archaeologists have found part of a victory inscription at Megiddo, dedicated to Shishak's triumph. The pharaoh left another record of this expedition sculptured on the "Bubastite Portal" of the great temple of Karnak.

SHOBACH
("expansion")
Captain of the army of Hadadezer, king

of Zobah in Syria, who was killed by King David in battle (II SAMUEL 10:16,18). In I Chronicles 19:16, he is called Shophach.

SHOBI
("captive")
Son of Nahash from Rabbah of the Ammonites. He showed kindness to David by bringing him supplies when he fled from Jerusalem to Mahanaim (II SAMUEL 17:27).

SISERA
("leader")
1. Canaanite commander of King Jabin's army of Hazor (JUDGES 4:2). The prophetess Prophetess and Judge Deborah was determined to establish Israelite power in the Jezreel Valley. She rallied several Israelite tribes, which rode out to face the Canaanite army at Mount Tabor under command of General Barak. As soon as Sisera's 900 chariots were given the order to advance, God unleashed a rainstorm that flooded the Jezreel Valley and stranded the chariots in the mud. Barak's militia made short work of them. Sisera then fled to the settlement of Heber the Kenite in the plain of Zaanaim. Jael, Heber's wife, brought him into her tent and fed him. After he fell asleep, Jael crept up to him and used a mallet to drive a tent peg through his temple (JUDGES 4:11-21; 5:24). Part of Deborah's song of victory includes a moving reference to Sisera's mother, waiting anxiously for her son to return, while her maids try to distract her (JUDGES 5:24-27).

2. Ancestor of temple servants who returned from the Babylonian exile with Zerubbabel (EZRA 2:53; NEHEMIAH 7:55).

SO
("a measure for grain")
King So is probably Osorkon IV (775–750 B.C.E.), who

was solicited by King Hoshea of Israel to join the rebellion against Assyria (II KINGS 17:4).

SOLOMON
("peaceful")

King Solomon (970 to 931 B.C.E.) was the son of King David and his favorite wife, Bathsheba (II SAMUEL 5:14). He was raised as a royal prince among many, but his chances of succeeding to the throne were improved when several of his half brothers, including

Flemish Baroque artist Frans Francken II (1581–1642) painted "Solomon and the Queen of Sheba."

Amnon and Absalom, were killed. Still, the son with the greatest legitimate claim was Adonijah, David's son by his wife Haggith, who was supported by Joab, David's senior general, as well as one of the high priests attending the Tabernacle, named Abiathar. So confident was Adonijah of his impending anointment that he decided to throw a celebration party at the springs of En-rogel, in the Kidron Valley, at which all of his brothers were invited—except Solomon. But Bathsheba had extracted David's promise that their son Solomon would succeed him. David moved quickly to preempt Adonijah's impending coronation. He ordered that Solomon be taken to the Gihon Spring and be anointed as king by

Zadok the priest (I KINGS 1:34). After King David died, Adonijah wanted permission to marry Abishag who had served King David as nurse and concubine in his old age. Rather than grant Adonijah permission to do so, Solomon ordered Benaiah to kill him. Benaiah also executed Joab, who had opposed Solomon's bid to the throne. When God appeared to Solomon in a dream, he asked God to give him a wise and understanding heart as well as the ability to judge good from bad (I KINGS 3:9). God was pleased to grant him his wish (I KINGS 3:11-12). According to the Books of Kings, Solomon became one of the wisest, wealthiest, and most powerful kings of the eastern lands. The most famous example of Solomon's just and wise ways was the case of two prostitutes disputing maternity of a baby. The king was able to identify the real mother by studying the reaction of each woman to the suggestion that the child be divided into two halves. Solomon also used his wisdom to create a modern administrative apparatus, dividing his realm into 12 districts that deliberately cut across tribal boundaries so as to further centralize power in Jerusalem. To pacify tribal sensibilities, he continued his father's policy of marrying wives from many tribes, as well as from those nations with whom he struck an alliance. One of these foreign wives was an Egyptian princess, daughter of Pharaoh (I KINGS 11:1); her father was probably Siamun of the 21st Dynasty (ca 978–959 B.C.E.). As wealth poured into his treasury, Solomon fulfilled God's promise to David: to build a true sanctuary to house the Ark of the Covenant. When this massive project was finished, a new Temple of white and gold had risen over Jerusalem. In addition to the Temple sanctuary proper, there were residential buildings for Solomon's staff, servants, and his extensive harem, although Pharaoh's daughter was housed in a separate pavilion for her private use (I KINGS 7:8). At the same time, Solomon built a ring of strongholds to protect his kingdom, with fortresses in Megiddo, Hazor, and Gezer. People came from all over to see the splendor of his court. Even the Queen of Sheba came for a visit and was amazed by the

magnitude of his wealth. His closest ally was Hiram, king of Tyre, who was a friend as well as a commercial partner. But Solomon's kingdom could not last forever. As soon as the old king died and was laid to rest, tribal support for a unified Israel began to crumble, and the kingdom split under his successor, King Rehoboam.

TABEEL
("God is good")

1. Father of a pretender to the throne of Judah, whose claim was supported by the kings of Syria and Israel in their war against King Ahaz (ISAIAH 7:6).

2. Governor of Samaria who wrote a letter to Artaxerxes, king of Persia, to prevent the reconstruction of the Temple in Jerusalem (EZRA 4:7).

TAHPENES
("Egyptian wife of the king")

Egyptian queen and wife of Pharaoh during the reign of King David. She married her sister to Hadad the Edomite, who had fled from David (I KINGS 11:19-20).

TAMAR
("palm")

1. Wife of Judah's elder sons Er and Onan, who both died before Tamar could have children. Judah refused to marry her to a third son for fear that he would die as well, so Tamar disguised herself as a prostitute and slept with Judah instead; she bore him twin sons, Perez and Zerah (GENESIS 38:6; RUTH 4:12).

2. Beautiful daughter of David and Maacah. Tamar was raped by her half brother Amnon, David's firstborn son by his wife, Ahinoam. Tamar's brother Absalom then killed Amnon during a sheepshearing festival, which forced him to go into hiding to escape David's wrath (II SAMUEL 13:1-32; I CHRONICLES 3:9).

3. Daughter of Absalom and granddaughter of King David (II SAMUEL 14:27).

TAMMUZ

(Syrian "sprout")

Akkadian sun god. In the Babylonian calendar, one month was dedicated to this god, beginning the summer solstice. He was also worshipped by people in Judah; the prophet Ezekiel describes women weeping for Tammuz at the Temple (EZEKIEL 8:14).

TAPHATH

("ornament")

Daughter of Solomon, and wife of Ben-abinadab who ruled over Dor (I KINGS 4:11).

TIBNI

Tibni, son of Ginath, who fought Omri for the throne of Israel. After years of battle, he was defeated and killed by Omri (I KINGS 16:21-22).

This eighth-century B.C.E. Assyrian bas-relief of Tiglath-pileser III is from Nimrud, Mesopotamia.

TIGLATH-PILESER III

("my confidence is the son of Esarra")

Also known as "Pul" in the Bible, Tiglath-pileser III (ca 745–727 B.C.E.) was a leading Assyrian king who was determined to reassert Assyrian control over Assyria's former vassal states, and to integrate them in an empire from the Tigris to the Nile. King Pekah of Israel and King Rezin of Syria realized that Tiglath-pileser was a major

threat, and restored the old Anti-Assyrian Coalition, combining Israel and Syria with the city-states of Ashkelon and Tyre. In response, King Ahaz of Judah entered an alliance between Judah and Tiglath-pileser himself. The Assyrian king then invaded Israel and dealt a crushing defeat to Pekah's coalition, capturing "Kedesh, Hazor, Gilead, and Galilee, [and] all the land of Naphtali, and he carried the people captive to Assyria" (II KINGS 15:29). King Pekah was assassinated by Hoshea, who succeeded him. Tiglath-pileser also invaded Syria, incorporating these lands as vassal states of the Assyrian Empire. Tiglath-pileser then returned north and focused his energies on suppressing Babylonia, which succumbed in 729 B.C.E. The king died two years later.

TIKVAH

("hope")

1. Son of Harhas who was the keeper of King Josiah's wardrobe, and father-in-law of the prophetess Huldah (II KINGS 22:14).

2. Father of Jahaziah, who opposed Ezra in his call for men of Judah to divorce their non-Jewish wives (EZRA 10:15).

TIRHANAH

Son of Caleb, the son of Hezron and his concubine Maacah, and leader of the tribe of Judah (I CHRONICLES 2:48).

TOAH

("bent")

Son of Zuph of the tribe of Levi and father of Eliab, and an ancestor of the prophet Samuel (I SAMUEL 1:1).

TOBIJAH

("good is the Lord")

A Levite sent out by King Jehoshaphat throughout Judah to teach the people the Torah (II CHRONICLES 17:8).

TOLA

("worm")

1. Eldest son of Issachar and grandson of Jacob and Leah, who went to Egypt with his grandfather Jacob (GENESIS 46:13).

2. Son of Puah and a member of the Issachar tribe, who served as Judge in Israel for 23

years after the death of Abimelech (JUDGES 10:1-2). He was buried in Shamir and succeeded by Jair.

URIAH

("God is my light")

1. A Hittite, the husband of Bathsheba whom David seduced. When Bathsheba found out she was pregnant, David summoned Uriah back from the field, so as to make it plausible that he had fathered Bathsheba's child, but that plot failed. David then decided to get rid of Uriah by ordering Joab to place him at the very front of a planned assault against the Ammonites, where he was certain to be killed (II SAMUEL 11:2–12:26).

2. A priest of the Temple during the reign of King Ahaz. While in Damascus to meet the Assyrian king, Ahaz saw an altar that so impressed him that he sent a model to Uriah, with instructions that it should replace the existing altar in the Temple. Isaiah called Uriah one of the witnesses to his prophecy of doom (ISAIAH 8:2).

3. Son of Shemaiah and a prophet from Kiriath-jearim, who foretold the destruction of the Temple. He had to flee to Egypt to escape arrest by King Jehoiakim, but he was seized in Egypt by Jehoiakim's agents and brought back to Judah for execution (JEREMIAH 26:20-3).

4. A Levite who stood with Ezra as he read the Torah to the people of Judah after the Babylonian exile (NEHEMIAH 8:4).

5. A priest of the family of Hakkoz, father of Meremoth, the priest appointed by Ezra to weigh the gold and silver brought back from Babylon, and to help repair Jerusalem's walls (EZRA 8:33; NEHEMIAH 3:4,21).

UZZAH

("strength")

1. Son of Shimei, a Levite descended from Merari, and father of Shimea (I CHRONICLES 6:29).

2. Son of Abinadab, who drove the cart

carrying the Ark of the Covenant from Gibeah to Jerusalem. When the oxen carrying the ark stumbled, Uzzah steadied the ark with his hand; but as soon as he touched the ark, he fell dead (I Chronicles 13:6-13; II Samuel 6:2-11).

This tablet, discovered in 1931, claims to be the headstone of the tomb of "Uzziah, king of Judah," though its historicity is debated.

UZZIAH
("strength of God")

1. A Levite and son of Uriel, also called Azariah (I Chronicles 6:24).
2. Father of Jonathan, one of David's supervisors in charge of the king's storehouses (I Chronicles 27:25).
3. Son of Amaziah by his wife, Jecoliah. He succeeded to the throne of Judah (ca 783–742 B.C.E.) at age 16 after his father was assassinated. The Books of Chronicles suggest that he was able to expand Judah's territory to the port of Elath (today's Eilat) at the expense of Edom, and that westward Judah now extended to Yabneh and Ashdod on the Mediterranean Sea (II Chronicles 26:2,6). Thus enlarged, Judah's economy grew, with "farmers and vinedressers in the hills and in the fertile lands" (II Chronicles 26:10). Uzziah himself, however, was struck with leprosy, which Chronicles interprets as punishment for his act of burning incense on the Temple altar—a rite only reserved for priests. For the remaining 11 years of his life, he ruled jointly with his son Jotham, who ascended the throne after Uzziah's death around 742 B.C.E. (II Kings 14:21; II Chronicles 26:1).

4. A priest of the sons of Harim, who had taken a foreign wife in the days of Ezra (Ezra 10:21).

ZABDI
("my gift")

1. Son of Zerah of Judah, and grandfather of Achan who took loot from Jericho against Joshua's orders (Joshua 7:1,17-18).
2. Son of Shimei and a leader of the tribe of Benjamin (I Chronicles 8:19).
3. One of David's officials in charge of his vineyards (I Chronicles 27:27).
4. Son of Asaph the minstrel; his grandson Mattaniah was responsible for the Thanksgiving prayer (Nehemiah 11:17). He is also called Zichri (I Chronicles 9:15).

ZABUD
("given")

Son of the prophet Nathan, who was one of the top officials in King Solomon's court and his closest friend (I Kings 4:5).

ZADOK
("righteous")

1. Son of Ahitub, of the line of Eleazer, and one of two high priests in the time of David (II Samuel 20:25; I Chronicles 24:3) and Solomon (I Kings 4:4). Zadok became sole high priest after Solomon exiled the other high priest Abiathar for supporting Adonijah, who had attempted to overthrow Solomon (I Kings 2:27,35; I Chronicles 29:22). From that time forward until the Maccabean revolt, all high priests were taken from the Zadok line.
2. Officer who led 22 soldiers from his clan to join David in Hebron (I Chronicles 12:28).
3. Father of Jerusha, who was wife of King Uzziah of Judah and mother of King Jotham (II Kings 15:33; II Chronicles 27:1).
4. Priest and son of Ahitub, father of Shallum, and an ancestor of Jehozadak, who was taken to Babylonia in captivity (I Chronicles 6:12).

5. Son of Meraioth and ancestor of Azariah, the first priest to settle in Jerusalem after the Babylonian exile (I Chronicles 9:11).
6. Descendant of Immer and a priest and scribe placed in charge of the distribution of tithes at the Temple by Nehemiah (Nehemiah 13:13).
7. Son of Baana, one of those who assisted in rebuilding the wall of Jerusalem (Nehemiah 3:4).
8. A leader of Judah who signed the covenant to observe the Law (Nehemiah 10:21).

ZALMUNNA
("shade")

One of the two kings of Midian who fled after their defeat at Ein Harod by Gideon. He was captured and executed (Judges 8:5-21).

ZECHARIAH
("remembered by the Lord")

1. One of the chiefs of the tribe of Reuben related to Joel (I Chronicles 5:7).
2. Son of Jeiel, a leader of the tribe of Benjamin and an uncle of King Saul (I Chronicles 8:31).
3. Son of Meshelemiah the Levite, he was a gatekeeper at the northern gate of the Tabernacle (I Chronicles 9:21).
4. A musician who performed on the harp when King David brought the Ark of the Covenant to Jerusalem (I Chronicles 15:18,20).
5. A priest in the time of David, appointed to blow the trumpet when King David brought the Ark of the Covenant to Jerusalem (I Chronicles 15:24).
6. Son of Isshiah, and a Levite serving in the Tabernacle (I Chronicles 24:25).
7. Son of Hosah, he was a Levite and gatekeeper the Tabernacle (I Chronicles 26:11).
8. Father of Iddo who was a leader of the half tribe of Manasseh in Gilead (I Chronicles 27:21).
9. One of five princes of Judah who were sent by King Jehoshaphat to teach the Torah to the people of Judah (II Chronicles 17:7).
10. Father of Jahaziel who prophesied that God would defeat the Ammonites and Moabites (II Chronicles 20:14).
11. One of Jehoshaphat's sons, who with his five brothers were killed by their eldest brother Jehoram when he became king of Judah (II Chronicles 21:2).

12. Son of Jehoiada, the high priest in the times of Ahaziah and Joash. After the death of Jehoiada, he boldly condemned both the king and the people for their rebellion against God, which so stirred up their resentment that they stoned him on orders of the king, and he died "in the court of the house of the Lord" (II CHRONICLES 24:20-2).

13. Son of Jeroboam II and the 14th king of Israel (743 B.C.E.), and the last from the house of Jehu. His reign lasted only six months as he was killed in a coup by Shallum, who seized the throne (II KINGS 10:30).

14. Father of Abi or Abijah, Hezekiah's mother (II KINGS 18:2).

15. A prophet who had "understanding in the seeing of God" in the time of King Uzziah, and who was much indebted to him for his wise counsel (II CHRONICLES 26:5).

ZEDEKIAH
("righteousness of God")

1. Last king of Judah. He was the third son of Josiah and brother of Jehoahaz. He ascended the throne at the age of 21 (598–586 B.C.E.) (II KINGS 23:31; 24:17-18). His original name was Mattaniah; but when Nebuchadnezzar placed him on the throne as the successor to Jehoiachin, he changed his name to Zedekiah. The prophet Jeremiah was his counselor (II KINGS 24:19-20; JEREMIAH 52:2-3). The kingdom was at that time a vassal state to Nebuchadnezzar; but, despite the strong protest of Jeremiah and others, Zedekiah entered into an alliance with Hophra (or Apries), king of Egypt, which resulted in a siege on Jerusalem. The siege lasted approximately 18 months, during which the city was plundered and laid to ruins (II KINGS 25:3; LAMENTATIONS 4:4,5,10). Zedekiah and his followers, attempting to escape, were made captive and taken to Riblah. There he witnessed his children put to death and was then taken to Babylon where he remained until his death (II KINGS 25:1-7; II CHRONICLES 36:12; JEREMIAH 32:4-5; 34:2-3; 39:1-7; 52:4-11; EZEKIEL 12:12). After the fall of Jerusalem, Nebuzaradan was sent to carry out its complete destruction (JEREMIAH 52:16). Gedaliah, with a Chaldean guard stationed at Mizpah, ruled over Judah (II KINGS 25:22,24; JEREMIAH 40:1-2,5-6).

2. Son of Chenaanah, one of 400 "prophets" who provided false counsel to King Ahab (I KINGS 22:11,24; I KINGS 18:10,23).

3. Son of Hananiah, one of the princes of Judah in the days of King Jehoiakim to whom Jeremiah's oracle was read by Baruch (JEREMIAH 36:12).

4. Son of Maaseiah, he was among the deportees sent to Babylon with King Jehoiachin, and who earned Jeremiah's wrath by falsely promising that the exile would be brief (Jeremiah 29:21).

An Old Russian Orthodox icon represents the prophet Zephaniah.

ZEPHANIAH
("God has protected")

1. A Kohathite and son of Tahath, he was an ancestor of Heman, King David's musician (I CHRONICLES 6:36).

2. Son of Cushi and one of the "minor prophets." He prophesied in the days of Josiah, king of Judah, and was contemporary of Jeremiah, with whom he had much in common. Zephaniah's oracles reflect a time before Josiah's religious reforms had been fully implemented. Zephaniah warns of God's impending judgment—"I will utterly sweep away everything from the face of the earth, says the Lord" (ZEPHANIAH 1:1)—but tempers this idea of a coming "day of wrath" with a promise of ultimate salvation, and "you shall fear disaster no more" (ZEPHANIAH 3:15).

3. Son of the priest Maaseiah, the "second priest" in the reign of Zedekiah (JEREMIAH 21:1). He supported Zedekiah's policy of pursuing a revolt against Babylonia, opposing the views of Jeremiah (JEREMIAH 29:25,26,29; 37:3; 52:24). He, along with some other captive Jews, was put to death by the king of Babylon at Riblah in the land of Hamath (II KINGS 25:21).

4. Father of Josiah, in whose home the prophet Zechariah ordered that Joshua the high priest should be crowned as leader (ZECHARIAH 6:10).

ZERUIAH
("guarded")

Sister of David and mother of his three nephews Abishai, Joab, and Asahel (II SAMUEL 2:18; I CHRONICLES 2:16).

ZIBA
("statue")

A servant in the household of Saul, whom David assigned to care for Saul's crippled son Mephibosheth. Ziba later betrayed Mephibosheth, gaining his property, but David ordered that half of all his lands be returned to Mephibosheth (II SAMUEL 9:2).

ZIBIAH
("deer")

A native of Beer-sheba, she was the wife of King Ahaziah of Judah and mother of King Joash (II KINGS 12:1; II CHRONICLES 24:1).

ZIMRI
("praiseworthy")

1. Son of Salu, a leader of the Simeon tribe, he took a woman from the Midian into his tent in full view of Moses and the Israelites. They were killed by Phinehas (NUMBERS 25:14).

2. Fifth king of the Northern Kingdom of Israel who reigned for only seven days in 885 B.C.E. Zimri, a commander of King Elah's army, murdered King Elah at Tirzah and assumed his throne. He was overthrown by Omri, and then perished in the palace fire he had set himself (I KINGS 16:8-20).

3. Son of Jehoaddah of the Benjamin tribe, and a descendant of King Saul (I CHRONICLES 8:36).

From Chronicles to Maccabees

*Thus says King Cyrus of Persia:
the Lord, the God of heaven,
has given me all the kingdoms of the earth,
and he has charged me to build
him a house at
Jerusalem in Judah.*

Ezra 1:3

*The Flemish painter Peter Paul Rubens (1577–1640) painted this
depiction of "Daniel in the Lion's Den" around 1615.*

THE BABYLONIAN EXILE TO THE MACCABEAN RESTORATION

Who Wrote the Books of Writings?

THE THIRD PRINCIPAL COLLECTION in Hebrew Scripture, known as *Ketuvim* or "Writings," contains a number of books that date from before and after the Babylonian exile. These include the Books of Chronicles, a parallel history of ancient Israel that is largely based on the Books of Samuel and Kings, as well as portions of Jeremiah, Isaiah, and Zechariah. The ideological perspective of the author of Chronicles is rigorously pro-Judah; the books ignore much of the material about the Northern Kingdom in Kings, and instead extol the example of the Davidic dynasty. It has been suggested that the author was possibly a Levite serving in Jerusalem, given his interest in Levitic individuals, viewpoints, and practices. The book was probably written after the exile, when Judah was administered by the Persian Empire.

The Books of Ezra-Nehemiah, which in most Christian Bibles follow Chronicles, originally formed one volume and cover the postexilic history from the fall of Babylon in 539 B.C.E. to the mid-fifth century B.C.E., when Judah was ruled as a Persian satrapy. They describe the efforts of two leaders, the priest **Ezra** and the governor **Nehemiah**, to restore a unique Jewish identity among the community after the trauma of the Babylonian exile, with a renewed focus on Temple worship and Torah obedience.

But the "Writings" collection also includes other books of which the dating is less certain, such as the so-called "Poetic Books" of Psalms, Proverbs, and Job. Though these books may contain elements that date as far back as the Davidic monarchy,

A painted enamel from Limoges ca 1550 depicts Judas Maccabee (above). British history painter Edwin Long (1829–1891) created this portrait of Queen Esther in 1878 (opposite).

they probably did not reach their final form until after the exile. This is also true of the so-called "Five Scrolls" *(Hamesh Megillot),* containing the Books of Song of Songs, Ruth, Lamentations, Ecclesiastes, and Esther.

Lastly, the "Writings" also include the Book of Ruth, which we encountered in Chapter 2, as well as the apocalyptic Book of Daniel. Though the book tells the story of **Daniel** and his companions during the exile in Babylon, modern scholarship has argued that the book only reached its final form in the second century B.C.E., during the suppression of Jewish practices by Syrian King **Antiochus IV Epiphanes** (175–164 B.C.E.).

The subsequent story of the Maccabean revolt against the Syrian kings is told in the Books of Maccabees. Originally written in Hebrew, the book is not included in the original canon of Hebrew Scripture, but it does appear in a Greek translation known as the Septuagint. Because the Septuagint formed the basis for the Christian "Old Testament," the Maccabees books are included in most Christian Bibles, although Protestant denominations consider them apocryphal, rather than an integral part of the Bible canon.

The "Writings" collection did not reach its final form until well into the second century C.E. That is why Jesus still refers to Hebrew Scripture as "the Law and the Prophets" (LUKE 16:16)—the first two divisions known as the Law *(Torah)* and the Books of the Prophets *(Nevi'im).* Nevertheless, Jesus was most likely familiar with some of the books in the emerging "Writings" collection, specifically the Psalms.

LEADING FIGURES IN THE BOOKS OF

CHRONICLES THROUGH MACCABEES

EZEKIEL

The forceful deportation of citizens from Judah to Babylon shocked the Hebrew nation to the core and led to a spiritual crisis. Why had God allowed this catastrophe to happen? How could Torah observance, including worship at the Temple, be sustained when the Temple lay in ruins? Would this mark the end of the great story of Israel?

These and other questions were addressed by the prophet Ezekiel, son of a Zadokite priest who ministered to refugees during the exile. As a "sentinel for the house of Israel" (EZEKIEL 3:17), Ezekiel had repeatedly warned of God's pending penalty for Judah's transgressions, including its fondness for idolatry (EZEKIEL 5:7-10). Now that this punishment had come to pass, Ezekiel's message turned to one of hope. In his visions, he saw Jerusalem, its Temple, and its kingdom restored to their former glory; his detailed description of the future Temple, provided by an angel serving as a guide, would later be consulted by the actual builders of the Second Temple (EZEKIEL 40-42).

The day would come, Ezekiel foretold, when God's dwelling place would once again be among them, when "I will be their God, and they shall be my people" (EZEKIEL 37:27). Ezekiel's gripping visions convinced his audience that the covenant was *not* broken, and that in due course, God would shepherd his people back to Israel.

This promise gave a new impetus to the need to preserve Hebrew customs and practices while the people lived in a foreign land. In fact, scholars believe that the Babylonian exile marks a crucial phase in the effort, begun by King Josiah many years earlier, to compile the many strands of Jewish history, ritual, and law into one comprehensive set of books. These books—Hebrew Scripture—would enable families to retain their unique identity and continue the rich liturgical life of their fathers and forefathers. Hence, from this time forward, modern scholars speak of the Hebrew nation as "Jews" (or *Yehudim,* possibly derived from "Judean") and refer to "Judaism" as a community in religious terms, no longer bound to a particular political entity or geographical location.

WISDOM LITERATURE

B ooks of Wisdom, as compared to Books of the Prophets, occupy a special place in the canon of Hebrew Scripture. While prophetic books are concerned with obedience to God's will in the face of national crisis, the wisdom literature is more concerned with the conduct of the individual. Examples include Proverbs, the Book of Job, the Book of Ecclesiastes, the Wisdom of Solomon, and the Wisdom of Ben Sira. Given his reputation for great wisdom, Solomon is traditionally credited with writing several of these; nevertheless, most works—such as Proverbs—were probably accumulated over many centuries as the expressions by leading sages, officials, and intellectuals (including, quite possibly, Solomon himself). In Proverbs, Wisdom is a woman who "love(s) those who love me, and those who seek me diligently find me" (PROVERBS 8:17).

The Song of Solomon has been characterized as a superb example of Jewish love poetry; some scholars believe it was sung during ancient Jewish weddings. The poem evokes the yearning of young lovers in often startlingly explicit language; nevertheless, it may also be seen as an allegory of God and his bride, the nation of Israel—and for Christians, of Christ and his Church.

By contrast, the Book of Ecclesiastes, which probably reached its final form in the third century B.C.E., is more philosophical in nature; it often elaborates on the temporal character and vanity of human existence. Among its many reflections is the famous verse "For everything there is a season, and a time for every matter under heaven" (ECCLESIASTES 3:1). ■

Pre-Raphaelite painter Edward Burne-Jones (1833–1898) created this stained glass of King Solomon holding the Temple of Jerusalem in 1890.

ca 562 B.C.E.	ca 550 B.C.E.	ca 546 B.C.E.	ca 539 B.C.E.
Babylonian King Nebuchadnezzar dies	King Cyrus II of Anshan conquers the kingdom of Media	King Cyrus II conquers the Lydian kingdom	Babylon surrenders to King Cyrus II

GEDALIAH

Compared to the comfortable lifestyle of Babylon, which was one of the most advanced cities of its time, life was considerably more difficult for the farmers and workers who were left behind in Judah to serve their new Babylonian lords. Virtually all of the towns had suffered considerable devastation; fields, wells, homes, and roads lay in ruins. In response, Babylonian regent Nebuzaradan organized a redistribution of land among the poor to help rebuild the agrarian economy (JEREMIAH 39:10). Nebuzaradan also named **Gedaliah**, son of Ahikam, as governor of Judah, charged with rebuilding the shattered nation. Gedaliah thereupon moved his court to Mizpah, where he was joined by a number of Judean officers who had survived the Babylonian onslaught.

The new governor urged these men to collaborate with the occupiers—a sentiment shared by Jeremiah—but his request fell on deaf

"Belshazzar's Feast" was painted by Dutch artist Rembrandt van Rijn (1606–1669) in 1635.

ears. Before long, a group of officers led by **Ishmael**, son of Elishama, who was related to Judah's former royal family, assassinated Gedaliah with the support of **King Baalis** of Ammon. But the coup failed in its ultimate objective—to restore Jewish control of Judah (JEREMIAH 41:1-10). Fearing Babylonian reprisals, much of Judah's remaining elite—including Jeremiah—fled to Egypt (II KINGS 25:25-26). Their fears were not unfounded; in retaliation, the Babylonians deported another group of Jews to Babylonia (JEREMIAH 52:30).

BELSHAZZAR

The next episode in the story takes place neither in Judah nor Babylon, but in the kingdom of Anshan, in what is today's Iran. This kingdom had been ruled by a dynasty that traced its origins to a legendary figure named Achaemenes (later the Persian dynasty

ca 552 B.C.E.	ca 520 B.C.E.	ca 515 B.C.E.	ca 508 B.C.E.
King Cambyses, son of Cyrus, conquers Egypt	Haggai and Zechariah are active during reign of Darius I	The Second Temple in Jerusalem is dedicated	The Greeks create a democratic constitution

CHAPTER 3: FROM CHRONICLES TO MACCABEES **173**

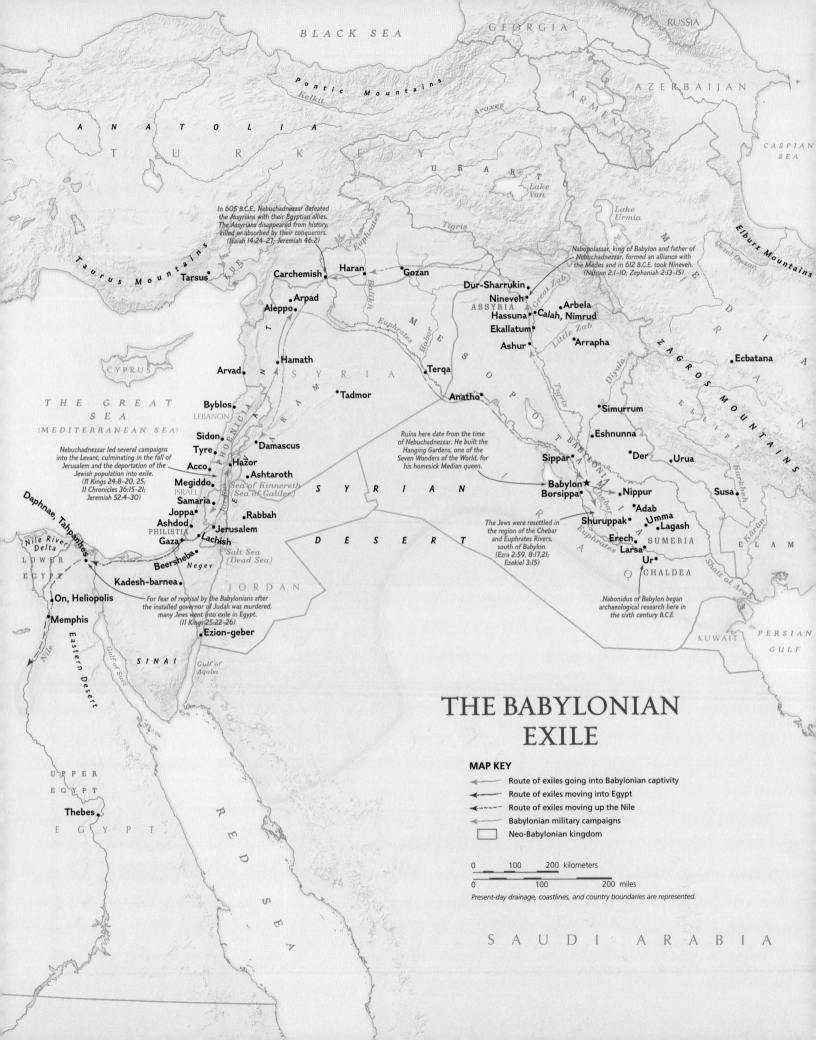

BLACK SEA

GEORGIA

RUSSIA

AZERBAIJAN

Pontic Mountains

Kelkit

ANATOLIA

TURKEY

ARMENIA

Araxes

URARTU

Lake Van

Lake Urmia

CASPIAN SEA

Elburz Mountains

Gezel Owzan

Taurus Mountains

Euphrates

Tigris

MEDIA

In 605 B.C.E., Nebuchadnezzar defeated
the Assyrians with their Egyptian allies.
The Assyrians disappeared from history,
killed or absorbed by their conquerors.
(Isaiah 14:24–27; Jeremiah 46:2)

Nabopolassar, king of Babylon and father of
Nebuchadnezzar, formed an alliance with
the Medes and in 612 B.C.E. took Nineveh.
(Nahum 2:1–10; Zephaniah 2:13–15)

Tarsus

Carchemish

Haran

Gozan

•Dur-Sharrukin

Nineveh

•Arbela

ZAGROS MOUNTAINS

•Arpad

Aleppo

ASSYRIA

Hassuna

•Calah, Nimrud

Great Zab

Ekallatum

Ashur

•Arrapha

Little Zab

Ecbatana

Hamath

Terqa

MESOPOTAMIA

Diyala

Arvad

SYRIA

•Tadmor

Anatho•

Tigris

•Simurrum

ELLIPI

CYPRUS

THE GREAT SEA
(MEDITERRANEAN SEA)

Byblos

LEBANON

PHOENICIA

•Eshnunna

Karkheh

Ruins here date from the time
of Nebuchadnezzar. He built the
Hanging Gardens, one of the
Seven Wonders of the World, for
his homesick Median queen.

Sidon

Tyre

•Damascus

Hazor

Acco

•Ashtaroth

Sippar

BABYLONIA

•Der

Urua

Susa

Nebuchadnezzar led several campaigns
into the Levant, culminating in the fall of
Jerusalem and the deportation of the
Jewish population into exile.
(II Kings 24:8–20, 25;
II Chronicles 36:15–21;
Jeremiah 52:4–30)

ARAM

Megiddo

ISRAEL

Sea of Kinnereth
(Sea of Galilee)

SYRIAN

Babylon★

Borsippa

Nippur

•Adab

•Umma

Lagash

ELAM

Samaria

Joppa

•Rabbah

DESERT

The Jews were resettled in
the region of the Chebar
and Euphrates Rivers,
south of Babylon.
(Ezra 2:59, 8:17,21;
Ezekiel 3:15)

Shuruppak

Ashdod

PHILISTIA

Jerusalem

Gaza

Lachish

Chebar

Euphrates

Erech

SUMERIA

Daphnae, Tahpanhes

Nile River Delta

LOWER EGYPT

Beersheba

Negev

Salt Sea
(Dead Sea)

JORDAN

Larsa

Ur•

CHALDEA

Kadesh-barnea

Nabonidus of Babylon began
archaeological research here in
the sixth century B.C.E.

Shatt al Arab

For fear of reprisal by the Babylonians after
the installed governor of Judah was murdered,
many Jews went into exile in Egypt.
(II Kings 25:22–26)

•On, Heliopolis

Memphis

Nile

Eastern Desert

Ezion-geber

SINAI

Gulf of Aqaba

KUWAIT

PERSIAN GULF

THE BABYLONIAN EXILE

UPPER EGYPT

RED SEA

Gulf of Suez

MAP KEY

→ Route of exiles going into Babylonian captivity

← Route of exiles moving into Egypt

←- Route of exiles moving up the Nile

← Babylonian military campaigns

▭ Neo-Babylonian kingdom

0   100   200 kilometers

0   100   200 miles

Present-day drainage, coastlines, and country boundaries are represented.

Thebes•

EGYPT

SAUDI ARABIA

THE BOOK OF DANIEL

Together with the Books of I Enoch and II Baruch, the Book of Daniel is one of the few apocalyptic books in the Hebrew canon. Though probably written in the second century B.C.E. during the reign of Antiochus IV, the story is set in the sixth century B.C.E., which enables its author (or authors) to include subsequent events as prophesies of the future. The first six chapters follow the story of a Jewish exile named Daniel and his Jewish companions during multiple time periods, from the reign of Nebuchadnezzar II to that of Persian King Darius. Daniel is called upon to explain Nebuchadnezzar's bizarre dreams, which pleases the king. But shortly thereafter, Daniel's companions are thrown into a furnace over their refusal to worship a pagan idol. Fortunately, they

A 16th-century Byzantine icon depicts a representation of the prophet Daniel.

stepped out of the flames completely untouched; not even their hair had been singed (DANIEL 3:27). The next episode takes place during the reign of Belshazzar, the co-regent of King Nabonidus; here, Daniel is required to explain mysterious words written on a wall. And finally, it is Persian King Darius who condemns Daniel to the lion's den, from which he emerges unscathed. In Chapters 7 through 11, Daniel is a prophet who receives multiple apocalyptic dreams and visions. Many feature strange animals, such as a leopard with four wings and four heads, which are believed to represent all of the foreign kings who once ruled over Israel. The message of Daniel's oracles is that God will deliver his people from oppression—including the Syrian persecutions under Antiochus IV. ■

---

would be referred to as the *Achaemenids*). Anshan was nominally a vassal kingdom of the Median Empire, which stretched from modern Turkey to the Persian Gulf, straddling much of the Babylonian Empire along its northeastern border. In 553 B.C.E., the king of Anshan, **Cyrus II** (559–529 B.C.E.), rose up against the Medes and defeated them. Cyrus then gradually took control of the vast Median Empire, defeating the last remaining monarch, King Croesus of Lydia, in 546 B.C.E. One story, probably apocryphal, relates how Croesus and Cyrus stood and watched as Cyrus's forces flooded into Sardis, the Lydian capital. "What are those men doing?" Croesus asked with astonishment. "They're plundering your city," Cyrus replied. Croesus turned to him and said, "No, *your* city. It's not mine any more."

Inevitably, Cyrus's next target was the Babylonian Empire, which had the misfortune of being ruled by a king named **Nabonidus** (ca 556–539 B.C.E.), who shared none of his predecessors' military acumen. Aware of his shortcomings, Nabonidus had decided

THE BOOK OF TOBIT

The apocryphal Book of Tobit relates the story of a Jewish exile named Tobit who lived with his wife, Anna, and son Tobias in Nineveh, capital of the Assyrian Empire. One day he traveled to Media to deposit some silver with his friend Gabael (TOBIT 1:14). Unfortunately, upon his return a swallow's droppings turned him blind. He then asked his son Tobias to retrieve his silver deposit from Media.

Tobias left on his journey accompanied by the archangel Raphael, who introduced himself as Azarias. After Tobias caught a fish, Raphael told him to keep the viscera; with these, Tobias met Sarah, the daughter of Raguel, and married her. Upon their return, a wedding feast was held, and Raphael revealed himself. All prostrated on the ground and praised God.

Tobias waited until both his parents had passed away, and then moved with his wife and children to Media. The message of the Book of Tobit is that God will abide by those who have faith in him, no matter how great their ill fortune. ■

to transfer much of his power to his son as co-regent. This was Belshar-usur (553–540 B.C.E.), who may have inspired the character of "**Belshazzar**" in the book of Daniel.

The book relates how Belshazzar threw a great feast, with wine served in vessels looted by Nebuchadnezzar from the Temple in Jerusalem. Suddenly, "the fingers of a human hand appeared and began writing" on the ornate wall of the banqueting hall: "*MENE, MENE, TEKEL,* and *PARSIN*" (DANIEL 5:5,25). None of the revelers could decipher the text, but Belshazzar's queen suggested that they summon Daniel.

DANIEL

Daniel was one of several highborn Jewish exiles who had been educated at the Babylonian court. Daniel was duly taken to the banqueting hall, where he instantly recognized the words. He turned to all who had gathered and explained that "*MENE,* God has numbered the days of your kingdom and brought it to an end; *TEKEL,* you

I returned to [the] sacred cities on the other side of the Tigris the sanctuaries of which have been ruins for a long time . . . and established for them permanent sanctuaries.

CYRUS THE GREAT, *The Cyrus Cylinder*

have been weighed on the scales and found wanting; *PERES,* your kingdom is divided and given to the Medes and Persians" (DANIEL 5:26-28). Daniel's prediction was promptly fulfilled, for "that very night," Belshazzar was assassinated (DANIEL 5:30).

According to the Bible, Belshazzar's successor, **King Darius**, then made Daniel one of the leading men of the kingdom, which provoked much envy from other courtiers. They decided to test Daniel's loyalty, and persuaded Darius to decree that for 30 days, everyone in the kingdom could worship only to statues of King Darius himself. Those who disobeyed would be thrown to the lions. The faithful Daniel ignored the decree and continued to pray to the Lord. His enemies gleefully reported this to the king, who had no choice but to throw him into a den of lions, but not without expressing the fervent wish that "your God, whom you faithfully serve, deliver you!" (DANIEL 6:16). The next morning, Darius rushed back to the cave, and was relieved to see that Daniel was indeed unharmed, for God's angel had "shut the lions' mouths." Those who had denounced Daniel were thrown into the den instead, and quickly devoured (DANIEL 6:22-24).

CYRUS II

But as God had foretold, the days of the Babylonian Empire were numbered. In 540 B.C.E., Cyrus was amassing his forces on the Babylonian border. Nabonidus rushed from his self-imposed exile to take command of his armies, but it was to no avail. Within the year, Cyrus had defeated the Babylonian army at Opis, and fought his way to the city of Babylon, which fell shortly thereafter. A tablet known as the "Verse Account of Nabonidus" suggests that the citizens of Babylon, fed up with their absentee monarch, simply opened

the gates. Cyrus's own chronicle, known as the Cyrus Cylinder, credits the supreme Babylonian god Marduk with his stupendous victory. Regardless, Cyrus was now the undisputed ruler of one of the greatest empires the world had ever known.

Given the long history of political rebellion in his new realm, Cyrus shrewdly calculated that his subjects could be enticed to pour their political aspirations into their national cult, if given the means to do so. A flourishing religion, sustained by a system of priests and sanctuaries, could grant these peoples a sense of autonomy, and thus discourage any thought of political rebellion. This is why, as documented on his cylinder, Cyrus actively encouraged the worship of indigenous gods throughout his domain, and even funded the "repair of their dwelling places," including those of the ancient Babylonian gods of Sumer and Akkad.

It also explains why Cyrus encouraged the restoration of Jewish worship in Judah. Unfortunately, most of the surviving religious elite of Judah were not in Jerusalem, but still in exile in Babylon, busy at work on completing the Deuteronomistic history of Israel. In response, the king declared that "the Lord . . . has charged me to build him a house at Jerusalem in Judah," and that all those still in Babylon would be "permitted to go up to Jerusalem in Judah, and rebuild the house of the Lord" (EZRA 1:2-3).

Filled with joy, many Jewish communities accepted the king's offer and embarked on the long voyage home, though many others did not. Some of these expatriate communities, though faithful to the Law, had prospered in Babylon, and enjoyed its highly sophisticated culture and lifestyle. Many others feared that a return to Jerusalem would disrupt the centers of Torah study they had so

A clay Cyrus Cylinder, dated to the sixth century B.C.E., describes the conquest of Babylon by Cyrus the Great.

ca 458 B.C.E.	ca 444 B.C.E.	ca 438 B.C.E.	ca 431 B.C.E.
Ezra undertakes his mission to Judah	Nehemiah, Artaxerxes' cup-bearer, travels to Judah	Parthenon is completed in Athens	Outbreak of the Peloponnesian War

JUDITH AND HOLOFERNES

"Judith Beheading Holofernes" is the work of Italian artist Michelangelo Merisi da Caravaggio (1573–1610). It was painted around 1599.

The story of **Judith** and **Holofernes** is found among the apocryphal works of the Septuagint, the Greek translation of Hebrew Scripture, which formed the basis for the Christian Old Testament. The purpose of the book is to inspire its readers with the courage and patriotism of its heroine, a widow named Judith, in the face of Babylonian aggression. According to the story, a military commander named Holofernes had been dispatched by King Nebuchadnezzar on a punitive expedition against Israel. The Babylonians soon besieged the Israelite town of Bethulia, where Judith lived. As its situation became desperate, Judith prayed to God, then put aside the sackcloth of her widowhood and "made herself very beautiful, to entice the eyes of all the men" (JUDITH 10:4). Passing bravely through the gates with only her maid as company, she was seized by a Babylonian patrol and taken to their camp, where all the soldiers "marveled at her beauty and admired the Israelites" (JUDITH 10:19). Holofernes, too, was deeply impressed, and invited her to stay. After three days had passed, Holofernes planned to seduce her after a lavish banquet, for he felt that "it would be a disgrace if we let such a woman go" (JUDITH 12:12). Late that night, as Judith was finally alone with Holofernes and the commander lay drunk on his bed, she seized his sword and cut off his head. The story has inspired countless artists, from the Italian Renaissance painter Andrea Mantegna to the 19th-century Austrian painter Gustav Klimt. ∎

ca 415 B.C.E.	ca 406 B.C.E.	ca 366 B.C.E.	ca 359 B.C.E.
The Torah, or Pentateuch, reaches its final form	Death of Euripides and Sophocles end the great era of Greek drama	Egypt revolts against Persian rule	Philip II of Macedon assumes power

① **Pasargadae** The Tomb of Cyrus at Pasargadae, inspired by Mesopotamian ziggurat designs, is believed to be the burial place of King Cyrus the Great, based on descriptions by Greek historians.

② **Persepolis** Persepolis ("City of Persians"), in today's Iran, was chosen by Cyrus the Great as the capital of the new Achaemenid Empire, although it was Darius the Great who built much of the palace complex.

③ **Lydia** A signature art of the Achaemenid dynasty was its virtuosity with precious metals, particularly the manufacture of beautifully detailed gold and silver artifacts, such as this gold armlet featuring griffins from Lydia.

④ **Susa** Ceremonial warriors appear in a relief from the palace of Darius the Great, wearing Median trouser suits. Such trousers were preferred for riding on horseback, particularly when going into battle.

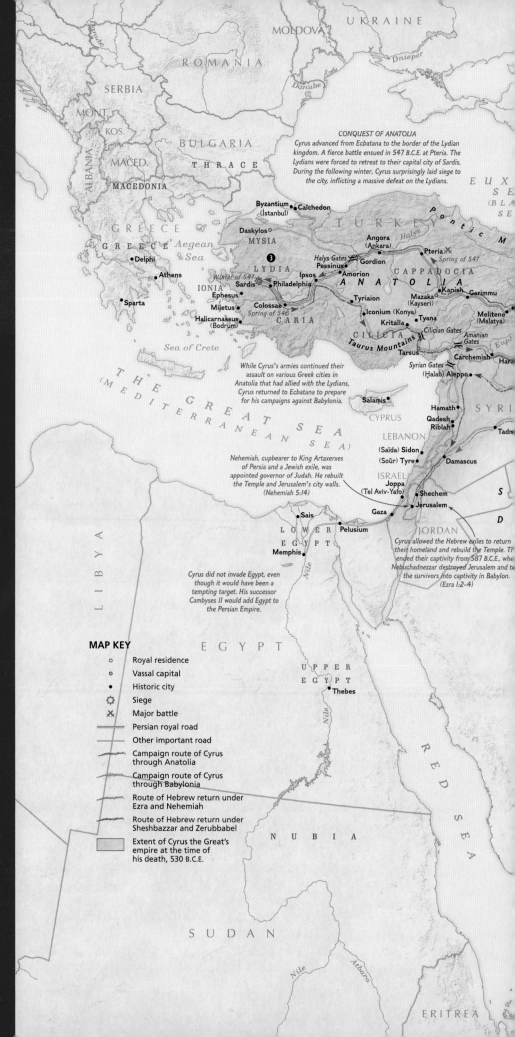

CONQUEST OF ANATOLIA
Cyrus advanced from Ecbatana to the border of the Lydian kingdom. A fierce battle ensued in 547 B.C.E. at Pteria. The Lydians were forced to retreat to their capital city of Sardis. During the following winter, Cyrus surprisingly laid siege to the city, inflicting a massive defeat on the Lydians.

While Cyrus's armies continued their assault on various Greek cities in Anatolia that had allied with the Lydians, Cyrus returned to Ecbatana to prepare for his campaigns against Babylonia.

Nehemiah, cupbearer to King Artaxerxes of Persia and a Jewish exile, was appointed governor of Judah. He rebuilt the Temple and Jerusalem's city walls. (Nehemiah 5:14)

Cyrus did not invade Egypt, even though it would have been a tempting target. His successor Cambyses II would add Egypt to the Persian Empire.

Cyrus allowed the Hebrew exiles to return to their homeland and rebuild the Temple. Th[is] ended their captivity from 587 B.C.E., whe[n] Nebuchadnezzar destroyed Jerusalem and t[ook] the survivors into captivity in Babylon. (Ezra 1:2-4)

MAP KEY
- ○ Royal residence
- ◉ Vassal capital
- ● Historic city
- ☼ Siege
- ✕ Major battle
- Persian royal road
- Other important road
- Campaign route of Cyrus through Anatolia
- Campaign route of Cyrus through Babylonia
- Route of Hebrew return under Ezra and Nehemiah
- Route of Hebrew return under Sheshbazzar and Zerubbabel
- Extent of Cyrus the Great's empire at the time of his death, 530 B.C.E.

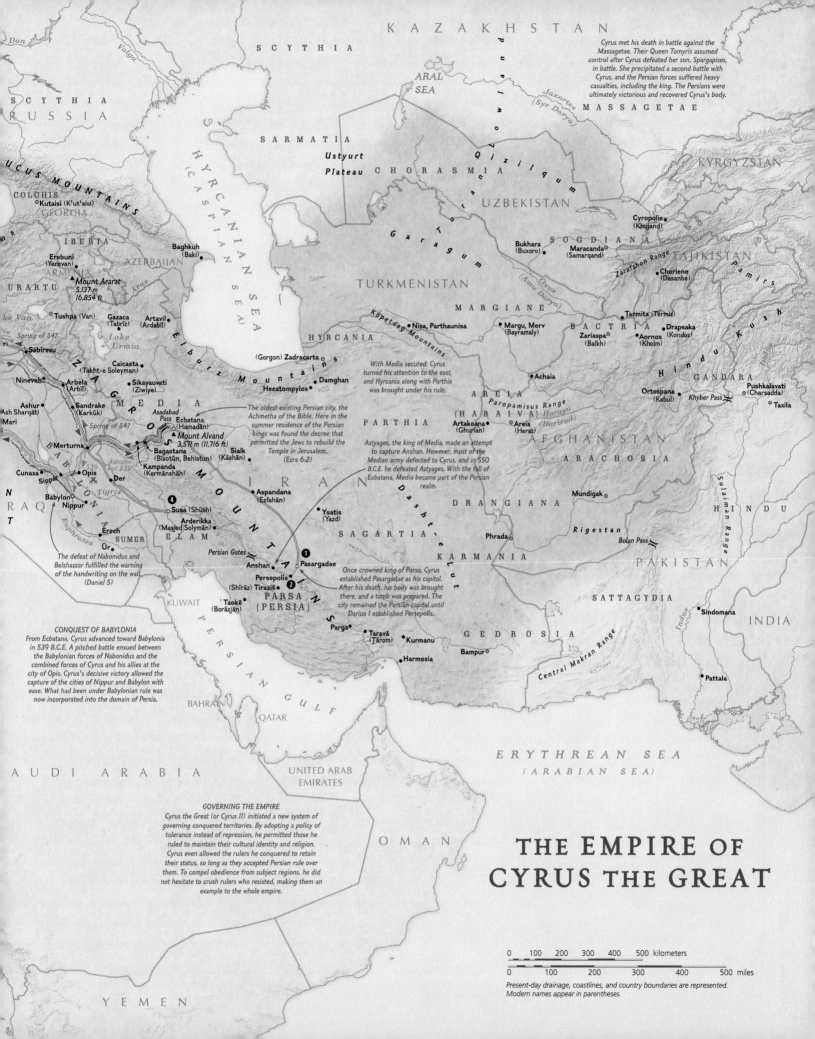

THE EMPIRE OF CYRUS THE GREAT

Cyrus met his death in battle against the Massagetae. Their Queen Tomyris assumed control after Cyrus defeated her son, Spargapises, in battle. She precipitated a second battle with Cyrus, and the Persian forces suffered heavy casualties, including the king. The Persians were ultimately victorious and recovered Cyrus's body.

With Media secured, Cyrus turned his attention to the east, and Hyrcania along with Parthia was brought under his rule.

Astyages, the king of Media, made an attempt to capture Anshan. However, most of the Median army defected to Cyrus, and in 550 B.C.E. he defeated Astyages. With the fall of Ecbatana, Media became part of the Persian realm.

The oldest existing Persian city, the Achmetha of the Bible. Here in the summer residence of the Persian kings was found the decree that permitted the Jews to rebuild the Temple in Jerusalem. (Ezra 6:2)

Once crowned king of Parsa, Cyrus established Pasargadae as his capital. After his death, his body was brought there, and a tomb was prepared. The city remained the Persian capital until Darius I established Persepolis.

The defeat of Nabonidus and Belshazzar fulfilled the warning of the handwriting on the wall. (Daniel 5)

CONQUEST OF BABYLONIA
From Ecbatana, Cyrus advanced toward Babylonia in 539 B.C.E. A pitched battle ensued between the Babylonian forces of Nabonidus and the combined forces of Cyrus and his allies at the city of Opis. Cyrus's decisive victory allowed the capture of the cities of Nippur and Babylon with ease. What had been under Babylonian rule was now incorporated into the domain of Persia.

GOVERNING THE EMPIRE
Cyrus the Great (or Cyrus II) initiated a new system of governing conquered territories. By adopting a policy of tolerance instead of repression, he permitted those he ruled to maintain their cultural identity and religion. Cyrus even allowed the rulers he conquered to retain their status, so long as they accepted Persian rule over them. To compel obedience from subject regions, he did not hesitate to crush rulers who resisted, making them an example to the whole empire.

0   100   200   300   400   500 kilometers
0   100   200   300   400   500 miles

Present-day drainage, coastlines, and country boundaries are represented. Modern names appear in parentheses.

painstakingly built. These communities would evolve into leading centers of Jewish exegesis in Persia, extending well into the era of Rabbinic Judaism.

SHESHBAZZAR AND ZERUBBABEL

The first caravan of 42,360 Jews that set out from Babylon on the 600-mile route to Jerusalem was led by a member of Judah's former royal house, named **Sheshbazzar.** Before his departure, King Cyrus was kind enough to give him more than 5,000 vessels and implements of silver and gold, which Nebuchadnezzar had looted from the Jerusalem Temple. Because Sheshbazzar's name is not attested anywhere else in the Bible, some scholars have identified him as Shenazzar, one of the sons of King Jehoiachin who was exiled to Babylon with his family (I Chronicles 3:18).

Once the exiles arrived in Judah, Sheshbazzar was installed as governor of Judah, now known as the subprovince of *Yehud,* part of the fifth Persian satrapy known as *'Abar nahara* ("Beyond the [Euphrates] River") (Ezra 5:14). Elsewhere in the Book of Ezra, however, the governor is identified as a man named **Zerubbabel**, another descendant of Jehoiachin. Indeed, both Sheshbazzar and Zerubbabel are credited with initiating the reconstruction of the Temple, which has led some scholars to assume that they are one and the same person (Ezra 5:2,16).

Based on Cyrus's original decree, which was found in the imperial archives in Ecbatana, the former capital of Media, the new Persian King Darius I (522–486 B.C.E.) formally authorized the funding for the new Temple (Ezra 6:2). A short time later, the foundations were finished, prompting joyful celebrations in Jerusalem.

The prophet Zechariah, a detail from the Vatican's Sistine Chapel ceiling by Michelangelo Buonarroti (1475–1564), was created between 1508 and 1512.

SYNAGOGUES

As the Jewish Diaspora—the dispersal of Jews throughout the Alexandrian Empire—spread, the need rose for local community halls where Jewish expatriates could meet to observe the Sabbath, celebrate Jewish festivals, and host other community functions. The result was the synagogue, from the Greek *synagogē* or "house of assembly"—*beit knesset* in Hebrew. These early synagogues usually consisted of a rectangular hall with benches on either side. The end wall facing Jerusalem contained a niche known as the "Ark," where the scrolls of the Torah were kept. One of the oldest such synagogues has been found in Egypt, dating to the third century B.C.E.

Eventually, the custom of building synagogues was also adopted in remote regions in Palestine proper—including in Wadi Qelt, southwest of Jericho; in Gamla, in the Golan; and in the casemate wall surrounding the Herodian mountain fortress of Masada on the Dead Sea. Though the original structure was built around 31 B.C.E., the Zealots—who took over the redoubt during the Jewish revolt against Rome in 66–70 C.E.—added plastered stone benches, running in four tiers along three sides, which held about 200 people. They also built a small attendant's room behind the Ark, where excavators found fragments of scrolls containing the Books of Ezekiel and Deuteronomy, as well as a potsherd inscribed with the phrase *me'aser kohen,* or "priest's tithe." A synagogue was not a sacred space, but a pastoral center used for readings, commentary, and other community events. ■

Haggai

But after the first blush of excitement, the work on the Temple seems to have stagnated. Part of the reason was that the Samaritans had interrupted the work, because they had been rebuffed from participating in the construction; "you have nothing to do with us in building a house to our God," Zerubbabel told them (EZRA 4:3). The Persian governor, **Rehum**, used the resulting fracas to recommend to the Persian king that work on the Temple be discontinued (EZRA 4:15). And indeed, as Judah's economy began to recover, farms prospered, and Jerusalem slowly rose from its ruins, perhaps the Temple became less of a priority. This stoked the wrath of a prophet named Haggai, about whom little is known other than that he composed his book during a five-month period in 520 B.C.E. "Is it a time for you yourselves to live in your paneled houses," Haggai thundered, "while this house lies in ruins? . . . You have sown much, and harvested little" (HAGGAI 1:4,5). Haggai's oracle coincided with an unexpected drought, and the prophet was quick to identify the Lord's anger as the cause. "Therefore the heavens above you have withheld the dew, and the earth has withheld its produce," he argued. His words must have had their intended effect, for shortly thereafter, Governor Zerubbabel and the high priest **Joshua** agreed to resume work on the Temple (HAGGAI 1:12-15).

Zechariah

Haggai's impatience was shared by the prophet Zechariah, "the son of Berechiah," who also pressed for a more energetic effort in rebuilding the Temple. In mystical visions reminiscent of the Book of Daniel, Zechariah saw great turmoil ahead, expressed in the apocalyptic imagery of horsemen and chariots, walls of fire, or a vision of the high priest Joshua standing before an angel and Satan; scholars believe these visions reflect the political upheaval in Persia following King Darius's accession to the throne.

But other oracles by Zechariah predict the return of a glorious Jewish kingdom. "I will return to Zion," says the Lord in one verse; "Jerusalem shall be called the faithful city, and the mountain of the Lord of hosts shall be called the holy mountain" (ZECHARIAH 8:3). The capital of Judah would once again become a wholesome,

THE FESTIVAL OF PURIM

The Book of Esther tells the story of a Persian grand vizier named Haman who planned "to destroy all the Jews . . . throughout the whole kingdom of Ahasuerus" (ESTHER 3:6). Queen Esther, warned of the conspiracy by her foster father, rushed to inform the king, who authorized all Jews to bear arms and defend themselves against the coming onslaught. Thus, the massacre was avoided, and all the plotters were killed (ESTHER 9:5). The event is celebrated in the Jewish feast of Purim, "on the fourteenth day of the month of Adar, as a day for gladness" (ESTHER 9:19). The word "purim" is the plural of "pur" or lot, which was thrown by Haman to determine the best date for staging the massacre. During the feast, the Book of Esther is read to the congregation, which traditionally engages in hissing and stamping of feet whenever the name of Haman is read. Purim is a happy feast involving much drinking and dancing, sharing delicious snacks as well as giving alms to the poor. Many Jews, particularly children, also dress up in costumes. ■

prosperous city, with streets "full of boys and girls playing in its streets." "And," says God, "they shall be my people, and I will be their God" (ZECHARIAH 8:5,8).

Under pressure of both Haggai's and Zechariah's urging, work on the Temple was once again pursued with vigor. It took five years, but around 515 B.C.E., the new Temple of Jerusalem was finally completed. The era of Second Temple Judaism (515 B.C.E.–70 C.E.) had begun.

Esther

King Darius died in 486 B.C.E. and was succeeded by **Xerxes I** (486–465 B.C.E.), the same Persian king who invaded Greece and sacked Athens, only to be defeated by a Greek fleet at the Battle of Salamis in 480 B.C.E. The outcome was far from decisive, however, and for the next two centuries, Persia and Greece would remain implacable foes while engaging in several proxy wars. The reason was largely economic: Both Greece and Persia vied for control of the lucrative Mediterranean trade, especially in the largely Hellenic territory of Asia Minor, which was experiencing rapid growth.

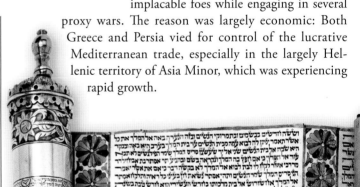

The Scroll of Esther was created by the 19th-century Iraqi School.

Spanish artist Francisco Collantes (1599–1656) painted "The Vision of Ezekiel" in 1630.

I decree that any of the people of Israel or their priests or Levites in my kingdom who freely offers to go to Jerusalem may go with you.

Many scholars believe that King Xerxes is the same as "**King Ahasuerus**" who appears in the Book of Esther. The book is unique in the Hebrew canon for several reasons, not in the least because it features a woman as the heroine in a story that is as skillfully written as any modern novel. Set amid the intrigue of the Persian court, the story relates how **Esther**, the adopted daughter of a Jewish exile living in "Shushan" (Susa), was introduced to the Persian king because of her extraordinary beauty. This was King Ahasuerus, who had decided to set aside his first wife, **Queen Vashti**. Esther "won his favor and devotion," and the king "set the royal crown on her head" (ESTHER 2:17).

Her stunning rise led to envy at the Persian court. The newly appointed grand vizier, an Ammonite named **Haman** (Ammon being the ancient enemy of Israel) began to plot "to destroy all the Jews . . . throughout the whole kingdom of Ahasuerus" (ESTHER 3:6). He ordered magicians to cast *pur,* or lots, in order to pick the right day for the planned massacre, and placed the provincial military on alert. Queen Esther, warned of the conspiracy by her foster father Mordecai, broke the news to the king, and identified Haman as the instigator. Enraged, Ahasuerus turned to Haman and cried, "Will he even assault the queen in my presence, in my own house?" (ESTHER 7:8).

Haman and his sons were dragged out to be hanged, but nothing could be done about Haman's planned massacre, because it had been issued as a royal decree. Moved by Esther's tearful pleading, the king then gave out another decree, authorizing all Jews in his kingdom to bear arms so as to defend themselves. Thus equipped, Jews were prepared when the militia came to murder them, and they "struck down all their enemies with the sword, slaughtering, and destroying them" (ESTHER 9:5). Ever since, that happy deliverance has been celebrated during the Jewish feast of Purim, "on the fourteenth day of the month of Adar, as a day for gladness" (ESTHER 9:19).

ARTAXERXES I

Xerxes died in a palace coup in 465 and was succeeded by King Artaxerxes I (465–425 B.C.E.). His rule was beset by threats from other powers in the region, notably Greece and a resurgent Egypt. At long last, the king negotiated a peace treaty with Athens and Argos in 449 B.C.E.

In the meantime, back in Judah, it was clear that the mere act of rebuilding the Temple had not restored the social and religious fabric of a once vibrant Hebrew community. For one thing, many prominent Jerusalem families still lived in Babylon; on the other hand, the province of Yehud had been colonized by many foreign immigrants from the Babylonian Empire. Over the past eight decades, these settlers had intermarried with native Jews or, more recently, with newly arrived Jews on their return from exile. The Hebrew nation of Judah had become a melting pot of many different cultures and religious practices.

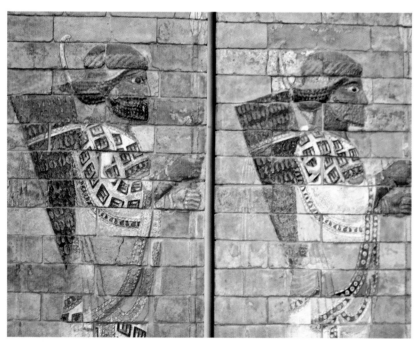

Archers, possibly members of the Persian Guard of the Immortals, march in lock step on a wall of molded enameled brick from Darius's palace ca 510 B.C.E. at Susa.

ca 285 B.C.E.	ca 280 B.C.E.	ca 280 B.C.E.	ca 259 B.C.E.
Ptolemy II begins rule; the Septuagint is written	The Pharos, famous lighthouse of Alexandria, is built	The new republic of Rome controls all of the Italian peninsula	The Zenon Papyri are written

THE HIGH PRIEST

The high priest was the supreme clerical figure of Temple Judaism and responsible for all rites and sacrifices associated with Temple worship. The first high priest was Aaron, brother of Moses (Exodus 28:1-2); future high priests had to be male descendants of Aaron (Leviticus 6:15). King Solomon, however, changed the succession line after he deposed the high priest Abiathar because of his support for his rival, Prince Adonijah. Instead, Solomon appointed a priest named Zadok, who had anointed him king. All subsequent high priests were therefore required to be descendants of Zadok, or "Zadokites"; some scholars believe this is the root of the word *Tzedoqim*, or Sadducees. Syrian King Antiochus IV broke the Zadokite line by appointing Menelaus, who unlike the previous high priests—Onias III and Jason— could not trace his lineage back to Zadok.

During the Herodian era, high priests were appointed based on their family's allegiance to Herod the Great personally; several, including the family of the Annas, had been brought in from Persia to ensure their total loyalty. During the Roman period, Roman prefects chose high priests for their political reliability.

The high priest was garbed in a sleeveless blue robe over which he wore a gold breastplate covered with 12 jewels, one for each of the Hebrew tribes. The robe's lower hem was fringed with tiny gold bells and tassels. The high priest was the only human being who was allowed to enter the Holy of Holies, the inner sanctum of the Temple, on Yom Kippur, the Day of Atonement. ◼

"Aaron the High Priest" is a work by British artist William Etty (1787–1849).

EZRA

This development was of great concern to a priest named Ezra, who ministered to the Jewish community of Babylon but was kept in touch about developments in Judah. It is possible that he served in some official capacity at the Persian court, because he was able to secure King Artaxerxes' support for an official mission "to make inquiries about Judah and Jerusalem according to the law of your God" (Ezra 7:14). With funds provided by the Persian treasury, Ezra traveled to Judah with an entourage of some five thousand souls, including officials, scribes, and servants, as well as many expatriate Jewish families (Ezra 8:1-14).

As soon as he arrived in Jerusalem, Ezra found to his astonishment that the "holy seed" of the Hebrew nation had been mixed with the "people of the lands," in violation of the Law that forbade Jews to marry non-Jewish spouses. Worse, much of the ancient Jewish customs and Temple rites had faded

THE FEAST OF HANUKKAH

The feast of Hanukkah, also known as the "Festival of Lights," commemorates the rededication of the Second Temple in 164 B.C.E., after the liberation of Jerusalem from Syrian rule by Maccabean leader Judas. Jewish historian Josephus wrote that Judas initiated an eight-day feast to celebrate the cleansing of the Temple. Hanukkah, too, is celebrated for eight nights and days, starting on the 25th day of Chislev—from late November through late December in the Gregorian calendar. During this period, each successive light on a nine-armed candelabra, known as the menorah, is lit. The ninth light, the *shamash*, is usually placed higher or lower than the other eight, and is used to provide illumination on all nights. Jewish tradition tells us that after the Maccabees entered the Temple, they found only enough sacred olive oil to burn the Temple menorah for one day; yet miraculously, it burned for eight days, enough time to press and prepare fresh sacred oil. ◼

away. In response, Ezra summoned all male Jews to assemble. When they had gathered in the driving rain, Ezra issued a stunning decree: All those who had married non-Jewish wives were to "make a confession to the Lord . . . (and) separate yourselves from the peoples of the land and from the foreign wives" (Ezra 10:11). Though it may have broken their hearts, the men obeyed and "sent them away with their children" (Ezra 10:44).

MALACHI

Ezra's concerns were shared by the prophet **Malachi**, who wrote the last book in the Jewish canon of Hebrew Scripture. Malachi, too, was deeply vexed by the high rate of mixed marriages involving foreign spouses, as well as the decline of sacrificial worship at the Temple. His oracles probably date from the latter period of Ezra's activity, but before the arrival of Nehemiah. Very little is known about the figure of Malachi himself (his name means "messenger" and may be a

ca 225 B.C.E.	ca 218 B.C.E.	ca 206 B.C.E.	ca 200 B.C.E.
Earliest known synagogue is built in Egypt	Hannibal invades Italy during the Second Punic War	The republic of Rome conquers Spain	Antiochus III defeats Ptolemy V: Judea is added to Seleucid Empire

Ottoman Sultan Suleiman the Magnificent built the walls of today's old city of Jerusalem around 1535.

pseudonym), but his fervor in denouncing religious laxity is no less than that of Haggai or Zechariah.

Indeed, Malachi placed part of the blame for this moral decay on the priesthood, who "have corrupted the covenant of Levi" by offering impure and blemished sacrificial animals, or convenient castaways that are "polluted food on my altar" (MALACHI 1:7; 2:8). Only by restoring true piety, said Malachi, will Judah once again be "a land of delight" (MALACHI 3:12).

To ensure that the Jewish nation would indeed embrace such a spiritual renewal, Malachi foretold that God would send "my messenger to prepare the way before me" (MALACHI 3:1). Near the end of the book, Malachi reiterated this theme, that God "will send you the prophet Elijah, before the great and terrible day of the Lord comes" (MALACHI 4:5).

The Christian tradition has identified Malachi's messenger as St. John the Baptist; indeed, in Matthew's Gospel, Jesus calls the Baptist "Elijah who is to come" (MARK 9:13).

NEHEMIAH

The efforts to restore an observant Jewish nation in Judah were continued by a Persian official of Jewish descent, named Nehemiah. Nehemiah served as a cupbearer to King Artaxerxes, and was thus able to solicit the king's support for a mission to Yehud that would help restore the native community, namely by rebuilding the city

proper. Nehemiah had been told that "the wall of Jerusalem is broken down, and its gates are destroyed by fire" (NEHEMIAH 1:3). Until the city was rebuilt, its social fabric would remain broken as well.

Several scholars believe the king's solicitous concern over such a small and relatively insignificant province was prompted by several revolts that had tormented the Persian Empire in preceding decades. Perhaps the king believed (as Cyrus had done) that the imposition of strict religious discipline would most likely curtail any seditious political activity. What's more, Artaxerxes was keenly aware that Judah was a strategic buffer state between Persia and an increasingly restless Egypt, while also poised on the crossroads of caravan routes that were vital to the Persian economy.

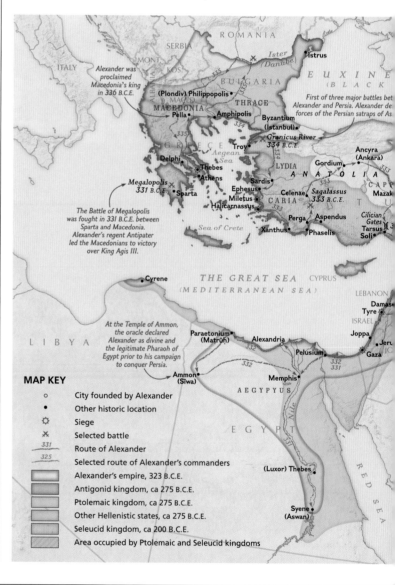

MAP KEY

○	City founded by Alexander
•	Other historic location
☼	Siege
✕	Selected battle
—331—	Route of Alexander
—325—	Selected route of Alexander's commanders
	Alexander's empire, 323 B.C.E.
	Antigonid kingdom, ca 275 B.C.E.
	Ptolemaic kingdom, ca 275 B.C.E.
	Other Hellenistic states, ca 275 B.C.E.
	Seleucid kingdom, ca 200 B.C.E.
	Area occupied by Ptolemaic and Seleucid kingdoms

ca 190 B.C.E.	ca 175 B.C.E.	ca 167 B.C.E.	ca 167 B.C.E.
Rome defeats Antiochus III, extending Roman control over Asia Minor	Antiochus IV ascends throne; proscribes all non-Greek cults in Syrian empire	Rome conquers Macedonia	Mattathias, a priest in Moderin, launches the Maccabean revolt

Installed as governor, Nehemiah organized a vast campaign to rebuild Jerusalem's walls. This activity provoked the ire of Judah's neighbors, including Samaria, Edom, and other fiefdoms east of the Jordan, who were quite content to see Jerusalem deprived of its defenses. Nehemiah was forced to have the construction areas patrolled around the clock, lest foreign raiders attempted to destroy the newly laid walls and kill the workers (NEHEMIAH 4:11,14).

The new governor was not satisfied with merely rebuilding Jerusalem's fortifications. When a famine struck, most farmers were forced to indenture their lands to buy grain to feed their families or to pay taxes. These peasants bitterly complained that "we are having to borrow money on our fields and vineyards to pay the king's tax" (NEHEMIAH 5:4). Nehemiah listened to their plight, gathered the officials and noblemen in the region, and ordered them to "[r]estore to them, this very day, their fields [and] their vineyards" (NEHEMIAH 5:10-11).

Eager to preserve the restoration of religious obedience in Judah, Nehemiah exercised his authority as governor to have all priests, officials, and the people, including "the gatekeepers, the singers, the temple servants and all those who . . . adhere to the law of God" solemnly sign the Covenant (NEHEMIAH 10:28). Judah had, in effect, become a Jewish theocracy—with a priestly elite, rather than a royal dynasty, ruling the nation on behalf of the Persian king. And so it

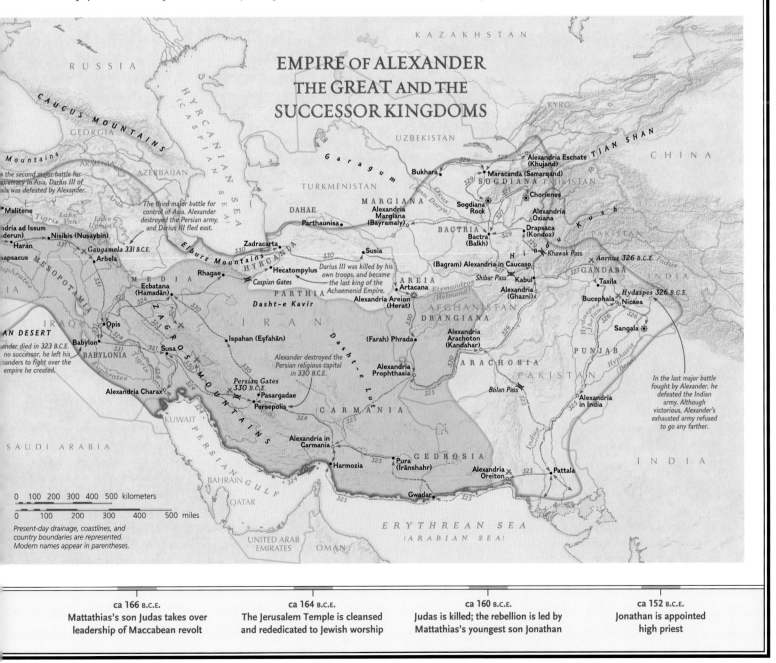

EMPIRE OF ALEXANDER THE GREAT AND THE SUCCESSOR KINGDOMS

0 100 200 300 400 500 kilometers

0 100   200   300   400   500 miles

Present-day drainage, coastlines, and country boundaries are represented. Modern names appear in parentheses.

ca 166 B.C.E.
Mattathias's son Judas takes over leadership of Maccabean revolt

ca 164 B.C.E.
The Jerusalem Temple is cleansed and rededicated to Jewish worship

ca 160 B.C.E.
Judas is killed; the rebellion is led by Mattathias's youngest son Jonathan

ca 152 B.C.E.
Jonathan is appointed high priest

THE SADDUCEES

Since the days of Ezra, power in Jerusalem had been held by the priesthood—the chief priests and priestly officials who served on the priestly council, or *Sanhedrin*, and supervised the rites of sacrifice at the Temple. Under Hasmonean rule, the priesthood was increasingly influenced by the Sadducees, or *Tzedoqim* in Hebrew. The Sadducees, who were believed to descend from the high priest Zadok, had reluctantly yielded their claim on the high priest's office—now taken by the Hasmonean kings—in return for gaining control of the priestly council, with jurisdiction over religious and other domestic matters. Their growing power was opposed by the Pharisees, a pious group of laymen and clergy who believed that instead of ritual sacrifice, the quintessential practice of Judaism was the application of the Law. Over time, the Sadducee party became a wealthy, conservative aristocracy that would welcome the Roman occupation. The power of certain Sadducee families in the Roman period is illustrated by the fact that the Romans appointed no less than seven members of the family of the Sadducee Annas—including his son-in-law, Caiaphas—to the office of high priest.

The Sadducees did not accept any Scripture beyond the Torah, or Law—including the Book of the Prophets—and did not believe in the immortality of the soul, an idea that was gaining currency among the Pharisees. In the Gospel of Luke, the Sadducees question Jesus on this very subject (LUKE 20:28-38). ∎

"Christ Before Caiaphas," painted by Italian artist Niccolo Frangipane (1563–1597), depicts Jesus standing before the high priest Caiaphas.

After Alexander son of Philip, the Macedonian . . . had defeated King Darius of the Persians and the Medes, he succeeded him as king.

1 MACCABEES 1:1

remained until a new power took control of the region, led by a young prince from the house of Macedon.

ALEXANDER THE GREAT

Since the fifth century B.C.E., Greek culture—its highly developed art and architecture, but also its literature, drama, and philosophy—had been percolating into the Persian Empire along the great trade routes between East and West, including those leading to the Persian province of Yehud. Devout Jews were offended by the Greek fondness for depicting human beings, often in the nude, but many others were seduced by the sophisticated Greek sense of style. Athens was the Paris of Antiquity: Even though it no longer controlled the Mediterranean politically, it continued to set the standard for modernity, art, architecture, and fashion—from painted vases to the construction of all-new *poleis,* or planned cities.

The seeping influence of "Hellenism" became a veritable flood when the young Macedonian **King Alexander** (356–323 B.C.E.) took his army of 40,000 soldiers and invaded Greece's ancient foe, Persia, in 334 B.C.E. After defeating King Darius III at the Battle of Issus in 333, Alexander rolled inexorably forward, first heading south into Syria, Phoenicia, Judah, and Egypt, before turning east to capture the great Persian cities of Babylon, Susa, and Persepolis. "He advanced to the ends of the earth," says the first Book of Maccabees. "He . . . ruled over countries, nations and princes, and they became tributary to him" (I MACCABEES 1:3,4).

But Alexander's reign was short-lived; even as the young blond warrior lay on his deathbed in 323, a fierce power struggle developed between his senior generals, known as the *Diadochi* or "successors." In the end, they agreed to break up Alexander's empire, each choosing a territory to which they had taken a fancy. Thus, **General Ptolemy**, who had been smitten by Egyptian culture, took Egypt; **General Seleucus** was awarded the heart of the Persian Empire; and **General Cassander** satisfied himself with Greece and Macedon. Soon, these generals—and their allies—went to war against each

ca 149 B.C.E.	ca 147 B.C.E.	ca 147 B.C.E.	ca 147 B.C.E.
Third Punic War between Rome and Carthage	Chinese dictionary of 10,000 characters is compiled by Hu Shin	The Romans destroy Corinth	Greece becomes the Roman province of Achaea

other to further expand their trophies, but by 301, the principal arrangements had been settled. Ptolemy was now King Ptolemy I Soter, founder of the Ptolemaic dynasty, who would rule with pharaonic splendor over Egypt, Judah, and Phoenicia from his new capital of Alexandria. Seleucus became the head of the Seleucid dynasty with control over Syria and Babylonia. Poised at the very fault line between these two great empires was tiny Judah, which retained its strategic role as the main intersection of overland trade routes.

Soon, trade was restored and began to grow exponentially as the Greek rulers introduced the *drachma,* a coin bearing the Attic owl, as standard currency throughout their realms. In its wake followed the wholesale movement of people, lured by the growing international prosperity. After Ptolemy I forcibly resettled a number of Jews from Jerusalem to Alexandria in 312, many other Jews followed voluntarily. The new Egyptian capital became the glittering jewel of the Ptolemaic Empire, a center of great learning epitomized by the Library of Alexandria.

Other Jews—not only merchants but also farmer-settlers and craftsmen—seized this opportunity to escape the rural plots of Judea and settle in the new cities along the Ionian coast of Asia Minor, today's Turkey. Thus began the first Diaspora, the first dispersal of Jews across the Mediterranean and Asia, not as a result of war or deportation, but prodded by economic opportunity.

Under Ptolemaic rule, the people of Judah—now called *Judea*—were left in peace, provided their fields were tended properly and agricultural tribute flowed south to boost the coffers of Alexandria. The Zenon Papyri, named after an official of the Ptolemaic court who conducted an audit in Judea around 258 B.C.E., give an inkling of the sheer variety of crops, fruits, and fish produced under Ptolemaic rule.

French artist Jean-Simon Berthélemy (1743–1811) painted "Alexander Cuts the Gordian Knot." It was prophesied that whoever loosed the knot would become ruler of all Asia.

THE SEPTUAGINT

As the Jewish community of Alexandria, capital of the Ptolemaic kingdom, continued to grow, demand rose for a Greek translation of Hebrew Scripture. According to the Letter of Aristeas (second century B.C.E.), King Ptolemy II (285–246 B.C.E.) was approached for funding the translation project. The king agreed, but remembered that his prisons still held many hundreds of Jewish prisoners of war, captured during military campaigns. He sent an emissary to the high priest Eleazar in Jerusalem and proposed an exchange: He would release the prisoners if the high priest sent him 72 learned scholars to produce the Greek translation. The result was a work known as the Septuagint—from the Latin word *septuaginta,* for "seventy." Given that the Septuagint is written in Alexandrian Greek, it is likely that the translation was actually carried out by Alexandrian scribes; the story of Jerusalem scholarship was simply maintained to make the translation more authoritative. ■

Tensions between Egypt and Syria, however, continued unabated. The two realms finally clashed in open warfare. Around 200 B.C.E., King Ptolemy V Epiphanes (203–181 B.C.E.) was defeated by King Antiochus III of Syria (223–187 B.C.E.). As part of the victor's spoils, Antiochus added Judea to the Seleucid Empire, plunging the province once again in turmoil.

SELEUCUS IV

The source of this turmoil was the Syrian treasury: It had been thoroughly depleted as a result of Antiochus's ill-advised attack on Greece, now a Roman dependency. The result was vigorous Roman intervention and Rome's demand for stiff reparation payments. By the time Antiochus's son Seleucus IV (187–175 B.C.E.) ascended the throne, the Seleucid Empire was tottering on the edge of bankruptcy. Seleucus then reverted to a desperate measure: He ordered all the temples

Dutch-born artist Gérard de Lairesse (ca 1640–1711) painted the "Expulsion of Heliodorus from the Temple" in 1674.

in his kingdom looted of their treasure—including the Temple that stood in the capital of the province of Judea.

Already, the Jewish population had chafed under the Syrian embrace of all things Greek. Whereas the Ptolemies had respected local customs and religious precepts, the Syrians believed that Hellenism—Greek civilization—would unify and integrate the highly diverse cultures in the Seleucid realm. Now, an even worse calamity loomed: the looting of the Second Temple by a Syrian official named **Heliodorus**. But as Heliodorus prepared to seize the Temple treasury, a miraculous apparition intervened, a "magnificently caparisoned horse, with a rider of frightening mien; it rushed furiously at Heliodorus and struck at him with its front hoofs" (II MACCABEES 3:24-25). The theft was prevented.

ca 135 B.C.E.	ca 133 B.C.E.	ca 112 B.C.E.	ca 106 B.C.E.
First activity at Qumran based on coins found at the site	Asia Minor becomes the eighth Roman province	Pharisees and Sadducees emerge in Judea	Roman orator and politician Cicero is born

JASON

After King Seleucus died and was succeeded by his brother Antiochus IV Epiphanes (175–164 B.C.E.), a power struggle ensued between contenders for the post of high priest at the Temple in Jerusalem. One contender was *Yeshua,* or Jesus, the brother of high priest **Onias III,** who changed his name to the Hellenized "**Jason.**" To secure the post, Jason offered Antiochus IV a bribe of "three hundred and sixty talents of silver." The fact that Onias III had strenuously opposed Seleucid efforts to rob the Temple treasury must have helped Jason's cause as well. Having ousted his brother and replaced him as high priest, Jason immediately set about to change Jerusalem "to the Greek way of life" (II MAC-CABEES 4:8,10).

"So they built a gymnasium in Jerusalem according to Gentile custom," adds the author of I Maccabees, "and removed the marks of circumcision, and abandoned the holy covenant . . . They sold themselves to do evil" (I MACCABEES 1:14-15). The crisis escalated further when another contender for the position of high priest, **Menelaus,** offered the king an even bigger bribe. This caused an outrage, not because of the bribe, but because Menelaus was not a descendant of Zadok, Solomon's high priest (as Jason evidently was); only Zadokites could aspire to become high priest. Jason was forced to flee to the Transjordan, where he secured financial assistance from the wealthy Tobiad family and prepared to recapture his former post by force, if necessary.

ANTIOCHUS IV EPIPHANES

As fate would have it, King Antiochus IV himself was in the area, having just been repulsed from Egypt by Roman and Egyptian forces. The growing civil war between the contestants for high priest gave him the pretext for marching into Jerusalem, pillaging the Temple, and venting his wrath on whomever did not support the pro-Greek faction.

Antiochus then took another fateful step: He decreed that the Jewish Law, including worship at the Temple, was to be suppressed. The holy sanctuary itself was converted to a temple dedicated to the Greek god Zeus; the altar in front of the Temple "was covered with abominable offerings" while the sanctuary proper was "filled with debauchery and reveling by the Gentiles, who dallied with prostitutes" (II MACCABEES 6:4). According to Jewish historian Josephus, who wrote in the latter part of the first century C.E., those who continued to observe Jewish rites were "whipped with rods, and their bodies torn to pieces," or crucified on the spot.

THE PHARISEES

The Pharisees—from the Hebrew *perushim,* or "separated ones"— were not a clerical group as is often assumed, but a coalition of pious laymen who "separated themselves" by scrupulously observing Covenant Law. What made them different from the Sadducees is their belief that the Law should be adapted to changing needs of their time. Whereas the Sadducees considered Hebrew Scripture a closed book, the Pharisees studied the Law and debated it extensively. Eventually, this led to a body of scriptural commentary known as the "Oral Law," which probably forms the basis of the third-century Mishnah. The Pharisees also believed in transferring the sanctity of the Temple, including its ritual purity, to the home, so as to observe God in all things. This is the reason why they debated such questions as what was considered "clean" or "impure," or what one was allowed to do on the Sabbath. Some scholars believe that this is the reason why the Pharisaic movement was largely an urban phenomenon, practiced by the affluent with plentiful access to water and ritual bathing pools, or *mikva'ot,* sometimes in their own homes.

The Pharisees also accepted the idea of the immortality of the soul, as well as the belief in the resurrection after Judgment Day—two concepts that would return in the teachings of Jesus. Under Hasmonean rule, the Pharisees exerted considerable power in Jerusalem as a counterweight to the growing influence of the Sadducees, but their political power waned under Herod the Great and subsequent Roman governors. ■

"The Pharisee and the Publican" is the subject of a sixth-century Byzantine mosaic in the Sant'Apollinare Nuovo, Ravenna, Italy.

ca 105 B.C.E.	ca 100 B.C.E.	ca 100 B.C.E.	ca 90 B.C.E.
College of Technology is founded in Alexandria	Gaius Julius Caesar is born	First Chinese ships reach India	Roman architect Vitruvius writes the *Ten Books of Architecture*

CHAPTER 3: FROM CHRONICLES TO MACCABEES **191**

Flemish painter Peter Paul Rubens (1577–1640) painted this depiction of "The Triumph of Judas Maccabeus" in 1635.

MATTATHIAS

The royal decree was not limited to Judea's capital. In the village of Modein, some 20 miles west of Jerusalem, a Seleucid officer was on hand to ensure that all villagers observed the pagan rites, rather than the worship of YHWH. One priest by the name of **Mattathias**, a descendant of a Levite named Hasmonaeus, refused to comply. Another villager stepped forward to make a pagan offering, perhaps fearing reprisals against himself and his family, but Mattathias grabbed the man and killed him. The priest then turned on the Syrian official and slew him as well.

This act of resistance galvanized what would become known as the Maccabean revolt. It was a spontaneous popular uprising against Syrian persecution, not because of the Syrian fondness for things Greek—the Hasmoneans themselves would often cloak their rule in Greek pomp—but because of their suppression of virtually every aspect of Jewish religious life, and the usurpation of the holy post of high priest. Leadership of the revolt soon passed from Mattathias to his son **Judas** (166–160 B.C.E.), a skilled and ruthless commander whose nom de guerre, we are told, was Maccabeus (from the Aramaic word *maqqaba,* or "hammer").

JUDAS MACCABEUS

As we saw, the history of ancient Israel is filled with uprisings against foreign oppression, most of which failed bitterly—as would be the case with two major revolts in the Roman period, the Jewish War of 66–70 C.E. and the Second Jewish War of 132–135 C.E. But the Maccabean revolt succeeded beyond all expectations. Avoiding open combat with the far superior Syrian army, Judas conducted a brilliant guerilla campaign that allowed him to molest and ultimately defeat Syrian forces in detail. In 164 B.C.E., he was able to

Now Maccabeus and his followers,
the Lord leading them on,
recovered the temple and the city;
they tore down the altars that had been built
in the public square by the foreigners,
and . . . purified the sanctuary.

II MACCABEUS 10:1-3

ca 82 B.C.E.	ca 76 B.C.E.	ca 73 B.C.E.	ca 71 B.C.E.
Following the Roman civil war, Sulla is declared dictator	Hasmonean King Alexander Jannaeus dies and is succeeded by his wife, Salome	Mithridates IV of Pontus rekindles war against Rome	The slave revolt under Spartacus is suppressed

THE EXTRA-CANONICAL WORKS

Some 13 religious works, written by Jewish authors between 300 B.C.E. and the late first century C.E., were not included in the final "canon" or composition of the Hebrew Scripture. Called "apocrypha" by Christian editors, these books include wisdom sayings, poetry, prayers, and histories that were, however, included in the Septuagint, the Greek translation of the Hebrew Scriptures. The Septuagint (including the apocrypha) then formed the basis for the "Old Testament," which is why much of this apocryphal literature does appear in Christian Bibles. Many of these works capture the unique zeitgeist of the Hebrew people under Syrian occupation and the Hasmonean restoration. They vividly show that despite the joy of liberation after the Maccabean revolt, the nation was increasingly polarized by the controversy of Hasmonean kings also serving as high priests, and the growing corruption of the priesthood. Whereas the first Book of Maccabees exalts the achievements of the Maccabees and their heirs, the Hasmonean kings, the second Book of Maccabees, which covers much of the same history, focuses instead on the restoration of the sanctity of Temple worship.

At the same time, these books depict a Jewish community struggling to come to terms with the growing influence of Greek culture, or Hellenism, under both Syrian and Hasmonean rulers. The author of *The Wisdom of Solomon,* which probably dates from the first century B.C.E., condemns all those following Greek customs as sybaritic revelers who "take [their] fill of costly wine and perfumes, and let no flower of spring pass [them] by" (WISDOM 2:7). ∎

A section from the scroll of Psalms from Qumran Cave 11 forms part of the Dead Sea Scrolls. The scrolls were found on the shore of the Dead Sea, from which they derive their name.

ca 70 B.C.E.
Roman poet Virgil is born

ca 68 B.C.E.
The Roman army captures Crete

ca 67 B.C.E.
Queen Salome dies and names her son, the high priest Hyrcanus II, as successor

ca 67 B.C.E.
Hyrcanus II, who favored the Pharisees, is deposed by his brother Aristobulus II

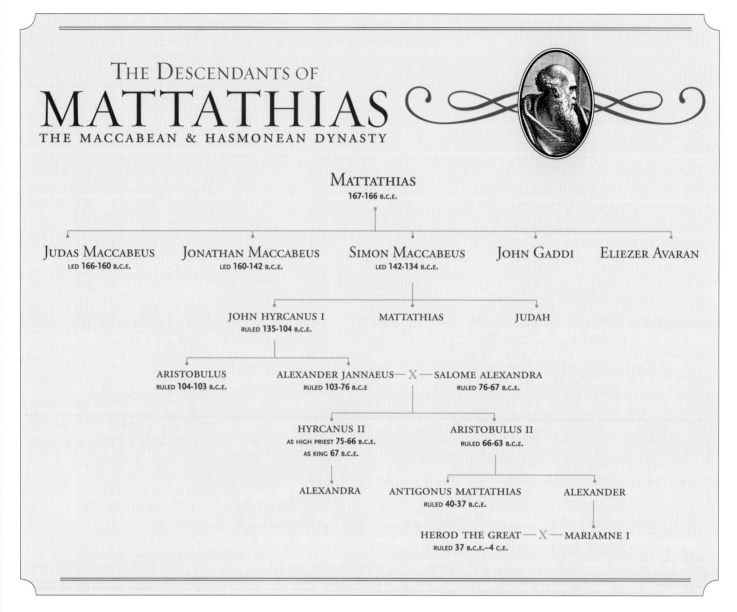

THE DESCENDANTS OF
MATTATHIAS
THE MACCABEAN & HASMONEAN DYNASTY

MATTATHIAS
167-166 B.C.E.

JUDAS MACCABEUS	JONATHAN MACCABEUS	SIMON MACCABEUS	JOHN GADDI	ELIEZER AVARAN
LED 166-160 B.C.E.	LED 160-142 B.C.E.	LED 142-134 B.C.E.		

JOHN HYRCANUS I
RULED 135-104 B.C.E.   MATTATHIAS   JUDAH

ARISTOBULUS
RULED 104-103 B.C.E.   ALEXANDER JANNAEUS — X — SALOME ALEXANDRA
RULED 103-76 B.C.E   RULED 76-67 B.C.E.

HYRCANUS II
AS HIGH PRIEST 75-66 B.C.E.
AS KING 67 B.C.E.   ARISTOBULUS II
RULED 66-63 B.C.E.

ALEXANDRA   ANTIGONUS MATTATHIAS
RULED 40-37 B.C.E.   ALEXANDER

HEROD THE GREAT — X — MARIAMNE I
RULED 37 B.C.E.–4 C.E.

capture Jerusalem, cleanse the Temple of all Greek idols, and solemnly restore the worship of YHWH—an event celebrated during the Jewish festival of Hanukkah (II MACCABEES 10:1-3).

That same year, Antiochus IV died, precipitating a clash between several contenders for the Syrian throne. One of them, the Seleucid **General Lysias**, revoked Antiochus's edict and restored full religious freedom to the citizens of Judea (II MACCABEES 11:15). It was a skillful move, for many Jewish factions—including the *Hasidim,* or "pious ones"—now abandoned the fight, given that their principal war aim had been satisfied. For the Maccabees, however, the ultimate goal was full political independence, and so Judas persevered (albeit with sharply reduced forces), only to be killed in the Battle of Elasa in 160 B.C.E. Judas's brother **Jonathan** (160–142 B.C.E.) then took up the torch and continued the guerilla campaign against the Seleucids.

JONATHAN MACCABEUS
Meanwhile, in Syria, the throne had been usurped by **Demetrius I** (162–150 B.C.E.), who sued for an armistice with Jonathan in

ca 65 B.C.E.	ca 63 B.C.E.	ca 63 B.C.E.	ca 63 B.C.E.
Roman poet Horace is born	Pompey defeats Mithridates IV, who commits suicide	Pompey conquers Syria and adds it to the Roman Empire	Gaius Octavius, the future Augustus, is born

152 B.C.E. The peace treaty granted Judea the status of an autonomous province within the Seleucid Empire, to be ruled by Jonathan as governor. Two years later, however, Demetrius was overthrown by another usurper called **Alexander Balas** (150–145 B.C.E.). Alexander had been careful to secure the support of both the Roman Republic and the Ptolemaic kingdom, by claiming to be "the son of Antiochus IV." Once on the throne, Alexander was more interested in debauchery than tradecraft, which enabled Demetrius's son Demetrius II to bring the Ptolemies over to his side and prepare a countercoup.

The turmoil in the Syrian capital of Antioch gave Jonathan the opportunity he had been waiting for. With Alexander too distracted by the ongoing power struggle, Jonathan's army captured Ashdod, Joppa, and Gaza along the Mediterranean coast, before swinging north to take large parts of Samaria and Galilee. This prompted another Syrian pretender, Antiochus VI, to order Jonathan's assassination, which was carried out by a general named **Trypho**.

Long before his death, however, Jonathan had alienated much of the Jewish population by assuming—with Alexander's support—the role of high priest. Even though Jonathan was of priestly stock—his father, Mattathias, had been a priest—he was not a descendant of Zadok; therefore, he was unfit to serve in this august post. What's more, many saw combining the role of governor, military commander, and high priest into one person as blasphemy. Jonathan's reckless move led to a split among many pious Jews and would create the factionalism that would persist well into the time of Jesus.

THE BOOK OF JOB

The story of Job has become synonymous with people enduring grave and ill-deserved misfortune. As in the case of the Book of Tobit, it challenges the traditional belief that a moral life will be rewarded with health, or that the righteous will always enjoy prosperity. Job's sufferings were the result of a test devised by Satan, to see if Job would abandon his faith if his blessings were taken from him. Thus, Job is plunged in penury, loses his children, and is left to lie in ashes, covered with boils and suffering great pain—all the while being mocked by his wife. Job endures his fate, longing for death, though firm in his belief that "my Redeemer lives" (JOB **19:25**). For his steadfastness, God restored his health and prosperity, and allowed him to start a new family. As such, the Book of Job tackles the difficult question of why a benevolent God can tolerate so much suffering in the world. ■

SIMON MACCABEUS

The leadership of the Jewish revolt now fell on the last surviving Maccabean brother, **Simon** (142–134 B.C.E.). In Syria, meanwhile, reigning King Demetrius II (145–140 B.C.E.) faced a powerful challenge from Trypho, Jonathan's assassin. Simon pledged his full support for Demetrius's crown, on condition that the king formally recognized Judea as an independent kingdom. Demetrius responded by suspending all tax collection in Judea in 142 B.C.E., effectively granting Simon's demand by default. The following year, Simon was acclaimed by a large assembly "of the priests and the people and of the elders of the land" as "their leader and high priest forever" (I MACCABEES 14:41).

Thus, 445 years after the capture of Jerusalem by Babylonian King Nebuchadnezzar, the Jews were free once again. For eight precious decades, the kingdom of David and Solomon would be restored in the form of the Hasmonean Dynasty.

The Maccabee Shrine in the Sankt Andreas Kirche in Cologne, Germany, is traditionally believed to hold the relics of the Maccabee brothers.

ca 62 B.C.E.	ca 54 B.C.E.	ca 48 B.C.E.	ca 47 B.C.E.
Founding of Florence	Caesar invades Britain	Caesar defeats Pompey at Pharsalia	Herod is appointed governor of Galilee by his father, Antipater

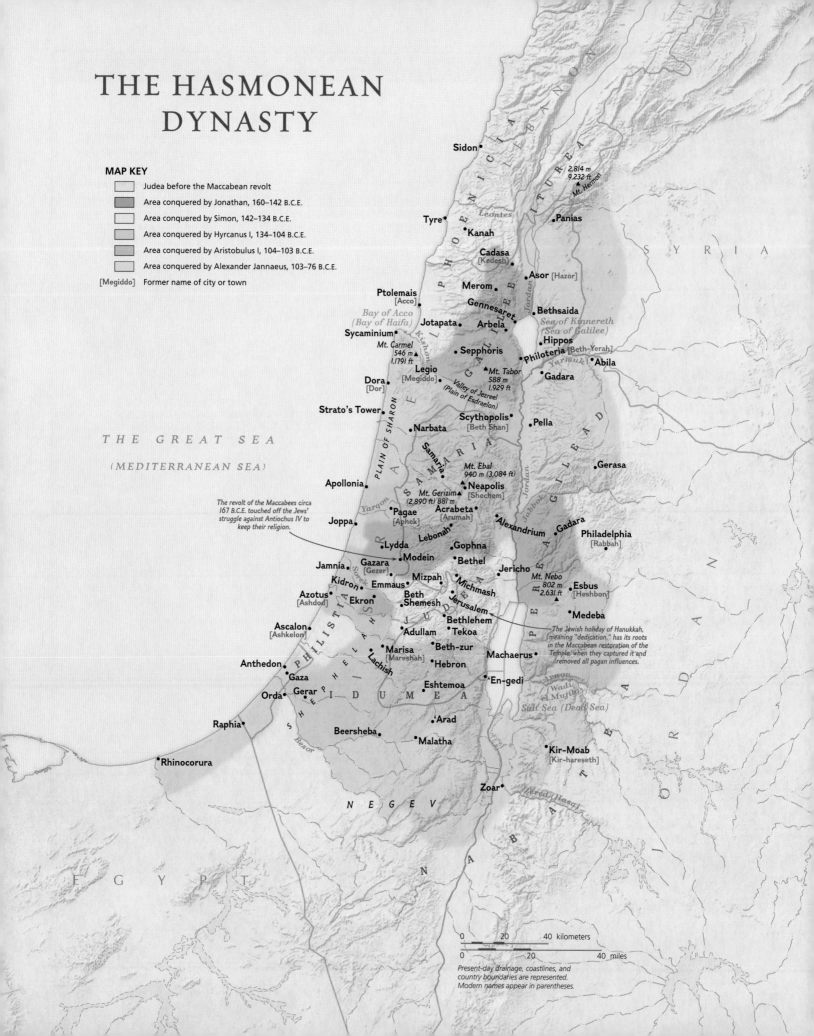

THE HASMONEAN DYNASTY

MAP KEY

Judea before the Maccabean revolt
Area conquered by Jonathan, 160–142 B.C.E.
Area conquered by Simon, 142–134 B.C.E.
Area conquered by Hyrcanus I, 134–104 B.C.E.
Area conquered by Aristobulus I, 104–103 B.C.E.
Area conquered by Alexander Jannaeus, 103–76 B.C.E.

[Megiddo]   Former name of city or town

Sidon

P H O E N I C I A

I T U R E A

2,814 m
9,232 ft
▲ Mt. Hermon

S Y R I A

Tyre

Leontes

Kanah

Panias

Cadasa
[Kedesh]

Asor [Hazor]

Merom

Bethsaida

Ptolemais
[Acco]

*Bay of Acco
(Bay of Haifa)*

G A L I L E E

Gennesaret

Jordan

Jotapata

Arbela

*Sea of Kinnereth
(Sea of Galilee)*

Sycaminium

Sepphoris

Hippos

Philoteria [Beth-Yerah]

Mt. Carmel
546 m ▲
1,1791 ft

Legio
[Megiddo]

▲ Mt. Tabor
588 m
1,929 ft

Yarmuk

Gadara

Abila

Dora
[Dor]

*Valley of Jezreel
(Plain of Esdraelon)*

G I L E A D

Strato's Tower

P L A I N   O F   S H A R O N

Scythopolis
[Beth Shan]

Pella

Narbata

Kishon

S A M A R I A

Mt. Ebal
940 m (3,084 ft)

Gerasa

Apollonia

Jordan

Mt. Gerizim
(2,890 ft) 881 m

Neapolis
[Shechem]

Jabbok

T H E   G R E A T   S E A

(MEDITERRANEAN SEA)

The revolt of the Maccabees circa
167 B.C.E. touched off the Jews'
struggle against Antiochus IV to
keep their religion.

Pagae
[Aphek]

Acrabeta
[Arumah]

Alexandrium

Gadara

Philadelphia
[Rabbah]

Joppa

Yarqon

Lebonah

Gophna

P E R E A

Lydda

Modein

Bethel

Jericho

Mt. Nebo
802 m
2,631 ft ▲

Esbus
[Heshbon]

Jamnia

Gazara
[Gezer]

Sorek

Mizpah

Michmash

Kidron

Emmaus

Azotus
[Ashdod]

Ekron

Beth
Shemesh

Jerusalem

J U D A E A

Bethlehem

Medeba

Ascalon
[Ashkelon]

P H I L I S T I A

Adullam

Tekoa

Marisa
[Mareshah]

Beth-zur

Machaerus

The Jewish holiday of Hanukkah,
meaning "dedication," has its roots
in the Maccabean restoration of the
Temple, when they captured it and
removed all pagan influences.

Anthedon

S H E P H E L A H

Lachish

Hebron

Gaza

Gerar

Eshtemoa

'En-gedi

*Arnon
Wadi
el-Mujib*

Orda

I D U M E A

Salt Sea (Dead Sea)

Raphia

Besor

'Arad

Beersheba

Malatha

Kir-Moab
[Kir-hareseth]

E G Y P T

N A B A T E A

N E G E V

Zoar

Nahal Hasa

T R A N S J O R D A N

0   20   40 kilometers

0   20   40 miles

*Present-day drainage, coastlines, and
country boundaries are represented.
Modern names appear in parentheses.*

Rhinocorura

THE ESSENES

During the polarization of Jewish society under the Hasmoneans, one group took an extreme view and withdrew from social life altogether. This community, called "the Essenes" by Josephus, formed a "commune" of sorts to pursue an ascetic lifestyle entirely based on Covenant Law. These Essenes were outraged by the Hasmonean usurpation of the office of high priest, which traditionally was reserved for descendants of the priest Zadok. This is why the Essenes referred to Jonathan Maccabeus and his "unqualified" successors as "the wicked priest" (*Kohein ha-Resha,* literally meaning "bad priest").

Withdrawn into their monastic retreats, the Essenes dressed in simple robes, prayed at regular intervals, and worked long hours tilling the desert soil. "They despise riches," Josephus

These remains of the Qumran settlement, dated between 150 B.C.E. and 70 C.E., are believed to have been inhabited by a sect, possibly related to the Essenes, who produced the Dead Sea Scrolls.

wrote, claiming that the movement numbered around 4,000 members, "and it is a law among them, that those who join must let whatever they have be shared with the whole order."

To the Essenes, physical and spiritual cleanliness were one and the same. They dug an elaborate network of cisterns to catch the rainfall, or to channel water from nearby springs, so that they could practice ritual immersion on a daily basis. On the Sabbath, they even withheld their bodily functions. The purpose of this ascetic lifestyle, practiced under the leadership of a "Teacher of Righteousness"—significantly, a Zadokite, was to bring the Essenes closer to God. For the Essenes, their sheltered community formed a new Temple, a *restored* Temple, just as their obedience to the Law represented a new form of sacrifice. ∎

THE HASMONEAN DYNASTY

Simon and his successors soon expanded Judea's territory to the legendary borders of David's kingdom. Simon had wisely dispatched a delegation to Rome to secure the recognition of the Roman Senate for his fledgling new kingdom, so that Judea's western flank was secure. With greatly expanded forces, Simon was able to defeat a halfhearted attempt by Antiochus VII to recapture Judea. In 135, however, he and his family fell victim to an assassination plot near Jericho, possibly engineered by the Syrian king himself. But the coup failed because one of Simon's sons, **John Hyrcanus**, escaped the assassins. John rushed to Jerusalem, where he was acclaimed as Judea's new leader and high priest; he then ruled for 30 years, during which he added Idumea and Samaria to Hasmonean territory.

Three other rulers would follow after John: his son Aristobulus (104–103 B.C.E.), the first to assume the title of "king"; his other son Alexander Jannaeus (103–76 B.C.E.), who married Aristobulus's widow Salome Alexandra; and finally, Salome Alexandra (76–67 B.C.E.) herself.

When Salome died, a power struggle erupted between her son and designated heir, Hyrcanus II (already serving as high priest) and her younger son Aristobulus II. Because Hyrcanus favored the political

faction of the Pharisees, the other party, the Sadducees, threw their support behind Aristobulus, who was able to capture the crown. Hyrcanus fled, but then asked King Aretas III of Nabataea, a territory roughly analogous to modern Jordan, to intervene. Aretas agreed, invaded Judah with his army, and laid siege to Jerusalem in 66 B.C.E. Judea was once again plunged in civil war.

These developments were of considerable concern to Rome. The Senate feared that the turmoil could spill over into Egypt, a vital supplier of grain to Rome's growing population. As it happened, the famous Roman General Pompeius (later known as Pompey the Great) had arrived in Damascus, fresh from defeating King Mithridates VI of Pontus (the northern coastal region of modern Turkey). Three separate delegations then rushed to the general in the hope of winning Rome's support: the Aristobulus faction; the Hyrcanus faction; and the Pharisees, who urged Pompey to get rid of the Hasmoneans altogether.

Pompey did neither; he simply marched into Judea, captured Jerusalem, and so put an end to Jewish independence. For the next 600 years, save for brief periods of rebellion, Palestine would be a dominion of Rome and its successor, Byzantium, until the Islamic conquest of 638 C.E.

ca 47 B.C.E.	ca 44 B.C.E.	ca 42 B.C.E.	ca 40 B.C.E.
Pompey is murdered in Egypt on orders of Cleopatra VII	Caesar is murdered in the Senate in Rome	Brutus and Cassius, murderers of Caesar, are defeated at Philippi	Herod is declared king of Judea in Rome

TREASURES OF THE PERSIAN AND GREEK AGE

Coinciding with the Persian and Greek occupation of Judea, the Hellenizing influence of Greek culture became widespread in the Levant. These Hellenistic influences made their way into Judea through Phoenicia, whose cultural and economic sphere stretched along the Mediterranean coast and across much of Galilee. This must have shocked the devout Jews of the region, who remained faithful to the Mosaic edict against "graven images." For the next 300 years, many practicing Jews would fight this new cultural imperialism with varying degrees of success until the arrival of a new and even greater imperialism—the reign of the Roman Caesars.

In the Persian realm, the Achaemenid dynasty of Persia continued to adorn its palaces at Pasargadae, Persepolis, and Susa with life-size, bas-relief sculptures that deliberately aimed to surpass their Assyrian predecessors. The Achaemenids also continued the Persian virtuosity in silver or gold objects, including a fondness for drinking cups fashioned in the shape of animals—such as the mythological winged lion that is the hallmark of Achaemenid rule. This artisan tradition was absorbed in the subsequent Parthian and Sassanid Empires, the last great Persian civilizations before the Muslim conquest.

Molded Enamel *Archers of the Persian Guard march on this wall of molded enameled brick from Darius's palace at Susa from ca 510 B.C.E.*

Gold Wreath *This beautiful gold wreath was found in the Crimea and is dated to the Hellenistic period around 300 B.C.E. Such gold wreaths have been found in Hellenistic tombs throughout the Mediterranean world.*

Persepolis Figurine *This figure appears on the western stairway facade of Darius's palace in Persepolis, added by Artaxerxes II in the late fifth century* B.C.E. *It once formed part of a procession of delegations bearing homage to the king.*

Glassware *A glass cup found in Palestine probably dates from the fourth century* B.C.E., *after improvements in core-forming techniques during the fifth century made the production of glass widespread.*

Silver Likeness *This Sassanid head, hammered from a single sheet of silver, was found in Iran and probably dates to the fourth century* C.E. *The elaborate crown suggests that the sitter was a king.*

Alexander Sarcophagus *A Greek depiction of Alexander the Great on his horse, routing the Persians, forms part of the so-called "Alexander Sarcophagus," dating from the late fourth century* B.C.E.

Achaemenid Gold *This fifth-century* B.C.E. *gold vessel in the shape of a lioness, probably crafted for royal use, demonstrates the mastery of Achaemenid artisans in precious metals.*

CHAPTER 3
WHO'S WHO

An Alphabetical Listing of Characters in the Books of Chronicles Through Maccabees

ABIJAH
("worshipper of God")

1. Second son of Samuel (I SAMUEL 8:2; I CHRONICLES 6:28). His conduct as a judge in Beersheba, along with that of his brother, led to popular discontent and ultimately provoked the people to demand a royal form of government.

"Samuel and His Sons Joel and Abijah" was produced by the French School in the 14th century.

2. Descendant of Eleazar, son of Aaron, and a chief of one of the 24 orders of priesthood, which David established (I CHRONICLES 24:10).
3. Son of Rehoboam, whom he succeeded on the throne of Judah (I CHRONICLES 3:10). He is also called Abijam (I KINGS 14:31; 15:1-8). He tried unsuccessfully to bring back the ten tribes to their allegiance.
4. Son of Jeroboam, the first king of Israel. He was severely ill as a child and, as per a prophet's divination, passed away in peace

and was greatly mourned by all of Israel (I KINGS 14:1-18).
5. Daughter of Zechariah and wife of Ahaz; also called Abi (II CHRONICLES 29:1; II KINGS 18:2).
6. Son of Becher, the son of Benjamin (I CHRONICLES 7:8).

ABISHUR
("father of protection")

One of the two sons of Shammai, of the tribe of Judah (I CHRONICLES 2:28-29).

ADAIAH
("witness of God")

1. Father of Queen Jedidah, the mother of King Josiah, native of Bozkath in the lowlands of Judah (II KINGS 22:1).
2. A Levite of the Gershonite branch, and ancestor of Asaph; a musician (I CHRONICLES 6:41).
3. A priest (I CHRONICLES 9:12; NEHEMIAH 11:12).
4. A Benjamite, son of Shimhi (I CHRONICLES 8:21).
5. A priest, son of Jehoram (I CHRONICLES 9:12; NEHEMIAH 11:12).
6. Father/ancestor of Maaseiah, one of the captains who supported Jehoiada (II CHRONICLES 23:1).
7. Two different descendants of Bani (EZRA 10:29,39).
8. Son of Joiarib, of the line of Pharez, within Judah's tribe (NEHEMIAH 11:5).

ADIEL
("ornament of God")

1. A prince of the tribe of Simeon, descended from the family of Shimei (I CHRONICLES 4:36).
2. A priest, father/ancestor of Maasai (I CHRONICLES 9:12).
3. Father/ancestor of Azmaveth, treasurer under David and Solomon (I CHRONICLES 27:25).

ADMATHA
("given by the highest")

One of the seven princes of Persia (ESTHER 1:14).

ADNA
("pleasure")

1. A priest, descendant of Harim in the days of Joiakim, Jeshua's son (NEHEMIAH 12:15).
2. One of the family of Pahath-moab, who returned with Ezra and married a foreign wife (EZRA 10:30).

ADNAH
("pleasure")

1. A Manassite who deserted Saul to join David's army on the road to Ziklag. He was one of David's captains, and fought at his side in the pursuit of the Amalekites (I CHRONICLES 12:20).
2. A military captain of 300,000 men of Judah, who were in Jehoshaphat's army (II CHRONICLES 17:14).

ADUEL

Son of Gabael, who was father to Tobiel, Tobit's father, "of the lineage of Asiel and tribe of Naphtali" (TOBIT 1:1).

AGIA

"The descendant of Solomon's servants" who returned with Zerubbabel to Jerusalem (I ESDRAS 5:34).

AGUR
("gathered")

Son of Jakeh; he is mentioned as an author of sayings in Proverbs (PROVERBS 30:1-9).

AHASUERUS
("king")

1. King of Persia, father of Darius the Mede (DANIEL 9:1).
2. King of Persia, who divorced his wife, Queen Vashti, and married Esther, cousin

Artist Antoine Coypel (1661–1722) painted this canvas of "Esther Before Ahasuerus" around 1697.

and ward of Mordecai. As revenge against a slight by Mordecai, his counselor Haman persuaded the king to issue an edict to kill all the Jews in his kingdom. However, Esther was able to persuade Ahasuerus to kill Haman and arm all Jews with weapons, thereby saving her people (ESTHER 1:1-3).

AHIO
("God's brother")
1. A Levite, son of Abinadab, who accompanied the Ark of the Covenant when it was brought out of his father's house by cart (II SAMUEL 6:3-4; I CHRONICLES 13:7).
2. One of the sons of Beriah, a Benjamite (I CHRONICLES 8:14).
3. One of the sons of Jeiel, the Gibeonite, and Maacah (I CHRONICLES 8:31; 9:37).

AKKUB
("insidious")
1. A descendant of Zerubbabel and son of Elioenai (I CHRONICLES 3:24).
2. One of the porters at the east gate of the Temple, whose ancestors returned from exile with Zerubbabel (EZRA 2:42-5).
3. A gatekeeper during the reign of Nehemiah (NEHEMIAH 11:19).
4. A Levite who assisted Ezra in explaining the Law to the people (NEHEMIAH 8:7).

ALCIMUS
("valiant")
Descendant of Aaron who became a high priest of Jerusalem with the help of King Demetrius and his army led by Bacchides. Alcimus's support of the Greeks led him to bitterly oppose the Maccabees. When Bacchides and his army returned to Antioch, Simon Maccabeus attacked and defeated Alcimus, driving him into Syria. With Demetrius's help, he eventually regained his priestly position in Jerusalem, but died soon afterward (I MACCABEES 7:4-50; 9:1,57; 2 MACCABEES 14).

A detail of Alexander the Great is from a mosaic in the House of the Faun in Pompeii, which was inspired by a painting by Philoxeilos of Entrea (356–323 B.C.E.).

ALEXANDER THE GREAT
King of Macedonia, who succeeded his father Philip, and died at the age of 32. He conquered a vast empire, which was divided among his generals after his death.

AMARIAH
("the Lord says")
1. Father of Ahitub and son of Meraioth, in the line of the high priests (I CHRONICLES 6:52,71).
2. High priest in the reign of Jehoshaphat (II CHRONICLES 19:11). He was the son of Azariah.
3. Head of a Levitical house of the Kohathites (I CHRONICLES 23:13; 24:23).
4. Head of one of the 24 courses (II CHRONICLES 31:15; NEHEMIAH 10:3; 12:2,13).
5. One of the sons of Bani in the time of Ezra (EZRA 10:42).
6. A priest who returned with Zerubbabel (NEHEMIAH 10:3; 12:2,13).
7. Descendant of Pharez (NEHEMIAH 11:4).
8. Ancestor of Zephaniah the prophet (ZEPHANIAH 1:1).

AMASAI
("burdensome")
1. A Levite, son of Elkanah, of the ancestry of Samuel (I CHRONICLES 6:25,35).
2. Leader of a body of men who joined David in the "stronghold," probably of Adullam (I CHRONICLES 12:18).
3. One of the priests appointed to precede the Ark ark on its removal from the house of Obed-edom (I CHRONICLES 15:24).
4. Father of a Levite named Mahath, one of the two Kohathites who took part in the cleansing of the Temple (II CHRONICLES 29:12).

AMASHAI
("the people's gift")
1. Son of Azarel, appointed by Nehemiah to reside at Jerusalem (NEHEMIAH 11:13).
2. A chieftain of Judah (NEHEMIAH 11:13).

AMMIZABAD
("people of the giver")
Son of Benaiah, who was a captain of the army under David (I CHRONICLES 27:6).

AMOK
One of the leaders of the priests and their associates in the days of Jeshua (NEHEMIAH 12:7,20).

ANAEL
Tobit's brother and Achiacharus's father, who was an official in Nineveh under Esar-haddon (TOBIT 1:21).

ANANIAH
("protected by Jehovah")
Son of Maaseiah (NEHEMIAH 3:23; 8:4).

ANDRONICUS
("conqueror")
1. An officer who was left as viceroy in Antioch by Antiochus Epiphanes during his absence (II MACCABEES 4:31-38).
2. Another officer of Antiochus Epiphanes, who was left on Gerizem (II MACCABEES 5:23).

ANNA
("gracious")
An aged widow, the daughter of Phanuel, who was a "prophetess," like Miriam, Deborah, and Huldah (II CHRONICLES 34:22).

ANTIOCHUS
("opponent")
Name of a number of kings of the Seleucid Empire of Syria, including:
1. Antiochus the Great, the "king of the north" (DANIEL 11:13-19). He was succeeded by his son, Seleucus Philopator (DANIEL 11:20).
2. Antiochus IV, surnamed "Epiphanes," who succeeded his brother Seleucus. Antiochus IV proscribed the Jewish religion and forced the Jews to make pagan sacrifices, which led to the Maccabean revolt.

APAME
A concubine of Darius and daughter of Bartacus the Illustrious (I ESDRAS 4:29).

APHERRA
Head of a family in the postexilic list; one of eight listed in I Esdras 5:34.

APOLLONIUS
1. Son of Thrasaeus and governor of Coele-Syria under the reign of King Seleucus. When Heliodorus robbed the Temple in Jerusalem, he supported Simon, the governor of the Temple, over Onias, the high

This marble bust is believed to represent Antiochus III (ruled 223–187 B.C.E.).

priest. He retired to Miletus when Antiochus Epiphanes became the new king (II MACCABEES 3:5).
2. Son of Apollonius (see previous entry), and raised in Rome with Demetrius, son of King Seleucus. Like his father, he became governor of Coele-Syria and Phoenicia. When Alexander Balas ousted Demetrius, he continued to support the toppled king (I MACCABEES 10:69).
3. Son of Menestheus and Antiochus Epiphanes's ambassador in Rome and Egypt. During a return from Egypt, he led an attack on Jerusalem with 22,000 men (I MACCABEES 1:29; II MACCABEES 4:21, 5:24-27).
4. Governor of Samaria during the reign of Antiochus Epiphanes. He was killed by Judas Maccabeus (I MACCABEES 3:10-11).
5. Son of Gennaeus and governor in Judea during the reign of Antiochus Eupator (II MACCABEES 12:2).

ARIARATHES OR ARATHES
King of Cappadocia. Educated in Rome, he declined to marry the sister of Demetrius Soter, as Rome has insisted. Rome declared war, drove Arathes from his kingdom and established Holofernes in his place. Arathes fled to Rome, and was granted a return to Cappadocia, where he played a role in the government. With time, he again was allowed to become king (I MACCABEES 15:22).

ARIEL
("lion of God")
1. One of the men Ezra sent to direct a caravan from Babylon to Jerusalem (EZRA 8:16).

A detail of Artaxerxes I (ruled 464–424 B.C.E.) comes from the Hall of 100 Columns in Persepolis, Iran.

2. Symbolic name that Isaiah gave to the city of Jerusalem (ISAIAH 29:1-2,7).

ARIUS
A king of Sparta, who wrote the letter to the high priest Onias that appears in I Maccabees (I MACCABEES 12:7,20-23).

ARSACES IV
Arsaces is the name assumed by many Parthian kings. Arsaces IV is mentioned in connection with the history of Demetrius, one of the Seleucid kings of Syria, and successor to Antiochus Epiphanes, the oppressor of the Jews, who caused the uprising against Syrian rule under the leadership of the Maccabees (I MACCABEES 14:1-3; 15:22).

ARSINOE III
Daughter of Berenice and Ptolemy II; sister/wife of Ptolemy IV.

ARTAXERXES
("righteous ruler")
Son of Xerxes and king of Persia for 40 years, who commissioned Ezra to restore religious observance in Judah. Artaxerxes also allowed Nehemiah to return to Jerusalem to help rebuild the city walls (EZRA 7:1; NEHEMIAH 2:1; 5:14).

ASAIAH
("whom God has made")
1. Prince of one of the families of the Simeonites during the reign of Hezekiah (I CHRONICLES 4:36).

2. A priest (II KINGS 22:14).

3. A Levite and chief of the family of Merari, who lived during the reign of David (I CHRONICLES 6:30). He took part in bringing the Ark from the house of Obed-edom to the city of David (I CHRONICLES 15:6,11).

4. Firstborn of "the Shilonite," who lived with his family in Jerusalem after the return from exile in Babylon (I CHRONICLES 9:5).

ASAPH
("collector")

1. A Levite, son of Berechiah, and one of the three leaders of David's choir. He was celebrated as a seer and musical composer. His sons were also poets and singers, who performed under their father as master (I CHRONICLES 6:39; 20:14; II CHRONICLES 29:30; EZRA 2:41; NEHEMIAH 12:46).

2. Father of Joah, and a scribe in the kingdom of Judah during the reign of Hezekiah (II KINGS 18:18,37; ISAIAH 36:3,22).

ASHHUR
("successful")

The "father of Tekoa," probably indicating he founded the village (I CHRONICLES 2:24; 4:5).

ASHPENAZ

Master of the eunuchs at the court of Nebuchadnezzar (DANIEL 1:3).

ASTYAGES

King of the Medes and predecessor of Cyrus (Bel and the Dragon). His wife was the daughter of Alyattes, king of Lydia. His daughter Mandane married Persian King Cambyses, and their son later became known as Cyrus the Great.

ATHENOBIUS

Friend of Antiochus VII, who was sent to Jerusalem by the king to protest against the occupation of Joppa and Gazara, and the citadel Jerusalem. His mission failed and he returned to Antiochus (I MACCABEES 15:28-36).

ATTAI
("timely")

1. Grandson of Sheshan through his daughter Ahlai, whom he gave in marriage to Jarha,

his Egyptian slave (I CHRONICLES 2:35,36). His grandson Zabad was one of David's mighty men (I CHRONICLES 11:41).

2. A Gadite warrior (I CHRONICLES 12:11).

3. Second son of King Rehoboam by Maacah, daughter of Absalom (II CHRONICLES 11:20).

ATTALUS
("increased")

King of Pergamum, and one of the kings whom Rome instructed to stop the persecution of the Jewish population (I MACCABEES 15:22).

ATTHARATES

A title assigned to Nehemiah, as usually conferred on a local or provincial Persian governor (NEHEMIAH 8:9; I ESDRAS 9:49).

ATUR OR ATER
("maimed")

1. Descendant of Hezekiah, who returned from the Babylonian exile with Zerubbabel (EZRA 2:16; NEHEMIAH 7:21).

2. A gatekeeper of the Temple who returned with Zerubbabel (EZRA 2:42; NEHEMIAH 7:45).

3. An Israelite who signed the covenant with Nehemiah (NEHEMIAH 10:17).

AZAREL
("God's helper")

1. A Korahite who entered the army of David at Ziklag (I CHRONICLES 12:6).

2. A musician in the temple appointed by lot; son of Heman (I CHRONICLES 25:4,18).

3. A captain of the tribe of Dan in the service of David (I CHRONICLES 27:22).

4. Son of Bani (EZRA 10:41).

5. Father of Amashai, a priest who lived in Jerusalem after the exile (NEHEMIAH 11:13).

6. A priest's son who played the trumpet when the wall was dedicated (NEHEMIAH 12:36).

AZARIAH
("whom God helps")

1. Son of Ethan from the tribe of Judah (I CHRONICLES 2:8).

2. Son of Jehu and descendant of Jarha, an Egyptian slave from Sheshan (I CHRONICLES 2:38-39).

3. Son of Ahimaaz, who became high priest after his grandfather Zadok during the reign of Solomon (I CHRONICLES 6:9; I KINGS 4:2).

4. Son of Hilkiah (I CHRONICLES 6:13-14; 9:11; EZRA 7:1,3).

5. Tenth king of Judah, also known as Uzziah. Azariah is possibly the son of Zephaniah, ancestor of Samuel the prophet (I CHRONICLES 6:36; 8:12; II KINGS 14:21; 15:1-27).

6. Son of Johanan, high priest during the

Azarel was one of the men who joined David in battle after the raid of Ziklag, as depicted in this 14th-century miniature.

reigns of Abijah and Asa (II CHRONICLES 6:10-11; 24:20-22).

7. Son of Obed, and prophet during the reign of Asa (II CHRONICLES 15:1,8; 23:3).

8. Son of Jehoshaphat (II CHRONICLES 21:2).

9. Another son of Jehoshaphat (II CHRONICLES 21:2).

10. King Uzziah of Judah, who in some texts is also known as Azariah (II CHRONICLES 22:6).

11. Son of Jeroham, one of the captains in Judah, who joined the conspiracy to overthrow Queen Athaliah (II CHRONICLES 23:1).

12. High priest during the reign of Uzziah, king of Judah, who beseeched the king not to burn incense on the altar, because this was reserved for priests (II CHRONICLES 26:17-20; II KINGS 14:21).

13. Leader of the Ephraim tribe (II CHRONICLES 28:12).

14. A Kohathite, and father of Joel during the reign of King Hezekiah, who obeyed Hezekiah's command to cleanse the Temple (II CHRONICLES 29:12).

15. A Merarite, and son of Jehallelel during the reign of Hezekiah, who obeyed Hezekiah's command to cleanse the Temple (II CHRONICLES 29:12).

16. Son of Hadok, and high priest during the reign of Hezekiah. He worked with the king

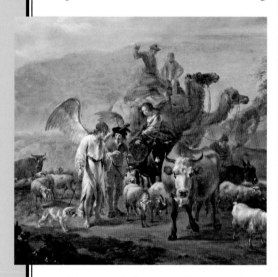

"The Return of Tobias," painted by artist Nicolaes Pietersz Berchem (1620–1683), features Tobias and the angel Raphael, who assumed the name Azarias.

to purify and restore the Temple (II CHRONICLES 31:10-13).

17. Son of Nathan, and captain of the guards during the reign of Solomon (I KINGS 4:5).

18. Hebrew name of Abednego. He was from the royal family of Judah, known for physical attractiveness, intelligence, and being religious (DANIEL 1:6-7,11,16,19).

19. Son of Hoshaiah and a leader of Judah after the Babylonian conquest. He urged that the people flee to Egypt (JEREMIAH 43:2-7).

20. Son of Maaseiah who repaired the wall of Jerusalem during the reign of Nehemiah (NEHEMIAH 3:23-24).

21. A captive who returned from Babylon with Zerubbabel (NEHEMIAH 7:7; 10:2).

22. A Levite who assisted Ezra in teaching the people the Law (NEHEMIAH 8:7).

23. A priest of Judah who signed the covenant with Nehemiah.

24. A priest of Judah who assisted with the dedication of the city wall (NEHEMIAH 10:2; 12:33).

AZARIAS

1. Man who put away his foreign-born wife (I ESDRAS 9:21; EZRA 10:21).

2. One of the leaders who stood with Ezra when he read the Law of Moses to the people in the Jerusalem marketplace (NEHEMIAH 8:4).

3. A name assumed by the angel Raphael (TOBIT 5:12; 6:6,13; 7:8; 9:2).

4. A general in the service of Judas Maccabee (I MACCABEES 5:18,56,60).

5. One of the three men thrown into the fiery furnace (DANIEL 1:6; 2:17).

AZAZIAH
("God has strengthened")

1. A Levite and harp player in the Temple (I CHRONICLES 15:21).

2. Father of Hoshea, who was made ruler over the Ephraimites (I CHRONICLES 27:20).

3. One of the Levites who took charge of the Temple tithes and offerings during the reign of King Hezekiah (II CHRONICLES 31:13).

AZMAVETH
("strong unto death")

1. One of David's 30 warriors from Bahurim, Azmaveth was the father of Jeziel and Pelet, two skilled archers who joined David's army at Ziklag. He became an overseer of the royal treasury (II SAMUEL 23:31; I CHRONICLES 8:36; 9:42; 10:3).

2. Son of Jehoaddah of the tribe of Benjamin; a descendant of King Saul (I CHRONICLES 27:25).

AZRIEL
("help of God")

1. Head of a house of the half tribe of Manasseh beyond Jordan (I CHRONICLES 5:24).

2. A Naphtalite, ancestor of Jerimoth, the

head of the tribe at the time of David (I CHRONICLES 27:19).

3. The father of Seraiah, an officer of Jehoiakim who was sent to arrest Jeremiah (JEREMIAH 36:26).

AZRIKAM
("help against the enemy")

1. Descendant of Zerubbabel, who was the son of Neariah from the royal family of Judah (I CHRONICLES 3:23).

2. Eldest son of Azel, descendant of Saul from the tribe of Benjamin (I CHRONICLES 8:38; 9:44).

3. A Levite and descendant of Shemaiah during the reign of Nehemiah, who resettled in Jerusalem after the Babylonian exile (I CHRONICLES 9:14; NEHEMIAH 11:15).

4. Commander in the palace of King Ahaz of Judah. He was killed by Zichri, a soldier in King Pekah's army during the attack on Judah (II CHRONICLES 28:7).

BACCHIDES

General and governor over the western part of the Seleucid kingdom during the reigns of Antiochus IV Epiphanes and Demetrius I Soter (I MACCABEES 7:8). He defeated the Maccabean army at the Battle of Elasa, where Judas Maccabeus was killed. He failed to defeat the Jewish warriors under command of Jonathan, the brother of Judas Maccabee (I MACCABEES 9:58).

BACENOR

Officer in Judas Maccabeus's army who fought against Gorgias, governor of Idumaea (II MACCABEES 12:35).

BAGOAS

A eunuch in the household of Holofernes, commander of the Babylonian army invading Judea. He took Judith under his wing, and later discovered the corpse of Holofernes after Judith had cut off his head (JUDITH 12:11; 13:1-3; 14:14).

BANI
("built")

1. A Gadite, and one of David's warriors (II Samuel 23:36).

2. A Levite and forefather of Ethan who played music in the Tabernacle during King David's reign (I Chronicles 6:46).

3. A leader of the tribe of Judah, whose descendants settled in Jerusalem after the exile (I Chronicles 9:4).

4. Ancestor of a family that returned with Zerubbabel from the Babylonian exile (Ezra 2:10; 10:29,34).

5. Father of Rehum, who helped rebuild the wall of Jerusalem (Nehemiah 3:17).

6. A Levite who helped Ezra explain the Law to the people (Nehemiah 8:7).

7. Father of Uzzi who supervised Temple services after the return from Babylon (Nehemiah 11:22).

BATH-SHUA
("daughter of wealth")

1. A Canaanite and wife of Judah. Mother to their three sons: Er, Onan, and Shelah (Genesis 38:1-5).

2. Daughter of Ammiel, also known as Bathsheba, the wife of Uriah who later became wife of David (I Chronicles 3:5).

BEDEIAH
("branch of God")

One of the men who divorced their foreignborn wives during the days of Ezra (Ezra 10:35).

BEELIADA
("who knows Baal")

Son of King David who was born in Jerusalem, also known as Eliada (II Samuel 5:16; I Chronicles 3:8; 14:7).

BELSHAZZAR
("the god Bel protects the king")

According to the Book of Daniel, he was the son of Nebuchadnezzar and his successor, though historically this is not the case. He invited a large group of guests to a great banquet where he and his princes drank out of silver and gold vessels that Nebuchadnezzar had taken from the Temple in Jerusalem. In the midst of their feast, a hand was seen writing a mysterious message on the wall, which the king's counselors were not able to understand. At the insistence of the queen, Daniel was brought in to interpret the cryptic writing. Later that night, the kingdom of the Babylonians came to an end, and Belshazzar was slain (Daniel 5:3,25; 7:1; 8:1).

BELTESHAZZAR
The Babylonian name given to Daniel by Nebuchadnezzar (Daniel 1:7).

BELTETHMUS
An official who helped compose a letter to King Artaxerxes opposing the rebuilding of Jerusalem, stating the people of Judah and Jerusalem would not pay tribute to him as king (I Esdras 2:16-19).

BERECHIAH
("blessed by God")

1. Fourth of five sons of Zerubbabel, from the Judah royal family (I Chronicles 3:20).

2. Son of Shimea, and father of Asaph, a musician during the reign of David (I Chronicles 6:39; 15:17).

3. A Levite and son of Asa, who ministered in the Temple after the return from exile (I Chronicles 9:16).

4. A gatekeeper of the Ark in the reign of King David (I Chronicles 15:23).

5. Son of Meshillemoth and one of the seven Ephraimite leaders during the reign of Ahaz. When King Pekah's army attacked Judah, Berechiah supported the prophet Oded, insisting that Pekah's captives be returned to Judah (II Chronicles 28:12).

6. Father of Meshullam, who helped rebuild the walls of Jerusalem (Nehemiah 3:4,30; 6:18).

7. Son of Iddo and father of Zechariah (Zechariah 1:1,7).

BERIAH
("excellent")

1. One of Asher's four sons, and father of Heber (Genesis 46:17).

2. Son of Ephraim, born after some of his brothers were murdered by the men of Gath (I Chronicles 7:20-23).

Italian artist Pietro Dandini (ca 1646–1712) painted the canvas "Belshazzar's Feast."

3. A Benjamite living in Aijalon who drove away the people of Gath with his brother Shema (I Chronicles 8:13).

4. A Levite, and son of Shimei, who served in the Tabernacle during King David's reign (I Chronicles 23:10-11).

BIGVAI
1. Head of a family that returned from Babylon with Zerubbabel with more than 2,000 people (Ezra 2:2,14; Nehemiah 7:7,19).

2. A leader of Judah who signed the covenant in the time of Nehemiah (Nehemiah 10:16).

BILDAD
("son of contention")

One of Job's three friends who was called "the Shuhite" (Job 2:11). Bildad, along with Job's other two friends, comforted Job in his grief by sitting with him for seven days and seven nights. When Job broke his silence, Bildad and his friends were surprised by Job's bitterness, tried to console him, and finally scolded him. The Lord ordered them to offer a burnt sacrifice as penance (Job 8:1; 18:1; 25:1).

BINNUI
("building")

1. A Levite and the father of Noadiah, who helped the priest Meremoth weigh the silver and gold vessels of the Temple brought back to Jerusalem by Ezra (Ezra 8:33).

2. Descendant of Pahath-moab who divorced his foreign-born wife during the days of Ezra (EZRA 10:30).

3. Head of a family who returned with Zerubbabel from Babylon (NEHEMIAH 7:15; 12:8).

4. A Levite who was the son of Henadad (NEHEMIAH 3:24). He assisted in repairing the wall of Jerusalem during the days of Nehemiah, and signed Nehemiah's solemn covenant (NEHEMIAH 10:9).

BISHLAM

("son of peace")

A Persian official in Samaria who together with Bishlam, Mithredath, Tabeel, and the rest of his associates wrote a letter to King Artaxerxes of Persia in protest against plans to rebuild the Temple in Jerusalem (EZRA 4:7).

BOAZ

Boaz was a wealthy relative of Elimelech, the father-in-law of Ruth. When Ruth's husband died, he was kind to her and eventually married her. He also acquired the estates of her deceased husband, Mahlon (RUTH 4:1). Their son Obed was King David's grandfather, who is also listed in the genealogies of the Gospels.

BUNNI

1. One of the Levites in the time of Nehemiah, who stood on a platform and prayed to God with other Levites (NEHEMIAH 9:4).

2. A Levite who was an ancestor of Shemaiah, one of the first Levites to settle in

Jerusalem after the return from the Babylonian exile (NEHEMIAH 11:15).

3. One of the leaders who signed Nehemiah's solemn covenant to divorce their foreign-born wives and to dedicate their firstborn to God, among other obligations (NEHEMIAH 10:15).

CARABASION

One of the sons of Bani, who had married foreign wives during the captivity (I ESDRAS 9:34).

CENDEBEUS

A general in the army of Antiochus VII who was appointed "captain of the seacoast" (I MACCABEES 16:4).

CHABRIS

Son of Gothoniel, and one of the three rulers of Bethulia in the time of Judith (JUDITH 6:15; 8:10; 10:6).

The painting titled "Ruth and Boaz" was painted by Dutch artist Aert de Gelder (1645–1727).

CHARMIS

Son of Melchiel and one of the three leaders of Bethulia (JUDITH 6:15; 8:10; 10:6).

A modern illustration depicts Cleopatra III, daughter of the Egyptian king Ptolemy VI Philometor.

CHELUB

Descendant of Judah, who was the brother of Shuah and the father of Mehir. His son Ezri was in charge of the workers who tilled the fields during the reign of King David (I CHRONICLES 27:26).

CHILION

("sickly")

Younger son of Elimelech and Naomi, and husband of Orpah, who moved to Moab with his parents and his brother Mahlon. Ten years after Chilion married Orpah, he died childless (RUTH 1:2,4-5; 4:9).

CLEOPATRA

Cleopatra III was the daughter of Egyptian King Ptolemy VI Philometor, who married Alexander Balas, a pretender to the Seleucid throne (I MACCABEES 10:57).

CONANIAH

("God has sustained")

One of the chiefs of the Levites in the time of Josiah, who gave the priests the cattle and oxen that had been donated for the Passover offerings (II CHRONICLES 35:9).

CYRUS II

King of Anshan who rose up against the Medes and ultimately took control of the Median and Babylonian Empires. He issued a decree authorizing the exiled Hebrews to return to their land, and also gave back the vessels and utensils of the Temple, which Nebuchadnezzar had brought to Babylon, to Sheshbazzar, leader of the returning captives. Cyrus encouraged the restoration of Jewish worship in Judah, and granted them leave to rebuild the Temple. These actions caused the prophet Isaiah to call him God's shepherd and God's anointed (II CHRONICLES 36:22).

DABRIA

One of five who wrote down the visions of Esdras (II ESDRAS 14:24).

DANIEL

("judge of God")

One of the great prophets of the late Old Testament era, whose book is one of the few apocalyptic texts in the Hebrew canon. According to the book, Daniel was taken captive by Nebuchadnezzar, king of Babylon, and elevated to high rank in the Babylonian and later Persian kingdoms. He was trained in the arts, letters, and wisdom in the Babylonian capital, and rose to high rank among Babylonian sages. Daniel was then called upon to explain Nebuchadnezzar's bizarre dreams, but shortly thereafter, his companions were thrown into a furnace over their refusal to worship a pagan idol. Fortunately, they stepped out of the flames completely untouched; not even their hair had been singed (DANIEL 3:27). During the reign of Belshazzar, the co-regent of King Nabonidus, Daniel was asked to explain mysterious words written on a wall: *"MENE, MENE, TEKEL,* and *PARSIN"* (DANIEL 5:5,25).

According to the book, Daniel also served as a high governmental official during the reigns of Cyrus, Cambyses, and Darius I. This provoked much envy from other courtiers. They persuaded Darius to decree that for 30 days, everyone in the kingdom could only worship statues of King Darius himself. Those who disobeyed would be thrown to the lions. Daniel ignored the decree and continued to pray to the Lord. His enemies reported this to the king, who had no choice but to throw him into a den of lions. The next morning, Darius rushed back to the den and was relieved to see that Daniel was unharmed, for God's angel had "shut the lions' mouths." Those who had denounced Daniel were thrown into the den instead, and were quickly devoured (DANIEL 6:22-24). In the last five chapters of the book, Daniel is a prophet who receives multiple apocalyptic dreams and visions. Many feature strange animals, such as a leopard with four wings and four heads, which are believed to represent all of the foreign kings that once ruled over Israel. The message of Daniel's oracles is that God will deliver his people from oppression. Scholars have argued that the Book of Daniel reached its final form during the Syrian persecutions under Antiochus IV in the second century B.C.E.

DARIUS I

King of Persia who expanded the Persian Empire, invaded Greece, and authorized the funding for the new Temple (EZRA 6:2).

DARIUS III

King of Persia who was defeated by Alexander the Great at the Battle of Issus in 333. Two years later, all of the Persian Empire had fallen to Alexander.

DELAIAH

1. Ancestor of a family that returned to Judah from Babylon with Zerubbabel (EZRA 2:60; NEHEMIAH 7:62).
2. Son of Mehetabel and the father of Shemaiah, a false prophet in the days of Nehemiah (NEHEMIAH 6:10).

DEMOPHON

Syrian general in Palestine under Antiochus

A Median officer pays homage to King Darius I in this limestone panel from ca 515 B.C.E.

V who harassed the Jews after a treaty had been signed between Lysias and Judas Maccabeus (II MACCABEES 12:2).

EDEN

("delight")

Son of Joah, and the father of Zerah (II CHRONICLES 29:12). Eden and Joah were among the Levites who gathered to make themselves ritually clean and to purify the Temple during the reign of King Hezekiah of Judah. Eden also helped to distribute offerings among the priests that the people had brought to the Temple (I CHRONICLES 6:21).

ELIASHIB

("God will restore")

1. A priest in the time of King David, who was responsible for the 11th turn of the service in the sanctuary (I CHRONICLES 24:12).
2. Son of Elioenai and one of the latest descendants of the royal family of Judah (I CHRONICLES 3:24).
3. Father of Jehohanan in whose home Ezra fasted to expiate the sins of Judah (EZRA 10:6).
4. A singer in the time of Ezra who divorced his foreign-born wife (EZRA 10:24).
5. A descendant of Zattu who divorced his foreign-born wife (EZRA 10:27).

6. A descendant of Bani who divorced his foreign-born wife (EZRA 10:36).

7. High priest at Jerusalem at the time of the rebuilding of the walls under Nehemiah (NEHEMIAH 3:1,20-21).

ELIEL
("my God is God")

1. One of the heads of the tribe of Manasseh on the east of Jordan (I CHRONICLES 5:24).

2. Descendant of Shimei who was a chief man in the tribe of Benjamin who lived in Jerusalem (I CHRONICLES 8:20).

3. Descendant of Shashak and a Benjamite chief who lived in Jerusalem (I CHRONICLES 8:22).

4. Mahavite warrior in King David's army who was renowned for his bravery (I CHRONICLES 11:46).

5. Another warrior in King David's army who was renowned for his bravery (I CHRONICLES 11:47).

6. One of 11 commanders from the tribe of Gad who left King Saul and joined David at Ziklag (I CHRONICLES 12:11).

7. A Kohathite Levite who was placed in charge of the transportation of the Ark from the house of Obed-edom to Jerusalem (I CHRONICLES 15:9,11).

8. A Levite in the time of Hezekiah who was in charge of the offerings made in the Temple (II CHRONICLES 31:13).

ELIHU
("he is my God")

1. Son of Barachel, "a Buzite" and one of Job's friends (JOB 32:2). Elihu made three speeches after his companions had finished their arguments, explaining to Job that God would forgive his sins if he repented, but Job insisted he was innocent (JOB CHAPTERS 32-37).

2. One of the captains from Manasseh who abandoned Saul and rallied to David at Ziklag (I CHRONICLES 12:20).

3. Descendant of Obed-edom, who was a doorkeeper at the gates of the Tabernacle during the reign of King David (I CHRONICLES 26:7).

ELIMELECH
("my God is king")

A wealthy man from Bethlehem and a relative of Boaz. Elimelech moved to the land of Moab with his wife, Naomi, and his two sons, one of whom married Ruth (RUTH 1:2-3; 2:1,3; 4:3).

ELIPHAZ
("God his strength")

1. One of Job's "three friends" who visited him during his suffering and entered into debate with him. His language is slightly more delicate and gentle than that of the other two, although he ascribes special sins to Job as the cause of his present predicament (I JOB 4:12-21; 15:12-16).

2. Son of Esau by his wife, Adah, and father of several Edomitish tribes (GENESIS 36:4,10-11,16).

ELZABAD
("whom God hath given")

1. One of the commanders from Gad who came across the Jordan to join David's forces (I CHRONICLES 12:12).

2. A Korhite Levite who was the son of Shemaiah and the grandson of Obed-edom, and served as one of the gatekeepers of the Tabernacle during the reign of King David (I CHRONICLES 26:7).

ESDRIS

A commander who served under Judas Maccabeus and distinguished himself in the Battle of Idumea against the Seleucid General Gorgias (II MACCABEES 12:36).

ESTHER
("a star")

Persian name of Hadassah, a Jewish girl who was orphaned and brought up by her cousin Mordecai, who had an office in the household of King Ahasuerus, king of Persia in "Shushan" (Susa). When Vashti was dismissed as queen, the king chose Esther for her beauty, not knowing her people or parentage. The newly appointed grand vizier named Haman began to plot "to destroy all the Jews . . . throughout the whole kingdom of Ahasuerus" (ESTHER 3:6). He ordered magicians to cast *pur,* or lots, in order to pick the right day for the planned massacre, and placed the provincial military on alert. Queen Esther, warned of the conspiracy by her father, broke the news to the king and identified Haman as the instigator. Haman was hanged, but nothing could be done about Haman's planned massacre because it had been issued as a royal decree. The king then gave out another decree, authorizing all Jews in his kingdom to bear arms so as to defend themselves. Thus equipped, Jews were prepared when the militia came to murder them and killed them all (ESTHER 9:5). The deliverance is celebrated during the Jewish feast of Purim (ESTHER 9:19).

ETHAN
("firm")

1. "The Ezrahite" of the tribe of Levi. One of the four sons of Mahol, he was distinguished for his wisdom and

"Esther, Queen of Persia Who Saved the Jews" was painted by Hermann Anschuetz (1802–1880).

is named as the author of the 89th Psalm (I Kings 4:31; I Chronicles 2:6).

2. Son of Kishi or Kushaiah; a Levite of the family of Merari during the reign of King David, and one of the leaders of the Temple music (I Chronicles 6:44; 15:17,19).

3. A Gershonite Levite, one of the ancestors of Asaph the singer (I Chronicles 6:42).

ETHANUS

One of the scribes who wrote for 40 days at the dictation of Ezra (II Esdras 14:24).

EUMENES
("well disposed")

King Eumenes II, king of Pergamum and Judas Maccabeus's ally, who defeated Antiochus III at the Battle of Magnesia. For his efforts, he was granted "India, Media, and Lydia" (I Maccabees 8:8).

EUPOLEMUS

A son of John and one of two emissaries sent by Judas Maccabeus to Rome to ask for the Senate's support against Demetrius (I Maccabees 8:17; II Maccabees 4:11).

EZRA
("help")

1. A priest among those who returned to Jerusalem under Zerubbabel (Nehemiah 12:1).

2. The priest and scribe who led the second group of exiles from Babylon to Jerusalem, and traditionally author of the book that bears his name. He was the son or grandson of Seraiah, and a descendant of Phinehas, Aaron's son (II Kings 25:18-21; Ezra 7:1-5). In the seventh year of the reign of Artaxerxes Longimanus, he obtained permission from the king for an official mission "to make inquiries about Judah and Jerusalem according to the law of your God" (Ezra 7:14). Ezra assembled about 5,000 exiles who were prepared to go up with him to Jerusalem. They rested for three days on the banks of the Ahava, and then commenced their march across the desert, which took four months.

As soon as he arrived in Jerusalem, Ezra found that the "holy seed" of the Hebrew nation had been mixed with the "people of the lands," in violation of the Law that

Spanish artist Pedro Berruguete (1450–1504) rendered this portrait of "The Prophet Ezra."

forbade Jews to marry non-Jewish spouses. Also, most of the ancient Jewish customs and Temple rites had been forgotten. In response, Ezra issued a decree that all those who had married non-Jewish wives were to "make a confession to the Lord . . . (and) separate yourselves from the peoples of the land and from the foreign wives" (Ezra 10:11). Ezra was also careful to have the whole people instructed in the Law of Moses; and in the Jewish tradition, his name is connected with the collecting and editing of the Pentateuch canon.

GABAEL

Ancestor of Tobit (Tobit 1:1).

GESHEM
("firmness")

Also known as Gashmu, Geshem was a chieftain who joined with Sanballat and

Tobiah in opposing the rebuilding of the wall of Jerusalem (Nehemiah 2:19; 6:1-2).

GILALAI
("dungy")

A priest in the days of Nehemiah, who was one of the many that walked behind Ezra in celebration of the dedication of the rebuilding of the walls of Jerusalem.

GINNETHON
("gardener")

One of the priests who signed Nehemiah's solemn covenant (Nehemiah 10:6).

GORGIAS

A general under Antiochus Epiphanes, who was appointed by Lysias to lead the army against Judea, where he defeated Judas Maccabeus (I Maccabees 3:38; 4:6; II Maccabees 8:9). In Jamnia, he also defeated the forces of Joseph and Azarias (II Maccabees 12:35).

HAGGAI
("festive")

One of the 12 minor prophets, Haggai was among the first to prophesy after the return from captivity in Babylon. Little is known of his personal history, but he may have been .one of the captives taken to Babylon by Nebuchadnezzar. Haggai, along with Zechariah, was able to inspire the people to continue rebuilding the Temple (Ezra 6:14). "Is it a time for you yourselves to live in your paneled houses," Haggai cried, "while this house lies in ruins? . . . You have sown much, and harvested little" (Haggai 1:4,5). Haggai's oracle coincided with an unexpected drought, and the prophet was quick to identify the Lord's anger as the cause. His words must have made an impact: Soon thereafter, Governor Zerubbabel and high priest Joshua agreed to resume work on the Temple (Haggai 1:12-15).

HAKKOZ
("the thorn")

Priest in charge of the seventh turn of the priestly services in the Tabernacle during the reign of King David (I CHRONICLES 24:10).

HAMAN

Chief minister or grand vizier of the Persian king Ahasuerus (ESTHER 3:1). After the failure of his attempt to destroy all the Jews in the Persian Empire, he was killed on the very gallows he had erected for the execution of Mordecai, Esther's adoptive father. Jewish congregations hiss whenever his name is mentioned on the day of Purim.

Jan Victors (1619–1676) painted this canvas of "Esther and Haman Before Ahasuerus" around 1635.

HANAN

("merciful")

1. Son of Shashak and a leader of Benjamin who lived in Jerusalem (I CHRONICLES 8:23).
2. Son of Azel, grandson of Eleasah, descendant of King Saul, and brother of Azrikam, Bocheru, Ishmael, Sheariah, and Obadiah (I CHRONICLES 8:38).
3. Son of Maacah, who was one of the brave soldiers in the army of King David (I CHRONICLES 11:43).
4. Ancestor of a family of Temple servants who had returned with Zerubbabel from the Babylonian exile (EZRA 2:46).
5. One of the Levites who explained the Law to the people in Jerusalem while standing on a wooden platform before the Water Gate (NEHEMIAH 8:7).

6. Two leaders of the same name who signed Nehemiah's solemn covenant (NEHEMIAH 10:22,26).
7. Son of Zaccur, and grandson of Mattaniah who was one of four people designated by Nehemiah to supervise the treasuries of the Temple, and distribute the offerings among the Levites and the priests (NEHEMIAH 13:13).
8. Son of Igdaliah, and man of God (JEREMIAH 35:4).

HANANI

("gracious")

1. One of the sons of Heman (I CHRONICLES 25:4,25).
2. A seer who rebuked Asa, king of Judah, and was imprisoned as a result (II CHRONICLES 16:7).
3. One of the priests who during the time of Ezra had married foreign wives (EZRA 10:20).
4. A brother of Nehemiah, who was made governor of Jerusalem by him (NEHEMIAH 1:2; 7:2).
5. A priest mentioned in Nehemiah 12:36.

HARIM

("consecrated")

1. Descendant of Adna, who was in charge of the third turn of services at the Tabernacle during the reign of King David (I CHRONICLES 24:8; NEHEMIAH 12:15).
2. Father of Malchijah, who repaired a sector of the walls of Jerusalem and the tower of the furnaces during the days of Nehemiah (NEHEMIAH 3:11).
3. One of the priests who signed Nehemiah's solemn covenant (NEHEMIAH 10:5).
4. One of the leaders who signed Nehemiah's solemn covenant (NEHEMIAH 10:27).

HASHABIAH

("whom God regards")

1. Son of Amaziah, a Levite (I CHRONICLES 6:45).
2. Son of Jeduthun, a Levite (I CHRONICLES 9:14).
3. The son of Kemuel, who was prince of the tribe of Levi during the time of David (I CHRONICLES 27:17).
4. A Levite, one of the leaders of his tribe,

who officiated for King Josiah at his great Passover feast (II CHRONICLES 35:9).
5. The fourth of the six sons of Jeduthun (I CHRONICLES 25:3).
6. One of the descendants of Hebron, the son of Kohath (I CHRONICLES 26:30).
7. A Levite who accompanied Ezra on the journey from Babylon (EZRA 8:19).
8. A chief priest who was in charge of the bullion and other valuables of the Temple at Jerusalem (EZRA 8:24); probably identical with the priest mentioned in Nehemiah 12:21.
9. Ruler of half of Keilah, who repaired a portion of the wall of Jerusalem under Nehemiah (NEHEMIAH 3:17).
10. One of the Levites who sealed the covenant after the return from captivity (NEHEMIAH 10:11; 12:24).
11. Son of Bunni, a Levite (I CHRONICLES 9:14; NEHEMIAH 11:15).
12. Son of Mattaniah, a Levite (NEHEMIAH 11:22).
13. A priest of the family of Hilkiah during the time of Joiakim, son of Jeshua (NEHEMIAH 12:21).

HASHUM

("enriched")

1. Ancestor of a family that returned with Zerubbabel from the Babylonian exile. His descendants divorced their wives during the days of Ezra (EZRA 2:19; 10:33).
2. One of the leaders who stood upon a pulpit of wood, next to Ezra, when the scribe read the law of Moses to the people in the marketplace (NEHEMIAH 8:4).
3. One of the leaders who signed Nehemiah's solemn covenant (NEHEMIAH 10:18).

HATHACH

One of the chamberlains of King Ahasuerus, who attended Esther and told her of Haman's plot (ESTHER 4:5-6; 9-10).

HATTUSH

1. Son of Shemaiah, brother of Igal, Bariah, Neariah, and Shaphat, and a descendant of King Jehoiachin. He returned with Ezra from the Babylonian exile (EZRA 8:2).
2. Son of Hashabiah, who was one of the men who helped repair the wall of Jerusalem during the days of Nehemiah (NEHEMIAH 3:10).

3. One of the priests who signed Nehemiah's solemn covenant (NEHEMIAH 10:4).

4. A priest who returned with Zerubbabel from the Babylonian exile (NEHEMIAH 12:2).

HELDAI
("worldly")

1. One of David's captains (I CHRONICLES 27:15).

2. An Israelite, who seems to have returned from the Babylon captivity (ZECHARIAH 6:10).

3. Also called Heled (I CHRONICLES 11:30) and Heleb (II SAMUEL 23:29).

A detail from "The Expulsion of Heliodorus from the Temple" was painted in the Vatican by Italian artist Raphael (1483–1520) in 1512.

HELIODORUS
("gift of the sun")

Officer of the Syrian king Seleucus IV (Philopator), who was charged to plunder the Temple in Jerusalem (II MACCABEES 3:21-28).

HELKAI

Descendant of Meraioth, who was the head of a priestly clan when Joiakim served as high priest during the time of Nehemiah (NEHEMIAH 12:15).

HERCULES

A Greek demigod, the son of Zeus and Alcmene, in whose honor King Hiram of Tyre built a temple (II MACCABEES 4:18-20).

HIERONYMUS

Syrian governor of Palestine during the reign of Antiochus V (II MACCABEES 12:2).

HILKIAH
("God's portion")

1. Father of Eliakim, head of King Hezekiah's household (II KINGS 18:37; ISAIAH 22:20; 36:22).

2. A high priest in the reign of Josiah who found an ancient scroll that contained "the Book of the Law," possibly the Book of Deuteronomy (II KINGS 22:4,8).

3. A Merarite Levite, son of Amzi, and ancestor of Ethan the musician who lived during the reign of King David (I CHRONICLES 6:45).

4. Another Merarite Levite, second son of Hosah, who served in the Tabernacle during the reign of King David (I CHRONICLES 26:11).

5. One of the leaders who stood with Ezra when he read the Law of Moses to the people in the Jerusalem marketplace (NEHEMIAH 8:4).

6. A priest of Anathoth, and father of the prophet Jeremiah (JEREMIAH 1:1).

7. Father of Gemariah, who was one of Zedekiah's envoys to Babylon (JEREMIAH 29:3).

HODAVIAH
("grandeur of God")

1. A member of the half tribe of Manasseh that settled east of the Jordan River, a mighty warrior and leader of his clan (I CHRONICLES 5:24).

2. Son of Hassenuah, father of Meshullam, and ancestor of Sallu (I CHRONICLES 9:7).

3. Ancestor of clan of Levites who returned with Zerubbabel from the Babylonian exile. He is also called Hodevah in Nehemiah 7:43.

HODIAH
("grandeur of God")

1. Naham's brother-in-law (I CHRONICLES 4:19), and a member of the tribe of Judah.

2. One of the Levites who explained the Law to the people as read by Ezra (NEHEMIAH 8:7), and who led their prayers (NEHEMIAH 9:5). One of the two Levites who sealed the

"Judith With the Head of Holofernes" is the work of Lucas Cranach the Elder (1472–1553) from ca 1530.

covenant of Nehemiah (NEHEMIAH 10:10,13).

3. One of the chiefs who sealed the covenant of Nehemiah (NEHEMIAH 10:18).

HOLOFERNES

A general of Nebuchadnezzar, king of the Assyrians, who was killed by the Hebrew heroine Judith during the siege of Bethulia (JUDITH 2:4).

HUPPAH

A priest in the time of David (I CHRONICLES 24:13).

IDDO
("God's friend")

1. Father of Abinadab, one of 12 officers responsible for King Solomon's household (I KINGS 4:14).

2. Descendant of Gershom, son of Joah (I Chronicles 6:21).

3. Son of Zechariah, ruler of the tribe of Manasseh, east of Jordan, in the time of David (I Chronicles 27:21).

4. A seer whose visions against Jeroboam, Rehoboam, and Abijah are described in the second Book of Chronicles, but have not otherwise survived (II Chronicles 9:29; 13:22).

5. Father or grandfather of the prophet Zechariah (Zechariah 1:1,7; Ezra 5:1).

6. Chief of the exiles in Casiphia, who sent priests and Levites to the Temple in Jerusalem (Ezra 8:17).

The arrest of Jeremiah by the chief priest Passhur, son of Immer, is depicted in this 16th-century engraving.

IMMER
("lamb")

1. Founder of an important family of priests, which had charge of the 16th course of the service at the Tabernacle (I Chronicles 24:14; Nehemiah 11:13).

2. Father of Pashhur, chief priest of the Temple who beat Jeremiah and put him in prison (Jeremiah 20:1).

ISHI
("salvation")

1. One of Judah's descendants, Appaim's son and Sheshan's father (I Chronicles 2:31). One of the great houses of Hezron.

2. A descendant of Judah, Zoheth, and Benzoheth's father (I Chronicles 4:20).

3. Head of a family of the tribe of Simeon in the days of King Hezekiah of Judah (I Chronicles 4:42).

4. One of the heads of the tribe of Manasseh on the east of Jordan (I Chronicles 5:24).

5. A symbolical name used in Hosea 2:16.

ISHMAIAH
("YHWH hears")

1. A mighty warrior from Gideon who left King Saul and joined David at Ziklag (I Chronicles 12:4).

2. Son of Obadiah, and the ruler of the tribe of Zebulun in the time of King David (I Chronicles 27:19).

ISMACHIAH
("God will sustain")

One of the Levites chosen to supervise the gifts, tithes, and offerings brought to the Temple (II Chronicles 31:13).

ISSHIAH
("God will lend")

1. A Levite, Izrahiah's son and Micah's brother, father of Zechariah, who was a descendant of Rehabiah (I Chronicles 24:21).

2. One of the soldiers who left King Saul and joined David at Ziklag (I Chronicles 12:6).

3. Descendant from Uzziel who served in the Tabernacle during the reign of King David (I Chronicles 23:20).

4. Descendant from Rehabiah who served in the Tabernacle during the reign of King David (I Chronicles 23:20).

ITHIEL
("God is with me")

1. A Benjamite, Jeshaiah's son and Maaseiah's father, who settled in Jerusalem after the exile (Nehemiah 11:7).

2. One of two people, Ithiel and Ucal, to whom Agur, Jakeh's son, delivered his discourse (Proverbs 30:1).

J

JAALAH
("wild goat")

A servant of Solomon whose descendants

returned from the Babylonian exile with Zerubbabel (Ezra 2:56).

JAASIEL
("made by God")

1. Mezobaite warrior, distinguished for his bravery (I Chronicles 11:47)

2. Abner's son, also called Jasiel, who served in King David's army (I Chronicles 27:21).

JAAZIEL
("comforted by God")

A Levitical musician who performed when the Ark was brought to Jerusalem (I Chronicles 15:18).

JADDUA
("known")

1. Son of Jonathan, a Levite who returned to Jerusalem after the exile (Nehemiah 12:11, 22).

2. A leader of the people of Judah who signed the covenant with Nehemiah (Nehemiah 10:21).

JAHATH

1. Son of Shimei, and grandson of Gershom, who served in the Tabernacle during the reign of King David (I Chronicles 23:10).

2. One of the sons of Shelomoth, of the family of Kohath, who served in the Tabernacle during the reign of King David (I Chronicles 24:22).

3. A Levite of the family of Merari, one of the supervisors repairing the Temple under Josiah (II Chronicles 34:12).

JAHAZIEL
("God will behold")

1. A Kohathite Levite, third son of Hebron (I Chronicles 23:19).

2. A Benjamite chief who deserted Saul to join David's army on the road to Ziklag (I Chronicles 12:4).

3. A priest in the reign of David who blew the trumpet after the transfer of the Ark to Jerusalem (I Chronicles 16:6).

4. Son of Zechariah, a Levite of the family of Asaph, who promised King Jehoshaphat that he would win a great victory against the Moabites and Ammonites (II Chronicles 20:14-17).

5. Father of Shecaniah who returned from exile in Babylon with Ezra (EZRA 8:5).

JAHZEIAH
("YHWH sees")
Son of Tikvah who was present when Ezra called upon the men of Judah to divorce their foreign-born wives (EZRA 10:15).

JARHA
Egyptian servant of Sheshan, to whom his master gave his daughter and heir in marriage (I CHRONICLES 2:34-35).

JASHOBEAM
("to whom the people return")
One of the chief commanders of David, he joined the king at Ziklag, where he distinguished himself by killing 300 Philistines with his spear (I CHRONICLES 11:11).

JAZIZ
("he will make prominent")
One of David's officers who was put in charge of David's flocks (I CHRONICLES 11:38).

JECONIAH
("whom God has appointed")
King of Judah and short-lived successor to Jehoiakim, who ruled under the name Jehoiachin. At the time of his accession, Jerusalem was unable to resist Nebuchadnezzar's army

(II KINGS 24:10-11). Jehoiachin, the queen mother, and all his servants and military officers surrendered to Nebuchadnezzar, who brought them as prisoners to Babylon. He remained in Babylon until his death (JEREMIAH 29:2; EZEKIEL 17:12; 19:9).

JEDAIAH
("known by God")
1. Son of Shimri, a Simeonite leader (I CHRONICLES 4:37).
2. A priest in Jerusalem during the reign of King David who was responsible for the second turn of service at the Tabernacle in Jerusalem. Some of his descendants returned to Jerusalem after the Babylonian exile (I CHRONICLES 24:7; EZRA 2:36).
3. The son of Harumaph who helped repair the walls of Jerusalem with Nehemiah (NEHEMIAH 3:10).
4. A priest in Jerusalem during the time of Nehemiah (NEHEMIAH 11:10).
5. A leader of Judah who returned to Jerusalem with Zerubbabel after the Babylonian exile, and was ordered by Zechariah to provide gold and silver for the crown to be worn by Joshua, the high priest (NEHEMIAH 12:7; ZECHARIAH 6:10,14).

JEHIEL
("God lives")
1. Father of Gibeon (I CHRONICLES 9:35).

2. One of David's warriors (I CHRONICLES 11:44).
3. A Levite who was appointed to conduct music when the Ark of the Covenant was moved from the house of Obed-edom to Jerusalem (I CHRONICLES 15:18,20).
4. Second son of Jehoshaphat, king of Judah, who was killed by his brother Jehoram (II CHRONICLES 21:2,4).
5. A Hachmonite who served as tutor to David's family toward the end of his reign (I CHRONICLES 27:32).
6. A Levite from the Heman family who was responsible for bringing offerings and tithes to the Temple during the reign of King Hezekiah (II CHRONICLES 29:14; 31:13).
7. A leader of Judah who donated sacrificial animals for Passover during the reign of King Josiah (II CHRONICLES 35:8).
8. Father of Obadiah, a leader of Judah who returned from exile in Babylon (EZRA 8:9).
9. Father of Shecaniah who confessed to Ezra that many men had married foreign-born wives (EZRA 10:2).
10. A priest and descendant of Harim who divorced his foreign-born wife (EZRA 10:21).
11. One of Elam's sons who divorced his foreign-born wife (EZRA 10:26).

JEHOHANAN
("God is gracious")
1. A Levite descendant of the Korah family who served as one of the doorkeepers to the Tabernacle (I CHRONICLES 26:3).
2. A military leader who commanded over 280,000 men in Judah during the reign of Jehoshaphat (II CHRONICLES 17:15).
3. Father of Ishmael, and captain of hundreds of soldiers who staged a coup against Queen Athaliah and installed Joash as king of Judah (II CHRONICLES 23:1).
4. Son of Eliashib who prayed after deciding that all those who had married foreign-born wives should divorce them (EZRA 10:6).
5. Father of Azariah (II CHRONICLES 28:12).
6. Son of Tobiah, one of the plotters who tried to sabotage Nehemiah's restoration of Jerusalem's walls (NEHEMIAH 6:18).
7. A chief priest of Judah during Joiakim's high priesthood (NEHEMIAH 12:13).

Jeconiah is depicted in this lunette fresco at the Vatican's Sistine Chapel, which was painted by Michelangelo Buonarroti (1475–1564).

8. One of the priests who sang hymns during the dedication of the Jerusalem wall (NEHEMIAH 12:42).

9. Son of Bebai who divorced his foreign wife (EZRA 10:28).

JEHOIARIB
("whom God defends")

Two priests of a family that had responsibility for the first turn of service at the Tabernacle during the reign of King David (I CHRONICLES 9:10; 24:7; NEHEMIAH 11:10).

JEHOZABAD
("God given")

1. A Korhite Levite, second son of Obed-edom, and one of the gatekeepers of the Tabernacle during the reign of David (I CHRONICLES 26:4,15).

2. A Benjamite captain during the reign of King Jehoshaphat of Judah (II CHRONICLES 17:18).

3. A servant of King Joash and son of the Moab woman Shomer, who was one of the King's assassins (II KINGS 12:21; II CHRONICLES 24:26).

JEIEL
("treasured of God")

1. A Reubenite leader of the house of Joel (I CHRONICLES 5:7).

2. A Benjamite leader living in Gibeon, and ancestor of Saul (I CHRONICLES 9:35).

3. Son of Hotham who with his brother Shama were renowned warriors in King David's army (I CHRONICLES 11:44).

4. A Merarite Levite who took part in Tabernacle services and played the harp when the Ark was brought to Jerusalem (I CHRONICLES 15:18; 16:5).

5. A Gershonite Levite and ancestor of Jahaziel who promised King Jehoshaphat that he would win a great victory against the Moabites and Ammonites (II CHRONICLES 20:14).

6. A scribe during the reign of King Uzziah (II CHRONICLES 26:11).

7. A Gershonite Levite who helped cleanse the Temple (II CHRONICLES 29:13).

8. One of the chiefs of the Levites during the reign of Josiah who donated many sacrificial animals for Passover (II CHRONICLES 35:9).

9. Son of Adonikam who formed part of the caravan of Ezra from Babylon to Jerusalem (EZRA 8:13).

10. Son of Nebo, who had taken a foreign wife and had to divorce her (EZRA 10:43).

JEKAMIAH
("whom God gathers/raises")

Son of Shallum, and a descendant of Jerahmeel, who was placed into the royal succession line after the short reign of Jehoiachin (I CHRONICLES 2:41; 3:18).

JEMIMAH
("dove")

The first of Job's three daughters born after his tribulations had ended (JOB 42:14).

JERAHMEEL
("mercy of God")

1. Firstborn son of Hezron, a brother of Caleb, and leader of the tribe of Judah (I CHRONICLES 2:9,25-26).

2. A Levite and son of Kish from a prominent Merari family who ministered at the Tabernacle during the reign of King David (I CHRONICLES 24:29).

3. An officer of King Jehoiakim in Judah, who arrested Baruch and burned Jeremiah's prophecies (JEREMIAH 36:26).

JEREMOTH
("moth established")

1. Son of Becher, also known as Jerimoth, who was renowned as a warrior (I CHRONICLES 7:8).

2. Son of Mushi, and grandson of Merari (I CHRONICLES 23:23; 24:30).

3. Son of Zariel who was appointed as leader of the Naphtali tribe under the reign of David (I CHRONICLES 27:19).

4. Descendant of Elam who divorced his foreign wife during the time of Ezra (EZRA 10:26).

5. Son of Zattu who divorced his foreign wife during the time of Ezra (EZRA 10:26).

JERIMOTH
("moth established")

1. Son of Bela, also known as Jeremoth, who was renowned as a warrior (I CHRONICLES 7:7).

2. A Benjamite who deserted Saul and joined King David at Ziklag (I CHRONICLES 12:5).

3. Son of Heman, a musician, and responsible for the second turn of service at the Tabernacle in Jerusalem during the reign of King David (I CHRONICLES 25:4,22).

4. Father of Mahalath, who was the wife of King Rehoboam (II CHRONICLES 11:18).

5. A Levite during the reign of Hezekiah who supervised the offerings and tithes at the Temple (II CHRONICLES 31:13).

JESHAIAH
("God has saved")

1. One of Hananiah's three sons, grandson of Zerubbabel, and a descendant of King David (I CHRONICLES 3:21).

2. One of the six sons of King David's musician Jeduthun, who was responsible for the eighth turn of service at the Tabernacle in Jerusalem (I CHRONICLES 25:3,15).

"The Tree of Jesse," from the Dome Altar, was painted by 15th-century German artist Absolon Stumme.

3. Eldest son of Rehabiah, father of Joram, and responsible for keeping the trophies captured by King David in battle (I CHRONICLES 26:25).

4. Son of Athaliah, and a member of the house of Elam who returned with Ezra from Babylon (EZRA 8:7).

5. A Levite from the Merari family who returned with Ezra to minister in the Temple (EZRA 8:19).

JESHUA
("savior")

1. Also known as Jeshuah, a priest who was responsible for the ninth turn of service at the Tabernacle in Jerusalem (I CHRONICLES 24:11; EZRA 2:36,40).

2. A Levite appointed by Hezekiah to distribute religious offerings (II CHRONICLES 31:15).

3. A Levite, son of Jozadak, a high priest after the Babylon captivity during the time of Zerubbabel, who was symbolically crowned in the Book of Zechariah (EZRA 2:2,6, 3:2-13; ZECHARIAH 3:1-9).

4. A Levite and father of Jozabad in the days of Ezra (EZRA 8:33).

5. Son of Pahath-moab, from the tribe of Judah, who returned from exile in Babylon with Zerubbabel (EZRA 2:6; NEHEMIAH 7:11; 10:14).

6. A Levite and son of Azaniah who signed Nehemiah's covenant (NEHEMIAH 10:9).

7. One of the leaders of Judah who explained the Law to the people in the marketplace in the time of Ezra (NEHEMIAH 8:7).

JESSE
("gift")

Father of David, son of Obed, and grandson of Boaz and Ruth. Jesse was a wealthy man in Bethlehem and raised sheep and goats. After David's conflict with Saul, he took his parents to Moab (ISAIAH 11:1,10; LUKE 3:32; MATTHEW 1:5-6; PSALMS 78:71; REVELATION 5:5; RUTH 4:17,22; I SAMUEL 16:11; 17:13-35; 22:3-4).

JETHER
("excels")

1. Father-in-law of Moses, also known as Jethro (EXODUS 4:18).

2. Oldest of Gideon's sons, who was ordered to kill the kings of Midian, Zebah, and Zalmunna (JUDGES 8:20).

3. Husband of Abigail, King David's sister, and the father of Amasa, a commander of Absalom's army who was killed by General Joab (I CHRONICLES 2:17; I KINGS 2:5,32; II SAMUEL 17:25).

4. Son of Jada, a descendant of Hezron from the Judah tribe who died childless (I CHRONICLES 2:32).

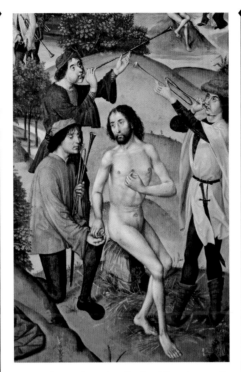

A naked Job is depicted in this detail from the triptych "Scenes From the Life of Job" by a Flemish artist working between 1466 and 1500.

5. One of the four sons of Ezra of the tribe of Judah (I CHRONICLES 4:17).

6. Leader of Asher, a family of warriors, and father of Jephunneh (I CHRONICLES 7:38).

JEUEL
("treasured")

1. Descendant of Zerah, and leader of a clan that returned to Jerusalem after the Babylonian exile (I CHRONICLES 9:6).

2. A Levite whose ancestors participated in the purification of the Temple during the reign of King Hezekiah (II CHRONICLES 29:13).

3. A man who returned from exile in Babylon with Ezra and helped rebuild Jerusalem (EZRA 8:13).

JOAKIM

1. High priest in Jerusalem who welcomed Judith back into the city after the death of Holofernes (JUDITH 4:6-15).

2. Husband of Susanna, a wealthy member of a Jewish community in Babylon. Two elders fell in love with Susanna, but when she rejected them they falsely accused her of adultery, only to be exonerated by Daniel (SUSANNA 1-63).

JOB

According to a story that Jewish tradition dates to the time of the patriarchs, Job was a prosperous man who lived in Uz. God and Satan tested Job to ensure he was a God-fearing man. After living in the midst of great wealth, his children and livestock were killed, and his possessions destroyed. He was also inflicted with physical sores on his body (JOB 2:7) Despite his suffering, he did not curse God until some friends came to comfort him. The friends convinced Job he had committed a sin at some point in his life and was being punished for it. However, God said they were wrong and restored his health and wealth (JOB 42:10).

JOHN HYRCANUS
("God favored")

One of the sons of Simon Maccabeus who escaped from the assassination plot against his father, and succeeded him as leader of newly independent Judea, while also serving as high priest. He was succeeded by his son Aristobulus I, who took the final step of assuming the title of king (I MACCABEES 16:18-22).

JOIAKIM
("God raises up")

Son of Jeshua and father of Eliashib, who served as high priest during the time of Ezra and Nehemiah (NEHEMIAH 12:10,12,26).

JOIARIB
("God will defend")

1. A teacher whom Ezra sent to Iddo to recruit Levites for the Temple in Jerusalem (EZRA 8:16).

2. Son of Zechariah, descendant of Judah, whose descendant Maaseiah was one of the first men of Judah to return from exile (NEHEMIAH 11:5).

A bronze prutah— *an ancient Jewish copper coin—of John Hyrcanus I dates from 135–104 B.C.E.*

3. A priest who returned with Zerubbabel to Jerusalem from the Babylonian exile. Also known as Jehoiarib (NEHEMIAH 11:10; 12:6,19).

JONATHAN
("God gave")
Youngest son of Mattathias and Maccabean leader after the death of Judas. Both the Syrian King Demetrius I and his opponent Alexander Balas maneuvered to have Jona-

"Jonathan Destroying the Temple of Dagon" is an engraving by French artist Gustave Doré (1832–1883).

than on his side (I MACCABEES 9:73–10:66). When Jonathan chose to ally himself with Alexander, he was appointed high priest. Combining the role of governor, military commander, and high priest into one person was seen by many as blasphemy. Jonathan's reckless move led to a split among many pious Jews and would create the factionalism that would persist well into the time. Three years later, as a reward for his services, Alexander conferred on him both the civil and military authority over Judea. In the conflict between Alexander and Demetrius II, Jonathan again supported Alexander, and in return received the gift of the city of Accaron with its territory (I MACCABEES 10:67-89).

After the fall of Alexander, Demetrius II summoned Jonathan to Ptolemais to answer for his attack on the Acra, but instead of punishing him, Demetrius granted him three districts in Samaria. The king also promised to withdraw the Syrian garrison from the Acra and other fortified places in Judea. When he failed to keep his word, Jonathan went over to the party of Antiochus VI, son of Alexander Balas, whose claims Tryphon was pressing. Jonathan was confirmed in all his possessions and dignities. Tryphon however, fearing that Jonathan might interfere with his plans, treacherously invited him to Ptolemais and killed him (I MACCABEES 11:19–12:48).

JOZABAD
("God bestows")
1. A Benjamite archer who deserted Saul's army and joined David's army at Ziklag (I CHRONICLES 12:4).
2. A leader of the Manasseh tribe, who deserted Saul's army and joined David at Ziklag (I CHRONICLES 12:20).
3. A Levite who supervised the offerings and tithes at the Temple during the reign of Hezekiah (II CHRONICLES 31:13).
4. A Levite who donated cattle for the Passover services during the reign of Josiah (II CHRONICLES 35:9).
5. A Levite and son of Jeshua during the reign of Ezra who was present when the gold and silver brought back from Babylon was weighed (EZRA 8:33).
6. A priest and father of Pashhur who divorced his foreign-born wife (EZRA 10:22).

JUDAS MACCABEUS
("the hammer")
Third son of the priest Mattathias who, after his father's death, was the leader of the Maccabean revolt against the Seleucids (I MACCABEES 3:8). Avoiding open combat with the far superior Syrian army, Judas conducted a brilliant guerilla campaign that allowed him to defeat the Syrian forces. In 164 B.C.E., he was able to capture Jerusalem,

cleanse the Temple of all Greek idols, and solemnly restore the worship of YHWH— an event celebrated during the Jewish festival of Hanukkah (II MACCABEES 10:1-3).

That same year, Antiochus IV died, precipitating a clash between several contenders for the Syrian throne. One of these, the Seleucid General Lysias, revoked Antiochus's edict and restored full religious freedom to the citizens of Judea (II MACCABEES 11:15). Many Jewish factions—including the Hasidim, or "pious ones"—now abandoned the rebellion, given that their principal war aim had been satisfied. For the Maccabees, however, the ultimate goal was full political independence, and so Judas persevered (albeit with sharply reduced forces), only to be killed in the Battle of Elasa in 160 B.C.E. Judas's brother Jonathan succeeded him.

JUDITH
("from Judah")
Young wife of Manasseh, a farmer of Bethulia. After her husband died of sunstroke, she did not remarry but lived quietly on the farm. When Bethulia was besieged by Babylonian forces led by a commander named Holofernes, Judith prayed to God, then put aside the sackcloth of her widowhood and "made herself very beautiful, to entice the eyes of all the men" (JUDITH 10:4). Passing through the gates with

This detail of Judas Maccabeus was painted by Italian artist Giacomo Jaquerio (1403–1453).

only her maid as company, she was seized by a Babylonian patrol and taken to their camp, where all the soldiers "marveled at her beauty and admired the Israelites" (JUDITH 10:19). Holofernes invited her to stay and planned to seduce her after a lavish banquet, for he felt that "it would be a disgrace if we let such a woman go" (JUDITH 12:12). Late that night, as Judith was finally alone with Holofernes and the commander lay drunk on his bed, she seized his sword and cut off his head.

KADMIEL
A Levite who returned from the Babylonian exile with Zerubbabel (EZRA 2:40; 3:9; NEHEMIAH 7:43).

KEREN-HAPPUCH
Youngest daughter of Job (JOB 42:14), who was born to him during the period of his reviving prosperity. She and her two sisters shared their father's inheritance with their brothers.

KEZIAH
Job's second daughter who was born to him after he regained his health and wealth (JOB 42:14). Her sisters were Keren-happuch and Jemimah. All three girls shared their father's inheritance with their brothers.

LASTHENES
A highly placed official under King Demetrius II Nicator (I MACCABEES 11:31-32). A letter addressed to Lasthenes, instructing him to exempt Judea from taxes, indicates that he was probably a finance minister of the kingdom. Josephus suggests that he was later successful in wresting the throne of Syria from the usurper Alexander Balas in favor of Demetrius (I MACCABEES 10:67).

LEMUEL
("dedicated to God")
A king of Massa, referred to in the Book of Proverbs, whose mother instructed him to abstain from pursuing women and drinking wine, but to judge righteously and protect the needy (PROVERBS 31:1-9).

LEVIATHAN
A sea monster with the body of a crooked serpent (JOB 41:1).

LUCIUS
A Roman consul who wrote a letter to Ptolemy Euergetes, confirming the leadership of Simon Maccabeus and granting the Jews the protection of Rome (I MACCABEES 15:16).

The sea monster known as "The Leviathan" was painted by Arthur Rackham (1867–1939) in 1908.

LYSIAS
("dissolving")
A Syrian general during the reign of Antiochus IV and Antiochus V. While campaigning, Antiochus IV left him in charge of the government and of his son, the later Antiochus Eupator. After Antiochus IV was killed and his son assumed the throne, Lysias wielded great power as regent. Lysias then led an army to suppress the revolt of Judas Maccabeus but was defeated at the Battle of Emmaus. Later on, however, he defeated the Maccabean forces, and briefly occupied

Jerusalem. He was then defeated by another pretender, Demetrius Soter, and killed by his own troops (I MACCABEES 3:32; 6:17; 7:2-4; II MACCABEES 10:11; 11:1; 14:2).

LYSIMACHUS
("scattering the battle")
Brother of the corrupt high priest Menelaus during the reign of Antiochus IV. When Menelaus was summoned to Antioch, he left Lysimachus as his deputy in Jerusalem. Lysimachus then robbed the treasures of the Temple, which caused an insurrection in which he met his death beside the treasury (II MACCABEES 4:29,42).

MAAI
An Asaphite musician who took part in the ceremony of the dedication of the walls (NEHEMIAH 12:36).

MAASEIAH
("work of God")
1. A Levite and one of the gatekeepers of the Tabernacle who sang and played musical instruments in front of the Ark of the Covenant (I CHRONICLES 15:18).
2. Son of Adaiah, and one of the army commanders who conspired to overthrow Queen Athaliah and place Joash on the throne (II CHRONICLES 23:1).
3. Record keeper in King Uzziah's army who was responsible for the army's organization (II CHRONICLES 26:11).
4. Son of King Ahaz of Judah, who was killed by Zichri when the armies of Israel and Syria invaded Judah (II CHRONICLES 28:7).
5. Governor of Jerusalem in the reign of King Josiah of Judah (II CHRONICLES 34:8).
6. Father of the priest Zephaniah, who was sent by King Zedekiah to Jeremiah to solicit his oracle about the prospects of the war against Nebuchadnezzar (JEREMIAH 21:1; 29:25).
7. Father of Zedekiah who was accused by Jeremiah of providing false oracles (JEREMIAH 29:21).

8. Son of Shallum, and one of the gatekeepers of the Temple in the time of Jeremiah (JEREMIAH 35:4).

9. Priest and descendant of the priest Jeshua who divorced his foreign-born wife (EZRA 10:18).

10. Descendant of Harim who divorced his foreign-born wife (EZRA 10:21).

11. Descendant of Pashhur who divorced his foreign-born wife (EZRA 10:22).

12. Descendant of Pahath-moab who divorced his foreign-born wife (EZRA 10:30).

13. Father of Azariah who helped repair the walls of Jerusalem (NEHEMIAH 3:23).

14. One of the leaders who stood next to Ezra when he read the Law of Moses to the people (NEHEMIAH 8:4).

15. Levite who explained the Law to the people after Ezra read it (NEHEMIAH 8:7).

16. Leader who signed Nehemiah's solemn agreement (NEHEMIAH 10:25).

17. Son of Baruch, and one of the first men of Judah to settle in Jerusalem after the return from the Babylonian exile (NEHEMIAH 11:5).

18. Son of Ithiel and one of the first men of Benjamin to settle in Jerusalem after the return from the Babylonian exile (NEHEMIAH 11:7).

19. Priest who played the trumpet at the dedication of the rebuilt walls of Jerusalem (NEHEMIAH 12:14).

20. Priest who participated in the dedication of the rebuilt walls of Jerusalem (NEHEMIAH 12:42).

MACRON

Son of Dorymenes and also known as Ptolemy, who was the governor of Coele-Syria and Phoenicia (II MACCABEES 8:8). He defected to the Seleucid monarchy, and was one of the commanders chosen by Lysias to suppress the Maccabean revolt, but was defeated by Judas Maccabeus instead. Later, he chose the side of Alexander Balas in the Syrian civil war (II MACCABEES 10:12). He fell in disfavor with Antiochus Eupator, and committed suicide by poison (II MACCABEES 10:13).

MAHLON
("sickly")

Son of Elimelech and Naomi and brother of Chilion. Both Mahlon and Chilion married Moabite wives, Ruth and Orpah, but died after ten years (RUTH 1:2).

MALACHI
("my messenger")

Author of the Book of Malachi, the last of the 12 books of the "Minor Prophets" (MALACHI 1:1). His oracles probably date from the latter period of Ezra's activity, but before the arrival of Nehemiah. Very little is known about the figure of Malachi himself (his name means "messenger" and may be a

This portrait of the prophet Malachi was painted by Italian artist Cristoforo Canozi da Lendinara (1449–1490).

pseudonym), but his fervor in denouncing religious laxity is no less than that of Haggai or Zechariah. Malachi, too, was deeply vexed by the high rate of mixed marriages involving foreign spouses, as well as the decline of sacrificial worship at the Temple. Malachi placed part of the blame for this moral decay on the priesthood, who "have corrupted the covenant of Levi" by offering impure and blemished sacrificial animals, or convenient castaways that are "polluted food on my altar" (MALACHI 1:7; 2:8). Only by restoring true piety, said Malachi, will Judah once again be "a land of delight" (MALACHI 3:12).

MALCHIJAH
("God is my King")

1. Son of Ethni, and father of Baaseiah, whose descendant Asaph was one of the leading musicians at the court of King David (I CHRONICLES 6:40).

2. Ancestor of the priest Adaiah (I CHRONICLES 9:12).

3. Priest in charge of the fifth turn of the priestly service in the Tabernacle, during the reign of King David (I CHRONICLES 24:9).

4. Descendant of Parosh who heeded Ezra's call to divorce his foreign-born wife (EZRA 10:25).

5. Son of Harim who heeded the call to divorce his foreign-born wife and repaired a sector of the walls of Jerusalem and the tower of furnaces during the days of Nehemiah (NEHEMIAH 3:11).

6. Son of Rechab who rebuilt the Dung Gate of Jerusalem during the days of Nehemiah (NEHEMIAH 3:14).

7. Son of a goldsmith who repaired a part of the walls of Jerusalem during the days of Nehemiah (NEHEMIAH 3:31).

8. A priest who signed Nehemiah's solemn covenant (NEHEMIAH 10:3).

9. A priest who blew the trumpet during the dedication of the rebuilt walls of Jerusalem, during the time of Nehemiah (NEHEMIAH 12:42).

MALCHIRAM
("my king is exalted")

One of the seven sons of King Jehoiachin, the last king of Judah, whose other sons were Salathiel, Hoshama, Pedaiah, Shenazzar, Jekamiah, and Nedabiah (I CHRONICLES 3:18).

MALLUCH
("ruling")

1. A Levite and forefather of Ethan who played music in the Tabernacle during King David's reign (I CHRONICLES 6:44).

2. A priest of Judah who returned from exile in Babylon with Zerubbabel (NEHEMIAH 12:2)

3. A descendant of Bani who heeded Ezra's call to divorce his foreign-born wife (EZRA 10:29)

4. A descendant of Harim who heeded Ezra's call to divorce his foreign-born wife (EZRA 10:32)

5. A priest who signed Nehemiah's solemn covenant (NEHEMIAH 10:4).

6. A leader of Judah who signed Nehemiah's solemn covenant (NEHEMIAH 10:27).

MANIUS

Titus Manius and Quintus Memmius were the legates of Rome who carried a letter to the Jewish people consenting to the terms that Lysias, a commander of Antiochus, granted to the Jews after his defeat (II MACCABEES 11:34).

MARESHAH
("summit")

1. Son of Caleb of the tribe of Judah (I CHRONICLES 2:42).

2. Son of Laadah and a leader of the tribe of Judah (I CHRONICLES 4:21).

MATTANIAH
("God's gift")

1. Son of King Josiah and Hamutal, also known as King Zedekiah (II KINGS 24:17). King Nebuchadnezzar from Babylon invaded Judah and defeated Judah after two years. King Zedekiah fled the city and was captured, forced to witness the slaying of his children, then blinded, after which he died in prison (II KINGS 24:17).

2. Son of Micah and a Levite who settled in the land of Judah after the return from the Babylonian exile (I CHRONICLES 9:15).

3. Son of Heman, and a Levite and member of a family of musicians who was in charge of the ninth turn of service that played musical instruments at the Tabernacle during the reign of David (I CHRONICLES 25:4).

4. Descendant of Asaph, and one of the Levites who purified the Temple during the reign of King Hezekiah of Judah (I CHRONICLES 29:13).

5. Descendant of Elam who heeded Ezra's call to divorce his foreign-born wife (EZRA 10:26).

6. Descendant of Zattu who heeded Ezra's call to divorce his foreign-born wife (EZRA 10:27).

7. Descendant of Pahath-moab who heeded Ezra's call to divorce his foreign-born wife (EZRA 10:30).

8. Descendant of Bani who heeded Ezra's call to divorce his foreign-born wife (EZRA 10:37).

9. Son of Mica (NEHEMIAH 11:17). A Levite from Jerusalem who was in charge of leading the thanksgiving prayers.

10. Son of Mica and ancestor of Uzzi (NEHEMIAH 11:22).

11. Levite who was a gatekeeper of the Temple during the days of Nehemiah (NEHEMIAH 12:25).

12. Son of Micaiah and ancestor of the priest Zechariah (NEHEMIAH 12:35).

13. Father of Zaccur and grandfather of Hanan who administered the treasures of Judah (NEHEMIAH 13:13).

MATTATHIAS

1. Jewish priest who launched the Maccabean revolt. In the village of Modein, some 20 miles west of Jerusalem, a Seleucid officer forced all villagers to conduct pagan rites, rather than the worship of YHWH. Mattathias, a descendant of a Levite named Hasmonaeus, refused to comply (I MACCABEES 2:22). Another villager stepped forward to make a pagan offering, perhaps fearing reprisals against himself and his family, but Mattathias grabbed the man and killed him. The priest then turned on the Syrian official and slew him as well. This act of resistance galvanized the Maccabean revolt. Leadership of the rebellion soon passed from Mattathias to his son Judas, a skilled and ruthless commander whose nom de guerre was "Maccabeus," from the Aramaic word *maqqaba,* or "hammer" (I MACCABEES 2:50).

2. Son of Absalom and one of the commanders who served under Jonathan Maccabeus, one of the leaders of the Maccabean revolt. Mattathias fought in the Battle of Hazor, where the Seleucids were defeated (I MACCABEES 11:70).

3. Youngest son of Simon the Maccabean who was murdered along with his father and his brother Judas by his brother-in-law Ptolemy, son of Abubus (I MACCABEES 16:12,4).

4. Envoy sent by the Syrian General Nicanor to parlay with Judas Maccabeus (II MACCABEES 14:19).

MATTENAI

1. Descendant of Hashum who divorced his foreign wife during the days of Ezra (EZRA 10:33).

2. Descendant of Bani who divorced his foreign wife during the days of Ezra (EZRA 10:37).

3. Descendant of Joiarib who served as priest during the tenures of Joiakim, the high priest, and Nehemiah (NEHEMIAH 12:19).

MATTITHIAH
("gift of God")

1. A Levite musician who played before Ark of the Covenant when it was carried from

"Mattathias Kills the Jewish Man About to Sacrifice to Zeus" is an engraving by French artist Gustave Doré (1832–1883).

the house of Obed-edom to its resting place in Jerusalem (I CHRONICLES 15:18).

2. One of the sons of Jeduthun, a musician of King David, who played the harp during the 14th turn of service at the Tabernacle (I CHRONICLES 25:3,21).

3. Eldest son of Shallum, of the family of Kohath, who settled in Jerusalem after he returned from the Babylonian exile and was in charge of the baked offerings (I CHRONICLES 9:31).

4. A leader of Judah who stood by Ezra while reading the Law out loud to the people (NEHEMIAH 8:4).

5. Descendant of Nebo who divorced his foreign-born wife (EZRA 10:43).

MEMMIUS

One of the Roman legates who brought a letter to the Hebrews after their victory over Lysias (II MACCABEES 11:34).

MENELAUS

High priest of the Temple in Jerusalem, who gained control of this office by bribing the Syrian King Antiochus IV. This caused an outrage among the population, not because of the bribe but because Menelaus was not a descendant of Zadok, Solomon's high priest, unlike the previous high priests, Onias III and Jason. Only Zadokites could aspire to become high priest. Menelaus was dismissed from office when Judas Maccabeus captured Jerusalem, and was later executed by the Seleucid General Lysias (II MACCABEES 4:23-39,43-50).

MERAIOTH

("rebellious")

1. Son of Zerahiah, father of Amariah, and ancestor of Ezra the scribe (I CHRONICLES 6:6; EZRA 7:3).

2. Son of Ahitub, father of Zadok, and ancestor of Azariah, a priest who settled in Jerusalem in Ezra's time (I CHRONICLES 9:11).

3. Ancestor of a priestly clan, whose leader was Helkai when Joiakim was high priest during the time of Nehemiah (NEHEMIAH 12:15).

MEREMOTH

("heights")

1. Son of the priest Uriah who counted and weighed the silver and gold utensils of the Temple, which Ezra had brought back from the Babylonian exile. He also helped repair the walls of Jerusalem, during the days of Nehemiah (EZRA 8:33; NEHEMIAH 3:4).

2. Descendant of Bani who divorced his wife, during the days of Ezra (EZRA 10:36).

Treasures from the Temple, received by the priest Meremoth, are shown in this engraving titled "Cyrus Restoring the Vessels From the Temple," by French artist Gustave Doré (1832–1883).

3. One of the priests who signed Nehemiah's solemn covenant (NEHEMIAH 10:5).

4. Priest who returned with Zerubbabel from the Babylonian exile (NEHEMIAH 12:3).

MESHEZABEL

("delivered by God")

1. Father of Berechiah, grandfather of Meshullam, who helped to repair the walls of Jerusalem (NEHEMIAH 3:4).

2. One of the leaders who signed Nehemiah's solemn agreement (NEHEMIAH 10:21).

3. Father of Pethahiah, and a leader of Judah in Nehemiah's time (NEHEMIAH 11:24).

MESHULLAM

("rewarded")

1. Grandfather of Shaphan, a scribe in the time of King Josiah (II KINGS 22:3).

2. Zerubbabel's son who led the return from Babylon to Judah (I CHRONICLES 3:19).

3. A Gadite in the reign of Jotham, king of Judah (I CHRONICLES 5:13).

4. A Benjamite, of the sons of Elpaal living in Jerusalem (I CHRONICLES 8:17).

5. A Benjamite, Sallu's father who settled in Jerusalem after the captivity (I CHRONICLES 9:7; NEHEMIAH 11:7).

6. A Benjamite who lived in Jerusalem after the captivity (I CHRONICLES 9:8).

7. Hilkiah's father and son of Zadok the priest, he was the grandfather of Azariah, the head of a priestly family who settled in Jerusalem after the captivity (I CHRONICLES 9:11; NEHEMIAH 11:11).

8. A priest, Meshillemith's son and an ancestor of Maasiai, who settled in Jerusalem after the captivity (I CHRONICLES 9:12).

9. A Kohathite or a family of Kohathite Levites, in the reign of Josiah (II CHRONICLES 34:12).

10. One of the leaders sent by Ezra to Iddo to gather Levites willing to return to Jerusalem and serving in the Temple (EZRA 8:16).

11. A leader who was present when Ezra called upon the men of Judah to divorce their foreign-born wives (EZRA 10:15).

12. Descendant of Bani who heeded Ezra's call to divorce his foreign-born wife (EZRA 10:29).

13. Berechiah's son who assisted in rebuilding the wall of Jerusalem. His daughter married Jehohanan, son of Tobiah (NEHEMIAH 3:4,30; 6:18).

14. Son of Besodeiah, who assisted Joiada the son of Paseah in restoring the old gate of Jerusalem (NEHEMIAH 3:6).

15. A leader who stood at the left hand of Ezra when he read the Law to the people (NEHEMIAH 8:4).

16. A priest who signed the covenant with Nehemiah (NEHEMIAH 10:7,20).

17. Head of a priestly family in the days of Joiakim (NEHEMIAH 12:13).

18. Head of the priestly family of Ginnethon in the days of Joiakim (NEHEMIAH 12:16).

19. A porter, descendant of Meshullam, in the days of Nehemiah (NEHEMIAH 12:25).

20. One of the leaders of Judah at the

dedication of the wall of Jerusalem (NEHE-MIAH 12:33).

MICHAEL
("who is like God?")

1. Father of Sethur, one of Moses' spies sent to Canaan to report its city and inhabitants' demographics (NUMBERS 13:13).

2. Leader of the tribe of Gad who lived in Bashan (I CHRONICLES 5:13).

3. Son of Jeshishai, and leader of a tribe who lived in Gilead (I CHRONICLES 5:14).

4. Son of Baaseiah, father of Shimea, and ancestor of Asaph, King David's musician (I CHRONICLES 6:40).

5. Son of Izrahiah and a leader in a clan of the tribe of Issachar. Members of the clan were famous warriors (I CHRONICLES 7:3).

6. Son of Beriah, the leader of a clan in Jerusalem (I CHRONICLES 8:16).

7. One of the captains who deserted Saul's army with his men and joined David at Ziklag (I CHRONICLES 12:20).

8. Son of King Jehoshaphat, who was killed by his brother Jehoram after Jehoshaphat died and Jehoram ascended the throne (II CHRONICLES 21:2).

9. Father of Omri, who was appointed a ruler of the Issachar tribe in the days of King David (I CHRONICLES 27:18).

10. Father of Zebadiah, and descendant of Shephatiah who returned from exile in Babylon (EZRA 8:8).

11. Traditionally, one of the four archangels and protector of the Hebrew people. Only

A detail of the archangel Michael appears in "Tobias and the Three Archangels" by Italian artist Francesco Di Gioanni Botticini (1446–1497).

after the Babylonian exile do these archangels assume names. For example, Michael is the angel referred to in Daniel's last vision as "the great prince who has charge of your people" (DANIEL 10:13; 12:1).

MIJAMIN
("auspicious")

1. Priest in charge of the sixth turn of the priestly service in the Tabernacle during the reign of King David (I CHRONICLES 24:9).

2. Descendant of Parosh who heeded Ezra's call to divorce his foreign-born wife (EZRA 10:25).

3. One of the priests who signed Nehemiah's solemn covenant (NEHEMIAH 10:7).

MIKLOTH
("rod")

Son of Jeiel and a leader of the tribe of Benjamin (I CHRONICLES 8:32).

MINIAMIN
("right hand")

1. A Levite who was responsible for distributing the gifts offered by the people among the other Levites during the days of King Hezekiah (II CHRONICLES 31:15).

2. Head of a clan of priests who lived in Jerusalem during the days of high priest Joiakim (NEHEMIAH 12:17).

3. One of the priests who played the trumpet during the dedication of the rebuilt walls of Jerusalem during the days of Nehemiah (NEHEMIAH 12:41).

MISPAR
("number")

One of the men who returned with Zerubbabel from the Babylonian exile (EZRA 2:2). He is also known as Mispereth (NEHEMIAH 7:7).

MITHREDATH OR MITHRADATES
("given by Mithra")

1. Treasurer of Cyrus, king of Persia, who was ordered to hand over the vessels of the Temple, which had been plundered by the Babylonians, to Sheshbazzar (EZRA 1:8).

2. A Persian officer stationed at Samaria during the days of Ezra, and one of the authors of a letter falsely accusing the Jews of preparing a rebellion against the king (EZRA 4:7).

MORDECAI
("belonging to Merodach")

Jair's son, of the tribe of Benjamin, who was carried into captivity with Jeconiah. He resided at Susa, the metropolis of Persia, and adopted his orphaned cousin Hadassah (Esther), whom he brought up as his daughter. When she was brought into the king's harem and made queen in place of the deposed Queen Vashti, he was promoted to an office in the court of King Ahasuerus, and was one of those who "sat in the king's gate" (ESTHER 2:21). While holding this office, he discovered a plot to kill the king, which was foiled. Mordecai later refused to bow down before Haman the Agagite, whom had been raised to the highest position at court; and Haman, offended by Mordecai, plotted his death in a wholesale destruction of the Jewish exiles throughout the Persian Empire (ESTHER 3:8-15). News of this plan reached Mordecai, who told Queen Esther, who stopped the attack. The Jews were saved, Mordecai was raised to a high rank, and

Haman was executed on the gallows he had built for Mordecai (ESTHER 6:2–7:10). In memory of this, Jews celebrate the feast of Purim (ESTHER 9:26-32).

MOZA
("exit")

1. Son of Caleb and Ephah, of the tribe of Judah and descendant of Hezron (I CHRONICLES 2:46).

2. Descendant of Saul and son of Zimri of the tribe of Benjamin (I CHRONICLES 8:36,37; 9:42,43).

NAARAH
("young girl")

One of the two wives of Ashhur, Tekoa's father (I CHRONICLES 4:5). They had four sons: Ahuzzam, Hepher, Temeni, and Haahashtari.

NAOMI
("my delight")

Elimelech's wife, mother of Mahlon and Chilion, and Ruth's mother-in-law. Naomi left Judea with her husband and two sons in a time of famine and went to the land of Moab. There, her husband and sons died. Heartbroken, Naomi prepared to move back to Bethlehem and told Ruth to return to her own family. Ruth decided to stay with her, saying, "Where you go, I will go" (RUTH 1:16). On her return to Bethlehem, Naomi wished to be known as Mara, "bitterness," instead of Naomi, "sweetness." In Bethlehem, Ruth sustained herself and her mother-in-law by gleaning kernels from the barley harvest (RUTH 1:2,20-21; 2:1).

NEHEMIAH
("consolation of God")

1. Hachaliah's son, a member of the Jewish exile community in Babylonia, and the cupbearer of King Artaxerxes Longimanus at Shushan, the winter residence of the kings of Persia, who would rise to become the Jewish governor of Judah.

During the king's reign, certain Jews arrived from Judea telling Nehemiah of the deplorable state of Jerusalem. He immediately decided to go to Jerusalem to try to better their condition, with the king's consent. Receiving an appointment as governor of Judea, he promised to return to Persia within a given time. Nehemiah's great achievement was the rebuilding of the walls of Jerusalem, and restoring that city to its former fortified state. Nehemiah's work elicited scorn and fear from the surrounding states. Sanballat and Tobiah conspired to attack the builders and stop the undertaking, but their attempt was defeated by Nehemiah. Various conspir-

"Nehemiah Looks Upon the Ruins of Jerusalem" was painted by James Jacques Joseph Tissot (1836–1902) between 1896 and 1902.

acies were contrived to remove Nehemiah and, if possible, to take his life; one that nearly succeeded was an attempt to make the king of Persia suspicious that Nehemiah would set himself up as an independent king once the walls were completed.

During his government, Nehemiah suppressed the demands of the nobles and the rich and saved many poor Jews from slavery. He refused his allowance as governor, in consideration of the people's poverty, and kept a table for 150 Jews who returned

from captivity. He made provisions for the maintenance of priests and Levites, as well as the worship of the Temple. He insisted that the sanctity of the precincts of the Temple be preserved, and expelled the high priest's family, who had contracted heathen marriages, from all sacred functions. Like Ezra, he rebuked Jews who had intermarried with foreigners. Lastly, he provided for keeping the Sabbath day holy.

2. One of the leaders who returned from the first expedition to Jerusalem from Babylon under Zerubbabel (EZRA 2:2; NEHEMIAH 7:7).

3. Azbuk's son who helped to repair the wall of Jerusalem (NEHEMIAH 3:18).

NER
("light")

Abiel's son and brother of Saul's father Kish, though he is described as King Saul's grandfather in Chronicles (I SAMUEL 14:50; I CHRONICLES 8:33).

NETHANIAH
("given of Jehovah")

1. One of Asaph's four sons, appointed by David to perform music in the Temple, who had responsibility for the fifth turn of service at the Tabernacle (I CHRONICLES 25:2,12).

2. Elishama's son, a member of the royal family of Judah, and father of Ishmael who murdered Governor Gedaliah (II KINGS 25:23,25).

3. A Levite sent by King Jehoshaphat to teach the Law to the people of Judah (II CHRONICLES 17:8).

4. Shelemiah's son, Cushi's grandson, and father of Jehudi, the official who read Jeremiah's prophecies to the princes of Judah (JEREMIAH 36:14).

NOGAH
("splendor")

Son of David, born in Jerusalem (I CHRONICLES 3:7; 14:6), though he is not included in the list of David's sons in the Book of Samuel (II SAMUEL 5:14,15).

NUMENIUS

Son of Antiochus and one of two envoys sent to Rome by Jonathan to renew the treaty of friendship (I MACCABEES 12:16).

OBED
("servant")

1. Son of Boaz and Ruth, father of Jesse and grandfather of David (RUTH 4:17; I CHRONICLES 2:12).

2. Son of Ephlal, grandson of Zabad, and father of Jehu (I CHRONICLES 2:37-38).

3. One of David's soldiers who was renowned for his bravery (I CHRONICLES 11:47).

4. One of the gatekeepers of the Temple; son of Shemaiah, the firstborn of Obed-edom (I CHRONICLES 26:7).

5. Father of Azariah, one of the captains of hundreds who joined with Jehoiada in the revolution against Athaliah (II CHRONICLES 23:1).

OBIL

An Ishmaelite who watched over the camels in David's palace (I CHRONICLES 27:30).

"Ruth and Obed" was painted by English painter Thomas Matthews Rooke (1842–1942) in 1876–1877.

ODED
("restoring")

1. Father of the prophet Prophet Azariah who ministered during the reign of Asa (II CHRONICLES 15:1).

2. A prophet in Samaria, at the time of Pekah's invasion of Judah. Oded went to Samaria and intervened on behalf of the captives, after which prisoners were returned (II CHRONICLES 28:9).

ONIAS

1. Onias I, a high priest in Jerusalem and ancestor of Simon the Just. Onias was a contemporary of the Spartan King Arius, who sent him a letter of friendship (I MACCABEES 12:7,20).

2. Son of the high priest Simon II, who succeeded his father as Onias III. During his reign as high priest, the Temple of Jerusalem was sacked by Heliodorus, an agent of Seleucus II. Onias prayed for intervention, which was granted when an apparition appeared to prevent the theft. Onias was later slain by Menelaus (II MACCABEES 4:34).

3. Onias IV, the high priest who was permitted to build a Jewish temple in Leontopolis by Egyptian King Ptolemy VI Philometor (II MACCABEES 4:21).

ORPAH
("mane")

Wife of Chilion, son of Naomi. After her husband's death, she accompanied her mother-in-law only part way to Bethlehem, then decided to return to her own tribe, the Moabites (RUTH 1:4; 2:4).

PAROSH
("flea")

Ancestor of one of the families from Judah, some of whom returned to Jerusalem from captivity in Babylon with Zerubbabel and others with Ezra. One descendant, Pedaiah, helped to rebuild the city, and other descendants were among those who signed the

Artist William Blake (1757–1827) painted "Naomi Entreating Ruth and Orpah to Return to the Land of Moab" in 1795.

covenant of Nehemiah (EZRA 2:3; 8:3; 10:25; NEHEMIAH 3:25; 7:8; 10:14).

PERSEUS

Son and successor of Philip III of Macedonia, who was the last king of Macedonia. A war with Rome ended in defeat and his capture at Pydna. Macedonia then became a Roman province, and Perseus was brought to Rome to die in captivity (I MACCABEES 8:5).

PETHAHIAH
("freed by God")

1. A priest during the reign of David who had responsibility for the 19th turn of service at the Tabernacle (I CHRONICLES 24:16).

2. A Levite in the time of Ezra, who agreed to divorce his foreign-born wife (EZRA 10:2). He is probably the same person mentioned in Nehemiah, who called on the people of Judah to confess their sins and praise God (NEHEMIAH 9:5).

3. Son of Meshezabel, and descendant of Zerah, who served as counselor to King Artaxerxes of Persia in the days of Nehemiah (NEHEMIAH 11:24).

PHASIRON

Leader of an Arab tribe whose descendants were killed by Jonathan in their tents, located in the wilderness near Bethbasi (I MACCABEES 9:66).

PHILIP

1. Greek king of Macedonia, and father of Alexander the Great (I MACCABEES 1:1).

2. King of Macedonia and father of Perseus, who was conquered by the Romans (I Mac-cabees 8:5).

3. Friend of the Syrian King Antiochus IV Epiphanes, who on his deathbed appointed Philip regent of the Seleucid kingdom until his younger son Antiochus came of age. He was upstaged by Lysias, who promptly crowned the boy king with himself as regent. Later, Philip captured the Syrian capital of Antioch when Lysias was busy fighting the Maccabees in Judea. Lysias rushed back and retook Antioch, after which Philip fled, probably to Egypt (I Mac-cabees 6:14-18; 55-63; II Mac-cabees 9:29).

PTOLEMY

Ptolemy VI Philometor, king of Egypt, during whose reign Egypt was twice invaded by the Syrian King Antiochus IV. Ptolemy VI then actively involved himself in the Syrian civil war, supporting the claim of Demetrius II. Ptolemy VI was favorably disposed to the idea of Jewish independence in Judea and allowed the high priest Onias IV to build a Jewish temple in Leontopolis (I Maccabees 1:18; 10:51-58; 11:1-18).

A gold coin depicts Ptolemy VI Philometor (ca 186–145 B.C.E.), king of Egypt during the Ptolemaic period.

R

RAM

("exalted")

1. Son of Hezron of the tribe of Judah, and ancestor of King David (RUTH 4:19; I CHRONICLES 2:9).

2. One of the sons of Jerahmeel and grandson of Hezron (I CHRONICLES 2:25,27).

3. Ancestor of Elihu, son of Barachel the Buzite, who debated with Job and his friends (JOB 32:2).

RAZIS

("father of the Hebrews")

A pious elder in Jerusalem, who was arrested by the Syrian General Nicanor for his opposition to the Syrian Hellenistic tendencies. To prevent himself from falling into the hands of Nicanor's soldiers, he stabbed himself and jumped off a tower wall (II Mac-cabees 14:37,42,43).

REHUM

("merciful")

1. A leader of Judah who returned from exile in Babylon with Zerubbabel (EZRA 2:2).

2. A Persian officer stationed at Samaria during the days of Ezra, and one of the authors of a letter falsely accusing the Jews of preparing a rebellion against the king (EZRA 4:8,9,17,23).

3. A Levite of the family of Bani, who assisted in rebuilding the walls of Jerusalem (NEHE-MIAH 3:17).

4. One of the leaders of Judah who signed the covenant with Nehemiah (NEHEMIAH 10:25).

REPHAIAH

("healed by God")

1. Son of Tola and Issachar's grandson, he and his family were a clan of renowned warriors (I CHRONICLES 7:2).

2. Descendant of David and a contemporary of Jerubbaal (I CHRONICLES 3:21).

3. Ishi's son, a captain of Simeon who, with his three brothers and 500 men, defeated the last of the Amalekites (I CHRONICLES 4:42).

4. Father of Eleasah, Binea's son and a descendant of Saul, who is also called Raphah (I CHRONICLES 8:37; 9:43).

5. Son of Hur and one of the repairers of the wall of Jerusalem under Nehemiah (NEHE-MIAH 3:9).

RHODOCUS

Maccabean soldier who betrayed Judas's battle plan to the Syrians when the fortress of Beth-zur was besieged (II MACCABEES 13:21).

RUTH

("friend")

A Moabitess, the wife of Mahlon and ancestress of David, whose wonderful story of love

This portrait of "Ruth," ancestor of David, was painted by French artist Charles Landelle (1821–1908) in 1886.

and loyalty is set in the time of the Judges. A famine had forced a man named Elimelech to leave his hometown of Bethlehem and take his wife, Naomi, and sons Mahlon and Chilion to the country of the Moabites. Elimelech died, whereupon Mahlon and Chilion both married local women. Mahlon chose a young woman named Ruth, but then died also. Heartbroken, Naomi prepared to move back to Bethlehem and told Ruth to return to her own family. Ruth decided to stay with her, saying, "Where you go, I will go" (RUTH 1:16).

In Bethlehem, Ruth sustained herself and her mother-in-law by gleaning kernels from the barley harvest. One day, she met the owner of a field named Boaz, who received her kindly. Naomi urged Ruth to return to Boaz at night and "uncover his feet"—an invitation to have relations with her. In response, Boaz promised to take care of her, a symbolic acceptance of marriage (RUTH 3:11). After they married, Ruth bore Boaz a son named Obed, the future father of Jesse, who would become the father of King David. Thus, Ruth was David's great-grandmother.

SALMA
("garment")
Leader of Judah, son of Hur and grandson of Caleb, Salma is the legendary founder of Bethlehem (I CHRONICLES 2:51).

SANBALLAT
("strength")
A Moabite from Horonaim who held a post in Samaria at the time Nehemiah was preparing to rebuild the walls of Jerusalem. He was opposed to the project and tried everything to stop it, including an assassination plot against Nehemiah (NEHEMIAH 4:2).

SAREA
One of the five who wrote down the visions of Esdras and were described as "trained to write swiftly." The others were Dabria, Selemia, Ethanus, and Asiel (II ESDRAS 14:24).

SELEMIA
One of the five who wrote down the visions of Esdras and were described as "trained to write swiftly." The others were Sarea, Dabria, Ethanus, and Asiel (II ESDRAS 14:24).

SELEUCUS IV PHILOPATOR
Syrian king and successor of Antiochus III. Originally well disposed toward the Jews, he sent a high official, Heliodorus, to Jerusalem to collect gold and silver from the Temple treasury. This theft was thwarted by the apparition of supernatural beings. He sent his son Demetrius to rescue his younger brother Antiochus IV Epiphanes, who was being held hostage in Rome. Seleucus was killed by Heliodorus, after which Antiochus IV seized the throne (DANIEL 11:20; I MACCABEES 7:1; II MACCABEES 3:2-6; 14:1).

SHADRACH
("command of Aku")
Babylonian name given to Hananiah, one of four princes of Judah taken to Babylon and held captive by Nebuchadnezzar. While in Babylon, Shadrach, Meshach, and Abednego refused to worship Babylonian idols, and were sent to a furnace as punishment. They were delivered by an angel and survived without any harm (DANIEL 1:6-7; 2:17,49; 3:12-30).

SHEBANIAH
("God has grown")
1. A Levite priest who blew the trumpet before the Ark of the Covenant during the reign of David (I CHRONICLES 15:24).
2. A Levite at the time of Ezra who prayed to God to forgive the sins of Judah and signed the agreement with Nehemiah (NEHEMIAH 9:4-5; 10:10).
3. A Levite priest who called upon the people

"Shadrach, Meshach, and Abednego in the Fiery Furnace" was painted by Simeon Solomon (1840–1905) in 1863.

of Judah to praise God during the public fast day instituted by Ezra; he later signed the covenant (NEHEMIAH 10:12).
4. A Levite priest who signed the agreement with Nehemiah; also known as Shecaniah (NEHEMIAH 10:4; 12:3,14).

SHECANIAH
("residence of God")
1. A priest during the reign of David who had responsibility for the tenth turn of service at the Tabernacle (I CHRONICLES 24:11).
2. A priest during the reign of Hezekiah who distributed the freewill offerings among the priests and Levites (II CHRONICLES 31:15).
3. Son of Jahaziel and head of a family that returned from exile in Babylon with Ezra (EZRA 8:5).
4. Father of Shemaiah, the priest who helped repair the walls of Jerusalem (NEHEMIAH 3:29).
5. Son of Arah and father-in-law of Tobiah, who tried to interfere with the rebuilding of Jerusalem's walls (NEHEMIAH 6:18).
6. A priest who returned from captivity with Zerubbabel (NEHEMIAH 12:3).

SHEPHATIAH
("judged by God")
1. Fifth son of David and Abital, who was born in Hebron (II SAMUEL 3:4; II CHRONICLES 3:3).
2. A Benjamite and warrior who joined David's army at Ziklag (I CHRONICLES 9:8; 12:5).
3. A prince and leader of the Simeonites during the reign of David (I CHRONICLES 37:16).
4. Son of Jehoshaphat, king of Judah, who was killed by his eldest brother Jehoram when he was crowned king (II CHRONICLES 21:2).
5. Ancestor of Zebadiah, son of Michael, who returned from exile in Babylon with Ezra (EZRA 8:8).
6. Name of two men whose ancestors returned to Jerusalem from Babylonian captivity with Zerubbabel (EZRA 2:4,57; 8:8; NEHEMIAH 7:9,59).
7. Son of Mahalalel of the tribe of Judah, father of Amariah, and an ancestor of Athaiah who settled in Jerusalem in the days of Nehemiah (NEHEMIAH 11:4).
8. A leader of Judah who urged King Zedekiah to kill Jeremiah for urging surrender to the Babylonian army. Given leave, they threw the prophet in a cistern, planning to let him die there (JEREMIAH 38:1-4).

SHEREBIAH

("flame of God")

A Levite who returned from Babylon to Jerusalem after Ezra's appeal to Iddo to send Levites to Judah. Sherebiah helped carry the silver and gold vessels from Babylon, assisted Ezra when the Law was read to the people, and signed the covenant (EZRA 8:17-18,24-30; NEHEMIAH 8:7; 9:4-5; 10:12; 12:8,24).

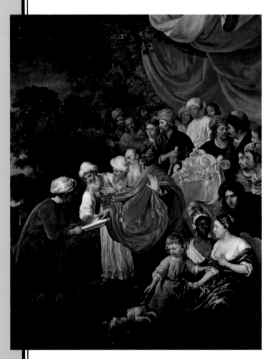

Dutch artist Jacob van Loo (ca 1614–1670) painted this canvas of "Zerubbabel Showing a Plan of Jerusalem to Cyrus." Zerubbabel is the Persian name for Sheshbazzar.

SHESHBAZZAR

("worshipper of fire")

Presumably, the Persian name of Zerubbabel, a member of Judah's former royal house, who led a caravan of exiles to Jerusalem. Before his departure, King Cyrus was kind enough to give him more than 5,000 vessels and implements of silver and gold, which Nebuchadnezzar had looted from the Jerusalem Temple (EZRA 1:8-11; 5:14-16; 6:14-18). Because Sheshbazzar's name is not attested outside the Book of Ezra, some scholars have identified him as either Zerubbabel or as Shenazzar, one of the sons of King Jehoiachin who was exiled to Babylon with his family (I CHRONICLES 3:18).

SHETHAR

("star")

One of the seven princes of Persia in the court of Ahasuerus (ESTHER 1:14).

SHIMRI

("watchman")

1. Father of Jedaiah, a leader of the tribe of Simeon who settled in Gedor during the reign of King Hezekiah (I CHRONICLES 4:37).
2. Father of Jediael, one of the "valiant men" of David's armies (I CHRONICLES 11:45).
3. Son of Hosah, a descendant from Merari, who served as one of the gatekeepers of the Tabernacle during the reign of David (I CHRONICLES 26:9-11).
4. A Levite and descendant of Elizaphan, who assisted with the purification of the Temple in the time of Hezekiah (II CHRONICLES 29:13).

SHIMSHAI

("bright")

Secretary of Rehum, Persian governor of the conquered provinces of Judea and Samaria. He wrote to Artaxerxes to persuade him to stop the Jews from rebuilding the temple (EZRA 4:8-9; 17-23).

TATTENAI

Persian governor who succeeded Rehum in Samaria and Judah during the reign of King Darius, and in the days of Zerubbabel (EZRA 5:3,6; 6:6,13). He questioned Zerubbabel's right to repair the Temple, but when Darius ordered the construction to proceed, he did not fail to support the project (I ESDRAS 6:3,7,27; 7:1).

THEODOTUS

1. One of the three ambassadors sent by Syrian General Nicanor to Judas Maccabeus to seek peace terms (II MACCABEES 14:19).
2. Commander of Egyptian forces in Syria who tried to assassinate King Ptolemy IV Philopator. The plot was preempted by a Jew named Dositheus who led the king away

and placed another man in his tent (III MACCABEES 1:2).

TOBIAH

("goodness of God")

1. Ancestor of a family who returned with Zerubbabel from the Babylonian exile. They were dismissed from the priesthood because they were unable to prove their Jewish ancestry (EZRA 2:60).
2. A Jew living in the Transjordan during the time of Nehemiah. Tobiah was a wealthy landowner with connections to some of the most prominent Jewish families. His son Johanan married the daughter of Meshullam who was the son of Berechiah (NEHEMIAH 6:18). He himself was the son-in-law of Shecaniah, the son of Arah (NEHEMIAH 6:17). When Tobiah and his allies found out that Nehemiah was going to Jerusalem to rebuild the defensive walls of Jerusalem, they were upset because it might seem that Nehemiah was planning a revolt against the Persian king. They fiercely opposed the construction even as Nehemiah continued to rebuild the walls. They even made attempts to capture Nehemiah, but these plots all failed. One day, the high priest Eliashib made the mistake of installing Tobiah in one of the chambers in the Temple complex during Nehemiah's absence. As soon as Nehemiah returned, he threw out all of Tobiah's belongings and ordered the room to be cleansed (NEHEMIAH 13:7-8).

TOBIAS

("God is good")

1. One of the Levites whom Jehoshaphat sent to teach in the cities of Judah (II CHRONICLES 17:8).
2. Father of Hyrcanus, who kept money in the treasury of the Jerusalem Temple (II MACCABEES 3:11).
3. Son and only child of Tobit and Anna from the tribe of Naphtali (TOBIT 1:9). According to the Book of Tobit, the family had been taken to Nineveh, the capital of the Assyrian Empire. There they continued to live according to the Torah, unlike many other Israelite refugees who embraced local customs. At night, Tobit went out to bury the dead left outside the city walls. One night,

"Departure of the Young Tobias" was created by French artist Pierre Parrocel (1670–1739) in 1733.

a swallow's droppings turned him blind. For this he was mocked; apparently, his many good deeds had failed to prevent his misfortune. Tobit asked his son to go to Media to retrieve Tobit's deposits of silver. Tobias left on the journey accompanied by the archangel Raphael, who introduced himself as a man named Azarias. After Tobias caught a fish, Raphael advised him to keep the viscera. With these, Tobias was later able to use the gall of the fish to cure his father's blindness. While in Ecbatana, he had met Sarah, daughter of Raguel, and married her. Upon their return, a wedding feast was held, and Raphael revealed himself. All prostrated themselves on the ground and praised God (TOBIT 12:7). Tobias waited until Tobit and Anna had passed away, then moved with his wife and children to Media.

4. Son of Josedec and one of the Jews who returned from Babylon to Jerusalem in the time of Zerubbabel, with silver and gold with which to make a crown (ZECHARIAH 6:10).

5. Son of Tobias the Elder (TOBIT 1:29).

TOBIT

A pious man of the tribe of Naphtali (TOBIT 1:1-6). He remained faithful to Jerusalem even when his ancestors broke away from the house of David and Jerusalem. He was taken captive during the days of Shalmaneser, but continued to perform many charitable deeds, giving bread and clothes to the needy and burying the dead (TOBIT 1:17). He stood in good favor with the king, traveling to Media to buy goods for him. While he was there, he deposited pouches of silver with his friend Gabael (TOBIT 1:14). When the situation changed and he was forced to flee, all of his belongings were confiscated and taken to the king's palace, leaving him only with his wife, Anna, and son Tobias (TOBIT 1:20). When he lost his eyesight and fell into great poverty, he prayed for death (TOBIT 2:10; 3:1-6). He asked his son Tobias to go to Media to retrieve his money with a companion and guide Azarias, who was the archangel Raphael. On the journey, Tobias caught a fish and Raphael encouraged him to keep the heart, liver, and gall. Tobias was then guided to the house of Sarah, daughter of Raguel of Ecbatana. He chased away the wicked demon Asmodeus from her bridal chamber, and later married her. They returned to Nineveh where the fish's gall was used to restore Tobit's eyesight (TOBIT 7:12; 8:3; 11:13).

TRYPHO

A commander of Syrian forces who usurped the Seleucid throne. He fomented unrest among the units that King Demetrius II was about to disband, took control of the Syrian capital of Antioch, and placed the young son of Alexander Balas on the throne as Antiochus VI. Through subterfuge, Trypho took Jonathan Maccabeus prisoner and later killed him. Jonathan's successor, Simon Maccabeus, threw his support behind Demetrius II. Soon thereafter, Trypho had Antiochus VI killed and took power himself. After a short, five-year reign, he was toppled by Antiochus VII. He fled to Orthosia but eventually committed suicide (I MACCABEES 11:39; 12:39-50).

ULAM
("porch")

1. A leader of the tribe of Manasseh and father of Bedan (I CHRONICLES 7:17).

2. Firstborn of Eshek, a leader of the tribe of Benjamin and descendant of the house of Saul (I CHRONICLES 8:39,40).

URIEL
("God is my light")

1. A Levite descended from Kohath, son of Tahath, and an ancestor of the prophet Prophet Samuel (I CHRONICLES 6:24).

Italian artist Bernardo Strozzi (1581–1644) painted this canvas of "The Healing of Tobit" in the early 1630s.

2. Head of a family descended from Kohath during the reign of David, who assisted in moving the Ark of the Covenant to Jerusalem, and later ministered in the Tabernacle (I CHRONICLES 15:5,11).

3. Uriel of Gibeah was the father of Maacah (or Micaiah), the favorite wife of King Rehoboam, mother of King Abijah (II CHRONICLES 13:2).

UZZI
("strong")

1. Son of Bukki and father of Zerahiah, a descendant of the priests Eleazar and Aaron, and an ancestor of Ezra the scribe (I CHRONICLES 6:5).

2. Son of Tola of the Issachar tribe, and brother of Rephaiah, Jeriel, Jahmai, Ibsam, and Shemuel, who were renowned warriors (I CHRONICLES 7:2).

3. Son of Bela and a grandson of Benjamin, who together with his brothers were brave men and heads of their clans (I CHRONICLES 7:7).

4. Son of Michri who was the father of Elah, one of the first members of the tribe of Benjamin to return from Babylon and settle in Jerusalem (I CHRONICLES 9:8).

5. Son of Bani and overseer of the Levites in the time of Nehemiah (NEHEMIAH 11:22).

6. A leader of a family of priests who were descendants of Jedaiah in the time of Joiakim the high priest (NEHEMIAH 12:19). He was one of the priests who celebrated the dedication of the rebuilt walls of Jerusalem (NEHEMIAH 12:42).

UZZIEL
("God is my strength")

1. Son of Kohath and grandson of Levi. One of his descendants of the same name was an uncle of Moses and Aaron (EXODUS 6:18).

2. Son of Ishi, and brother of Pelatiah, Rephaiah, and Neariah. He and his brothers led 500 men who defeated the last surviving Amalekites at Mount Seir, and settled in the region (I CHRONICLES 4:42).

3. Son of Bela, grandson of Benjamin, and brother of Ezbon, Uzzi, Jerimoth, and Iri, who were renowned for their bravery (I CHRONICLES 7:7).

4. A Levite who was a member of a family

of musicians (I CHRONICLES 25:4). He was in charge of the 11th turn of service that played musical instruments in the Tabernacle during the reign of David. He was also called Azarel (I CHRONICLES 25:18).

5. Descendant of Jeduthun, King David's musician, and one of the Levites who gathered to purify the Temple during the reign of King Hezekiah of Judah (II CHRONICLES 29:14).

6. Son of Harhaiah and member of a family of goldsmiths who helped to repair the walls of Jerusalem during the days of Nehemiah (NEHEMIAH 3:8).

VAIZATHA

Youngest son of Haman the Agagite, who plotted to kill all the Jews in the Persian Empire. The plot was preempted, and Haman and his sons were killed (ESTHER 9:9).

VANIA

Descendant of Bani who heeded Ezra's call to divorce his foreign-born wife (EZRA 10:36).

"Queen Vashti Leaving the Royal Palace" was painted by Italian artist Filippino Lippi (ca 1457–1504).

VASHTI
("beautiful")

Wife of Ahasuerus, king of Persia. She refused to appear in front of the king during a banquet, for which the king divorced her. A royal decree was issued that banned her from ever appearing in front of the king (ESTHER 1:9). Ahasuerus selected Esther as her replacement; Esther then helped foil Haman's plot to kill the Jews of Persia.

ZABAD
("gift")

1. Son of Nathan, father of Ephlal, and descendant of Jarha, the Egyptian slave who married the daughter of his master Sheshan (I CHRONICLES 2:36).

2. Son of Tahath, and a leader of the tribe of Ephraim (I CHRONICLES 7:21).

3. Son of Ahlai, one of King David's brave warriors (I CHRONICLES 11:41).

4. Son of Shomer, also known as Jozachar, who was involved in the plot to kill King Joash (II CHRONICLES 24:26).

5. Descendant of Zattu who divorced his foreign-born wife during the days of Ezra (EZRA 10:27).

6. Descendant of Hashum who divorced his foreign-born wife during the days of Ezra (EZRA 10:33).

7. Descendant of Nebo who divorced his foreign-born wife during the days of Ezra (EZRA 10:43).

ZABDIEL
("gift of God")

1. Father of Jashobeam who was a commander of King David's army who served in the first month of the year (I CHRONICLES 27:2).

2. Supervisor of 128 priests who served in Jerusalem during the days of Nehemiah (NEHEMIAH 11:14).

ZARIUS

Brother of King Jehoiakim according to the first Book of Esdras (I ESDRAS 1:38-48).

ZEBADIAH
("God had given")

1. Son of Beriah and a leader of the tribe of Benjamin in Jerusalem (I CHRONICLES 8:15).

2. Son of Elpaal and a leader of the tribe of Benjamin in Jerusalem (I CHRONICLES 8:17).

3. Son of Jeroham of Gedor, and brother of Joelah, a Benjamite warrior who deserted King Saul's army and joined David at Ziklag (I CHRONICLES 12:7).

4. Son of Meshelemiah, one of the gatekeepers of the Tabernacle during the reign of King David (I CHRONICLES 26:2).

5. Son of Asahel and nephew of Joab, who became commander of King David's army that served in the fourth month, with 24,000 men under his command (I CHRONICLES 27:7).

6. A Levite sent by King Jehoshaphat in the third year of his reign to teach the Laws of God in the cities of Judah (II CHRONICLES 17:8).

7. Son of Ishmael and King Jehoshaphat's official "in charge of all the king's matters," including the army and taxes, excluding religious matters (II CHRONICLES 19:11).

8. Son of Michael, and a descendant of Shephatiah who returned with Ezra from Babylon as the head of 60 males of his clan (EZRA 8:8).

9. Descendant of the priest Immer who divorced his foreign-born wife in the days of Ezra (EZRA 10:20).

ZECHARIAH
("God has remembered")

A postexilic prophet of Judah and the 11th of the 12 minor prophets. Like Haggai, Zechariah was impatient with the progress on the rebuilding of the Temple, and pressed for a more energetic effort. In mystical visions reminiscent of the Book of Daniel, Zechariah saw great turmoil ahead, expressed in the apocalyptic imagery of horsemen and chariots, walls of fire, or a vision of the high priest Joshua standing before an angel and Satan; scholars believe these visions reflect the political upheaval in Persia following King Darius's accession to the throne. But other oracles by Zechariah predict the return of a glorious Jewish kingdom. "I will return to Zion," says the Lord in one verse; "Jerusalem shall be called the faithful city, and the mountain of the Lord of hosts shall be called the holy mountain" (ZECHARIAH 8:3). The capital of Judah would once again become a wholesome, prosperous city, with streets "full of boys and girls playing in its streets." "And," says God, "they shall be my people, and I will be their God" (ZECHARIAH 8:5,8).

ZERAH
("rising light")

1. Son of Reuel and grandson of Esau, and a leader of the desert tribe of Edom (GENESIS 36:13,17; I CHRONICLES 1:37).

2. Son of Judah and Judah's daughter-in-law, Tamar. At birth, the hand of Zerah burst out, and the midwife put a scarlet thread around his wrist. His twin brother Perez was born first, however (GENESIS 36:33; I CHRONICLES 1:44).

3. Son of Iddo and a descendant of Levi's son Gershom (I CHRONICLES 6:21).

4. Son of Adaiah the Levite, and an ancestor of King David's musician Asaph (I CHRONICLES 6:41).

5. A commander of Ethiopia who fought against King Asa of Judea but was utterly defeated (II CHRONICLES 14:9-15).

ZERESH
("gold")

Wife of Haman the Agagite. When Haman told her of being forced by King Ahasuerus to pay homage to Mordecai, a Jew, Zeresh prophesied that Haman would fall, and Mordecai would triumph (ESTHER 5:10,14; 6:13).

ZERUBBABEL
("seed of Babylon")

Son of Pedaiah or Shealtiel, and a relative of King Jehoiachin, who may be identical with the man known as Sheshbazzar (I CHRONICLES 3:19; EZRA 1:8,11). Zerubbabel led the first caravan of 42,360 Jewish exiles from Babylon to Jerusalem. Before his departure, King Cyrus gave him more than 5,000 vessels and implements of silver and gold, which Nebuchadnezzar had looted from the Jerusalem Temple. Once in Judah, Zerubbabel was installed as governor of Judah, and he is credited with initiating the reconstruction of the Temple. The work was interrupted by Samaritans, after they had been rebuffed from participating in the construction; "you have nothing to do with us in building a house to our God," Zerubbabel said (EZRA 4:3). Persian Governor Rehum used the fracas to recommend to the Persian king that work on the Temple be discontinued (EZRA 4:15). But after King Darius mounted the throne, Zerubbabel and the high priest Jeshua initiated a new campaign to continue the Temple project, prodded by the Prophets Haggai and Zechariah.

"Job on the Dung Hill" is an engraving by French artist Gustave Doré (1832–1883). One of the friends who came to comfort him was Zophar.

ZIZA
("prominence")

1. Shiphi's son, a chief of the Simeonites in the reign of Hezekiah (I CHRONICLES 4:37).

2. King Rehoboam's son by his favored wife, Maacah, Absalom's granddaughter (II CHRONICLES 11:20).

ZOPHAR
("departing" or "sparrow")

One of the three friends of Job who came to console him in his distress. He is called a Naamathite, or an inhabitant of a place called Naamah (JOB 2:11; 11:1; 20:1; 42:9).

THE FOUR GOSPELS

*And you, Bethlehem,
in the land of Judah . . .
from you shall come
a ruler who is to shepherd
my people Israel.*

GOSPEL OF MATTHEW 2:6 (AFTER MICAH 5:2)

*The "Adoration of the Magi" is the work of the Cologne artist known as
Master of St. Severin (ca 1480–1520). It was painted around 1515.*

THE LIFE OF JESUS
Who Wrote the Four Gospels?

THE FOUR GOSPELS form the core of the New Testament (NT), the principal book of Christian Scripture. The New Testament is sometimes called "The New Covenant," because Christians believe that Jesus is the fulfillment of the promise of the "Old" Testament (or Hebrew Scripture). According to this covenant, God sent his Son, Jesus the Christ, to spread the "good news" (the meaning of "gospel," or "goodspell," *euangelion* in Greek) of a New Kingdom of God, and the promise of eternal redemption.

Although Matthew's is the first Gospel in the New Testament canon, the oldest Gospel is actually that of Mark. Mark arranged the acts and sayings of Jesus in a narrative that propels the impetus of the story toward the climax of the Crucifixion. The other Gospels followed his example; it is believed that Matthew and Luke copied as much as 60 percent of Mark's story into their own narratives.

Nevertheless, the Gospel accounts do not always agree with one another. This raises the question of whether the evangelists were either eyewitnesses themselves or had access to eyewitness accounts of the events they wrote about. Many scholars assume that the evangelists relied on a variety of sources that had been circulating for several decades. John's Gospel even identifies its source, in the form of testimony by Jesus' "beloved disciple," and adds that "we know that his testimony is true" (JOHN 21:24). What's more, it appears that none of the evangelists wrote in Palestine proper, but in other areas in the Roman Empire.

Not much is known about the evangelist Mark. Bishop Papias of Hierapolis in Phrygia (now Turkey) wrote that Mark's work was inspired by Peter's teaching. Unfortunately, the Gospel's author is nowhere identified in the work itself, so we may never know for certain.

In contrast to Mark's narrative, the evangelists Luke and Matthew produced their Gospels in a style that betrays their education and experience with the Greco-Roman literary models. Matthew often adds stylistic flourishes to a particular saying of Jesus. Luke is a skillful author who frames his story with historical references, and imbues the narrative with dramatic tension.

Matthew's Gospel has been dated anywhere from the early 70s to the mid-80s of the first century. Given this date, it is unlikely (though not impossible) that the author is the disciple "Matthew" who worked as a tax collector in Capernaum until Jesus called him to his ministry (MATTHEW 9:9).

According to the same majority opinion, Luke possibly wrote his Gospel between 70 and 85 C.E. A physician named Luke appears in Paul's letters and other New Testament writings, which prompted some Church fathers to assume that the evangelist was a doctor (COLOSSIANS 4:14; II TIMOTHY 4:11). However, the Gospel text itself does not suggest such, particularly in scenes of Jesus' healing.

According to Church tradition, the author of Luke was also responsible for the Book of the Acts of the Apostles, and this suggestion is widely accepted, given the obvious stylistic similarities between the two books. Both Luke and Matthew use material that does not appear in Mark at all. Since the 1970s, scholars have tried to reconstruct this hypothetical source, known as "Q" (based on the German word for "source," or *Quelle*).

Given the evident similarities between Mark, Matthew, and Luke, their works are sometimes referred to as the Synoptic Gospels (from the Greek word *sunoptikos,* meaning "seen together").

By contrast, the Gospel of John is different from the preceding Gospels in terms of style and content. Short citations by Jesus in the former Gospels evolve into extensive monologues in John. Arguably written between 90 and 110 C.E., John's work is known as the "spiritual Gospel" in which Jesus appears in metaphorical terms like "Light of the World" and the "Bread of Life." Recently, some scholars have argued that John's Gospel does include original historical material.

An anonymous Cologne artist painted this elegant Gothic panel of the Annunciation ca 1300.

THE ROMAN EMPIRE

Map labels (by region):

Caledonia — Hadrian's Wall

Hibernia

North Sea

Germania — *Vistula*, *Sarmati...*

BRITANNIA — Eburacum, Deva, Lindum, Viroconium, Isca Silurum, Glevum, Camulodunum, Verulamium, Londinium, Dubrae, Noviomagus, Isca Dumnoniorum

ATLANTIC OCEAN

MAGNA GERMANIA *12 B.C.E.–9 C.E.* — ☆ *Teutoburgerwald 9 C.E.*, Noviomagus, Vetera, ❶ Colonia Agrippinensis, Bonna

GERMANIA INFERIOR — Portus Itius, Gesoriacum, Bagacum, Augusta Treverorum, *Vangiones 436 C.E.*, Mogontiacum

Juliobona, Rotomagus, Noviodunum, Durocortorum, *Catalaunian Plain 451 C.E.*, Lutetia

Augustodurum, Cenabum

LUGDUNENSIS — Darioritum, Juliomagus, Portus Namnetum, Caesarodunum, Limonum, Augustodunum

Gallia

AQUITANIA — Mediolanum, Burdigala

GERMANIA SUPERIOR — Argentorate, *Alesia 52 B.C.E.* ☆, Vesontio, Aventicum

BELGICA

Castra Regina, Carnuntum, Vindobona, Brigetto, Aquincum

RAETIA — Curia, Augusta Vindelicum, Cambodunum, Iuvavum

NORICUM — Teurnia, Virunum, Savaria

☆ *Nedao 454 C.E.*, Apulum, Sarmizegetusa Regia

PANNONIA SUPERIOR — Siscia, Mursa

PANNONIA INFERIOR

DACIA — Viminacium, Singidunum, Sirmium

Alps — **ALPES GRAIAE ET POENINAE** — Octodurum, Axima; **ALPES COTTIAE** — Segusio; **ALPES MARITIMAE** — Cemenelum

Lugdunum (Lyons), Vienna, *Ticinus 218 B.C.E.*, Mediolanum, Cremona, *Lake Garda*

Trebbia 218 B.C.E. ⚔, Placentia, Genoa, *Po*, Bononia, Ravenna, Ariminum

NARBONENSIS — Tolosa, Nemausus ❷, Arausio, Arelate, Narbo, Massilia, Forum Julii ⚓

Florentia, Pisae, *Metaurus River 207 B.C.E.* ⚔, Ancona, Arretium, *Sentinum 295 B.C.E.* ⚔, *Lake Trasimeno 217 B.C.E.*, Perusia, Castrum Novum, Saturnia, **ITALIA**, Cosa, Veii, ★ Rome, Ostia

CORSICA — Aleria

SARDINIA — Olbia, Carales

MACEDONIA — *Cynoscephalae 197 B.C.E.* ⚔, Heraclea, *Pydna 168 B...*, Thess..., Stobi, Philippop...

EPIRUS — Ambracia, *Actium 31 B.C.E.*, Nicopolis

ACHAEA — Corinth

DALMATIA — Salonae

MOESIA SUPERIOR — *Naissus 269 C.E.* ☆, Serdic..., Oescus

Illyricum, *Adriatic Sea*, Dyrrhachium, Apollonia, Brundisium

Beneventum, Capua, Puteoli, Misenum, Neapolis, Pompeii, *Caudine Forks 321 B.C.E.* ⚔, Taranto, Paestum, *Heraclea 280 C.E.*, Thurii, Croton

Cannae 216 B.C.E. ★, Corfinium

LUSITANIA — Brigantium, Lucus Augusti, Legio VII Gemina, Asturica, Bracara Augusta, Portus Cale, Salamantica, Scallabis, Emerita Augusta, Olisipo, Pax Julia, *Tagus*

TARRACONENSIS — Pompaelo, Clunia, Numantia, Caesaraugusta, Dertosa, Tarraco, Barcino, *Ilerda 49 B.C.E.*, Emporiae, Rhodae, Toletum, Saguntum, Valentia, *Hispania*, *Ebro*

BAETICA — *Baecula 208 B.C.E.* ⚔, Corduba, Carthago Nova, *Italica*, *Ilipa 206 B.C.E.* ⚔, Hispalis, Malaca, Gades, Carteia, Tingis

Balearic Islands, Palma

Mediterranean Sea

Tyrrhenian Sea

Mylae 260 B.C.E. ⚔, Messana, Rhegium, Panormus, Catana, **SICILIA**, *Drepanum 249 B.C.E.* ⚔, *Lilybaeum 218 B.C.E.* ⚔, *Agrigentum 261 B.C.E.* ⚔, Syracuse, *Ecnomus 256 B.C.E.* ⚔

Ionian Sea

Bagradas 255 B.C.E. ⚔, Utica, Carthage, Hippo Regius, Thugga, *Zama 202 B.C.E.* ⚔, Hadrumetum, Thapsus

Cartennae, Caesarea, Sitifis, *Cirta 203 B.C.E.* ⚔

MAURETANIA TINGITANA — Rusaddir, Sala, Volubilis

MAURETANIA CAESARIENSIS — Portus Magnus ⚓, Lambaesis, Thamugadi, Theveste

AFRICA — Sabratha, Oea, Leptis Magna, Charax

Cy..., Ptolemais

Legend

- ▪ Roman Territory, 201 B.C.E.
- ▫ Gains by 100 B.C.E.
- Area ruled by the time of Julius Caesar's death, 44 B.C.E.
- Area ruled by the time of Caesar Augustus's death, 14 C.E.
- Gains by Emperor Trajan 117 C.E.
- Region temporarily held by Rome, with dates
- Vassal of Rome
- ⌁⌁⌁ Fortified frontier
- — Roman road

- ⊙ Provincial capital
- ∪ Legion headquarters
- ⚓ Major naval base
- ⚔ Battle of the Samnite Wars (343–290 B.C.E.)
- ⚔ Battle of the 1st Punic War (264–241 B.C.E.)
- ⚔ Battle of the 2nd Punic War (218–202 B.C.E.)
- ⚔ Battle of the Macedonian Wars (214–148 B.C.E.)
- ⚔ Battle of the Roman-Germanic Wars (113 B.C.E.–439 C.E.)
- ⚔ Battle of Julius Caesar's Civil War (49–45 B.C.E.)
- ☆ Other major battle

Scale:
0 50 100 150 200 250 kilometers
0 50 100 150 200 250 miles

Present-day drainage and coastlines are represented.
Modern names appear in parentheses.

1 Cologne Founded by the Romans in 50 C.E., Cologne was the capital of the Roman province of Germany Inferior and headquarters of the Roman legions; it boasted this monumental city gate.

2 Nîmes The Pont du Gard, built in the first century C.E., formed part of the 31-mile Roman aqueduct system that carried water from springs at Uzès to the Roman colony of Nemausus (today's Nîmes).

3 Miletus These remains of the second-century C.E. Roman baths illustrate the importance of Miletus, one of the main cities of Lydia on Asia Minor, during the Roman period. Paul visited the city around 57 C.E.

4 Alexandria The recently excavated Roman amphitheater in Alexandria, Egypt, was built after the destruction of the Kitos War in 115 C.E. by Emperor Hadrian.

Map labels:
Dnieper
Don
Volga
Caspian Sea
Scythia
Olbia
Panticapaeum
BOSPORAN KINGDOM
Pityus
Caucasus Mts.
Chersonesus
Lake Sevan
Black Sea
Trapezus
ARMENIA 114–117 C.E.
Lake Van
Lake Urmia
Tomis
Tropaeum Traiani
urostorum
Sinope
Amisus
Pompeiopolis
Satala
Amastris
Zela
Megalopolis
Nicopolis 48 B.C.E.
Tigranocerta
Heraclea Pontica
Gangra
BYTHINIA ET PONTUS
CAPPADOCIA
Amida
ASSYRIA 116–117 C.E.
ple
Hadrianopolis (Adrianople)
Byzantium (Constantinople)
Nicomedia
Ancyra
Caesarea
Melitene
Edessa
Carrhae 53 B.C.E.
Samosata
MESOPOTAMIA 115–117 C.E.
CIA
Perinthus
Nicaea
Prusa
Cyzicus
Dorylaeum
Asia Minor
GALATIA
Antiochia
Iconium
Cyrrhus
Tarsus
Antiochia
Dura Europos
Euphrates
Tigris
ASIA
Pergamum
Magnesia 190 B.C.E.
Smyrna
Aphrodisias
LYCIA
CILICIA
Seleucia
Laodicea
SYRIA
Palmyra
Ephesus
Attalia
Raphaneae
Miletus
Emesa
Cnidus
Myra
Salamis
Tripolis
Heliopolis
Rhodus
CYPRUS
Damascus
Paphos
Tyrus
CRETA
Gortyn
Caparcotna
Caesarea
Bostra
Sea
JUDAEA
Dead Sea
Jerusalem
Gaza
Petra
ARABIA
Nicopolis
Pelusium
Alexandria
Memphis
Oxyrhynchus
Hermopolis
Nile
Red Sea
AEGYPTUS
Ptolemais
Coptus
Thebae
RENE

LEADING FIGURES IN THE GOSPELS OF
MATTHEW, MARK, LUKE, AND JOHN

The Roman aqueduct in Caesarea, on the Mediterranean coast of today's Israel, was built by Herod the Great between 22 and 10 B.C.E.

KING HEROD

The Nativity narratives of Luke and Matthew are set in the waning days of Herod the Great, king of the Jewish kingdom often referred to as Roman "Palestine," even though strictly speaking, the region was not called as such until after the suppression of the Second Jewish Revolt in 135 C.E. Ironically, Herod and his family were not Jewish by birth, but Idumean by origin. Idumea, known as "Edom" in the Hebrew Scriptures, was a largely pagan region roughly equivalent to today's Negev desert and southern Jordan. After Hasmonean King John Hyrcanus conquered the territory in 125 B.C.E., its population was told to convert to Judaism, though most families probably continued to worship according to their ancestral rites. This may explain why, as soon as Herod was installed as king of Palestine by force of Roman arms around 37 B.C.E., Herod indulged in the construction of cities and temples dedicated to Roman emperors and

deities. He even built theaters for gladiatorial contests with wild animals, which—as the Jewish historian Josephus tells us—"greatly offended the Jews." Perhaps in an effort to placate his observant Jewish subjects, around 22 B.C.E., Herod embarked on a project to extend the Second Temple in Jerusalem into one of the largest sanctuaries in the Roman world. Because the Temple was built on a hill, he created a vast floating esplanade supported by strong supporting walls. One of these has survived and is revered today as the Western Wall, the holiest place in Judaism. Herod's project was still under construction when Jesus and his disciples visited the Temple on the eve of Passover around 30 C.E.

At the same time, tensions between Herod and the **Sadducees** rose as the Sadducees sought to have full authority over Temple operations, which were previously in the hands of the Hasmoneans. Herod then began to favor émigré priestly families from Babylonia for all his key

HEROD'S TOMB

According to Josephus, Herod was buried in his palatial fortress of Herodion in the Judean Desert. For many years, archaeologists searched in vain to find the king's tomb until a team of Israeli archaeologists led by Ehud Netzer resumed excavations on the hill in May 2007. They first uncovered the remains of an extensive palace, including a large swimming pool, as well as a monumental stairway that led to a mausoleum. This mausoleum consisted of a *tholos,* a circular structure surrounded by 18 columns. Nearby, three sarcophagi were found. One was carved from pink Jerusalem limestone and adorned with numerous floral motifs, which Netzer believed may have contained Herod's body; however, no human remains were found. Netzer returned to the Herodion in 2010 for further excavations, but was injured in a fall and died two days later. ∎

ca 50 B.C.E.	ca 49 B.C.E.	ca 48 B.C.E.	ca 47 B.C.E.
Caesar and Pompey compete for control of Rome	Caesar crosses the Rubicon and takes his legion onto native Roman soil	Caesar defeats Pompey at Pharsalia	Antipater's son Herod is appointed governor of Galilee

appointments—including the high priest—because their loyalty to their benefactor was unquestioned.

Despite the treasures Herod lavished on the Temple, the resentment of his subjects grew. In response, Herod created a police state that suppressed any form of discontent or challenge to his rule. According to Matthew, Herod ordered a massacre of "all the children in and around Bethlehem who were two years old or under," so as to eliminate the child whom magi from the East had called "the child who has been born king of the Jews" and thus a potential rival to his dynasty (MATTHEW 2:2,16). This event is not attested in any other literature of the period, but apparently Matthew's audience had no trouble crediting King Herod with such an abominable decree.

ZECHARIAH

It was "in the days of King Herod of Judea," says the Gospel of Luke, that the angel **Gabriel** had appeared to an elderly man named **Zechariah**, a member of the "priestly order of Abijah" who served God in the Temple (LUKE 1:5). Zechariah was married to **Elizabeth**, who herself was of priestly stock and a descendant of Aaron, but the couple was childless. When Zechariah saw the angel he was terrified, but Gabriel put him at ease, saying, "Do not be afraid, Zechariah, for your prayer has been heard. Your wife Elizabeth will bear you a son, and you will name him John." The angel also foretold that the boy would be "filled with the Holy Spirit," and would minister to the "people of Israel . . . with the spirit and power of Elijah" (LUKE 1:13,16-17). Zechariah could not believe the angel's words, knowing that he and his wife were advanced in age. So Gabriel struck him deaf and mute, until the day that his son would be born. And indeed, when Zechariah emerged from the Temple, he was unable to speak.

The elegant polychrome terra-cotta figure of a woman dates from the first century C.E.

MARY

Not long thereafter, "in the sixth month," the angel Gabriel was sent on another mission, this time to a town called Nazareth in Galilee. Here lived a young girl named **Mary**, who was betrothed to a man by the name of **Joseph**, of the house of David. Gabriel appeared before Mary in her house in Nazareth, and said, "Do not be afraid, Mary, for you have found favor with God." And the angel continued, "You will conceive in your womb and bear a son, and you will name him Jesus. He will be great, and will be called the Son of the Most High" (LUKE 1:30-31). The name

THE WORLD AROUND THE YEAR 1

The life and times of Jesus of Nazareth coincided with major changes in Palestine and, indeed, the known world at the time. The Roman civil war prompted by the assassination of Julius Caesar (ruled 49–44 B.C.E.) ultimately led to the establishment of an Imperial monarchy founded by Augustus (ruled 27 B.C.E.–14 C.E.), in which the power of the Roman Senate slowly faded away. The new position of Roman emperor, equipped with unbridled personal power, figures prominently in the Gospel stories. It is Augustus who presided over the breakup of Herod's kingdom into four regions, to be governed by three of Herod's sons and his sister. One of these, Herod Antipas, was placed in charge of Galilee. Augustus also ordered a global census in the Gospel of Luke, and dismissed Archelaus, the son of Herod who ruled over Judea, from his post. The emperor then turned Judea into a Roman province. The fifth Roman governor or "procurator" of this province, a man named Pilate of the House house of the Pontii, would sit in judgment of Jesus. Herod Antipas, meanwhile, undertook the building of a new city on the ruins of Sepphoris, located some six miles from Nazareth; some scholars believe it is possible that both Joseph and his son Jesus, noted for their skill in woodwork, would have been involved in this construction. Later, Herod Antipas ordered the arrest of John the Baptist, and his subsequent execution. Luke wrote that Herod was also briefly involved in the hearings in Jerusalem to determine Jesus' guilt, but that the tetrarch sent Jesus back to Pilate when Jesus gave him no answer (LUKE 23:9). ■

Discovered in Sepphoris, this colorful mosaic featuring geometric motifs probably dates from a later phase of this Galilean city, possibly around the third century C.E.

ca 47 B.C.E.	ca 46 B.C.E.	ca 46 B.C.E.	ca 46 B.C.E.
Library of Alexandria is destroyed by fire	Herod suppresses a rebellion led by Hezekiah the Galilean	Northern Africa is added to the Roman Empire	Julius Caesar introduces the Julian calendar of 365 days

KINGDOM OF HEROD THE GREAT

MAP KEY

- ···· District or region boundary
- Herod's Kingdom
- Roman province of Syria
- Nabatean Kingdom
- • / ○ City of the Decapolis / location uncertain
- ○ Location uncertain
- ⊙ Herodian fortress

THE GREAT SEA *(MEDITERRANEAN SEA)*

Expanded by Herod the Great and named in honor of his patron, Caesar Augustus, this city was known for its splendid buildings. It would become a Roman administrative center.

Herod the Great built a large acropolis on the ancient location of Samaria and renamed the city Sebaste, the Greek version of "Augustus."

The birthplace of Herod the Great, an Idumean. He built magnificent fountains and baths to beautify the city.

The Decapolis was a commercial league whose member cities enjoyed a measure of autonomy within the Roman province.

As a way of garnering favor with his subjects, Herod instituted a great building program. Jerusalem benefited, receiving a new market, amphitheater, theater, a new building where the Sanhedrin could convene, and a new royal palace. In 20 B.C.E. reconstruction began on the Temple.

Herod the Great constructed an elaborate monument and temple over the traditional tomb of the patriarchs.

Once a treasure-house fortress of the Hasmoneans, it had been torn down by the Romans. Herod the Great rebuilt it as a fortress and prison.

Sidon
Damascus
Mt. Hermon 2,814 m / 9,232 ft
Tyre
Kanah
Raphana
Achzib
Cadasa
Asor
GAULANITIS
Merom UPPER GALILEE
BATANEA
Ptolemais
Capernaum
Bethsaida
Bay of Acco (Bay of Haifa)
Jotapata
Arbela
Sea of Kinnereth (Sea of Galilee)
Sycaminium
Hippos
AURANITIS
Mt. Carmel 546 m / 1,791 ft
Philoteria
Gebae
Nazareth
Abila
Dora
Mt. Tabor 588 m / 1,929 ft
Gadara
Edrei
Legio
Caesarea
Scythopolis
Pella
Narbata
Dion
Gerasa
Sebaste
Mt. Ebal 940 m / 3,084 ft
Amathus
Apollonia
Neapolis
Mt. Gerizim 881 m / 2,890 ft
Antipatris
Lebonah
Alexandrium
Gadara
Joppa
Phasaelis
Philadelphia
Lydda
Bethel
Archelais
Jericho
Gazara
Mizpah
Cyprus
Esbus
Emmaus
Jerusalem
Kidron
Zorah
Mt. Nebo 802 m / 2,631 ft
Azotus
Beth Shemesh
Bethlehem
Medeba
Hyrcania
Ascalon
Herodium
Salt Sea (Dead Sea)
Marisa
Beth-zur
Machaerus
Anthedon
Lachish
Hebron
Gaza
Eshtemoa
En-gedi
Masada
Raphia
Beersheba
Malatha
Kir-Moab

PHOENICIA
LEBANON
ITUREA
SYRIA
Leontes
Hula Valley
Jordan
LOWER GALILEE
Kishon
Yarmuk
DECAPOLIS
PLAIN OF SHARON
SAMARIA
JORDAN
Yarqon
Jabbok
Jordan
JUDEA
PEREA
Sorek
SHEPHELAH
PHILISTIA
IDUMEA
Besor
NEGEV
Arnon
NABATEA
Zered
EGYPT

0   20   40 kilometers
0   20   40 miles

Present-day drainage, coastlines, and country boundaries are represented. Modern names appear in parentheses.

"Jesus," or "Yeshua" in Aramaic, is, like "Joshua" or "Hosea," a contraction of *Yehoshuah,* meaning "YHWH is salvation," and a common name in ancient Judea and Galilee.

Mary said to the angel, "How can this be, since I am a virgin?" Gabriel replied, "the Holy Spirit will come upon you, and the power of the Most High will overshadow you" (LUKE 1:34-35). And to prove his point, the angel added that "your relative Elizabeth in her old age has also conceived a son . . . for nothing will be impossible with God." Mary then set out to visit her cousin Elizabeth; when Elizabeth saw Mary and heard her voice, she thought: "the babe in my womb leaped for joy" (LUKE 1:42-44).

JOSEPH

But what of Mary's fiancé, the man called Joseph? Matthew's Gospel gives us Joseph's side of the Nativity story. Where Joseph lived is not entirely clear; Matthew implies that he lived in Bethlehem, whereas John states that he hailed from Nazareth. When Joseph learned that Mary was pregnant, even though they hadn't been wed, he "planned to dismiss her quietly" because he was "unwilling to expose her to public disgrace." But before he could cancel the wedding, "an angel of the Lord" appeared to him in a dream and said, "Joseph, son of David, do not be afraid to take Mary as your wife, for the child conceived in her is from the Holy Spirit" (MATTHEW 1:21).

Artist Rogier van der Weyden (ca 1400–1464) sets this visualization of the Annunciation in the richly appointed home of a Flemish burgher.

GALILEE

Throughout much of the history of ancient Israel, Galilee was very different from Judea. With an annual rainfall of up to 44 inches a year, the mountains in the north gave the region plenty of water—which explains Galilee's fecundity. It was also blessed with a large freshwater lake, the Sea of Galilee, shaped in the form of a harp, *kinor* in Hebrew; in Hebrew Scripture, it is called Lake Kinneret (NUMBERS 34:11). Timber was sparse except for olive trees, a native species, often found in family-tended orchards. Olive trees are tenacious and can grow for hundreds of years, but their wood is gnarly and ill suited for fine carpentry.

Located far to the north, Galilee had always been surrounded by foreign, i.e., *pagan,* territory: Phoenicia to the northwest, Syria to the north, and Nabatea to the east. The idea of an enclave

The rolling fields of the Beit Netofa Valley, near Nazareth, appear to be as lush as they were in the days of Jesus.

surrounded by foreigners may be the root of the word "Galilee" *(ha-galil),* a shortening of the Hebrew *galil ha-goyim,* meaning "circle of the peoples." Matthew, citing Isaiah, calls the region "Galilee of the Gentiles" (MATTHEW 4:15; ISAIAH 9:1-2).

According to Josephus, almost everyone in Galilee was involved in agriculture, given the exceptional fertility of the Beit Netofa and Nahal Sippori valleys. Josephus lists 204 towns and villages in Galilee, based on which archaeologists have extrapolated that the total population must have ranged between 150,000 and 250,000 people. Nazareth is not included in this list, which suggests it was a small hamlet that—like all other satellite villages in the area—depended on the markets of Sepphoris, the capital of the province, to sell its produce. ∎

ca 45 B.C.E.	ca 44 B.C.E.	ca 44 B.C.E.	ca 44 B.C.E.
Roman Tower of the Winds, a water and solar clock, is built in Athens	**Julius Caesar is assassinated by conspirators Brutus and Cassius**	**Herod imposes massive taxes on Galileans to raise funds for Cassius**	**Mount Etna on Sicily erupts**

In those days a decree went out from Emperor Augustus that all the world should be registered.

GOSPEL OF LUKE 2:1

As Mary's pregnancy advanced, says Luke, a decree went out from Emperor Augustus that all the world should be registered (LUKE 2:1). The purpose of such a census was not to gauge the demographic makeup of a province, but to establish a detailed inventory of individuals and their property. Only in this manner could Rome determine a reasonable assessment of what a given region was worth, and what it could be expected to yield in taxes. This was important, because Roman governors outsourced tax collection to free agents; without a census, they had no way of establishing whether or not these tax collectors were cheating.

Because Joseph's family had come from Bethlehem in Luke's depiction of the events, Joseph had no choice but to take his pregnant wife and set out on the long journey to Bethlehem. When they arrived there, they found that all the inns were full. The only shelter available was that of a stable, and there, Mary gave birth to **Jesus**. She "wrapped him in bands of cloth, and laid him in

The "Adoration of the Magi" was painted by Italian artist Sandro Botticelli (ca 1445–1510) around 1478.

ca 43 B.C.E.	ca 43 B.C.E.	ca 43 B.C.E.	ca 42 B.C.E.
First compilation of the Ayurveda, a Hindu medical treatise	Octavian, Antony, and Lepidus form a triumvirate in Rome	Roman poet Ovid is born	Caesar's assassins Brutus and Cassius are defeated at the Battle of Philippi

a manger" (LUKE 2:6-7). Soon a group of shepherds arrived, who had been sleeping in the nearby fields until summoned by an angel to go see "the Messiah, the Lord" (LUKE 1:11).

MAGI FROM THE EAST

The shepherds were not the only ones who came to pay homage to the newborn child. According to Matthew, the birth summoned the arrival of three **magi**, or "wise men from the East." At many courts in the East, including ancient Babylon and Persia, learned astrologers often served as priestly advisers, practiced in the art of magic. In the later Christian tradition, the three magi have also been interpreted as kings. Back in Jerusalem, however, King Herod's suspicions were aroused by the news that a new "king" had been born. He summoned the magi and asked them to let him know where this child was so that "I may also go and pay him homage." A bright star then led the magi until it stopped "over the place where the child was," and "upon entering the house, they saw the child with Mary his mother" (MATTHEW 2:11). They knelt down before the child in the manger and "offered him gifts of gold, frankincense, and myrrh." But before they could set out on their return journey, the magi were warned in a dream not to return to Herod, and so they left by another road (MATTHEW 2:12).

Herod was furious when he found out that the magi had departed without telling him the location of the newborn child. To ensure that the child would not survive, he ordered that all the children in and around Bethlehem under two years of age be killed forthwith—an event known as the "Massacre of the Innocents," which only appears in Matthew's Gospel. Fortunately, an angel appeared to Joseph in a dream and said, "Get up, take the child and his mother, and flee to Egypt." Joseph did as the angel told him, and took his new family to Egypt, where he remained until an angel appeared once again to tell him it was safe to return.

However, says Matthew, when Joseph heard that Herod's son **Archelaus** was ruling

The three magi appear in a sixth-century C.E. mosaic of the Sant'Apollinare Nuovo in Ravenna, Italy.

over Judea, he was afraid to go there—no doubt in the belief that Archelaus would be as ruthless a tyrant as his father. Instead, Joseph and his young family traveled north and settled in Galilee. At this point, the Gospels of Matthew and Luke once again converge, for it is in Nazareth that Jesus would spend the years of his childhood.

For seven days after the birth of her male child, Mary was considered ritually impure (LEVITICUS 12:2). This enabled her to slowly recover from the strain of birth, while the women in her village helped her cope with the joys and chores of motherhood. On the eighth day, the baby Jesus underwent *berit,* or ritual circumcision (GENESIS 17:10-12). "After eight days had passed," Luke says, "it was time to circumcise the child" (LUKE 2:21). Joseph formally named his child, thus acknowledging him as his offspring.

SIMEON

For 33 days after giving birth, Mary was not allowed to touch anything holy. Then, to restore her state of purity, Mary and

THE EDUCATION OF JESUS

Luke's story of the 12-year-old Jesus debating scholars in the Temple has raised a question: Where would a child from a rural family have received such an education? Paul was educated by Gamaliel, one of the leading Pharisaic sages of his day, but such tutelage was beyond the means of Jesus' parents, who were poor. The Palestinian and Babylonian Talmuds state that the Pharisee Simeon ben Shetah (103–176 B.C.E.) ordered every town to have a *Bet ha-Sefer,* or "House of the Book," where young boys could be taught in the Law. This, however, was more of a pious ideal than actual practice. Only later, after the destruction of the Temple in 70 C.E., did itinerant teachers, or rabbis, begin to visit villages to teach Scripture. Nevertheless, Jesus' own knowledge of Jewish oral tradition must have been considerable because he is often referred to as rabbi, or teacher, in the Gospels. ■

ca 42 B.C.E.	ca 40 B.C.E.	ca 40 B.C.E.	ca 40 B.C.E.
The Roman Empire is divided between Octavian, Mark Antony, and Lepidus	Parthians invade Palestine in support of Antigonus, a pretender to the throne	Herod flees to Rome and persuades the Senate to declare him king of all Palestine	Mark Antony donates 200,000 scrolls from Pergamon to the Library of Alexandria

CHAPTER 4: THE FOUR GOSPELS **241**

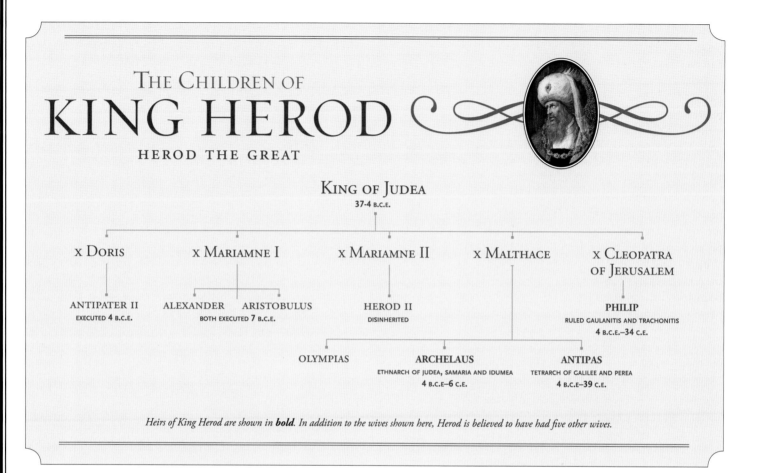

THE CHILDREN OF
KING HEROD
HEROD THE GREAT

KING OF JUDEA
37-4 B.C.E.

x DORIS	x MARIAMNE I	x MARIAMNE II	x MALTHACE	x CLEOPATRA OF JERUSALEM

ANTIPATER II
EXECUTED 4 B.C.E.

ALEXANDER   ARISTOBULUS
BOTH EXECUTED 7 B.C.E.

HEROD II
DISINHERITED

PHILIP
RULED GAULANITIS AND TRACHONITIS
4 B.C.E.–34 C.E.

OLYMPIAS

ARCHELAUS
ETHNARCH OF JUDEA, SAMARIA AND IDUMEA
4 B.C.E–6 C.E.

ANTIPAS
TETRARCH OF GALILEE AND PEREA
4 B.C.E–39 C.E.

Heirs of King Herod are shown in **bold**. *In addition to the wives shown here, Herod is believed to have had five other wives.*

Joseph went to Jerusalem to present an offering of purification in the Temple, as prescribed by the Book of Leviticus. In a roundabout way, Luke confirms that Mary and Joseph were poor because they offered "a pair of turtledoves or two young pigeons" instead of a lamb, the lesser sacrifice allowed for couples of limited means (LUKE 2:22-24; LEVITICUS 12:6-8). In the Temple was a devout Jew, who had been told that he would not die without seeing "the Lord's Messiah." His name was **Simeon**. When he saw Mary and her baby, he took the child in his arms, saying, "Master, now you are dismissing your servant in peace, according to your word; for my eyes have seen your salvation, which you have prepared in the presence of all peoples, a light for revelation to the Gentiles and for glory to your people Israel" (LUKE 2:29-32).

JESUS

And then, says Luke, "the child grew and became strong, filled with wisdom; and the favor of God was upon him" (LUKE 2:40). Before long, the young boy would have helped his father Joseph with his daily work, because male children in Galilee were expected to follow in the trade of their fathers. Mark tells us that, years later, when Jesus returned to his native Nazareth after the launch of his ministry, the people of his hometown were astonished by his words. "Is this not the carpenter, the son of Mary and brother of James?" they asked (MARK 6:3). Mark uses the word *tektōn,* which although traditionally translated as "carpenter" actually means a "worker" or "journeyman" in stone, wood, or metal. Workable wood fit for carpentry was rare and expensive in Lower Galilee, and probably beyond the reach of most peasants. What Galilee did have, in abundance, was fertile land, thanks to its deep water tables, which captured and held rainfall, augmented by wells. According to first-century Jewish historian Josephus, almost everyone in Galilee sustained himself with agriculture. Indeed, many of Jesus' future parables would use the language of the fields and orchards, rather than that of a carpentry shop. This has prompted some scholars to suggest that Joseph was a farmer, who perhaps augmented his income with his

ca 39–37 B.C.E.	ca 38 B.C.E.	ca 37 B.C.E.	ca 36 B.C.E.
Herod lands in Palestine and battles Antigonus for control of Judea	Mark Antony returns to Egypt	Herod conquers Jerusalem; Antigonus is executed	Herod appoints his brother-in-law Aristobulus III as high priest

woodworking skills. As such, Jesus would have witnessed the rites of cultivation—sowing, reaping, and harvesting—early on.

Around 6 C.E., the Tetrarch of Galilee, **Herod Antipas**, decided to rebuild the provincial capital of Sepphoris, which had been thoroughly destroyed ten years earlier, during a revolt in the aftermath of King Herod's death. Because Sepphoris was located less than six miles from Nazareth, it has been suggested that Joseph and Jesus were employed in building this new city. Construction labor in Galilee was scarce, given that neither the Hasmoneans nor King Herod had ever bothered to build anything of note in the province. It was not unusual for rulers of the Roman era to simply conscript labor from among surrounding villages and hamlets. What's more, it might explain why Mark calls Jesus a *tektōn*. On the other hand, Sepphoris is not mentioned in the Gospels, perhaps because it was a garrison town, and we don't know whether Jesus, like his father, had any special construction skills.

A Roman plate from late antiquity shows a fisherman cleaning his freshly caught fish.

Luke says that when Jesus was 12 years old—around 8 C.E., if we assume that Jesus was born in the last year of King Herod's reign—his parents took him to Jerusalem once more. The occasion for this journey was the Passover festival. They stayed in Jerusalem, visited the Temple, and eventually got ready to return home. Because they were traveling among other pilgrims from Galilee, including friends and relatives, Joseph and Mary were not surprised when they did not see Jesus walking nearby. But when they had gone a day's journey without seeing him, they became worried. They searched high and low for their son, and decided to rush back to Jerusalem. After three days, they found their 12-year-old sitting in the Temple, engrossed in debate with scholars and teachers of the Law.

Apparently, the learned men were amazed with Jesus' knowledge and understanding of the Torah. Relieved and upset in equal measure, Mary told him, "Why have you treated us like this? Look, your father and I have been searching for you in great anxiety."

"Christ in the House of His Parents" was painted by English Pre-Raphaelite artist John Everett Millais (1829–1896) in 1849. His mother, Mary, kneels at Jesus' side.

ca 35 B.C.E.	ca 34 B.C.E.	ca 32 B.C.E.	ca 32 B.C.E.
Aristobulus III is drowned on orders of Herod	Dalmatia is added to the Roman Empire	Herod launches war against Nabatea	Octavian and the Roman Senate declare war on Cleopatra and Mark Antony

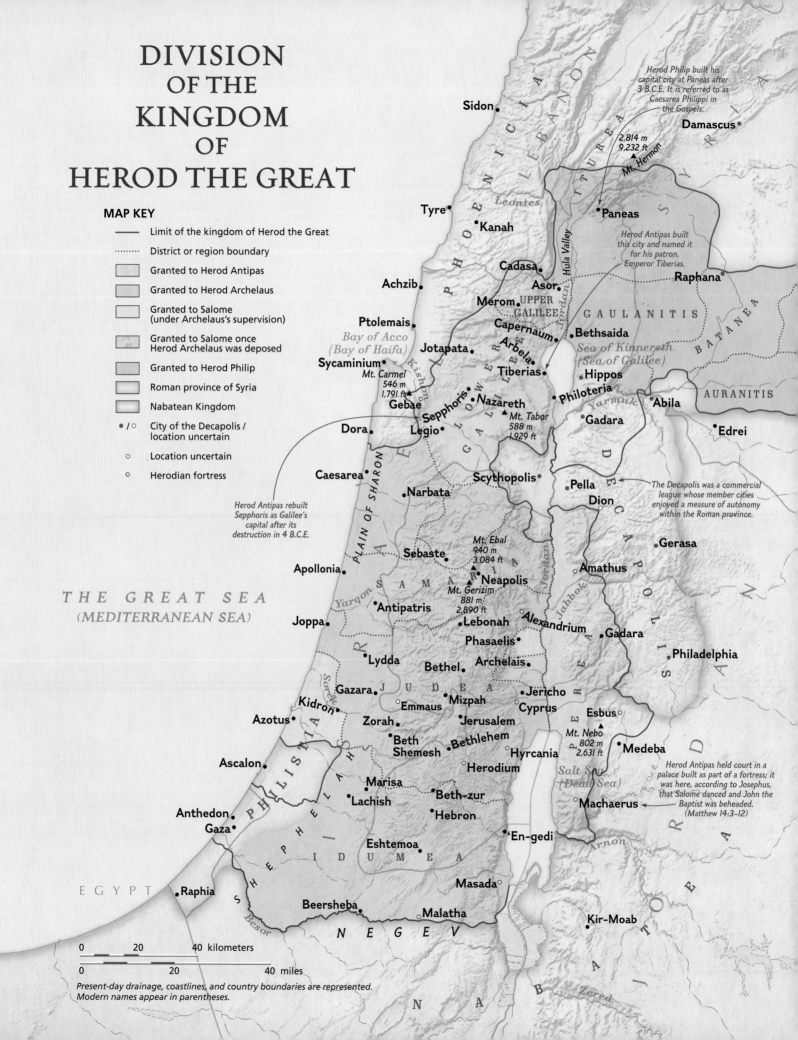

DIVISION OF THE KINGDOM OF HEROD THE GREAT

MAP KEY

—— Limit of the kingdom of Herod the Great

········ District or region boundary

Granted to Herod Antipas

Granted to Herod Archelaus

Granted to Salome (under Archelaus's supervision)

Granted to Salome once Herod Archelaus was deposed

Granted to Herod Philip

Roman province of Syria

Nabatean Kingdom

● / ○ City of the Decapolis / location uncertain

○ Location uncertain

◉ Herodian fortress

Herod Philip built his capital city at Paneas after 3 B.C.E. It is referred to as Caesarea Philippi in the Gospels.

Herod Antipas built this city and named it for his patron, Emperor Tiberias.

Herod Antipas rebuilt Sepphoris as Galilee's capital after its destruction in 4 B.C.E.

The Decapolis was a commercial league whose member cities enjoyed a measure of autonomy within the Roman province.

Herod Antipas held court in a palace built as part of a fortress; it was here, according to Josephus, that Salome danced and John the Baptist was beheaded. (Matthew 14:3-12)

THE GREAT SEA
(MEDITERRANEAN SEA)

Present-day drainage, coastlines, and country boundaries are represented. Modern names appear in parentheses.

Labels on map

Sidon
Damascus
Tyre
Kanah
Mt. Hermon 2,814 m 9,232 ft
Paneas
Raphana
Cadasa
Achzib
Asor
Merom
UPPER GALILEE
GAULANITIS
BATANEA
Ptolemais
Capernaum
Bethsaida
Bay of Acco (Bay of Haifa)
Jotapata
Arbela
Sea of Kinnereth (Sea of Galilee)
Sycaminium
Tiberias
Hippos
Mt. Carmel 546 m 1,791 ft
Nazareth
Philoteria
AURANITIS
Gebae
Sepphoris
Gadara
Abila
Dora
Legio
Mt. Tabor 588 m 1,929 ft
Edrei
PLAIN OF SHARON
Caesarea
Scythopolis
Pella
Narbata
Dion
Apollonia
Sebaste
Mt. Ebal 940 m 3,084 ft
Amathus
Gerasa
Neapolis
Mt. Gerizim 881 m 2,890 ft
DECAPOLIS
Joppa
Antipatris
Lebonah
Alexandrium
Gadara
Lydda
Phasaelis
Philadelphia
Gazara
Bethel
Archelais
Jericho
Cyprus
Esbus
Emmaus
Mizpah
Kidron
Zorah
Jerusalem
Medeba
Azotus
Beth Shemesh
Bethlehem
Hyrcania
Mt. Nebo 802 m 2,631 ft
Ascalon
Herodium
Salt Sea (Dead Sea)
Marisa
Beth-zur
Machaerus
Anthedon
Lachish
Hebron
Gaza
Eshtemoa
En-gedi
IDUMEA
Raphia
Masada
Kir-Moab
Beersheba
Malatha
NEGEV
EGYPT
PHILISTIA
SHEPHELAH
JUDEA
SAMARIA
PEREA
NABATEA
Leontes
Hula Valley
Jordan
Yarmuk
Jabbok
Yarkon
Sorek
Besor
Arnon
Zered
PHOENICIA
LEBANON
ITUREA
SYRIA

Scale

0   20   40 kilometers
0   20   40 miles

Jesus looked up and replied, "Why were you searching for me? Did you not know that I must be in my Father's house?" (LUKE 2:48-49).

JOHN THE BAPTIST

The Gospels do not provide us any additional information about Jesus' childhood and adolescence. Luke and Matthew pick up the story when Jesus decides to go down to the Jordan to join the movement of **John the Baptist**, while the Gospels of Mark and John simply begin their story with this signal encounter between Jesus and John.

The fact that all four Gospels devote considerable time to Jesus' time with John the Baptist is significant. According to Josephus, John the Baptist was a major dissident of his time who railed against the corruption of Jewish society and urged repentance. John "was a good man," Josephus says, "who exhorted the Jews to exercise virtue, both in terms of righteousness toward one another and piety toward God, and so come to baptism." Apparently, John's message was successful, for Josephus claims that "crowds flocked to him, and they were greatly moved by his words." Mark agrees with that assessment; "people from the whole Judean countryside and all the people of Jerusalem were going out to him," Mark says, and were "baptized by him in the river Jordan, confessing their sins" (MARK 1:5).

With his eye for historical accuracy, Luke dates the beginning of John's activity "in the fifteenth year of the reign of **Emperor Tiberius**, when **Pontius Pilate** was governor of Judea, and Herod was ruler of Galilee" (LUKE 3:1). Luke here refers to Herod Antipas, the son of Herod the Great, who was appointed Tetrarch of Galilee and Perea in 4 B.C.E. Tiberius succeeded Augustus in 14 C.E., and Pontius Pilate assumed his office as Roman prefect in Judea in 26 C.E.; by modern reckoning, Luke is probably talking about the year 29 C.E.

John was quite a sight to behold. "John wore clothing of camel's hair with a leather belt around his waist, and his food was locusts and wild honey," Matthew says, evoking the image of a modern Elijah, whom the Book of Kings described as "a hairy man, with a leather belt around his waist" (MATTHEW 3:4; II KINGS 1:8). The allusion reminded Matthew's audience of God's promise that "I will send you the prophet Elijah

before the great and terrible day of the Lord comes" (MALACHI 4:5). And now, that day had come.

Jesus asked to be baptized by John and to be cleansed of his sins, in imitation of John's other followers. John protested, "I need to be baptized by you, and do you come to me?" (MATTHEW 3:14). But Jesus insisted, and thus John took him to the clean, flowing waters of the Jordan and baptized him. As Jesus emerged from the water, says Mark, "he saw the heavens torn apart and the Spirit descending like a dove on him. And a voice came from heaven, 'You are my Son, the beloved; with you I am well pleased'" (MARK 1:10-11).

The "Baptism of Christ" by Renaissance artist Andrea del Verrocchio (1436–1488) features an angel at far left painted by the young Leonardo da Vinci (1452–1519).

This verse—which combines the Psalms ("You are my Son," from Psalms 2:7) with Isaiah ("My chosen, in whom my soul delights," from Isaiah 42:1)—is repeated almost verbatim in all the other Gospels (MATTHEW 3:17, LUKE 3:22, and JOHN 1:32-33).

We don't know how long Jesus stayed with John, but sometime after 29 C.E., Herod Antipas must have decided that he could no longer tolerate John's activity as a prominent dissident preacher. Mark, whose example is followed by other evangelists, states that the reason for John's arrest was the Baptist's vehement criticism of Antipas's second marriage to a woman named "Herodias, his brother Philip's wife." It is not clear whether Mark is referring to his half brother Philip, Tetrarch of the Gaulanitis, or his nephew Herod Philip I, son of King Herod and Mariamne. To complicate matters further, Herodias herself was Antipas's niece, because she was the daughter of another of King Herod's sons, Aristobulus. Either way, the family

THE TOMB OF JOHN THE BAPTIST

Mark says that after John the Baptist was killed on orders of Herod Antipas, "his disciples . . . took his body and laid it in a tomb" (MARK 6:29). This tomb has never been found, although in 2005, archaeologist Shimon Gibson claimed that he had discovered a cave near Ain Karim, which he associated with John's baptism. It is true that John's movement survived the Baptist's arrest and continued well into the second century, penetrating as far as Asia Minor (ACTS 19:1-4). As a postscript, Josephus tells us that around 35 C.E., King Aretas invaded Perea, the territory ruled by Herod Antipas, to seek revenge for the tetrarch's divorce from his daughter. Antipas's army was destroyed. Josephus adds that when word of the defeat spread in Palestine, many people were pleased, for they "thought that the destruction of Herod's army came from God, as just punishment for what he had done to John [the Baptist]." ∎

relationship was uncomfortably close, and John did not hesitate to tell the tetrarch that "it is not lawful for you to have your brother's wife," citing the prohibition against such a marriage in Leviticus 18:16 (MARK 6:18).

The historian Josephus, on the other hand, claims that John was arrested because his movement was growing at an alarming rate. "By putting [John the Baptist] to death," Josephus wrote, "[Antipas] would prevent any mischief he might cause." Mark provides further detail on the Baptist's form of execution. His Gospel relates how Herodias's daughter delighted her stepfather on his birthday with her seductive dancing. Antipas was so entranced that he offered her "whatever she wished," even "half of my kingdom." The daughter—whose name, according to Josephus, was Salome—ran to her mother, who told her to ask "for the head of John the Baptist on a platter." Antipas had no choice but to accede to her wish (MARK 6:17-28).

THE KINGDOM OF GOD

Much of Jesus' teachings advanced the notion of a Kingdom of God. Several Jewish factions had talked about such a kingdom in preceding decades. For some, it expressed the idea of a nation governed by Jewish Law and ruled by a true Davidic king, rather than a Herodian tyrant or a Roman despot. But to Jesus, the Kingdom of God—or Kingdom of Heaven, a term that piously avoids using the name of "God"—would mean something different: not a political entity, but a new compact for the social and spiritual renewal of Jewish society. It is possible that Jesus saw his vision of God's kingdom as a return to the quintessential virtues of the Law: compassion toward one another, solidarity within one's community, and

Italian Renaissance artist Raphael (1483–1520) painted "Christ's Charge to St. Peter" around 1516 as a cartoon, a preparatory drawing, for the Vatican's Sistine Chapel.

unconditional love and faith in God. "Do not think that I have come to abolish the Law or the Prophets," Jesus says emphatically; "I have come not to abolish, but to fulfill" (MATTHEW 5:17).

For Jesus, the Kingdom of God was not something that could be imposed from above by force of arms. "The kingdom of God is not coming with things that can be observed," Jesus says in the Gospel of Luke; "for in fact, the kingdom of God is *among you*" (LUKE 17:20-21). Healing the sick was an important aspect of Jesus' vision, for it illustrated the power of faith, love, and compassion that would bring about this kingdom. The miracles were living proof that the Kingdom of God, and God's personal intervention, was at hand. ∎

ca 30 B.C.E.	ca 29 B.C.E.	ca 28 B.C.E.	ca 28 B.C.E.
Egypt is annexed as a Roman province, ending its 3,000-year independence	Herod places his beloved wife, Mariamne I, on trial	Herod's theater in Jerusalem is inaugurated	Chinese imperial astronomers create first record of sunspots

PHILIP

John's arrest left his movement in disarray. According to the Gospel of John, this is when three of the Baptist's disciples—**Philip**, **Andrew**, and Andrew's brother **Simon**—gravitated to Jesus as their new teacher. Significantly, all three were from the north, from a town called Bethsaida. Bethsaida lay east of the Jordan River in the Gaulanitis, just across the border from Galilee; as such, it was governed by **Herod Philip**, and not by Herod Antipas. The town may thus have given the group a temporary refuge until it became clear that Antipas was not planning to arrest the disciples of the Baptist as well.

Philip would become a prominent disciple in the Gospel of John. On the way to Galilee, he met a man named **Nathanael** and told him that "we have found him about whom Moses in the law and also the prophets wrote, Jesus son of Joseph from Nazareth." Nathanael scoffed, "Can anything good come out of Nazareth?" (JOHN 1:43,45-46). Nevertheless, after he met Jesus, Nathanael became a disciple as well; some scholars believe that Nathanael is synonymous with the **Apostle Bartholomew** in the Synoptic Gospels.

In John's Gospel, Philip was put in charge of the provisioning of Jesus' traveling group. One day, when a large group had gathered to

Jacopo Bassano (ca 1510–1592) painted "The Miraculous Draught of Fishes" around 1545. The disciple Philip is shown next to Jesus.

hear the rabbi speak, Jesus turned to Philip and asked casually, "Where are we to buy bread for these people to eat?" Shocked, Philip looked at Jesus and said, "Six months' wages would not buy enough bread for each of them to get a little!" Naturally, Jesus said this "to test him," for shortly thereafter he multiplied a basket of loaves and fish and fed 5,000 people (JOHN 6:5-11).

The other Gospels, however, present a different narrative about the aftermath of John's arrest. In their story, Jesus prepared for his ministry by moving into the desert for 40 days—perhaps an allusion to the 40 years of preparation that the Israelites spent in the desert before moving into the Promised Land. While in the desert, Jesus was tempted by **Satan**, but resisted him.

SIMON PETER

Jesus and his small group of followers now moved to Capernaum, where Jesus chose his Apostles from among the local fishermen according to the Synoptic Gospels. Two of these were "**James [the] son of Zebedee** and his brother **John**, in the boat with their father **Zebedee**" (MATTHEW 4:21). The Greek word *apostolos* is derived from

1 Capernaum The synagogue of ancient Capernaum, built of blocks of white limestone, has been dated to the early fourth century c.e., although some scholars believe it was built on top of an older synagogue structure.

2 Bethsaida These remains of dwellings, built of basalt stone, in the ancient city of Bethsaida were excavated from 1987 onward by a group of universities from the United States, Germany, and Poland.

3 Tabgha Some scholars believe that this gently sloping hill on the shores of the Sea of Galilee near Tabgha served as the location of Jesus' Sermon on the Mount.

4 Magdala Reeds and shrub cover the western shore of the Sea of Galilee near the remains of the ancient town of Magdala, with the modern town of Migdal in the distance.

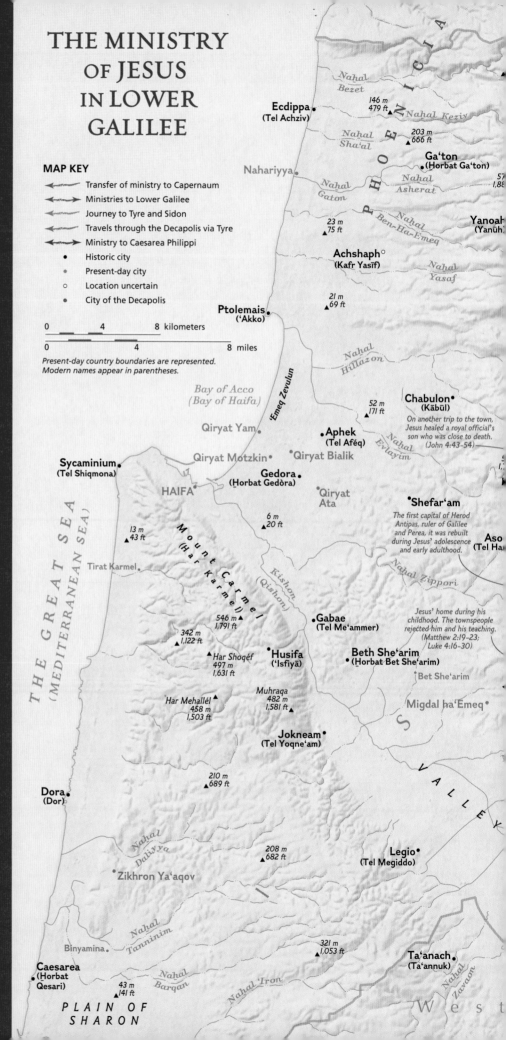

THE MINISTRY OF JESUS IN LOWER GALILEE

MAP KEY

⟵ Transfer of ministry to Capernaum
⟵ Ministries to Lower Galilee
⟵ Journey to Tyre and Sidon
⟵ Travels through the Decapolis via Tyre
⟵ Ministry to Caesarea Philippi

● Historic city
● Present-day city
○ Location uncertain
● City of the Decapolis

0   4   8 kilometers
0   4   8 miles

Present-day country boundaries are represented.
Modern names appear in parentheses.

Ecdippa
(Tel Achziv)
146 m
479 ft

203 m
666 ft

Nahariyya

Ga'ton
(Horbat Ga'ton)

Yanoah
(Yanūh)

Achshaph ○
(Kafr Yasīf)

23 m
75 ft

21 m
69 ft

Ptolemais
('Akko)

Bay of Acco
(Bay of Haifa)

Chabulon
(Kābūl)
On another trip to the town, Jesus healed a royal official's son who was close to death. (John 4:43–54)

52 m
171 ft

Qiryat Yam

Aphek
(Tel Aféq)

Qiryat Motzkin

Qiryat Bialik

Sycaminium
(Tel Shiqmona)

Gedora
(Horbat Gedòra)

Qiryat Ata

HAIFA

Shefar'am
The first capital of Herod Antipas, ruler of Galilee and Perea, it was rebuilt during Jesus' adolescence and early adulthood.

Aso
(Tel Ha

13 m
43 ft

6 m
20 ft

Tirat Karmel

546 m
1,791 ft

Gabae
(Tel Me'ammer)

Jesus' home during his childhood. The townspeople rejected him and his teaching. (Matthew 2:19–23; Luke 4:16–30)

342 m
1,122 ft

Har Shoqéf
497 m
1,631 ft

Husifa
('Isfiyā)

Beth She'arim
(Horbat Bet She'arim)

Bet She'arim

Har Mehallél
458 m
1,503 ft

Muhraqa
482 m
1,581 ft

Migdal ha'Emeq

Jokneam
(Tel Yoqne'am)

210 m
689 ft

Dora
(Dor)

208 m
682 ft

Legio
(Tel Megiddo)

Zikhron Ya'aqov

321 m
1,053 ft

Ta'anach
(Ta'annuk)

Binyamina

Caesarea
(Horbat Qesari)

43 m
141 ft

PLAIN OF SHARON

Cadasa
(Tel Qedesh)

To Caesarea Philippi
and returning
to Capernaum
To Tyre
and Sidon

Lake
Hula

From
Tyre and Caesarea Philippi

▲ Har Avital
1,204 m
3,950 ft

540 m
1,772 ft

82 m
269 ft

160 m
525 ft

504 m
1,654 ft

▲ Har Yosifon
981 m
3,219 ft

Har Addir
1,006 m
3,301 ft

Nahal Keziv

Gischala
(Jīsh)

885 m
2,904 ft

Har Ben Zimra

Asor
(Tel Hazor)

Nahal Dishon

Nahal Hazor

372 m
1,221 ft

G A U L A N I T I S

Har Merom
1,208 m
3,963 ft

Merom

Was taught his "good news of
the kingdom" and healed
...des, large crowds from the
...nding regions followed him
...from place to place.
(Matthew 4:23–25)

After his resurrection, Jesus met the
disciples in Galilee and commissioned
them to "go make disciples of all nations."
(Matthew 28:16–20)

CAPERNAUM
Called "his own town," Capernaum
was where Jesus based his
ministries, and many of his miracles
were performed there. A frontier
town between the lands of Antipas
and Philip, the city was astride an
important trade route that would
have helped spread his message
throughout the region.
(Matthew 9:1)

Har Ha'ari
1,047 m
3,435 ft

Har Hillel
1,071 m
3,514 ft

Bersabe
(Horbat Be'er Sheva')

One possible location where the
feeding of the multitude
could have taken place.
(Matthew 14:13–21; 15:32–39)
Jesus healed many when he
and the disciples visited.
(Mark 6:53–56)

•Zefat

Jesus denounced the cities most
of his miracles had been
performed in because of their
lack of repentance. He also
included Bethsaida and
Capernaum in his judgment.
(Matthew 11:20–24)

435 m
1,427 ft

A likely location where the
feeding of the multitude and the
multiplication of the loaves and
fishes took place.
(Matthew 14:13–21; 15:32–39)

Nahal Meshushim

Hanania
(Zomet
Hananya)

Har Kena'an
486 m
1,595 ft

Chorazin
(Korazim)

Nahal Daliyyot

Gamala
(Gamla)

Har Kammon
598 m
1,962 ft

Har Hazon
584 m
1,916 ft

Tradition places the Sermon
on the Mount here.

Bethsaida
(Zomet Bet Zayda)
❷

Bethsaida was the
hometown of disciples
Peter, Andrew, and Philip.
(John 1:44)

Jesus healed a blind man
by spitting on his eyes and
laying his hands on him.
(Mark 8:22–26)

Mary Magdalene was from here.
She was one of several women
who had been healed or cleansed,
and who provided support for
Jesus and the disciples.
(Luke 8:2–3)

Capernaum
(Kefar Nahum)
❶

Nahal Kanaf

Jesus performed his first
miracle here, turning water
into wine at a wedding.
(John 2:1–11)

Heptapegon / Tabgha
('En Sheva')
❸

After sending the disciples
on ahead by boat, Jesus
walked on the water out to
them during the night.
(Matthew 14:22–33)

...pata
...fat)

Har Netofa
526 m
1,726 ft

Nahal Zalmon

Gennesaret
(Ginnosar)

Cana
(Horbat Qana)

Magdala / Taricheae
(Migdal)
❹

Sea of
Kinnereth,
Lake Tiberias
(Sea of Galilee)

Gergesa
(Kursi)

Nahal Samakh

151 m
495 ft

Horns of Hattin
(Qarne Hittim)
326 m
1,070 ft

•**Arbela**
(Horbat Arbel)

A possible site where Jesus cast
out demons that entered swine,
which then rushed down the slope
to drown in the water. Another
possible place is near the city
of Gadara south of the Yarmuk River.
(Luke 8:26–39)

Haré Tir'an ▲ 548 m
1,798 ft

261 m
856 ft

Aphek
(Afiq)

Nahal Yiftahel

Tiberias
(Teverya)

Bethmaus
(Horbat Bet Ma'on)

Hippos
(Horbat Susita)

S Y R I A

...horis
...ori)

•**Garis**
(Kefr Kanna)

Taking his ministry to the
towns of the region, Jesus
cleansed a leper, and his fame
spread throughout Galilee.
(Mark 1:38–45)

Hammath
(Hammat)

Nahal Raqqad

Yarmuk

-hepher
Mash-had)

Har Yona

532 m
1,745 ft

The second capital of Herod Antipas,
whom Jesus called "that fox." He ruled
Galilee and Perea in Jesus' time.
(Luke 13:32)

144 m
472 ft

Shaken by a sudden storm,
the disciples despaired until
Jesus awoke and "rebuked
the wind and the waves,"
quieting the maelstrom.
(Matthew 8:23–27)

368 m
1,207 ft

Nazerat 'Illit

A possible site of the
Transfiguration. Jesus also healed
an epileptic boy in the area.
(Matthew 17:1–13; 17:14–22)

Sennabris

Philoteria
(Tel Bet Yerah)

•**Nazareth** (Nazerat)

Exaloth
(Iksāl)

Mt. Tabor
588 m
1,929 ft

Big'at Yavne'el

Har Yavene'el

Emmatha
(Hammat Gader)

368 m
1,207 ft

565 m
1,854 ft

497 m
302 ft

Big'at Kesullot

•**Endor**
('En Dor)

Jesus brought the dead son
of a widow back to life before
the whole funeral procession.
(Luke 7:11–17)

368 m
1,207 ft

Gadara
(Umm Qays)

335 m
1,099 ft

D E C A P O L I S

Jordan

fula 'Illit

•**Nain**
(Nein)

Giv'at Hamore
515 m
1,690 ft

Nahal Tavor

Wādī 'Arab

...fula

Shunem
(Sūlam)

147 m
482 ft

Ramot Yissakhar

Kamon
(Qam)

...G

J E Z R E E L

Jesus healed a deaf and
mute man in the Decapolis.
(Mark 7:31–37)

377 m
1,237 ft

The Decapolis was a commercial
league whose member cities
enjoyed a measure of autonomy.

eel, Esdradela
(Yizre'el)

Haré Gilboa

Nahal Harod

Wādī Taiyiba

•**Ephron**
(At Tayyibah)

497 m
1,631 ft

Scythopolis
(Bet She'an)

Jordan

...ank

As Jesus passed along the Sea of Galilee, he saw Simon and his brother Andrew casting a net into the sea . . . And Jesus said to them, "Follow me and I will make you fish for men."

GOSPEL OF MARK 1:16-17

the Aramaic *shaliach,* which means "delegate." In addition to the aforementioned disciples, Jesus also chose "Bartholomew, and **Matthew**, and **Thomas**, and **James son of Alphaeus**, and **Thaddaeus**, and **Simon the Cananaean**, and **Judas Iscariot**, who betrayed him" (MARK 3:18-19).

Matthew wrote that Simon's mother-in-law had a house in Capernaum, where she lay sick in bed with a fever. Jesus healed her, and the house thereupon became the base of Jesus ministry; often it was mobbed by the sick or the possessed who were clamoring to be healed (MATTHEW 8:14). The remains of an octagonal structure discovered in the 1920s may be an ancient Byzantine church that, as early pilgrim records attests, was built over the house.

Just a few steps from this house stands a beautifully restored synagogue. Though recent studies have shown that the synagogue dates from the fourth century, it could have been built over the remains of an older synagogue that served as the scene of Jesus' first public appearance. In 1981, Franciscan archaeologists uncovered the foundations of a basalt structure that probably dates to the first century C.E.

According to Mark, "He entered the synagogue and taught," and "they kept on asking one another, 'What is this? A new teaching—with authority?' " And at once, "his fame began to spread throughout the surrounding region of Galilee" (MARK 1:27-28).

Italian artist Bernardino Luini (ca 1480–1532) painted this portrait of "The Magdalen," depicting Mary Magdalene, around 1525.

How to cope with this fame? Mark reports that Simon went looking for Jesus and eventually found him absorbed in prayer. "Everyone is looking for you," Simon said. Jesus turned to him and replied, "Let us go into the neighboring towns, so that I may proclaim the message there also." Thus was launched the ministry of Jesus in Galilee.

By this time it was clear that Simon would become Jesus' first Apostle, his "right hand man." In the Gospel of John, Jesus tells Simon, "You are to be called Cephas." The word *kephas* is a transliteration of the Aramaic word *kêfa,* which means "stone" or the more familiar "rocky"; in Christian literature, it would be translated into *Petros,* or **Peter**. Later, Jesus designated Simon Peter as the leader of the Apostolic mission, saying, "You are Peter, and on this rock I will build my Church" (MATTHEW 16:17-18).

Jesus then took his followers and led them on an extended campaign through the towns and villages of Galilee. His choice of fishermen as disciples gave him access to a boat, which the Gospels suggest was owned by a partnership between Peter, Andrew, and the sons of Zebedee.

The message he brought was that of a new kingdom—not in a political but in a social and spiritual sense, where people would return to the covenantal tenets of faith in God and compassion to one another under God's benevolent rule. This Kingdom of God message was effectively summarized in his Sermon on the Mount, which drew thousands of people from the surrounding communities. As Jesus had promised in his opening sermon in Capernaum, quoting Isaiah, his purpose was to "bring good news to the poor" (LUKE 4:18). Whereas most of Jesus' contemporaries saw the reign of God as a future promise to be realized by a redeemer or Messiah, many Gospel passages suggest that Jesus saw the kingdom as something to be accomplished in his lifetime (MARK 1:15; LUKE 17:21).

MARY MAGDALENE

It is likely that Jesus' visits to townships around the Sea of Galilee may have included a place called Magadan or

ca 23 B.C.E.
Herod's palace in Jerusalem and the Herodion fortress in the Judean desert are built

ca 22 B.C.E.
Construction begins on the harbor of Caesarea Maritima on the Mediterranean coast

ca 21 B.C.E.
Work begins on the expansion of the Second Temple in Jerusalem

ca 19 B.C.E.
Construction of the Pont du Gard as part of the aqueduct of Nîmes

THE TOWN OF MAGDALA

The excavations of the residential section of ancient Magdala by the Universidad Anáhuac México Sur are ongoing. This is the town of Mary Magdalene.

Among recent archaeological discoveries in Israel, none is more exciting than the still ongoing excavation of Magdala, the town of Mary Magdalene. Magdala (or *Tarichaea* in Greek) is located on the northwest bank of the Sea of Galilee at the foot of the Arbel Cliff. During the early Roman period, it was renowned for its fish processing industry. The current excavations, led by the Universidad Anáhuac México Sur in collaboration with the Israeli Antiquities Authority, have revealed that the town reached its peak in the decades before the birth of Jesus. It had an extensive commercial area close to the port, and farther inland, a large residential area near a synagogue. The western section was predominantly Jewish, whereas the eastern area, close to the area of major economic activity, was more Roman. Most residences were multifamily, as was typical in Galilee, and built with local materials such as basalt and limestone, though a few show traces of plaster covering. Except for ritual and public spaces, the floors consisted of packed earth. To date, the excavation team led by Marcela Zapata Meza has unearthed scores of objects, including domestic and ritual pottery, oil lamps, amphorae, glass objects, fishnet weights, nails, spoons, bells, and bone dice, as well as grinding stones—all from roughly the time of Jesus. Magdala's synagogue is being excavated by Israeli archaeologist Dina Avshalom-Gorni, who has recovered a carved stone representing the seven-branched lampstand known as a menorah. It is believed to be one of the oldest synagogues discovered in Israel proper. ∎

Magdala, a major center of the local fish industry. In the Talmud, the place is known as *Magdala Nunayya* (Magdala of the Fishes), while in Greek it was called *Tarichaea* (Fish Salters). In fact, Magdalene fish sauce was a favorite condiment throughout Palestine and beyond.

One of Jesus' followers came from Magdala. Given that Mary was a very common name, the Gospels refer to her as **Mary Magdalene**. Mary may have come into contact with Jesus because of his healing powers. "Seven demons had gone out of her," says Luke without referring to an actual exorcism (LUKE 8:2). This may suggest that Mary suffered from a chronic disease, which in Antiquity was often associated with bad spirits. Mary defied the stereotype of a young Jewish woman in first-century Galilee. Whereas unwed women were usually restrained from leaving their home without a relative as an escort, Mary went boldly where Jesus went, and together with other women "provided for them out of their own resources" (LUKE 8:2-3). This may indicate that Mary's family was well-to-do, which would also explain her greater freedom of movement.

THE MIRACLES OF JESUS

Biblical scholars have discovered that stories of Jesus' miracles appear in the oldest oral strata about Jesus—the earliest traditions that were collected and edited by the evangelists. Jesus lived in a society that, unlike ours, strongly believed in magic and miraculous phenomena as a reflection of the supernatural powers that controlled people's lives. According to Josephus, exceptional men and women, possessed by the Spirit of God, were expected to be capable of supernatural "signs." Similarly, the Babylonian Talmud describes numerous rabbis who had the gift of producing either rain or drought through prayer. Many scholars distinguish between the healing miracles, including exorcisms, and the nature miracles. A close analysis shows that the healing stories follow a predictable format and vocabulary, whereas the nature miracles have a less recognizable pattern. This may suggest that the healing stories reflect historical events observed by eyewitnesses, whereas the nature miracles may carry a more symbolic message. ∎

As the months passed, Mary became one of Jesus' most loyal followers. She, together with another small group of women, stood fearlessly at Jesus' cross after all the Apostles had gone in hiding (MARK 15:40-41).

Mary Magdalene is often depicted in Western art as "the penitent Magdalene," even though there is no evidence anywhere in the Gospels that Mary Magdalene lived a sinful or promiscuous life. Nevertheless, by the third century, she had become fully assimilated with the unnamed woman in Luke, "a sinner," who bathes Jesus' feet with her tears, and dries them with her hair (LUKE 7:38). By the sixth century, Pope Gregory I declared Mary Magdalene to be a "fallen woman" guilty of "forbidden acts." Only in 1969 did Pope Paul VI explicitly separate the figure of Mary Magdalene from the "sinful woman" character.

JAIRUS'S DAUGHTER
As Jesus' ministry progressed, it became evident that many of the crowds who followed Jesus were more interested in seeing a miracle performed than in hearing his teachings.

THE TRAVELS OF JESUS BEYOND GALILEE

MAP KEY

- Ruled by Herod Antipas
- Ruled by Herod Philip
- Roman province of Judaea
- Roman province of Syria
- Imperial estate
- Nabatean Kingdom
- .... District or region boundary
- ← Route of Joseph, Mary, and Jesus during Herod's time
- ← Return route from Egypt
- ← Probable routes for regular trips to Jerusalem
- • / ○ City of the Decapolis / location uncertain

On a trip to the area around Tyre and Sidon, Jesus healed the daughter of a Gentile woman. (Matthew 15:21-28)

Simon Peter gave his great confession, "You are the Messiah, the Son of the living God." Jesus had asked who the people thought he was. (Matthew 16:13-20)

After Herod's death Joseph returned from Egypt, settling in Nazareth in Galilee. (Matthew 2:19-23)

Joseph was required to travel to Bethlehem to be counted in the Roman census, as he was of the line of King David. (Luke 2:1-5)

Jesus encountered a Samaritan woman at Jacob's Well. He spoke to her of his "living water" that would be "a spring of water gushing up to eternal life" for any who would drink. (John 4:1-42)

On one journey to Jerusalem, Jesus healed ten lepers who cried out to him as he was entering a village. (Luke 17:11-19)

Joseph and Mary brought the baby Jesus to the Temple to dedicate him as the Law of Moses required. (Luke 2:22-24)

In response to questioning Pharisees, Jesus taught them about the sanctity of marriage. (Matthew 19:1-12)

Warned in a dream, Joseph took his family to Egypt to escape Herod's wrath. (Matthew 2:13-14)

THE GREAT SEA (MEDITERRANEAN SEA)

Sidon
Damascus
2,814 m 9,232 ft Mt. Hermon
Tyre
Kanah
Caesarea Philippi (Paneas)
Cadasa
Asor
Raphana
Ecdippa
Merom
GAULANITIS
Jotapata
Capernaum
Bethsaida
Ptolemais
Arbela
Bay of Acco (Bay of Haifa)
Tiberias
Sea of Kinnereth (Sea of Galilee)
Sycaminium
Hippos
Mt. Carmel 546 m 1,791 ft
Nazareth
Philoteria
Gabae
Abila
Sepphoris
Mt. Tabor 588 m 1,929 ft
Gadara
Dora
Legio
Caesarea
Scythopolis
Pella
Narbata
Ginae
Dion
Gerasa
Mt. Ebal 940 m 3,084 ft
Sebaste
Neapolis
Amathus
Apollonia
Sychar
Antipatris
Mt. Gerizim 881 m 2,890 ft
Joppa
Lebonah
Phasaelis
Gadara
Lydda
Archelais
Philadelphia
Bethel
Jamnia
Gazara
Jericho
Esbus
Jerusalem
Bethany
Mt. Nebo 802 m 2,631 ft
Azotus
Bethlehem
Medeba
Ascalon
Herodium
Marisa
Beth-zur
Machaerus
Lachish
Hebron
Salt Sea (Dead Sea)
Anthedon
En-gedi
Gaza
Eshtemoa
Raphia
Masada
Beersheba
Malatha
Kir-Moab
NEGEV
EGYPT

PHOENICIA
LEBANON
Leontes
ITUREA
SYRIA
GALILEE
Kishon
Jordan
SAMARIA
DECAPOLIS
Yarmuk
Jabbok
PLAIN OF SHARON
Yarqon
Sorek
SHEPHELAH
JUDEA
PEREA
Arnon
Zered
NABATEA

0   20   40 kilometers
0   20   40 miles

Present-day drainage, coastlines, and country boundaries are represented. Modern names appear in parentheses.

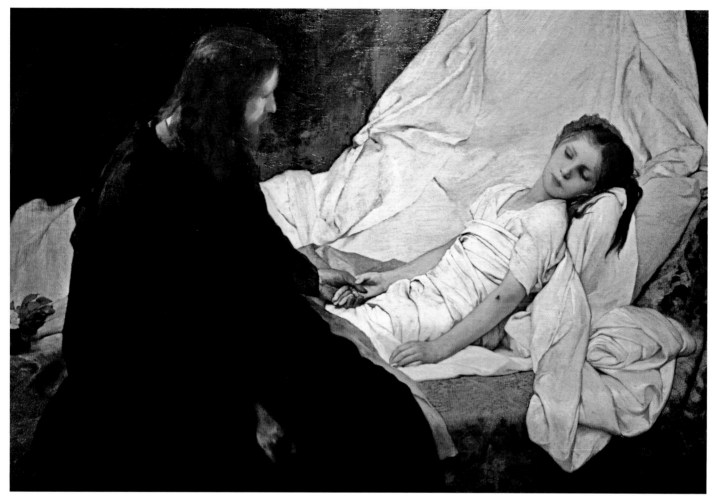

As Mark attests, Jesus' fame as a man able to perform miraculous signs (*semeioi* in Greek) had tremendous resonance in an age that believed in supernatural phenomena as a reflection of divine will. According to Josephus, people were prepared to accept a prophet's bona fides only if he was able to perform a supernatural act—preferably an exorcism. Jesus' first miracle in Capernaum was such an exorcism, and he would perform many more in the months to come (MARK 5:1-13).

Many of Jesus' miracles, moreover, are echoes of miraculous events in Hebrew Scripture, particularly those performed by the prophets Elijah and Elisha, who the evangelists often cited. Jesus' multiplication of loaves and fish to feed the five thousand, for example, has a parallel in Elijah's multiplication of meal and oil for the widow at Zarephath (I KINGS 17:14). Similarly, the instances of Jesus healing a leper (i.e., MARK 1:41) are comparable to the story

"The Raising of Jairus's Daughter" was painted by Prague-born Austrian artist Gabriel Max (1840–1915) around 1878. Jairus, a synagogue leader, had begged Jesus to heal his child.

of Elisha curing Naaman, a leprous commander of the Syrian army (II KINGS 5:14), while Elisha's conversion of Jericho's toxic wells into fresh water (II KINGS 2:21) is echoed in Jesus' conversion of water into wine in Cana (JOHN 2:9).

Another notable example is the miracle that took place when Jesus "crossed in the boat to the other side," meaning the western shore of the Sea of Galilee.

Here, Jesus was met by a large crowd, including a man named **Jairus**, "one of the leaders of the synagogue." He fell at Jesus' feet and begged him, "My daughter is at the point of death. Come and lay your hands on her, so that she may be made well, and live" (MARK 5:21-24). Jesus was delayed, however, and soon the news arrived that the young girl had died. "Don't trouble the Teacher further," the crowd told Jairus, but Jesus went over to his house nevertheless. He ordered the wailers to leave, went to the girl's room, and said to her

ca 8 B.C.E.	ca 7 B.C.E.	ca 6 B.C.E.	ca 5 B.C.E.
Herod reconciles with Augustus	Alexander and Aristobulus are tried by their father, Herod, and executed	Herod moves to curb the influence of the Pharisees	Antipater II, Herod's heir, is charged with treason. Antipas is named heir instead

lifeless body, *Talitha cum!*—which means in Aramaic, "Little girl, get up!" Immediately, color reappeared on the girl's cheeks, and she woke and rose.

This powerful miracle, which some believe parallels Elijah's breathing life into a widow's dead son (I KINGS 17:22), showed Jesus as a man who not only controlled life, but also even death—a foreshadowing of his Resurrection.

THE MESSIAH

During Jesus' journeys in Lower Galilee, a mysterious event took place. Taking his most trusted disciples—Peter, James, and John—Jesus ascended a hill where "he was transfigured before them, and his clothes became dazzling white." As the Apostles looked up in amazement, Jesus was joined by two heavenly figures: Moses and Elijah. These prophets are the leading protagonists of the Law *(Torah)* and the Prophets *(Nevi'im),* the two principal divisions of Hebrew Scripture as it was known in Jesus' time. High above came a voice, which said,

PONTIUS PILATE

Pontius Pilate is an enigmatic figure. What little we know about him (outside the Gospels) comes from Josephus and the Jewish author Philo of Alexandria, who both lived in the first century, as well as Roman records. Pilate was a member of the equestrian family of the Pontii; therefore, he did not belong to the elite senatorial class, which usually provided governors for overseas service. By custom, Roman *equites,* or "knights," were appointed to senior administrative and military posts of the Imperial government, but rarely to the top position of running an overseas province. Some scholars believe it is significant that in the very year of Pilate's appointment, 26 C.E., Emperor Tiberius withdrew from active life, leaving the running of the government to the captain of his Praetorian Guard, Lucius Aelius Sejanus. Pilate was the fifth procurator of Judea, having succeeded Valerius Gratus, and was dismissed from office in 36 C.E. for excessive cruelty toward his subjects. ■

"This is my Son, the beloved; listen to him!" (MARK 9:3-7).

The purpose of the Transfiguration is to present Jesus as the fulfillment of Hebrew Scripture, one of the cardinal ideas of the canonical Gospels. Another motive for this highly unusual event may be to help the faithful imagine the Resurrection of Jesus, because the actual Resurrection is neither observed nor described in any of the Gospels. Traditionally, the Transfiguration is said to have occurred on Mount Tabor in the Jezreel Valley, although some believe that Mount Hermon, today located at the juncture between Israel, Lebanon, and Syria, would have been the place.

In the latter phase of his ministry, Jesus ventured beyond the traditional boundaries of Lower Galilee and into the predominantly pagan territories located around his native region. One reason, perhaps, was that according to Luke, his teachings were beginning to attract people from far-flung areas such as "Judea, Jerusalem, and the coast of Tyre and Sidon" (LUKE 6:17), in contrast to the opposition he encountered in Galilee. For example, Jesus traveled to the "country of the Gerasenes" beyond the eastern shore of the Sea of Galilee, where Jesus exorcised a man possessed by demons (MARK 5:1-13). This territory formed part of the Decapolis, a federation of ten predominantly Hellenistic cities in what is today southern Syria and the north part of Jordan. "Gerasenes" may refer to Gerasa, today's Jerash, which was a leading trade nexus for caravan roads between Damascus in the north and Petra in the south, or to another, less prominent Greek city called Gadara, today's Umm Qays.

Jesus then pushed north toward the coastal territory of Phoenicia, today's Lebanon, which was likewise largely Gentile (MARK 7:24). Here he traveled in the region of Tyre, which was one of the principal harbors on the Mediterranean coast, as well as the city of Sidon. Perhaps Jesus was intrigued by the question of why Gentiles from these sophisticated Greek cities would travel to Galilee to hear him speak. In Tyre, he was impressed with a local woman who had heard Jesus make an oblique reference to Gentiles as "dogs." "Even the dogs under

The triumphal gate of the Hellenistic city of Gerasa—modern Jerash, Jordan—led to the main forum, where the religious, civic, and commercial facilities of the city could be found.

ca 4 B.C.E.	ca 4 B.C.E.	ca 4 B.C.E.	ca 4 B.C.E.
Young demonstrators remove the golden eagle from the Temple as a Roman symbol	Putative date of birth of Jesus	Antipater II is executed	Herod dies; Augustus confirms Herod's will dividing his kingdom among his sons

He came down with them and stood on a level place, with a great crowd of his disciples and a great multitude of people from all over Judea, Jerusalem, and the coast of Tyre and Sidon.

GOSPEL OF LUKE 6:17

the table eat the children's crumbs," she pointed out. Jesus assured her that her daughter, who was possessed by a demon, was now healed (MARK 7:27-30).

Jesus then moved northeast, toward the rolling hills of the Golan. Here was a town called Caesarea Philippi, center of the cult of the Greek god Pan, which a few years later would be expanded into a splendid Greco-Roman city. In this Gentile place, on the threshold of returning to his native land, Jesus felt a need to assess the impact of his ministry. "Who do people say that I am?" he asked. Some disciples said, "John the Baptist." Others said, "Elijah." Still others hedged their bets and said, "One of the prophets." Only Simon Peter stood up and proclaimed, "You are the **Messiah**" (MARK 8:30). In Matthew, Jesus warmly praises Simon Peter for his acumen, adding a pun on Peter's nickname (*Petros* in Greek, or "rock"): "You are Peter, and on this rock I will build my church" (MATTHEW 16:17-18). But he also swore his disciples to silence, ordering them "not to tell anyone that he was the Messiah" (MATTHEW 16:20).

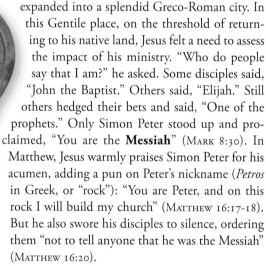

This olive lamp with a gladiator in its middle is typical of terra-cotta lamps in use throughout the Roman Empire.

Sometime at the beginning of the Jewish month of Nisan, possibly in the year 30 C.E., Jesus decided to travel with his Apostles to Jerusalem for the Passover feast. The Synoptic Gospels only refer to one Passover feast, which suggests that Jesus' ministry was relatively short—around 18 months or so. John's Gospel, on the other hand, describes no less than five journeys to Jerusalem, often prompted by one of the major pilgrim festivals, including no less than three Passovers, one Feast of Tabernacles, and one Hanukkah festival (JOHN 2:13; 5:1; 6:4; 10:22; 11:55).

It is possible that Jesus felt his time in Galilee had run its course. In one unusual outburst, he scolded the cities that had formed the "triangle" of his ministry. "Woe to you, Chorazin!" he cries in Luke

Dutch artist Rembrandt van Rijn (1606–1669) painted this intimate and human portrait of Jesus between 1648 and 1650.

THE MESSIAH

The purpose of the Synoptic Gospels is to present Jesus as the Messiah (*Mashiach* in Hebrew, or "anointed one," "Christos" in Greek) as foretold in the Scriptures. The idea of a Kingdom of God had been circulating for some time, for example, in the Book of Daniel (7:27) or the Psalms of Solomon (18:6-8). There was no agreement on what kind of a savior this Messiah would be. Some saw him as a descendant of King David; as the archangel Michael; or by contrast, as "one like a son of man," a normal human being. The Dead Sea Scrolls speak of *two* Messiahs: a warrior king and "branch of David," and a priest, the "Messiah of Aaron." Others envisioned a military leader, such as Simon bar Kokhba, the leader of the Second Jewish Revolt against the Romans in 132–135 C.E. John the Baptist also described the Messiah in militant terms, as a man whose "winnowing fork is in his hand, to clear his threshing floor . . . but the chaff he will burn with unquenchable fire" (LUKE 3:17). To Jesus, however, the Kingdom of God was not a political but a social and spiritual entity. Nevertheless, Jesus was aware of the political overtones of the Messiah title. In Matthew's Gospel, Jesus "sternly ordered the disciples not to tell anyone that he was the Messiah" (MATTHEW 16:20). Instead, Jesus himself referred to himself as the Son of Man, perhaps inspired by the eschatological visions of the Book of Daniel. ■

ca 4 B.C.E.	ca 4 B.C.E.	ca 4 B.C.E.	ca 3 B.C.E.
Herod's son Antipas assumes title of tetrarch of Galilee and Perea	While Archelaus, new ruler of Judea, is in Rome, a rebellion erupts	Judas, son of Hezekiah of Galilee, leads a revolt in Galilee	The Jewish revolts are suppressed by Roman forces; Sepphoris is burned

Their fear was not without justification. As they crossed from Galilee into Samaria, they entered Roman territory, which for the past four years had been governed by a new Roman procurator named Pontius Pilate. Soon after his arrival in Judea, Pilate had embarked on a deliberate policy of confrontation with his Jewish subjects, possibly in the belief that the privileges Augustus granted to Jewish subjects (such as being absolved of sacrificing to the statue of the emperor) should be abrogated. As it happened, there was no one to constrain Pilate's obstinacy because his immediate superior, Lucius Aelius Lamia, governor of Greater Syria, was not in Antioch but in Rome. In 28 C.E., just two years before Jesus' reported journey to Jerusalem, the tensions between Pilate and his Judean subjects erupted in a massacre of Jewish pilgrims in the Temple; Jesus obliquely refers to this bloodbath in the Gospel of Luke (LUKE 13:1).

We can therefore imagine the apprehension of Jesus' followers; they probably knew that all Roman forces around the Temple would be on high alert during Passover. And indeed, as they were making their way down south, Pilate himself was traveling from his residence in Caesarea to Jerusalem, accompanied by reinforcements, to personally supervise the security arrangements for the Passover festival.

ZACCHAEUS

As he was approaching Jerusalem, Jesus passed through Jericho, a city that straddled several caravan routes between Syria, Arabia, and the Mediterranean. Its strategic position had resulted in several toll stations; in the Roman era, a tax was assessed each time goods moved from one jurisdiction to the next. One tax collector in the city, says

ROMAN PREFECTS OF THE
FIRST PROCURATORSHIP OF

JUDEA

COPONIUS
6-9 C.E.

MARCUS AMBIVULUS
9-12 C.E.

ANNIUS RUFUS
12-15 C.E.

VALERIUS GRATUS
15-26 C.E.

PONTIUS PILATE
26-36 C.E.

MARCELLUS
37 C.E.

MARULLUS
37-41 C.E.

Spanish artist El Greco—born Doménikos Theotokópoulos (1541–1614)—painted "Christ Healing the Blind" in 1578.

and Matthew. "Woe to you, Bethsaida! If the powerful deeds performed among you had been done in Tyre and Sidon, they would have changed their ways long ago, sitting in sackcloth and ashes!" (MATTHEW 11:21; LUKE 10:13). "And you, Capernaum," Jesus continued, addressing the town that had served as his home and base, "will you be exalted to heaven? No, you will be brought down to Hades" (LUKE 10:15). Clearly, Jesus was disappointed with the response to his teachings in this region. Perhaps he felt that Judea would be more receptive to his Kingdom of God program.

What's more, to preach in Jerusalem at Passover meant he would preach to the Jewish nation at large, for soon thousands of Jews from all over Palestine and the Diaspora would converge on Jerusalem for the great festival. Thus, Jesus embarked on his fateful journey to Jerusalem, and "those who followed," said Mark, "were afraid" (MARK 10:32).

ca 2 C.E.	ca 4 C.E.	ca 5 C.E.	ca 6 C.E.
Augustus's grandson and heir Lucius dies	Augustus's other grandson Gaius is killed; Augustus adopts Tiberius	First use of the adjustable caliper in China	Archelaus is removed from office and banished to Vienne, Roman Gaul

Michelangelo Caravaggio (1571–1610) painted this canvas of sisters Martha and Mary, who lived in Bethany, around 1598.

Luke, was a wealthy man named **Zacchaeus**. When Jesus began to attract a crowd, Zacchaeus, who was short in stature, climbed into a sycamore tree, hoping to see Jesus as he passed by. Jesus looked up and said, "Zacchaeus, hurry and come down; for I must stay at your house today." Overwhelmed by Jesus' presence, Zacchaeus meekly promised to atone for his sins. "Half of my possessions, Lord, I will give to the poor," the tax collector said, "and if I have defrauded anyone of anything, I will pay back four times as much" (LUKE 19:1-8). This buoyed the spirits of the Apostles; here, at last, was a man willing to help build the Kingdom of God.

BARTIMAEUS

Another man was eagerly waiting for Jesus to pass. This was a blind beggar named **Bartimaeus**, son of Timaeus, who as usual was sitting by the roadside, hoping for alms. As he sensed that Jesus was near, he called out, "Jesus, Son of David, have mercy on me"—the first public declaration of Jesus as the Messiah, since the Messiah was expected to descend from King David. The people around Bartimaeus told him to be quiet, but he cried out even louder, "Son of David, have mercy on me!" Jesus summoned him, and asked, "What do you want me to do for you?" "My teacher," the blind man responded, using the honorific rabbi, "let me see again." "Go," Jesus replied, "your faith has made you well" (MARK 10:46-52).

MARY AND MARTHA

The last and final stop before reaching Jerusalem was a small township called Bethany. Here, according to a supplemental story in the Gospel of John, lived two sisters named **Mary** and **Martha** with

ca 6 C.E.	ca 6 C.E.	ca 6 C.E.	ca 6 C.E.
Augustus annexes Judea as a Roman province; first procurator is Coponius	Quirinius, the new governor of Syria, initiates a census in Judea	Annas (Ananus ben Seth) is appointed high priest by Quirinius	The Roman census provokes a new revolt; party of the Zealots is formed

THE ROAD TO JERUSALEM

MAP KEY

- Ruled by Herod Antipas
- Ruled by Herod Philip
- Roman province of Judaea
- Roman province of Syria
- Imperial estate
- Nabatean Kingdom
- .... District or region boundary
- ⟵ Route of Jesus to Jerusalem
- • / ○ City of the Decapolis / location uncertain

Sidon

Damascus

2,814 m
9,232 ft
Mt. Hermon

PHOENICIA

LEBANON

ITUREA

SYRIA

Tyre

Leontes

**Caesarea Philippi
(Paneas)**

Kanah

Cadasa

Raphana

Ecdippa

Asor

Merom

GAULANITIS

Ptolemais

Jotapata

Capernaum

Bethsaida

*Bay of Acco
(Bay of Haifa)*

Arbela

*Sea of Kinnereth
(Sea of Galilee)*

Sycaminium

Tiberias

Hippos

Mt. Carmel
546 m
1,791 ft

Nazareth

Philoteria

Abila

Gabae

GALILEE

Sepphoris

Mt. Tabor
588 m
1,929 ft

Gadara

Dora

Legio

Kishon

Caesarea

Scythopolis
Pella

PLAIN OF SHARON

Narbata

Ginae

Dion

THE GREAT SEA
(MEDITERRANEAN SEA)

DECAPOLIS

Gerasa

Mt. Ebal
940 m
3,084 ft

Neapolis

Sebaste

Amathus

Apollonia

SAMARIA

Sychar

Mt. Gerizim
881 m
2,890 ft

*Zacchaeus, a chief
tax collector, was
converted.
(Luke 19:1–10)*

Yarqon

Antipatris

PEREA

Jabbok

Lebonah

Gadara

Joppa

Phasaelis

Philadelphia

Lydda

Bethel

Archelais

*Blind Bartimaeus is
given sight by Jesus.
(Mark 10:46–52)*

Jamnia

Gazara

Jericho

Sorek

Jerusalem

Esbus

Azotus

SHEPHELAH

**Bethany
(Al 'Ayzarīyah)**

Mt. Nebo
802 m
2,631 ft

Medeba

JUDEA

*Jesus entered the city to the praising
cries of "Hosanna," meaning "save us"
in Hebrew. He would later be turned
over to authorities, crucified, then
buried, and resurrected in the city.
(Matthew 21:9)*

Bethlehem

Herodium

*Jesus raised Lazarus
from the dead after four
days in the tomb.
(John 11:1–44)*

Ascalon

Marisa

Beth-zur

Machaerus

Lachish

Hebron

*Salt Sea
(Dead Sea)*

Anthedon

'En-gedi

Gaza

Eshtemoa

*Jesus was anointed in the
house of Simon the Leper.
(Matthew 26: 6–13; Mark
14:3–9; John 12:1–8)*

EGYPT

Masada

Arnon

Raphia

Beersheba

Malatha

Kir-Moab

NEGEV

NABATEA

Besor

Zered

0   20   40 kilometers

0   20   40 miles

*Present-day drainage, coastlines, and country boundaries are represented.
Modern names appear in parentheses.*

their brother **Lazarus.** From the Gospel accounts, it appears that Jesus was a close and loving friend, and perhaps a relative. In first-century Palestine, friendship—and particularly friendship with people in other towns—was often defined in terms of blood relations. Their house now served as the setting for two important events.

The first, which appears in the Gospel of Luke, relates how Jesus began to teach as soon as he entered the house. Mary "sat at the Lord's feet and listened to what he was saying," in another example of Jesus' extraordinary concern to invite both men and women in his entourage. While Mary sat and listened, however, her sister Martha had to work twice as hard to get the house ready for Jesus' stay. Exasperated, she turned to Jesus and said, "Lord, do you not care that my sister has left me to do all the work by myself? Tell her then to help me." But Jesus replied, "Martha, Martha, you are worried and distracted by many things; there is need of only one thing. Mary has chosen the better part, which will not be taken away from her" (LUKE 10:39-42). Jesus' response had a twofold meaning: that spirituality trumped material concerns, but also that women disciples should be treated on equal terms as men.

LAZARUS

The Gospel of John adds another story about the Bethany family. When Jesus was still on the road, "across the Jordan," Lazarus fell

"The Raising of Lazarus" is the work of the Italian Mannerist artist Mirabello Cavalori (1520–1572).

Making a whip of cords he drove all of them out of the Temple . . . [and] poured out the coins of the money changers and overturned their tables.

GOSPEL OF JOHN 2:15

ill, and his sisters feared for his life. They sent an urgent message to Jesus, saying, "Lord, he whom you love is ill" (JOHN 11:3). Surprisingly, Jesus did not proceed to Bethany right away. He stayed on the east bank of the Jordan for two more days before leisurely making his way to the Bethany residence. By the time Jesus got there, Lazarus had been in his tomb for four days. Confused and distraught, Martha chided him, saying, "Lord, if you had been here, my brother would not have died." Mary, the more sensitive one, simply burst into tears, weeping so bitterly that Jesus "was greatly disturbed in spirit and deeply moved" (JOHN 11:17-33).

Taking charge of the situation, Jesus ordered for the stone of Lazarus's tomb to be removed, and cried out in a loud voice, "Lazarus, come out!" And immediately "the dead man came out, his hands and feet bound with strips of cloth, and his face wrapped in a cloth." According to John, this was the moment when the "**chief priests**" and the "**Pharisees**" called a meeting of the Jewish council, the **Sanhedrin**, to plot Jesus' arrest and execution (JOHN 11:39-47).

THE MONEY CHANGERS

Shortly thereafter, the Gospels tell us, Jesus made a triumphant entry into Jerusalem, seated on a colt. "Many people spread their cloaks on the road," says Mark, "and others spread leafy branches that they had cut in the fields." Some were shouting, "Hosanna! Blessed is he who comes in the name of the Lord!" (MARK 11:7-10). Jesus' destination was the forecourt of the Temple, but, says Mark, "as it was already late, he went out to Bethany with the twelve" (MARK 11:11).

When Jesus did finally reach the Temple during his next visit to Jerusalem, he was in for a shock. The Temple forecourt had been

Tyrian silver shekels, dated around 68 C.E., were the only type of currency permitted within the Temple of Jerusalem.

---

ca 6 C.E.	ca 9 C.E.	ca 9 C.E.	ca 12 C.E.
Antipas, now known as Herod Antipas, begins the rebuilding of Sepphoris	The Roman legions led by Varus are destroyed by the Cherusci in the Teutoburg Forest	Marcus Ambivulus succeeds Coponius as procurator of Judea	Annius Rufus succeeds Marcus Ambivulus as procurator of Judea

Spanish artist El Greco—born Doménikos Theotokópoulos (1541–1614)—painted "Christ Cleaning the Temple" before 1570.

These words, "a den of robbers," struck a chord. Two years before, Pilate (and, conceivably, the high priest **Caiaphas**) had been accused of illegally appropriating funds from the Temple treasury to build a Roman aqueduct. That Jesus was actually quoting from Jeremiah's Temple Sermon may have escaped them. Indeed, as soon as "the chief priests and the **scribes** heard it, they kept looking for a way to kill him" (MARK 11:18; JEREMIAH 7:11).

JUDAS ISCARIOT

For the time being, however, Jesus and his Apostles were still at large. The streets of Jerusalem were packed with pilgrims, which would have frustrated attempts by the Temple guards to track down Jesus. It was the 14th of Nisan, the eve of Passover, but any thought of Jesus going back to Bethany to celebrate the Passover meal was, for the moment, out of the question; no doubt the city gates were still heavily guarded. Jesus sent two of his disciples to find a place where they could stay; they would follow a man with a jar, and when he reached his house, they were to ask where the teacher could celebrate Passover with his disciples (MARK 14:14). It was as Jesus had foretold, and before long they were ushered into a large upper room. This may be the same place where, according to the Book of Acts, the disciples met after the Crucifixion (ACTS 12:12-13).

converted into a bazaar where **money changers** did brisk business converting Roman currency into Temple shekels, and where a variety of sacrificial animals could be purchased. Why was Jesus surprised? The sale of Paschal Lambs was necessary, because every family was expected to sacrifice a lamb on the eve of the Passover festival. To purchase these animals, one had to convert one's cash into Temple shekels, because foreign currency—notably Roman coins—carried an image of the emperor, and such graven images were prohibited within the confines of the Temple. The answer is, as some scholars have surmised, that this commerce usually took place on the Mount of Olives, in a market called *Chanut,* far away from the Temple complex. This would explain why Jesus was deeply aggrieved by this unseemly trade, for he "began to drive out those who were selling and those who were buying in the temple, and he overturned the tables of the money changers and the seats of those who sold doves." Raising his voice, Jesus said, "Is it not written, 'My house shall be called a house of prayer for all the nations?' But you have made it a den of robbers" (MARK 11:15-17).

As soon as they were settled, Jesus made a shocking announcement: "One of you will betray me, one who is eating with me" (MARK 14:18). That man was **Judas Iscariot.** The term "Iscariot" has been linked to the term *sicarius,* which is Latin for "dagger man," an epithet sometimes associated with the Jewish party of the **Zealots.** Other scholars believe that "Iscariot" simply means that Judas hailed from Kerioth, a town in southern Judea. This would have set him apart from the other Apostles, who were Galilean, because Kerioth was located in Judea. Jesus was right; while Temple guards were scouring Jerusalem for a trace of the Galilean rabbi, Judas had approached the chief priests and offered to lead them to Jesus. Delighted, the priests offered Judas money for this information— 30 pieces of silver, a princely sum (MARK 14:11; MATTHEW 26:15).

Now, as they were reclining at the table while their supper was being served, the Apostles watched as Jesus broke bread, blessed it, and gave it to the disciples, saying, "Take, eat; this is my body."

ca 14 C.E.	ca 15 C.E.	ca 15 C.E.	ca 16 C.E.
Augustus dies and is succeeded by Tiberius (14–37 C.E.)	Valerius Gratus succeeds Annius Rufus as procurator of Judea	Ishmael ben Fabus is appointed high priest in Jerusalem	Tiberius's adopted son Germanicus defeats German tribes along the Rhine

Then Jesus took a cup, and after giving thanks he gave it to them, saying, "Drink from it, all of you; for this is my blood of the covenant, which is poured out for many for the forgiveness of sins." With this, Jesus instituted the *Eucharist,* a Greek word that means "thanksgiving." It would be reenacted in many early Christian communities in commemoration of Jesus until the rite became the quintessential liturgical sacrament of Mass.

After the meal was concluded and night had fallen, the group left Jerusalem and went to the Mount of Olives, to a place called Gethsemane (MARK 14:36). Jesus was in a somber mood. "You will all become deserters," he said. Peter indignantly denied it. "I will not!" he said. Jesus turned to him and replied, "Truly I tell you, this day, this very night, before the cock crows twice, you will deny me three times" (MARK 14:27-30).

The origin of the name "Gethsemane" may be the word *gatshemanim* ("press of oils"); such oil presses were usually placed in a cave to provide a constant temperature for the oil-producing process. Fourth-century author Egeria wrote that she had visited such a cave (rather than a garden) on the Mount of Olives during her pilgrimage in the Holy Land.

In search of solitude, Jesus now moved away from the rest and threw himself to the ground, praying, "My Father, if it is possible, let this cup pass from me; yet not what I want but what you want" (MATTHEW 26:39). He then went looking for his disciples,

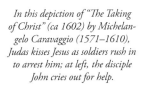

In this depiction of "The Taking of Christ" (ca 1602) by Michelangelo Caravaggio (1571–1610), Judas kisses Jesus as soldiers rush in to arrest him; at left, the disciple John cries out for help.

ca 16 C.E.	ca 17 C.E.	ca 17 C.E.	ca 18 C.E.
Eleazar, son of Annas, is appointed high priest in Jerusalem	Herod Antipas begins construction of a new city on the Sea of Galilee, called Tiberias	Simon ben Camithus is appointed high priest in Jerusalem	Joseph Caiaphas, son-in-law of Annas, is appointed high priest in Jerusalem

but found that all had fallen asleep. So had most of the other people around him. On Passover night, the Mount of Olives would have been covered with sleeping pilgrims and their families, because they didn't have the means to secure an inn in the city. This is why the Temple guards had insisted that Judas point out Jesus to them from among the crowd. Judas did so by kissing his master on his cheek—a traditional sign of respect—and by saying, "Greetings, Rabbi!" (MATTHEW 26:49). In Luke's Gospel, one of the disciples took his sword and cut off the ear of "the slave of the high priest." "No more of this," Jesus said sternly, and restored the ear to the man's head (LUKE 22:51). And then they arrested him and led him away.

CAIAPHAS

Custom dictated that Jesus should have been locked up in the Temple stockade until such time that the full Sanhedrin could hear his case. This is exactly what happened to Peter, John, and other Apostles upon their arrest (ACTS 4:3; 5:17). But instead, Jesus was taken directly to the Jerusalem residence of the high priest Joseph Caiaphas. This was highly unusual, for a number of reasons. First, it was the eve of

Passover, one of the holiest nights on the Jewish liturgical calendar, when the high priest and other priestly officials would be expected to celebrate the festival with their families, rather than adjudicating the case of a rural rabbi from Galilee. Second, while Caiaphas's residence was probably quite comfortable, if not luxurious, it was unlikely that his home would have been large enough to accommodate the full quorum of 72 members on the Sanhedrin, even assuming that these members would have allowed themselves to be summoned on such short notice. The hastily organized indictment of Jesus as described in Mark's account—which would form the basis for all subsequent Gospels—was conducted under cloak of darkness, which suggests that Caiaphas was eager to dispense with Jesus as soon as possible, and to do so behind closed doors, without the full Sanhedrin present.

John states that Jesus was first questioned by **Annas**, Caiaphas's father-in-law who had previously served as high priest, and as head of the Annas family was probably considered a leading authority on religious matters. Following a brief hearing, Jesus was then referred to Caiaphas (JOHN 18:13-24).

At that moment, Caiaphas had served some 12 years in office, having succeeded his brother-in-law Eleazar ben Ananus, one of

THE CAIAPHAS INDICTMENT

Why did Caiaphas order an immediate hearing on Jesus' fate at his own residence? One answer is that Caiaphas wanted to preempt any more violent demonstrations like Jesus' attack on the money changers, which would undoubtedly have provoked Roman forces. Another motive might be that Caiaphas expected the Pharisee faction of the Sanhedrin to come to Jesus' defense. The Gospels attest that Joseph of Arimathea and Nicodemus, both members of the Sanhedrin, were in sympathy with Jesus' teachings (MARK 15:43; JOHN 19:38). Caiaphas's fear was not unfounded; some months later, when Peter and the Apostles were brought before the Sanhedrin, the noted Pharisee Gamaliel defended them and ultimately secured their release (ACTS 5:34-39). Indeed, it is unlikely that the indictment by Caiaphas

involved "the full council" as Mark suggests. The Mishnah states that no trial by the Sanhedrin could take place at night, or during a festival. Even *if*

Caiaphas had been able to convene the full Sanhedrin, including scribes, in his house, they may not have fit in his home. Formal meetings of the Sanhedrin usually took place in a hall known as the *Lishkat La-Gazit* ("Chamber of Hewn Stones"), located in the Stoa of the Temple. Indeed, in John's Gospel, the chief priests or members of the Sanhedrin are not present at all. In 1990, archaeologists discovered several ossuaries from the first century C.E. The most elaborate of the boxes bore an Aramaic inscription: *Yehoseph bar Qypa* or "Joseph Caiaphas." It is possible that this ossuary belonged to the high priest who indicted Jesus. ■

According to the inscription, this elaborate ossuary contained the bones of the high priest Caiaphas, or "Yosef bar Caifa."

ca 19 C.E.	ca 22 C.E.	ca 23 C.E.	ca 24 C.E.
Tiberius's adopted son Germanicus dies	Start of the Eastern Han dynasty in China	Tiberius's son Drusus dies, leaving Tiberius without an heir	Greek geographer Strabo writes his *Geography*, first comprehensive geographical treatise of the Earth

Dutch artist Gerard van Honthorst (1592–1656) painted "The Denial of St. Peter" around 1623. A servant girl identified Peter as being with Jesus, and Peter dismissed her.

another, not made with hands" (MARK 14:58). Inflammatory rhetoric, perhaps, but hardly grounds for prosecution, because countless prophets in Hebrew Scripture had said the same thing, warning that the Jerusalem Temple would face imminent destruction.

Caiaphas then tried a different tack and asked Jesus flat out, "Are you the Messiah?" According to Mark, Jesus replied, "I am," and then cited from the Book of Daniel and the Psalms: "You will see the Son of Man seated at the right hand of 'the Power,' and 'coming with the clouds of heaven'" (PSALMS 110:1; DANIEL 7:13-14).

This is what Caiaphas needed to hear. He knew that the Romans had no interest in the minutiae of Jewish exegesis, but words like "the right hand of the power" would get their attention. The high priest tore his clothes and said, "Why do we still need witnesses?" In his view, Jesus had incriminated himself.

Then they seized him and led him away, bringing him into the high priest's house.

GOSPEL OF LUKE 22:54

Annas's five sons to become high priest. Caiaphas was facing a difficult situation. Without the full backing of the Sanhedrin, a high priest did not have the power to single-handedly order a man's death. His only other option was to refer the whole matter to the local Roman government. This would be a very controversial move, because over preceding decades, the Sanhedrin had fought hard to retain its autonomy in domestic matters, without any interference from the Roman authorities. The other and even more fundamental problem was that Jesus was only guilty of disturbing the peace, and perhaps of blasphemy, in the Temple forecourt, but neither of these warranted Roman intervention, let alone a sentence of death.

To make matters worse, the indictment hearing as described by Mark did not go according to plan. The various eyewitnesses did not agree. "We heard him say," said one, "I will destroy this temple that is made with hands, and in three days I will build

THE HIGH PRIEST'S SERVANT GIRL

While these proceedings were taking place, Peter was sitting outside in the courtyard, torn between the need to defend Jesus and his fear of being arrested as well. So he sat with the guards, who had lit a fire to keep themselves warm. The month of Nisan usually falls in March or early April, when nights in Jerusalem can be very cold. Around them, Caiaphas's servants came and went, attending to the needs of this sudden influx of visitors. One of these was a servant girl who passed Peter and stopped in her tracks. Looking intently at him, she said, "You also were with Jesus, the man from Nazareth." Flushed, and doubtlessly aware of the stares of the guards around him, Peter said hotly, "I do not know or understand what you are talking about," and walked away into the forecourt to the residence, just as a cock began to crow. But the servant girl wouldn't let it go. She turned to bystanders, who were probably following this exchange with rising interest, and said, "This man is one of them." Peter again dismissed her. But now others were taking a close look as well, and confirmed what the girl had said. Peter began to curse, and for the third time denied it. Then the cock crowed again, and Peter remembered what Jesus had said to him. He broke down and wept (MARK 14:66-72).

ca 26 C.E.	ca 26 C.E.	ca 26 C.E.	ca 28 C.E.
Tiberius withdraws from government, passing power to Sejanus	Pontius Pilate is appointed to succeed Valerius Gratus as procurator of Judea	Pilate provokes massive protests by staging emblems of the emperor near the Temple	Rumors circulate of Pilate using money from the Temple treasury to build an aqueduct

❶ Gethsemane This garden on the Mount of Olives is located close to the traditional place of Gethsemane, the place where Jesus was arrested.

❷ Sisters of Zion The Convent of the Sisters of Zion is believed to mark the location of the Antonia Fortress, one of the places where Pilate could have sat in judgment.

❸ Holy Sepulcher The Church of the Holy Sepulcher is traditionally identified as the location of Golgotha, where Jesus was crucified and buried.

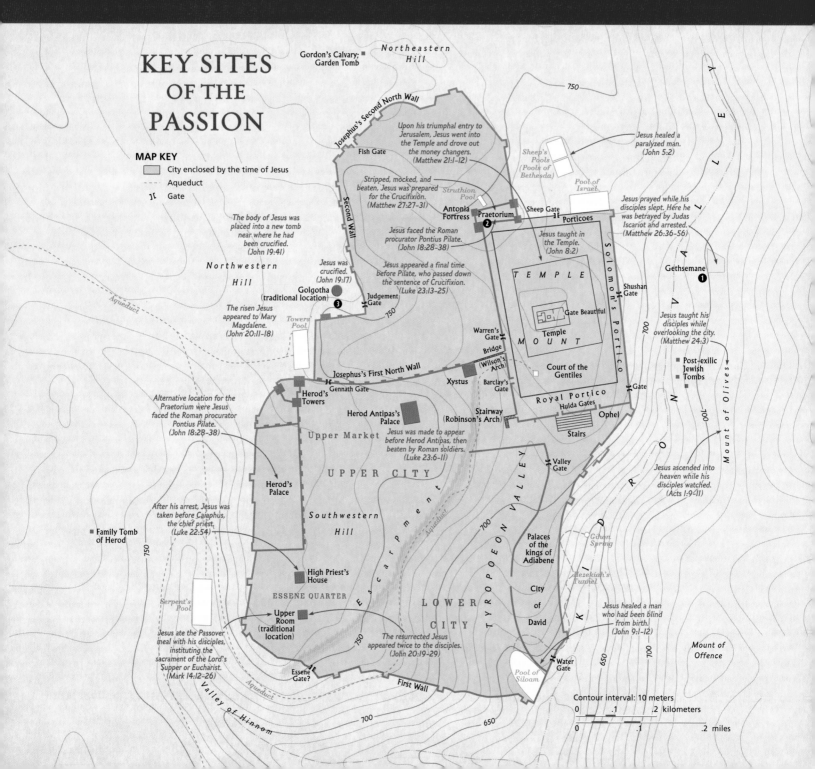

KEY SITES OF THE PASSION

MAP KEY

▨ City enclosed by the time of Jesus

- - - Aqueduct

⊥⊏ Gate

Gordon's Calvary; Garden Tomb

Northeastern Hill

Josephus's Second North Wall

Fish Gate

750

Upon his triumphal entry to Jerusalem, Jesus went into the Temple and drove out the money changers. (Matthew 21:1-12)

Sheep's Pools (Pools of Bethesda)

Jesus healed a paralyzed man. (John 5:2)

Pool of Israel

Stripped, mocked, and beaten, Jesus was prepared for the Crucifixion. (Matthew 27:27-31)

Struthion Pool

Second Wall

Antonia Fortress

Praetorium ❷

Sheep Gate

Porticoes

The body of Jesus was placed into a new tomb near where he had been crucified. (John 19:41)

Jesus faced the Roman procurator Pontius Pilate. (John 18:28-38)

Jesus prayed while his disciples slept. Here he was betrayed by Judas Iscariot and arrested. (Matthew 26:36-56)

T E M P L E

Jesus taught in the Temple. (John 8:2)

Solomon's Portico

Northwestern Hill

Jesus was crucified. (John 19:17)

Jesus appeared a final time before Pilate, who passed down the sentence of Crucifixion. (Luke 23:13-25)

Gethsemane ❶

Golgotha (traditional location) ❸

Judgement Gate

750

Shushan Gate

The risen Jesus appeared to Mary Magdalene. (John 20:11-18)

Towers Pool

Warren's Gate

Gate Beautiful

M O U N T

Temple Mount

Jesus taught his disciples while overlooking the city. (Matthew 24:3)

Aqueduct

Josephus's First North Wall

Bridge (Wilson's Arch)

Barclay's Gate

Court of the Gentiles

Post-exilic Jewish Tombs

Gate

Herod's Towers

Gennath Gate

Xystus

Royal Portico

Hulda Gates

Herod Antipas's Palace

Stairway (Robinson's Arch)

Ophel

Upper Market

Jesus was made to appear before Herod Antipas, then beaten by Roman soldiers. (Luke 23:6-11)

Stairs

Alternative location for the Praetorium were Jesus faced the Roman procurator Pontius Pilate. (John 18:28-38)

U P P E R   C I T Y

Valley Gate

Escarpment

Jesus ascended into heaven while his disciples watched. (Acts 1:9-11)

Herod's Palace

Mount of Olives

Southwestern Hill

700

Palaces of the kings of Adiabene

After his arrest, Jesus was taken before Caiaphas, the chief priest. (Luke 22:54)

■ Family Tomb of Herod

Gihon Spring

Hezekiah's Tunnel

City of David

750

High Priest's House

ESSENE QUARTER

L O W E R   C I T Y

TYROPOEON VALLEY

K I D R O N

Jesus healed a man who had been blind from birth. (John 9:1-12)

Serpent's Pool

Upper Room (traditional location)

Jesus ate the Passover meal with his disciples, instituting the sacrament of the Lord's Supper or Eucharist. (Mark 14:12-26)

The resurrected Jesus appeared twice to the disciples. (John 20:19-29)

750

Water Gate

Mount of Offence

Essene Gate?

Aqueduct

First Wall

Pool of Siloam

650

Valley of Hinnom

700

650

Contour interval: 10 meters

0   .1   .2 kilometers

0   .1   .2 miles

PONTIUS PILATE

As dawn broke, the drama shifted to the praetorium where Pontius Pilate had taken residence for the duration of Passover. The praetorium was literally the residence of the *praetor,* or provincial governor, and usually the most prestigious building in town (MARK 15:15-6; MATTHEW 27:27). Scholars are divided over the location of the praetorium. Either it was set up in the old palace of Herod, which stood in the southwestern part of the city near today's Jaffa Gate, or in the Antonia Fortress, the Herodian citadel adjacent to the Temple complex, where Roman forces were in bivouac.

As Mark describes it, Jesus was brought before Pilate; the charge was read—claiming to be the Messiah, "the King of the Jews"—and Jesus' response, "You say so," was noted for the record (MARK 15:2). Pilate then asked if the prisoner had anything more to say in his defense,

THE TRIAL OF JESUS

The Gospels of Matthew, Luke, and John describe a full "trial" presided by Pilate, though scholars believe that they are mostly based on the brief description Mark provided. The question is whether Jesus, as a colonial subject, would have merited such a trial. Legal proceedings under the *Ius Civile,* Roman civil law, were reserved only for Roman citizens. Colonials were judged under a more arbitrary set of rules, loosely known as the *Ius Gentium*—the "law of nations." Originally, this law had been drafted for crimes committed by foreigners on Roman soil. During the Imperial period, the law was extended as a form of "colonial law" to Roman overseas territories. *Praetors* who ruled under this law essentially rendered judgment as they saw fit without the bothersome details of a full Roman trial. It is therefore possible that Mark's account of a brief hearing before Pilate is closer to history than the more elaborate versions in the other Gospels. ■

given that the chief priests—serving as *delatores,* or accusers, in Roman parlance—were accusing him "of many things." Jesus made no further reply, which essentially sealed his verdict. Under Roman colonial law, anyone with ambitions to become the king of Judea was by definition a political rebel, and by custom, rebels were automatically condemned to death by crucifixion.

BARABBAS

Before Jesus was taken away to his execution, however, Pilate decided to give the "crowd," which had gathered outside the praetorium, a say in the matter. As Mark puts it, "at the festival he used to release a prisoner for them, anyone for whom they asked" (MARK 15:6). Some scholars have argued that such an amnesty would be out of character for Pilate, and that as a striking token of mercy, it would have been mentioned by Josephus,

Italian artist Antonio Ciseri (1821–1891) painted this view of Pilate showing the scourged Jesus to the crowds in 1880. The painting is known as "Ecce Homo."

ca 28 C.E.	ca 28-29 C.E.	ca 29 C.E.	ca 29 C.E.
Pilate suppresses a massive demonstration in Jerusalem; a massacre ensues	John the Baptist begins his movement in the Jordan; Jesus joins him	John the Baptist is arrested by Herod Antipas and later beheaded	Jesus leads three of John's disciples back to Galilee and begins his ministry

This detail of Pilate washing his hands over Jesus' fate is taken from the so-called "Lyversberg Passion" triptych by an unknown master. It was painted between 1460 and 1490.

French artist William-Adolphe Bouguereau (1825–1905) painted "The Flagellation of Our Lord Jesus Christ" in 1880, after exhaustive research on Roman scourging methods.

A group of soldiers then led Jesus into the courtyard of the palace, and scourged him. They clothed him in a purple cloak, and after twisting some thorns into a crown, forced the crown on his head. They struck and spat upon him, then knelt down in mocking homage, saying "Hail, King of the Jews!" When they had tired of their cruel game, they dressed him again in his clothes and led him out to be crucified (MARK 15:16-20).

SIMON OF CYRENE

Artist depictions of Jesus on his way to Golgotha, "the place of the skull," invariably show him carrying a full cross. It is true that the Romans usually forced prisoners to carry the instrument of their death themselves. There was no set "design" for such a cross, and as Roman documents indicate, crucifixions used a variety of cross configurations, including a simple upright stake. However, a full-size wooden cross, able to hold the weight of a man, is extremely heavy; some estimates put it at 300 pounds, well beyond the strength of the average Palestinian man in Antiquity.

Romans typically used a killing ground outside the city walls that could be routinely used for public executions. In Judea, moreover, wood was sparse and expensive. This has given rise to the theory that the execution grounds in Jerusalem, on the mount of Golgotha, had a set of upright wooden stakes erected for permanent use. If this was the case, then prisoners only carried the crossbeam, or *patibulum* in Latin. This crossbeam was likewise intended for repeated use, but it could be affixed to, and removed from, the upright gibbet fairly easily. Even so, the patibulum would still have weighed at least 75 pounds.

Weakened as a result of the scourging, and suffering from acute blood loss, Jesus would undoubtedly have struggled to carry this heavy beam through the narrow and uneven streets of Jerusalem. Perhaps he stumbled. According to Mark, the Romans forced a bystander, **Simon of Cyrene** (a city in North Africa), to take up Jesus' crossbeam and carry it for him (MARK 15:21). Mark refers to Simon as "the father of Alexander and Rufus." An ossuary discovered in 1941 among the tombs of the Kidron Valley, and bearing the inscription "Alexander (son) of Simon," may provide a historical attestation of this person.

The exact route that Simon and Jesus would have taken to Golgotha is impossible to ascertain, because Jerusalem was thoroughly

had it occurred. Others, however, point to evidence of amnesties elsewhere in the Roman Empire; Pliny the Younger, in one of his epistles, wrote that certain prisoners "were released upon their petition to the proconsuls, or their lieutenants." Indeed, it is possible that Pilate would, on occasion, have tried to ingratiate himself with his restless subjects. As it happened, says Mark, the prison contained various "rebels who had committed murder during the insurrection," perhaps referring to the massive protest around 28 C.E. that Pilate had so bloodily suppressed.

One of these prisoners was a convicted murderer called **Barabbas**. Turning to the crowd, Pilate offered them a choice: "Do you want me to release for you the King of the Jews?" But, says Mark, the chief priests had infiltrated the crowd, and told them to choose Barabbas instead. Pilate then asked, "What do you wish me to do with the man you call the King of the Jews?" They shouted back, "Crucify him!" (MARK 15:7-13; MATTHEW 27:16-26). Taken aback, Pilate asked, "Why, what evil has he done?" But the crowd shouted back, "Crucify him!" And so Pilate, "wishing to satisfy the crowd," released Barabbas; and after flogging Jesus, he handed him over to be crucified. In Matthew's Gospel, Pilate even used a bowl of water so he could "wash his hands" of the entire affair, saying, "I am innocent of this man's blood; see to it yourselves" (MATTHEW 27:24).

ca 30 C.E. Jesus is tried and crucified on orders of Pilate during the Passover festival	ca 34–35 C.E. Jewish followers of Jesus, led by Jesus' brother James, are increasingly marginalized	ca 35 C.E. The disciple Stephen is stoned to death by a mob	ca 35–40 C.E. Saul (that is, Paul) halts his persecution of Jewish Christians and joins the movement

destroyed—not once, but twice—by vengeful Roman armies following Jewish rebellions in 70 and 135 C.E. But most scholars accept that the Church of the Holy Sepulcher, today located in the western part of Jerusalem's Old City, just north of the old Roman *decumanus,* is the place of Jesus' Crucifixion and burial.

Mark says that the procession of Jesus and the other condemned men reached Golgotha "on the third hour," roughly around nine o'clock in the morning. Here, a special detail of Roman *immunes,* or army specialists, trained in crucifixion procedures, took over. They stripped Jesus, forced him down on the ground, and stretched his arms along the length of the crossbeam. They then nailed his arms to the wood, driving a long iron nail through the spot just below the wrist, between the radius and ulna bones of the upper forearm. Most paintings show Jesus nailed to the cross through his palms, but the soft tissue of a human hand is not strong enough to carry the weight of an adult man. The soldiers then took either side of the crossbar, raised it high over their heads, and slammed it into the open notch of

THE VIA DOLOROSA

The Via Dolorosa, or "Road of Sorrows," is the presumed path of Jesus on his way to Golgotha, the place of his execution, located in today's Old City in Jerusalem. It contains 14 so-called Stations of the Cross, although the last stations, 10 through 14, are contained within the Church of the Holy Sepulcher. The exact route, however, has traditionally been subject to intense debate because Jerusalem was entirely destroyed in 135 C.E. by Emperor Hadrian. This is why fragments of the chiseled limestone of Herod's Temple complex appear throughout structures in Jerusalem. The tradition of a Good Friday procession along the Via Dolorosa began in the Byzantine era. As more and more churches were built in Jerusalem, a variety of Via Dolorosa routes began to proliferate. Only in the 18th century did an agreed-upon route emerge, as defined by the Franciscans who since 1350 have been in charge of most holy Christian sites in Israel. ■

the nearest stake, suspending Jesus above the ground. Lastly, Jesus' ankles were squeezed into a small wooden block, shaped in the form of a U, and nailed to the cross.

In this posture, suspended by one's arms, it becomes very difficult to breathe. In order to breathe, the condemned must lift himself up; by lifting himself up, he puts strain on his nailed arms and feet, further adding pain to his torment. Thus, the agony of crucifixion is largely self-inflicted.

The purpose of public crucifixions was to serve as a deterrent for any individuals contemplating political agitation. To drive this message home, the Romans affixed a sign to Jesus' cross, which read, mockingly: "The King of the Jews." Two other men, condemned as "bandits," were crucified and set up on his right and left (MARK 15:26-27).

MARY, MOTHER OF JAMES

The Apostles, the core of Jesus' following, had fled. But three women remained steadfast by Jesus' side—another example of the uniquely

THE PARABLE OF THE GOOD SAMARITAN

In many of his teachings, Jesus uses parables, essentially allegorical stories that illustrate the point Jesus wished to make. Many of these parables use the metaphorical language of the field and the cycle of sowing and reaping; others are drawn from contemporary life that Jesus observed around him. One famous parable was inspired by the fact that many roads swarmed with thieves and militia, possibly as the result of two peasant revolts in 4 B.C.E. and 6 C.E. Once, said Jesus, a man "was going down from Jerusalem to Jericho, and fell into the hands of robbers, who stripped him, beat him, and went away, leaving him half dead" (LUKE 10:30). Two people, a priest and a Levite, passed the unconscious man and ignored him. Only the third passerby, a **Samaritan,** bandaged his wounds and took him to an

inn, where he gave the innkeeper money to pay for the victim's recovery. Jesus asked, "Which of these three, do you think, was a neighbor to the man who fell into the hands of the robbers?" The answer was, "The one who showed him mercy." Jesus nodded and said, "Go and do likewise" (LUKE 10:30-37). The purpose of the story was twofold: to illustrate the power of compassion, a key pillar of Jesus' Kingdom of God teachings, and also to denounce prejudice. Most Jews considered Samaritans—the native population of Samaria—untouchables, because they had intermarried with Babylonian settlers after the region's conquest by the Assyrian King Sargon II. ■

"The Good Samaritan Heals the Traveler," painted by Dutch artist Nicolaes Roosendael (1634–1686) around 1665, depicts the well-known parable.

prominent role Jesus' female followers played in the Gospels. They are "Mary Magdalene and **Mary the mother of James the Younger** and of **Joses**, and **Salome**" (MARK 15:40). We know Mary Magdalene; Salome is arguably the mother of Zebedee's sons, an identification that is confirmed in Matthew's Gospel (and a further indication of this family's close involvement with Jesus' ministry). The reference to the other Mary is more difficult to decipher. Earlier in his Gospel, Mark stated that Jesus had four brothers, "James and Joses and **Judas** and **Simon**" (MARK 6:3). This would indicate that the woman at the foot of the cross is none other than Mary, the mother of Jesus. But why Mark would not identify her as such, and instead refer to her other sons, James and Joses? The answer is not clear. Mary appears twice more in Mark's Passion story, but once again she is described as either "Mary the mother of Joses" or "Mary the mother of James," respectively (MARK 15:46; 16:1). Luke, too, refers to this eyewitness as "Mary the mother of James" (LUKE 24:11).

The fourth Gospel, that of John, identifies three individuals at Jesus' cross: "his mother, and his mother's sister, Mary the wife of **Clopas**, and Mary Magdalene" (JOHN 19:25). The Greek name for Clopas is **Alphaeus**. If John is correct, then *both* the mother of Jesus *and* the mother of James, son of Alphaeus, would have been standing at the cross—a tradition that is followed by most painters in Western and Eastern Orthodox art. How this bears on Mark's description is uncertain. Lastly, John's text also indicates that "Mary the wife of Clopas (c.q., Alphaeus)" was the sister of Mary, the mother of Jesus.

THE BELOVED DISCIPLE

The Gospel of John then says: "When Jesus saw his mother and the disciple whom he loved standing beside her, he said to his mother, "Woman, here is your son." Then he said to the disciple, "Here is your mother" (JOHN 19:26-27).

The "Deposition from the Cross" is the product of the workshop of the Master of St. Lawrence, painted ca 1425. It depicts Jesus being removed from the cross, surrounded by grief-stricken supporters.

This verse has given rise to another mystery, namely, which beloved disciple is Jesus referring to? John states that there were only three women standing at the cross, so the most obvious candidate would be Mary Magdalene. Why then would Jesus call the Magdalene "your son?" Some have interpreted this as Jesus' deliberate attempt to elevate her to the status of a male Apostle; support for this theory comes from the Gospel of Thomas, in which Jesus says about Mary Magdalene: "Behold, I shall lead her, that I may make her male, in order that she also may become a living spirit like you males."

Many authors, however, have argued that Jesus is referring to the man who appears elsewhere in this Gospel as "the beloved disciple," whom Christian tradition has identified as John the Evangelist himself (JOHN 13:23-25). Others believe that this Gospel is referring to the emerging *ekklesia,* the community of early Christians, and that Jesus charges Mary to serve as their patroness.

JOSEPH OF ARIMATHEA

At noontime, says Mark, darkness came over the whole land, and three hours later, Jesus cried out with a loud voice, *"Eloi, Eloi, lema sabachthani?"* which means, "My God, my God, why have you forsaken me?"—a well-known Jewish cry of anguish from the Book of Psalms (MARK 15:33-34; PSALMS 22:1). He then "gave a loud cry" and breathed his last. Jesus' body hung lifeless on the cross. His agony had lasted six hours—a mercifully short time, to judge by Roman sources. The other condemned men were arguably still alive by sunset, for in the Gospel of John, the Romans then began to break their legs (JOHN 19:32). Without the use of their legs, the victims could not push themselves up to breathe, and thus slowly suffocated. Jesus was already dead, but one soldier used his lance to pierce Jesus' side, just to make sure (JOHN 19:34).

ca 40 C.E.	ca 40 C.E.	ca 41 C.E.	ca 41 C.E.
One of the first Christian churches is built in Corinth	Greek sailors use monsoon winds to sail to southern India	Agrippa I, grandson of Herod the Great, is appointed king of Roman Judea	Emperor Claudius confirms the right of Jews to observe their religious practices in the Empire

In the meantime, however, a prominent Jew had secured an audience with Pilate. His name was **Joseph of Arimathea**. Mark describes him as a member of the Sanhedrin, as we previously noted, and quite possibly a follower of Jesus, because he too was "waiting expectantly for the kingdom of God" that Jesus had talked about (MARK 15:43). He asked Pilate for the body of Jesus, which was a bold request indeed; the condemned were usually deposited in a tomb reserved for the executed, or worse, in a pit to serve as carrion. Pilate was surprised to hear that Jesus was already dead, knowing that crucified men could live for a day or more. He summoned the **centurion**, and the officer did confirm that Jesus had been dead for some time. Only then did Pilate grant Joseph his request.

Joseph "brought a linen cloth" and used it to wrap Jesus' body, possibly with the help of the three women, before placing it in a tomb "that had been hewn out of a rock." Such tombs were expensive; quite possibly it was a cavern that Joseph had intended as his own burial place. Luke adds that it was a "rock-hewn tomb where no one had ever been laid" (LUKE 23:53). The Gospel of John adds another character to the scene, a man named **Nicodemus**, who brought "a mixture of myrrh and aloes, weighing about a hundred" to anoint the corpse and thus cover the odors of incipient decomposition (JOHN 19:39). The Synoptic Gospels, however, clearly indicate that the body was not anointed because the burial party was simply running out of time. Night was falling, ushering in the Sabbath, when funerary services were prohibited.

Bone dice from the Roman period are perhaps similar to the dice that the soldiers rolled to divide the garments of Jesus.

This is why, "when the Sabbath was over," the three woman who had witnessed the Crucifixion once again returned to the tomb, this time carrying "spices so that they might go and anoint him" (MARK 16:1). As they approached the tomb, they were worried how they were going to roll away the heavy stone at the entrance to the tomb. But when they arrived, they saw that "the stone, which was very large, had already been rolled back." Inside was a young man, dressed in a white robe, who said, "Do not be alarmed; you are looking for Jesus of Nazareth, who was crucified. He has been raised; he is not here" (MARK 16:6). The women were seized with "terror and amazement," but the man continued: "Tell his disciples and Peter that he is going ahead of you to Galilee; there you will see him, just as he told you." The women then fled from the tomb, and "they said nothing to anyone, for they were afraid" (MARK 16:6-8).

Michelangelo Caravaggio (1571–1610) painted "The Incredulity of St. Thomas" ca 1603. Thomas said he must see the marks on Jesus' body to believe he had risen from the dead.

THOMAS

Soon after this event, sightings of the risen Jesus were reported throughout Judea and Galilee. Sometimes Jesus appeared as a man of flesh and blood; at other times, he was an ephemeral being. In the Gospel of John, Jesus revealed himself to Mary Magdalene but told her "not to hold on to me, because I have not yet ascended to the Father" (JOHN 20:17). Luke relates how two of Jesus' followers were traveling on the road to Emmaus when they met a stranger who hadn't heard about the tragic Passover events. Perplexed, the two followers told him "about Jesus of Nazareth, who was a prophet mighty in deed and word." Later that evening, when the stranger broke bread and blessed it, their eyes were opened and they recognized Jesus, who vanished from their eyes (LUKE 24:13-31).

In another story from John's Gospel, the fearful Apostles had locked themselves in a house, when suddenly Jesus appeared among them and said, "Peace be with you." He then showed them his hands and his side. After Jesus disappeared, Thomas the Apostle joined them and could not believe that Jesus had risen. "Unless I see the mark of the nails in his hands, and put my finger in the mark of the nails in his side," he said, "I will not believe." A week later, the disciples were once again in the house when Jesus reappeared before them. Turning to Thomas, Jesus said, "Put your finger here and see my hands. Reach out your hand and put it in my side. Do not doubt but believe." And Thomas believed (JOHN 20:19-28).

Gold Cups *Solid gold cups such as this fine sample from the early Roman period (first century C.E.), found near Knidos, today's Turkey, are rare.*

Silver Mirror *This lovely silver mirror with handle, crafted in the first century, was excavated in Cologne, Germany.*

Glass Flask *The introduction of the glassblowing technique in Palestine around 50 B.C.E. revolutionized glassmaking, as shown by this delicate Roman flask.*

Hair Combs *Combs of this type have been found in both Palestine and Egypt throughout the period of Roman occupation.*

Golden Jewelry *This bracelet featuring facing lion heads was excavated in Greece, a Roman province since the second century B.C.E.*

Terra-Cotta Vessel *In sharp contrast to the Roman glass flask, this terra-cotta vessel is more typical of the simple earthenware most Judeans used in the first century C.E.*

TREASURES OF THE ROMAN AGE

Cameo Pendant *This first-century cameo depicts Emperor Augustus wearing the rayed crown of the sun god.*

T he arrival of the Romans in Palestine, following Pompey's conquest of 63 B.C.E., introduced the upper classes of Judea to the refinement of Roman art, including glassware, silverware, and other fine implements. Even before the Early Imperial period, affluent Romans had begun to advertise their cultural sophistication by filling their homes with fashionable decorative arts produced throughout the new Roman possessions. Foremost among these was Greece, which—although a Roman province since the mid-second century B.C.E.—continued to hold Romans in thrall with its exquisite sense of style. Greek artisans catered to this need with a large number of workshops that produced everything from red-figure vases to fine jewelry, as well as copies of classical Greek statuary and paintings—most of which are now lost. By contrast, glassware was a uniquely Roman specialty that slowly percolated throughout the Roman Empire, in part because of the revolutionary invention of the blowpipe.

The artistry of these fine Roman artifacts stands in sharp contrast to the humble earthenware that the less affluent—the vast majority of workers and peasants—continued to use throughout Palestine in the period of Roman occupation.

Silver Strainer *In the ancient world, wine was usually diluted with water prior to consumption, as attested by this first-century C.E. silver wine strainer from an affluent Roman household.*

Terra-Cotta Plates *These two simple terra-cotta plates are typical of the type peasant families in Judea and Galilee used during the first century C.E.*

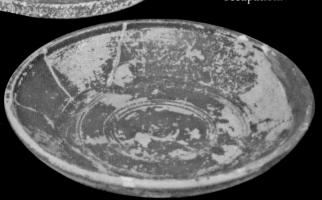

Glass Urn *This lovely glass container from the first century C.E. reveals the sheer artistry of Roman glassmaking made possible by the introduction of the blowpipe.*

CHAPTER 4
WHO'S WHO

An Alphabetical Listing of Characters in the Gospels of Matthew, Mark, Luke, and John

ALEXANDER
("defender of men")
Son of Simon of Cyrene, who was compelled by the Romans to bear the cross for Jesus (MARK 15:21). An ossuary discovered in 1941 among the tombs of the Kidron Valley, and bearing the inscription "Alexander (son) of Simon," may provide powerful attestation of this individual.

ALPHAEUS
("thousand")
1. Father of the Apostle James the Younger (MATTHEW 10:3; MARK 3:18; LUKE 6:15; ACTS 1:13). The Hebrew version of "Alphaeus" is Cleophas, or Clopas. John refers to a woman named "Mary, the wife of Clopas," who stood by the cross of Jesus; this may suggest that this Mary was the mother of James (JOHN 19:25).
2. Father of Levi the tax collector; Levi was later known as the Apostle Matthew (MARK 2:14).

ANDREW
("manly")
One of Jesus' first Apostles and Simon Peter's brother (JOHN 1:40; MATTHEW 4:18). According to the Gospel of John, Andrew was born in Bethsaida, served as a disciple of John the Baptist, and was the first disciple chosen by Jesus. He then brought his brother Simon to Jesus, having told him, "We have found the Messiah" (JOHN 1:38-41). According to the Gospel of Mark, Jesus spotted Andrew and Simon "casting a net into the sea—for they were fishermen." Jesus said to them, "Follow me and I will make you fish for men" (MARK 1:16-17). Andrew brought the boy with loaves and fishes to Jesus' attention, which he then used to feed 5,000.

While Peter, James, and John stand out in the Synoptic Gospels, Andrew and Philip appear to have considerable prominence in the Gospel of John.

ANNAS
("gracious")
High priest of the Temple in Jerusalem, appointed at age 36 in 6 C.E. by the Romans, though later deposed by Roman procurator Valerius Gratus. By the Mosaic Law, the high priesthood was held for life; thus, even though the Romans had deposed Annas, he still may have commanded considerable respect (NUMBERS 3:10). This may explain why according to the Gospel of John, Jesus was first brought before Annas, and after a brief questioning was sent to Caiaphas (JOHN 18:19-23). As it happened, Caiaphas was married to Annas's daughter, and was therefore his son-in-law. He was raised to the office of priesthood himself in 18 C.E. In fact, no less than eight members of Annas's family held this supreme office, which underscores the close ties of the family to the Herodian dynasty as well as to the Romans. According-ing to the Book of Acts, Annas was president of the Sanhedrin when Peter and John were brought before this council (ACTS 4:6).

ANTIPATER
("in place of the father")
Father of King Herod, and founder of the Herodian dynasty. He formed part of an embassy sent by the Jewish people to renew a peace treaty with the Romans (I MACCABEES 12:16; 14:22).

ARCHELAUS
("prince of the people")
Son of Herod the Great by Malthace, a Samaritan woman, and ethnarch of Judea, Samaria, and Idumea from 4 B.C.E. to 6 C.E. (MATTHEW 2:22). He was probably educated along with his brother Antipas at Rome, and was named by his father, Herod the Great, as one of his successors. Consequently, at Herod's death, his kingdom was divided between his three sons, Antipas, Archelaus, and Philip. Neither inherited the coveted

Artist James Jacques Joseph Tissot (1836–1902) created the painting depicting "Annas and Caiaphas" ca 1886–1894.

title of king; instead, Archelaus had to accept the title of ethnarch, "ruler of the people." In the ninth or tenth year of his reign, his brothers brought a complaint against him on the grounds of tyranny. As a consequence, Archelaus was banished to Vienne in Gaul, where he is said to have died ten years later; meanwhile, his territory became a Roman province, to be ruled by a Roman procurator. In the Gospel of Matthew, Joseph and Mary turned aside on their way back from Egypt for fear of Archelaus and settled in Galilee, which was ruled by Archelaus's brother Herod Antipas.

A bronze coin with a boat dates from the period of Herod Archelaus, king of Judea (ruled 4 B.C.E.–6 C.E.).

ARETAS

King of Aram-Damascus (Syria), and father-in-law of Herod Antipas, son of Herod the Great. His daughter returned to Aretas when Herod Antipas decided to marry Herod Philip's wife, Herodias. This led to a war between Aretas and Herod Antipas, during which Herod's army was defeated (ACTS 9:25; II CORINTHIANS 11:32; LUKE 3:19-20; MARK 6:17; MATTHEW 14:3).

AUGUSTUS

("venerable")

Gaius Octavius, or Octavian, later known as Caesar Augustus, was the first Roman emperor during whose reign Jesus was born (LUKE 2:1). According to Luke, his decree that "all the world should be taxed" was the occasion of Jesus' being born, according to prophecy, in Bethlehem (MICAH 5:2). Octavian's father was Gaius Octavius; his mother was Atia, daughter of Julia and the sister of Julius Caesar. Upon the assassination of Julius Caesar, Octavian learned he was to be his heir, and was taken into the triumvirate with Antony and Lepidus, who divided jurisdiction over the empire among themselves. This led to a struggle for supreme power, which ended in favor of Octavian at the Battle of Actium. On this victory, he was saluted

as imperator by the Senate, who conferred the title of Augustus on him. The first link binding him to New Testament history is his treatment of King Herod after the Battle of Actium. The king, who had chosen Antony's side, found himself pardoned, taken into favor, and confirmed in his power. After Herod's death, Augustus divided his dominions, almost exactly according to Herod's dying directions, among his sons. Augustus died in Nola in Campania in his 76th year. Before his death, he designed Tiberius as his heir (LUKE 3:1).

B

BARABBAS

("son of the father")

A robber or murderer whom Pilate proposed to condemn to death, instead of Jesus (JOHN 18:40; MARK 15:7; LUKE 23:19). Turning to "the crowd" that had gathered in front of him, Pilate offered them a choice: "Do you want me to release for you the King of the Jews?" Anticipating this, "the chief priests stirred up the crowd to have him release Barabbas for them instead." Pilate then asked, "What do you wish me to do with the man you call the King of the Jews?" They shouted back, "Crucify him!" (MARK 15:7-13;

MATTHEW 27:16-26). Mark claims that it was Pilate's custom to grant such amnesties, that "at the festival he used to release a prisoner for them" (MARK 15:6), but this is not attested in any documents of the period that specifically refer to Pilate. Some historians question why Pilate would have risked releasing a convicted "rebel" at the beginning of the volatile week of Passover. Others, however, point to evidence that, on occasion, other Roman governors did publicly pardon malefactors, or that people were occasionally released on special holy days.

BARACHIAH

("God blessed")

Father of Zechariah, who according to Matthew was "murdered between the temple and the altar" (MATTHEW 23:35).

BARTHOLOMEW

("son of Tolmai")

One of the 12 Apostles, an "Israelite indeed" (JOHN 1:47), and believed by some to have been the same person as Nathanael (MATTHEW 10:3; ACTS 1:13). In the Synoptic Gospels, Philip and Bartholomew are always mentioned together, while Nathanael is never mentioned; in the fourth Gospel, Philip and Nathanael are similarly mentioned together, but nothing is said of Bartholomew. Bartholomew was one of the disciples to whom Jesus appeared at the Sea of Tiberias after his Resurrection (JOHN 21:2), and was also a witness of the Ascension (ACTS 1:4,12-13).

BARTIMAEUS

("son of Timaeus")

A blind beggar in Jericho who sat by the wayside begging as Jesus passed out of Jericho on his journey to Jerusalem. His blindness was cured on the grounds of his faith. Matthew refers to two blind men outside Jericho who were healed, but he does not provide names (MARK 10:46; MATTHEW 20:30).

BEELZEBUL (OR BAALZEBUB)

("lord of the flies")

Name given to Satan, "the prince of demons." In the Gospels, the scribes of Jerusalem accused Jesus of being "possessed by

Pontius Pilate offers the crowd a choice between releasing Jesus or Barabbas in this illustration from the Codex of Predis of 1476.

Beelzebul" (MATTHEW 10:25; MARK 3:22). The character may be the same as Baal-zebub, the god of the Philistine city of Ekron (II KINGS 1:2).

BELOVED DISCIPLE

The Gospel of John makes four references to the "beloved disciple," a character who does not appear in the other three Gospels—those of Matthew, Mark, and Luke—at least not under that title. Jesus is obviously very attached to this Apostle. Several times, John reiterates that this is someone "whom Jesus loved." It is he who reclines next to Jesus at the Last Supper and asks Jesus, at Peter's urging, who of the 12 will betray him. After Jesus has been nailed to the cross, Jesus looks down at Mary and the beloved disciple and says to Mary, "Woman, here is your son," and, to the disciple, "Here is your mother." And, says John, "from that hour the disciple took her into his own home" (JOHN 19:26-27). Later on, when John's Gospel tells us that the Apostles have returned to Galilee to resume their old trades, the disciple is one of the seven fishermen who net a miraculous catch of 153 fish.

The one name that is conspicuously missing from these narratives is John, son of Zebedee, which has fueled speculation that the Gospel is, in fact, referring to this Apostle as "the beloved disciple." Tradition has further suggested that John, son of Zebedee, is one and the same as John the Evangelist, but the dating of John's Gospel makes this less certain. If it is true that the Gospel of John was written in the last decade of the first century C.E., it is unlikely that it could have been written by a direct contemporary of Jesus. John's Gospel does state that its account is based on the testimony of "the beloved disciple," and adds in its final paragraphs that "this is the disciple who is testifying to these things and has written them, and we know that his testimony is true." There is, therefore, every reason to suggest that the author of the Gospel of John may have had access to a written testimonial attributed to the beloved Apostle from Jesus' immediate circle.

CAESAR

Title assumed by Roman emperors after Julius Caesar. In the New Testament, this title is given to various emperors as sovereigns of Judea without their accompanying distinctive proper names (JOHN 19:15; ACTS 17:7). The Jews were expected to pay tribute to Caesar imperator; all Roman citizens

Dutch artist Gerard van Honthorst (1592–1656) painted "Christ Before Caiaphas" around 1617.

had the right of appeal to him (MATTHEW 22:17; ACTS 25:11). All Caesars, or emperors, referred to in the New Testament are Augustus, Tiberius, Claudius, and Nero (LUKE 2:1; 3:1; 20:22; ACTS 11:28; 25:8; PHILIPPIANS 4:22).

CAIAPHAS

Annas's son-in law and Jewish high priest from 18 to 36 C.E., during the reign of Tiberius, while Pilate was procurator of Judea and Samaria. Thus, he was in office at the beginning of Jesus' public ministry, during his condemnation and his Crucifixion (LUKE 3:2; MATTHEW 26:3,57; JOHN 11:49;

18:13-14). He was believed to be a member of the Sadducees, and as high priest the person who presided over the indictment of Jesus. According to the Gospels, Caiaphas had no power to condemn a man to death, and therefore sent Jesus to Pilate, the Roman governor, to pronounce the sentence against him (MATTHEW 27:2; JOHN 18:28).

CENTURION
("hundred")

A centurion, *ekatóntarchos* in Greek, was an officer in charge of a hundred soldiers in the Roman army, roughly comparable to the modern rank of sergeant major. There were 60 centurions in each legion of 6,000 men.

1. Centurion at Capernaum, who came to Jesus with a message that his servant was gravely ill. Jesus said to him, " 'I will come and cure him,' but the centurion answered, 'Lord, I am not worthy to have you come under my roof; but only speak the word, and my servant will be healed.'" Jesus, amazed by the faith of one who was clearly not a Jew, replied, "Truly I tell you, in no one in Israel have I found such faith" (MATTHEW 8:6-10). And, says Matthew, the servant was healed that very moment.

2. Centurion on Golgotha, who was the eyewitness at the moment of Jesus' death. Executions were usually carried out by a detail of Roman *immunes,* or army specialists, trained in crucifixion procedures, under command of a centurion. Sometime later that day, Joseph of Arimathea petitioned Pilate for the release of Jesus' body. "Pilate," says Mark, "summoning the centurion . . . asked him whether he had been dead for some time" (MARK 15:45). The centurion confirmed that Jesus was indeed dead.

CHIEF PRIESTS

The Gospels sometimes refer to the "chief priests" (MATTHEW 2:4; 26:3). The priesthood itself was a large society of clergymen, some 7,200 in number, who were divided into 24 courses, or families. Sixteen of these were Zadokite and eight were descendants of Ithamar. Each family group was responsible for one week of service in the Temple, so each family served for at least two weeks a year, in addition to festivals. Some 200 senior priests with direct responsibility for the sacrificial rites supervised the actual Temple operations, as well as the Temple treasury and the gathering of various tithes from across the Jewish world. It is possible that many of these chief priests were either close allies or relatives of the Annas dynasty, which controlled the office of the high priest for much of the first century.

CHUZA
("the seer")
The house steward of Herod Antipas (LUKE 8:3).

CLEOPAS
("of a renowned father")
One of the two disciples with whom Jesus conversed on the way to Emmaus about the day of the Resurrection (LUKE 24:18). The name is probably a contraction of the Greek "Cleopatros."

CLOPAS
Name of the husband of Mary, one of the women who stood by the cross of Christ. Because Clopas is the Hebrew version of Alphaeus, it is possible that Clopas was also the father of the Apostle James the Younger (MATTHEW 10:3; JOHN 19:25).

ELIAKIM
("raised up by God")
1. Son of Hilkiah, deputy of Hezekiah (II KINGS 18:18; 19:2; ISAIAH 36:3,11,22; 37:2).
2. Original name of Jehoiakim, king of Judah (II KINGS 23:34; II CHRONICLES 36:4).
3. A priest (NEHEMIAH 12:41).
4. Son of Melea (LUKE 3:30).
5. Son of Abiud (MATTHEW 1:13).

ELIZABETH
("the oath of God")

A detail from a triptych by a Flemish artist working between 1466 and 1500 shows Mary and her cousin Elizabeth.

Wife of Zechariah, cousin of Mary, and mother of John the Baptist (LUKE 1:5-60). The angel Gabriel appeared to Elizabeth's husband, who was a member of the "priestly order of Abijah" (LUKE 1:5). Zechariah was taken aback by the angel's appearance, so Gabriel said, "Do not be afraid, Zechariah, for your prayer has been heard." And Gabriel continued: "Your wife Elizabeth shall bear you a son, and you will name him John. You will have joy and gladness, for he will be great in the sight of the Lord" (LUKE 1:13-15). Indeed, Elizabeth gave birth to a son despite her advanced age.

Gabriel then brought Mary the news that she, too, would give birth to a son, named Jesus. When Mary protested that she was a virgin, the angel Gabriel replied that "the Holy Spirit will come upon you, and the power of the Most High will overshadow you" (LUKE 1:34-35). So as to underscore God's power, the angel added that "your relative Elizabeth in her old age has also conceived a son . . . for nothing will be impossible with God." Mary then set out to visit her cousin Elizabeth; when Elizabeth saw Mary and heard her voice, she thought: "the babe in my womb leaped for joy" (LUKE 1:42-44).

ESSENES
One of the religious factions in late Second Temple Judaism, in addition to the Sadducees and Pharisees. During the polarization of Jewish society under the Hasmoneans over the controversy whether a Jewish king could also serve as high priest, one group withdrew from social life altogether. This community, called "the Essenes" by the Jewish historian Josephus, formed a monastic community to pursue an ascetic lifestyle entirely based on Covenant Law. They were outraged by the Hasmonean usurpation of the office of high priest, which traditionally was reserved for descendants of the priest Zadok. The Essenes dressed in simple robes, prayed at regular intervals, and worked long hours tilling the desert soil. They dug an elaborate network of cisterns to catch the rainfall, or to channel water from nearby springs, so that they could practice ritual immersion on a daily basis. On the Sabbath, they even withheld their bodily functions. The purpose of this ascetic lifestyle, practiced under the leadership of a "Teacher of Righteousness" (significantly, a Zadokite), was to bring the Essenes closer to God.

Several scholars have suggested that John the Baptist may have been a member of the community of Qumran, which in itself could have been a faction within the Essene movement. Both John and the Essenes advocated the sharing of possessions, and subsisted on a spartan diet. What's more, both John and Jesus were referred to as teachers, as was the leader of the Qumran community (LUKE 3:12; JOHN 3:26).

HELI
("ascending")
Father of Joseph, husband of Mary (LUKE 13:23).

HEROD ANTIPAS
Tetrarch of Galilee and Perea from 4 B.C.E. to 39 C.E. whose reign coincided with the time of Jesus' boyhood and adulthood in Galilee.

Antipas was a son of Herod the Great by his Samaritan wife, Malthace, and brother of Archelaus and Philip (MATTHEW 2:22). He first married the daughter of Aretas, a king of Arabia, then divorced her to marry Herodias, the wife of his half brother, Herod Philip. In revenge, King Aretas invaded Herod's territory and defeated him. A passage from Josephus attributes this defeat as retribution for Antipas's murder of John the Baptist (MATTHEW 14:4). Prompted by his wife, Antipas traveled to Rome to meet with Caligula to secure further power, but instead he was banished to Lugdunum for the rest of his life (MARK 6:14). Like his father, Herod Antipas was responsible for major building projects, including the reconstruction of Sepphoris and the building of a new city on the Sea of Galilee, called Tiberias.

HEROD PHILIP
("horse-loving")
Tetrarch of Iturea, Gaulanitis, and Trachonitis from 4 B.C.E. to 34 C.E., and the only son of Herod who retained his position until his death. Philip was the son of Herod the Great by his wife, Mariamne, the daughter of Simon, the high priest. According to the Gospel of Mark, he was married to Herodias, the sister of Agrippa I, by whom he had a daughter, Salome; though later, Herodias divorced Philip to marry Philip's half brother Herod Antipas, a marriage that was denounced by John the Baptist (MARK 6:17; MATTHEW 16:13; LUKE 3:1). Historically, however, Philip was married to Salome, the daughter of Antipas and Herodias.

HEROD THE GREAT
("hero-like")
Governor of Galilee and later king of Judea, including of all the Jewish territories. Herod was the second son of Antipater, an Idumean Julius Caesar chose to appoint as epitropos, or chief minister, of Judea during the reign of Hyrcanus II, the last Hasmonean king and a vassal of Rome.

Antipater divided his territories among his sons, placing Herod in charge of the government of Galilee and, later, Coele-Syria. During the Roman civil war between Octavian and Mark Antony on the one hand, and Caesar's assassins, Brutus and Cassius, on the other, Antipater and Herod chose the side of Cassius. One reason may have been that Cassius was in closer proximity to Judea, having established himself in Syria to raise new legions to defeat Mark Antony. Herod levied punishing taxes on the Galilean farmers and thus raised the funds that Cassius needed to raise his legions. Later, when Judea was invaded by the Parthians, the Roman Senate confirmed Herod as king of Judea, and equipped him with a Roman army with which he proceeded to oust the Parthians as well as all those factions opposed to him, and established his 33-year rule.

During this period, Herod enjoyed a greater autonomy and latitude than any other Roman vassal king in the region, while enriching Judea and Samaria with many vainglorious building projects. Chief among these was the new harbor complex at Caesarea, on the Mediterranean coast, and the vast expansion of the Second Temple precinct. He also built strong defensive redoubts at strategic points around his kingdom, including the fortresses of Masada, Herodion, and Machaereus. In the Gospel of Matthew, Herod is depicted issuing an edict to slay all firstborn Jewish sons in Bethlehem, because he felt threatened by the prophecy of the birth of the "King of the Jews," although this event is not attested in the other Gospels, nor in the literature of the period (MATTHEW 2:1-22; LUKE 1:5; ACTS 23:35).

"King Herod the Great" was painted by James Jacques Joseph Tissot (1836–1902).

Elisabetta Sirani (1638–1665) painted the canvas "Herodias With the Head of John the Baptist."

In May 2007, a team of Israeli archaeologists led by Ehud Netzer announced that they had located a tomb halfway up the hill of the Herodion, which they claim once held Herod's body.

HERODIAS
("feminine version of Herod; hero-like")
Daughter of Aristobulus, a son of Mariamne and Herod the Great, and consequently sister of Agrippa I. According to Josephus, she married Herod Beothus, a private citizen living in Rome, but the Gospels of Mark and Matthew claim that she first married the Tetrarch Philip, and later wed the Tetrarch Herod Antipas, her step-uncle. In the Gospels, she is the one who suggests that her daughter Salome ask for the head of John the Baptist, because John had denounced her marriage to Antipas (MATTHEW 14:8-11; MARK 6:24-28; LUKE 3:19).

J

JAIRUS
A ruler of the synagogue at Capernaum who beseeched Jesus to come and heal his

daughter who was gravely ill. Before Jesus could go to his house, the news arrived that the daughter had already died. "Why trouble the teacher any further?" the people said. Nevertheless, Jesus set out for Jairus's house. When they arrived, the house was full of people weeping and wailing loudly. But Jesus said, "Why do you make a commotion and weep? The child is not dead, but sleeping." He ordered everyone out of the house, and asked the child's father and mother to take him to the dead girl's room. And, says Mark, "he took her by the hand and said to her, *'Talitha cum,'*" which means, "Little girl, get up!" And immediately the girl got up and began to walk about (MARK 5:22; MATTHEW 9:18,23-26; LUKE 8:41).

JAMES, BROTHER OF JESUS
("supplanter")

The Gospel of Mark records how the people of Nazareth said to one another, "Is this not the carpenter *(tektōn),* the son of Mary and brother of James and Joses and Judas and Simon, and are not his sisters here with us?" (MARK 6:3). Ten years after the Crucifixion, James had become the leader of the "church in Jerusalem," as distinct from the Christian communities in Asia Minor, which included both Jews and Gentiles (ACTS 12:17). An observant Jew himself, James was not in a position to deny Paul his mission among the Gentiles, but he did insist that Gentile converts abstain from idolatry and illicit sexual activity, and pledged not to eat any meat of an animal that had been strangled or still contained any blood (ACTS 15:20).

JAMES, FATHER OF JUDAS

James, father (or brother) of Judas the disciple, who may be the disciple known in the Gospel of John as Thaddaeus—to distinguish him from Judas Iscariot. This Judas only appears in the Gospel of Luke (LUKE 6:16).

JAMES, SON OF ALPHAEUS

One of the 12 Apostles in the Synoptic Gospels (MARK 2:14). Some scholars believe he is identical to James, son of Clopas, given that Clopas is the Hebrew name of Alphaeus.

JAMES, SON OF CLOPAS

James, son of Clopas, was the disciple whose mother Mary is mentioned as being witness to the Crucifixion (JOHN 19:25). It is possible that James, son of Clopas, and James, son of Alphaeus, are one and the same.

JAMES, SON OF ZEBEDEE

James, son of Zebedee, was one of Jesus' 12 Apostles, with his brother John. The Gospel of Matthew depicts Jesus walking along the shore of the Sea of Galilee until he saw two brothers, "James [the] son of Zebedee and his brother John, in the boat with their father Zebedee, mending their nets" (MATTHEW 4:18-21). "And," says the Gospel of Mark, "they left their father Zebedee in the

This drawing of Jesus was made by Leonardo da Vinci (1452–1519) as a study for his "Last Supper" around 1495.

boat with the hired men, and followed him" (MARK 1:20; 3:14; MATTHEW 10:2). According to Luke, James and John, sons of Zebedee, "were partners *(koinōnoi)* with Simon," which may suggest that they fished in partnership, perhaps having a joint lease on a boat. Later, James and John were present, together with Peter, during the Transfiguration of Jesus on Mount Tabor (MARK 9:3-7). Matthew relates how later in Jesus' ministry, the mother of James and John actively lobbied for the advancement of her sons,

insisting that "these two sons of mine will sit, one at your right hand and one at your left, in your kingdom," to which Jesus responds, "You do not know what you're asking" (MATTHEW 20:20-22). In the Synoptic Gospels, Peter, James, and John are the most prominent disciples. According to Josephus and the Book of Acts, King Agrippa I (ruled 37–44 C.E.) ordered the execution of James, the son of Zebedee, around 44 C.E. during the suppression of Jewish Christians in Judea (ACTS 12:2).

JESUS

Like "Joshua" or "Hosea," the name Jesus, or "Yeshua" in Aramaic, is a contraction of *Yehoshuah,* meaning "YHWH is salvation"; as such, it was a very common name in Judea and Galilee. According to the Gospels of Matthew and Luke, Jesus was born in Bethlehem to Mary and Joseph during the reign of King Herod. Before, the angel Gabriel had appeared to Mary and told her she would conceive and give birth to a child, and to name the child "Jesus." While in Bethlehem, and unable to find a room in the inn, Mary gave birth in a stable (LUKE 2:6-7). According to the same Nativity accounts, magi came from the east with gifts to see the child that was born the "King of the Jews." In Matthew's Gospel, Joseph had a dream in which an angel told him to take his wife and son and flee to Egypt, as Herod was planning on killing Jesus by ordering all male babies to be murdered; after their Egyptian sojourn, they moved to Nazareth.

When Jesus was 12 years old, he went to Jerusalem for Passover with his parents. After the festival, Mary and Joseph started the journey back to Nazareth, but realized Jesus was not with them. Jesus had remained in Jerusalem, talking with scholars in the Temple. Those in the Temple were impressed by Jesus' intelligence and understanding.

When Jesus was about 30 years old, he was baptized by John in the Jordan River. This event is one of the few episodes in Jesus' life reported in all four Gospels, with few differences. After John's arrest by Herod Antipas, some of John the Baptist's disciples gravitated to Jesus, who took them back to

Galilee. There, he launched his ministry with a sermon in the synagogue of Capernaum. He then preached all around Galilee, culminating in his major discourse, the Sermon on the Mount. During this time, he performed many healing miracles, many reported across the Gospels, as well as nature miracles, which have less attestation.

At some point in his campaign, Jesus felt that he had failed to move the Galileans to repent and embrace his vision for a "Kingdom of God" on earth. "Woe to you, Chorazin!" he cries in the Gospels of both Luke and Matthew; "woe to you, Bethsaida! If the powerful deeds performed among you had been done in Tyre and Sidon, they would have changed their ways long ago, sitting in sackcloth and ashes!" (MATTHEW 11:21; LUKE 10:13).

This is when Jesus decided to travel to Jerusalem, the spiritual heart and center of the country. As the Passover festival drew near, Jesus entered Jerusalem to cheering crowds. But shortly thereafter, while in the Temple, Jesus was incensed by the trade in currency and sacrificial animals, which had been moved into the Temple forecourt. He overthrew the tables of the money changers, crying, "you have made it a den of robbers" (JEREMIAH 7:11; MARK 11:15-17). According to Mark, this event made him a wanted man, for as soon as "the chief priests and the scribes heard it, they kept looking for a way to kill him" (MARK 11:18). Following the Last Supper with his disciples, he was betrayed in the Garden of Gethsemane by a kiss from Judas Iscariot, and arrested. Jesus was questioned by a faction of the Sanhedrin, the priestly council presided by the high priest Caiaphas, and subsequently condemned by Pontius Pilate, the Roman procurator of Judea.

After these hearings, Jesus was scourged and sent to Calvary. The Roman soldiers wrote "King of the Jews" on his cross as passersby mocked him. The Gospels offer different versions of Jesus' final moments; according to Mark, Jesus cried out with a loud voice, *"Eloi, Eloi, lema sabachthani?"* which means, "My God, my God, why have you forsaken me?" (MARK 15:33-34).

Following his death, Joseph of Arimathea asked that Jesus' body be removed from the cross. His body was wrapped in clean cloth and taken to a tomb for burial.

A few days after the body was placed in the tomb, some of his followers discovered the tomb to be empty. According to the Gospels, Jesus then appeared before several disciples after this death (ACTS 1:1-11; 7:55; 9:10-18; 10:37-38; 19:4; I CORINTHIANS 11:23-26; JOHN

This panel of John the Baptist is the work of the German artist Georg Pencz (1500–1550).

1:28-37,46; 2:13-20; 3:34; 6:58-59; 7:16,42; 10:40-42; 13:26-27; 14:10; 18:1-36; 19:2-27; 20:12-15; LUKE 1:5,31-38; 2:1-22,41,52; 3:1-23; 4:16; 9:18-36,22; 23:7-28; 24:4; MARK 1:9-11; 6:3,8; 9:2-8; 14:22-61; 15:17-39; 16:5-9; MATTHEW 1:1-12,19-20; 2:1-23; 3:13-17; 4:18-20 11:27; 13:55; 17:1-9; 27:29-66; 28:5; PSALMS 118:25-26; TIMOTHY 3:16).

JOANNA
("grace of God")

1. Ancestor of Jesus, son of Rhesa, and grandson of Zerubbabel; he is also known as Hananiah (I CHRONICLES 3:19; LUKE 3:27).
2. Wife of Chuza, the steward of Herod Antipas (LUKE 8:3).

JOHN, SON OF ZEBEDEE
("graced by God")

An Apostle, born to Zebedee and his wife, Salome, and brother of James. The Gospel of Matthew depicts Jesus walking along the shore of the Sea of Galilee until he saw two brothers, "James [the] son of Zebedee and his brother John, in the boat with their father Zebedee, mending their nets" (MATTHEW 4:18-21). "And," says the Gospel of Mark, "they left their father Zebedee in the boat with the hired men, and followed him" (MARK 1:20; 3:14; MATTHEW 10:2). Later, James and John were present, together with Peter, during the Transfiguration of Jesus on Mount Tabor (MARK 9:3-7). Matthew relates how later in Jesus' ministry, the mother of James and John actively lobbied for the advancement of her sons, insisting that "these two sons of mine will sit, one at your right hand and one at your left, in your kingdom," to which Jesus responds, "you do not know what you're asking" (MATTHEW 20:20-22).

According to tradition, John continued to play a prominent role in the early Church after Jesus' death and Resurrection. In the Book of Acts, he was present when Peter healed the lame man near the Temple and was subsequently arrested, together with Peter, and thrown in prison. Later, he may have followed Paul's example and left Palestine for other centers of Christian activity. It is therefore plausible, as Church church teachings suggest, that John eventually wound up in

Italian artist Marco Basaiti (1470–1530) painted "The Calling of the Sons of Zebedee." Zebedee had two sons—John and James—who were disciples of Jesus.

Ephesus, in modern-day Turkey. In his Letter to the Galatians, written around 53 C.E., Paul explicitly refers to John as the Apostle who supported his preaching and conversion activities among the Gentiles.

JOHN THE BAPTIST
("graced by God")
Born six months before Jesus, John was the son of Zacharias, a priest of Abijah, and Elisabeth, daughter of Aaron. His birth was foretold by the angel Gabriel. Born a Nazarite, John spent his young adult life in Judah. As an adult, John preached the coming of a Messiah and warned his audience that "even now the ax is lying at the root of the trees; every tree therefore that does not bear good fruit is cut down and thrown into the fire" (LUKE 3:9). His words inspired many, resulting in thousands being baptized by him in the Jordan River. According to Matthew, John lived in the desert and "wore clothing of camel's hair with a leather belt around his waist, and his food was locusts and wild honey,"

evoking the image of Elijah, who was likewise described as "a hairy man, with a leather belt around his waist" (MATTHEW 3:4; II KINGS 1:8). The allusion to Elijah reminded Matthew's audience of God's promise that "I will send you the prophet Elijah before the great and terrible day of the Lord comes" (MALACHI 4:5).

Several scholars have linked John the Baptist to the community of Qumran near the Dead Sea, whose members, the Essenes, are believed to have written the Dead Sea Scrolls. The Qumranite community texts insist that members hand over their property and possessions "to the hand of the man who is the examiner over the possessions of the many." Similarly, John the Baptist told his listeners that "Whoever has two coats must share with anyone who has none; and whoever has food must do likewise" (LUKE 3:10-11). Both the Qumranites and John the Baptist lived far from Judea's urban centers, in search of an ascetic lifestyle, subsisting on a spartan diet. What's more, the Qumran concept of a teacher/prophet who leads his people to repentance resonates strongly with the portrayal of John the Baptist and Jesus in the Gospels, who are also referred to as teachers (LUKE 3:12; JOHN 3:26).

Jesus heard of John's fame and traveled from Galilee to the Jordan to be baptized by John. John, however, was arrested for denouncing the marriage of Herod Antipas to Herodias. He was taken to the castle of Machaerus as a prisoner and later beheaded (I CHRONICLES 24:10; LUKE 1:5,15; 3:8-19; MATTHEW 3:1-12; 14:3-12). In his teachings, Jesus often paid homage to John the Baptist, telling the crowds, "I tell you, among those born of women no one is greater than John" (LUKE 7:28).

JOHN THE EVANGELIST
("graced by God")
Author of the Gospel of John, which offers not only the most lyrical but also the most theologically sophisticated account of Jesus' life and deeds. In John, Jesus delivers long discourses that dwell at length on key themes of Christian theology, often using poetic allegories such as the "bread of life" and "light of this world." The Gospel of John has traditionally been credited to either the Apostle

"John, son of Zebedee," or the Apostle John, "the disciple [whom] Jesus loved." If it is true that the Gospel of John was written in the last decade of the first century C.E., it is unlikely that it could have been written by a contemporary of Jesus. Nevertheless, there is much material in this Gospel that does not appear in any of the Synoptic Gospels, which suggests that John may have used authentic sources about Jesus to which none of the other evangelists may have had access. Indeed, the Gospel itself makes no claim about its authorship, but it does state that

St. John the Evangelist appears in this stained glass window from the Cathedral of St. Peter in Trier, Germany, dating from 1520.

its account is based on the testimony of "the beloved disciple," and adds in its final paragraphs that "this is the disciple who is testifying to these things and has written them, and we know that his testimony is true." There is, therefore, every reason to suggest that the author of the Gospel of John may have had access to a written testimonial attributed to an Apostle from Jesus' immediate circle.

JOSEPH
("increase")

Father of Jesus, husband of Mary, who hailed from the lineage of David. Joseph's original place of residence is not clear; Matthew implies that Joseph lived in Bethlehem,

"St. Joseph," the father of Jesus, is the work of Spanish artist Jusepe de Ribera (1591–1652) from ca 1635.

rather than Nazareth. Only John specifically states that Joseph was "from Nazareth," but he offers no further details. Joseph is the central figure in Matthew's Nativity account. When he was told that Mary was pregnant, though they hadn't been wed yet, he "planned to dismiss her quietly" because he was "unwilling to expose her to public disgrace." But before Joseph could cancel the wedding, "an angel of the Lord appeared to him in a dream and said, 'Joseph, son of David, do not be afraid to take Mary as your wife, for the child conceived in her is from the Holy Spirit'" (MATTHEW 1:21). According to Luke, Joseph took Mary to Bethlehem in response to a Roman census, but Matthew suggests that Joseph and Mary lived

in Bethlehem all along. The star that led the magi from the east stopped "over the place where the child was," and "upon entering the house, they saw the child with Mary his mother" (MATTHEW 1:24). Later on in Matthew's story, after Joseph and Mary had fled to Egypt to escape from King Herod's massacre of the innocents, an angel appeared to Joseph, telling him it was safe to return. "But," says Matthew, "when he heard that Archelaus was ruling over Judea in place of his father Herod, he was afraid to go there." Instead, they traveled north and settled in Galilee.

The Gospel of Mark describes Joseph as a *"tektōn,"* which in the King James Bible is translated as "carpenter," though its true meaning refers to a skilled worker in either stone, wood, or metal. Because Jesus' parables often use the language of agriculture, rather than carpentry, it has been suggested that Joseph was a farmer, like most Galileans, but perhaps augmented his income with woodworking.

Joseph accompanied Mary and Jesus to Jerusalem when Jesus was 12 years old, which is the last reference to Joseph. He died most likely before Jesus, because unlike Mary, he is not mentioned in the accounts of Jesus' ministry and Crucifixion (JOHN 19:25; LUKE 2:4; 3:23; MATTHEW 1:16; 13:55).

JOSEPH OF ARIMATHEA
("increase")

A native of Arimathea and member of the Sanhedrin. Mark adds that Joseph himself was "waiting expectantly for the kingdom of God," which suggests that Joseph was supportive of Jesus' ministry (MARK 15:43). John calls him "a disciple of Jesus" (JOHN 19:38). After Jesus' death, he asked permission from the procurator Pilate to take possession of the body, which was granted. He then wrapped the body in linen and buried Jesus in the tomb he had prepared for himself. Joseph then "rolled a stone against the door of the tomb" and went on his way (JOHN 19:39; LUKE 23:50-55; MARK 15:46; MATTHEW 27:57).

JOSES
("exalted")

1. Son of Eliezer, in the genealogy of Christ (LUKE 3:29).
2. One of the brothers of Jesus, mentioned in the Gospel of Mark (MARK 6:3).

JUDAS
("praise")

1. Son of Jacob, husband to Tamar, and father to Perez and Zerah (MATTHEW 1:2-3).
2. Judas Iscariot. One of Jesus' 12 Apostles who betrayed him to the Sanhedrin for 30 pieces of silver. What made Judas's act of betrayal even more grievous is that he identified Jesus to the arrest squad by way of a kiss, traditionally a sign of love and respect for one's teacher. John suggests that before his betrayal, Judas enjoyed Jesus' trust, because he was entrusted with the group's "money box" (JOHN 12:6).

Mark identifies Judas by his full name: Judas Iscariot. The term "Iscariot" has been linked to the term *sicarius,* which is Latin for "daggerman," an epithet sometimes

"The Kiss of Judas" is a detail from a fresco painted by Giotto di Bondone (ca 1266–1337) around 1305.

associated with the Jewish party of the Zealots. On the other hand, "Iscariot" may simply indicate that Judas hailed from Kerioth, a town in southern Judea. This would, however, have set him apart from the other Apostles, who were Galilean, because Kerioth in located in Judea.

Judas felt remorse and attempted to return the payment to the priests, which was refused. Matthew writes that Judas subsequently hanged himself. The Book of Acts argues that he fell to his death in a field he had bought with the silver, while Bishop Papias claims he was crushed by a chariot (MATTHEW 26:15; 27:5; ACTS 1:18).

LAZARUS
("God helps")
1. Known by an abbreviated version of Eleazar, Lazarus was the brother of Mary and Martha in Bethany. He was resurrected by Jesus after being entombed for three days. After dining with Jesus, Israelite priests sought to kill Lazarus and Jesus (JOHN 11:1-14,38-44; 12:1-18).
2. A beggar (LUKE 16:19-31).

LEVI
("adhesion; joined")
One of the Apostles, the son of Alphaeus (MARK 2:14; LUKE 5:27,29), also called Matthew (MATTHEW 9:9). See **Matthew**.

LUKE
The author of the Gospel of Luke is traditionally associated with a man called Luke, who traveled with Paul on his journey to Greece and accompanied him on his last voyage to Jerusalem. He is sometimes identified with the "beloved physician" referred to in Paul's Letter to the Colossians (COLOSSIANS 4:14). This has prompted some to suggest that Luke was trained in medicine, quite possibly in Antioch in Syria, and that he became a Gentile convert to Christianity under Paul's tutelage. However, the Gospel text itself does not suggest that the author was a doctor.

Italian painter Fra Angelico (1387–1455) painted the "Resurrection of Lazarus" in 1450.

Of all the evangelists, Luke was most concerned about framing his story in its proper historical setting, such as dating events by the reigning emperor. He explicitly referred to certain accounts that "were handed on to us by those who from the beginning were eyewitnesses and servants of the word" (LUKE 1:2). What's more, Luke claimed that "many other authors" before him had tried to organize the reports of Jesus. This implies not only that Luke had access to *several* sources, but also that these traditions were, in one way or another, inadequate or conflicting, for Luke continued by saying that "after investigating everything," he saw the need to compose "an *orderly* account" (LUKE 1:1-3).

Luke's Greek was influenced by the "biblical" style of the Septuagint, the Greek translation of the Hebrew Scriptures composed in Alexandria, Egypt. This has prompted some to suggest that "Luke" wrote for a Diaspora Judeo-Christian community somewhere in the Mediterranean region. The author of Luke is also traditionally credited with writing the Book of Acts of the Apostles; given the similarity in style and theological perspective, scholars widely accept this suggestion.

LYSANIAS
A Roman governor of Abilene during the reign of Tiberius (LUKE 3:1).

MAGI
According to Matthew, the birth of Jesus in Bethlehem summons the arrival of three "wise men from the East." At many courts in the east, including ancient Babylon and Persia, learned astrologers often served as priestly advisers, practiced in the art of magic. In the centuries since, the three magi have also been interpreted as kings. A bright star led the magi from the east until it stopped "over the place where the child was," and "upon entering the house, they saw the child with Mary his mother" (MATTHEW 1:24). The magi knelt down for the baby Jesus and "offered him gifts of gold, frankincense, and myrrh." This is possibly an illusion to Isaiah's vision of nations rendering tribute to Jerusalem: "A multitude of camels shall cover you . . . they shall bring gold and frankincense, and proclaim the praise of the Lord" (MATTHEW 2:11; ISAIAH 60:6). Herod's suspicions were aroused by the news that a new "king" had been born. When the magi stopped at his palace on their way, Herod asked them to let him know where this newborn babe was, so that "I may also go and pay him homage." But the magi were warned in a dream not to return to Herod, and so they left for their own country by another road (MATTHEW 2:12).

MALCHUS
Servant to the high priest Caiaphas. Peter cut off his right ear in the Garden of Gethsemane, but the man was healed by Jesus (JOHN 18:10; MATTHEW 26:51; MARK 14:17; LUKE 22:49-51).

MARK
Author of the Gospel of Mark, arguably the first and oldest Gospel about the life and deeds of Jesus. It was probably written sometime between 66 and 70 C.E., following the outbreak of the Jewish Rebellion in Roman Judea. Mark's Gospel does not provide any information about Jesus' youth and adolescence. Instead, his story begins when Jesus

joins the group of John the Baptist in the Jordan—that is, when Jesus was already past 30 years of age.

The author of this Gospel has traditionally been identified as [John] Mark, the friend of Paul and later of the Apostle Peter, who visited the community at Colossae and is also mentioned in the closing greetings of Peter's letter from Rome (COLOSSIANS 4:10; I PETER 5:13). Bishop Irenaeus wrote around 185 C.E. that Mark was the "disciple and

Simon Vouet (1590–1649) painted "Martha Reproofs her Vain Sister Mary Magdalen" in 1621.

interpreter" of Peter, which suggests that this Mark spoke Latin, Greek, and Aramaic (because all four Gospels were written in a Greek patois known as *koiné*). But the actual text of the Gospel of Mark does not mention a Mark, nor does it identify its author. Christian tradition holds that the Gospel of Mark was written in the city of Rome. Careful study of the Gospels of Matthew and Luke indicate that these evangelists copied as much as 60 percent of Mark's story into their own narrative.

MARTHA

Sister of Lazarus and Mary, who lived in Bethany. Martha welcomed Jesus and his disciples into their home as they traveled.

She felt responsible for the guests' well-being, and was upset when her sister Mary was more interested to sit with Jesus and listen to his words. She decided to complain to Jesus about her sister's neglect of her duties. "Lord, do you not care that my sister has left me to do all the work by myself?" she asked. "Tell her then to help me." But Jesus corrected her, saying, "Martha, Martha, you are worried and distracted by many things; there is need of only one thing" (LUKE 10:40-42). Martha returns in the Gospel of John when her brother Lazarus was gravely ill, but Jesus did not rush to Bethany to heal him. Indeed, Jesus only arrived when Lazarus had been in his tomb for four days. Martha chided him, saying, "Lord, if you had been here, my brother would not have died." Jesus replied, "Your brother will rise again" (JOHN 11:17-33). Jesus cried out in a loud voice, "Lazarus, come out," and promptly "the dead man came out, his hands and feet bound with strips of cloth, and his face wrapped in a cloth." According to John, this was the moment when the Jewish Sanhedrin decided on Jesus' arrest and execution (JOHN 11:39-47).

MARY, MOTHER OF JESUS

Wife of Joseph and mother of Jesus. Prior to marrying Joseph, while she lived in Nazareth with her parents, the angel Gabriel appeared to her and told her she would soon be with child. When Mary replied that she was still a virgin, Gabriel replied that "the Holy Spirit will come upon you, and the power of the Most High will overshadow you," adding that "your relative Elizabeth in her old age has also conceived a son . . . for nothing will be impossible with God" (LUKE 1:34-35). Mary visited her cousin Elizabeth, who was indeed with child as well.

According to Luke, in whose Gospel

Mary is the central character in the Nativity story, Joseph took Mary to Bethlehem in response to a decree from Augustus, requiring all to be counted in a census. While there, they found that all the inns were filled. So they sought shelter in a stable, and while there, "the time came for her to deliver her child. And she gave birth to her firstborn son and wrapped him in bands of cloth, and laid him in a manger" (LUKE 2:6-7). According to the same Nativity account, magi came from the east with gifts to see the child that was born the "King of the Jews."

Matthew suggests that Joseph and Mary lived in Bethlehem all along. The star that led the magi from the East east stopped "over the place where the child was," and "upon entering the house, they saw the child with Mary his mother" (MATTHEW 1:24). Later on in Matthew's story, after Joseph and Mary had fled to Egypt to escape King Herod's massacre of the innocents, an angel appeared to Joseph, telling him it was safe to return. "But," says Matthew, "when he heard that Archelaus was ruling over Judea in place of his father Herod, he was afraid to go there." Instead, they traveled north and settled in Galilee. In Luke's Gospel, Mary and Joseph travel to Jerusalem a month after Jesus' birth to present an offering of purification in the Temple, as prescribed by Leviticus. Luke confirms that Mary and Joseph were poor because they offered "a pair of turtledoves or two young pigeons," usually allowed for poor couples (LUKE 2:22-24; LEVITICUS 12:6-8).

Mark suggests that Mary had more children by Joseph, and that Jesus ultimately had four brothers, "James and Joses and Judas and Simon," as well as at least two sisters (MARK 6:3). Some scholars, however, defend the Catholic tradition of the perpetual virginity of Mary by noting that the term "brother" (*adelphos* in Greek) was often used within a clan to refer to close relatives or cousins. When Jesus was 12 years old, he went to Jerusalem for Passover with his parents. After the festival, Mary and Joseph started the journey back to Nazareth, but realized Jesus was not with them. Jesus had remained in Jerusalem, talking with scholars in the Temple.

Mark suggests that Mary was one of the women who stood at the cross following Jesus' Crucifixion (MARK 15:40; LUKE 1:32-35,46-56; 2:1-7,41-52; MATTHEW 1:21; 2:11).

MARY, WIFE OF CLOPAS

Wife of Clopas and the mother of James the Younger and Joses (MATTHEW 27:56). She is mentioned as one of the women who was standing by the cross at the Crucifixion of Jesus. On the third day after the Crucifixion, Mary went with Mary Magdalene and Salome to the tomb with "spices, so that they might go and anoint him" (MARK 16:1). When they arrived, they found that the stone had been rolled back. Inside, they found a young man, dressed in a white robe, who said, "Do not be alarmed; you are looking for Jesus of Nazareth, who was crucified. He has been raised; he is not here" (MARK 16:6). Mary and the other women were terrified, but the man said, "Tell his disciples and Peter that he is going ahead of you to Galilee; there you will see him, just as he told you." And, Mark adds, the women fled from the tomb, and they said nothing to anyone, for they were afraid" (MARK 16:6-8).

MARY MAGDALENE

As her name indicates, Mary came from Magdala, which was a thriving center of the Galilean fish processing industry (MATTHEW 27:56). Jesus drove out the seven demons that possessed her, which may suggest that Mary suffered from a disease such as epilepsy; in Antiquity, people with epilepsy were often thought to be possessed by spirits (LUKE 8:2). Mary then followed Jesus throughout Galilee and onto Jerusalem.

Mary defied the stereotype of a young Jewish woman in first-century Galilee. Whereas unwed women were usually restrained from leaving their home without a relative as an escort, Mary went boldly where Jesus went. The fact that she was still unmarried, even though she was presumably an adult, was like-wise highly unusual. One answer may be that Mary Magdalene was an affluent woman, who by virtue of her wealth had achieved a certain level of

independence. This is supported by Luke, who states that she belonged to a group of women who "provided for them out of their own resources" (LUKE 8:2-3).

Mary Magdalene was present at Jesus' Crucifixion. On the third day after the Crucifixion, Mary Magdalene went with Mary and Salome to the tomb with "spices, so that they might go and anoint him" (MARK 16:1). When they arrived, they found that the stone had been rolled back. Inside, they found a young man, dressed in a white robe, who said, "Do not be alarmed; you are looking for Jesus of Nazareth, who was crucified. He has been raised; he is not here" (MARK 16:6). Mary and the other women were terrified, but the man said, "Tell his disciples and Peter that he is going ahead of you to Galilee; there you will see him, just as he told

you" (MARK 16:6-8). In John's Gospel, Mary wants to embrace Jesus after the Resurrection, but he stops her, saying, "Do not hold on to me, because I have not yet ascended to the Father" (JOHN 20:17).

Mary Magdalene is often depicted in Western art as "the penitent Magdalene." There is no evidence anywhere in the Gospels that Mary Magdalene lived a sinful or promiscuous life, but by the third century, she had become fully assimilated with the unnamed woman in Luke, "a sinner," who bathes Jesus' feet with her tears, and dries them with her hair (LUKE 7:38). By the sixth century, Pope Gregory I declared Mary Magdalene to be a "fallen woman" guilty of "forbidden acts"—attributes of a prostitute. In 1969, Pope Paul VI explicitly separated the figure of Mary Magdalene from the "sinful woman" character.

MARY OF BETHANY

Mary lived in the town of Bethany with her sister Martha and her brother Lazarus (LUKE 10:39). When Jesus and his disciples went to Bethany, they were welcomed into their home. While Martha prepared dinner, Mary sat at the feet of Jesus and listened to his teachings. Martha complained about her sister and told Jesus to tell Mary to help her instead. Jesus corrected her, saying, "Martha, Martha, you are worried and distracted by many things; there is need of only one thing" (LUKE 10:40-42).

When Lazarus got sick, the sisters sent Jesus a message urging him to come. When Jesus arrived at last, he found that Lazarus had already been buried. Martha told Jesus that if he had been on time, Lazarus would not have died. Mary then burst into tears, weeping so bitterly that Jesus "was greatly

The painting titled "Mary Magdalen" by Flemish artist Quentin Matsys (ca 1465–1530) was probably completed by 1525.

disturbed in spirit and deeply moved" (JOHN 11:17-33). Jesus then ordered for the stone to be removed, and he called to Lazarus to come out. And immediately "the dead man came out, his hands and feet bound with strips of cloth, and his face wrapped in a cloth." According to John, this was the moment when the Jewish Sanhedrin decided on Jesus' arrest and execution (JOHN 11:39-47).

MATTATHA
("gift of God")
Son of Nathan and grandson of David in the genealogy of Jesus (LUKE 3:31). His son was Menna.

MATTATHIAS
("gift of God")
1. Son of Amos, the father of Joseph, and an ancestor of Jesus (LUKE 3:25).
2. Son of Semein, the father of Maath, and an ancestor of Jesus (LUKE 3:26).

MATTHAN
("gift of God")
Grandfather of Joseph, the husband of Mary (MATTHEW 1:15).

MATTHAT
("gift of God")
1. Son of Levi, the father of Heli, and an ancestor of Jesus (LUKE 3:24).
2. Son of Levi, the father of Jorim, and an ancestor of Jesus (LUKE 3:29).

MATTHEW
("gift of God")
Christian tradition attributes the Gospel of Matthew to the tax collector named Levi whom Jesus found in the customs house in Capernaum and subsequently called to join him as an Apostle (MARK 2:14; MATTHEW 9:9). Levi was thereafter known as Matthew. The Gospel text itself, however, never identifies its author. What's more, the Matthew Gospel is written in an erudite and elegant Greek, which may have been beyond the abilities of a tax collector in a small township like Capernaum. Bishop Papias of Hierapolis (Asia Minor) wrote in the early second century C.E. that Matthew had compiled

a collection of sayings by Jesus, written in Hebrew. It is therefore plausible that the anonymous author of Matthew's Gospel had access to such a "sayings" document as one of his putative sources, which may have led to the Gospel's attribution to Matthew later on. Matthew's Gospel may have been produced in Antioch in Syria, because Ignatius, bishop of Antioch, is able to cite passages from this work as early as 110 C.E.

"St. Matthew and the Angel" is the work of Dutch artist Barent Fabritius (1624–1673) from ca 1656.

MELCHI
("my king")
1. Son of Jannai, the father of Levi, and an ancestor of Jesus (LUKE 3:24).
2. Son of Addi, the father of Neri, and an ancestor of Jesus (LUKE 3:28).

MESSIAH
("Anointed One")
Messiah, or *Mashiach,* denotes a king who has been anointed as a legitimate ruler. In Jewish eschatology, particularly in the intertestamental period, the term "Messiah" came to signify a future ruler of the Davidic line who would oust foreign occupiers, restore Jewish independence, and rule Israel as a Kingdom

of God, governed by the Torah. There was, however, no agreement on what kind of a savior this Messiah would be. Some saw him as a descendant of King David. In Daniel, he is described as the archangel Michael or by contrast, as "one like a son of man," a normal human being. The Dead Sea Scrolls speak of *two* Messiahs: a warrior king and "branch of David," and a priest, the "Messiah of Aaron." Others envisioned a military leader, such as Simon bar Kokhba, the leader of the Second Jewish Revolt against the Romans in 132–135 C.E. John the Baptist likewise described the Messiah in militant terms, as a man whose "winnowing fork is in his hand, to clear his threshing floor . . . but the chaff he will burn with unquenchable fire" (LUKE 3:17). In Matthew, Jesus welcomed the title of Messiah but "sternly ordered the disciples not to tell anyone," perhaps because he was aware of its volatile political ramifications (MATTHEW 16:20). Instead, Jesus himself referred to himself as the Son of Man, perhaps inspired by Daniel's eschatological visions.

MONEY CHANGERS
Pilgrims entering the Temple to deposit tithes or offer an animal sacrifice had to convert their coins into the Tyrian shekels, the only currency accepted within the Temple. Originally, the sale of sacrificial lambs during Passover may have taken place at some distance from the Temple precinct, in a market called *Chanut* on the Mount of Olives. Based on references by Philo as well as Josephus, all sacrificial animals, including doves, goats, and lambs, would have been kept well away from the Temple until the actual moment of sacrifice, to prevent the Temple pavement from being covered with animal waste. The high priest Caiaphas may have decided to change this custom and bring the market inside the Temple to exert greater control over the quality of the lambs being sold, or to prevent any animals from being injured in the crush of being taken by the pilgrims from the Mount of Olives to the Temple. This may explain why Jesus was surprised when seeing the commercial activity in

Dutch painter Rembrandt Harmensz van Rijn painted "Christ Driving the Moneychangers from the Temple" around 1626.

the Temple forecourt, and why he decided to "cleanse the Temple" by overturning the tables of the money changers (MARK 11:15-17).

NATHANAEL
("God gave")
A disciple of Jesus who was born in Cana (JOHN 1:45). Some believe that Nathanael and Bartholomew are the same person (MATTHEW 10:3; ACTS 1:13). In the Synoptic Gospels, Philip and Bartholomew are always mentioned together, while Nathanael is never mentioned; in the fourth Gospel, Philip and Nathanael are similarly mentioned together, but nothing is said of Bartholomew. Specifically, John's Gospel states that on the way to Galilee, Philip met a man named Nathanael and told him that "we have found him about whom Moses in the law and also the prophets wrote, Jesus son of Joseph from Nazareth." Nathanael was

not impressed and scoffed, "Can anything good come out of Nazareth?" Jesus found out about Nathanael's comment, and told him, "Here is truly an Israelite in whom there is no deceit!" (JOHN 1:45-47). At that point, Nathanael followed Jesus and became one of the 12 disciples.

NICODEMUS
("conqueror of the people")
According to the Gospel of John, Nicodemus was a Pharisee and a member of the Sanhedrin who came to Jesus at night to learn more about his teachings. He asked Jesus, "Rabbi, we know that you are a teacher who has come from God; for no one can do these signs that you do apart from the presence of God." Jesus answered him, "Very truly, I tell you, no one can see the kingdom of God without being born from above" (JOHN 3:1). Later on, Nicodemus defended Jesus against other Pharisees, saying, "Our law does not judge people without first giving them a hearing to find out what they are doing, does it?" (JOHN 7:51). After the Crucifixion, Nicodemus came to the aid of Joseph of Arimathea who had secured the body of Jesus to help with the burial, "bringing a mixture of myrrh and

Flemish artist Jacob Jordaens (1593–1678) painted "Christ Instructing Nicodemus," who was a Pharisee and member of the Sanhedrin.

aloes, weighing about a hundred pounds" (JOHN 19:39).

PETER
("rock")
Son of Jonas or John, the man originally known as Simon hailed from Bethsaida in the Gaulanitis, just on the border of Galilee (MATTHEW 4:18). Like his brother Andrew, Peter was a fisherman, but the two brothers spent some time with John the Baptist in the Jordan, where they met Jesus. After John's arrest, Simon and Andrew traveled back to Galilee with Jesus, where they plied their fishing trade in partnership with John and James, the sons of Zebedee; they also became disciples of Jesus.

Simon's mother-in-law had a house in Capernaum. His mother was sick, but Jesus healed her (MARK 1:29-31). Her home then became the base of Jesus' Galilean ministry. Jesus gave Simon a new name: "You are to be called Cephas." The Greek word *kephas* is a transliteration of the Aramaic word *kêfa,* which means "stone" or the more familiar "rocky"; in Christian literature, it would be translated into Petros, or Peter. Later, he designated Peter as the leader of the Apostolic mission, saying, "You are Peter, and on this rock I will build my church" (MATTHEW 16:17-18).

Like his fellow Galileans, Peter spoke Aramaic, the native tongue of first-century Palestine, with an accent that marked him as a man from Galilee. Matthew notes that while Peter was warming his hands by a fire in the courtyard of Caiaphas's palace, he was promptly recognized as one of Jesus' followers by his speech. "Certainly you are also one of them," a servant girl told Peter, "for your accent betrays you" (MATTHEW 26:73).

Throughout Jesus' ministry, Peter served as the senior Apostle, and was present at many miracles performed by Jesus. In Luke, for example, Peter told Jesus that they had "toiled all night long, and not caught anything." Jesus urged him to throw his nets

Marco Zoppo (1433–1478) painted this portrait of St. Peter in 1468. Peter, one of Jesus' Apostles, was crucified upside down.

once again. Their nets found such a huge catch that "many ships from nearby" rushed to the scene to help (LUKE 5:4-7). He was also chosen to be present, together with James and John, when Jesus underwent the Transfiguration (MARK 9:3-7). Furthermore, when during a journey to Caesarea Philippi, Jesus asked his disciples the question, "Whom do people say I am?" Only Peter gave the right answer: "You are the Messiah" (MARK 8:30). Nonetheless, Peter's abandonment of Jesus in his hour of greatest need, following his arrest on the Mount of Olives, is a severe indictment in the Gospels of the man's character. Once before, Jesus had chided Peter as a man "of little faith" when he had ordered him to walk on water toward him. Even though he denied Jesus three times in the courtyard of the building where Jesus was indicted, he held his first place among the Apostles. According to the Book of Acts, he continued to preach following the Crucifixion, had the power to heal the sick, and was the first to bring the Gospel to the Gentiles (ACTS 15:7). In Joppa, he brought a woman named Tabitha back to life, in a close parallel

to Jesus' miraculous resuscitation of Jairus's daughter (ACTS 9:40).

Tradition holds that Peter was arrested during the pogroms against Christians in Rome following the great fire of 64 C.E. According to Church legend, Peter was condemned to be crucified, but he insisted that he be crucified upside down, lest he die in the same position as Jesus. He was buried on the right bank of the Tiber River, called the Ager Vaticanus, where the Church of St. Peter would later arise.

PHANUEL
("face of God")
Father of Anna, the prophetess of the tribe of Asher (LUKE 2:36).

PHARISEES
The Pharisees (from the Hebrew *perushim* or "separated ones") were a coalition of priests and pious laymen who "separated themselves" by scrupulously observing Covenant Law. What made them different from the Sadducees is their belief that the Law should be adapted to changing needs of their time. Whereas the Sadducees considered Hebrew Scripture a closed book, the Pharisees studied the Law and debated it extensively. Eventually, this led to a body of scriptural commentary known as the "Oral Law," which probably forms the basis of the third-century Mishnah.

James Jacques Joseph Tissot (1836–1902) painted "The Pharisees Question Jesus." The Pharisees were a group of priests and pious laymen.

Under Hasmonean rule, the Pharisees exerted considerable power in Jerusalem as a counterweight to the growing influence of the Sadducees, but their political power waned under Herod the Great and subsequent Roman governors.

The Pharisees believed in transferring the sanctity of the Temple, including its ritual purity, to the home, so as to observe God in all things. This is the reason why they debated such questions as to what was considered "clean" or "impure," or what one was allowed to do on the Sabbath. The Gospels depict the Pharisees as Jesus' adversaries, but in truth, they had much in common with Jesus. Among other things, the Pharisees accepted the idea of the immortality of the soul, as well as the belief in the resurrection after Judgment Day—two concepts that would return in Jesus' teachings.

PHILIP
("lover of horses")
One of the 12 Apostles who was from Bethsaida, as were Simon Peter and Andrew, and who had originally joined John the Baptist in the Jordan (MATTHEW 10:3). In the Gospel of John, Philip enjoys considerable prominence. He readily responded when Jesus first addressed him, and he is the one who brought Nathanael to Jesus (JOHN 1:43,45-46). In the Book of Acts, he is listed as being present at the election of Matthias before the Pentecost. According to the Gospel of John, he was responsible for the provisioning of Jesus' traveling group of Apostles, and was stunned to be told to feed the 5,000 who had come to hear Jesus speak. Philip is often confused with the man described in the Book of Acts as one of seven deacons charged with distributing food among the community of disciples (ACTS 6:5). According to one legend, Philip is said to have preached in Phrygia and

This rendering of "The Apostle Philip" is the work of French artist James Jacques Joseph Tissot (1836–1902).

died at Hierapolis, though it is not clear whether this refers to Philip the Apostle or Philip the deacon.

PONTIUS PILATE

Fifth Roman procurator of Judea, Samaria, and Idumea, after these territories were incorporated as a Roman crown province (Luke 3:1). Pilate's term ran from 26 to 36 C.E., during which time he lived in the procurator's residence at Caesarea, but often traveled to Jerusalem during Jewish festivals to enforce law and order.

Pilate, who hailed from the house of Pontii, was not of senatorial rank, but a member of the knightly (or "equestrian") class. Soon after his arrival in Judea, he embarked on a deliberate policy of provocation and confrontation with his Jewish subjects. In this, he had considerable latitude because his superior, Lucius Aelius Lamia, governor of Greater Syria, was not in Antioch but in Rome. As such, Pilate presided over several massacres of Jews, notably in Jerusalem around 28 C.E.; Jesus obliquely refers to this massacre in the Gospel of Luke (Luke 13:1).

All Gospels state that Jesus was brought up on charges before Pilate, and that it was Pilate who condemned him to the cross. The oldest Gospel, that of Mark, portrays Pilate as a sympathetic official who is reluctant to order Jesus' death, which may have been motivated by the fact that Mark wrote in Rome for a Roman audience. The theme of Pilate's compassion is further elaborated upon in the other Gospels, notably in the Gospel of John. However, contemporary records, including those of Josephus and Philo, depict Pilate as a man of wanton cruelty who was eventually dismissed from office because of his brutality against the Jewish people—notably, the violent suppression of a religious gathering of Samaritans.

QUIRINIUS

Gaius Publius Sulpicius Quirinius was a longtime friend of Julius Caesar who served under Augustus in the legion that defeated Mark Antony. He completed a term as governor in Galatia and Pamphylia in Asia Minor before being appointed as governor of Greater Syria, which included the recent Roman acquisitions of Judea, Samaria, and Idumea. Quirinius's first decision as governor was to order a census to assess the property values in all of the regions now under his control. This census is described in the Gospel of Luke as the reason why Joseph and Mary had to travel to Bethlehem (Luke 2:2).

RUFUS
("red")

Son of Simon, and brother of Alexander (Mark 15:21). Simon carried Jesus' cross on his way to Golgotha.

SADDUCEES
("followers of Zadok")

Since the return from the Babylonian exile, power in Jerusalem had been held by a priesthood—the chief priests and priestly officials who served on the priestly council, or *Sanhedrin,* and supervised the rites of sacrifice at the Temple. Under Hasmonean rule, the priesthood was increasingly influenced by the party of the Sadducees, or *Tzedoqim* in Hebrew. The Sadducees, who were believed to descend from the high priest Zadok, had reluctantly yielded their claim on the high priest's office to the Hasmonean monarchy, in return for gaining control of the priestly council, with jurisdiction over religious and other domestic matters. Their growing power was opposed by the Pharisees, a pious group of laymen and clergy who believed that instead of ritual sacrifice, the quintessential practice of Judaism was the application of the Law. Over time, the Sadducee party became a wealthy, conservative aristocracy that welcomed the Roman occupation. The power of certain Sadducee families in the Roman period is illustrated by the fact that the Romans appointed no less than seven members of the family of the Sadducee Annas (including his son-in-law, Caiaphas) to the office of high priest. The Sadducees did not accept any Scripture beyond the Torah, or Law—including the Book of the Prophets—and did not believe in the immortality

"The Question of the Sadducees" was painted by British artist Harold Copping (1863–1932). The Sadducees questioned Jesus on the subject of immortality.

of the soul, an idea that was gaining currency among the Pharisees. In the Gospel of Luke, the Sadducees question Jesus on this very subject (LUKE 20:28-38).

SALOME
("peaceable")

1. Wife of Zebedee, and mother of James and John (MARK 15:40). She witnessed the Crucifixion of Jesus with Mary Magdalene and with "Mary," who may have been Jesus' mother. On the third day after the Crucifixion, she went with the other two women to Jesus' tomb, bringing sweet spices to anoint the body.

2. Daughter of Herodias, who danced for her stepfather Herod Antipas with such guile that Herod promised to give her whatever she wished. Prodded by her mother Herodias, Salome asked for the head of John the Baptist. Though the Gospel of Mark does not identify her by name, the Jewish historian Josephus does (MARK 6:17-28).

SAMARITANS

A community living in Samaria who followed traditional Jewish precepts but believed that Mount Gerizim, rather than Jerusalem, was the holy place of Israelites. Samaritans claimed their descent from the tribes of Ephraim and Manasseh, the two sons of Joseph. Numbering some million people in Roman times, Samaritans were considered "untouchables" by Jews in Jesus' day. This prejudice went back to the time of the Assyrian King Sargon II (ruled 721–705 B.C.E.), who invaded Israel and deported the population to the north (II KINGS 17:6). Their homes, fields, and cattle were appropriated by Babylonian settlers, many of whom came from Cuthah in Babylonia. Over time, these foreign farmers assimilated with the remaining Jewish population in Samaria, and eventually adopted Jewish cultic practice and faith. Samaritans were often scathingly referred to as "Cuthaeans," after the ancient city of Cuthah in Babylonia.

Apparently, the prejudice was mutual. Luke relates how an advance party sent by Jesus to prepare his way "entered a village of the Samaritans to make ready for him; but they did not receive him" (LUKE 9:52-53). The indignant Apostles asked Jesus to punish the village by raining down fire from heaven, but Jesus refused. The antipathy between Jews and Samaritans makes Jesus' parable of the Good Samaritan, who showed compassion toward a Jewish victim, even more poignant (LUKE 10:30-37).

In 36 C.E., a man claiming to be the Messiah planned to mark the Passover festival by leading a group of followers to the holy mountain of Mount Gerizim, where they would find sacred vessels Moses buried. Pilate interpreted this pilgrimage as a political demonstration, and ambushed the worshippers. This massacre was reported to Pilate's superior, Governor Vitellius in Antioch, Syria, who removed Pilate from office and sent him back to Rome.

SANHEDRIN

The Sanhedrin was the 70- or 72-member Jewish council charged with overseeing religious and domestic matters. Since the Hasmonean period, control over the Sanhedrin was contested by two parties: the Sadducees, an aristocratic priestly community, and the predominantly lay brotherhood known as the Pharisees (although many Pharisees were priests as well). Faced with Sadducee opposition, the Hasmonean kings struck a compromise: The Sadducees were given majority control of the Sanhedrin

James Jacques Joseph Tissot (1836–1902) painted "The Morning Judgement," an illustration from "The Life of Our Lord Jesus Christ" (1886–1894).

as well as the administration of the Temple and its sacrificial system, in return for Sadducee support of the Hasmonean regime, including the right of Hasmonean kings to either appoint high priests or to serve as such themselves. King Herod continued the arrangement, and appointed a number of high priests during his reign, favoring émigré Babylonian families. Still, during the early first century, the Sanhedrin was deeply divided between the Sadducee majority, "being filled with jealousy," and a highly vocal minority of Pharisees who sought to curtail Sadducee power at every opportunity. According to the Book of Acts, the Sanhedrin began to suppress the Apostolic movement after Jesus' Crucifixion by imprisoning some of the Apostles. Meetings of the Sanhedrin usually took place in a special hall known as the *Lishkat La-Gazit,* or the "Chamber of Hewn the Stones," located in the Stoa section of the Temple.

SATAN

Leader of fallen angels and God's adversary. Satan appears in the Gospels during the temptation of Jesus, when Satan promised Jesus that he would give him all the kingdoms in the world if only he would worship him. Elsewhere in the New Testament, he is called "the dragon" and "the old serpent" (REVELATION 12:9; 20:2), and is denounced as "the spirit that now works in the children of disobedience" (EPHESIANS 2:2).

SCRIBES

A "scribe," an individual often referred to in the Gospels, was a professional writer skilled in preparing a variety of legal documents, who catered to the vast majority of illiterate peasants in Palestine. A scribe was essentially a notary public who could prepare forms of marriage, divorce, sale, credit, or rent. Given that these legal documents followed the Torah, the Jewish Law, scribes were of necessity steeped in the precepts of Mosaic legislation. As such, they are often presented by Mark as the educated opposition to Jesus, together with the Pharisees and Sadducees (MARK 1:21-22).

SIMEON

A devout Jew living in Jerusalem, who had been told that he would not die without seeing "the Lord's Messiah." A month after Jesus' birth, Mary and Joseph went to Jerusalem to present an offering of purification in the Temple, as prescribed by Leviticus (LUKE 2:22-24). Simeon met them at the Temple and took the child in his arms, saying, "Master, now you are dismissing your servant in peace, according to your word; for my eyes have seen your salvation, which you have prepared in the presence of all peoples, a light for revelation to the Gentiles and for glory to your people Israel" (LUKE 2:29-32).

SIMON, BROTHER OF JESUS

According to the Gospel of Mark, Simon was one of Jesus' four brothers (MARK 6:3). The Gospel of John notes that near the end of Jesus' ministry, "Jesus' own brothers" did not believe in him.

SIMON, FATHER OF JUDAS

In the Gospel of John, Judas Iscariot who betrays Jesus is identified as the son of Simon (JOHN 6:71; 13:2).

SIMON OF CYRENE

Father of Alexander and Rufus (MATTHEW 27:32), who was compelled by the Romans to bear Jesus' cross when Jesus succumbed on the way to Golgotha (MARK 15:21).

SIMON PETER

Before being renamed *Kephas* or "Petros," Jesus' first and foremost disciple, the Apostle Peter was known as Simon. See **Peter.**

SIMON THE APOSTLE

One of the 12 Apostles, who was known as "the Cananaean," an Aramaic word that means "the zealous one" (MATTHEW 10:4; MARK 3:18); Luke uses the Greek version, "Zelotes" or "the Zealot" (LUKE 6:15; ACTS 1:13). It is unclear if this cognomen has any relationship to the religious party of the Zealots.

SIMON THE LEPER

A leper living in Bethany who entertained Jesus at his house. During the meal, a woman came in with an alabaster jar of precious ointment, which she poured on Jesus' head. Some complained that this was a waste of a very expensive liquid with ointment, but Jesus replied, "Why do you trouble the woman? She has performed a good service for me. For you always have the poor with you, but you will not always have me. By pouring this ointment on my body she has prepared me for burial" (MATTHEW 26:6-13; MARK 14:3-9).

German painter Albrecht Dürer (1471–1528) created "Saint Simeon [or Simon] and Saint Lazarus" in 1503.

SIMON THE PHARISEE

Luke's version of Simon the Leper, in whose house a woman comes to anoint Jesus' head, is set in Galilee, not Bethany, and Simon is a Pharisee, not a leper. The woman wept and washed Jesus' feet with her tears, then wiped them with the hair of her head, after which she kissed his feet and anointed them (LUKE 7:36-38). When Simon the Pharisee disapproves, Jesus tells the parable of the two debtors: " 'One owed five hundred denarii, and the other fifty. When they could not pay, he canceled the debts for both of them. Now which of them will love him more?' Simon answered, 'I suppose the one for whom he canceled the greater debt.' Jesus said to him, 'You have judged rightly.' Then turning toward the woman, he said to Simon, 'Do you see this woman? I entered your house; you gave me no water for my feet, but she has bathed my feet with her tears and dried them with her hair . . . You did not anoint my head with oil, but she has anointed my feet with ointment. Therefore, I tell you, her sins, which were many, have been forgiven; hence she has shown great love' " (LUKE 7:41-47).

SUSANNA
("lily")
In the Gospel of Luke, Susanna, Joanna, Mary Magdalene, and other women accompanied Jesus and the other 12 disciples in his ministry in Galilee (LUKE 8:3).

TAX COLLECTOR
Officials responsible for collecting taxes, called *telones* or *architelones* in the Gospels. After the territories of Judea, Samaria, and Idumea were incorporated into the Roman Empire as a crown province in 6 C.E., Rome could no longer rely on the old Herodian administration to collect the "tribute," or taxes, that were its due as occupying power. The local Roman governor, however, did not have the administrative apparatus to collect the taxes from every individual; therefore, this activity was outsourced to free agents. The purpose of the census ordered by Quirinius, governor of Greater Syria, which is mentioned in Luke as the reason for Joseph's and Mary's journey to Bethlehem, was to arrive at accurate property values so that these freelance tax collectors could be held to account.

Tax collectors, or "publicans," were the only officials in Galilee with capital, and it was to them, ironically, that farmers had to turn for personal loans when they were unable to pay their taxes. Their land was pledged as collateral; when the loan was inevitably not repaid, their land was foreclosed upon. This is one reason why Jesus'

contemporaries so heartily despised these officials; another reason is that they habitually cheated on taxpayers, as is evident from John the Baptist's sermon (LUKE 3:12-14). It is also why Jesus singled out tax collectors as people whom he had to convert in order for them to realize the Kingdom of God on earth. Time and again, Jesus is criticized for consorting with these people; while on the

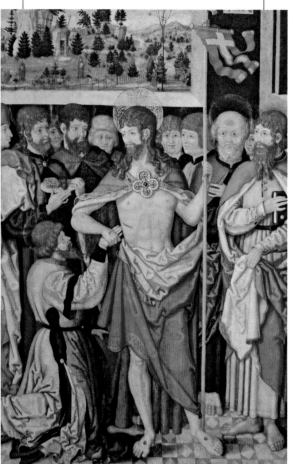

This detail of a painting by German artist Wilhelm Stetter (1487–1552) shows Thomas probing the wounds of Christ.

road to Jerusalem, he even told a tax collector named Zacchaeus that he will stay at his house (LUKE 19:5). Zacchaeus confessed that "if I have defrauded anyone of anything, I will pay back four times as much" (LUKE 19:1-8).

THADDAEUS
Son of James, and one of the 12 Apostles

according to the Gospels of Matthew and Mark (MATTHEW 10:3; MARK 3:18). In the Gospels of Luke and John, as well as the Book of Acts, he is known as Judas. John refers to "Judas [not Iscariot]" to distinguish him from the Apostle who betrayed Jesus (JOHN 14:22).

THEOPHILUS
("friend of God")
Addressee of the Gospel according to Luke, and of the Book of Acts of the Apostles. In Acts, he is called "most excellent," which suggests that Theophilus had a high social standing and may have been an official of sorts (ACTS 23:26). The idea that Theophilus was the "sponsor" of both Luke and Acts further confirms the Church tradition that both works were written by the same author.

THOMAS
("twin")
One of the 12 Apostles according to the Gospel of Mark, which is repeated in the Gospels of Matthew and Luke (MARK 3:18-19). Thomas is depicted in the Gospel of John as a loyal but simple disciple, who often asks for clarifications. When Jesus travels to Bethany upon hearing that Lazarus is gravely ill, Thomas says, "Let us go also, that we may die with him" (JOHN 11:16). The name "Thomas" has become synonymous with a disbeliever. After the Resurrection, he refused to believe that Jesus had risen, until Jesus appeared and allowed him to touch his wounds (JOHN 20:27). Thomas was with Peter and other disciples on the Sea of Galilee when Jesus appeared to them for the last time.

TIBERIUS
Successor of Caesar Augustus and second Roman emperor, who reigned from 14 to 37 C.E. Tiberius was the son of Tiberius Claudius Nero and Livia, who became a stepson of Augustus when Livia married him. Tiberius became emperor at age 55 and distinguished himself in various military

This Roman bust of the Emperor Tiberius was carved after his death in 37 C.E.

campaigns, while proving himself an able administrator of civil affairs. Luke dates the birth of Jesus to the 15th year of Tiberius's reign (LUKE 3:1). Sometime after 14 C.E., Herod Antipas, tetrarch of Galilee, built a new city on the shores of the Sea of Galilee and named it Tiberias in the emperor's honor. In 26 C.E., the year when Pontius Pilate was appointed prefect to Judea, Tiberius chose to retire from active government on the island of Capri, leaving the empire in the hands of the commander of the Praetorian Guard, Lucius Aelius Sejanus.

TIMAEUS
("defiled")
Father of blind Bartimaeus in Jericho, whose sight was restored by Jesus. Bartimaeus then became the first person to publicly proclaim Jesus as the Messiah (MARK 10:46).

ZACCHAEUS
("pure")
A wealthy tax collector near Jericho, who was short in stature and climbed up into a sycamore tree to see Jesus as he approached the city. Jesus looked up and said, "Zacchaeus,

hurry and come down; for I must stay at your house today" (LUKE 19:1-5). Zacchaeus proved to be a willing convert. "Look, half of my possessions, Lord, I will give to the poor," the tax collector exclaimed, "and if I have defrauded anyone of anything, I will pay back four times as much" (LUKE 19:1-8).

ZEALOTS
The Hellenization of the Jewish kingdom under the Herodians and the subsequent Roman occupation produced a religious party that may have split from the Pharisaic faction, and sought full religious and political freedom without any compromise. Born from the tax revolts of the early part of the century, the Zealots became a potent organization with its own militant wing of *sicarii* (*sikarioi* in Greek), meaning "dagger men." During the regime of the Roman procurator Gessius Florus who, says Josephus, ruled "like an executioner rather than a governor," the Zealots launched a rebellion against the Roman occupation that became known as the First Jewish Rebellion of 66–70 C.E.

ZEBEDEE
("abundant; portion")

A fisherman of Galilee, the father of the Apostles James the Great and John (MATTHEW 4:21), and the husband of Salome (MATTHEW 27:56; MARK 15:40).

ZECHARIAH
("Jehovah is remembered")
Father of John the Baptist and husband of Elizabeth. The angel Gabriel appeared to Zechariah, who was a member of the "priestly order of Abijah" (LUKE 1:5). Zechariah was taken aback by the angel's appearance, so Gabriel said, "Do not be afraid, Zechariah, for your prayer has been heard." And Gabriel continued: "Your wife Elizabeth shall bear you a son, and you will name him John. You will have joy and gladness, for he will be great in the sight of the Lord" (LUKE 1:13-15). Zechariah could not believe the angel's words, knowing that he and his wife were advanced in age. So Gabriel struck him deaf and mute, until the day that his son would be born. And indeed, when Zechariah emerged from the Temple, he was unable to speak until Elizabeth gave birth to a son. According to a legend, Zechariah was later killed in the Temple on orders of Herod.

"Christ and the Family of Zebedee" was painted by Italian artist Bonifacio de' Pitati (1487–1553). Zebedee was the father of two of Jesus' Apostles.

From Acts of the Apostles to Revelation

*You will receive power
when the Holy Spirit has come upon you;
and you will be my witnesses
in Jerusalem, in all Judea and Samaria,
and to the end of the earth.*

ACTS OF THE APOSTLES 1:8

*"The Pentecost," by French artist Jean Restout (1663–1702), depicts
the dramatic events that took place during this feast, which is
celebrated 50 days after Passover.*

THE GROWTH OF EARLY CHRISTIANITY

Who Wrote the New Testament?

THE NEW TESTAMENT is the principal Scripture of Christianity. In addition to the Gospels of Matthew, Mark, Luke, and John, the New Testament also includes the Book of the Acts of the Apostles, which covers the early development of the Christian Church; the Epistles (or Letters) attributed to Paul; additional apostolic letters; and the apocalyptic Book of Revelation. The name "New Testament" (*diatheke* in Greek) is really the translation of the Hebrew *berith,* the New "Covenant," because Christians believe that Jesus Christ is the ultimate fulfillment of the covenant promise of the Old Testament.

According to Church tradition, the author of the Gospel of Luke wrote the Book of the Acts of the Apostles, which most modern scholars accept. Stylistically, Acts and the Gospel of Luke have much in common; what's more, both books were apparently commissioned by the same sponsor, a man named Theophilus (Acts 1:1).

The oldest written source about Jesus is not the Gospel literature, but the letters (or Epistles) written by Paul. The purpose of these missives was to bolster the faith of the early Christian congregations, and to adjudicate whenever tensions arose among their different constituencies. Paul dictated some of these letters himself; others were written on his behalf or by anonymous authors claiming Paul's authority.

In the subsequent decades of Christianity's astonishing growth, however, many other Christian documents began to circulate, including a variety of "gospels," "acts," and "apocalypse" documents. These were often attributed to Jesus' disciples so as to bolster their credibility. An official canon of Christian writings, similar to the canon of Hebrew Scripture, was urgently needed.

Around 180 C.E., Bishop Irenaeus of Lyons (140–ca 203 C.E.) proposed an anthology that included the Gospels of Matthew, Mark, Luke, and John, as well as the Pauline Epistles. Indeed, the earliest manuscripts of the New Testament, dating to around 200, contain only these texts. The Christian theologian Tertullian of Carthage (ca 155–220 C.E.) agreed with Irenaeus's collection and coined the phrase "New Testament," because Jesus was the living proof of God's new covenant with mankind.

Almost a century later, Bishop Eusebius of Caesarea (263–339 C.E.) and his friend and colleague Pamphilius (ca 260–309 C.E.) took the next step in creating a formal New Testament canon of Christian documents, all written in Greek, which was the lingua franca of the era. This canon was comprised of the four Gospels chosen by Irenaeus; the Book of the Acts of the Apostles; the Epistles of Paul; the Epistles of Peter; and the "Apocalypse of John," known today as Revelation. At the same time, both Irenaeus and Eusebius rejected a number of Gnostic documents, such as the Gospel of Thomas and the Gospel of Peter as the work of "heretics." Other writings, including the Acts of Paul, the Apocalypse of Peter, the Epistle of Barnabas, and the Didache (or the Teachings of the 12 Apostles), were likewise omitted as sources of questionable authority.

The debate over the final composition of the New Testament would continue well into the Middle Ages, with much of the argument focused on the authority of the Epistle of James and the Book of Revelation, until the Council of Trent (1545–1563) by and large affirmed Eusebius's compilation. Thus, by the end of the fourth century, Christianity had arrived at the final canon of its Scripture, inclusive of an updated version of the Septuagint that was adopted as the "Old Testament"—presenting the world with the Christian Bible as we know it today.

"St. Paul Writing His Epistles" was painted by 16th-century French artist Valentin de Boulogne (1591–1632).

LEADING FIGURES IN THE BOOKS OF
ACTS OF THE APOSTLES THROUGH REVELATION

This hall, located on Mount Zion, is traditionally believed to be the location where Jesus and his disciples shared the Last Supper, and where the Apostles met during Pentecost.

MATTHIAS

Fifty days, or seven weeks, after Passover, Jewish pilgrims from all over the Roman world once again traveled to Jerusalem for the feast of Shavuot ("weeks" in Hebrew) or *Pentecost,* a Greek word meaning "fiftieth." It presented Jesus' followers with an opportunity to revive Jesus' ministry and to preach to thousands of worshippers, if they chose to do so. Already, says Acts, Jesus had appeared several times after his Resurrection, "speaking about the kingdom of God" (ACTS

1:3). He urged the Apostles to stay in Jerusalem, rather than be dispersed across Galilee, and to wait until "the Holy Spirit" would come upon them.

But they acutely felt the loss of Jesus' charismatic presence when, as Acts tells us, Jesus was finally lifted into heaven. They returned to the "room upstairs where they had been staying," possibly the same room where Jesus had celebrated the Last Supper, and spent their days in prayers and debate. Because Judas Iscariot was no longer with them, they debated who should replace him. It was agreed that this new disciple should have been a part of the movement from the very beginning. Two followers qualified as such: **Joseph Barsabbas** (also known as Justus) and a man named **Matthias**. They prayed, cast lots, and finally elected the follower named Matthias.

Outside, the streets of Jerusalem had begun to fill with the throngs of Pentecost worshippers when something unusual happened. Suddenly the house where they were staying was filled with "a sound like the rush of a violent wind," while "divided tongues, as of fire appeared among them" (ACTS 2:2-3). Thus infused with the Holy Spirit, the Apostles were emboldened to abandon their hiding place and begin to preach openly to the multitudes. The crowds, says Acts, were astonished. Even those from foreign lands could understand what the Apostles were saying, for they were speaking in other languages, "as the Spirit gave them ability." All were "amazed and perplexed" that Galileans knew so many foreign languages; some sneered and said, "They are filled with new wine" (ACTS 2:7-13).

And suddenly from heaven there came a sound like the rush of a violent wind, and it filled the entire house where they were sitting.

ACTS OF THE APOSTLES 2:2

ca 10 C.E.	ca 26–28 C.E.	ca 30 C.E.	ca 30 C.E.
Possible birth date of Paul	Putative date of Jesus' baptism by John in the Jordan River	Jewish writer Philo is active in Alexandria, Egypt	Putative date of Jesus' Crucifixion in Jerusalem

PETER

The Pentecost event had made Peter a changed man. Hearing the sneers from the crowd, he rose and countered that he and his fellow Apostles were not drunk for it was "only nine o'clock in the morning." If anything, they were drunk with the "new wine" of the Holy Spirit. He then went on to articulate what would become the guiding principle of the Apostolic mission: that Jesus of Nazareth, a man "with deeds of power, wonders and signs," had risen, so that the "entire house of Israel [would] know with certainty that God has made him both Lord and Messiah."

But what did this mean? If this Jesus, the Messiah, was no longer among the living, how could this be of any benefit to the people of Israel? Peter replied that even though Jesus had ascended into the heavens, his power remained undiminished: "Repent, and be baptized, every one of you in the name of Jesus Christ so that your sins may be forgiven; and you will receive the gift of the Holy Spirit." The term "Jesus Christ" signified that Jesus was *Christos* or "the Anointed One," the Greek translation of Messiah.

Many responded to Peter's call, says Acts; eventually, they added up to some 3,000 people in all. These new followers were welcomed into the Apostolic circle and introduced to its rites, including the practice of "fellowship . . . the breaking of bread and the prayers." The believers were also called upon to "sell their possessions and goods and distribute the proceeds to all, as any had needed"—a practice not dissimilar from that the Essenes used (ACTS 2:38-45).

In every other respect, however, these early followers continued to live as practicing Jews. They prayed in the Temple, observed the Sabbath, and followed the precepts of the Torah (ACTS 2:45; 15:5). Peter is even credited with performing miracles in the Temple, such as healing the lame man at the "Beautiful Gate"—possibly, the Nicanor Gate that separated the Court of the Women from the Temple precinct proper. Following this miracle, Peter and the Apostle John preached in Solomon's Portico, the large colonnade to the east of the esplanade, and baptized many as disciples of Jesus.

Flemish painter Peter Paul Rubens (1577–1640) painted this depiction of "St. Peter as Pope."

ANNAS AND HIS FAMILY

The priestly elite, including "the captain of the Temple and the Sadducees" observed this development with growing alarm. They had assumed that by crucifying Jesus, they had crushed his Messianic

| ca 37 C.E. | ca 37 C.E. | ca 38 C.E. | ca 40 C.E. |
| Tiberius dies; succeeded by Gaius Caligula | Pontius Pilate is recalled to Rome | Jewish pogroms in Alexandria | One of the earliest Christian communities founded in Corinth |

CHAPTER 5: FROM ACTS OF THE APOSTLES TO REVELATION   299

THE GNOSTIC GOSPELS

In the decades of Christianity's astonishing growth, many other Christian documents began to circulate, including a variety of "gospels," "acts," and "apocalypses"—writings often attributed to disciples in Jesus' inner circle so as to bolster their credibility (a common practice in Antiquity). Most of these documents were written from the second to the third century C.E., and some articulate ideas that ran counter to the theology Paul and his followers espoused. This includes the Gospel documents produced by so-called "Gnostic" circles. A large number of these texts were discovered near the Egyptian hamlet of Nag Hammadi in 1945. The Gnostic followers of Jesus did not adhere to the emphasis on Jesus' death and Resurrection as the quintessential redemptive act of his ministry. Instead, they believed that Jesus taught a new form of spirituality, a total surrender to the divine spirit within themselves, which ultimately led to a secret knowledge (*gnosis* in Greek) of God, and they attributed this orientation to leading men among the Apostles. Among the most famous of noncanonical texts is the Gospel of Thomas. It is not a "gospel" in the traditional sense, nor a truly "Gnostic" one, for it only provides a listing of specific sayings by Jesus, without any attempt to interpret these in a theological context. "Sayings documents" of this type were often used in Antiquity to disseminate the teachings of a noted sage. As such, the Gospel of Thomas bears a notable resemblance to the sayings document known as "Q," which, though never found, is believed to have been a source for the Gospels of Matthew and Luke. ∎

This page is taken from the Codex Tchacos, *an ancient Coptic papyrus containing Gnostic texts including "The Gospel of Judas."*

movement. The news of Jesus' Resurrection came as an unwelcome challenge, because the Sadducees (unlike the Pharisees) firmly rejected the possibility of eternal life. Before long, Peter and John were arrested and placed into custody.

When the new day dawned, the family of Annas—including the former high priest himself, as well as "Caiaphas, **Jonathan** and **Alexander**, and all who were of the high priestly family"—assembled to hear the case (Acts 4:5-6). This is additional evidence of the extraordinary interest that Annas's family seemed to have in suppressing the movement, because Annas and Caiaphas were involved with the indictment of Jesus as well. We're not quite sure who "Jonathan and Alexander" are, though Jonathan is possibly the son of Annas who would succeed Caiaphas as high priest upon the latter's dismissal in 36 C.E.

Peter and John were brought before this tribunal and thoroughly interrogated, but no hard proof of any seditious activity could be found, and thus they were duly released.

ARAMAIC

The Apostles spoke Aramaic, a Semitic language closely related to Hebrew and Phoenician. The Gospels contain 26 Aramaic words spoken by Jesus, including *Abba*, an Aramaic term of strong relation that Jesus used to address God the Father. While on the cross, Jesus cries out *"Eloi, Eloi, lama sabachthani?"*—an Aramaic quote from Psalm 22:1, which means "Lord, Lord, why have you forsaken me?" The Apostles probably spoke Aramaic with a strong Galilean accent. Matthew notes that while Peter was warming his hands by a fire in the courtyard of Caiaphas's palace, he was promptly recognized as one of Jesus' followers because "your speech gives you away." It is possible that Jesus and his disciples may also have picked up a few words of Greek. The Gospels suggest that he could converse with a centurion, as well as the prefect, Pontius Pilate, who would have spoken Greek. ∎

Nevertheless, Annas would bide his time and wait for the proper opportunity to destroy the movement once and for all.

ANANIAS AND SAPPHIRA

Among the many followers the Apostles had welcomed into their midst was a group of Jews referred to as "Hellenists" in Acts. These were most likely Greek-speaking Jews from Alexandria, Asia Minor, or other locations in the Roman Empire, as compared to the followers from Palestine (referred to as "Hebrews" in Acts) who spoke Aramaic. Soon, tensions emerged between these factions for a number of reasons, one of which was the accusation that widows among the Greek faction did not receive the same share of food that Hebrew widows did (Acts 6:1). As we saw, the Apostolic mission was a commune of sorts, in which all possessions and food were shared equally. Those who refused to do so could be punished harshly. One couple, **Ananias**

ca 41 C.E.	ca 41 C.E.	ca 41 C.E.	ca 43 C.E.
Agrippa I, grandson of Herod the Great, is appointed king of Roman Judea	Emperor Claudius confirms the right of Jews to observe their religious practices in the empire	Caligula is assassinated and succeeded by Claudius	Founding date of London

and **Sapphira**, had sold a piece of property but kept back some of the proceeds for themselves. When Ananias was confronted with these facts, he dropped down and died. A few hours later, his wife Sapphira was brought in and interrogated about the actual sale price of the property. She refused to divulge the truth, and was likewise struck dead. And, says Acts, "a great fear seized the whole church" (ACTS 5:1-10).

STEPHEN

With these tensions growing, certain Hellenists started to distance themselves from the obedience shown by Hebrew followers toward the Temple. By this time, many followers in the Diaspora had long since built their liturgical life around the synagogue, rather than the Temple. Their animosity, however, was principally targeted toward

the Sadducees, the priestly elite who controlled Temple operations and who were despised by many Jews as Roman collaborators. One outspoken leader of the Greek community, a man named **Stephen**, began to agitate against Temple worship altogether, arguing that God does not dwell in "buildings built by human hands" (ACTS 7:48). These tensions threatened to split the Apostolic community, for many other followers—not only the "Hebrews" but also many freedmen from North Africa and Asia Minor—remained faithful to Temple worship (ACTS 6:9).

In due course, Stephen was denounced to the Sanhedrin for "speaking blasphemous words against Moses and God." This was the opportunity Annas and Caiaphas had been waiting for. According to Acts, Stephen was arraigned before the high priest and the council, and denounced. Stephen countered his accusers with a lengthy speech, ending with the assertion that "the Most High does not dwell in houses

The painting titled "The Death of Ananias" was created by Italian artist Raphael (1483–1520) in 1515.

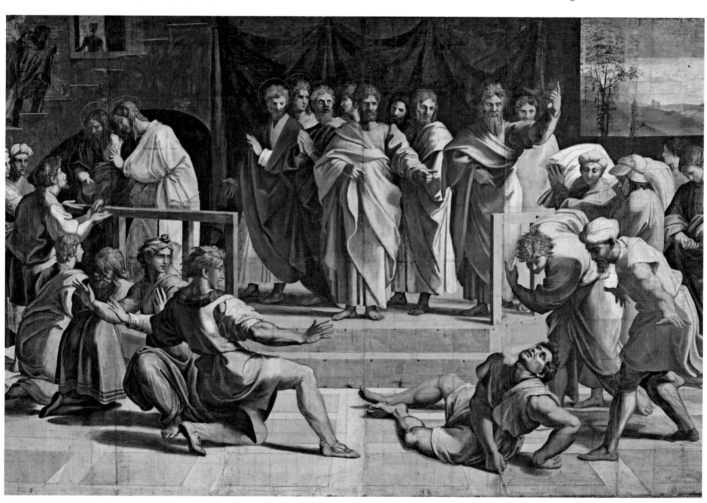

ca 43 C.E.
Roman invasion of Britain

ca 44 C.E.
King Agrippa I dies; Judea reverts back to a Roman province

ca 44 C.E.
Cuspius Fadus is appointed Roman procurator of Judea

ca 46 C.E.
Tiberius Alexander replaces Cuspius Fadus as Roman procurator of Judea

"The Martyrdom of Saint Stephen" is the work of Spanish artist Juan de Juanes (1510–1579). Accused of blasphemy, Stephen was stoned to death.

made with human hands." "You stiff-necked people," Stephen cried, "which of the prophets did your ancestors not persecute?" Just like them, Stephen said, "You have become (the) betrayers and murderers" of "the Righteous One" (ACTS 7:58).

Stephen's words caused an uproar. "With a loud shout," says Acts, "they dragged him out of the city and began to stone him," in a striking parallel with the mob that denounced and condemned Jesus during his trial. It is perhaps remarkable that no Roman procurator is featured in this story. Some believe Pilate would not have bothered to return to Jerusalem for Stephen's trial, while other authors have tried to date this event to 36 C.E., after Pilate's removal from office, and before the arrival of the new Roman prefect, Marcellus, in 37 C.E.

Stephen's murder marked a new phase in the conflict between the Sadducee leadership and the Apostolic mission. What had begun as mere harassment of Jesus' followers now turned into an all-out "persecution." As a result, Jerusalem ceased to be the nexus of the movement while the Apostles were "scattered throughout the countryside of Judea and Samaria" (ACTS 8:1). Many of the Greek disciples fled to Cyprus, Phoenicia, and Syria, specifically the city of Antioch on the Orontes, which in the decades to come would emerge as a major center of Christian activity.

> *Now when the apostles at Jerusalem heard that Samaria had accepted the word of God, they sent Peter and John to them.*
>
> ACTS OF THE APOSTLES 8:14

PHILIP

One of the disciples who moved to Samaria was a man called **Philip** (not to be confused with the Apostle Philip), whose name may indicate that he was a member of the Greek-speaking group of Jewish Christians. Acts identifies him as one of seven deacons charged with distributing food among the community of disciples—a necessary task, because many of the disciples were widows or immigrants without income, and all possessions were to be shared (ACTS 6:5). Samaria, as we have seen, was a territory that many Jews avoided and where, apparently, the feeling was mutual. According to the Gospel of Luke, Jesus had once sent an advance party to the region, which "entered a village of the Samaritans to make ready for him; but they did not receive him" (LUKE 9:52-53). Enraged by their rejection, the Apostles urged Jesus to punish the village by raining down fire from heaven, but Jesus refused.

Imagine, therefore, the astonishment with which the remaining Apostles in Jerusalem received the news of Philip's resounding success in this territory. His preaching was so well received that "unclean spirits, crying out with loud shrieks, came out of many who were possessed, and many others who were paralyzed or lame were cured." This led to "great joy in that city," quite possibly the

An anonymous Saxon goldsmith crafted this gilded figure of the disciple Philip around 1350.

ca 47 C.E.	ca 48 C.E.	ca 52 C.E.	ca 54 C.E.
Birth of Greek historian Plutarch	Ventidius Cumanus replaces Tiberius Alexander as Roman procurator of Judea	Antonius Felix replaces Ventidius Cumanus as Roman procurator of Judea	Claudius dies and is succeeded by Nero, son of his wife, Agrippina

THE VATICAN

According to Church tradition, Peter was buried on a hill on the right bank of the Tiber River, called the Ager Vaticanus. In 324 C.E., Constantine the Great built the first basilica of St. Peter to mark this spot. It reportedly had a stairway that led to the crypt where pilgrims could touch the tomb of St. Peter. The current St. Peter's basilica, designed by Bramante and Michelangelo, was begun in 1506 and completed more than a century later. In the early 1940s, while World War II raged throughout Europe, Pope Pius XII ordered archaeologists to excavate the area right under the altar to determine if the tomb of St. Peter could still be found. The excavation was conducted in great secrecy, lest for some reason the tomb could not be located. After several years of persistent excavation, the scientists did discover the remains of a white marble shrine, placed against a red stucco wall. This appears to correspond to a description of Peter's tomb, written by a second-century pilgrim named Gaius. The shrine was enclosed in marble, which archaeologists dated to the time of Constantine the Great. The grave under the aedicule itself was empty. Within one of the nearby stucco walls, however, the team discovered the remains of a man approximately 60 years of age. In 1950, Pius XII went on radio to declare that the bones of St. Peter had been found, although the Pope admitted that "it is impossible to prove with certainty that they belong to the Apostle." ∎

The current St. Peter's Basilica in the Vatican was completed in 1626; it was based on designs by Bramante (1444–1514) and Michelangelo (1475–1564).

ca 57 C.E.	ca 58 C.E.	ca 58 C.E.	ca 58 C.E.
Paul writes his Letter to the Romans	Putative date of Paul's arrest in Jerusalem and transfer to Caesarea	Roman poet Juvenal is born	Emperor Ming-Ti introduces Buddhism to China

Dutch artist Rembrandt van Rijn (1606–1669) painted "The Baptism of the Eunuch" in 1626. Philip encountered the Ethiopian eunuch on the road to Gaza.

whom the Samaritans had always considered a prophet because of his ability to perform amazing feats. Simon was therefore deeply impressed when he saw Peter and John lay their hands on the disciples, who thereupon received the "Holy Spirit." Simon took the Apostles aside and offered them money if they gave him the power to transmit the Holy Spirit as well. Peter angrily denounced him, "for I see that you are in the gall of bitterness and the chains of wickedness" (ACTS 8:18-23).

An angel then instructed Philip to turn south "to the road that goes down from Jerusalem to Gaza." Philip did as he was told, and traveled across the Shephelah hills toward Gaza. Along the way, he met a highly placed **eunuch** from the court of Candace, Queen of Ethiopia, who was in charge of her treasury. A devout man, though a Gentile, the eunuch was reading from the Book of Isaiah when Philip ran up to him and offered to explain the passage he was reading, which was Isaiah 53:7-8: "Like a sheep he was led to the slaughter." Philip told the eunuch about Jesus, and the Ethiopian agreed to be baptized—thus foreshadowing the future Apostolic mission to the Gentiles (ACTS 8:26-38).

Next, Philip traveled to "Azotus" (today's Ashdod) and turned north, moving up the coast while passing through "all the towns until he came to Caesarea." This heavily Romanized city and residence of the Roman procurator now became his base of operations (ACTS 8:40). Here, he led the growing Christian community while raising four daughters, each of whom "had the gift of prophecy" (ACTS 21:9).

TABITHA

While Philip made his way to Caesarea, Peter had left Samaria and turned west toward Lydda, a village located close to today's Lod, some nine miles from the coast. Here he healed a man named **Aeneas**, who had been paralyzed for eight years, with the words "Aeneas, Jesus Christ heals you; get up and make your bed!" (ACTS 8:34).

city of Sebaste, which had been built by Herod on the ruins of ancient Samaria (ACTS 8:7-8).

Philip's extraordinary work prompted a visit by Peter and John, who wanted to see this Christian community of Samaritans themselves. One of the new followers was a magician named **Simon**,

ca 60 C.E.	ca 60 C.E.	ca 62 C.E.	ca 62 C.E.
Porcius Festus replaces Antonius Felix as Roman procurator of Judea	Putative date of Paul's embarkation for Rome	Heron of Alexandria designs a steam engine, water clock, water fountain, and odometer	Lucceius Albinus replaces Porcius Festus as Roman procurator of Judea

The Italian Early Renaissance painter Masolino (ca 1383–ca 1447) painted the fresco "Healing of the Cripple and Raising of Tabitha" between 1424 and 1428.

Not far from Lydda was Joppa, one of the oldest cities in Judea, whose port had been in almost continuous use since the second millennium B.C.E.; today, it's a suburb of Tel Aviv called Jaffa. Here lived a woman named **Tabitha** (an Aramaic name; *Dorcas* in Greek, which means "gazelle"), who was "devoted to good works and acts of charity." When she fell ill and died, the local community grieved deeply until some followers heard that Peter was just a few miles away in Lydda. They went over and prevailed on Peter to come to Joppa. In a close parallel to Jesus' miraculous resuscitation of Jairus's daughter, Peter ordered all of the wailing women out of Tabitha's house, then knelt down at the woman's body and prayed. At last, he said, "Tabitha, get up," and the woman opened her eyes and sat up (ACTS 9:40).

CORNELIUS

Peter decided to stay in Joppa, enjoying the hospitality of a man named **Simon**, who was a tanner. Then, as now, its location on the Mediterranean Sea made Joppa a pleasant place to linger. One day, after Peter went up to the roof to pray, he fell into a trance. He saw a large sheet being lowered with various unclean animals, while a voice said, "What God has made clean, you must not call profane" (ACTS 10:10-15). Peter was deeply puzzled by the vision. He was still trying to make sense of it when several men arrived with a request for Peter to travel to Caesarea. They explained that a man named **Cornelius**, a centurion of the Italian cohort who was a God-fearing man, urgently desired to see him (ACTS 10:1).

Up to this point, the Apostles—like other observant Jews—generally refrained from close contact with Gentiles, because they did not honor the purity laws, particularly with regard to kosher food and drink. What's more, Jesus himself had always avoided Gentile cities, focusing his ministry on "the lost sheep of Israel." Now, however, Peter began to understand the vision he had just experienced. Clearly, God was telling him that what was previously considered unclean, including social relations with Gentiles, was no longer so. Thus, he agreed to go to Caesarea.

CORNELIUS CENTURION

According to Acts, a "centurion of the Italian cohort" named Cornelius, who was a "God-fearing man," urgently wished to see Peter (ACTS 10:1). The reference to "the Italian cohort" has confused scholars. A *cohors II Italica* is known to have been stationed in Syria in 63 C.E., but no Roman documents place it in Joppa, and certainly not between 41 and 44, when Judea was briefly ruled by King Herod Agrippa. It is possible that Luke is simply referring to a cohort made up of Italian soldiers, rather than local recruits and auxiliaries—as was often the case with Roman forces in Judea. On the other hand, the term "God-fearing" (or its Jewish parallel, *yir'ei Hashem*—"fearers of the Name") is well known, for in Scripture it refers to a Gentile with great sympathy and admiration for the Jewish religion, though not a practicing Jew himself. ■

Upon entering the centurion's house, Peter said, "You yourselves know that it is unlawful for a Jew to associate with or to visit a Gentile; but God has shown me that I should not call anyone profane or unclean" (ACTS 10:28). Cornelius and those with him were then baptized—the first Gentiles, together with the Ethiopian eunuch, to be welcomed as believers in Christ. But many practical questions about the idea of having Gentiles in the Christian movement remained. These would only come to the fore with the rise of another Apostle—a man who never knew Jesus, but who of all the disciples would exert the greatest influence on the growth of early Christianity: Paul of Tarsus.

SAUL

The principal sources for the life of Paul are the Book of Acts, and the Epistles written by Paul himself, or written on his behalf (or under his name) by his disciples. These Epistles are actually the oldest Christian documents extant today. The Epistles to the Thessalonians are commonly believed to be among Paul's first letters, whereas "Romans" and (if authentic) "Colossians" should be dated near the end of Paul's ministry, between 57 and 58 C.E.

Paul, then known as **Saul**, was probably born around 10 C.E. in the city of Tarsus, in the province of Cilicia on Asia Minor. In his Letter to the Philippians, Paul provides some biographical details: He belonged to the tribe of Benjamin and was trained as a Pharisee (PHILIPPIANS 3:5). The Book of Acts says that he was a pupil of the distinguished Pharisaic scholar Gamaliel, who may be the same Gamaliel who intervened on Peter's behalf during his hearing in front of the Sanhedrin. Paul also confessed that "as to zeal" he worked as "a persecutor of the church"; in his Letter to the Galatians, he adds that because of this zeal he was able to advance "beyond many among my people of the same age" (GALATIANS 1:14). He was probably one of the orchestrators of Stephen's stoning; Acts tells us that witnesses to the execution "laid

Paul, previously known as Saul, cries out in alarm in this painting of "The Conversion of St. Paul on the Road to Damascus" by Michelangelo Caravaggio (1571–1610).

ca 65 C.E.	ca 66 C.E.	ca 66-70 C.E.	ca 67 C.E.
Seneca is ordered by Nero to commit suicide	Outbreak of the Jewish Rebellion in Palestine against the Romans	Mark writes his Gospel, the oldest of the four canonical Gospels	General Vespasian arrives in Galilee to suppress the Jewish Rebellion

their coats at the feet of a young man named Saul," and that "Saul approved of their killing him" (ACTS 7:58; 8:1).

Saul soon asked permission to extend his dragnet beyond Judea and into Damascus in Syria, where a number of Jewish Christians had presumably found refuge. He was keen to find "any who belonged to the Way, men or women," and "bring them bound to Jerusalem" (ACTS 9:2). But as Saul set out on his journey, an intervention took place. Suddenly, a light from heaven flashed around him. Saul fell to the ground and heard a voice saying, "Saul, why do you persecute me?" (ACTS 9:4). Saul scrambled to his feet but, unable to see, was led to Damascus, where a disciple named **Ananias** was told in a vision to look after him. Ananias was reluctant, for he knew Saul's reputation as ruthless enforcer, a man who "has authority from the chief priests to bind all who invoke your name." But God told him that he had chosen Saul "to bring my name before the Gentiles."

This 12th-century gilded Byzantine medallion depicts St. Peter.

As soon as Ananias laid his hands on Saul, "something like scales fell from his eyes," and Saul could see again (ACTS 9:18). Saul, now renamed Paul, was baptized; soon thereafter, he began to proclaim Jesus in the synagogues, saying, "He is the Son of God."

Jerusalem's priestly circles were stunned by Paul's sudden turnabout. He was placed under surveillance, and a conspiracy was formed to kill him. But, says Acts, his disciples spirited him over the Damascus city walls at night by lowering him in a basket, from where he made his way to Jerusalem (ACTS 9:25).

Once he arrived, he was received in the Apostolic community with suspicion. Many disciples thought he was a fifth columnist, trying to infiltrate the movement; some Hellenist radicals even tried to kill him. In his Letter to the Galatians, however, Paul offers a different narrative. "I did not confer with any human being, nor did I go up to Jerusalem to those who were already Apostles before me," he insists; instead, he "went away at once into Arabia," there to contemplate

ROMAN JERUSALEM

The layout of today's Old City of Jerusalem has little in common with the Jerusalem that Jesus knew. After suppressing the second Jewish Revolt (131–135 C.E.), the Roman Emperor Hadrian decreed that Jerusalem should be demolished, lest it become the rallying point for another Jewish rebellion. Most Jews who had survived the fighting were forcibly removed. To seal Jerusalem's destruction, Hadrian then ordered a pagan city to be built on top of the rubble, which he named Aelia Capitolina. "Aelius" was the name of Hadrian's gens, or tribe; and "Capitolinus" referred to Jupiter Capitolinus, the chief god in Roman mythology. Hadrian even ordered a temple to Jupiter built on top of the place where the Jewish Second Temple had stood.

This Roman colonnade of the Cardo Maximus formed part of Aelia Capitolina, the Roman city built on the ruins of ancient Jerusalem.

As in most Roman cities, the city was designed using a grid pattern anchored on a main avenue running north to south, known as the cardo, which was bisected at right angles by a decumanus running east to west; remnants of the cardo boulevard were excavated in the Jewish Quarter after the 1960s. Hadrian's city planners soon realized that the Tyropoeon Valley running inside the ancient city walls required a secondary cardo running parallel toward the east. Both the primary and secondary cardo streets are preserved to this day in the course of the Suq Khan ez-Zeit and Al-Wad streets. Both main streets converged, then as now, in a large square in front of the city's principal gate, the Damascus Gate, which in Roman times was a large reinforced city gate. ■

ca 68 C.E.	ca 69 C.E.	ca 69 C.E.	ca 70 C.E.
Emperor Nero commits suicide and is succeeded by Galba	Rome is ruled by three emperors in succession: Galba, Otho, and Vitellius	Vespasian acclaimed emperor	Titus captures Jerusalem and destroys the Second Temple

1 Paphos The St. Paul's pillar in an early Christian basilica on Cyprus is the place where, according to tradition, Paul was tied and scourged by the Roman governor of Paphos before his conversion to Christianity.

2 Ephesus In the theater of Ephesus, Paul's companions became embroiled in a dispute with artisans selling statuettes of Artemis in the Temple of Artemis, who felt business was threatened by Paul's conversion efforts.

3 Athens Upon arrival in Athens, Paul preached on a hill known as the Areopagus (foreground), from where his listeners had an impressive view of the ancient Acropolis.

4 Corinth Ruins of the temple of Apollo still stand in ancient Corinth, the Greek city that Paul first visited between 51 and 52 C.E., and where he stayed for 18 months, possibly during the governorship of L. Iunius Gallio.

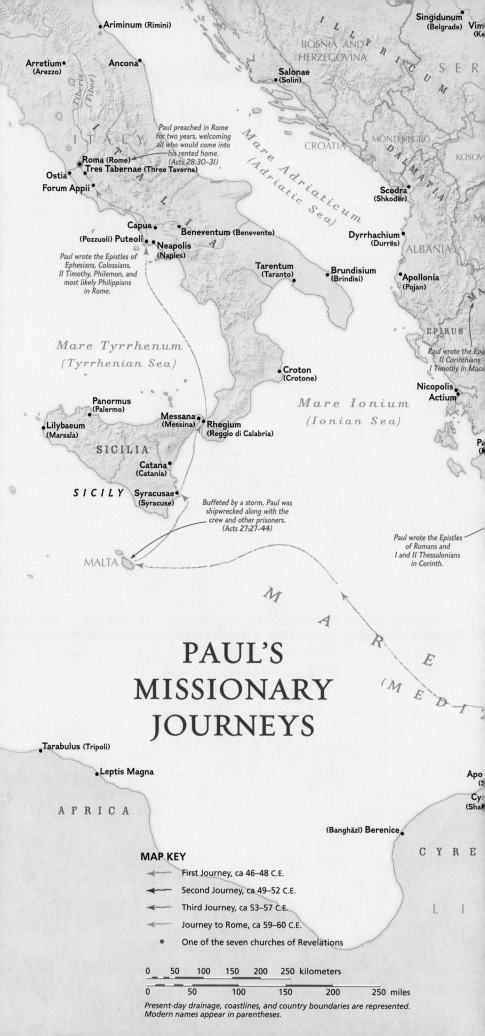

Ariminum (Rimini)

Singidunum (Belgrade) Vim (K.

ILLYRICUM

BOSNIA AND HERZEGOVINA

SER

Arretium (Arezzo)

Ancona

Salonae (Solin)

CROATIA

MONTENEGRO DALMATIA

KOSO

Paul preached in Rome for two years, welcoming all who would come into his rented home. (Acts 28:30-31)

Mare Adriaticum (Adriatic Sea)

Roma (Rome)
Tres Tabernae (Three Taverns)

Ostia
Forum Appii

Scodra (Shkodër)

Dyrrhachium (Durrës)

ALBANIA

Capua

Beneventum (Benevento)

(Pozzuoli) Puteoli

Neapolis (Naples)

Tarentum (Taranto)

Brundisium (Brindisi)

Apollonia (Pojan)

Paul wrote the Epistles of Ephesians, Colossians, II Timothy, Philemon, and most likely Philippians in Rome.

EPIRUS

Mare Tyrrhenum (Tyrrhenian Sea)

Croton (Crotone)

Paul wrote the Ep II Corinthians I Timothy in Mac

Panormus (Palermo)

Lilybaeum (Marsala)

Messana (Messina)

Rhegium (Reggio di Calabria)

Nicopolis Actium

Mare Ionium (Ionian Sea)

SICILIA

Catana (Catania)

SICILY

Syracusae (Syracuse)

Buffeted by a storm, Paul was shipwrecked along with the crew and other prisoners. (Acts 27:27-44)

Paul wrote the Epistles of Romans and I and II Thessalonians in Corinth.

MALTA

MARE (MEDI

PAUL'S MISSIONARY JOURNEYS

Tarabulus (Tripoli)

Leptis Magna

Apo (S

Cy (Sha

AFRICA

(Banghāzī) Berenice

CYRE

LI

MAP KEY

→ First Journey, ca 46–48 C.E.

→ Second Journey, ca 49–52 C.E.

→ Third Journey, ca 53–57 C.E.

→ Journey to Rome, ca 59–60 C.E.

• One of the seven churches of Revelations

0   50   100   150   200   250 kilometers

0   50   100   150   200   250 miles

Present-day drainage, coastlines, and country boundaries are represented. Modern names appear in parentheses.

DACIA
ROMANIA

Danuvius (Danube)

MOESIA

BULGARIA

• Tomis (Constanţa)
• Civitas Tropaeensium (Adamclisi)

• Durostorum (Silistra)

• Novae (Svishtov)

• Nicopolis ad Istrum (Nikyup)

• Odessus (Varna)

• Serdica (Sofia)

preached in the
que, but some Jews
a mob, which rioted.
l Silas left for Berea.
(Acts 17:1–9)

• Philippopolis (Plovdiv)

THRACIA

Paul and Silas were thrown into
prison after they cast an evil spirit
out of a slave girl, costing her owners
her abilities. They were miraculously
freed by an earthquake.
(Acts 16:16–40)

PONTUS EUXINUS
(BLACK SEA)

• Sinope (Sinop)

(Amasra) Amastris

• Amisus (Samsun)

Pontic Mountains

• Amaseia (Amasya)

PONTUS

Bosporus

Thessalonica (Thessaloníki)
Philippi • Neapolis (Kavála)
• Abdera
Amphipolis (Amfípoli)
Apollonia
rea (Véria)

Thásos
Samothrace
Imbros
Lemnos

Hellespont
(Dardanelles)

Perinthus (Marmaraereğlisi)
Byzantium (Istanbul)
Chalcedon (Kadıköy)
Nicomedia (Kocaeli)

Heraclea Pontica (Ereğli)

BITHYNIA

Sangarius

TURKEY

Halys

Cyzicus

Lampsacus (Lâpseki)

After a night vision of a man from
Macedonia begging him for help, Paul
left for the region to preach there.
(Acts 16:9–10)

PHRYGIA

• Ancyra (Ankara)

• Gordium (Gordion)

GALATIA

CAPPADOCIA

Alexandria Troas
Assos

Adramyttium (Edremit)

Lesbos

(Mitilíni) Mytilene

Pergamum (Bergama)

Thyatira (Akhisar)

Sardis

Smyrna (Izmir)

ASIA

Philadelphia (Alaşehir)

Home of a great temple
to Artemis (Diana); a riot
ensued when Paul
preached against idols.
(Acts 19:23–41)

ANATOLIA
(ASIA MINOR)

Pisidian Antioch (Yalvaç)

PISIDIA

Apamea (Dinar)

• Archelais (Aksaray)

• Caesarea Cappadociae (Kayseri)

• Tyana

Iconium (Konya)

• Melitene (Malatya)

After preaching and healing, Paul was
stoned by a crowd stirred up by hostile
Jews and left for dead outside the city.
He returned to continue the ministry.
(Acts 14:8–20)

• Samosata (Samsat)

COMMAGENE

Ephesus
Mæander

Laodicea (Denizli)
Colossae (Honaz)

LYCAONIA

Lystra
Derbe

Portae Ciliciae
(Cilician Gates)

CILICIA

• Edessa (Şanlıurfa)

• Zeugma

Euboea

Athenae (Athens)

Ándros

Miletus

Sámos

The son of a Jewish woman and a
Greek man, Timothy joined Paul
on his second journey.
(Acts 16:1–3)

PAMPHYLIA

Perga

Attaleia (Antalya)
Side

Taurus Mountains

Tarsus

Issus

Alexandria ad Issum (Iskenderun)

Antiochia (Antioch)

• Aleppo (Ḥalab)

Euphrates

Halicarnassus (Bodrum)

Cos

Cnidus

LYCIA

Paul's (Saul) home city. He was a
Pharisee who persecuted the church
before he was converted.
(Acts 9:11, Philippians 3:5–6)

Seleucia Tracheotis (Silifke)

Seleucia Pieria (Samandağ)

A strong bastion of early
Christianity, Antioch sponsored
all three of Paul's journeys.
(Acts 13:3, 15:40, 18:22–23)

SYRIA

Cyclades

Náxos

After reasoning with
some of the philosophers
of the Areopagus,
several were converted.
(Acts 17:20–34)

rta
rti)

Rhodes

Rhodes

Patara

Myra (Kale)

Mare Creticum
(Sea of Crete)

Santorini

CRETA

Phenice, Phoenix
Crete
Gortyn
Lasea

Cnossus (Knosós)

Cauda (Gávdos)

Fair Havens

Cape Salmone
(Akrotírio Pláka)

Paul rebuked a false prophet named
Bar-jesus before the Roman proconsul.
The pretender was struck with blindness,
and the proconsul was converted.
(Acts 13:6–12)

CYPRUS

Cyprus

Salamis

Disciples of Jesus
Christ were first called
"Christians" in Antioch.
(Acts 11:26)

Paphos (Kouklia)

(Tripoli) Tripolis

(Jbail) Byblos

PHOENICIA

LEBANON

(Saïda) Sidon

Damascus

ABILENE

On his way to imprison
Christians in Damascus,
Saul (renamed Paul)
was converted after a
miraculous encounter
with Christ.
(Acts 9:1–19)

MARE
INTERNUM
(MEDITERRANEAN SEA)

Peter, Paul, and Barnabus met with other
Christian leaders to repudiate a sect that said
new Gentile converts needed to obey the Law
of Moses. In unity, they agreed that salvation
was by faith in Christ alone, no works of the
Law were required.
(Acts 15:1–21)

(Soûr) Tyre

('Akko) Ptolemais

Lacus
Tiberias
(Sea of
Galilee)

• Bostra (Buşra ash Shām)

Caesarea

ISRAEL

Antipatris

Neapolis (Nablus)

Jerusalem

Gaza

JUDAEA

Lacus Asphaltites
(Dead Sea)

NABATAEA

JORDAN

Alexandria (El Iskandarîya)

Paraetonium (Maţrûh)

Pelusium

OFF TO ROME
After returning to Jerusalem on
completion of his third mission, Paul
was imprisoned after the Jews accused
him of inciting riots. Tried before the
Roman authorities and King Agrippa, he
appealed his case to Caesar, as was the
right of any Roman citizen.
(Acts 21–26)

Daphnae (Kôm Dafana)

Terenuthis

AEGYPTUS

Heliopolis

Memphis

Nilus (Nile)

EGYPT

SINAI

• Petra

Aelana (Al 'Aqabah)

SAUDI
ARABIA

"The Conversion of the Proconsul Sergius Paulus" is a work by Italian artist Raphael (1483–1520). Sergius Paulus summoned Barnabas and Paul to hear the word of God.

his role in the Apostolic mission, before meeting Peter and **James** three years later (GALATIANS 1:17). Whatever the case may be, Paul eventually returned to his native town of Tarsus.

BARNABAS

In the meantime, an exciting development had taken place. Christian refugees who had fled to Antioch, capital of Roman Syria, had built a flourishing community that was attracting a steady stream of converts. It was here that the term "Christians" was coined to identify Christ's disciples (ACTS 11:21). *Christianos* in Greek literally means "follower of Christ."

The Jerusalem group decided to send one of its disciples to find out more about this Christian group. The choice fell on a man from Cyprus named Joseph, who had donated all his possessions to the Jerusalem church, and had been renamed **Barnabas** by his fellow followers. Barnabas made his way to Antioch and found there were indeed "a great many people" who had joined the Church. In fact, Barnabas felt overwhelmed, and wanted someone to help him. He remembered that there was a follower in nearby Tarsus, in Cilicia, named Paul; according to Acts, Barnabas

ca 73 C.E.	ca 73 C.E.	ca 75 C.E.	ca 75 C.E.
Besieged by the Roman Tenth Legion, the Jewish Zealots on Masada commit mass suicide	Yohanan ben Zakkai establishes a new Jewish religious academy in Yabneh	Putative date of the book *The Jewish War* by Josephus	Vespasian begins the construction of the Colosseum

had met Paul during the latter's brief visit to Jerusalem. Barnabas went to Tarsus and asked Paul to help him with the mission in Antioch. Paul agreed, and thus embarked on a mission that would ultimately take him to the far corners of the eastern Roman Empire and into the city of Rome itself.

PAUL

Accompanied by a third disciple called **John Mark**, Paul and Barnabas first traveled to Cyprus, Barnabas's native region, where Paul preached in synagogues from Salamis to Paphos, the Cypriot capital. The visit was very successful; Paul was even able to convert the Roman proconsul, **Sergius Paulus** (ACTS 13:12). They then crossed over to Perga on the Pamphylian coast, where John Mark decided to return to Jerusalem. From there, Paul and Barnabas traveled to another city, also called Antioch, though located in Pisidia. Here, however, their preaching met with fierce opposition from the local Jewish community, which forced them to divert to Iconium in Roman Lycaonia, only to be rebuffed once again. Rumors of a plot to assassinate them propelled the travelers to Lystra, where Paul healed a lame person. Astonished, the crowd shouted, "The gods have come down to us in human form!" (ACTS 14:10-11). The local Jewish community, however, was less impressed and tried to stone Paul. The two then moved on to Derbe, where people were more receptive to their preaching. From there, they retraced their steps to Perga, and embarked for their home base in Antioch in Syria.

Along the way, Paul made an interesting discovery. Apparently, many Gentiles were interested in becoming followers of Christ as well. As we saw, Peter had baptized a small number of Gentiles, but these followers were "God-fearing" people who embraced Judaism as well as baptism. Paul, however, had found that

Many of the Asia Minor provinces featured Greco-Roman cities where elegant Roman tableware, such as this first-century bronze vessel, was widely available.

THE SYNAGOGUE

The word "synagogue" comes from the Greek *synagogē*, which means "assembly" or "gathering." Josephus refers to synagogues as *proseuchai* (singular *proseuchè*), which means "prayer house." Some early synagogues have been found in Jericho, Magdala, and Gamla, which some scholars believe date to the first century B.C.E., and on Masada. In smaller villages, however, Sabbath services may have taken place in a prominent location out in the open, in the village square, or in one of the homes—usually the larger one—of a village elder. The Book of Acts confirms this when it relates how Paul and his companions "went [on the Sabbath day] outside the gate by the river, where we supposed there was a place of prayer" (ACTS 16:13). Some of the most prominent Galilean synagogues, including the ones in Capernaum and Chorazin, appear to have been built in the fourth century C.E., during the heyday of Rabbinic Judaism in the region. ■

many Gentiles were attracted to Christian spirituality without wanting to adopt Jewish customs as well. In fact, certain precepts of the Torah, such as circumcision and the kosher dietary laws, were a strong deterrent for many Gentiles. This raised the question whether a convert to Christ should also be expected to become Jewish. Did the imitation of Christ require one to follow the Jewish Law as well?

For the Apostles in Jerusalem, who were all practicing Jews, faith in Christ was inseparable from Jesus' own example as a Jewish rabbi. But Paul disagreed. He believed that the Jewish rite of circumcision had been replaced by baptism and faith in Christ. "Real circumcision is a matter of the heart," he wrote in his Letter to the Romans; "it is spiritual, not literal" (ROMANS 2:29). As far as the Jewish Law was concerned, Paul told the Galatians, "a person is justified not by the works of the Law but through faith in Jesus Christ" (GALATIANS 2:16). By doing so, Paul deliberately separated the early Christian movement from its Jewish roots, perhaps in the belief that there were many more Gentile than Jewish prospects in the Empire. And in the end, this is exactly what happened.

This synagogue was built by Zealot rebels fighting the Roman Tenth Legion on the Herodian fortress of Masada between 70 and 73 C.E.

French artist Jean-Leon Gerome (1824–1904) painted this canvas entitled "The Christian Martyrs' Last Prayer" in 1883. The setting is in Rome.

PROVINCE OF PALESTINA
CIRCA 135 C.E.

MAP KEY

Roman province of Palestina
Roman province of Syria
Roman province of Arabia
○   Location uncertain
[Jerusalem]   Former city name

MARE INTERNUM
(MEDITERRANEAN SEA)

Emperor Hadrian made an effort to desecrate areas venerated by early Christians. He had a temple to Venus built over the place of Jesus' Crucifixion, the site now covered by the Church of the Holy Sepulchre. In Bethlehem, he constructed a pagan shrine on the site revered as the place of Christ's birth, where the Church of the Nativity now resides. Those efforts, coupled with an unbroken line of Christian bishops in Jerusalem up to Hadrian's time, make it likely that the traditional sites for those events are correct.

Emperor Hadrian founded a new city on the ruins of Jerusalem. A temple to the god Jupiter was built on the Temple Mount.

Sidon
Damascus •

2,814 m
9,232 ft
Mt. Hermon

S Y R I A

Tyre •
Kanah •

• Caesarea Philippi
(Paneas)

Cadasa •
Asor •
Raphana •

Ecdippa •
Merom •

GAULANITIS

Ptolemais •
Jordan

*Bay of Acco
(Bay of Haifa)*
Jotapata •
Capernaum •
• Bethsaida

Sycaminium •
Mt. Carmel
546 m
1,791 ft
Arbela •
*Lacus Tiberias
(Sea of Galilee)*

Gabae •
Sepphoris •
Nazareth •
Tiberias •
• Hippos

Dora •
Legio •
Mt. Tabor
588 m
1,929 ft
Philoteria •
Gadara •
• Abila

Kishon
Yarmuk

Caesarea •

Scythopolis •
• Pella

Narbata •
Ginae •

Dion ○

Plain of Sharon

Mt. Ebal
940 m
3,084 ft

Apollonia •
Sebaste •
Neapolis •
• Amathus

Gerasa •

Yarqon
Mt. Gerizim
881 m
2,890 ft
Jordan
Jabbok

Joppa •
Antipatris •
Lebonah •

Phasaelis •
• Gadara

Lydda •
Archelais •
Philadelphia •

Bethel •

S H A R O N

Sorek
Jamnia •
Gazara •
Emmaus •
Jericho •
Esbus •

Azotus •
Aelia Capitolina •
[Jerusalem]
Bethany •
Mt. Nebo
802 m
2,631 ft
Medeba •

Bethlehem •

Ascalon •
*Lacus Asphaltitis
(Dead Sea)*

Marisa •
Beth-zur •

S H E P H E L A H

Lachish •
Hebron •

Anthedon •
Eshtemoa •
En-gedi •

Gaza •

Arnon

Beersheba •

Kir-Moab •

Raphia •

J O R D A N

N E G E V

E G Y P T

Zered (Hasa)

0   20   40 kilometers

0   20   40 miles

Present-day drainage, coastlines, and country boundaries are represented. Modern names appear in parentheses.

JAMES

When word of Paul's activity among the Gentiles reached the Apostolic group in Jerusalem, which was now led by James, it was met with deep concern. Certain members argued that "unless you are circumcised according to the custom of Moses, you cannot be saved" (ACTS 15:1). James is also known as **James the Just** in some traditions, to distinguish him from James the Apostle. In the Gospel of Thomas, for example, the disciples asked Jesus: "We know that you will depart from us; who is it who will lead us?" Jesus replied, "Wherever you have come from, go to James the Just, for whom heaven and earth came to be" (THOMAS 12).

Paul was asked to come to Jerusalem to explain himself. There are two records of this Jerusalem Conference, in Acts as well as in the Epistle to the Galatians, and both differ in details (ACTS 11:27-30; GALATIANS 2:1-10). Many scholars agree, however, that the meeting probably took place in the latter part of the 40s, and that it resulted in a compromise. Paul could minister to Jews and Gentiles throughout the Mediterranean world if he so wished, but James and his followers would limit themselves to preaching among the circumcised. The only condition that James asked of Paul was that Gentile converts adhere to the so-called Laws of Noah, which Leviticus imposed on any foreigners living on Israel's soil (LEVITICUS 17:10): namely, to abstain from idolatry; illicit sexual activity; and any meat of an animal that had been strangled or still contained any blood (ACTS 15:20).

Dutch artist Rembrandt van Rijn (1606–1669) painted this portrait of "Timothy and his Grandmother" in 1648. Timothy would become Paul's assistant.

TIMOTHY

Buoyed by the outcome of the Jerusalem Conference, Paul embarked on a second and even more ambitious mission. While Barnabas went back to Cyprus, Paul left for Derbe, Lystra, and Antioch of Pisidia, to visit the communities he and Barnabas had founded on their first journey. He was accompanied by a disciple known as **Silas** (though Paul referred to him using the Latinized version of "Silvanus"), who together with Paul would suffer imprisonment in Philippi until an

earthquake shook the prison and broke their chains; in Christian art, Silas is often depicted with a broken chain in his hands.

In Lystra, they were joined by another follower named Timothy. Thus began another close partnership, for Timothy would soon become Paul's assistant, confidante, and protégé. Paul called him his "'own son in the faith." Born of a Jewish mother and Greek father, however, Timothy was not circumcised. This put Paul's thesis of Gentile acceptance to the test. In the end, Timothy agreed to be circumcised just so that he would be welcomed in Jewish communities, which Paul continued to visit as well.

Paul had originally planned to travel the western part of Asia Minor, but a vision took him from Troas across the Aegean Sea to the port of Neapolis, in Macedonia. Here, the narrative in Acts changes from the third to the first person ("we immediately tried to cross over to Macedonia"), which, some authors believe, suggests that Luke, the presumed author of Acts, had now joined Paul and Timothy on their journey (ACTS 16:10).

The exact chronology of Paul's subsequent journey is subject to debate, but it is likely that he formed Christian communities in Philippi and Thessalonica, until a mob in Thessalonica forced him to flee to Beroea (I THESSALONIANS 1:8; ACTS 17:5-10). He then made his way to Athens, where he debated with Epicurean and

Giovanni Paolo Panini (1691–1765) created this evocative work entitled "The Apostle Paul Preaching on the Ruins" in 1744.

ca 96 C.E.
Domitian is assassinated and succeeded by Nerva

ca 98 C.E.
Nerva dies and is succeeded by Trajan

ca 110 C.E.
Oldest known use of paper for writing in China

ca 116 C.E.
Trajan extends Roman Empire into Parthia

316 NATIONAL GEOGRAPHIC WHO'S WHO IN THE BIBLE

A limestone fragment from Corinth reads, "Erastus, in return for his aedileship, laid [this pavement] at his own expense." This may be "Erastus, the city treasurer" referred to in Paul's Letter to the Romans.

Stoic philosophers in the Agora, the central marketplace, before preaching on a hill known as the Areopagus. He told the crowd that he had found an altar in the city, which was dedicated "to an unknown God." "What therefore you worship as unknown," Paul said, "this I proclaim to you now" (ACTS 17:23).

From Athens, Paul traveled on to Corinth, where he remained for 18 months. Based on his later Letter to the Corinthians (I AND II), written from about 54 C.E. onward, the Christian congregation in Corinth was mostly Gentile. According to Acts, a group of Jews accused Paul of "persuading people to worship God in ways that are contrary to the law." The presiding judge, a man named Gallio who was "proconsul of Achaia," dismissed the charge, given that it was not pertinent to Roman law (ACTS 18:12-17). Early in the 20th century, archaeologists discovered an inscription in the Temple of Apollo in Delphi that refers to a governor named "L. Iunius Gallio" from 52 C.E. This has been very helpful for scholars in trying to date Paul's journeys.

Sometime after 54 C.E., Paul left on a third journey using the city of Ephesus as his base. He then returned to Corinth and wrote his famous Epistle to the Romans. In the closing of this letter, Paul conveys the greetings of several disciples, including "Timothy, my co-worker"; several others whom Paul calls "my relatives"; and a follower known as "Erastus, the city treasurer" (ROMANS 16:23). In 1929, excavators found a first-century limestone fragment in Corinth inscribed with the words "Erastus, in return for his aedileship, laid [this pavement] at his own expense."

According to the first Letter to Timothy (ostensibly sent by Paul to his assistant, but probably written much later), Paul told Timothy to remain in Ephesus to prevent "heresy" from affecting the church in Ephesus (I TIMOTHY 1:3-4). He then made his way back to Jerusalem.

AGRIPPA I

Over the past decades, Judea had undergone some important changes. In 37 C.E., Emperor Gaius Caesar, nicknamed "Caligula" (ruled 37–41 C.E.), had given **Herod Agrippa I** (ruled 37–44 C.E.), a grandson of Herod the Great, control over the former tetrarchy of Philip. When Herod Antipas, ruler of Galilee and Perea, fell from grace in 39 C.E., Agrippa received his territories as well. Soon thereafter, Caligula declared himself a living god, and ordered that subjects throughout the Empire—including Jerusalem—should offer sacrifices to him. Many Jews in Judea balked at this decree and prepared to revolt, which was only preempted by Caligula's assassination in 41 C.E.

Caligula's successor, Emperor **Claudius**, extended Agrippa's territory by adding Judea, Samaria, and

A Roman bust found in Cologne depicts the Roman Emperor Gaius Caligula (ruled 37–41 C.E.).

ca 117 C.E.
Putative date of Tacitus's
Histories

ca 117 C.E.
Trajan is succeeded by Emperor
Hadrian

ca 122 C.E.
Hadrian's Wall is built in Britain

ca 131 C.E.
Outbreak of the Second
Jewish Rebellion, known as the
Bar Kokhba Revolt

CHAPTER 5: FROM ACTS OF THE APOSTLES TO REVELATION   **317**

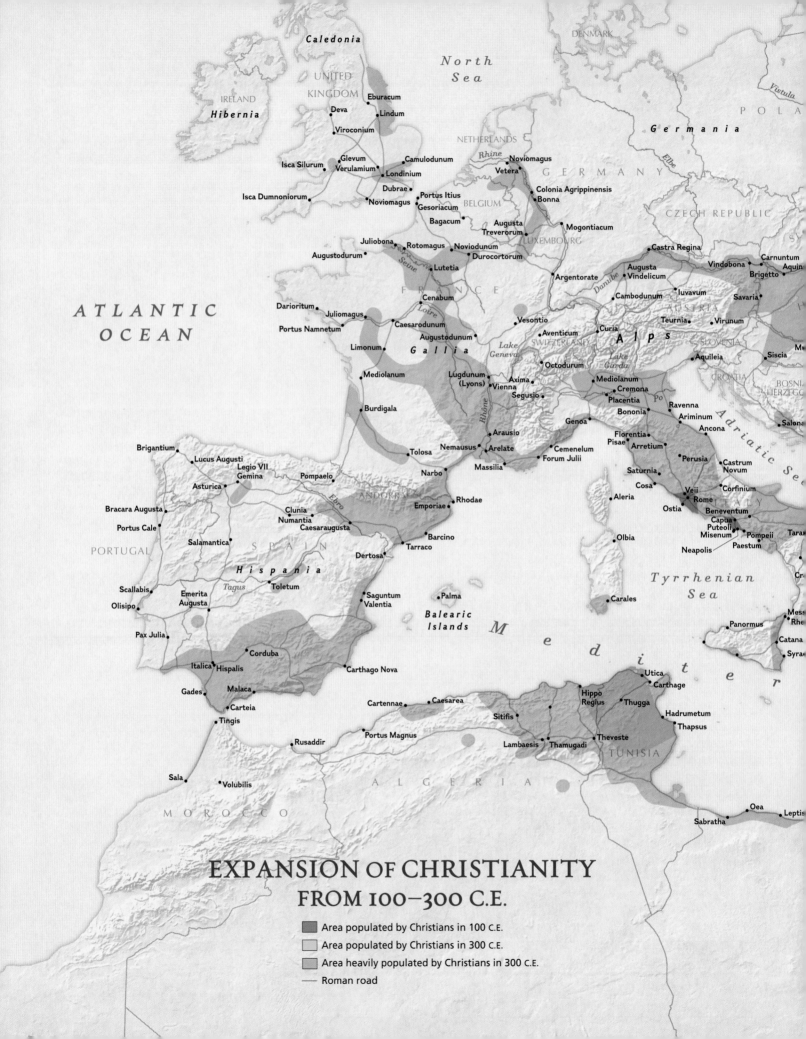

Caledonia

North Sea

IRELAND
UNITED KINGDOM

Hibernia

DENMARK

POLA

Germania

Eburacum
Deva · Lindum
Viroconium
Glevum · Camulodunum
Isca Silurum · Verulamium
Londinium
Isca Dumnoniorum
Dubrae
Noviomagus

NETHERLANDS
Rhine
Noviomagus
Vetera
GERMANY
Colonia Agrippinensis
Bonna

BELGIUM

LUXEMBOURG

CZECH REPUBLIC

Mogontiacum

Castra Regina

Germania

Vistula

Portus Itius
Gesoriacum
Bagacum
Augusta Treverorum

Juliobona
Rotomagus · Noviodunum
Augustodurum · Lutetia
Durocortorum
Argentorate

Augusta Vindobona
Vindelicum
Carnuntum
Aquin
Brigetto
Cambodunum · Iuvavum
Savaria

Gallia

Darioritum
Juliomagus
Portus Namnetum
Cenabum
Caesarodunum
Augustodunum

Vesontio
Aventicum
SWITZERLAND
Curia

Augusta
AUSTRIA
Teurnia · Virunum
SLOVENIA

ATLANTIC
OCEAN

Limonum

Lake Geneva

Alps
Mediolanum
Cremona
Aquileia
Siscia
CROATIA

Mediolanum
Lake Garda

BOSNIA
HERZEG

Burdigala

Lugdunum
(Lyons)
Axima
Vienna
Segusio
Octodurum

Placentia
Bononia
Po
Ravenna
Ariminum
Salona

Adriatic Se

Arausio
Nemausus · Arelate
Tolosa
Narbo
Massilia

Genoa
Cemenelum
Forum Julii

Florentia
Pisae · Arretium
Saturnia
Cosa

Ancona

Perusia
Castrum
Novum
Corfinium
Veii
Aleria
Rome
Ostia
ITALY
Beneventum
Capua
Puteoli
Misenum · Pompeii
Neapolis · Paestum

Tara

Brigantium
Lucus Augusti
Legio VII
Gemina
Asturica
Pompaelo
ANDORRA
Emporiae
Rhodae

Bracara Augusta
Portus Cale
PORTUGAL
Salamantica
Clunia
Numantia
Caesaraugusta
Barcino
Tarraco
Dertosa

SPAIN
Hispania
Tagus
Toletum

Tyrrhenian Sea

Olbia

Carales

Panormus

Messi
Rhe
Catana
Syra

Scallabis
Olisipo
Emerita
Augusta
Pax Julia

Saguntum
Valentia
Palma
Balearic Islands

Mediter

Corduba
Italica · Hispalis
Gades
Malaca
Carteia
Tingis

Carthago Nova

Cartennae · Caesarea
Sitifis

Utica
Carthage
Hippo
Regius
Thugga

ean

Rusaddir
Portus Magnus

Lambaesis · Thamugadi
TUNISIA
Theveste

Hadrumetum
Thapsus

Sala
Volubilis

MOROCCO

ALGERIA

Oea
Leptis
Sabratha

EXPANSION OF CHRISTIANITY
FROM 100–300 C.E.

Area populated by Christians in 100 C.E.

Area populated by Christians in 300 C.E.

Area heavily populated by Christians in 300 C.E.

— Roman road

KAZAKHSTAN

Volga

RUSSIA

Don

Dnieper

UKRAINE

Sarmatia

Scythia

Caspian Sea

TURKMENISTAN

Dniester

Olbia

Panticapaeum

Caucasus Mts.

GEORGIA

AZERBAIJAN

ROMANIA

Apulum

Troesmis

Chersonesus

Pityus

Lake Sevan

ARMENIA

Azer.

Sarmizegetusa Regia

Tomis

Black Sea

Trapezus

Lake Van

Lake Urmia

Singidunum

Durostorum

Tropaeum Traiani

Sinope

Satala

Viminacium

Oescus

Novae

Danube

Amisus

Pompeiopolis

Megalopolis

Tigranocerta

IRAN

Parthia

SERBIA

BULGARIA

Amastris

Heraclea Pontica

Gangra

Zela

TURKEY

Serdica

Hadrianopolis (Adrianople)

Byzantium (Constantinople)

Ancyra

Caesarea

Melitene

Amida

Philippopolis

Perinthus

Nicomedia

Nicaea

Edessa

Nicopolis

KOSOVO

Stobi

Cyzicus

Prusa

Dorylaeum

Samosata

MACED.

Dyrrhachium

Heraclea

Thessalonica

Asia Minor

Antiochia

Iconium

Cyrrhus

Tigris

Euphrates

Ctesiphon

Pergamum

Tarsus

Antiochia

Dura Europos

Ambracia

Smyrna

Aphrodisias

Seleucia

SYRIA

Palmyra

IRAQ

Nicopolis

Delphi

Ephesus

Miletus

Attalia

Laodicea

Raphaneae

Corinth

Athens

Aegean Sea

Cnidus

Rhodus

Myra

Salamis

Tripolis

Emesa

Sparta

CYPRUS

Paphos

Heliopolis

Damascus

LEBANON

Tyrus

Bostra

Gortyn

Caparcotna

Caesarea

West Bank

Dead Sea

SAUDI

Jerusalem

ISRAEL

JORDAN

ARABIA

Gaza

Gaza Strip

Petra

Mediterranean Sea

Nicopolis

Pelusium

Ptolemais

Cyrene

Alexandria

Memphis

LIBYA

Oxyrhynchus

Hermopolis

Nile

Red Sea

Ptolemais

Coptus

Thebae

EGYPT

0   50   100   150   200   250 kilometers

0   50   100   150   200   250 miles

Present-day drainage and coastlines are represented.
Modern names appear in parentheses.

RULERS OF ROMAN
JUDEA

KING AGRIPPA I
41-44 C.E.

CUSPIUS FADUS, PROCURATOR
44-46 C.E.

TIBERIUS ALEXANDER, PROCURATOR
46-48 C.E.

VENTIDIUS CUMANUS, PROCURATOR
48-52 C.E.

ANTONIUS FELIX, PROCURATOR
52-60 C.E.

**AGRIPPA II,
RULER OF GALILEE AND PEREA**
53-70 C.E.

PORCIUS FESTUS, PROCURATOR
60-62 C.E.

LUCCEIUS ALBINUS, PROCURATOR
62-64 C.E.

GESSIUS FLORUS, PROCURATOR
64-66 C.E.

Idumea. For a brief time, therefore, Agrippa found himself ruling over a territory that was roughly the size of his grandfather's kingdom, stirring Jewish hopes for a full restoration. Regrettably, Agrippa died in Caesarea in 44 C.E. Because his son, also called Marcus Julius Agrippa, was only 17 years old, Emperor Claudius decided to change Judea back into a Roman province. It was now known as Syria Palaestina, governed by a Roman procurator, **Cuspius Fadus** (ruled 44–46 C.E.).

Four years later, however, Claudius deemed Agrippa's son to be sufficiently mature to be given rule over some smaller territories, including Philip's old tetrarchy, as **Agrippa II** (ruled 48–70 C.E.). Around this time, Rome was struck by civil unrest. According to Roman historian

A Roman bust from Cologne depicts the Roman Emperor Claudius (ruled 41–54 C.E.).

Suetonius, this was blamed on Jewish Christians, because "the Jews were constantly causing *disturbances* at the instigation of *Christ* (or 'Chrestus,' as Tacitus called him, which was a more common name in Rome)." Claudius issued a decree evicting all Jews from Rome—though in due course, many Jewish families began to drift back (ACTS 18:2).

Thus it was that upon his return to Jerusalem, Paul found a city filled with tension. In Rome, sentiment had turned against Jews, while many Judeans bemoaned the loss of their autonomy to a Roman procurator. To make matters worse, these prefects were hopelessly inept or corrupt;

ca 132 C.E.	ca 135 C.E.	ca 135 C.E.	ca 138 C.E.
Chinese astronomer Zhang Heng develops a planetarium	The Second Jewish Rebellion is suppressed	Emperor Hadrian razes Jerusalem and builds a new city, Aelia Capitolina, in its place	Emperor Hadrian dies and is succeeded by Antoninus Pius

in the span of 16 years, Judea would be ruled by no less than five different procurators.

ANTONIUS FELIX

Paul was welcomed back by James and the Apostles, but they warned Paul that word of his proselytizing efforts in Asia Minor had spread, and that presumably "you teach all the Jews living among the Gentiles to forsake Moses" (ACTS 21:21). They urged Paul to discredit those rumors by going to the Temple and making a sacrifice in full view of all gathered there. Nevertheless, a group of "Jews from Asia" (presumably, Asia Minor) stirred up the crowd, and falsely accused him of taking a Gentile past the *soreg,* the sacred enclosure surrounding the Temple precinct (ACTS 21:27-29). Paul was arrested and remanded in the Antonia Fortress. For some, this was not enough, and a plot was hatched to kill him.

This golden aureus was struck during the reign of Emperor Claudius (ruled 41–54 C.E.).

The Roman commander of the fortress, **Claudius Lysias**, found out about the plot and quickly dispatched Paul to the Roman procurator, **Antonius Felix** (ruled 52–60 C.E.) in Caesarea. He also wrote a note to Felix, which said that Paul "was accused concerning questions of their law, but was charged with nothing deserving death or imprisonment" (ACTS 23:28).

Procurator Felix was a freedman and brother of Claudius's secretary of the treasury; according to Josephus, the brothers owed their freedom to the emperor himself. His rule in Judea was characterized by brutality and corruption; according to Acts, Felix did nothing to advance Paul's case, but summoned him often for "conversations," in the hope that he would be offered a bribe in return for Paul's freedom (ACTS 24:26). Because Paul refused to accommodate him, he was left to languish in prison for two years until Felix was replaced by **Porcius Festus** (ruled 60–62 C.E.). Felix did not, as yet, fade from history; he had married a Judean princess, Drusilla, who was the daughter of Agrippa I. Felix was thus the brother-in-law of Agrippa II. Drusilla bore him a son, Marcus Antonius Agrippa, as well as a daughter named Antonia Clementiana. Drusilla had the misfortune of staying in Campania when Mount Vesuvius erupted on August 24, 79, and she died in the cataclysm.

AGRIPPA II

At this time, around the year 60 C.E., the chief priests in Jerusalem once again demanded that Paul stand trial before the Sanhedrin.

This portrait of St. Paul is by Italian artist Bartolomeo Montagna (1450–1523) from 1482. Jews such as Antonius Felix did not welcome Paul when he returned to Jerusalem.

The outline of the Circus Maximus in Rome is still visible near the ruins of the Domus Augustana, a wing of Domitian's imperial palace on Palatine Hill.

NERO'S PERSECUTIONS

The Roman historian Tacitus tells us that after the great fire of Rome in 64 C.E., Emperor Nero put hundreds of Christians to death as part of public entertainment. "Some, dressed in the skin of wild animals, were torn to pieces by dogs," Tacitus writes; "others were crucified, or made into torches that were ignited after dark so as to function as lanterns. Nero provided his Gardens for the spectacle, and staged displays in the Circus." Quite possibly, the gardens that Tacitus is referring to were located on Nero's property on the Esquiline Hill, where he would later build his sumptuous *Domus Aurea,* or "Golden House." The property had once been owned by Maecenas, whose wealth was legendary. The location of the Circus is debated. Today, guides at the Roman Colosseum will sometimes tell pious tourists that this was the place where Christians were thrown to the lions. Yet the Colosseum, more properly called the Flavian Amphitheater, was built some eight years *after* the fire—not by Nero but by Emperor Vespasian. It is likely that Tacitus was referring to the Circus Maximus, which was a favorite venue for chariot racing, and included a track of more than 550 yards. Built before the time of Julius Caesar, in the days of the republic, the Circus Maximus was the biggest venue for staging large public entertainments in the mid-60s. After the fire, Nero himself extended the racetrack by some 100 yards. ∎

As a Roman citizen, however, Paul maintained his right of *provocatio,* of being heard by the emperor, or more properly the "emperor's tribunal" in Rome (ACTS 25:10).

The case gained such notoriety that the new procurator, Festus, felt compelled to refer the matter to Agrippa II (ACTS 25:13–22). Five years earlier, the new Roman **Emperor Nero** (ruled 54–68 C.E.) had extended Agrippa's northern territory with a number of cities in Galilee, including Tiberias, as well as Perea. Agrippa had also been granted the right to choose the high priest, which gave him considerable leverage in religious matters. Thus, it was not unusual that the Roman procurator decided to consult with Agrippa II about Paul, though technically the case did not fall under his jurisdiction.

This Roman bust depicts the Roman Emperor Nero (ruled 54–68 C.E.).

Paul then made a lengthy presentation before both Festus and Agrippa, which prompted the latter to wonder if Paul was trying to turn him into a Christian. Paul replied, "I pray to God that not only you but also all who are listening to me today might become such as I am—except for these chains." Agrippa then got up and took his leave; but as an aside, he told Festus, "This man could have been set free if he had not appealed to the emperor" (ACTS 26:28–29).

Finally, later that year, Paul was embarked with other prisoners on a ship for Rome. During the voyage, the vessel was hit by a heavy squall, which stranded Paul and other survivors on the beach at Malta. From there, an Egyptian grain ship eventually deposited him at Puteoli, in the bay of Naples. Paul then made his way to Rome, awaiting his hearing at the emperor's court. He "lived there two whole years at his own expense," says Acts, writing letters to the faithful and receiving visitors, but the details of what happened after that are uncertain (ACTS 28:30).

ANANUS

Porcius Festus died suddenly in 62 C.E. His designated replacement was **Lucceius Albinus**, who at the time was still residing in Rome. As preparations were made for the new Roman procurator to sail to Caesarea, Judea experienced a temporary power vacuum. As it happened, there was a change in the office of high priest as well. Agrippa II, who was wont to appoint and fire high priests at will, dismissed the sitting high priest,

ca 180 C.E.	ca 185 C.E.	ca 185 C.E.	ca 192 C.E.
Marcus Aurelius dies; Commodus reigns as sole emperor	Bishop Irenaeus proposes an anthology of the Gospels of Matthew, Mark, Luke, and John	Chinese astronomers observe a supernova in the constellation Centaurus	Emperor Commodus is murdered; Septimius Severus succeeds in 193

Joseph Cabi ben Simon, and appointed **Ananus**, the son of Annas (or Ananus in Latin) instead. The antipathy of Annas's family toward the Jerusalem church was still alive. As Josephus tells us, Ananus won the Sanhedrin's backing to indict "James, the brother of Jesus known as Christ and several others on the charge of breaking the Law," giving us an important attestation of the early Jerusalem church in a non-Christian source. James was thrown off the Temple parapet and stoned to death. The early Christian movement in Palestine was now without a leader. Within a decade, it would all but cease to exist.

NERO

While Paul was presumably still under house arrest in Rome, the city was devastated by a great fire. Some Romans suspected that Emperor Nero had set the fire himself, so as to clear large parts of the city for a design he himself had helped create. Perhaps to counter these rumors, Nero tried to pass the blame on to Rome's Christian

THE EMERGING CHURCH

Many early Christians, including Paul, were convinced that Christ would return in their lifetime. This expectation delayed the development of a formal Church organization, because Christ himself would come and establish his new kingdom. Soon, however, the question of how to administer the growing Christian communities became urgent. Paul had written to the Corinthians that "God has given the first place to apostles, second to prophets, and third to teachers" (I CORINTHIANS 12:28). Consequently, certain Christian communities began to appoint priestly leaders, or *presbyters*, on the strength of their ability and faith. Eventually, these prelates claimed that their authority derived from the apostolate itself, and so the title of bishop emerged. After the Council of Nicaea, held in 325, the bishopric of Rome was increasingly recognized as the leading authority, closely followed by the bishops of Antioch, Alexandria, and Constantinople. The bishop of Rome adopted the Roman name for supreme priest, which was *Pontifex Maximus*, or Pope. ∎

communities. The Roman historian Tacitus (ca 56–117 C.E.) relates how Christians were arrested, interrogated, and swiftly condemned. Clement I, a Christian bishop living in Rome near the end of the first century, claims that Peter had the misfortune of visiting the city during this period and was swept up in the persecution. According to Church legend, Peter was condemned to be crucified, but he insisted on being crucified upside down, lest he die in the same position as Jesus. Peter was buried in a rural spot on the right bank of the Tiber River, called the Ager Vaticanus.

The Christian theologian Tertullian of Carthage (ca 160–220 C.E.) wrote that Paul was also put to death at this time. According to Church tradition, other Apostles would eventually die a martyr's death as well, in either Palestine or Asia Minor, with the exception of John, son of Zebedee. If that is true, then by 65 C.E., just one year before the outbreak of the Jewish Rebellion in Palestine, all the principal leaders of the early Christian Church had been killed.

"The Crucifixion of St. Peter" was painted in the Brancacci Chapel in Florence, Italy, by Filippino Lippi (1457–1504). Peter was crucified during the reign of Emperor Nero.

ca 193 C.E.	ca 200 C.E.	ca 215 C.E.	ca 220 C.E.
Emperor Septimius Severus permits a persecution of Christians by local Roman officials	The Huns invade Afghanistan	The Baths of Caracalla are built in Rome	End of the Han Dynasty in China

THE CHRISTIAN CATACOMBS

Although Christianity was outlawed in the Roman Empire, Christian burials had to be conducted in secret. Many Christians, regardless of class, did what the poor of Rome had done for some time, and began to carve burial niches underneath the city, known as catacombs. Most of these catacombs were dug in the soft volcanic rock along the main roads leading to Rome, such as the Via Appia, the Via Ostiense, and the Via Tiburtina. The dead were wrapped in linen and placed in *loculi*, or burial niches, while wealthier families commissioned large subterranean tombs, decorated with columns and friezes. Many others contained simple though moving paintings that illustrate key phases of worship. In Rome alone, excavators have identified more than 60 catacomb networks, some equipped with galleries across multiple levels down to a depth of 60 feet. Here, Christian families would not only bury their dead, but also gather to pray, and sometimes to celebrate the Eucharist.

After the emancipation of the Christian faith by Gallienus and later by Constantine the Great, wealthy Christian patrons could return to Roman burial practices and thus commission sculptors to create fine sarcophagi. These marble coffins then became the favorite form of burial, because Christianity expressly forbade the Roman practice of cremation. One of the earliest examples is the sarcophagus from the Villa Felice in Rome. Carved around 312 C.E., it shows scenes of St. Peter and Christ, including the entry of Jesus into Jerusalem, riding a donkey. ■

An early Christian sarcophagus, dated around 312 C.E., shows the entry of Jesus in Jerusalem from the Villa Felice in Rome.

| ca 220 C.E.
First Goth invasions of the
Roman Empire | ca 221 C.E.
Roman citizenship is conferred
on every person in the empire | ca 249 C.E.
Emperor Decius initiates a persecution
of all individuals, including Christians,
who refuse to worship Roman gods | ca 261 C.E.
Emperor Gallienus ends
persecution of Christians |

JOHN OF PATMOS

Against the backdrop of this intensive political upheaval, the author known as John of Patmos is believed to have written the Book of Revelation (so called after the first word in the book, *apokalypsis,* which is Greek for "revelation" or "unveiling"). Christian tradition has identified this John as the son of Zebedee, one of the 12 Apostles, as well as the author of the Gospel of John. However, in the book, John explicitly refers to the "twelve names of the twelve apostles of the Lamb" without making any effort to associate himself with this group (REVELATION 21:14). Instead, the author merely calls himself a servant of God who, while staying on the island of Patmos, was visited by an angel of the Lord (REVELATION 1:1). What's more, John of Patmos dedicates his work to seven churches located on Asia Minor, all of which (except for Ephesus) were not known as Christian communities in Paul's time. This suggests that John was an itinerant missionary or leader/preacher working well after Paul's work in the region. The seven cities are Ephesus (near today's Selçuk), Smyrna (today's Izmir), Pergamum (near today's Bergama), Thyatira (today's Akhisar), Philadelphia (today's Alaşehir), and Laodicea on the Lycus (near today's Eskihisar), all in what is the western region of Turkey today.

The Book of Revelation follows the format of Jewish apocalyptic writings as the experience of a prophet or seer who is allowed to glimpse heavenly secrets and future events. Its principal purpose is revealed in the opening of the book: a message from the risen Jesus to churches who are suffering under persecution, urging them to remain steadfast in faith. As

"The Vision of St. John" is the work of the Master of the Johannes Vision, who was active in Cologne between 1450 and 1470.

DATING THE BOOK OF REVELATION

Revelation depicts a time of severe Christian persecution, which has led some scholars to date it to the reign of Emperor Domitian. Bishop Eusebius, an early historian of the Church, confirms that Domitian condoned the oppression of Jewish and Gentile Christians, though recent research suggests that some of this hostility may have been the result of tensions among these Jewish and Christian communities proper. Others believe the book should be dated to the persecutions by Nero in the wake of the great fire. The numeric code of the "beast" in Revelation, "666" (REVELATION 13:18), is widely believed to refer to Nero, just as the book's references to "Babylon" probably alluded to Rome. Nero's persecution of Christians, however, was largely limited to the city of Rome and would not have extended to Asia Minor. Another theory holds that Revelation may have been composed over many decades, from the 60s to the 90s. ∎

such, the book assures its audience that Jesus is ultimately in control of world history, notwithstanding Satan's efforts to challenge him at every turn, for only Jesus is able to break the seven seals on the scroll of destiny (REVELATION 5:5). Although the world must first pass through an age of war, pestilence, and false prophets, it will ultimately be redeemed by angels, proclaiming a new Jerusalem, a golden age ruled by God.

Like the Book of Daniel, Revelation tells its story with a cast of often bizarre beings and phenomena. Some, like the many-horned beast that rises from the ocean, are inspired by Daniel, while the description of the four horsemen may have been derived from Ezekiel, and the locusts with teeth like lions may have their origin in Joel. In all, scholars have identified some 348 references from Hebrew Scripture, with Isaiah, Ezekiel, Daniel, Enoch, and Psalms being the most prominent.

---

ca 269 C.E.
The Library of Alexandria is partly burned

ca 271 C.E.
The compass is developed in China

ca 300 C.E.
Bishop Eusebius codifies the first canon of the New Testament

ca 313 C.E.
Constantine the Great issues the decree of Milan, tolerating all religions including Christianity

San Vitale *One of the treasures of early Byzantine art is the Church of San Vitale in Ravenna, Italy. Its presbytery, begun in 527 and completed 20 years later, is covered with beautiful mosaics using themes from the Old and New Testament.*

The Good Shepherd
This fifth-century statue of the Good Shepherd was found in Işiklar, Turkey. The representation became a popular motif for depicting Christ, possibly because of its appearance in older, pagan traditions.

Villa Felice *Marble coffins became the favorite form of burial for wealthy Christian families, because Christianity forbade the Roman practice of cremation. This sarcophagus from Rome's Villa Felice is one of the earliest examples. Carved around 313 C.E., it shows scenes of Jesus and Peter on the eve of the Passion.*

Hagia Irene *The Hagia Irene, or Church of Holy Peace, is one of the first Christian churches built after Christianity was formally tolerated as a Roman religion by Constantine the Great in 313. Though it suffered extensive damage during the Nika Revolt in 532, it was restored by Emperor Justinian in 548, and has survived to this day.*

San Marco Basilica *Anonymous artists created this mosaic of Mary enthroned with the child Jesus and flanked by John and Mark the Evangelists in the narthex of the San Marco Basilica in Venice around 1200.*

Belgian St. Oda *In Europe, artists focused their skills on creating elaborate reliquaries for the remains of revered saints, such as this reliquary of the Belgian St. Oda, whose shrine was located in Amay, today located in the Walloon province of Liège.*

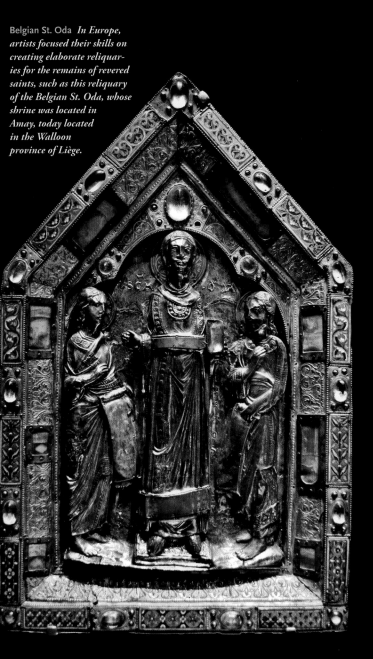

TREASURE OF THE CHRISTIAN ERA

The emancipation of Christianity, beginning with Emperor Gallienus and culminating with Constantine the Great and Theodosius II, unleashed a powerful flowering of Christian art throughout the Roman Empire, soon to be called the Byzantine Empire. In Rome, sculptors who had previously carved sarcophagi with pagan figures were now allowed to turn to Christian themes. Among others, the idea of Jesus as the "Good Shepherd" became a popular motif in early Christian art. In Visigoth Spain, tombs were now proudly adorned with the Christian monogram of the Greek letters chi and rho, the first two letters of the Greek word "Christos." And in Constantinople, the new capital of the Roman Empire, Constantine's architects searched for the perfect design of a Christian sanctuary, and settled on the Roman basilica type, previously used for civic functions and the courts. Amazingly, one of the first of these Christian "churches" has survived to this day, in the form of the basilica of Hagia Irene ("Holy Peace"), in the city now known as Istanbul, Turkey. Two centuries later, this paradigm found its most beautiful expression in the sixth-century Basilica of San Vitale, covered with scintillating Byzantine mosaics.

In Europe, by contrast, Christian art searched for indigenous roots through the veneration of reliquaries, containing the remains of native saints. Some of these early medieval reliquaries are works of a deep and moving piety, heralding the early Romanesque style.

Visigoth Plaque *This fifth-century plaque from Spain, which once covered a columbarium or grave niche, proudly proclaims the deceased as a Christian by using the chi and rho monogram, the first two characters of "Christos."*

CHAPTER 5
WHO'S WHO
An Alphabetical Listing of Characters in the Books of
Acts of the Apostles to Revelation

A "Christian" fighting for his life was painted by John Millar Watt (1895–1975).

ABADDON
("destruction")

The Hebrew name of "the angel of the bottomless pit" (REVELATION 9:11). In Greek, his name is Apollyon, which means "destroyer." The Hebrew name is also used as a term for utter destruction (JOB 26:6; 28:22; 31:12; PROVERBS 15:11; 27:20).

ACHAICUS

One of the three Corinthians who visited Paul in Ephesus (I CORINTHIANS 16:17).

AENEAS

A paralytic who was confined to his bed for eight years until he was healed by Peter (ACTS 9:33-34).

AGABUS

A prophet who predicted that a famine would take place in Judea (ACTS 11:27-28). Josephus does mention a famine that occurred in Judea in the reign of Claudius, while Tiberius Alexander was procurator, which swept away many of the inhabitants. Many years afterward, Agabus met Paul in the house of the deacon Philip at Caesarea, and warned him of the dangers that awaited him in Jerusalem should he persist (ACTS 21:10-12).

AGRIPPA I

Son of Aristobulus and Bernice, grandson of Herod the Great, Herod Agrippa I (ruled 37–44 C.E.) was given control over the former tetrarchy of Philip by Emperor Gaius Caesar, nicknamed "Caligula." When Herod Antipas, Agrippa's uncle, fell from grace in 39 C.E., Agrippa received Galilee and Perea as well. Caligula's successor, Emperor Claudius, extended Agrippa's territory by adding Judea, Samaria, and Idumea. For a brief time, therefore, Agrippa ruled as king over a territory that was roughly the size of

his grandfather's kingdom, stirring Jewish hopes for a full restoration. According to Acts, Agrippa persecuted the Christian community in Judea, imprisoned Peter, and ordered the execution of the Apostle James, son of Zebedee. He died in Caesarea in 44 C.E.

AGRIPPA II

Son of Herod Agrippa I, and great-grandson of Herod I the Great. In 48, Agrippa II was deemed to have been sufficiently matured

This canvas of the prophet St. Agabus was painted by Spanish painter Fray Juan Bautista Mayno (1569–1649).

to be given rule over a few minor territories, including Philip's old tetrarchy, as Agrippa II (ruled 48–70 C.E.). Several years later, the new Roman Emperor Nero (ruled 54–68 C.E.) extended Agrippa's territory with a number of cities in Galilee including Tiberias, as well as Perea. Despite the fact that Judea was under Roman rule, Agrippa gradually became recognized as the region's de facto puppet king, for example, by spending a fortune restoring and beautifying parts of Jerusalem. He also enlarged the city of Caesarea Philippi, renaming it Neronias in that emperor's honor. Agrippa was given the right to choose the high priest, which gave him additional authority in religious matters. When Paul argued for this innocence, Agrippa told the procurator, Festus, "This man could have been set free if he had not appealed to the emperor" (ACTS 26:28–29). Agrippa II died without producing an heir, thus ending the Herodian dynasty.

ALEXANDER
("defender of men," after Alexander the Great)
1. A relative of Annas the high priest, possibly his son, who was present when Peter and John were examined before the Sanhedrin (ACTS 4:6).
2. A Jew at Ephesus put forward by his countrymen during the tumult raised by Demetrius the silversmith, to plead their cause with the mob (ACTS 19:33). He was later reproached by Paul as one who, together with one Hymenaeus, let go of "faith and good conscience," and so "shipwrecked their faith" (I TIMOTHY 1:19-20).
3. "Alexander the coppersmith," mentioned as having caused Timothy much trouble (II TIMOTHY 4:14).

AMPLIATUS
("enlarged")
The Latin version of the Greek name Amplias, a member of the Christian community in Rome, to whom Paul sent greetings (ROMANS 16:8). He is designated "my beloved in the Lord." A common name in the Early Imperial period, it is found twice in the cemetery of Domitilla; the earlier inscription is over a cell from the end of the first century or the beginning of the second century.

ANANIAS
("God has favored")
1. A disciple in Jerusalem, and Sapphira's husband (ACTS 5:1–11). Ananias sold his goods for the benefit of the Church but he kept back a part of the price, without telling the Apostles. His wife knew of the deception. When it was discovered, Peter denounced the fraud and Ananias fell down and died.
2. A Christian in Damascus who became Paul's instructor (ACTS 9:10). He was "a devout man according to the law, having a good report of all the Jews which dwelt" at Damascus (ACTS 22:12).
3. The high priest who presided over Paul's hearing (ACTS 23:2). This high priest became enraged at Paul's declaration, "I have lived in all good conscience before God until this day" and had an attendant hit him on the mouth. Paul quickly replied, "God will strike you, you whitewashed wall!" Being reminded that Ananias was the high priest, Paul said, "I did not realize, brothers, that he was the high priest" (ACTS 23:5).

ANDRONICUS
("conqueror")
A Christian in Rome (ROMANS 16:7).

ANNA
("gracious")
1. A "prophetess" in Jerusalem (LUKE 2:36). She was of the tribe of Asher.
2. A devout widow (LUKE 2:36,37).

ANTIPAS
("like the father")
1. A martyr at Pergamos, and according to tradition, the bishop of that place (REVELATION 2:13).
2. Herod Antipas, a son of Herod the Great by his Samaritan wife, Malthace, and tetrarch of Galilee and Perea until 39 C.E. (LUKE

The painting "The Feast of Herod" is from the Italian School in the 16th century. Herod Antipas was the son of Herod.

23:7). Antipas ordered the beheading of John the Baptist at the instigation of Herodias, the ex-wife of Herod Philip, whom he had married (MATTHEW 14:1-12). According to Luke, Pilate sent Jesus to him for interrogation (LUKE 23:7). The wife of Chuza, his house steward, was one of Jesus' disciples (LUKE 8:3).

APELLES
("called")
A Christian disciple in Rome to whom Paul sends greetings in Romans 16:10.

APOLLOS
("given by Apollo")
An Alexandrian Jew who was baptized a Christian under the tutelage of Aquila and Priscilla. He preached with the Apostle Paul at Corinth and later Ephesus (ACTS 18:24–28; 19:1; I CORINTHIANS 1:12; 3:4–7).

APOLLYON
("destroyer")
Known as the "angel of the abyss" and the "king of the locusts," Apollyon is the Greek version of the Hebrew word "Abaddon." According to the Book of Revelation,

Apollyon is the king of a horde of demonic horsemen, represented by locusts, who arise from the abyss to torment earth's inhabitants (REVELATION 9:11).

APPHIA
("fruitful")
A female Christian of Colossae, possibly the wife of Philemon, who is mentioned in a letter to Philemon by Paul (PHILEMON 1:22,25).

AQUILA
("eagle")
A native of the Greek territory Pontus, Aquila met Paul in Corinth and later accompanied him to Ephesus. At one time, Aquila had lived in Rome with his wife, Priscilla, but they were forced to flee as a result of an edict by Emperor Claudius, banning all Jews from the city (ACTS 18:2; 26:1; I CORINTHIANS 16:19).

ARCHIPPUS
("master of horses")
A Christian teacher in Colossae whom Paul called his "fellow soldier." He was a member of Philemon's family, probably his son (COLOSSIANS 4:17; PHILEMON 1:2).

ARISTARCHUS
("the best ruler")
A Thessalonian who accompanied Paul on several missionary journeys, including voyages to Asia Minor and Rome (ACTS 19:29; 20:4; 27:2). He was imprisoned with Paul in Rome (COLOSSIANS 4:10; PHILEMON 1:24).

ARISTOBULUS
("good counselor")
A Roman whose household is mentioned in Paul's Letter to the Romans (ROMANS 16:10).

ARTEMAS
("gift of Artemis")
A companion of Paul. Paul wrote Titus to say he was going to send Artemas to Crete, so Titus could visit Paul in the winter at Nicopolis (TITUS 3:12).

ARTEMIS
Not to be confused with the Greek hunter-goddess Artemis known as Diana to the Romans, the Ephesian Artemis was an ancient mother-goddess depicted as a female figure with many breasts or eggs, denoting her fertility. Her prominent temple in Ephesus contained many sacred paintings and sculptures and was rebuilt three times. There was a treasury behind her shrine containing the wealth of many nations. Her idol is said to have fallen from the sky. In Acts, Paul's preaching led to a protest by silversmiths who made their living selling silver figurines of the goddess's cult statue. Their spokesperson, a man named Demetrius, said "there is danger not only that this trade of ours may come into disrepute but also that the temple of the great goddess Artemis will be scorned, and she will be deprived of her majesty that brought all Asia and the world to worship her" (ACTS 19:24–27). Paul's companions were dragged to the city's theater, which still exists; eventually they were released, whereupon Paul left for Macedonia.

ASYNCRITUS
("incomparable")
A Christian to whom Paul sent his greetings in a letter to the Christians in Rome (ROMANS 16:14). Arguably, Asyncritus, Phlegon, Hermas, Patrobas, and Hermes formed a small group within the larger Christian community of Rome.

BAR-JESUS
("son of Jesus")
Also known as Elymas, Bar-Jesus was a son of Joshua, a false prophet and magician who lived in Paphos (ACTS 13:6).

BARNABAS
("son of encouragement")
A name given by the Apostles to Joseph, a man from Cyprus, who had donated all his possessions to the Jerusalem church, and in return had been renamed Barnabas (Aramaic for "son of the prophet"). He introduced the recently converted Saul to the Apostles in Jerusalem. When word reached Jerusalem that there was a flourishing community of believers in Antioch, capital of Roman Syria, the Apostles decided to send

"St. Paul Preaching Before the Temple of Diana at Ephesus" was painted by Adolf Pirsch (1858–1929) in 1885. Also known as Artemis, she was an ancient mother-goddess.

Barnabas to investigate. Barnabas enlisted Paul's help, because Paul was in Tarsus at the time. Paul agreed, thus embarking upon his ministry that would take him to places throughout the Roman Empire. Barnabas consulted with the Apostles on the relationship of non-Jews within the church (ACTS 4:36; 9:27; 11:19-26; 13:2; 15:1,36-41; 26:17).

BARSABBAS
("son of Sabbas")
1. Surname of Joseph, also called Justus Barsabbas. After the Crucifixion of Jesus, he was proposed as a candidate for the apostleship left vacant by the death of Judas Iscariot. However, he was not awarded the position (ACTS 1:15-26).
2. Surname of Judas. Judas, with Silas, was a delegate from the church in Jerusalem to the non-Jewish Christians of Antioch, Syria, and Cilicia. They were appointed to convey the decree regarding the behavior of non-Jewish Christians with regard to the Jewish Law. Silas and Barsabbas accompanied Paul and Barnabas to Antioch, and stayed in the city to preach (ACTS 15:40-41).

BERNICE
("brings victory")
Eldest daughter of Agrippa I. After her first husband died, she was married to her uncle Herod, king of Chalcis. After his death and the outbreak of the Jewish Revolt, she moved with her brother Agrippa II to Rome, where their close relationship sent many tongues wagging, prompting a satire by Juvenal. She was present when Paul was allowed to make a presentation to Festus and Agrippa II (ACTS 2:5,13,23; 25:13,23; 26:30).

BLASTUS
("sprout")
Chamberlain to King Herod Agrippa I (ACTS 12:20).

CANDACE
A Queen of Ethiopia who had a eunuch in her court who served as her treasurer.

French painter Theodore Chasseriau (1819–1856) created this study for "St. Philip Baptising the Eunuch of the Queen of Ethiopia." The queen's name was Candace.

Ethiopia was a successful nexus of commerce between Africa and Asia Minor at the time. Her treasurer traveled to Jerusalem, and, upon his return journey, met the deacon Philip. The eunuch was reading from the Book of Isaiah when Philip ran up to him and offered to explain the passage he was reading, which was Isaiah 53:7-8: "Like a sheep he was led to the slaughter." Philip told the eunuch about Jesus, and the Ethiopian agreed to be baptized—thus foreshadowing the future Apostolic mission to the Gentiles (ACTS 8:26–38).

CARPUS
("fruit, wrist")
A Christian who kept Paul's cloak and priceless books and parchments during Paul's stay in Troas (II TIMOTHY 4:13). During Paul's imprisonment, Paul wrote to Timothy, asking him to bring the items that he had left with Carpus.

CENTURION
("hundred")
A centurion, *ekatóntarchos* in Greek, was an officer in charge of a hundred soldiers in the Roman army, roughly comparable to the modern rank of sergeant major. Each legion of 6,000 men had 60 centurions. Cornelius, the first Gentile to be converted by Peter, was a centurion (ACTS 10:28).

CHLOE
("green")
A female Christian who lived in Corinth (I CORINTHIANS 1:11). Some members of her household had told Paul of the divided state of the Corinthian church.

CLAUDIA
A woman who, along with Eubulus, Pudens, and Linus, sent well wishes to Timothy (II TIMOTHY 4:21).

CLAUDIUS
1. Fourth Roman emperor who extended Agrippa's reign to a size comparable to the kingdom of Herod the Great. He also dealt with several famines, arising from unfavorable harvests (ACTS 11:28-30). When Rome was struck by civil unrest, Claudius issued a decree evicting all Jews from Rome—though in due course, many Jewish families began to drift back (ACTS 18:2). After the death of Agrippa, Claudius decided to turn Judea back into a Roman

This marble bust of Emperor Claudius (10 B.C.E.–54 C.E.) from Thasos dates to the first century C.E.

province, because Agrippa's son was only 17 years old. It was now known as Syria Palaestina, once again governed by a Roman procurator, the first of whom was Cuspius Fadus (ruled 44–46 C.E.).
2. Claudius Lysias was the commander of the Antonia Fortress, the headquarters of the Roman army in Jerusalem (ACTS 23:26). During Paul's last visit to Jerusalem, he was set upon by a mob and put by the Romans in protective custody in the Antonia Fortress, given that he was a Roman citizen. When Claudius Lysias heard that there was a plan to kill Paul, he sent him to Felix, the procurator in Caesarea, with a note stating that Paul "was accused concerning questions of their law, but was charged with nothing deserving death or imprisonment" (ACTS 23:28).

CLEMENT
("merciful")
A Christian from Philippi who worked with Paul when the latter was in Philippi (PHILIPPIANS 4:3). He was assisted by two women, Euodias and Syntyche.

COLOSSIANS
Members of the Christian congregation Colossae, to whom the Letter to the Colossians is dedicated. Colossae was located in Phrygia (today's Turkey) on the Lycus River, some 12 miles south of Laodicea. The Christian community here was reportedly founded by Epaphras, who told Paul about the growing church in the city while the latter was a prisoner in Rome. Paul never visited the city; in his Letter to Philemon, he expressed his desire to visit the place once he was freed from prison, which never came to pass. The letter may have been written by an anonymous follower after Paul's death, yet under his name so as to bolster its authority.

CORINTHIANS
Members of the Christian congregation of Corinth, capital of Achaia or Roman Greece, to whom the first and second letter of Paul to the Corinthians is dedicated. This congregation was predominantly Gentile, and included members such as Prisca and Aquila, Achaicus, Fortunatus, Crispus, and

Gaius. Paul also refers to "Erastus, the city treasurer" (ROMANS 16:23). In 1929, excavators found a first-century limestone fragment in Corinth inscribed with the words "Erastus, in return for his aedileship, laid [this pavement] at his own expense." The first Letter to the Corinthians is usually dated around 54 or 55 C.E., while the second letter, written partly in response to the activity of rival Jewish-Christian preachers in the city, should be dated around one or two years later.

CORNELIUS
A Roman centurion of the Italian cohort who was stationed in Caesarea (ACTS 10:1). When an angel came to him in a night vision and told him to send two servants and a soldier to fetch Peter from Joppa, he did what the angel asked. On the night that the men went to get Peter, Peter himself had a vision. He saw a large sheet being lowered with various unclean animals, while a voice said, "What God has made clean, you must not call profane" (ACTS 10:10-15). Peter was deeply puzzled by the vision when the men arrived with a request for Peter to travel to Caesarea. As soon as Peter arrived in Caesarea, Cornelius fell at his feet. It was when Peter told Cornelius to stand up that Peter understood the meaning of his vision: that no man was unclean. Cornelius told Peter

"The Vision of Cornelius the Centurion" is the work of Dutch artist Gerbrand van den Eeckhout (1621–1674). It dates from 1664.

about his own vision, and when Cornelius and his friends started to speak in different tongues and magnify God, Peter baptized them. Cornelius thus became the first Roman to be baptized by Peter.

CRESCENS
A companion of Paul in Rome, who left him to go to Galatia (II TIMOTHY 4:10).

CRISPUS
Head of the synagogue in Corinth. He converted to Christianity, and was baptized by Paul (ACTS 18:8).

DAMARIS
("gentle")
An Athenian woman who became a believer after hearing Paul explain his doctrine in front of the Areopagus, where the Athenian council met to debate philosophical issues and legal cases. Dionysius is believed to be Damaris's husband (ACTS 17:34).

DEMAS
Companion of Paul while the latter was under arrest in Rome. He was present when Paul sent his letters to the Colossians, and to Philemon. In both these letters, Paul conveys the greetings of Demas, along with those of Luke, "the beloved physician" (COLOSSIANS 4:14). In Paul's Letter to Timothy (if indeed it was written by Paul), he expresses his disappointment with Demas for having forsaken Paul due to his "love for this present world" (TIMOTHY 4:10).

DEMETRIUS
("belonging to Demeter")
1. A silversmith in the city of Ephesus who earned his living making and selling silver

"Saint Dionysius the Areopagite" is by the Greek icon painter Kostos Loudovikos (b. 1961).

statuettes of the Greek goddess Artemis of Ephesus (ACTS 19:24). He felt the missionary activities of Paul were reducing the demand for idols, and thus threatened his livelihood. Demetrius instigated a riot against Paul and his companions, but he was told by the town official if he had complaints against Paul, he should follow the legal procedure and bring the matter to court.

2. Bearer of the third letter of John the Elder, which was addressed to Gaius (III JOHN 1:12).

DIONYSIUS

Member of the Areopagus, the high council of Athens, which met on Mars Hill to debate philosophical issues and legal cases. Dionysius became a believer after hearing Paul explain his doctrine in front of the Areopagus. Damarius is believed to be Dionysius's wife (ACTS 17:34).

DIOTREPHES
("nourished")
An elder of the Christian community to which Gaius, the addressee of the third letter of John, belonged. Diotrephes had attacked John's authority and was rebuked by John for his pride, and for his refusal to receive messages and offer hospitality (III JOHN 1:9).

DORCAS

Doras is the Greek name of Tabitha. She was a Christian convert, known for her charity and good deeds, who lived in Joppa. When she got sick and died, Peter, who was staying in the neighboring town of Lydda, was asked to come to Joppa. As soon as he arrived, he was taken to Dorcas's room in the upper floor, where several women were crying and wailing. Peter asked the women to leave the room. He then knelt and prayed, and he said, "Tabitha, arise." Dorcas came back to life (ACTS 9:36).

DRUSILLA

Daughter of Agrippa I and Jewish wife of the Roman procurator, Antonius Felix (ruled 52–60 C.E.) in Caesarea (ACTS 24:24). Procurator Felix was a freedman and brother of Claudius's secretary of the treasury; according to Josephus, the brothers owed their freedom to the emperor himself. The fact that Felix was appointed procurator despite having married a Jewess demonstrates Claudius's tolerance toward Jews, despite his decree to remove Jews from Rome following disturbances there. Drusilla was present when her husband sent for Paul, and heard him explain his faith (ACTS 24:24). She then accompanied her husband back to Rome, where the Imperial authorities interrogated him for his cruelty and poor government of the Judean province. Drusilla bore Felix a son, Marcus Antonius Agrippa, as well as a daughter named Antonia Clementiana. Drusilla and her son had the misfortune of staying in Campania when Mount Vesuvius erupted on August 24, 79, and they died in the cataclysm.

E

ELYMAS
Arabic name of the false prophet or sorcerer Bar-Jesus who opposed Paul's preaching in Cyprus. He was struck with blindness after Paul cursed him. Elymas then converted to Christianity (ACTS 13:8).

EPAENETUS
("praised")
A Christian in Rome whom Paul calls "well-beloved." Paul mentions Epaenetus in his letter to the Christians of Rome as being one of the first converts to Christianity in Achaia, modern-day Greece (ROMANS 16:5).

EPAPHRAS
("lovely")
A Christian who preached in the city of Colossae and was a friend of Paul (COLOSSIANS 1:7); he may in fact have been the founder of the Christian community of Colossae. He remained with Paul in Rome, while Paul was imprisoned; indeed, Paul calls him his "fellow prisoner" (PHILEMON 1:23).

EPAPHRODITUS
("fair")
A Christian who brought messages to Paul from the city of Philippi to Rome, where Paul was imprisoned. Paul referred to Epaphroditus as "my brother" (PHILIPPIANS 2:25).

This miniature is taken from a 16th-century version of "St. Paul's Epistle to the Ephesians."

EPHESIANS

Members of the Christian community of Ephesus, a leading port city on the Ionian coast of Asia Minor, to whom the Letter to the Ephesians is dedicated. Scholarship has cast considerable doubt on Paul's authorship, given that the style and theological viewpoints in this Epistle are markedly different from the letters that are undoubtedly from the hand of Paul. The Ephesian community was largely composed of Gentiles, who experienced little or no kinship with Jewish Christians or indeed the Jewish roots of Christianity. Scholars usually date this letter, written by a Christian disciple, to between 80 and 95 C.E.

ERASTUS

("beloved")

1. One of the attendants of Paul at Ephesus who went with Timothy to Macedonia (ACTS 19:22).

2. City treasurer of Corinth. In the closing of his Letter to the Romans, Paul conveys the greetings of several disciples, including a follower known as "Erastus, the city treasurer" (ROMANS 16:23). In 1929, excavators found a first-century limestone fragment in Corinth inscribed with the words "Erastus, in return for his aedileship, laid [this pavement] at his own expense."

EUBULUS

("good-willer")

One of the four people who sent greetings to Timothy in what is presumably the last letter written by Paul (II TIMOTHY 4:21).

EUNICE

("victorious")

Mother of Timothy, who was a Jewish woman married to a Greek (ACTS 16:1; II TIMOTHY 3:15). Thus, Timothy was not circumcised, but Timothy later agreed to undergo this procedure so as to facilitate his movement in Jewish communities.

EUODIA

("fragrant")

A Christian woman in Philippi (PHILIPPIANS 4:2; PHILEMON 4:2).

EUTYCHUS

("fortunate")

A young man of Troas who fell from an

Sir Edward Burne-Jones (1833–1898) created this stained glass picture of St. Timothy and Eunice, his mother.

open window on the third floor of the house where Paul was preaching, and was "taken up dead." Paul restored him to life (ACTS 20:9-12).

FELIX

("happy")

Antonius Felix was the Roman procurator of Judea from 52 to 60 C.E. Felix was a freedman and brother of Claudius's secretary of the treasury; according to Josephus, the brothers owed their freedom to the emperor himself. Paul was brought before Felix in Caesarea and remanded to prison. According to Acts, Felix did nothing to advance Paul's case, but summoned him often for "conversations," in the hope that he would be offered a hefty bribe in return for Paul's freedom (ACTS 24:26). Because Paul refused to accommodate him, he was left to languish in prison for two years until Felix was replaced by Porcius Festus (ruled 60–62 C.E.). On his return to Rome, the Jews in Caesarea accused Felix of cruelty. He would have been condemned if his brother Pallas had not prevailed with Emperor Nero to spare him. The wife of Felix was Drusilla, daughter of Herod Agrippa I.

FESTUS

Porcius Festus (ruled 60–62 C.E.) was Felix's successor as procurator of Judea, appointed by Nero (ACTS 24:27). A few weeks after Festus reached Judea, he heard the cause of Paul, who had been left a prisoner by Felix, in the presence of Herod Agrippa II and Bernice his sister. Because of his appeal to the emperor's tribunal, Paul was sent to Rome. It has been suggested that Festus, after being in office less than two years, died in Judea.

FORTUNATUS

("fortunate")

One of the three Corinthians, the others being Stephanas and Achaicus, who were at Ephesus when Paul wrote his first Letter to the Corinthians (I CORINTHIANS 16:17). A Fortunatus is mentioned at the end of the extracanonical first Epistle of Clement to the Corinthians; they may be one and the same person.

GAIUS

1. Paul's companion in his travels and his host at Corinth. Gaius was baptized by Paul and would serve as his host once again during his second journey to that city (I CORINTHIANS 1:14; ROMANS 16:23).

2. A Macedonian whose life, along with Aristarchus, was in danger from the mob at Ephesus that was threatening Paul (ACTS 19:29).

3. A Galatian born in Derbe who accompanied Paul on his last journey to Jerusalem (ACTS 20:4).

4. A Christian of Asia Minor to whom John addressed his third epistle (III JOHN 1:1).

5. Gaius Caesar, son of Germanicus and a member of the Julio-Claudian dynasty, who as third emperor of Rome and ruled from 37 to 41 C.E. Gaius is commonly known by his nickname "Caligula," or "little soldier's boot," given to him by his father's soldiers while campaigning. Gaius gave a grandson of Herod the Great, Herod Agrippa I (ruled 37–44 C.E.), control over the former tetrarchy of Philip, including the Gaulanitis. When Herod Antipas, tetrarch of Galilee and Perea, fell from grace in 39 C.E., Agrippa received these territories as well. Soon thereafter, Caligula declared himself a living god, and ordered that subjects throughout the empire—including Jerusalem—should offer sacrifices to him. Many Jews in Judea prepared for war, which was only preempted by Caligula's assassination in 41 C.E.

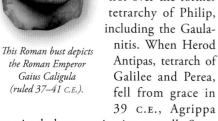

This Roman bust depicts the Roman Emperor Gaius Caligula (ruled 37–41 C.E.).

GALATIANS

Members of the Christian community of Galatia, which today designates a large area around Ankara, capital of Turkey, but in Paul's day extended toward the Mediterranean and included such cities as Lystra and Iconium. The Letter to the Galatians is generally regarded as written by Paul himself. In it, he summoned all of his rhetorical powers to combat the influences of other Jewish-Christian preachers, who had arrived in the area and were telling recently baptized Gentiles that they should be circumcised (GALATIANS 5:2-12), observe the Sabbath (GALATIANS 4:10), and adhere to other precepts of the Jewish Law, including food preparation (GALATIANS 4:17). Although there is no agreement on the dating of the letter, many scholars tend to place it in the early part of the 50s.

GALLIO

Junius Annaeus Gallio was the Roman proconsul of "Achaia" (or Greece) when Paul arrived in Corinth (ACTS 18:12). Gallio was the brother of Lucius Annaeus Seneca, the eminent philosopher who served as tutor and sometime minister of Emperor Nero. He is spoken of by his contemporaries as "sweet Gallio," and is often described as a most popular and affectionate man. When the Jews brought Paul before his tribunal on the charge of persuading "men to worship God contrary to the law," he refused to listen to them, and "drove them from the judgment seat" (ACTS 18:13-16).

GAMALIEL

("God's reward")

1. Son of Pedahzur and a captain of the tribe of Manasseh at the census at Sinai (NUMBERS 1:10; 7:54,59; 20:20). He commanded his tribe's army on the march through the wilderness (NUMBERS 10:23).

2. Son of rabbi Simeon and grandson of the famous rabbi Hillel the Elder. Gamaliel was a Pharisee and celebrated doctor of the law, noted for his learning, and served

"The Apparition of Gamaliel to the Priest Lucien" is from the Altarpiece of St. Stephen and was painted by Michael Pacher (1435–1498) around 1470.

as president of the Sanhedrin during the reigns of Tiberius, Caligula, and Claudius. The Mishnah calls him one of the greatest rabbis, arguing that "Since Rabban Gamaliel the Elder died, there has been no more reverence for the law, and purity and piety died out at the same time" (SOTAH 15:18). According to Acts, Gamaliel intervened on the Apostles' behalf during their hearing before the council on the charge of preaching the Resurrection of Jesus. If their work or counsel was of man, Gamaliel argued, it would come to nothing; but if it was of God, they could not destroy it, and therefore ought to be on their guard lest they should be "found fighting against God" (ACTS 5:34-40). Acts also states that Paul was once one of Gamaliel's disciples (ACTS 22:3), though this continues to be the subject of scholarly debate. Whereas Gamaliel always counseled temperance and tolerance, Paul was known as an uncompromising individual, fiercely devoted to his beliefs. Gamaliel is assumed to have died about 18 to 20 years before the destruction of Jerusalem in 70 C.E.

HERMAS

A Christian to whom Paul sent greetings in his Letter to the Romans (ROMANS 16:14).

HERMES

1. Greek god of boundaries who moved easily between the domain of mortals and gods as both divine messenger and intercessor; the Romans called him Mercury. After Paul healed a cripple in the city of Lystra, witnesses in the crowds shouted in the Lycaonian language, "The gods have come down to us in human form!" Barnabas was called Zeus, and Paul was readily identified as Hermes "because he was the chief speaker" (ACTS 14:10-12).
2. The name of a Roman Christian to whom Paul sent greetings in his Letter to the Romans (ROMANS 16:14).

HERMOGENES
("born of Hermes")

A companion of the Apostle Paul in Asia Minor, who eventually abandoned him because of the many trials they encountered (II TIMOTHY 1:15).

HERODION
(form of "Herod," "hero-like")

A Roman Christian whom Paul greets and calls his "kinsman" in his Letter to the Romans (ROMANS 16:11).

HYMENAEUS
("belonging to marriage")

Name of a person who appears twice in the correspondence between Paul and Timothy, where he is labeled as a heretic or "false teacher." Apparently, Hymenaeus was a believer in Christ who taught "that the resurrection is past already," and that by contrast, true resurrection was within oneself, once the soul awoke from sin (I TIMOTHY 1:20; II TIMOTHY 2:17-18). Scholars have interpreted these teachings as an early form of Gnosticism, which focused on the spirituality of Jesus' teachings as a

Hans Memling (ca 1433–1494) painted "St. John the Evangelist at Patmos" from the "Mystic Marriage of St. Catherine" triptych, which dates to 1479.

conduit to finding divine knowledge within oneself, and rejected the idea of physical resurrection.

JAMBRES

One of the two magicians at the court of Pharaoh in ancient Egypt, who according to the Book of Exodus opposed Moses. The actual name appears only in the New Testament (II TIMOTHY 3:8) and in Targum Pseudo-Jonathan, Exodus 7.

JANNES

One of the two magicians at the court of Pharaoh in ancient Egypt, who according to the Book of Exodus opposed Moses. The actual name appears only in the New Testament (II TIMOTHY 3:8).

JASON

A Christian who served as host of Paul and Silas in Thessalonica. A Jewish mob attacked him in the hopes of capturing Paul. When they were unable to find him, they instead brought Jason before the ruler of the city. It is possible that the same Jason accompanied Paul and his kinsmen from Thessalonica to Corinth (ACTS 17:5-9; ROMANS 16:21).

JESUS JUSTUS

A Jewish Christian, and a disciple of Paul in Rome (COLOSSIANS 4:11).

JOHN OF PATMOS

Author of the Book of Revelation, who according to Christian tradition was exiled to the Greek island of Patmos during the Roman persecution of Christians during the reign of Domitian (REVELATION 1:9). The same tradition also identifies this John as the son of Zebedee, one of the 12 Apostles, who also wrote the Gospel of John and the Letters of John in the New Testament canon. Modern scholars question this identification, given that the Greek style and grammar of the Gospel of John is highly developed and thus beyond the skill of a simple fisherman from Capernaum (most fishermen were, in fact, illiterate). What's more, if the Book of Revelation was indeed written during the reign of Domitian, who ruled from 81 to 96 C.E., then obviously John the disciple must have lived to a very old age, well into his 90s, which was more than double the average life expectancy in first-century Palestine. Some authors have argued that perhaps these works were written by members of a so-called "Johannine community" inspired by the life and sayings of John the Apostle. On the other hand, John (or "Johanan") was a very common name in Palestine.

JOHN THE ELDER
("graced by God")

Author of three letters in the New Testament, who is traditionally identified as the evangelist who wrote the Gospel of John. There are indeed remarkable similarities between the letters and the Gospel in terms of thematic material; what's more, the first Book of John appears to use extensive citations from this Gospel. Nevertheless, the differences in writing style between the first Book of John and the second and third Books of John have led some scholars to conclude that these were written by different authors. A putative date for the Letters of John is near the end of the first century, possibly in Ephesus.

The Via Recta, or Straight Street, in Damascus— shown here in a print from 1900—was the street where, according to Acts, Ananias met Saul in the house of Judas.

JOSEPH BARSABBAS
("son of Sabba")
Joseph Barsabbas reportedly accompanied the Apostles during their journeys with Jesus and was present at John's baptism. After Jesus' Crucifixion, he was suggested as a candidate to replace Judas Iscariot but lost to Matthias (ACTS 1:15-26).

JUDAS
("celebrated")
1. Judas, alternative spelling for Judah, son of Jacob (MATTHEW 1:2).
2. Son of Simon, surnamed Iscariot, one of the 12 Apostles, who betrayed Jesus to his enemies (MATTHEW 10:4).
3. Judas of Galilee, who in 6 C.E. led a resistance movement against the Romans in response to the tax census ordered by Quirinius, the governor of Greater Syria, in the newly annexed province of Judea. According to Josephus, Judas and "Zadok the Pharisee" then formed the Zealot movement, the "fourth sect" in Palestine after the Sadducees, Pharisees, and Essenes; this Zealot movement is believed to have instigated the Jewish Revolt of 66–70 C.E. Gamaliel referred to Judas the Galilean in his defense of the Apostles before the Sanhedrin (ACTS 5:37).
4. Judas of Damascus, a Jew who sheltered Saul when he was struck blind on the road to that city. Ananias, a Christian, went to the house and restored Saul's sight (ACTS 9:11).
5. Brother of Joseph Barsabbas and an elder member of the Christian council in Jerusalem. Together with Silas, he was asked to take a letter to the people of Antioch to explain what Law observance was required of Gentiles who wished to be baptized. Judas and Silas were instructed to "impose . . . no further burden than these essentials: that you abstain from what has been sacrificed to idols and from blood and from what is strangled and from fornication." These precepts, known as the Noahide Laws, were traditionally imposed on all Gentiles living in Israel (ACTS 15:22).

JUDE
("celebrated")
Brother of James and of Jesus, a "servant of Jesus Christ" who according to Christian tradition was the author of the Letter of Jude in the canon of the New Testament (JUDE 1:1). Jude traveled throughout Palestine as an itinerant preacher and missionary of the Apostolic movement. Though disputed, scholars have recently upheld the attribution of this letter to Jesus' brother. If this is true, then the Letter of Jude, which was apparently written in response to the teachings of certain Christian dissidents preaching great moral latitude, could be considered the oldest document in the New Testament.

JULIA
A Christian woman in Rome, possibly

the spouse of Philologus, to whom Paul sent greetings in his Letter to the Romans (ROMANS 16:15).

JULIUS

A centurion of the so-called Augustan cohort in the Roman army, who was in charge of Paul and other prisoners during the sea voyage from Caesarea to Rome. When the boat was shipwrecked and the soldiers of the guard detail prepared to kill the prisoners to prevent their escape, Julius intervened and allowed all occupants to swim to shore, saving Paul in the process (ACTS 27:1-3,43).

JUNIAS

A Christian at Rome to whom Paul sent greetings in his Letter to the Romans. Junias as well as a man named Andronicus were called "kinsmen" by Paul, which may suggest they were fellow Jews and not necessarily blood relatives; he also indicated that they were imprisoned at one time. Furthermore, Paul stated that "they were in Christ before me," which suggests that they were founders or members of the Christian community in Rome that existed well before Paul's time (ROMANS 16:7).

JUSTUS
("just")

1. One of the candidates who was nominated with Matthias to succeed Judas as the 12th Apostle (ACTS 1:23), also called Joseph Barsabbas.

2. A Christian at Corinth with whom Paul lodged (ACTS 18:7).

3. A Christian of Jewish origin who was mentioned by Paul in his Letter to the Colossians as someone who was a comfort to him while he was in prison in Rome (COLOSSIANS 4:11).

LINUS
("derived from flax")

This statue of St. Luke was carved by Venetian sculptor Niccolò di Piero Lamberti (1370–1451).

One of four people who sent greetings to Timothy in the last letter written by Paul (II TIMOTHY 4:21). The placement of the name may indicate that Linus was the son of Pudens and Claudia.

LOIS
("agreeable")

Mother of Eunice and the grandmother of Timothy, who lived in Lystra (II TIMOTHY 1:5).

LUCIUS
("illuminative")

Lucius, or Lucius of Cyrene, was a Christian

teacher at Antioch who preached and organized the Church church during the year that Paul lived in Antioch as well (ACTS 13:1). He is possibly the same person that Paul mentions in his Letter to the Romans, where he is referred to as his kinsman (ROMANS 16:21).

LUKE

A faithful companion of Paul, who since the late second century has been credited as the author of the Gospel of Luke and the Acts of the Apostles (COLOSSIANS 4:14). Luke was reportedly born at Antioch in Syria, where he studied medicine. He joined Paul on his second journey from Troas to Philippi. Six years later, he returned with Paul from Philippi to Jerusalem, and then accompanied him on his last journey from Caesarea to Rome. He remained with Paul during his captivity in prison and is mentioned by Paul in his Letter to Philemon. The identification of Luke, the companion of Paul as Luke, the author of the third Gospel, has not found universal support among scholars. One reason is the problem of dating: Paul and Luke traveled to Rome between 60 and 62 C.E., whereas the Gospel of Luke is generally dated to the 80s. There is some evidence that the author of Luke and Acts was a physician (compare LUKE 8:42-48 with MARK 4:24-34), but it is quite slim, particularly when it comes to scenes of Jesus' healing.

LYDIA

A woman of Thyatira who made her living selling purple cloth. While Paul was staying in Philippi, he went out of the city with his companion to preach to a group of women, which included Lydia. She was converted through Paul's preaching and baptized along with the other members of her household. She then persuaded Paul to be a guest in her house during his stay in Philippi (ACTS 16:14).

LYSIAS
See **Claudius Lysias.**

M

MANAEN

One of the prophets and teachers in the Antioch church, who was active during the year when Paul lived in Antioch. According to Acts, Manaen was "a member of the court of Herod the ruler," which either suggests that he was raised at the court of the Tetrarch Herod Antipas, or that he or his father served Herod Antipas as a courtier (ACTS 13:1).

This portrait of St. Mark was created by Giovanni Francesco Barbieri Guercino (1591–1666).

MARK

Son of Mary, a leading Christian in Jerusalem whose house served as a meeting place for the early Apostolic movement. Mark was originally known by his Jewish name of Johanan, or "John," and later adopted the Roman surname of Mark, or "Marcus." John Mark traveled with Barnabas and Paul through Asia Minor and the Greek islands, preaching the Gospel and making new converts. Among others, he visited the community at Colossae (COLOSSIANS 4:10). While in Perga, Mark decided to return to Jerusalem. Paul and Barnabas then fell out over the question whether they should take John Mark along on the second journey they were planning. The two longtime companions split: Mark and Barnabas left for Cyrus, which was Barnabas's native region, while Paul took Silas on his long overland journey through Syria and Asia Minor. Ten years later, Paul and John Mark appear to have reconciled, and Mark is referred to as a "fellow worker." In other references, Paul noted that Mark was a fellow prisoner in Rome (ACTS 12:12). Mark then became a close companion of Peter; in the first Letter of Peter from Rome, he sends the greetings of "my son Mark." Bishop Papias of Hierapolis said around 120–130 C.E. that Mark was the "disciple and interpreter" of Peter, who "handed down to us in writing the things that Peter had proclaimed," which led to the identification of John Mark as the author of the Gospel. But the actual text of the Gospel does not mention a Mark, nor does it identify its author.

MARY

Mother of John Mark, and sister of Barnabas (COLOSSIANS 4:10). Along with her brother, she sold her land and gave the proceeds of the sale into the treasury of the Church church (ACTS 4:37; 12:12). Her house in Jerusalem served as the meeting place for the disciples, possibly beginning with the Last Supper and lasting throughout the early period of the Apostolic mission.

MATTHIAS

After the Passion events and death of Judas Iscariot, the Apostles debated who should replace him. It was agreed that this new disciple should have been a part of the movement from the very beginning. Two followers qualified: Joseph Barsabbas (also known as Justus) and a man named Matthias. They prayed, cast lots, and finally elected the follower named Matthias (ACTS 1:23).

"St. Matthias" is the work of the English School from the 19th century. Matthias became an Apostle after the death of Judas.

MNASON

An "early disciple" from Cyrus, in whose house Paul and other disciples stayed on Paul's last journey to Jerusalem (ACTS 21:16).

N

NARCISSUS

A Christian to whose family Paul sent greetings in his Letter to the Romans (ROMANS 16:11).

NEREUS

A Christian who Paul named and sent greetings to in his Letter to the Romans (ROMANS 16:15).

NICANOR

One of the seven deacons, "men of good standing, full of the Spirit and of wisdom," who were chosen to serve tables and distribute food to the needy, in response to a complaint that Greek widows in the Jerusalem community were not receiving their fair share (ACTS 6:3,5).

In Ephesus, where Paul befriended a Christian named Onesiphorus, Tiberius Julius Aquila later built the famous Library of Celsus.

NICOLAUS

One of the seven deacons, "men of good standing, full of the Spirit and of wisdom," who were chosen to serve tables and distribute food to the needy, in response to a complaint that Greek widows in the Jerusalem community were not receiving their fair share (ACTS 6:3,5).

NYMPHA (OR NYMPHAS)

A Christian saluted by Paul in his Letter to the Colossians as a member of the church of Laodicea (COLOSSIANS 4:15).

OLYMPAS

A Roman Christian whom Paul greets in his Letter to the Romans (ROMANS 16:15).

ONESIMUS

An escaped slave from Colossae whom Paul met in Rome and subsequently converted to Christianity. Onesimus became Paul's assistant and confessed that in addition to running away from his master, Philemon, he had also robbed him. Eventually he returned to Philemon with a letter from Paul, begging for forgiveness and for receiving Onesimus as a brother in Christ. "I appeal to you for my child, Onesimus," Paul wrote, "whose father I have become in my imprisonment" (COLOSSIANS 4:9; PHILEMON 1:10).

ONESIPHORUS

("bringing profit")

A Christian who befriended Paul during his stay in Ephesus. Later, Onesiphorus visited Paul while he was imprisoned in Rome, and brought him food, drink, and news from the outside (II TIMOTHY 1:16).

PARMENAS

One of the seven deacons who along with Stephen, Philip, Prochorus, Nicanor, Parmenas, and Nicolas, "men of good standing, full of the Spirit and of wisdom," were chosen to serve tables and distribute food to the needy, in response to a complaint that Greek widows in the Jerusalem community were not receiving their fair share (ACTS 6:3,5).

PATROBAS

("father's life")

A Christian at Rome to whom Paul sent salutations in his Letter to the Romans (ROMANS 16:14). Roman historian Tacitus refers to a wealthy former slave named Patrobas, who was freed after serving Nero and subsequently executed under Galba (Tacitus, *History* i.49; ii.95).

PAUL

Born in Tarsus around 10 C.E. and originally named Saul, Paul was a member of the tribe of Benjamin and a Pharisee (PHILEMON 3:5; ACTS 23:6). Acts states that he was a pupil of the distinguished Rabbi Gamaliel, who may be the same Gamaliel who intervened on Peter's behalf during his hearing in front of the Sanhedrin. Paul confessed that "as to zeal," he worked as "a persecutor of the church"; in his Letter to the Galatians, he adds that this zeal had enabled him to advance "beyond many among my people of the same age" (GALATIANS 1:14). He may have been one of the orchestrators of Stephen's stoning; Acts tells us that witnesses to the execution "laid their coats at the feet of a young man named Saul," and that "Saul approved of their killing him" (ACTS 7:58; 8:1).

Having received permission to track Christians "into cities abroad," Paul (or

French artist Eustache Le Sueur (1616–1655) painted "Paul Preaching in Ephesus" in 1649.

Saul as he was called at that time) journeyed to Damascus. Suddenly, a light from heaven flashed around him. Saul fell to the ground and heard a voice saying, "Saul, why do you persecute me?" Saul scrambled to his feet but, unable to see, was led to Damascus, where a disciple named Ananias was told in a vision to look after him. As soon as Ananias laid his hands on Saul, "something like scales fell from his eyes," and he could see again (Acts 9:18). Saul, now renamed Paul, was baptized, and soon began to proclaim Jesus in the synagogues.

According to Acts, Paul made his way to Jerusalem, where he met the Apostles (Acts 9:25). In his Letter to the Galatians, however, Paul claims that he did not go to Jerusalem to see "those who were already Apostles before me," but spent three years contemplating his role in the Apostolic mission, spending time in Arabia (Galatians 1:17). Paul eventually returned to his native town of Tarsus.

Barnabas, sent on a special mission to Antioch, needed help with this rapidly growing community. He went to Tarsus to seek Paul and brought him to Antioch as an assistant. As the Church grew, Paul and Barnabas, with John Mark as their attendant, left on the first missionary tour. They sailed from Seleucia to Cyprus. Here, Sergius Paulus, the Roman proconsul, was converted. The missionaries then crossed to the mainland and arrived at Perga (Acts 13:13). Although John Mark returned to Jerusalem, Paul and Barnabas proceeded through Pamphylia, Pisidia, and Lycaonia, returning by the same route and founding Christian communities where they went. From Perga, they returned to Antioch.

After remaining in Antioch for "a long time," a controversy broke out in the church over the obedience of baptized Gentiles to the Jewish Law. Paul believed that a baptized Gentile need not become a Jew as well: He wrote "a person is justified not by the works of the Law but through faith in Jesus Christ"

(Galatians 2:16). Paul and Barnabas were sent to consult the Church at Jerusalem. It was decided that Paul could minister to Jews and Gentiles throughout the Mediterranean world if he so wished, but that James and his followers in Jerusalem would limit themselves to preaching among the circumcised

"Elymas the Sorcerer Struck Blind Before Sergius Paulus" is the work of Giulio Clovio (1498–1578). Sergius Paulus was the proconsul of Cyprus.

(Acts 15:1-21). After a short rest at Antioch, Paul said to Barnabas: "Let us go again and visit our brothers in every city where we have preached the word of the Lord, and see how they do." But Paul and Barnabas quarreled over the question whether they should take Mark as well. Unable to resolve the matter, they separated and never met again. Paul, however, would afterward speak kindly about Barnabas, and would send for Mark in Rome (Colossians 4:10; II Tim 4:11).

Paul then took Silas, instead of Barnabas, on his second missionary journey. He went by land, revisiting the churches he had

already founded in Asia Minor, but he also longed to enter into "regions beyond," and traveled on to Phrygia and Galatia (Acts 16:6). He then turned to Bithynia, but the Spirit guided him in another direction. He traveled to the shores of the Aegean and arrived at Troas, where he saw, in a vision, a man who cried, "Come over, and help us" (Acts 16:9). Paul saw this as a message from God and set sail across the Hellespont. This led him into Europe, carrying the Gospel into the Western world. In Macedonia, he founded Christian communities in Philippi, Thessalonica, and Berea. Paul then passed into Achaia, Roman Greece. He reached Athens and continued on to Corinth, where he remained a year and a half. While in Corinth, he wrote his two epistles to the church of Thessalonica, and then sailed for Syria. He was accompanied by Aquila and Priscilla, whom he left at Ephesus. He landed at Caesarea, went up to Jerusalem, and continued on to Antioch (Acts 18:20-23).

Around 54 c.e., Paul began his third missionary tour. He journeyed to the "upper coasts" of Asia Minor, and made his way to Ephesus, where he worked for at least two years. With his assistants, he carried the Gospel to Colossae in Laodicea and other places they could reach. The silversmiths of Ephesus organized a riot against Paul, and he left the city for Troas, and then met Titus in Macedonia (II Corinthians 2:12). He sailed to Jerusalem.

At the feast of Pentecost, he was attacked by a mob in the Temple and arrested. He appealed to the emperor, claiming the privilege of a Roman citizen to be heard by an Imperial tribunal, and was detained in Caesarea for two years (Acts 25:11). Finally, Paul and other prisoners were embarked on a ship for Rome. During the voyage, the vessel was hit by a heavy squall, which stranded Paul and a number of other survivors on the beach at Malta. From there, an Egyptian grain ship eventually deposited him at Puteoli, in the bay of Naples. Paul slowly made his way to Rome, awaiting his hearing at the emperor's court. He "lived there two whole years at his own expense," writing letters to the faithful. His rooms were visited by many anxious inquirers, both Jews and Gentiles (Acts 28:23,30-31). After the burning of Rome, which Nero saw fit to attribute to the Christians, a persecution broke out against the Christians. According to Church tradition, Paul was seized, condemned, and delivered to the executioner, though the historical details are uncertain (Acts 28:30).

A Greek Orthodox icon depicts Saint Philemon. Paul addressed an epistle to him.

PERSIS

A Christian woman in Rome to whom Paul sent greetings (Romans 16:12). She is spoken of as "beloved," and as having "labored much in the Lord."

PHILEMON

Name of the Christian to whom Paul addressed his epistle on behalf of Onesimus. Philemon was a native of Colossae, and a person of some note among the citizenry. He is called a "fellow-worker," which indicates that he was a fellow Christian. Apphia, who is also mentioned, may have been his wife, and "Archippus our fellow soldier" was probably his son. The letter served to ask Philemon to forgive his runaway slave, Onesimus. As such, the document revealed an unusual quality of Paul: as a supplicant, asking for forgiveness "for my child, Onesimus" with all the charm Paul could muster (Philemon 1:2; Colossians 4:9). The Letter to Philemon is the only epistle in the New Testament addressed to an individual, rather than a community.

PHILETUS
("amiable")

At Ephesus, Philetus and Hymenaeus claimed that the "resurrection was past already" (II Timothy 2:17-18). Scholars have interpreted these teachings as an early form of Gnosticism, which focused on the spirituality of Jesus' teachings as a conduit to finding divine knowledge within oneself, and rejected the idea of physical resurrection.

PHILIP
("lover of horses")

1. One of the 12 Apostles who was from Bethsaida, as were Simon Peter and Andrew, and who originally joined John the Baptist in the Jordan (John 1:44). In the Gospel of John, Philip enjoys considerable prominence. He readily responded when Jesus first addressed him, and he is the one who brought Nathanael to Jesus (John 1:43,45-46). In the Book of Acts, he is listed as being present at the election of Matthias before the Pentecost. According to the Gospel of John, he was responsible for the provisioning of Jesus' traveling group of Apostles, and was stunned to be told to feed the 5,000 who had come to hear Jesus speak (Matthew 10:3; Mark 3:18; John 6:5-7; 12:21-22; 14:8-9; Acts 1:13). Nothing certain is known of his later life. Tradition states that he preached in Phrygia and died in Hierapolis.

2. One of the seven deacons, "men of good standing, full of the Spirit and of wisdom," who were chosen to serve tables and distribute food to the needy, in response to a complaint that Greek widows in the Jerusalem community were not receiving their fair

"The Martyrdom of St. Philip" was painted by Jusepe de Ribera (ca 1590–1652) in 1639.

share (Acts 6:3,5). He was one of those who were "scattered abroad" by the persecution that arose after the death of Stephen. He went first to Samaria, where he was an evangelist (Acts 8:5-13). While there, he received a divine command to go south, along the road leading from Jerusalem to Gaza. These towns were connected by two roads. The one Philip was directed to take led through Hebron. It was also a minimally inhabited district, and hence called "desert." Along the road, he was overtaken by the chariot of an Ethiopian man, the eunuch or chief officer of Queen Candace, who was at that moment reading a portion of the prophecies of (Isaiah 53:6-7). Philip began conversing with him and expounded these verses, preaching the words of Jesus. The eunuch received the message and believed. He was then baptized, and "went on his way rejoicing." By the Spirit, Philip instantly vanished from the sight of the eunuch after the baptism. He was next found at Azotus, where he continued his evangelistic work until he came to Caesarea. He is not mentioned again for about 20 years, still at Caesarea when Paul and his companions were on the way to Jerusalem (ACTS 21:8).

PHILIPPIANS

Members of the Christian community of Philippi, a city in the Roman province of Macedonia originally founded by Philip II, father of Alexander the Great, in 356 B.C.E. According to Acts, Paul visited the city accompanied by Silas, Timothy, and Luke, which led to the foundation of a Christian congregation. As the first congregation founded on European soil, Paul remained deeply attached to this Christian community; according to Acts, he would pay the city two additional visits, around 56 and 57 C.E. There is no agreement as to the date of this letter. If sent from Ephesus, it would have been written around 54 C.E., but if it was sent from Caesarea or Rome, as a growing number of scholars have argued, it would have been sent at least four to six years later.

PHLEGON

("burning")

A Christian to whom Paul sent greetings in his Letter to the Romans (ROMANS 16:14).

PHOEBE

("bright")

A "deaconess of the church at Cenchrea," the port of Corinth. She was the bearer of Paul's Letter to the Romans. Paul commended her to the Christians in Rome "for she has been a benefactor of many, and of myself as well" (ROMANS 16:1-2).

PHYGELUS

("fugitive")

A Christian disciple in Asia who deserted Paul after his second imprisonment, perhaps in Troas (II TIMOTHY 1:15). After Paul was arrested, many other Christians may have abandoned him for fear of being arrested as well.

PRISCA OR PRISCILLA

Wife of Aquila, who with her husband became a follower of the Apostle Paul (ACTS 18:2; ROMANS 16:3). At one time, Aquila and Priscilla had lived in Rome, but they were forced to flee as a result of an edict by the Emperor Claudius, banning all Jews from the city (ACTS 18:2; I CORINTHIANS 16:19).

This illustration of Priscilla, also known as Prisca, is taken from "Women of the Bible" by Harold Copping (1863–1932) in 1927.

PROCHORUS

One of the seven deacons, "men of good standing, full of the Spirit and of wisdom," who were chosen to serve tables and distribute food to the needy, in response to a complaint that Greek widows in the Jerusalem community were not receiving their fair share (ACTS 6:3,5).

PUBLIUS

("common")

The "chief man," probably the governor, of the island of Malta ("Melita"), who took in Paul and his companions when they shipwrecked off the island (ACTS 28:7-8).

PUDENS

("bashful")

A Christian in Rome, who sent greetings to Timothy (II TIMOTHY 4:21).

QUARTUS

("fourth")

A Christian man in Corinth who asked to send greetings to the Christian community of Rome (ROMANS 16:23). Some traditions identify him as an early disciple of Jesus.

REPHAN

An idol worshipped secretly by the Israelites in the wilderness, possibly corresponding to Baal or Molech (ACTS 7:43).

RHODA

("rose")

Name of a maid in the household of Mary, mother of John Mark, who announced the arrival of Peter after his release from prison (ACTS 12:13).

ROMANS

Members of the Christian community in Rome, to whom Paul's Letter to the Romans is dedicated. There is evidence to suggest that the Roman congregation of Christians predates Paul's missionary work and remained faithful to their Jewish roots. In Corinth, Paul met a Jewish Christian couple, Aquila and Priscilla, who together with other Jews had been expelled from Rome by decree from Emperor Claudius, in response to civil disturbances in the city over "Chrestus." As a result, Paul's Letter to the Romans is perhaps the most carefully articulated statement of his theological views, seeking a balance between Gentile Christians and Christians who remained faithful to the Jewish Law. The letter is usually dated around 57 C.E., before his return to Jerusalem.

RUFUS
("red")

A Christian to whom Paul sent greetings in his Letter to the Romans. Paul calls him "chosen in the Lord" and also salutes Rufus's mother, whom he considers as his own (ROMANS 16:13).

SAPPHIRA
("beautiful")

Wife of Ananias. The couple had sold a piece of property to donate to the Jerusalem church, but kept some of the proceeds for themselves. When Ananias was confronted with these facts, he dropped down and died. A few hours later, his wife Sapphira was brought in and interrogated about the actual sale price of the property. She refused to divulge the truth, and was likewise struck dead. And, says Acts, "a great fear seized the whole church" (ACTS 5:1-10).

SCEVA

Head of a community of priests, "the sons of Sceva," in Ephesus, who conducted an unsuccessful exorcism in the name of "Jesus whom Paul preaches" during Paul's second visit to that town (ACTS 19:13-17). By contrast, Paul conducted many healings and exorcisms in Ephesus.

SECUNDUS
("second")

A Christian of Thessalonica who accompanied Paul on his final trip from Greece to Jerusalem (ACTS 20:4).

SERGIUS PAULUS

The proconsul of Cyprus when Paul visited that island with Barnabas on his first missionary tour (ACTS 13:7). He is described as an intelligent man, eager for information from all sources within his reach. Paul was able to overcome the opposition of a magus or false prophet called Bar-Jesus, and was allowed to baptize the proconsul.

SILAS

Also called Silvanus, Silas was a prominent member of the Christian Church in Jerusalem. He and Judas were chosen by the Church church to accompany Paul and Barnabas on their return from the council of Apostles and deliver the council's decision with regard to the observance of the Law by baptized gentiles. Judas and Silas were instructed to "impose . . . no further burden than these essentials: that you abstain from what has been sacrificed to idols and from blood and from what is strangled and from fornication." These precepts, known as the Noahide Laws, were traditionally imposed on all Gentiles living in Israel (ACTS 15:22). Silas was also chosen to accompany Paul on his second missionary in Corinth. Later, he carried Peter's letter to Christians in Asia Minor. Together with Paul, he would suffer imprisonment in Philippi until an earthquake shook the prison and broke their chains; in Christian art, he is often depicted with a broken chain in his hands (ACTS 15:22,32-33,40; 16:19-24; 17:10,14; 18:5; II CORINTHIANS 1:19; PETER 5:12; I THESSALONIANS 1:1).

SIMON OR SIMEON
("hearing")

1. A teacher and disciple in the church of Antioch (ACTS 1:1-3).
2. Name by which James referred to the Apostle Peter (ACTS 15:14).
3. A magician, known as Simon Magus, with a strong reputation for magic among the Samaritans. Simon was deeply impressed when he saw Peter and John lay their hands on newly baptized followers, who thereupon received the "Holy Spirit." Simon took the Apostles aside and offered them money if

French painter Nicolas Poussin (1594–1665) painted "The Death of Sapphira," who was the wife of Ananias.

This painting of "Peter's Confrontation With Simon Magus" was painted by Avanzino Nucci (ca 1552–1629) in 1620. Simon Magus was known as a magician by the Samaritans.

they gave him the power to transmit the Holy Spirit as well. Peter angrily denounced him, "for I see that you are in the gall of bitterness and the chains of wickedness" (ACTS 8:9-24).

4. A Christian and tanner from Joppa, who offered Peter the hospitality of his home (ACTS 9:43; 10:6,17,32).

SOPATER

Possibly the same individual as Sosipater, Sopater was a Christian from the town of Beroea, in northern Greece, who accompanied Paul on his return from Corinth to Jerusalem (ACTS 20:4-6; ROMANS 16:21).

SOSTHENES

1. Head of the synagogue in Corinth, who was beaten by a mob in front of Gallio, the local Roman governor, after Sosthenes refused to testify against Paul at the instigation of the local Jewish congregation (ACTS 18:12-17).

2. A Christian covert Paul mentions in the first Letter to the Corinthians (I CORINTHIANS 1:1-2). Some sources believe that this is the same Sosthenes who refused to act against Paul in Corinth, though this idea does not have universal support.

STEPHANAS
("crown")
A Christian in Corinth who was baptized by Paul (I CORINTHIANS 1:16; 16:15-16).

STEPHEN
("crown")
One of seven deacons, and head of the community of "Greek" followers who began to distance themselves from the obedience shown by Hebrew followers toward the Temple. These tensions threatened to split the Apostolic community, for many other followers—not only the "Hebrews" but many freedmen from North Africa and Asia Minor—remained faithful to Temple worship (ACTS 6:9).

In due course, Stephen was denounced to the Sanhedrin for "speaking blasphemous

This oil painting of "The Martyrdom of St. Stephen" was painted by Jacques Stella (1596–1657) in 1623. Stephen was accused of blasphemy and stoned to death.

words against Moses and God." According to Acts, Stephen was arraigned before the high priest and the council, and was denounced. Stephen countered his accusers

with a lengthy speech, ending with the assertion that "the Most High does not dwell in houses made with human hands." "You stiff-necked people," Stephen cried, "which of the prophets did your ancestors not persecute?" Just like them, Stephen said, "You have become (the) betrayers and murderers" of "the Righteous One" (ACTS 7:58).

Stephen's words caused an uproar. "With a loud shout," says Acts, "they dragged him out of the city and began to stone him." Some authors have tried to date this event to 36 C.E., after Pilate's removal from office, and before the arrival of the new Roman prefect, Marcellus, in 37 C.E. Stephen's murder marked a new phase in the conflict between the Sadducee leadership and the Apostolic mission. What had begun as mere harassment of Jesus' followers now turned into an all-out "persecution" (ACTS 6:3-15; 7:54-60; 8:1-2; 22:20).

SYNTYCHE
("accident")
A Christian woman in Philippi who was involved in a disagreement with another Christian woman by the name of Euodia. Paul was grateful to both women for helping him and his fellow worker, Clement, spread the word of God; he beseeched them in his Letter to the Philippians to put aside their differences (PHILIPPIANS 4:2).

TABITHA
("gazelle")
A Christian convert who lived in Joppa. She was known for her good works; in Greek, she was called "Dorcas." When she got sick and died, Peter, who was sent for from Lydda, prayed over the dead body and said, "Tabitha, arise." She opened her eyes, sat up, and came back to life (ACTS 9:36).

TERTIUS
("third")

A Christian who wrote the Letter to the Romans, which Paul dictated to him, and in which he added his own personal greetings (ROMANS 16:22).

TERTULLUS

Roman prosecuting attorney who was retained by the high priest Ananias to present the charges against Paul in Caesarea before the Roman procurator Antonius Felix. Tertullus stood up before Felix and eloquently accused Paul of sedition, incitement, and profanation of the Temple. Paul, however, was able to refute these charges with equal eloquence (ACTS 24:1).

THESSALONIANS

Members of the Christian congregation in Thessalonica (today's Thessaloniki), capital of the Roman province of Macedonia, to whom Paul dedicated his Letters to the Thessalonians. The Thessalonians were predominantly Gentile, which is why Paul's first letter draws heavily from Greek culture while refraining from discussions of the Jewish Law. It is generally believed to be Paul's oldest extant letter, written around 50 C.E., while the second Letter to the Thessalonians, if genuinely from Paul's hand, was probably written shortly thereafter.

THEUDAS
("God-given")

Name of an insurgent mentioned in Gamaliel's speech before the Jewish council (ACTS 5:36). He headed about 400 men who rebelled against the Romans in the mid-40s. He was killed, and his followers scattered. Gamaliel also refers to Judas the Galilean, but his rebellion is dated to 6 C.E.

TIMON

One of the seven deacons who along with Stephen, Philip, Prochorus, Nicanor, Parmenas, and Nicolas, "men of good standing, full of the Spirit and of wisdom," were chosen to serve tables and distribute food to the needy, in response to a complaint that Greek widows in the Jerusalem community were not receiving their fair share (ACTS 6:3,5).

TIMOTHY
("honoring God")

Son of a Greek man and Jewish woman named Eunice (II CORINTHIANS 1:1). He was Paul's companion, fellow worker, and messenger who eventually became Paul's confidante and protégé. Born of a Jewish mother and Greek father, however, Timothy was not circumcised. This put Paul's thesis of Gentile acceptance to the test. In the end, Timothy agreed to be circumcised, so as to facilitate his movements among Jewish communities, which Paul continued to visit as well. Timothy, along with Silas, accompanied Paul to several cities where they converted many of the listeners. While Paul was in Asia, he sent Timothy to Macedonia, and later to Thessalonica to strengthen the faith of the people. He returned with positive reports for Paul about the work he had done in Thessalonica.

In Paul's first Letter to the Corinthian church, he refers to Timothy as his beloved son who he is sending to teach the principles of Christian life. He asks the people to treat Timothy with respect. Paul describes Timothy as someone who shares his thinking and who focuses on the work of Jesus.

There are two letters to Timothy, ostensibly sent by Paul to his assistant, but probably written much later. In these, Paul tells Timothy to remain in Ephesus to prevent "heresy" from affecting the church in Ephesus (I TIMOTHY 1:3-4).

TITIUS JUSTUS

A Gentile who worshipped God, and whose house was next to the synagogue (ACTS 18:7).

TITUS

A faithful Greek companion of Paul and an addressee of one of his letters (II CORINTHIANS 2:13). Titus, along with Paul and Barnabas, went from Antioch to Jerusalem to consult with the Apostles and elders over the question of whether Gentiles should be circumcised. Paul's refusal to order Titus to be circumcised became a symbol of his great determination to accept Gentiles into the Church. Paul then sent Titus on many missions to several cities; when Paul was in Macedonia, Titus joined him (II CORINTHIANS 7:6). Titus was close to the Corinthian church, and was overjoyed when Paul was able to resolve some of his problems with the Corinthians. The last mission that Paul charged Titus with was to organize a Christian community in Crete.

This stained glass window of St. Timothy from the Chapel of Saint Sebastian in Alsace dates to ca 1160.

"The Triumph of Titus" was created by British painter Sir Lawrence Alma-Tadema (1836–1912) in 1885.

TROPHIMUS

A Gentile convert who, along with Tychicus, was one of Paul's travel companions during his third missionary journey (ACTS 20:4). When Trophimus became sick in Miletus, Paul was forced to leave him behind. He accompanied Paul on his final trip to Jerusalem along with Secundus, Aristarchus, Gaius of Derbe, Timotheus, Tychicus, and Sopater of Berea. He unwittingly caused Paul to be imprisoned. When Paul was seen taking Trophimus to the Temple in Jerusalem, they accused Paul of defiling the Temple by bringing a Gentile into the holy place. Paul was seized, dragged out of the Temple, and put into custody. The commander of the Roman troops, Claudius Lysias, then sent Paul to Caesara.

TRYPHAENA

Tryphaena and Tryphosa were two Christian women to whom Paul sent greetings in his Letter to Romans (ROMANS 16:12).

TRYPHOSA

("luxuriating")

Tryphosa and Tryphaena were two Christian women to whom Paul sent greetings in his Letter to Romans (ROMANS 16:12).

TYCHICUS

("fortunate")

One of Paul's companions and helpers, whom Paul called "a beloved brother and faithful servant of the Lord." He traveled to Ephesus and later to Colossae, carrying two letters from Paul, one to the Christian community of that city, and the other one to Philemon. During Paul's final journey, Tychicus traveled with him from Greece to Jerusalem (ACTS 20:4).

TYRANNUS

Teacher in Ephesus in whose school Paul preached. Before, Paul had taught in a synagogue, trying to convince the Ephesians about Jesus as the Messiah, but after three months, the opposition to his conversion efforts had hardened. Paul then decided to hold his discussions in the hall of Tyrannus. It was not in vain, for Ephesus would ultimately become the anchor of the "seven churches" in Asia Minor.

URBANUS

A man in Rome whom Paul sent greetings as "our fellow-worker in Christ" (ROMANS 16:3,6).

ZEALOTS

The Hellenization of the Jewish kingdom under the Herodians and the subsequent Roman occupation produced a religious party that may have split from the Pharisaic faction, and sought full religious and political freedom without any compromise. Born from the tax revolts of the early part of the century, the Zealots became a potent organization with its own militant wing of *sicarii* (*sikarioi* in Greek), meaning "dagger men." During the regime of the Roman procurator Gessius Florus who, says Josephus, ruled "like an executioner rather than a governor," the Zealots launched a rebellion against the

A relief inside the Arch of Titus depicts the menorah from the Second Temple being taken by Roman soldiers after their victory over Zealot defenders of Jerusalem in 70 C.E.

Roman occupation that became known as the Jewish War of 66–70 C.E.

ZENAS

A lawyer who was asked by Paul in his Letter to Titus to come and meet him in Nicopolis, on the Dalmatian coast of the Adriatic, accompanied by a scholar named Apollos. The reason for this request is not known (TITUS 3:13).

EPILOGUE
Early Christianity and Rabbinic Judaism After the Fall of Jerusalem

VESPASIAN AND THE JEWISH WAR

In 66 C.E., just two years after the great fire of Rome, a cataclysmic event took place with long-lasting consequences for both Judaism and Christianity. Long-simmering tensions between Jews and their Roman occupiers in Judea led to riots, and finally an all-out war. The Roman procurator, Gessius Florus, was partly to blame, because he had reportedly stolen 17 talents from the Temple treasury. Against all odds, the Jewish rebels succeeded in defeating the Roman forces in Judea and occupied Jerusalem, prompting Agrippa II to flee. Soon the revolt spread to Galilee and Samaria; reinforcements sent by the Roman governor of Syria, Cestius Gallus, were decimated in the Beth Horon pass.

It took several months for Rome to recognize the extent of the disaster. At long last, Emperor Nero sent several legions under command of General Vespasian, who landed in Ptolemais (today's Acre) in April 67. Two years later, with Rome once again convulsed by civil war, Vespasian was declared emperor by his own legion (69–79 C.E.). The general's son, Titus, was charged with prosecuting the war against the rebels.

By the summer of 70, Titus had thrown a siege around Jerusalem while his soldiers steadily fought their way toward the last holdout of the Zealots, the Temple precinct. In the melee, the Temple was burned to the ground.

With Jerusalem in Roman hands, one of Titus's legions, the Tenth, moved farther south into the Judean desert in search of the last outpost of the Zealots, who had retreated to the Herodian fortress of Masada. Along the way, the Romans destroyed the community in Qumran, though its members were able to hide most of their sacred scrolls in caves in the surrounding hills; these would be discovered in the 20th century as the "Dead Sea Scrolls."

With Palestine now fully pacified, Vespasian moved quickly to reestablish Roman control. Judea, Samaria, and Idumea, as well as parts of Perea and some coastal areas, were combined into a new Roman province of "Judaea." Agrippa II, who had remained loyal to the Romans throughout the rebellion, was rewarded with a rump state consisting of parts of Galilee and Phoenicia, but upon his death in 92 C.E., these were also added to Roman Judea.

All Jews who had survived the Roman siege were evicted from Jerusalem and forbidden to return, though recent research has cast doubt on the degree to which this edict was enforced. At the same time, the war had also compelled many Jewish Christians to flee; according to Church tradition, many settled in the city of Pella, located just across the Jordan River in the Decapolis.

YOHANAN BEN ZAKKAI

The destruction of the Temple threw the Jewish religious factions in disarray. With sacrificial operations at the Temple now terminated, the Sadducees lost their raison d'être and faded away. The Zealots, the party that—according to Josephus—had instigated the rebellion, were most likely suppressed. But a core element of the Pharisees may have survived. Yohanan ben Zakkai, a pupil of the renowned Rabbi Hillel and leader of

The sixth-century basilica of San Vitale in Ravenna—one of the oldest Byzantine churches in Italy—contains one of the best preserved mosaics from the Justinian era with themes from the Old and New Testament.

a rabbinical school in Jerusalem, had always advocated peace with Rome. The Romans took notice. When Yohanan petitioned the Roman legate for permission to establish a new religious school in Yabneh on the Mediterranean coast, his request was granted.

The Yabneh School became a leading academy of Jewish scholars, rabbis, and rabbinical students, who continued the Pharisaic tradition of scriptural debate and legislative commentary. Today, many scholars believe that Yohanan's circle was, in fact, largely composed of Pharisees.

In time, Yohanan was even allowed to restore the Jewish tribunal, known as the Beth Din ("house of judgment") to rule on domestic matters, just as the Sanhedrin had done before the rebellion. Thus, under Yohanan's guidance, Yabneh became the foundation of Jewish spiritual recovery.

Another key influence on the Jewish Restoration was the Diaspora, the far-flung Jewish communities throughout the Roman Empire. For centuries, these Jews had developed a liturgical life that was largely independent from the Temple in Jerusalem, and instead revolved around the synagogue as a center of prayer, study, and social events. Their example would soon be followed in Palestine, as many towns began the construction of synagogues.

CHRISTIANITY UNDER THE EARLY PRINCIPATE

Significantly, Emperor Vespasian never revoked the status of Judaism as an officially permitted religion, but that did not apply to the growing Christian communities in Asia Minor, Greece, and the Italian peninsula itself. Christianity remained an outlaw cult. Fortunately, Vespasian did not concern himself with religious persecution, and neither did his son Titus, who had many Jewish friends and, according to the Roman historian Tacitus, even considered marrying Berenice, the sister of Agrippa II.

But Titus's brother Domitian, who succeeded him in 81 C.E., had other ideas. An obstinate man, Domitian (ruled 81–96 C.E.) was devoted to the worship of Jupiter, the chief Roman god, and that of Minerva,

The necropolis of Beth She'arim ("House of Strangers"), with more than 20 cave systems and countless sarcophagi, was one of the most prominent Jewish burial grounds in late Antiquity.

The central crossing of the Church of the Holy Sepulcher in Jerusalem, known as the Catholikon Dome, was originally built during the 12th-century Crusader period.

goddess of wisdom and commerce. All cults who challenged the official Roman religion were forbidden. Bishop Eusebius of Caesarea (263–339 C.E.), an early historian of the Church, wrote that Domitian launched severe persecutions of both Jews and Christians, though this is not attested in any Roman documents of the period. In places where oppression did occur, Christians sometimes clamored to be martyred as a matter of honor—as in the case of Bishop Ignatius, who was arrested around 110 C.E. and eagerly awaited his death in the arena.

Indeed, modern scholars still debate whether the Roman oppression of Christians was a matter of state policy, or the result of local frictions. Some of the most able emperors of the second century, including Trajan (ruled 98–117) and Hadrian (ruled 117–138), were not interested in harassing communities that were essentially peaceful, tolerant, and often noted for their charitable works. In many cities, Christians were caring for the sick, the poor, or the unemployed. When one of his governors, the younger Pliny (61–ca 112 C.E.), boasted of his pursuit of Christians in Bithynia, Emperor Trajan berated him, calling Pliny's reliance on anonymous denunciations "unworthy of our times."

THE SECOND JEWISH REVOLT

Emperor Hadrian (ruled 117–138) also adopted a policy of temperance, but when the Jews of Palestine once again rose in revolt in late 131 under the leadership of Simon bar Kokhba ("son of a star"), Hadrian came down with all of Rome's might. The revolt was defeated, and in 135, Jerusalem was literally wiped off the map. To ensure its utter destruction, Hadrian ordered a new Roman city, Aelia Capitolina, to be built in its place. All Jews were evicted, and this time the decree was enforced; Jews were only permitted to return once a year, to mourn the destruction of the Temple.

The turmoil also affected the Yabneh School founded by Yohanan ben Zakkai. After Emperor Antoninus Pius (138–161 C.E.) reinstated Judaism as a permitted religion, the academy moved from Yabneh to Beth She'arim; then Sepphoris; and finally to Tiberias, on the Sea of Galilee. Here, Simeon ben Gamaliel (135–175 C.E.), grandson (or great-grandson) of Rabbi Gamaliel who had once taught Paul, was permitted to form a new Sanhedrin. At the head of this council stood a patriarch, a position that eventually became a hereditary office for those of Davidic pedigree. In time, the Sanhedrin acquired a considerable amount of local autonomy, which in turn fostered an impression of Jewish self-rule, thus calming Judea's restless population.

THE MISHNAH

Something similar was happening among the Jewish communities in Persia, now ruled by Parthians who took control of the Persian Empire in the second century B.C.E. Here too, Parthian governors saw the wisdom of delegating local authority to prominent clerics who were sensitive to the unique needs and practices of Judaism. Eventually, this led to the institution of the office of *Exilarch,* or patriarch, of the Jewish community in Babylon. Academies soon followed, such as the academy at Pumbeditha (near today's Fallujah in Iraq), founded by Judah ben Ezekiel (220–299 C.E.).

In Palestine, the patriarchate continued to legislate Jewish life based on an ongoing discussion of the Law. Most of this Oral Law material was organized in a collection known as the Mishnah ("teaching") in the early third century. Written mostly in Hebrew, and believed to have been edited by Rabbi Yehudah HaNasi ("the Prince"), the Mishnah was an attempt to provide a systematic reference for legal arguments and precepts based on the Torah.

Upon his death around 217, Yehudah was buried in the necropolis of Beth She'arim, a prominent Jewish burial ground until the fourth century.

This bust of Constantine I (306–337 C.E.) was taken from a colossal statue of the emperor.

THE GROWTH OF CHRISTIANITY IN THE SECOND CENTURY

Although Christianity was banned, it still grew rapidly thanks to countless missionaries who carried the Gospel beyond the orbit of Paul's original journeys. Many of these Christians were not clerics but sailors, soldiers, officials, and traders who used the excellent Roman land and sea routes to bring word of the Christian faith throughout the Empire.

At this stage, Christianity was not yet a unified movement but a proliferation of disparate groups. Some were observant Jews; others were Gentiles who followed the precepts of Paul; and others again were Gnostic groups whom the Church would later brand as dissidents or heretics.

In the third century, the incidence of Roman persecutions increased. Rome faced a growing number of external threats and, in reaction, turned to pious worship of its gods. Emperor Decius (ruled 249–251) insisted that all citizens prove their patriotism by sacrificing to the Roman gods. Fortunately the decree was suspended by Emperor Gallienus (ruled 260–268). By the time Constantine the Great (ruled 306–337) granted Christianity official status in 313, the Church had penetrated into all corners of the Empire, from Britain to Bostra, from Cappadocia to Carthage, and from Antioch to Dura-Europos on the Euphrates River. ◈

The Hagia Sophia in Istanbul, Turkey—the last monumental masterpiece of Roman architecture—was built as a basilica by Emperor Justinian I between 532 and 537 C.E.

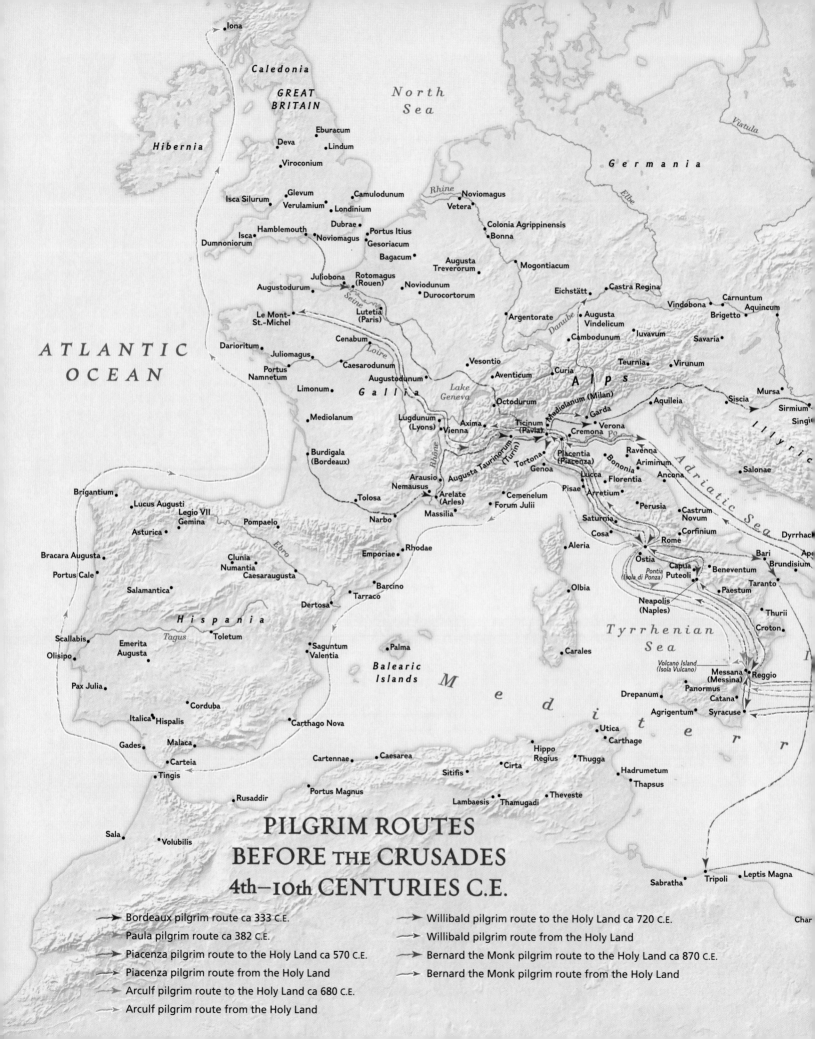

Iona

Caledonia

**GREAT
BRITAIN**

*North
Sea*

Hibernia

Germania

Deva
Lindum
Eburacum
Viroconium

Rhine
Noviomagus
Vetera

Isca Silurum
Glevum
Verulamium
Camulodunum
Londinium

Colonia Agrippinensis
Bonna

Isca
Dumnoniorum
Hamblemouth
Noviomagus
Portus Itius
Gesoriacum

Dubrae

Augusta
Treverorum

Mogontiacum

Vistula

Bagacum

Castra Regina
Eichstätt

Carnuntum

Juliobona
Rotomagus
(Rouen)
Noviodunum
Durocortorum

Vindobona
Brigetto
Aquincum

Augustodurum

Seine

Le Mont-
St.-Michel
Lutetia
(Paris)

Argentorate
Danube
Augusta
Vindelicum
Iuvavum
Savaria

Darioritum
Cenabum
Loire

Vesontio
Curia
Teurnia
Virunum

Mursa

Augustodunum
Caesarodunum

Aventicum

Alps
Garda

Aquileia
Siscia
Sirmium
Singi

Gallia
Lugdunum
(Lyons)
Axima
Vienna
Mediolanum (Milan)
Verona

Illyric

**ATLANTIC
OCEAN**

Juliomagus
Portus
Namnetum

Limonum

Mediolanum

*Lake
Geneva*
Octodurum
Ticinum
(Pavia)

Cremona

Po
Ravenna

Adriatic Sea

Burdigala
(Bordeaux)

Rhône
Augusta Taurinorum
(Turin)
Tortona
Genoa
Placentia
(Piacenza)
Bononia
Ariminum

Salonae

Arausio
Nemausus

Lucca
Florentia
Ancona

Brigantium
Lucus Augusti
Legio VII
Gemina
Pompaelo
Tolosa
Narbo
Arelate
(Arles)
Massilia
Cemenelum
Forum Julii
Pisae
Arretium
Perusia
Castrum
Novum
Corfinium

Dyrrhac

Asturica
Clunia
Numantia
Caesaraugusta
Rhodae
Emporiae

Saturnia
Cosa
Rome

Bracara Augusta
Ebro
Aleria

Ostia
Capua
Puteoli
Beneventum

Bari
Ap

Portus Cale
Salamantica
Barcino
Tarraco
Dertosa

Olbia

*Pontia
(Isola di Ponza)*
Neapolis
(Naples)
Paestum

Brundisium
Taranto

Scallabis
Emerita
Augusta
Tagus
Toletum

Hispania

Thurii
Croton

Olisipo
Saguntum
Valentia
Palma

Carales

*Volcano Island
(Isola Vulcano)*
Messana
(Messina)
Reggio

Pax Julia

Corduba

*Balearic
Islands*

Drepanum
Panormus
Catana

Italica
Hispalis
Carthago Nova

Med
iterr

Agrigentum
Syracuse

Gades
Malaca
Carteia
Tingis

*Tyrrhenian
Sea*

I

*M
e
d
i
t
e
r
r*

Rusaddir
Portus Magnus
Cartennae
Caesarea
Sitifis
Cirta
Hippo
Regius
Thugga

Utica
Carthage

Hadrumetum
Thapsus

Sala
Volubilis

Lambaesis
Thamugadi
Theveste

PILGRIM ROUTES
BEFORE THE CRUSADES
4th–10th CENTURIES C.E.

Sabratha
Tripoli
Leptis Magna

Char

→ Bordeaux pilgrim route ca 333 C.E.

→ Paula pilgrim route ca 382 C.E.

→ Piacenza pilgrim route to the Holy Land ca 570 C.E.

→ Piacenza pilgrim route from the Holy Land

→ Arculf pilgrim route to the Holy Land ca 680 C.E.

→ Arculf pilgrim route from the Holy Land

→ Willibald pilgrim route to the Holy Land ca 720 C.E.

→ Willibald pilgrim route from the Holy Land

→ Bernard the Monk pilgrim route to the Holy Land ca 870 C.E.

→ Bernard the Monk pilgrim route from the Holy Land

Sarmatia

Dnieper

Scythia

Caspian Sea

Dniester

C a u c a s u s   M t s.

Volga

Don

Olbia

Lake Sevan

Chersonesus

B l a c k   S e a

Trapezus

Lake Van

Lake Urmia

Apulum

Troesmis

Sinope

Amisus

Satala

Sarmizegetusa Regia

Tomis

Pompeiopolis

Durostorum

Tropaeum Traiani

Amastris

Zela

Megalopolis

Tigranocerta

Danube

Oescus

Novae

Heraclea Pontica

Gangra

P a r t h i a

Amida

T h r a c e

Serdica

Hadrianopolis (Adrianople)

Constantinople

Ancyra

Caesarea

Melitene

Edessa

Harran

Philippopolis

Nicomedia

Samosata

Nicopolis

Perinthus

Nicaea

Prusa

Dorylaeum

Cyrrhus

Stobi

Cyzicus

A s i a

Antiochia

Iconium

M i n o r

Antiochia

Aleppo

Heraclea

Pergamum

Tarsus

Seleucia

Chalcis

Palmyra

Thessalonica

Smyrna

Aphrodisias

Perga

Laodicea

Raphaneae

Emesa

Aegean

Ambracia

Delphi

Ephesus

Attalia

Antaradus

Heliopolis

Nicopolis

Athens

Miletus

Patara

Myra

Salamis (Constantia)

Tripolis

Corinth

Cnidus

Cyprus

Sidon

Damascus

Sparta

Rhodus

Paphos

AREA ENLARGED

Cythera (Kithira)

Rhodes

Bostra

Candia

Jerusalem

Dead Sea

Gortyn

Crete

S e a

n   e   a   n

Petra

Pelusium

Alexandria

Clymsa

Cyrene

Ptolemais

Memphis

Qubba, Babyon

Pharan

Mt Sinai 2,285 m 7,497 ft

Oxyrhynchus

Hermopolis

Nile

Ptolemais

Thebae

Coptus

0   50   100   150   200   250 kilometers

0   50   100   150   200   250 miles

Present-day drainage and coastlines are represented.
Modern names appear in parentheses.

Tyre

Leontes

Kanah

Ecdippa

Cadasa

Asor

Merom

Ptolemais

Jotapata

Capernaum

Bethsaida

Bay of Acco (Bay of Haifa)

Arbela

Jordan

Sycaminium

Sephoris

Tiberias

Sea of Galilee

Nazareth

Dora

Legio

Mt. Tabor 588 m 1,929 ft

Gadara

THE GREAT SEA (MEDITERRANEAN SEA)

Caesarea

Narbata

Ginae

Scythopolis

Pella

P L A I N   O F   S H A R O N

Sebaste

Neapolis

Willibald took side trips to Jericho, Hebron, and Gaza.

Sychar

Amathus

Yarqon

Antipatris

Lebonah

Jabbok

Joppa

Lydda

Bethel

Jericho

Azotus

Sorek

Jerusalem

Bethany

Paula died in Bethlehem.

Ascalon

Lachish

Bethlehem

Salt Sea (Dead Sea)

Hebron

S H E P H E L A H

Gaza

Eshtemoa

En-gedi

Besor

Arnon

Beersheba

Masada

Malatha

N E G E V

Elusa

0   20   40 kilometers

0   20   40 miles

CHARTING THE ROUTES TO THE HOLY LAND

JERUSALEM IN THE BYZANTINE ERA

Constantine's Edict of Milan of 313, by which Christianity became an official religion of the Roman Empire, also turned Roman Palestine into a major destination for pilgrims. Now known as the "Holy Land," it would be visited by thousands of faithful in the centuries to come. A major building program, initiated by Constantine's mother, the Empress Helena, created churches and shrines at key sites featured in the Gospels throughout the region. At the same time, Hadrian's city of Aelia Capitolina reverted back to "Jerusalem"—albeit in a thoroughly Christian mold. A sixth-century mosaic from a Byzantine church in Madaba, Jordan, is a snapshot of Jerusalem from that period, with the central Cardo Maximus, or main Roman boulevard, running across the city.

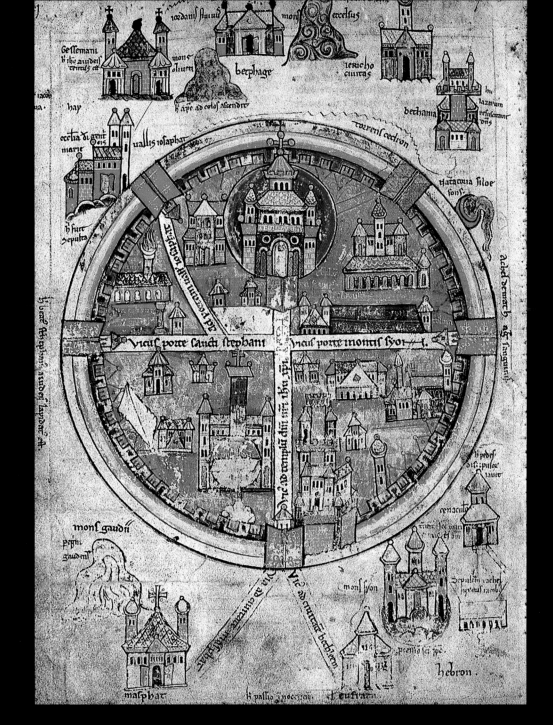

CRUSADER JERUSALEM

In 637, the Muslim caliph 'Umar ibn al-Khattab defeated Byzantine Emperor Heraclius and captured Jerusalem. Control of the Holy Land passed to the Islamic Empire. Initially, the new Muslim administration respected Jewish and Christian worship, but this changed when the Fatimid caliph Al-Hakim (985–1021) ordered the destruction of all churches and synagogues throughout his domain. The Church of the Holy Sepulcher was torn down in 1008. In 1073, the Seljuqs ousted the Fatimids from Jerusalem and massacred the Jews and Christians in the city. In response, Pope Urban II called for a Crusade to free the Holy Land from Muslim rule, which succeeded in 1099. This 12th-century Crusader map shows the newly restored Church of the Holy Sepulcher at the city's center.

ALEXANDRIA, GATEWAY TO THE HOLY LAND

In 1275, the last Crusaders were evicted from the Holy Land by the Mamluk sultan Baibars. The Mamluks retained control of Palestine until in 1517, when Jerusalem fell to the Ottoman Turks, who would remain in charge for another 400 years. Still, many Christians and Jews longed to see Palestine, often traveling to Alexandria because of its superior sea links. From Alexandria, some pilgrims traveled as far as Mount Sinai and St. Catherine's

Monastery, deep in the Sinai desert, before turning east toward Palestine. Following the invention of the movable block printing press, cartographers began to cater to the near-insatiable interest in the mysterious Middle East with the publication of woodcut prints, which were subsequently hand-colored, as in this view of Alexandria from Braun and Hogenberg's *Civitates Orbis Terrarum VI* of 1617.

THE HOLY LAND UNDER THE OTTOMANS

Ottoman rule cast a long shadow over the Holy Land, as Palestine was plunged into a prolonged period of official neglect. Christian churches and Jewish synagogues crumbled while pilgrims fought off Barbary pirates, thieves, and heatstroke. While traveling in Palestine itself, they often suffered appalling conditions in local inns. Back in Europe, however, these deprivations only added to the allure and magic of the Holy Land. Until the 16th century, maps

of Palestine were largely driven by the cartographer's imagination, but superior exploration techniques steadily gave maps a more geographical character. An excellent example is the 1572 map of Egypt and Palestine from the *Theatrum Orbis Terrarum* by Flemish cartographer Abraham Ortelius (1527–1598). By the time of Ortelius's death, "Theater of the World," generally considered to be the first modern atlas, had been published 25 times.

APPENDIX

THE HEBREW SCRIPTURES (TANAKH)

THE LAW (TORAH)	THE PROPHETS (NEVI'IM)	THE WRITINGS (KETUVIM)
Genesis	*Former Prophets:*	Psalms
Exodus	Joshua	Proverbs
Leviticus	Judges	Job
Numbers	Samuel (I and II)	Song of Solomon
Deuteronomy	Kings (I and II)	Ruth
	Latter Prophets:	Lamentations
	Isaiah	Ecclesiastes
	Jeremiah	Esther
	Ezekiel	Daniel
	Twelve Minor Prophets:	Ezra-Nehemiah
	Hosea	Chronicles (I and II)
	Joel	
	Amos	
	Obadiah	
	Jonah	
	Micah	
	Nahum	
	Habakkuk	
	Zephaniah	
	Haggai	
	Zechariah	
	Malachi	

THE BOOKS OF THE OLD TESTAMENT

Genesis	Isaiah	*Deuterocanonical/Apocryphal:*
Exodus	Jeremiah	Tobit
Leviticus	Lamentations	Judith
Numbers	Ezekiel	Esther
Deuteronomy	Daniel	The Wisdom of Solomon
Joshua	Hosea	Ecclesiasticus
Judges	Joel	Baruch
Ruth	Amos	Letter of Jeremiah
I Samuel	Obadiah	*Additions to Daniel, including:*
II Samuel	Jonah	Prayer of Azariah
I Kings	Micah	Song of Three Jews
II Kings	Nahum	Susanna
I Chronicles	Habakkuk	Bel and the Dragon
II Chronicles	Zephaniah	I Maccabees
Ezra	Haggai	II Maccabees
Nehemiah	Zechariah	I Esdras
Esther	Malachi	Prayer of Manasseh
Job		Psalm 151
Psalms		III Maccabees
Proverbs		II Esdras
Ecclesiastes		IV Maccabees
Song of Solomon		

THE BOOKS OF THE NEW TESTAMENT

THE GOSPELS	Tradtional Attribution	Possible Date
Matthew	Matthew (Levi)	75–90 C.E.
Mark	Mark, Peter's interpreter	66–70 C.E.
Luke	Luke, Paul's attendant	75–90 C.E.
John	John (disciple)	85–100 C.E.

ACTS	Tradtional Attribution	Possible Date
Acts of the Apostles	Luke, Paul's attendant	75–90 C.E.

PAULINE EPISTLES	Tradtional Attribution	Possible Date
Letter to the Romans	Paul	56–57 C.E.
First Letter to the Corinthians	Paul	54–55 C.E.
Second Letter to the Corinthians	Paul	55–56 C.E.
Letter to the Galatians	Paul	50–56 C.E.
Letter to the Ephesians	Paul (pseudonymous)	80–95 C.E.
Letter to the Philippians	Paul	54–55 C.E.
Letter to the Colossians	Paul	57–61 C.E.
First Letter to the Thessalonians	Paul	50–51 C.E.
Second Letter to the Thessalonians	Paul	50–51 C.E.
First Letter to Timothy	Paul (pseudonymous)	90–110 C.E.
Second Letter to Timothy	Paul (pseudonymous)	90–110 C.E.
Letter to Titus	Paul (pseudonymous)	90–110 C.E.
Letter to Philemon	Paul	54–55 C.E.
Letter to the Hebrews	Paul (pseudonymous)	60–95 C.E.

GENERAL EPISTLES	Tradtional Attribution	Possible Date
Letter to James	James, brother of Jesus	50–70 C.E.
First Letter of Peter	Peter (pseudonymous)	70–90 C.E.
Second Letter of Peter	Peter (pseudonymous)	80–90 C.E.
First Letter of John	John (disciple)	ca 100 C.E.
Second Letter of John	John (disciple)	ca 100 C.E.
Third Letter of John	John (disciple)	ca 100 C.E.
Letter of Jude	Jude, brother of Jesus	45–65 C.E.

PROPHECY	Tradtional Attribution	Possible Date
Revelation	John (disciple)	70–100 C.E.

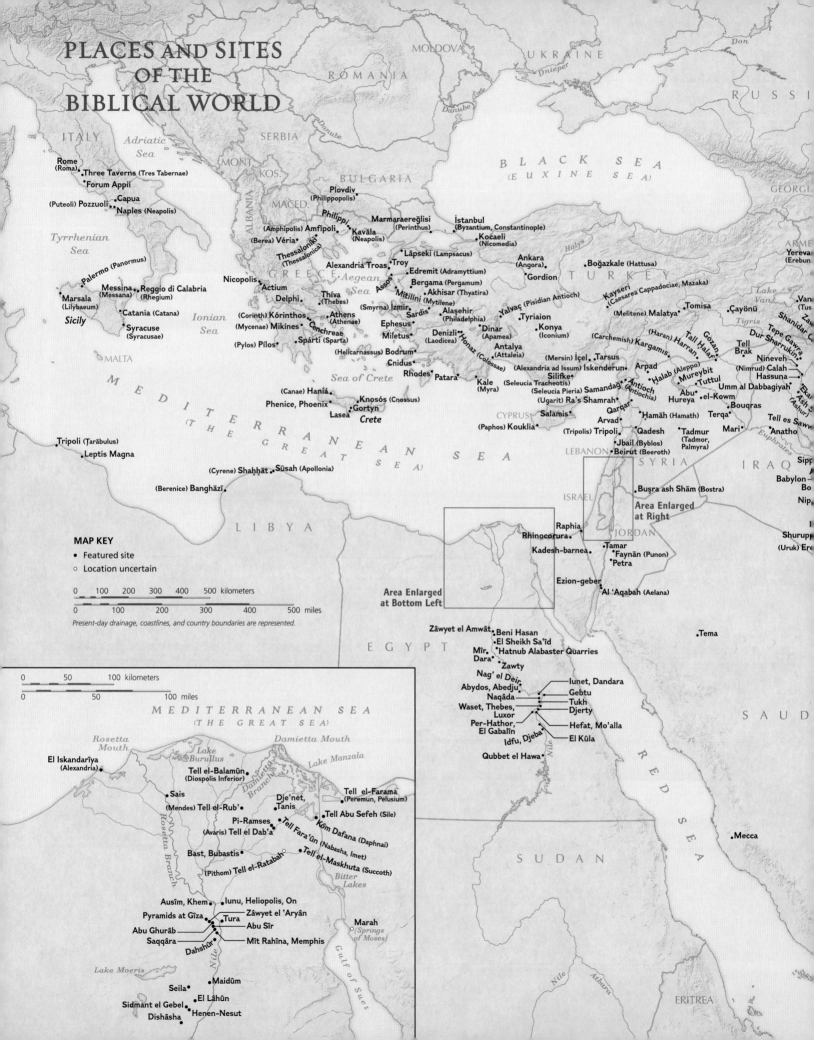

PLACES AND SITES
OF THE
BIBLICAL WORLD

Featured site

MAP KEY
- Featured site
- ○ Location uncertain

| 0 | 100 | 200 | 300 | 400 | 500 kilometers |
| 0 | 100 | 200 | 300 | 400 | 500 miles |

Present-day drainage, coastlines, and country boundaries are represented.

MONT.
KOS.
ROMANIA
MOLDOVA
UKRAINE
Don
RUSSI
SERBIA
MACED.
BULGARIA
GEORGI
BLACK SEA
(EUXINE SEA)
ARME
Yereva
(Erebun)

ITALY
Adriatic Sea
Rome (Roma)
Three Taverns (Tres Tabernae)
Forum Appii
Capua
(Puteoli) Pozzuoli
Naples (Neapolis)

Plovdiv (Philippopolis)
Philippi
(Amphipolis) Amfipoli
Kavăla (Neapolis)
(Berea) Véria
Thessaloníki (Thessalonica)
Marmaraereğlisi (Perinthus)
İstanbul (Byzantium, Constantinople)
Kocaeli (Nicomedia)

Tyrrhenian Sea
Palermo (Panormus)
Messina (Messana)
Reggio di Calabria (Rhegium)
Marsala (Lilybaeum)
Catania (Catana)
Syracuse (Syracusae)
Sicily
MALTA

GREECE
Aegean Sea
Nicopolis
Actium
Delphi
(Corinth) Kórinthos
(Mycenae) Mikínes
(Pylos) Pílos
Thíva (Thebes)
Athens (Athenae)
Cenchreae
Spárti (Sparta)
(Pylos) Pílos

Lâpseki (Lampsacus)
Alexandria Troas
Troy
Assos
Edremit (Adramyttium)
Bergama (Pergamum)
Mitilíni (Mytilene)
Akhisar (Thyatira)
İzmir (Smyrna)
Sardis
Alaşehir (Philadelphia)
Ephesus
Miletus
Denizli (Laodicea)
Bodrum (Helicarnassus)
Cnidus
Rhodes
Patara
Kale (Myra)

Ankara (Angora)
Gordion
TURKEY
Kayseri (Caesarea Cappadociae, Mazaka)
Yalvaç (Pisidian Antioch)
Tyriaion
Konya (Iconium)
Dinar (Apamea)
Honaz (Colossae)
Antalya (Attaleia)
(Mersin) İçel
(Alexandria ad Issum)
Silifke (Seleucia Tracheotis)
Tarsus
İskenderun
Samandağ (Seleucia Pieria)
(Ugarit) Ra's Shamrah
Antioch (Antiochia)

Boğazkale (Hattusa)
Tomisa
Melitene) Malatya
Çayönü
Van (Tus
Zaw
Shanidar Ca
Tepe Gawra
Dur Sharrukin
(Haran) Harran
Gozan
Tall Halaf
Tell Brak
Nineveh
(Nimrud) Calah
Hassuna
Abu Hureya
el-Kowm
Umm al Dabbagiyah
Bouqras
Terqa
Tell es Sawr
Anatho
(Carchemish) Kargamıș
Halab (Aleppo)
Mureybit
Tuttul
Arpad
Ebl
Ash
Ashur

Ionian Sea
MEDITERRANEAN SEA (THE GREAT SEA)

Tripoli (Tarābulus)
Leptis Magna
(Cyrene) Shahhât
Sūsah (Apollonia)
(Berenice) Banghāzī

LIBYA

Sea of Crete
(Canae) Haniá
Phenice, Phoenix
Lasea
Knosós (Cnossus)
Gortyn
Crete

CYPRUS
(Paphos) Kouklia
Salamis

Qarqar
Hamāh (Hamath)
Arvad
(Tripolis) Tripoli
Qadesh
Tadmur (Tadmur, Palmyra)
Mari
Mari
Euphrates
IRAQ
Sipp
Babylon
Bo
Nip

LEBANON
Jbail (Byblos)
Beirut (Beeroth)
ISRAEL
SYRIA
Buşra ash Shām (Bostra)

Area Enlarged at Right

JORDAN
Raphia
Rhinocorura
Kadesh-barnea
Tamar
Faynān (Punon)
Petra
Ezion-geber
Al 'Aqabah (Aelana)

Area Enlarged at Bottom Left

EGYPT

SAUD

Tema

Zâwyet el Amwât
Beni Hasan
El Sheikh Sa'îd
Mîr,
Dara
Hatnub Alabaster Quarries
Zawty
Nag' el Deir
Abydos, Abedju
Naqâda
Waset, Thebes,
Luxor
Per-Hathor, El Gabalîn
Idfu, Djeba
Qubbet el Hawa
Iunet, Dandara
Gebtu
Tukh
Djerty
Hefat, Mo'alla
El Kûla

RED SEA

Mecca

SUDAN

Inset map (bottom left)

| 0 | 50 | 100 kilometers |
| 0 | 50 | 100 miles |

MEDITERRANEAN SEA
(THE GREAT SEA)

Rosetta Mouth
Damietta Mouth
Lake Burullus
Lake Manzala
El Iskandarîya (Alexandria)
Tell el-Balamûn (Diospolis Inferior)
Sais
(Mendes) Tell el-Rub'
Dje'net, Tanis
Tell el-Farama (Peremun, Pelusium)
Tell Abu Sefeh (Sile)
Pi-Ramses
(Avaris) Tell el Dab'a
Tell Fara'ûn (Nabasha, Imet)
Kôm Dafana (Daphnai)
Bast, Bubastis
(Pithom) Tell el-Ratabah
Tell el-Maskhuta (Succoth)
Bitter Lakes
Rosetta Branch
Damietta Branch
Ausîm, Khem
Iunu, Heliopolis, On
Pyramids at Gîza
Tura
Zâwyet el 'Aryân
Abu Ghurâb
Abu Sîr
Saqqâra
Dahshûr
Mît Rahîna, Memphis
Marah (Springs of Moses)
Gulf of Suez
Lake Moeris
Seila
Maidûm
Sidmant el Gebel
El Lâhûn
Dishâsha
Henen-Nesut
Nile

SAUDI

SUDAN
Nile
Atbara
ERITREA

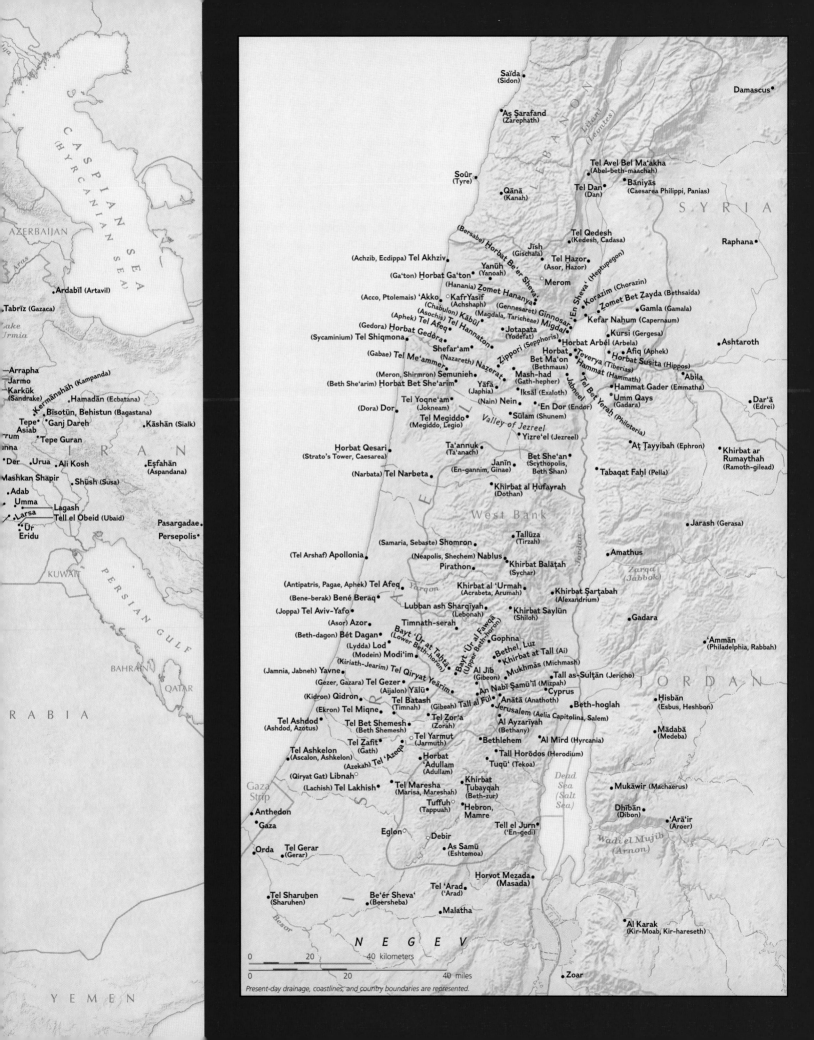

Saïda
(Sidon)

Damascus

Aş Şarafand
(Zarephath)

Tel Avel Bel Ma'akha
(Abel-beth-maachah)

Soûr
(Tyre)

Qānā
(Kanah)

Tel Dan
(Dan)

Bāniyās
(Caesarea Philippi, Panias)

S Y R I A

Tel Qedesh
(Kedesh, Cadasa)

Raphana

(Bersabe) Horbat Be'er Sheva'
(Achzib, Ecdippa) Tel Akhziv

Jīsh
(Gischala)

Yanūh
(Yanoah)

Tel Hazor
(Asor, Hazor)

(Ga'ton) Horbat Ga'ton

Zomet Hananya

En Sheva' (Heptapegon)

Korazim (Chorazin)

Zomet Bet Zayda (Bethsaida)

(Hanania)

Merom

(Acco, Ptolemais) 'Akko
KafrYasīf
(Achshaph)

Ginnosar
(Gennesaret)

Gamla (Gamala)

(Chabulon)

Magdala, Taricheae) Migdal

Kefar Nahum (Capernaum)

(Aphek) Tel Afeq

(Asochis) Tel Hannaton Kābūl

Jotapata
(Yodefat)

Kursi (Gergesa)

(Gedora) Horbat Gedora

Horbat Arbél (Arbela)

Afiq (Aphek)

(Sycaminium) Tel Shiqmona

Zippori (Sepphoris)

Teverya
(Tiberias)

Horbat Susita (Hippos)

Shefar'am

Horbat
Bet Ma'on
(Bethmaus)

Hammat
(Hammath)

Ashtaroth

(Gabae) Tel Me'ammer
(Nazareth) Nazerat

Mash-had
(Gath-hepher)

Tel Bet Yerah
(Philoteria)

Hammat Gader (Emmatha)

(Meron, Shimron) Semunieh

Yafā
(Japhia)

Iksāl
(Exaloth)

Umm Qays
(Gadara)

Abila

(Beth She'arim) Horbat Bet She'arim

(Nain) Nein

'En Dor
(Endor)

Dar'ā
(Edrei)

Tel Yoqne'am
(Jokneam)

(Dora) Dor

Sūlam
(Shunem)

Yizre'el (Jezreel)

At Tayyibah (Ephron)

Khirbat ar
Rumaythah
(Ramoth-gilead)

Valley of Jezreel

Horbat Qesari
(Strato's Tower, Caesarea)

Ta'annuk
(Ta'anach)

Bet She'an
(Scythopolis,
Beth Shan)

Tabaqat Fahl (Pella)

(Narbata) Tel Narbeta

Janīn
(En-gannim, Ginae)

Khirbat al Hufayrah
(Dothan)

West Bank

Jarash (Gerasa)

Tallūza
(Tirzah)

(Samaria, Sebaste) Shomron

Amathus

(Tel Arshaf) Apollonia

(Neapolis, Shechem) Nablus

Pirathon

Khirbat Balātah
(Sychar)

Khirbat Sartabah
(Alexandrium)

Khirbat al 'Urmah
(Acrabeta, Arumah)

Gadara

(Antipatris, Pagae, Aphek) Tel Afeq

Khirbat Saylūn
(Shiloh)

(Bene-berak) Bené Beráq

Lubban ash Sharqīyah
(Lebonah)

'Ammān
(Philadelphia, Rabbah)

(Joppa) Tel Aviv-Yafo

Timnath-serah

Bayt 'Ur al Fawqā
(Upper Beth-horon)

(Asor) Azor

Gophna

(Beth-dagon) Bét Dagan

Bayt 'Ur at Tahtā
(Lower Beth-horon)

Bethel, Luz

(Lydda) Lod

Khirbat at Tall (Ai)

(Modein) Modi'im

Al Jib
(Gibeon)

Mukhmās (Michmash)

Tall as-Sultān (Jericho)

(Kiriath-Jearim) Tel Qiryat Yeārim

(Jamnia, Jabneh) Yavne

An Nabī Samū'īl (Mizpah)

Cyprus

J O R D A N

(Gezer, Gazara) Tel Gezer

(Aijalon) Yālū

Tall al Fūl

Anātā (Anathoth)

Beth-hoglah

Hisbān
(Esbus, Heshbon)

(Kidron) Qidron

(Gibeah)

Jerusalem (Aelia Capitolina, Salem)

(Ekron) Tel Miqne

Tel Batash
(Timnah)

Tel Zor'a
(Zorah)

Mādabā
(Medeba)

Tel Ashdod
(Ashdod, Azotus)

Tel Bet Shemesh
(Beth Shemesh)

Al Ayzarīyah
(Bethany)

Tel Zafit
(Gath)

Tel Yarmut
(Jarmuth)

Bethlehem

Al Mird (Hyrcania)

Tel Ashkelon
(Ascalon, Ashkelon)

Horbat
'Adullam
(Adullam)

Tall Horōdos (Herodium)

Mukāwir (Machaerus)

(Azekah) Tel 'Azeqa

Tuqū' (Tekoa)

Dead
Sea
(Salt
Sea)

(Qiryat Gat) Libnah
(Lachish) Tel Lakhish

Tel Maresha
(Marisa, Mareshah)

Khirbat
Tubayqah
(Beth-zur)

Dhībān (Dibon)

'Arā'ir (Aroer)

Gaza
Strip

Tuffuh
(Tappuah)

Hebron,
Mamre

Tell el Jurn
('En-gedi)

Wadi el Mujib
(Arnon)

Anthedon

Eglon

Debir

As Samū
(Eshtemoa)

Gaza

Orda

Tel Gerar
(Gerar)

Horvot Mezada
(Masada)

Tel 'Arad
('Arad)

Tel Sharuhen
(Sharuhen)

Be'ér Sheva'
(Beersheba)

Malatha

N E G E V

0   20   40 kilometers

0   20   40 miles

Zoar

Present-day drainage, coastlines, and country boundaries are represented.

CASPIAN SEA
(HYRCANIAN SEA)

AZERBAIJAN

Ardabīl (Artavil)

Aras

Tabrīz (Gazaca)

Lake
Irmia

Arrapha

Jarmo

Karkūk
(Sandrake)

Kermānshāh (Kampanda)

Hamadān (Ecbatana)

Tepe
Asiab

Bīsotūn, Behistun (Bagastana)

Kāshān (Sialk)

Ganj Dareh

I R A N

Tepe Guran

Der

Urua

Ali Kosh

Esfahān
(Aspandana)

Mashkan Shapir

Shūsh (Susa)

Adab

Umma

Lagash

Pasargadae

Larsa

Tell el Obeid (Ubaid)

Ūr

Eridu

Persepolis

KUWAN

P E R S I A N   G U L F

BAHRAIN

QATAR

A R A B I A

Y E M E N

FURTHER READING

CHAPTER 1 FROM GENESIS TO DEUTERONOMY

Bertman, Stephen. *Life in Ancient Mesopotamia*. New York: Oxford University Press, 2005.

Bietak, M. *Avaris, the Capital of the Hyksos: Recent Excavations at Tell el-Daba*. London: British Museum Press, 1996.

Clayton, Peter A. *Chronicle of the Pharaohs*. London: Thames & Hudson, 1994.

Cline, Eric: *From Eden to Exile: Unraveling Mysteries of the Bible*. Washington, D.C.: National Geographic Society, 2006.

Collon, Dominique. *Ancient Near Eastern Art*. London: Trustees of the British Museum, 1995.

Coogan, Michael D., ed. *The Oxford History of the Biblical World*. New York: Oxford University Press, 2001.

Davies, W. D., et al. *The Cambridge History of Judaism* (vols. I–III). Cambridge: Cambridge University Press, 1999.

Gardner-Wilkinson, J. *The Ancient Egyptians: Their Life and Customs* (vols. I–II). London: Studio Editions, 1994.

Hallo, William W., and William K. Simpson. *The Ancient Near East: A History*. Fort Worth, TX: Harcourt Brace, 1998.

Isbouts, Jean-Pierre. *The Biblical World: An Illustrated Atlas*. Washington, D.C.: National Geographic Society, 2007.

Lewis, Jon E. *Ancient Egypt*. New York: Carroll & Graf Publishers, 2003.

Rainey, Anson F. *Egypt, Israel, Sinai: Archaeological and Historical Relationships in the Biblical Period*. Tel Aviv: Tel Aviv University, 1987.

Roaf, Michael. *Cultural Atlas of Mesopotamia and the Ancient Near East*. Abingdon: Andromeda Oxford, 2004.

Shanks, Hershel. *Ancient Israel: From Abraham to the Roman Destruction of the Temple*. Washington, D.C.: Biblical Archaeology Society, 1999.

CHAPTER 2 FROM JOSHUA TO KINGS

Ackerman, Susan. *Under Every Green Tree: Popular Religion in Sixth-Century Judah*. Atlanta, GA: Scholars Press, 1992.

Cline, Eric. *The Battles of Armageddon: Megiddo and the Jezreel Valley From the Bronze Age to the Nuclear Age*. Ann Arbor, MI: University of Michigan Press, 2002.

Coote, R. B., and K. W. Whitelam. *The Emergence of Early Israel in Historical Perspective*. Sheffield: Almond Press, 1987.

Eynikel, E. *The Reform of King Josiah and the Composition of the Deuteronomistic History*. Leiden: E. J. Brill, 1996.

Finkelstein, Israel, and Neil Asher Silberman. *The Bible Unearthed: Archeology's New Vision of Ancient Israel and The Origin of Its Sacred Texts*. New York NY: The Free Press, 2001.

Finkelstein, Israel, and Neil Asher Silberman. *David and Solomon: In Search of the Bible's Sacred Kings and the Roots of the Western Tradition*. New York NY: The Free Press/Simon & Schuster, 2006.

Fritz, Volkmar, et al. *The Origins of the Ancient Israelite States*. Sheffield: Sheffield Academic Press, 1996.

Mitchell, T. C. *The Bible in the British Museum: Interpreting the Evidence*. London: British Museum Press, 1988.

Silberman, Neil Asher, et al. *The Archeology of Israel: Constructing the Past, Interpreting the Present*. Sheffield, England: Sheffield Academic Press, 1997.

Vanderhooft, D. S. *The Neo-Babylonian Empire and Babylon in the Latter Prophets*. Atlanta: Scholars Press, 1999.

Vaughn, Andrew G., and Ann E. Killebrew, eds. *Jerusalem in Bible and Archaeology: The First Temple Period*. Atlanta: Society of Biblical Literature, 2003.

Yadin, Y. *Hazor: The Discovery of a Great Citadel of the Bible*. London: Weidenfeld and Nicholson, 1975.

CHAPTER 3 FROM CHRONICLES TO MACCABEES

Bosworth, A.B. *Conquest and Empire: The Reign of Alexander the Great*. New York: Cambridge University Press, 1988.

Carter, C. E. *The Emergence of Yehud in the Persian Period*. Sheffield: Sheffield Academic Press, 1999.

Chancey, Mark A. *Greco-Roman Culture and the Galilee of Jesus*. Cambridge: Cambridge University Press, 2005.

Harrington, Daniel. *The Maccabean Revolt: Anatomy of a Biblical Revolution*. Wipf & Stock Publishers, 2009.

Horsley, Richard A. *Galilee: History, Politics, People*. Harrisburg, PA: Trinity Press, 1995.

King, Philip J., and Lawrence E. Stager. *Life in Biblical Israel*. Louisville, KY: Westminster John Knox Press, 2002.

Maier, Paul L, ed. *Josephus: The Essential Works,* translation. Grand Rapids, MI: Kregel Publications, 1994.

Schiffman, Lawrence H. *Reclaiming the Dead Sea Scrolls: The History of Judaism, the Background of Christianity, the Lost Library of Qumran*. New York: Doubleday, 1995.

Stemberger, Günter. *Jewish Contemporaries of Jesus: Pharisees, Sadducees, Essenes*. Minneapolis: Fortress Press, 1995.

Chapter 4 The Four Gospels

Borg, Marcus J. *Jesus: Uncovering the Life, Teachings, and Relevance of a Religious Revolutionary.* San Francisco: HarperSanFrancisco, 2006.

Chancey, Mark A. *The Myth of a Gentile Galilee.* Cambridge: Cambridge University Press, 2002.

Chilton, Bruce. *Rabbi Jesus.* New York: Image/Doubleday, 2000.

Chilton, Bruce. *Mary Magdalene: A Biography.* New York: Image/Doubleday, 2006.

Crossan, John Dominic. *Jesus: A Revolutionary Biography.* New York: HarperCollins Publishers, 1994.

Crossan, John Dominic, and Jonathan L. Reed. *Excavating Jesus: Beneath the Stones, Behind the Texts.* New York: HarperCollins, 2001.

Ehrman, Bart. *Jesus: Apocalyptic Prophet of the New Millennium.* New York: Oxford University Press, 1999.

Evans, Craig. *Jesus and his World: The Archaeological Evidence.* Louisville: Westminster John Knox Press, 2012.

Hezser, Catherine. *Jewish Literacy in Roman Palestine.* Tübingen, Germany: Mohr Siebeck, 2001.

Horsley, Richard A. *Jesus and Empire: The Kingdom of God and the New World Disorder.* Minneapolis: Fortress Press, 2003.

Humphrey, Hugh M. *From Q to "Secret" Mark: A Composition History of the Earliest Narrative Theology.* London: T and T Clark, 2006.

Isbouts, Jean-Pierre. *In the Footsteps of Jesus: A Chronicle of His Life and the Origins of Christianity.* Washington, D.C.: National Geographic Society, 2012.

Levine, Amy-Jill, ed. *Historical Jesus in Context.* Princeton: Princeton University Press, 2006.

McCane, Byron R. *Roll Back the Stone: Death and Burial in the World of Jesus.* Harrisburg, PA: Trinity Press International, 2003.

Meier, John P. *A Marginal Jew: Rethinking the Historical Jesus* (vols. 1, 2, and 3). New York: Doubleday, 1994.

Oakman, Douglas E. *Jesus and the Economic Questions of His Day.* Queenstown, Ontario: Edwin Mellen Press, 1986.

Reed, Jonathan. *Archaeology and the Galilean Jesus: A Re-Examination of the Evidence.* Harrisburg, PA: Trinity Press International, 2002.

Reed, Jonathan L. *The HarperCollins Visual Guide to the New Testament.* New York: HarperCollins, 2007.

Safrai, Ze'ev. *The Economy of Roman Palestine.* London: Routledge, 1994.

Sanders, E. P. *Jesus and Judaism.* Philadelphia: Fortress, 1985.

Senior, Donald. *Jesus: A Gospel Portrait.* Mahwah, NJ: Paulist Press, 1992.

Stemberger, Günter. *Jewish Contemporaries of Jesus: Pharisees, Sadducees, Essenes.* Minneapolis: Fortress, 1995.

Chapter 5 From Acts of the Apostles to Revelation

Archer, Léonie J. *Her Price is Beyond Rubies: The Jewish Woman in Graeco-Roman Palestine.* Sheffield, England: JSOT Press, 1990.

Chilton, Bruce. *Rabbi Paul: An Intellectual Biography.* New York: Image/Doubleday, 2005.

Ehrman, Bart D. *Lost Christianities: The Battles for Scripture and the Faiths We Never Knew.* Oxford: Oxford University Press, 2003.

Elsner, Jas. *Imperial Rome and Christian Triumph.* New York: Oxford University Press, 1998.

Evans, Craig A., ed. *The World of Jesus and the Early Church.* Peabody, MA: Hendrickson Publishers, 2011.

Goodman, Martin. *State and Society in Roman Galilee, A.D. 132–212.* Totowa, NJ: Rowman and Allanheld, 1983.

Ilan, Tal. *Jewish Women in Greco-Roman Palestine.* Peabody, MA: Hendrickson, 1996.

Jeffers, James S. *The Greco-Roman World of the New Testament Era: Exploring the Background of Early Christianity.* Downers Grove, IL: InterVarsity Press, 1999.

Kee, Howard Clark. *The Beginnings of Christianity: An Introduction to the New Testament.* London: T and T Clark, 2005.

Magnes, Jodi. *Stone and Dung, Oil and Spit: Jewish Life in the Time of Jesus.* Grand Rapids: Eerdmans, 2011.

Neusner, Jacob. *Judaism When Christianity Began: A Survey of Belief and Practice.* Louisville: John Knox Press, 2002.

Neusner, Jacob. *The Mishnah: A New Translation.* New Haven: Yale University Press, 1988.

Pagels, Elaine. *Beyond Belief: The Secret Gospel of Thomas.* New York: Random House, 2003.

Pagels, Elaine. *The Gnostic Gospels.* New York: Random House, 1979.

Porter, Stanley, ed. *Paul and his Theology.* Pauline Studies, vol. 3. Leiden, Holland: Brill, 2006.

Robinson, J. M., gen. ed. *The Nag Hammadi Library.* Leiden: EJ Brill, 1977.

Udoh, Fabian E. *To Caesar What Is Caesar's: Tribute, Taxes, and Imperial Administration in Early Roman Palestine (63 B.C.E.–70 C.E.).* Providence: Brown Judaic Studies, 2005.

ABOUT THE AUTHOR

Dr. Jean-Pierre Isbouts is a humanities scholar and graduate professor in the doctoral programs at Fielding Graduate University in Santa Barbara, California. Dr. Isbouts has published widely on the origins of Judaism, Christianity, and Islam, including two best sellers: *The Biblical World,* published by the National Geographic Society in 2007, and *In the Footsteps of Jesus,* published by the National Geographic Society in 2012. His other books include *Young Jesus: Restoring the Lost Years of a Social Activist and Religious Dissident* (Sterling, 2008); *From Moses to Muhammad: The Shared Origins of Judaism, Christianity and Islam* (Pantheon, 2010); and *The Mysteries of Easter,* published by the National Geographic Society in early 2012. An award-winning filmmaker, Dr. Isbouts has also produced a number of programs, including *Charlton Heston's Voyage Through the Bible* (GoodTimes, 1998), *The Quest for Peace* (Hallmark, 2003), and *Young Jesus* (PBS, 2008). His website is www.jpisbouts.org.

BOARD OF ADVISERS

ERIC H. CLINE is professor of Classics and Anthropology and serves as the chair of the Department of Classical and Near Eastern Languages and Civilizations at the George Washington University in Washington, D.C. A prolific researcher and author with 14 books and nearly 100 articles and book reviews to his credit, Dr. Cline is an experienced field archaeologist. He has directed or participated in 28 seasons of excavation and survey in Israel, Egypt, Jordan, Cyprus, and Greece.

STEVEN FELDMAN works with early career scholars in helping them transform dissertations into publishable academic books. Previously, he served as web editor and director of educational programs for the Biblical Archaeology Society and managing editor of both *Biblical Archaeology Review* and *Bible Review,* published by the Society. Feldman holds a master's degree from the University of Chicago Divinity School.

BRUCE CHILTON is the Bernard Iddings Bell professor of religion at Bard College, chaplain of the college, and executive director of the Institute of Advanced Theology. Dr. Chilton founded two journals, the *Bulletin for Biblical Research* and the *Journal for the Study of the New Testament,* as well as the monograph series *Studying the Historical Jesus* series (Eerdmans). Some of his books include *Rabbi Jesus: An Intimate Biography* (Doubleday); *Rabbi Paul: An Intellectual Biography* (Doubleday); *Mary Magdalene: A Biography* (Doubleday); and *The Way of Jesus* (Abingdon).

CRAIG EVANS is the Payzant Distinguished Professor of New Testament Studies at Acadia Divinity College of Acadia University in Nova Scotia, Canada. He is the author and editor of more than 60 books and hundreds of articles and reviews, including *The World of Jesus and the Early Church* and *Jesus and His World: The Archaeological Evidence.*

ACKNOWLEDGMENTS

This book encapsulates nearly 20 years of research in the culture, literature, archaeology, and art of the Hebrew Scriptures and the New Testament. I would like to thank Lisa Thomas, senior editor at National Geographic's Book Division, for developing the concept for this book in the first place, and for her unerring support throughout this long and intensive effort. I once again enjoyed an outstanding editorial team at National Geographic, led by my wonderful editor Barbara Payne. Specifically, I must thank Kay Hankins and Carol Norton for their beautiful layouts, Matt Propert for his excellent photo research, Carl Mehler for his wonderful maps, and Heather McElwain for her gentle copy edit.

Special thanks are due to the panel of distinguished scholars who reviewed the manuscript, namely Bruce Chilton, Bernard Iddings Bell professor of religion at Bard College; Eric Cline, professor of Classics and Anthropology at the George Washington University; Professor Craig Evans at Acadia Divinity College in Wolfville, Nova Scotia; and Steven Feldman, who previously served as web editor and director of educational programs for the Biblical Archaeological Society.

I must also thank my six outstanding doctoral students at Fielding Graduate University who contributed many hours of research in the composition of the *Who's Who* index entries, including Deirdre E. Bradley, M. Rockelle Gray, Joanna I. Hesketh, Kelly Usselman, Molly M. Wagner, and Lauren N. White; their hard work is deeply appreciated.

I have profited from the research of many other scholars, notably the recent published work of Marcus Borg, Mark Chancey, Bruce Chilton, Eric Cline, John Dominic Crossan, Craig Evans, David Fiensy, K. C. Hanson, Richard Horsley, Zvi Gal, Peter Garnsey, John P. Meier, Fabian Udoh, and Jonathan Reed. I also wish to thank my pastor, Monsignor Lloyd Torgerson of St. Monica's Church in Santa Monica, California, for his spiritual guidance. Needless to say, any errors in the narrative are mine, and mine alone.

I would also like to thank my agent, Peter Miller, and his staff at Global Lion Management. And finally, I must express my deepest gratitude to my family for their patience and understanding, and particularly to my wife, Cathie, my muse and indefatigable companion during our many journeys through the Middle East.

Jean-Pierre Isbouts

ILLUSTRATIONS CREDITS

ARNY = Art Resource, NY; BAL = The Bridgeman Art Library; GI = Getty Images

All photographs courtesy of Pantheon Studios, Inc., unless otherwise noted:

Cover (UPLE), bpk, Berlin/Staatliche Museen/ARNY; Cover (UPCTR), Jerry L. Thompson/ARNY; Cover (UPRT), Cameraphoto Arte, Venice/ARNY; Cover (LO), Scala/Ministero per i Beni e le Attività culturali/ARNY.

1, Detail from one of the Bible Windows depicting Solomon and the Queen of Sheba (stained glass), English School (20th century)/Canterbury Cathedral, Kent, UK/BAL; 2-3, "The Garden of Eden With the Fall of Man," ca 1615 (oil on panel), Brueghel, Jan (1568–1625) & Rubens, P. P. (1577–1640)/Mauritshuis, The Hague, The Netherlands/BAL.

INTRODUCTION: 13, Sistine Chapel ceiling and lunettes, 1508–1512 (fresco) (post-restoration), Buonarroti, Michelangelo (1475–1564)/Vatican Museums and Galleries, Vatican City/BAL.

CHAPTER 1: 24 (LE), Adam and Eve, 1537 (panel), Cranach, Lucas, the Elder (1472–1553)/Kunsthistorisches Museum, Vienna, Austria/BAL; 24 (RT), Adam and Eve, 1537 (panel), Cranach, Lucas, the Elder (1472–1553)/Kunsthistorisches Museum, Vienna, Austria/BAL; 25, "Noah's Sacrifice," 1847–1853 (oil on canvas), Maclise, Daniel (1806–1870)/Leeds Museums and Galleries (Leeds Art Gallery) U.K./BAL; 29, "The Sacrifice of Isaac," 1603 (oil on canvas), Caravaggio, Michelangelo Merisi da (1571–1610)/Galleria degli Uffizi, Florence, Italy/Alinari/BAL; 30 (LO), Pantheon Studios, Inc., Courtesy of Glumik; 36 (INSET), "The Dismissal of Hagar," 1660s (oil on canvas), Fabritius, Barent (1624–1673)/Ferens Art Gallery, Hull Museums, UK/BAL; 37, Alfredo Dagli Orti/The Art Archive at ARNY; 43, Large Passover plate (brass), Israeli School (20th century)/The Israel Museum, Jerusalem, Israel/BAL; 46, "Moses With the Tablets of the Law" (oil on canvas), Reni, Guido (1575–1642)/Galleria Borghese, Rome, Italy/Giraudon/BAL; 54 (LE), Aaron throwing down the rod that God has given Moses (gouache on paper), English School (20th century)/Private Collection/© Look and Learn/BAL; 54 (RT), "Abraham and Sarah Before Abimelech," 1681 (oil on canvas), Roos, Johann Heinrich (1631–1685)/Allen Memorial Art Museum, Oberlin College, Ohio, USA/Gift of Dr. Alfred Bader in memory of Wolfgang Stechow/BAL; 56, Samuel Killing Agag, "King of the Amalekites" (oil on panel), Troyen, Rombout van (ca 1605–1650)/Musée des Beaux–Arts, Dunkirk, France/Giraudon/BAL; 57, Punic civilization, Terra-cotta statuette of god Baal Hammon on the throne from Thinissut, Tunisia, fourth century B.C.E./De Agostini Picture Library/G. Dagli Orti/BAL; 58, "Jacob parting From Benjamin," English School (20th century)/Private Collection/© Look and Learn/BAL; 60 (UP), Erich Lessing/ARNY; 60 (LO), "The consecration of Eleazar as High Priest," Hole, William Brassey (1846–1917)/Private Collection/© Look and Learn/BAL; 61, "Eliezer of Damascus," 1860 (oil on canvas), Dyce, William (1806–1864)/Minneapolis Institute of Arts, MN, USA/The Putnam Dana McMillan Fund/BAL; 62, Eve (oil on panel), Cranach, Lucas, the Elder (1472–1553)/Koninklijk Museum voor Schone Kunsten, Antwerp, Belgium/© Lukas—Art in Flanders VZW/Photo: Hugo Maertens/BAL; 63, "The Apparition of Gamaliel to the Priest, Lucien," from the Altarpiece of St. Stephen, ca 1470 (oil on panel), Pacher, Michael (1435–1498)/Musée d'Art et d'Archéologie, Moulins, France/Giraudon/BAL; 64, © RMN-Grand Palais/ARNY; 65 (LE), "Victory O Lord," 1871 (oil on canvas), Millais, Sir John Everett (1829–1896)/Manchester Art Gallery, UK/BAL; 65 (RT), DEA Picture Library/GI; 66, Cameraphoto Arte, Venice/ARNY; 67 (LE), "Jacob's Ladder," ca 1490 (oil on panel), French School (15th century)/Musée du Petit Palais, Avignon, France/BAL; 68, "Joseph and His Brethren Welcomed by Pharaoh." Gouache on board. 12⅛ x 8⅝" (30.8 x 21.9 cm). Gift of the heirs of Jacob Schiff. X1952-138. Photo: John Parnell. The Jewish Museum, New York /ARNY; 69, "Judith and Holofernes," 1599 (oil on canvas) (detail of 79578), Allori, Cristofano (1577–1621)/Palazzo Pitti, Florence, Italy/BAL; 70, "Lot and His Daughters," ca 1650 (oil on canvas), Guercino (Giovanni Francesco Barbieri) (1591–1666)/Gemäuldegalerie Alte Meister, Dresden, Germany/© Staatliche Kunstsammlungen Dresden/BAL; 71, "Meeting Between Abraham and Melchizedek" (oil on canvas), French School (17th century)/Musée des Beaux-Arts, Rennes, France/Giraudon/BAL; 72, Erich Lessing/ARNY; 73, Window depicting Naphtali (stained glass), English School (14th century)/Wells Cathedral, Somerset, UK/BAL; 75 (LE), Gianni Dagli Orti/The Art Archive at ARNY; 75 (RT), DEA/A. Dagli Orti/GI; 76, DEA/A. Dagli Orti/GI; 77, "Massacre of the Hivites by Simeon and Levi" (litho), English School (19th century)/Private Collection/The Stapleton Collection/BAL; 78, By kind permission of the Trustees of the Wallace Collection, London/ARNY; 79, Erich Lessing/ARNY.

CHAPTER 2: 80-81, Pantheon Studios, Inc./Courtesy SMK Foto/Statens Museum for Kunst; 82, Eileen Tweedy/The Art Archive at ARNY; 84, "Joshua Commanding the Sun," English School (19th century)/Private Collection/© Look and Learn/BAL; 100, David, ca 1440 (bronze), Donatello (ca 1386–1466)/Museo Nazionale del Bargello, Florence, Italy/BAL; 101, © RMN-Grand Palais/ARNY; 103, I Kings 2:10-11 The Death of David, and 2:19-25 Bathsheba asks Solomon for Abishag to marry Adonijah, from the Nuremberg Bible (Biblia Sacra Germanaica) (colored woodcut), German School (15th century)/Private Collection/The Stapleton Collection/BAL; 104, "The Visit of the Queen of Sheba to King Solomon," illustration from *Hutchinson's History of the Nations,* early 1900s (color litho), Poynter, Sir Edward John (1836–1919) (after)/Private Collection/BAL; 105, The Imperial Crown made for the coronation of Otto I, the "Great" (912–73) showing one of four enamel plaques representing King Solomon as the symbol of Wisdom, West German, late tenth century with later additions (gold, precious stones, pearls, and enamel)/Kunsthistorisches Museum, Vienna, Austria/BAL; 107 (LE), Wikipedia; 107 (RT), Statuette of King Necho, Late Period (bronze), Egyptian 26th Dynasty (664–525 B.C.E.)/Brooklyn Museum of Art, New York, USA/Charles Edwin Wilbour Fund/BAL; 108, Wikipedia; 109, "Elisha Raising the Son of the Shunamite," 1881 (oil on canvas), Leighton, Frederic (1830–1896)/Leighton House Museum, Kensington & Chelsea, London, UK/BAL; 112, The Prophet Hosea, predella of an altarpiece by Gherardo Starnina, known as Master of the Bambino Vispo (ca 1360–before 1413), panel/De Agostini Picture Library/BAL; 116, Wikipedia; 120, "The Prophet Amos," 1535 (oil on panel), Juan de Borgona (ca 1470–ca 1535)/Museo Catedralicio, Cuenca, Spain/BAL; 126, Album/ARNY; 127 (LE), SuperStock/SuperStock; 127 (RT), "The Death of Absalom," Hole, William Brassey (1846–1917)/Private Collection/© Look and Learn/BAL; 128 (LE), Adonijah, Uptton, Clive (1911–2006)/Private Collection/© Look and Learn/BAL; 128 (RT), "Elijah Rebuking Ahab," Gow, Mary L. (1851–1929)/Private Collection/© Look and Learn/BAL; 129, Wikipedia; 130, "The Feast of Absalom" (oil on canvas), Preti, Mattia (Il Calabrese) (1613–1699)/Private Collection/Photo © Agnew's, London, UK/BAL; 131 (LE), Figurine of Asherah, Canaanite, 999–600 B.C.E. (clay), Bronze Age (2000–600 B.C.E.)/Private Collection/Photo © Zev Radovan/BAL; 131 (RT), "Joash Saved From the Massacre of the Royal Family," 1867 (oil on canvas), Levy, Henri Leopold (1840–1904)/Musée des Beaux-Arts, Arras, France/Giraudon/BAL; 132 (LE), "Barak and Deborah" (oil on canvas), Solimena, Francesco (1657–1747)/Private Collection/BAL; 132 (RT), "The Toilet of Bathsheba," 1710 (oil on copper), Verkolje, Nicolaes (1673–1746)/Private Collection/Johnny Van Haeften Ltd.,

London/BAL; 133, Deborah, Landelle, Charles (1821–1908)/Private Collection/© Look and Learn/BAL; 134, Samson and Delilah, Caravaggio, Michelangelo (1571–1610) (follower of)/Hospital de Tavera, Toledo, Spain/BAL; 135 (LE), "Elijah Visited by an Angel" from the Altarpiece of the Last Supper, 1464–1468 (oil on panel), Bouts, Dirck (ca 1415–1475)/St. Peter's, Louvain, Belgium/Giraudon/BAL; 135 (RT), "The Prophet Elisha Rejecting Gifts From Naaman," 1637 (oil on canvas), Grebber, Pieter Fransz de (ca 1600–1653)/Frans Hals Museum, Haarlem, The Netherlands/Index/BAL; 136, Window depicting Gideon's Fleece (stained glass), French School (13th century)/Laon Cathedral, Laon, France/BAL; 137, "David Victorious Over Goliath," ca 1600 (oil on canvas), Caravaggio, Michelangelo Merisi da (1571–1610)/Prado, Madrid, Spain/BAL; 138, "The Infant Samuel Brought by Hannah to Eli," 17th century (oil on canvas), Eeckhout, Gerbrandt van den (1621–1674)/Ashmolean Museum, University of Oxford, UK/BAL; 139 (LE), "The Healing of Hezekiah," miniature from the *Psalter of Paris,* manuscript, tenth century/De Agostini Picture Library/G. Dagli Orti/BAL; 139 (RT), Scala/ARNY; 140, By kind permission of the Trustees of the Wallace Collection, London/ARNY; 141, "The Philistines hang Saul's body from the walls of Beth-Shan; the valiant men of Jabesh-Gilead remove the body; they burn the bodies of Saul and his three sons; an Amalekite brings the crown to David, with tidings of Saul's death." France (probably Paris), ca 1250. MS. M.638, f. 35v. The Pierpont Morgan Library/ARNY; 142, "Jehoiakim Burning the Roll," English School (20th century)/Private Collection/© Look and Learn/BAL; 143 (LE), Jehu (engraving), English School (19th century)/Private Collection/© Look and Learn/BAL; 143 (RT), Sistine Chapel Ceiling: The Prophet Jeremiah (pre-restoration), Buonarroti, Michelangelo (1475–1564)/Vatican Museums and Galleries, Vatican City/BAL; 144, "Jeroboam Sacrificing to the Golden Calf," 1752 (oil on canvas), Fragonard, Jean-Honoré (1732–1806)/École Nationale Supérieure des Beaux-Arts, Paris, France/Giraudon/BAL; 145 (UP), Erich Lessing/ARNY; 145 (LO), Jezebel, 1896, Shaw, John Byam Liston (1872–1919)/© Russell-Cotes Art Gallery and Museum, Bournemouth, UK/BAL; 146, Table Base with the Story of Jonah (Jonah swallowed and cast up by the Big Fish). Roman, Early Byzantine, early fourth century. Marble, white. Overall: 19½ x 24 x 13¼ in. (49.5 x 61 x 33.7 cm) Base: 9⅝ x 10¼ in. (24.4 x 26 cm) weight: 181 lb (82.1 kg). The Metropolitan Museum of Art, Gift of John Todd Edgar, 1877 (77.7). Image copyright © The Metropolitan Museum of Art. Image source: ARNY; 147 (LE), "Moses and Joshua Descending From the Mount," Dixon, Arthur A. (1872–1959)/Private Collection/© Look and Learn/BAL; 147 (RT), "The Death of King Josiah at Megiddo," Hole, William Brassey (1846–1917)/Private Collection/© Look and Learn/BAL; 150, "Merodach Sets Forth to Attack Tiamat," illustration from *Myths of Babylonia and Assyria* by Donald A. Makenzie, 1915 (color litho), Wallcousins, Ernest (1883–1976) (after)/Private Collection/The Stapleton Collection/BAL; 151, Detail of the Prophet Micah, from the exterior of the right wing of the Ghent Altarpiece, 1432 (oil on panel) (see 472381, 472325), Eyck, Hubert (ca 1370–1426) & Jan van (1390–1441)/St. Bavo Cathedral, Ghent, Belgium/© Lukas—Art in Flanders VZW/Photo: Hugo Maertens/BAL; 152, © RMN-Grand Palais/ARNY; 153 (LE), Ms H 7 fol.114r Nahum announcing the destruction of Nineveh, from the Bible of Jean XXII (vellum), French School (15th century)/Musée Atger, Faculté de Médecine, Montpellier, France/Giraudon/BAL; 153 (RT), Alfredo Dagli Orti/The Art Archive at ARNY; 154, Window depicting the prophet Obadiah, ca 1270–1275 (stained glass), French School (13th century)/Church of St. Urbain, Troyes, France/Giraudon/BAL; 156, Innis, Caroline. Caleb, Achsah and Othniel, 1827. Watercolor on paper, 23½ x 20½ in. (59.7 x 52.1 cm). Gift of Mrs. Edith G. Halpert, JM 33-54. The Jewish Museum, New York/ARNY; 157, "Rahab and the Spies," English School (20th century)/Private Collection/© Look and Learn/BAL; 158, bpk, Berlin/Skulpturensammlung und Museum für Byzantinische Kunst, Staatliche Museen, Berlin, Germany/Joerg P. Anders/ARNY; 159 (RT), Erich Lessing/ARNY; 160 (RT), © The Trustees of the British Museum/ARNY; 161, bpk, Berlin/Gemäldegalerie, Staatliche Museen, Berlin, Germany/Joerg P. Anders/ARNY; 162, © RMN-Grand Palais/ARNY; 163 (UP), "The Death of Sisera" (oil on canvas), Palma Il Giovane (Jacopo Negretti) (1548–1628)/Musée d'Art Thomas Henry,

Cherbourg, France/Giraudon/BAL; 163 (LO), Gianni Dagli Orti/The Art Archive at ARNY; 164, "Solomon and the Queen of Sheba" (oil on canvas), Francken, Frans II the Younger (1581–1642)/Musée des Beaux-Arts, Quimper, France/BAL; 165, Erich Lessing/ARNY; 166, Epitaph of King Uzziah of Judah (limestone)/Israel Museum, Jerusalem, Israel/The Ridgefield Foundation, New York, in memory of Henry J. and Erna D. Leir/BAL; 167, Public Domain image from Wikimedia Commons.

CHAPTER 3: 171, © RMN-Grand Palais/ARNY; 172, King Solomon holding the temple, 1890 (stained glass), Burne-Jones, Sir Edward Coley (1833–1898)/Leigh, Staffordshire, UK/Ann S. Dean, Brighton/BAL; 175, Erich Lessing/ARNY; 178 (UP), Aleksandar Todorovic/Shutterstock; 181, Esther Scroll and Case, Baghdad, Iraq (pen & ink with tempera on parchment), Iraqi School (19th century)/The Israel Museum, Jerusalem, Israel/BAL; 182-183, "The Vision of Ezekiel," 1630 (oil on canvas), Collantes, Francisco (1599–1656)/Prado, Madrid, Spain/BAL; 185, "Aaron the High Priest" (oil on board), Etty, William (1787–1849)/Sunderland Museums & Winter Garden Collection, Tyne & Wear, UK/© Tyne & Wear Archives & Museums/BAL; 188, "Christ Before Caiaphas," Frangipane, Niccolo (fl.1563–1597)/Galleria e Museo Estense, Modena, Italy/BAL; 189, Erich Lessing/ARNY; 190, "The Expulsion of Heliodorus From the Temple," 1674 (oil on canvas), Lairesse, Gerard de (1640–1711)/Private Collection/Johnny Van Haeften Ltd., London/BAL; 192, "The Triumph of Judas Maccabeus," 1635 (oil on canvas), Rubens, Peter Paul (1577–1640)/Musée des Beaux-Arts, Nantes, France/Giraudon/BAL; 193, Section from the Psalms Scrolls, Qumran cave 11, ca 30–50 (parchment)/The Israel Museum, Jerusalem, Israel/BAL; 200, Ms 22 Samuel and his sons Joel and Abijah (vellum), French School (14th century)/Bibliothèque Sainte-Genevieve, Paris, France/Archives Charmet/BAL; 201 (LE), "Esther Before Ahasuerus," before 1697 (oil on canvas), Coypel, Antoine (1661–1722)/Louvre, Paris, France/Giraudon/BAL; 201 (RT), Alexander the Great (356–323 B.C.E.) from The Alexander Mosaic, depicting the Battle of Issus between Alexander and Darius III (399–330 B.C.E.) in 333 B.C.E., floor mosaic removed from the Casa del Fauno (House of the Faun) at Pompeii, after a fourth-century B.C.E. Hellenistic painting by Philoxenos of Eritrea (mosaic) (detail of 154003), Roman (first century B.C.E.)/Museo Archeologico Nazionale, Naples, Italy/Giraudon/BAL; 202 (UP), Bust of Antiochus III (223–187 B.C.E.), replica of an original from third century B.C.E. (marble), Greek/Louvre, Paris, France/BAL; 202 (LO), Artaxerxes I (464–24 B.C.E.) receiving a grandee in "Median" dress while Other Dignitaries look on, detail from the west entrance to the Hundred Column Hall (stone) (photo), Achaemenid (fifth century B.C.E.)/Persepolis, Iran/BAL; 204, "The Return of Tobias," ca 1670–1680 (oil on canvas), Berchem, Nicolaes Pietersz. (1620–1683)/Musée des Beaux-Arts, Pau, France/Giraudon/BAL; 205, "Belshazzar's Feast," Danini, Pietro (ca 1646–1712)/Pushkin Museum, Moscow, Russia/BAL; 206 (LE), Erich Lessing/ARNY; 206 (RT), ARNY; 207, A Median officer paying homage to King Darius I (ca 550–486 B.C.E.) from the Treasury, ca 515 B.C.E. (limestone) (see also 279364), Achaemenid (550–330 B.C.E.)/Persepolis, Iran/Giraudon/BAL; 208, "Esther" (oil on canvas), Anschuetz, Hermann (1802–80)/Pushkin Museum, Moscow, Russia/BAL; 209, Scala/ARNY; 211 (RT), Judith with the head of Holofernes, ca 1530 (panel), Cranach, Lucas, the Elder (1472–1553)/Kunsthistorisches Museum, Vienna, Austria/BAL; 214, The Tree of Jesse, from the Dome Altar, 1499 (tempera on panel) (see 145501-15), Stumme, Absolon (15th century)/Hamburger Kunsthalle, Hamburg, Germany/BAL; 215 (RT), Prutah of John Hyrcanus I, 129–104 B.C.E. (bronze), Hasmonean (140–37 B.C.E.)/Israel Museum, Jerusalem, Israel/BAL; 216 (RT), "The Nine Worthies and the Nine Worthy Women," detail of Judas Maccabeus, 1418–1430 (fresco), Jaquerio, Giacomo (fl.1403–1453)/Castello della Manta, Saluzzo, Italy/Alinari/BAL; 217, "The Leviathan," 1908 (color litho), Rackham, Arthur (1867–1939)/Bibliothèque des Arts Décoratifs, Paris, France/Archives Charmet/BAL; 218, Alinari/ARNY; 221, Gianni Dagli Orti/The Art Archive at ARNY; 222, Tissot, James Jacques Joseph (1836–1902) and Followers. "Nehemiah Looks Upon the Ruins of Jerusalem," ca 1896–1902. Gouache on board. 9¼ x 7⁷/₁₆ in. (23.6 x 18.9 cm) Gift of the heirs of Jacob Schiff, X1952-378. Photo by John Parnell. The Jewish Museum, New York/ARNY; 223 (LE), Tate, London/ARNY; 223 (RT), "Naomi entreating Ruth and Orpah to return to the land of Moab," from a series of 12 known as "The Large Colour Prints," 1795, Blake, William (1757–1827)/Victoria & Albert Museum, London, UK/The Stapleton Collection/BAL; 224 (RT), "Ruth," 1886 (oil on canvas), Landelle, Charles (1821–1908)/Shipley Art Gallery, Gateshead, Tyne & Wear, UK/© Tyne & Wear Archives & Museums/BAL; 225, "Shadrach, Meshach and Abednego in the Fiery Furnace," 1863 (w/c), Solomon, Simeon (1840–1905)/Private Collection/© Mallett Gallery, London, UK/BAL; 226, "Zerubbabel Showing a Plan of Jerusalem to Cyrus" (oil on canvas), Loo, Jacob or Jacques van (ca 1614–1670)/Musée des Beaux-Arts, Orleans, France/Giraudon/BAL; 227 (LE), "Departure of the Young Tobias," 1733 (oil on canvas), Parrocel, Pierre (1670–1739)/Musée des Beaux–Arts, Marseille, France/Giraudon/BAL; 227 (RT), "The Healing of Tobit," early 1630s, Strozzi, Bernardo (1581–1644)/Hermitage, St. Petersburg, Russia/BAL; 228, "Queen Vashti leaving the royal palace" (oil on panel), Lippi, Filippino (ca 1457–1504)/Museo Horne, Florence, Italy/Giraudon/BAL.

CHAPTER 4: 242, "Herod and Herodias at the Feast of Herod" (oil on panel) (detail of 222483), Francken, Frans the Elder (1542–1616)/Musee Municipal, Dunkirk, France/Giraudon/BAL; 251, Courtesy Marcela Zapata Meza, Universidad Anáhuac México Sur; 274, "Annas and Caiaphas," illustration for *The Life of Christ,* ca 1886–1894 (w/c & gouache on paperboard), Tissot, James Jacques Joseph (1836–1902)/Brooklyn Museum of Art, New York, USA/BAL; 275 (LE), Erich Lessing/ARNY; 275 (RT), Album/ARNY; 278 (LE), "Herod" (21 b.c.e.–39 c.e.), illustration for *The Life of Christ,* ca 1886–1894 (w/c & gouache on paperboard), Tissot, James Jacques Joseph (1836–1902)/Brooklyn Museum of Art, New York, USA/BAL; 278 (RT), "Herodias, With Head of John the Baptist," Sirani, Elisabetta (1638–1665)/Burghley House Collection, Lincolnshire, UK/BAL; 281 (LE), "The Calling of the Sons of Zebedee" (panel), Basaiti, Marco (1470–1530)/Galleria dell' Accademia, Venice, Italy/BAL; 282 (RT), "The Betrayal of Christ," detail of the kiss, ca 1305 (fresco) (detail of 65199), Giotto di Bondone (ca 1266–1337)/Scrovegni (Arena) Chapel, Padua, Italy/BAL; 283, Scala/ARNY; 284, Erich Lessing/ARNY; 287 (LE), "Christ Driving the Moneychangers From the Temple," 1626 (oil on canvas), Rembrandt Harmenszoon van Rijn (1606–1669)/Pushkin Museum, Moscow, Russia/BAL; 287 (RT), "Christ Instructing Nicodemus" (oil on canvas), Jordaens, Jacob (1593–1678)/Musée des Beaux-Arts, Tournai, Belgium/BAL; 288 (RT), "The Pharisees Question Jesus," illustration for *The Life of Christ,* ca 1886–96 (gouache on paperboard), Tissot, James Jacques Joseph (1836–1902)/Brooklyn Museum of Art, New York, USA/BAL; 290 (LE), "The Question of the Sadducees," Copping, Harold (1863–1932)/Private Collection/© Look and Learn/BAL; 290 (RT), "The Morning Judgement," illustration from *The Life of Our Lord Jesus Christ,* 1886–1894 (w/c over graphite on paper), Tissot, James Jacques Joseph (1836–1902)/Brooklyn Museum of Art, New York, USA/Purchased by Public Subscription/BAL; 291, "Saint Simeon and Saint Lazarus," ca 1503 (oil on panel) (see also 498671), Dürer or Duerer, Albrecht (1471–1528)/Alte Pinakothek, Munich, Germany/BAL; 293 (RT), Scala/ARNY;

CHAPTER 5: 294-295, © RMN-Grand Palais/ARNY; 301, V&A Images, London/ARNY; 302 (LE), Erich Lessing/ARNY; 305, Scala/ARNY; 323, Alfredo Dagli Orti/The Art Archive at ARNY; 328 (LE), "Christian Fights for His Life," Watt, John Millar (1895–1975)/Private Collection/© Look and Learn/BAL; 328 (RT), "St. Agabus" (oil on canvas), Maino or Mayno, Fray Juan Batista (1569–1649)/© The Bowes Museum, Barnard Castle, County Durham, UK/BAL; 329, "The Feast of Herod" (oil on canvas), Italian School (16th century)/Musée des Beaux-Arts, Caen, France/Giraudon/BAL; 330, "St. Paul Preaching Before the Temple of Diana at Ephesus," 1885 (oil on canvas), Pirsch, Adolf (1858–1929)/Private Collection/Photo © Bonhams, London, UK/BAL; 331 (LE), Study for

"St. Philip Baptising the Eunuch of the Queen of Ethiopia" (oil on canvas), Chasseriau, Theodore (1819–1856)/Musée de la Ville de Paris, Musée du Petit-Palais, France/Giraudon/BAL; 331 (RT), Bust of Emperor Claudius (10 b.c.e.–54 c.e.) from Thasos (marble), Roman (first century c.e.)/Louvre, Paris, France/Giraudon/BAL; 332, Pantheon Studios, Inc./Courtesy The Walters Art Museum; 333 (UP), Banque d'Images, ADAGP/Art Resource, NY © 2013 Artists Rights Society (ARS), New York/ADAGP, Paris; 333 (LO), V&A Images, London/ARNY; 334, St. Timothy and Eunice (stained glass), Burne-Jones, Sir Edward Coley (1833–1898)/Birmingham Museums and Art Gallery/BAL; 335 (LE), Caligula, Gaius Julius Caesar (12–41). Roman Emperor (37–41). Bust. Marble. Carlsberg Glyptotek Museum. Copenhagen. Denmark/Photo © Tarker/BAL; 335 (RT), "The Apparition of Gamaliel to the Priest, Lucien," from the Altarpiece of St. Stephen, ca 1470 (oil on panel), Pacher, Michael (1435–1498)/Musée d'Art et d'Archéologie, Moulins, France/Giraudon/BAL; 336, "St. John the Evangelist at Patmos," from the Mystic Marriage of St. Catherine triptych, 1479 (right wing) 1479 (oil on panel), Memling, Hans (ca 1433–1494)/Memling Museum, Bruges, Belgium/BAL; 339 (LE), "Saint Mark" (oil on copper), Guercino (Giovanni Francesco Barbieri) (1591–1666) (studio)/Private Collection/Photo © Christie's Images/BAL; 339 (RT), St. Matthias, English School (19th century)/Private Collection/© Look and Learn/BAL; 342 (LE), Wikipedia; 342 (RT), "The Martyrdom of St. Philip," 1639 (oil on canvas), Ribera, Jusepe de (lo Spagnoletto) (ca 1590–1652)/Prado, Madrid, Spain/Giraudon/BAL; 343, "Priscilla," illustration from *Women of the Bible,* published by The Religious Tract Society, 1927 (color litho), Copping, Harold (1863–1932)/Private Collection/BAL; 344, "The Death of Sapphira" (oil on canvas), Poussin, Nicolas (1594–1665)/Louvre, Paris, France/Giraudon/BAL; 345 (RT), "The Martyrdom of St. Stephen," ca 1623 (oil on copper), Stella, Jacques (1596–1657)/Fitzwilliam Museum, University of Cambridge, UK/BAL; 346, © RMN-Grand Palais/ARNY.

Charting the Routes to the Holy Land: 356, Map of Jerusalem, detail from the Madaba Mosaic Map (photo)/Church of Saint George, Ma'daba, Jordan/Photo © Zev Radovan/BAL.

INDEX

Boldface indicates illustrations.

Ahitub (son of Phinehas) 129, 130
Aiah (father of Rizpah) 56, 150, 158
Aiah (son of Zibeon) 56
Alcimus 201
Alexander (son of Simon of Cyrene) 268, 274, 289, 291
Alexander Balas 195, 202, 216, 217, 227
Alexander the Great 188–189, 201, 206, 207, 223; "Alexander Sarcophagus" **199**; family tree 194; mosaic **201**; painting **189**; time line 180–181
Alphaeus 270, 274, 283
Amalek 54, 56, 78, 85, 147
Amasa (son of Hadlai) 130
Amasa (son of Jether/Ithra) 126, 130, 145, 215
Amaziah (Levite, father of Hashabiah) 210
Amaziah (name of multiple characters) 130
Amaziah, King (son of Joash) 106, 107, 130, 142, 144, 166
Amittai (father of Jonah) 130, 146
Ammiel (father of Bathsheba) 56, 205
Ammiel (name of multiple characters) 56
Ammihud (descendant of Pharez) 56, 205
Ammihud (name of multiple characters) 56
Amnon (son of David) **90–91**, 97, 101, 127, 129, 130, **130,** 146, 164
Amnon, King (son of Shimon) 106, 121, 130, 142, 147
Amon (name of multiple characters) 130
Amos 107, 108, 112–113, 120, 121, 130, 143, 151; paintings **120, 131**
Amoz 130, 140
Amram (name of multiple characters) 56
Amram (son of Kohath) 47, 54, 56, 68, 69, 71, 72, 151
Amraphel (Hamite king) 56
Amraphel (king of Shinar) 56
Anah (son of Seir) 56, 60
Anah (son of Zibeon) 56, 74
Ananias 300–301, **301,** 307, 329, 337, 341, 344, 346
Andrew (Apostle) 247, 250, 274, 287, 288, 342
Aner 56
Annas 261, 262, 269, 274, **274,** 299–301, 323, 329
Aquila 329, 330, 332, 341, 343, 344
Aram (son of Kemuel) 56, 69
Aram (son of Shem) 56, 63, 65, 78

Aram (son of Shomer) 56
Aramaic (language) 287, 300
Araunah 130–131
Archelaus. *see* Herod Archelaus
Ard 57
Arioch (name of multiple characters) 57
Armoni 131, 150, 158
Arpachshad (name of multiple characters) 57
Asa, King 62, 108, 131, 133, 149, 229; alliance with Ben-hadad I 132; defeat of Zerah 79; invasion of Israel 133; pact with Omri 107, 155; portrait **108**; rebuked by seer 210; reign of 101, 106, 108; sons 142, 205
Asahel 127, 131, 145, 147, 167, 229
Asenath 37, 57, 62, 68–69, 71, 75, 150
Asher 36, 41, 57, 64, 73, 76, 79, 93, 138, 141, 205
Asherah (Baal's consort) 109, 144
Asherah (mother goddess) 57, 97, 149
Ashima 131
Ashkenaz 57, 63
Ashtoreth 131, **131**
Ashur (Assyrian deity) 111
Ashur/Ashhur (son of Hezron and Abijah) 65, 131, 203, 222
Ashur/Ashhur (son of Shem) 131
Asshur 57
Athaliah 107, 131, **131,** 142, 143, 145, 150, 155, 203, 213, 214, 217, 223
Azahiah 61, 104, 106, 107, 109, 129
Azarel (Korahite) 203, **203**
Azzur (father of Hananiah) 131, 137
Azzur (father of Jaazaniah) 131, 141
Azzur (leader of Judah) 131

Baal (Phoenician deity) 57, 108, 113, 128, 131, 132, 135, 136, 144, 145; altar to 89; cult 38, 109, 157; idol 343; priests 109, 150
Baal (Reubenite) 57
Baal Hammon (Phoenician deity) **57**
Baal-Hanan 57
Baalis 131, 172
Baana (father of Zadok) 132, 166
Baana (son of Ahilud) 131–132

Baanah (Netophathite) 132
Baanah (son of Rimmon) 132, 157
Baanah/Banna (man who accompanied Zerubbabel) 132
Baanah/Banna (son of Hushai) 132
Baasha 132, 134, 143, 144
Balaam 57, 58, 75, 79
Balak 57, 58
Barabbas 265, 268, 275, **275**
Barak 132, **132,** 141, 163
Barnabas 11, **310,** 310–311, 330–331, 336, 339, 341, 344, 346
Barsabbus, Joseph 298, 337, 338, 339
Bartholomew (Apostle) 247, 250, 275, 287
Bartimaeus 257, 275, 293
Baruch (priest) 132
Baruch (son of Col-hozeh) 132, 218
Baruch (son of Neriah) 122, 123, 132, 136, 146, 149, 160, 161, 167, 214
Baruch (son of Zabbai) 132
Basemath (daughter of Elon) 62
Basemath/Bashemath (daughter of Ishmael) 55, 58, 70, 161
Basemath/Bashemath (daughter of Solomon) 58
Bathsheba (daughter of Ammiel) 56, 102, 126, 128, 132, 153, 164, 165, 205; paintings **102, 132**; woodcut **103**
Becher 58, 61, 145, 155, 200, 214
Beelzebub or Baalzebub 275–276
Beeri (father of Hosea) 58, 139
Beeri (father of Judith) 58
Bel 132
Bela (father of Ahijah) 129
Bela (son of Azaz) 58
Bela (son of Benjamin) 57, 58, 63, 152, 214, 228
Bela (son of Beor) 58
Beloved Disciple 233, 270, 276, 281
Ben-Abinadab 132
Ben-Hadad (King of Damascus) 128, 132, 133, 138, 142
Ben-Hesed 133
Ben-Hur 133
Benaiah (father of Pelatiah) 133, 156
Benaiah (name of multiple characters) 133
Benaiah (son of Jehoiada) 132–133, 142, 145, 163, 164
Benaiah the Pirathonite 133, 201
Benjamin 37–43, 57–69, 58, **58,** 75, 93, 134, 152, 155, 200, 228

I

Ishmael (son of Abraham) 20, 29, 33–39, 55, 64–66, 76; daughter 39, 58, 70, 149; in Judaism and Islam 34, 37; Ka'bah construction 37, 66; paintings of **37, 66**; sons 36, 56, 60, 63, 66, 68, 69, 71–73, 78, 137

Ishmael (son of Azel) 210

Ishmael (son of Elishama) 131, 136, 141, 154, 173, 222

Ishmael (son of Nethaniah) 61, 222

Ishvi (son of Asher) 141

Ishvi (son of Saul) 141

Israel (name given to Jacob) 39, 41, 66, 67

Issachar (son of Jacob) 36, 39, 41, 66, 70, 93, 157, 165, 224

Ithra (father of Amasa) 130. *See also* Jether (son of Ezrah)

Ittai (Benjamite) 141

Ittai (Philistine) 141

Izhar 66, 69

Jaazaniah (captain who accompanied Hohanan ben-Kareah) 141

Jaazaniah (Maacathite) 141

Jaazaniah (son of Azzur) 131, 141

Jaazaniah (son of Jeremiah) 141

Jaazaniah (son of Shaphan) 141, 161

Jabal 23, 24, 55, 66, 70

Jabesh 141

Jabin (king of Hazor, called "the king of Canaan") 64, 88, 93, 133, 141

Jabin (king of Hazor, organized confederacy of northern princes) 85, 141

Jachin (name of multiple characters) 66

Jacob 28, 36–43, 58, 62, 64, 66–71, 73, 75–77; blessing of grandsons 62, 71, 150; daughter Dinah's rape and 39, 60, 67, 77, 97; dream of ladder 39, 67, **67,** 106, 144; God's covenant with 39, 50, 67; inheritance of birthright 38–39, 62, 66–67, 75; paintings of **38, 41, 58, 67**; sons 39, 41–42, 76, 77, **77**, 93, 136

Jael 64, 138, 141, 163, **163**

Jair (eighth Judge of Israel) 89, 141, 165

Jair (father of Elhanan) 141, 148

Jair (father of Mordecai) 77, 141, 163

Jair (son of Segub) 141

Jairus 251, 253, 278–279, 288, 305

Jalam 36, 67

James (name of multiple characters) 279

James, son of Alphaeus (Apostle) 250, 270, 274, 277, 279

James, son of Zebedee (Apostle) 247, 250, 279, 281, **281,** 287, 290, 293, **293**, 328

Jamin (name of multiple characters) 67

Japheth 26, 57, 63, 64, 67, 73

Japhia (king of Lachish) 141

Japhia (son of David) 142

Jashen 142

Jecoliah 142

Jedidah 142, 200

Jehoahaz (king of Israel, son of Jehu) 111, 112, 142, 143; lineage 106; time line 107

Jehoahaz (king of Judah, son of Jehoram) 129, 142

Jehoahaz (king of Judah, son of Josiah) 122, 137, 142, 154, 167; lineage 106

Jehoiachin (king of Judah) 135, 136, 142, 154, 180, 210, 213, 214, 218, 226, 229; exiled to Babylon 123, 142, 167, 180, 213, 226; lineage 106; surrender to Nebuchadnezzar 123, 142, 154, 213

Jehoiada 132, 133, 142–145, 149, 155, 167, 200, 223

Jehoiakim (king of Judah) 61, 122–123, 134, 142, 143, 154, 156, 214, 228; Jeremiah's prophecies burned 136, **142,** 214; original name 142, 277; prophets and 120, 123, 136, 160, 161, 162, 165, 204; time line 119

Jehoram (king of Israel) 109, 111, 129, 142, 143, 145, 151; lineage 106; time line 104

Jehoram (king of Judah) 107, 129, 131, 142, 143, 166, 213, 221, 225; lineage 106; time line 105

Jehoram (priest) 142, 200

Jehoshaphat (king of Judah) 129, 131, 135, 142–143, 147, 151–152, 203, 212–214, 221; lineage 106; teachers sent out by 61, 73, 128, 142, 152, 154, 155, 162, 165, 166; time line 104

Jehoshaphat (name of multiple characters) 142

Jehosheba 142, 143

Jehu (king of Israel) 111–112, 134, 135, 142, 143; coup led by 109, 145, 154;

detail from black obelisk **111**; engraving **143**; lineage 106; time line 105

Jehu (name of multiple characters) 143

Jehu (son of Obed) 143, 155

Jehucal (Jucal) 143, 161

Jehudi 143, 154, 161, 222

Jephthah 63, 89, 140, 143

Jeremiah (chief of tribe of Manasseh) 144

Jeremiah (father of Hamutal) 137, 144

Jeremiah (father of Jaazaniah) 141

Jeremiah (Gadite/Benjamite) 144

Jeremiah (prophet) 9, 120–123, 134, 136, 137, 143–144, 146, 152; accused of treason 140, 161; arrest 137, 204, **212**; Baruch and 123, 132, 146, 149, 160, 167; conflicts with false prophets 129, 217; engraving **212**; father 121, 211; flight into Egypt 146, 173; imprisonment 144, 147, 149, 150, 212; King Zedekiah and 134, 137, 149, 167; at Mizpah 132, 136, 144; mosaic **121**; oracles 136, 137, 152, 161, 162, 167, 217; paintings **123, 143**; prophecies 123, 137, 154, 161, 214, 222; Temple sermon 122, 143, 260; thrown into cistern 225; uncle 160

Jeroboam I (king of Israel) 105–107, 129, 144, **144**, 163, 167, 212; golden calves commissioned 51, 106, 144; lineage 106; son 73, 100; time line 100

Jeroboam II (king of Israel) 112, 121, 130, 131, 144; death 113; lineage 106; son 167; time line 108

Jeroham (father of Azariah) 144, 203

Jeroham (father of Elkanah) 61, 144

Jeroham (name of mutiple characters) 144

Jeroham of Gedor 144, 229

Jerusha 144, 148, 166

Jeshurun 67

Jesus 233–271, **279,** 279–280; arrest of **261,** 264; attack on money changers 259, 260, **260,** 262, **262,** 280, 286–287, **287**; baptism **245,** 279, 281; betrayal by Judas **261,** 280, 282, **282**; birth 140, 240–241, 254, 279, 283, 284; Caiaphas and **188,** 263, 274, 276, **276**; childhood and adolescence 77, 241–245, **243,** 279, 282, 284; crown of thorns **266–267,** 268; Crucifixion 264, 268–270, **270,** 276, 285; education 241; Last Supper 260–261, 276, 280; ministry in lower Galilee: map 248–

249; miracles 246, 251, 253, **253,** 254, **256,** 280, 286, 287, 288; multiplication of loaves and fish 109, **244,** 247, 253, 274; parable of the Good Samaritan 269, 290; Pontius Pilate and 265, **265, 266–267,** 275, **275,** 276, 280, 289; questioning by Sadducees 188, **188, 290**; Resurrection 63, 254, 271, 280, 285, 292, 300, 335; scourging of 265, 268, **268**; time line 254, 265, 268; tomb 271, 282; Transfiguration **8,** 254, 279, 281, 288; trial of 265

Jether (father-in-law of Moses) 215. *See also* Jethro

Jether (leader of Asher) 215

Jether (son of Ezrah) 62, 215

Jether (son of Gideon) 215

Jether (son of Jada) 215

Jether the Ishmaelite 126, 215

Jethro 47, 50, 51, 64, 67–68, 72, 79, 89, 138, 215; alternative names 65, 75; painting of **67**

Jetur 36, 68

Jeush (son of Bilhan) 68

Jeush (son of Esau) 36, 68

Jeush (son of Rehoboam) 68

Jeush (son of Shimei) 68

Jezebel 107–109, 128, 131, 135, 142–145, **145,** 152, 155

Jezreel (name of multiple characters) 145

Jezreel (son of Hosea) 113, 145

Jidlaph 68

Joab (name of multiple characters) 145

Joab (son of Zeruiah) 97, **101,** 101–103, 127, 130–133, 137, 145, 153, 155; killing of Amasa 130, **145,** 215; Uriak and 102, 132, 165

Joanna 280, 292

Joash (father of Gideon) 136, 145

Joash (king of Judah) 111, 130, **131,** 138, 145, 149, 167, 213, 214, 217, 228; lineage 106; time line 106–107

Joash (name of multiple characters) 145

Jobab (king of Edom) 68, 79

Jobab (name of multimple characters) 68

Jochebed 47, 54, 56, 68, 71, 72

Joel (descendant of Reuben) 145, 166

Joel (Kohathite Levite) 146, 204

Joel (name of multiple characters) 145–146

Joel (prophet) 120, 157, 325

Joel (son of Pediah) 146, 158

Joel (son of Samuel) 145, **200**

Johanan (father of Azariah) 146, 203

Johanan (son of Kareah) 146, 147

Johanan (son of Tobiath) 146, 228

John, son of Zebedee (Apostle) 247, 250, 276, 279, 280–281, **281,** 287, 290, 293, **293,** 323, 325, 336

John of Patmos 325, 336

John the Baptist 245–246, 278, **278, 280,** 281, 290, 292; arrest and murder of 237, 246, 265, 278, 279, 281, 329; baptism of Jesus **245,** 279, 281; description of the Messiah 255, 286; Essenes and 277; in the Jordan 279, 284, 287, 288, 342; parents and birth 237, 277, 293; time line 265; tomb 246

John the Elder 333, 336–337

John the Evangelist 270, 276, **281,** 281–282, **327,** 336, **336**

Jokshan 37, 55, 59, 68

Joktan 64, 68, 74, 76, 161

Jonadab 146

Jonah (prophet) 78, 120, 130, 146, **146**

Jonathan (chief priest) 147, 189; time line 187, 189

Jonathan (name of multiple characters) 146–147

Jonathan (son of King Saul) 96, 97, 135, 146, 150, 159

Jonathan (son of Mattathias) 194–195, 197, 216, **216,** 219, 222, 223, 226

Joram (name of multiple characters) 147

Joram (son of Ahab) 142, 147

Joseph (father of Jesus) 77, 237–243, 275, 277, 279, **282,** 282–292, 289

Joseph (man from Cyprus) 310, 330–331

Joseph (of the Issachar tribe) 65; Potiphar's wife and 75, **75**

Joseph (son of Jacob) 39–43, 64, 67–70, **68,** 74–77, 79, 93, 121, 136; coat 41, **41,** 42; family tree 37

Joseph (son of Mattathias) 286

Joseph of Arimathea 262, 270–271, 276, 280, 282, 287

Joses 270, 279, 282, 284, 285

Joshua (high priest) 167, 181, 209, 213, 229

Joshua (name of multiple characters) 147

Joshua (son of Nun) 54, 60, 68, **82, 84,** 84–87, 147, **147,** 157; curse 55, 139; kings put to death by 128, 133, 157; lands divided by 93, 147; original name 140

Josiah (king of Judah) 19, 83, 117, 120, 121, 131, 147–148; battle of Megiddo 107, 117, 122, 143, **147,** 148, 154; book of the Law and 121, 126, 147, 211; destruction of Molech sites 72, 152; Jeremiah and 121, 122, 143; lineage 106; Passover feast 73, 162, 207, 210, 214; time line 117

Jotham (king of Judah) 117, 140, 144, 148, 166, 220; lineage 106; time line 111

Jotham (son of Gideon) 148

Jubal 23, 24, 55, 66, 69, 70, 93

Judah (son of Jacob) 39, 41, 43, 62, 69, 70, 74–77, 93, 138, 164, 205, 229; also known as Judas 282, 337; family tree 36; painting **78**

Judas (brother of Jesus) 270, 279, 284

Judas (brother of Joseph Barsabbas) 337, 344

Judas (son of Jacob). *See* Judah

Judas (son of James) 279

Judas Iscariot (Apostle) 250, 260–262, 280, 282–283, 291, 292, 331, 337; betrayal of Jesus **261,** 280, 282, **282**

Judas Maccabaeus 192, **192,** 194, 202, 204, 207–209, **216,** 216–220, 226; family tree 194; Hanukkah and 185, 216; painted enamel depicting **171**; time line 187

Judas of Damascus 337

Judas of Galilee 337, 346

Jude 337

Judith (daughter of Beeri) 58, 69, **69**

Judith (wife of Manasseh) 177, **177,** 204, 211, **211,** 215, 216–217

K

Kaiwan (star god) 148

Kedar 36, 69

Kedemah 36, 69

Kemuel (father of Hashabiah) 69, 210

Kemuel (son of Nahor) 56, 69

Kemuel (son of Shiptan) 69

Kenan 24, 69

Kenaz (brother of Caleb) 148, 156, 160

Keturah 36, 47, 54, 55, 59, 60–71, 76, 79, 89, 161; family tree 37

Tertius 346
Thaddaeus (Apostle) 292
Thomas (Apostle) 271, **271**, 292, **292**
Tiberius (Roman emperor) 245, 254, 292–293, **293**; time line 256, 260, 262–263, 299
Tibni 136, 165
Tidal 78
Tiglath-pileser III (king of Assyria) 104, 113, 116, 117, 157, 162, 165; bas-reliefs **113, 114, 165**; time line 111
Tikvah (son of Harhas) 165, 213
Timaeus 257, 293
Timna (concubine of Esau's son Eliphaz) 78
Timna (daughter of Seir) 64, 78
Timna (leader of Edom) 78
Timna (son of Eliphaz, grandson of Esau) 78
Timon 346
Timothy **315**, 315–317, 334, **334**, 338, 346, **346**
Tirhanah 165
Titius Justus 346
Titus (companion of Paul) 330, 341, 346, 347, **347**
Toah 165
Tobijah 165
Tola (son of Issachar) 157, 165, 224, 228
Tola (son of Puah) 89, 165

Urbanus 347
Uri 58, 65, 78
Uz (name of multiple characters) 78
Uzziah (king of Judah) 116–117, 130, 142, 144, 166, 203, 204; leprosy 117, 166; lineage 106; portrait **116**; time line 108; Uzziah Tablet 117, **166**

Vatican **211**, 303, **303**; Sistine Chapel **213**
Via Dolorosa ("Road of Sorrows"), Jerusalem 269

Zaavan 78
Zabdi (name of multiple characters) 166
Zabud 166
Zacchaeus 256–257, 292, 293
Zaccur (father of Shammua) 78, 161
Zaccur (name of multiple characters) 78–79
Zaccur (son of Hammuel) 76, 78, 162
Zaccur (son of Mattaniah) 79, 210, 219
Zadok (father of Jerusha) 144, 166
Zadok (father of Shallum) 160, 166
Zadok (high priest) 60, 102, 126, 129, 130, 164, 166, 185, 188, 191, 220, 289
Zadok (name of multiple characters) 166
Zadok (son of Baana) 132, 166
Zalmunna 136, 166, 215
Zaphenath-Paneah 79
Zebedee 247, 250, 276, 279, 281, 287, 290, 293, **293**, 336
Zebulun (son of Jacob) 36, 39, 41, 62, 70, 79, 93
Zechariah (father of Jahaziel) 166, 212
Zechariah (father of John the Baptist) 237, 277, 293
Zechariah (king of Israel) 113, 120, 141, 160, 167; lineage 106
Zechariah (name of multiple characters) 166–167
Zechariah (priest who blew trumpet) 147, 162, 166
Zechariah (prophet) 11, 167, 180, 181, 212, 218, 229; time line 173
Zechariah (son of Isshiah) 166, 212
Zechariah (son of Jehoiada) 145, 167
Zedekiah (king of Judah) 123, 134, 137, 143, 144, 146, 154, 167, 217, 225; original name 150, 219; time line 106, 120
Zedekiah (name of multiple characters) 167
Zedekiah (prophet) 149, 167, 217
Zelophehad 71, 74, 79
Zenas 347
Zephaniah (father of Josiah) 167
Zephaniah (prophet) 120, 136, 149, 167, **167**, 201
Zephaniah (son of Maaseiah) 129, 162, 167, 217

Zephaniah (son of Tahath) 167
Zephi 79
Zerah (Ethiopian) 79, 108, 229
Zerah (father of Calcol) 133
Zerah (father of Heman) 64
Zerah (father of Jobab) 68, 79
Zerah (name of multiple characters) 79, 229
Zerah (son of Eden) 207
Zerah (son of Judah) 74, 77, 79, 164, 166, 229, 282
Zeruiah 127, 131, 145, 167
Ziba 167
Zibiah 167
Zichri 61, 62, 79, 146, 149, 166, 204, 217
Zillah 24, 70, 72
Zilpah 36, 41, 57, 79, 136
Zimran 37, 55, 79
Zimri (commander of Israel) 79, 106, 107, 134, 155, 167
Zimri (father of Carmi) 59
Zimri (son of Jehoaddah) 79, 167, 222
Zimri (son of Salu) 74, 79, 167
Zipporah 47, 50, 61, 63, 68, 79, **79**
Zohar 62, 79
Zuar 79
Zur 59, 79

‹125›
YEARS

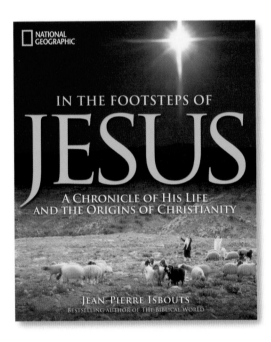
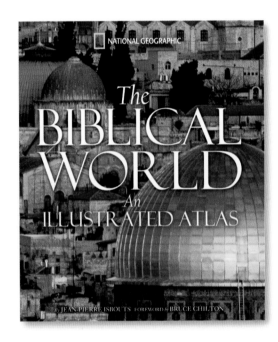